Ebenezer Henderson

The Book of the Twelve Minor Prophets

Translated from the original Hebrew, with a commentary, critical, philological, and

exegetical

Ebenezer Henderson

The Book of the Twelve Minor Prophets
Translated from the original Hebrew, with a commentary, critical, philological, and exegetical

ISBN/EAN: 9783337419462

Printed in Europe, USA, Canada, Australia, Japan

Cover: Foto ©Lupo / pixelio.de

More available books at **www.hansebooks.com**

THE BOOK

OF

THE TWELVE

MINOR PROPHETS,

TRANSLATED FROM THE ORIGINAL HEBREW.

WITH

A COMMENTARY,

CRITICAL, PHILOLOGICAL, AND EXEGETICAL.

BY

E. HENDERSON, D.D.

WITH

A BIOGRAPHICAL SKETCH OF THE AUTHOR,

By E. P. BARROWS,
HITCHCOCK PROFESSOR IN ANDOVER THEOLOGICAL SEMINARY.

Andover:
WARREN F. DRAPER.
BOSTON: GOULD & LINCOLN. NEW YORK: HURD & HOUGHTON.
PHILADELPHIA: SMITH, ENGLISH, AND COMPANY.
CINCINNATI: G. S. BLANCHARD.

1866.

i

PUBLISHER'S NOTE.

THE increasing demand for the English edition of Dr. Henderson's Commentary on the Minor Prophets, suggested an application to the author for permission to reprint it in this country. The following note contains his very kind and courteous consent:

MR. DRAPER:
  Dear Sir,—
    Impressed with a sense of your honorable conduct in consulting me prior to the reprinting of a cheaper edition of my Commentary on The Minor Prophets, I feel no hesitation in granting you the sanction you desire, on the terms specified in your letter of November 4, 1856.
    I remain, dear Sir,
      Yours truly,
        E. HENDERSON, D. D.
MORTLAKE, Surrey, Nov'r 20, 1856.

P. S. Enclosed you will find a list of corrections, copied from my husband's memoranda.   S. H.

Not only have the corrections referred to been made in the present edition, but it was found desirable, also, to verify all the quotations in the Oriental languages, so that the whole work has now been thoroughly revised. This, with other causes, has contributed to delay the publication till the present time. We have to regret that, meanwhile, the venerable author has ceased from his labors, and passed to his reward.

It seems fitting that a short biographical sketch of his useful and eventful life should accompany this volume, as a tribute to his memory among those who will receive the benefits of his studies and labors, but who may not have access to the full biography prepared by his friends.

BIOGRAPHICAL SKETCH OF THE AUTHOR.

The lamented death of the author of the present Commentary occurred while the plates were in process of preparation for an American edition of the work. It seems highly proper, therefore, that a brief sketch of his life and character be prefixed to it. The writer of this, not having access to original sources of information, has drawn his materials from the "Memoir of the Rev. E. Henderson," by his daughter, Thulia S. Henderson, which has lately been published in London.

EBENEZER HENDERSON was born on the 17th day of November, 1784, at Dunfermline, an ancient borough in the eastern part of Scotland, situated in the county of Fife, a little north of the Firth of Forth, and well known as the residence of Anne of Denmark, and the birthplace of King Charles the First. He was the youngest son of George and Jean Henderson. His father was an agricultural laborer, and belonged to the Secession-body of Scotch Presbyterians. "Two years at Dunfermline," the memoir tells us, "and one year and a half at Dunduff, formed the sum-total of his schooling" in the days of his boyhood.[1] Then, at twelve years old, it was resolved that he should be initiated into some trade. But it happened to him, as it has to others whom Providence had foreordained to fill religious and literary spheres, that one attempt after another proved abortive. First he was placed with an elder brother to learn the trade of a clock-and-watch-maker. But here he staid only long enough to gain such an insight into the craft as was afterwards of no little use to him in his missionary wanderings, where recourse to a professed artisan for the rectification of his timepiece was impossible. He was next placed as an apprentice to a boot-and-shoe-maker for the space of three years. Of his progress in this business nothing is known. Only it is certain that "he had not yet found the niche in which he was to take his stand."

[1] Memoir, p. 13.

For this a spiritual preparation was needed. This, through the grace of the Holy Spirit, he received in the deep religious awakening that took place in connection with the labors of Robert and James Haldane, the latter of whom visited Dunfermline in company with Mr. Aikman.

"A saw-pit at the top of Chalmers' Street, and an open place in Woodhead Street, are remembered in connection with various out-door preachings to an assembled multitude. Many of the ungodly were awakened, and the godly were stirred up to works of good-doing. Sunday Schools were established, and they rapidly flourished. Of the 'six' that are recorded as having been in a prosperous state within the parishes of Dunfermline as early as 1798, there was one in which were enrolled the names of Ebenezer Henderson and Douglas Cusine (pronounced Cousin), — the two who are remembered as having borne the palm for diligence and attention."[1]

This little incident shows the original aptitude of our author for the pursuits of a scholar. The precise time of his first open profession of religion is not known. But there is abundant evidence that from this period he devoted himself with all his soul to the service of Christ. The needful preparation for future duty was freely granted him in the Seminary in Edinburgh, which had been originated, and was still supported, by the generosity of Mr. Robert Haldane. The course of instruction was brief, extending only through two years. But this was then thought to be the utmost that was compatible with the urgent demand for home and foreign laborers. "Dr. Henderson always urged the importance of a prolonged collegiate course; and doubtless felt that had his own preparatory studies been of longer continuance, he might have gone forth better equipped for his work."[2] So speaks the memoir; to which may be added, that it was only by a severe and long process of self-training, continued after he left the Seminary, that he was enabled to qualify himself for the work of a translator of the holy Scriptures, and a commentator on their contents, in which he became so distinguished. The class of 1803 — the fifth in order of institution — was the one which he joined. We need not be surprised when we find one of his surviving fellow-students bearing testimony that he was at that time "more of a linguist than a theologian; more given to literature than to divinity."[3] No one can read his commentaries, so rich in oriental lore, without perceiving at a glance that it was the side of sacred literature rather than of systematic theology to which he was drawn by the natural affinities of his mind. To him the memoir justly applies the remark made of one of his contemporaries, the late Rev. Alexander Dewar: "He could comprehend and

---

[1] Memoir, p. 17.   [2] P. 23.   [3] Rev. James Kennedy, of Inverness.

seize the leading features of a complicated question, though he rarely, if ever, dealt in barren abstractions; strong, broad good sense was a distinguishing element of his mind; he was a man of facts and fundamental principles."[1]

In the vacations the seminary students were sent out on preaching-tours. We find him in the summer recess of 1804 appointed to visit the Orkney Islands, which lie off the northern extremity of Scotland. Thus was inaugurated that remarkable series of northern missions to which the providence of God, contrary to his own original intentions, had appointed him.

In the second year of his seminary life he was called to the foreign service, in the following way: The Rev. John Paterson, pastor of a church at Cambuslang, and the Rev. Archibald McLacy, pastor at Kircaldy, having been invited by the two Congregational churches in Edinburgh to go forth as missionary agents, resigned their charges, and came to Edinburgh for a brief course of preparatory study with special reference to the service to which they had devoted themselves. Their destination was India. But Mr. McLacy being by the circumstances of his family detained at home, Mr. Paterson's friends urged him to select from among the seminary students a man for his colleague. As he surveyed the assembled class, he said of Mr. Henderson, then but twenty-one years of age, and with whom he had no previous acquaintance, "This is the man for me." Thus commenced between the two missionaries a life-long friendship. As soon as Mr. Henderson made known his willingness to embark in this cause, his services were accepted, and the missionaries elect were set apart by the imposition of hands, with prayer and fasting, at an evening service in the Tabernacle, Leith Walk, on August 27, 1805.

But God, who understood perfectly the sphere in which these his two servants could best labor, had destined both to a northern instead of a tropical field. Here the following extract from a letter which he wrote on the subject some twelve years later, is perfectly in place:

"When I originally devoted myself to the Redeemer's service, and entered on a course of study preparatory to engaging in it, I had no specific station or sphere of labor in view; but was determined, in reliance on his promised grace, cheerfully to proceed to whatever place he should be pleased to point out to me, whether at home in my native country, or among the heathen in a distant land. Accordingly, when our dear brother Paterson requested me to accompany him to India, it was a matter of no great difficulty for me to give my consent to his proposal."[2]

---

[1] Memoir, p. 25.   [2] P. 37.

This delightful passage shows that he was willing to be guided. And let it be said, for the encouragement of all youthful candidates, that God will certainly guide all who are willing to be guided, into the field in which they can serve him to the best advantage. The two missionary brethren had marked out India for their field, but God sent them into northern Europe.

The directors of the East India Company were at that time, as is well known, hostile to missionary labors among the people whom they ruled. Messrs. Carey and Marshman, with some coadjutors, were indeed carrying on their good work without molestation, but with no open sanction on the part of the directors. Such a sanction the Messrs. Haldane openly sought for themselves and others, and were decidedly refused, and the door was thus closed to their intended enterprise. "The British possessions," says the memoir, "were not approachable by a Christian missionary in a British vessel. But there were Danish ships in which such men could embark; there were Danish settlements where they could effect a landing, and whence they could proceed to some neighboring districts, whose governors might be disposed, if not to sanction, at least to ignore the efforts that might be made."[1] They accordingly repaired to Copenhagen, in the hope of securing a passage thence to Serampore. But here disappointment awaited them. One vessel only was to sail that season, and every berth was preëngaged. They offered to go in the steerage; even that was full.

Meanwhile they found all around them a field white for the harvest. Although as yet ignorant of the Danish language, they had already commenced a service in the English tongue the second Sabbath after their arrival. Next they procured the translation into Danish of a tract entitled "The One Thing Needful," and forthwith set it in active circulation. Their English congregation increased, and they had secured, early in November, the translation and printing of one thousand copies of the "Great Question Answered." Still hoping to be able the ensuing spring to embark for Serampore, they earnestly urged upon their friends at home the importance of not leaving their present field unoccupied when they should be withdrawn from it. In reply they received a letter informing them that but one of the two fields, India or Denmark, could be at present occupied, and urging that they should consent to remain in their present position. They complied; and thus they found themselves, without any planning of their own, inaugurated into the Danish field. The two friends soon separated, Mr. Paterson remaining in Copenhagen, and Mr. Henderson going to Elsineur.

[1] Memoir, p. 41.

At Elsineur he gave lessons, in private families and classes, in the English language, while at the same time he sedulously devoted himself to the acquisition of the Danish, and the other northern languages, which, when once mastered, would greatly enlarge the circle of his influence. As the sphere of his vision widened, he turned his thoughts towards Sweden, and he and his companion determined to gain satisfactory information concerning the spiritual condition of this kingdom, as well as of Denmark. Mr. Henderson repaired to Helsingburgh in the southern part of Sweden, with a supply of religious publications. Next, he and his colleague journeyed through Skonen, leaving tracts at Lund and Malmö, in the hands of such as were likely to translate them into Swedish. After this they undertook an exploring tour in Denmark. Crossing the Great Belt and the Little Belt, they advanced as far as the Moravian settlement at Christiansfeld, in Schleswig. In one respect this journey was of striking importance, by bringing them personally into connection with the British and Foreign Bible Society, and also turning their attention towards Iceland. Learning that the Fünen Evangelical Society was purposing to print two thousand copies of the New Testament for their long-neglected fellow-subjects in Iceland, they ventured to suggest that five thousand instead of two thousand should be the number struck off for the first instalment. The Danes not having courage for this, it was determined that assistance should be sought from London. The two friends accordingly wrote directly to the managers of the Bible Society in the British metropolis, who agreed to defray the cost of the additional three thousand copies.

The war which took place in 1807 between England and Denmark, compelled the two missionaries to withdraw to Sweden. Mr. Henderson took up his residence at Gottenburgh, while Mr. Paterson proceeded to Stockholm, where he was eminently successful in organizing systematic efforts for the circulation of Swedish Bibles and tracts. The ensuing summer of 1808, the two friends travelled in Sweden and Lapland, inquiring into the state of the parishes, and scattering the seeds of divine truth. Having reached Tornea, at the head of the Gulf of Bothnia, they entered Finland, and, turning around the gulf, proceeded till they were close upon Wasa, when the approach of a Russian army compelled them to a hasty retreat back around the head of the same gulf. In October they reached their respective stations, after a journey of two thousand three hundred miles. This tour gave them an affecting insight into the spiritual wants of the people. In many parishes there was on an average only one Bible in every eighth house,—the wealthy and middle classes only being able to possess a copy, while the cottagers remained, from poverty, destitute of this treasure.

During all Mr. Henderson's residence in Denmark and Sweden, he was, along with his missionary labors, busily prosecuting his studies in Hebrew and Greek, as well as in German, Danish, and Swedish. We have already seen how he first became interested in the enterprise for furnishing Iceland with the word of God. Of the five thousand copies of the Icelandic New Testament that had been printed, as noticed above, fifteen hundred had been sent off before the breaking out of the war between England and Denmark. The remaining three thousand five hundred were lying in store, ready for shipment. For some time the prosecution of the enterprise was unavoidably interrupted. But at last, in 1810, it seemed possible to resume it. The Bible Society having authorized one of the two missionaries to visit Iceland in person, while the other should forward the printing of the Bibles that were to follow, Mr. Henderson was designated for the tour in Iceland. This occasioned a preliminary visit to England, where he spent the summer of 1810 among his old friends. He returned to Sweden in October, but various circumstances delayed his visit to Iceland, so that he was at liberty to spend two years more at Gottenburgh.

"It was early in the year 1811, and probably as the result of arrangements made with the Edinburgh publisher, or with some Edinburgh friend, when in Scotland during the previous summer, that Mr. Henderson's earliest literary production, the first fruits of his German studies, left the press; viz., a translation of Roos's 'Exposition of Daniel.'"[1] The rules laid down by Roos as canons for the interpretation of prophecy were adopted and adhered to by Dr. Henderson to the last; and thus this initial work seems to have exerted an important influence upon him as an expounder of prophecy.

But to return to the Icelandic Bible. Mr. Paterson was about to start for Russia on a Bible mission, and it became necessary, to expedite the work, that Mr. Henderson should obtain leave of entrance into Denmark, and then repair to Copenhagen, where he could urge on the printer and the reviser of the press in their daily work. His application the King of Denmark referred to the Chancery. The Chancery, after some delay, sent the petition back to his majesty, with a strong recommendation that it should be granted, and the royal assent was accordingly given. But annoying delays occurred in connection with the printing that remained to be done, as well as heavy expenses arising from the depreciation of the Danish currency, and the exorbitant war prices charged upon every article of food.

"The two years which were thus spent by him in the Danish capital, would have been tedious, had there not been great facilities in that city for the continuance of other labors. The translation of 'The Warning Voice,' and 'The End of Time' into Icelandic, was effected beneath his eye, as also that of the tract entitled 'Serious Considerations' into Danish. In preparation for

[1] Memoir, p. 84.

his contemplated journey, he was studying the language and ecclesiastical history of Iceland."[1]

So the memoir; and in addition to this, it adds that he was also prosecuting vigorously the study of Hebrew. "A Morocco Jew," says he, in a letter dated Dec. 1, 1812, "who has a beautiful pronunciation, reads a Hebrew chapter with me the one day, and I read an English chapter with him the other. I begin to speak a little with him in Hebrew."[2] Having received a suggestion from his friend Mr. Paterson, when on a visit to him in Sweden in March 1814, that when his Icelandic mission was completed he "might find bible-work to do in the regions to the north and west of Russia," he immediately began to turn his attention to the languages of those regions. About the same time, also, we find that he began the study of Arabic. He speaks of it as "remarkably easy, the structure being so much like the Hebrew, and there being so many Hebrew words in it." "The Grammar," he says, "will be an easy task. Its richness in words will be the principal difficulty."[3]

An object which Mr. Henderson earnestly desired to see effected before leaving the country was the organization of the earliest Bible Society in Denmark. This good work he was permitted to see accomplished under very favorable auspices, one of the rooms of the episcopal palace being offered for the purpose, and the meeting being attended by several men of high eminence. Soon after "this launching of Denmark's life-ark," all the needful preparations having been at last made, Mr. Henderson embarked for Iceland on the eighth of June, 1814. "The freight of Bibles," says the memoir, "had been subdivided, and the several packages forwarded during the spring to seven of the principal Icelandic ports, — an arrangement adopted by reason of the difficulty that would have attended their transmission across the interior of the island. The treaty of Kiel, in January 1814, had effectually done away with the restrictions and risks incident to the late war; and the Icelandic ship-owners had displayed a patriotic liberality in conveying the books free of expense."[4] After a five weeks' passage, he arrived in safety at Reykiavik, on the south-western coast of Iceland, and was well received by Bishop Vidalin, by his step-son, Sysselmand Thorgrimson, by Mr. Knudsen the Danish merchant, and several men of note in the Icelandic metropolis.

Mr. Henderson's printed account, entitled "Iceland, or the Journal of a Residence in that Island,"[5] is so copious, and so well known to the public, that it is not necessary to enter into the details of his journeyings. Suffice it to say, that in three journeys, each from Reykiavik as a point of departure, he explored the whole island, travelling not less than two thousand six hun-

[1] Memoir, p. 117. [3] P. 132. [5] In two vols. 8vo. Edinburgh, 1818.
[2] P. 118. [4] P. 137.

dred miles, ascertaining the spiritual condition of the people, and everywhere making efficient arrangements for the distribution of the word of God.

"In almost every hamlet there was new proof that such effort was needed; in each hamlet, proof also that the effort would meet with response on the part of willing purchasers. Here was a parish in which a folio Bible, greatly injured by use, had all its defective pages accurately supplied by the pen of a common peasant; and there another, whose lent copy had so long been retained by the islanders of Grimsey, that the right of its possession had become a disputed point. One copy in an island; two in a parish; twelve among two hundred people; six among two hundred and fifty; a clergyman seeking for seventeen long years to possess a copy of his own, and hitherto unable to secure the treasure; peasants who had offered, but offered in vain, to the amount of five-and-twenty shillings for a copy;—such are the incidents that crowd upon the page. The Testaments sent over in 1807 and 1812, were traced to their destination, but were found to have gone a very little way towards meeting the extensive demand. * * * The general intelligence of the people rendered their need of Scripture the more obvious. In a parish of four hundred, where all who were above eight years old had been taught to read, there might well be a universal desire for the Book of books."[1]

In the month of July, 1815, the initial steps were taken at Reykiavik which resulted in the formation of the Icelandic Bible Society, an institution which still exists, and, according to the latest communications, received several years since, had issued in all above ten thousand Bibles and Testaments. Having finished his work of exploration, Mr. Henderson sailed for Copenhagen, where he arrived Sept. 6, 1815. In bringing to a close the notice of this visit to Iceland, it is pertinent to add, that, while zealously and energetically executing his commission as agent of the British and Foreign Bible Society, he improved every opportunity to make himself acquainted with the remarkable natural phenomena of that wonderful island.

"He, in consequence, visited and inspected with ardent and indefatigable zeal the awfully sublime, yea, often terrific scenes, which abound in that land of volcanoes, in which often a strange conflict is seen between the elements of fire and water—between boiling hot springs and all the cold and freezing changes of snow and ice. There we find our traveller climbing up and descending mountains, standing between thundering masses of melting lava and rushing floods, and exhibiting an indomitable courage, amounting, in the opinion of his hardy Icelandic guides, to almost a provocation of dangers so immediate and threatening, that even a spectator at a distance could scarcely refrain from mingled feelings of admiration of his courage and calm self-possession, amidst surrounding scenes of horror, and of disapproval and

[1] Memoir, p. 155.

condemnation of a spirit of presumption, exposing health and life to needless risk and sacrifice. * * * Yet this very boldness, nay, rashness, enabled him to witness and describe scenes which few, if any, of his predecessors in travel had dared to approach so near, and to observe so closely."[1]

It should be added that Mr. Henderson, being a good Icelandic scholar, was thus enabled freely to converse with all classes of the native population, from the learned clergy and gentry to the illiterate farmer and day-laborer. "Thus joyfully and manfully proceeding on his errand of mercy, he was treated by high and low, by the clergy and the laity, in the most respectful manner. He was most kindly and hospitably entertained, often accompanied part of the way by those who had afforded him in their houses every accommodation and comfort in their power; or provided with safe guides, and dismissed with prayers, benedictions, and other affecting marks of the liveliest gratitude and Christian affection, by our Icelandic brethren, — and which they desired to evince to one who had been sent to them from a far distant nation as a messenger of peace, and an angel of mercy, with the gift of that Holy Book, which had already proved to millions, and would in time to come prove to generations yet unborn, an inexhaustible source of the purest instruction, and the most solid consolation."[2]

From his return to Copenhagen in September 1815, to October of the following year, Mr. Henderson was assiduously employed in journeying through Denmark and the adjacent regions of Pomerania and northern Germany, being, as he expressed it, "constantly on the wing." Wishing for a season of rest, he had already bespoken his passage to Leith, in Scotland, with the hope of spending some time among his friends at home, when he received notice of an appointment to visit St. Petersburgh, on an agency for the British and Foreign Bible Society. A letter written to Mr. Paterson under date of October 22, 1816, gives a delightful revelation of his feelings in view of this sudden change in his plans, and of his whole-hearted devotion to the cause of Christ. He says:

"What a complete change has instantaneously been effected in my plans! I imagined my continental labors were at a close for this season; had spent about eight days with my friends here in Altona; bespoke my passage on board one of the smacks for Leith; made every needful preparation for my departure, and was fondly dreaming of domestic enjoyments, when all at once I heard a voice behind me saying, ' This is the way, walk ye in it.' I ' turned to the voice that spake unto me,' and behold, my path was plain before me. Instead of Edinburgh, I was to regard St. Petersburgh as the place of my destination. On Sabbath last, after preaching my first sermon on

---

[1] Rev. Dr. Steinkopff, as quoted in memoir, p. 105.
[2] Dr. Steinkopff, as quoted above, p. 106.

Lot's wife, I received two letters from London, one five, the other only six days old, urging the necessity of my repairing without a moment's delay to St. Petersburgh, with the view of strengthening your hands in the work of the Lord."[1]

Of course he complied without hesitation, and wrote to the committee in London: "Had I not come to the determination instantly to comply with your request, how could I have borne the cutting reflection, 'Demas hath forsaken me, having loved the present world?'"[2]

In the middle of December we find him in the Russian capital, where his labors, after he had been duly initiated by Mr. Paterson (who was preparing for a temporary absence), date from about the commencement of the year 1817. Here he entered upon "another man's line of things made ready to his hand," for Mr. Paterson was an efficient Bible agent.

"The task was multiform. It consisted in seeing to the corrections of the proofs as they left the press, and in superintending the town-issue of those Scriptures, or portions of Scripture, that were already in stock; in transmitting copies, when needful, to the associations already formed in various parts of the empire, and in corresponding with the Astrachan and other missionaries about the translations or reëditions that were yet needed. French, Greek, Moldavian, Georgian, Calmuc, and other Bibles were in progress. Archimandrites and princes had to be consulted; translators had to be conferred with; paper, types, and binding had to be cared for; the depôt to be looked after; and committee-meetings, of several hours in duration, to be attended."[3]

How efficient was the Russian Bible Society at this period, may be inferred from the fact, that in a letter dated St. Petersburgh, June 8, 1817, Dr. Henderson states that from the establishment of the society, to the present time, its committee had "either published, or engaged in publishing, no fewer than *forty-three* editions of the sacred Scriptures, in *seventeen* different languages, forming a grand total of one hundred and ninety-six thousand copies."[4] Much of the success of the good cause he attributes to the warm patronage then extended by the Emperor Alexander to the Bible cause.

An incident that occurred during this visit to St. Petersburgh deserves a passing notice, as a further illustration of his self-denying missionary spirit. He received in January 1817 a very urgent and unexpected call to join the mission which had been projected by the London Missionary Society to the town of Irkutsk, in Siberia. Immediately he set apart a day for solemn self-examination and prayer with reference to his duty. The record he has left of this, shows how deep down into his soul the true spirit of Christianity had penetrated. The result of this prayerful deliberation was a decision to go on

---

[1] Memoir, p. 205.   [2] P. 205.   [3] P. 208.   [4] P. 219.

the mission, though he thereby renounced the fondly-cherished hope of a visit to his native country. But scarcely was this determination formed before he was called to reconsider it, on account of the strenuous efforts of the Bible Society to retain him in their employment; and this cost him a severer struggle than the first. But, with the same simplicity of purpose with which he had formed the resolve to go on the Irkutsk mission, he renounced it, and continued his labors in the service of the Bible Society.

During the residence in St. Petersburgh that has just been noticed, he received from Copenhagen a document, sealed with the triangle and the seven-stringed lyre of the Scandinavian Literary Society, nominating him one of its corresponding members. In the month of June following, a diploma was forwarded from Kiel, conferring upon him the title of Doctor in Philosophy.

The return of Dr. Paterson, in August, left him at liberty to revisit his native land, where he arrived in December, taking Stockholm, Copenhagen, and other places belonging to the field of his former labors, on his route.

The earliest news that reached Dr. Henderson upon his return to England was the tidings of his mother's death. His father's decease had occurred during his Icelandic explorations. Repairing to Edinburgh, he wrote the concluding part of his work on Iceland, and superintended the printing of the same. In the end of April, 1818, his volumes left the press, bearing a dedication to Prince Christian Frederic, of Denmark. So favorably were they received, that a second edition was soon called for, and an abridgment was published at a later date in the United States.

Soon afterwards (May 19) he was united in marriage to Miss Susannah Kennion, the daughter of Mr. John Kennion, in whom he found a companion of cultivated mind and congenial spirit, every way worthy of himself. The ensuing summer he spent in travelling for the Bible Society through England and Scotland. On Monday, Sept. 28, he, with his companion, set sail from Leith, on his third continental journey. It was intended that after revisiting the Hanoverian and Holstein auxiliaries, he should winter at Copenhagen, then pass, viâ Norway, to St. Petersburgh, and finally take up his abode at Astrachan, on the Caspian Sea, where rooms were already assigned him in the Mission House, and whither the bulk of his luggage was at once forwarded, to await his expected arrival. Such was the plan. He was now in the zenith of his popularity and influence as a Bible agent, and to human appearance everything promised a favorable issue. But, as in the beginning of his missionary career, so now he had to learn once more that God's ways are not man's ways. To him it happened, as it has to many other eminent servants of God, that, in the full tide of success, a series of reverses was to be encountered, by which his Christian activity should be turned into another channel, where, doubtless, God saw that his labors could best subserve the cause of his kingdom. When, in carrying out the plan above sketched, the time had arrived for his long-planned journey to Norway, he started from Gottenburgh on this expedition "in a small country conveyance, so low built that its structure naturally suggested a notion of perfect security. "It is hardly bigger than a wheelbarrow; if it were upset, you could scarcely be hurt, was the remark casually made."[1] But he had that very day to learn that

> "Safety consists not in escape
> From dangers of a frightful shape."

About mid-day, the little vehicle was upset, and the traveller's shoulder and the radius of the fore-arm were dislocated and otherwise injured. Unable to bear the motion of a carriage, he was conveyed to the river near by, and taken back along the Gotha Elf. Eventually, the bones in the fore-arm lost their power of flexion and rotation, and the delay which the accident had occasioned left no time for the journey to Norway.

Dr. Henderson proceeded to St. Petersburgh, which place was reached on the 11th of September, 1819. The studies which occupied the closing months of 1819, like those of the preceding winter at Copenhagen, consisted in the mastering of the Turkish, Tatar, and Persic languages, all of which would be needed for his anticipated Astrachan labors, upon which he hoped to enter the ensuing season. But a delay of a whole year was occasioned by the death of Dr. Paterson's wife, which made it necessary that the bereaved husband should have a temporary respite from his services at the Russian capital. It was not till March 1821 that Drs. Paterson and Henderson could arrange to start with Mr. Seroff, one of the committee, on their projected visit of exploration. Leaving St. Petersburgh, they proceeded, by Novgorod and Tver, to Moscow; thence, by Kalouga and Koursk, to Pultawa, the field so fatal to the Swedish hero; thence, by Tchernigov and Kiev, to Odessa, on the Black Sea. After this they made an eight days' Crimean trip, spending the Sabbath at Akhtiar, the modern *Sevastopol*. Thence they journeyed eastward to Taganrog, on the Sea of Azof, where Dr. Henderson was seized with an ague which clung to him with pertinacity during all the remainder of his journey. Crossing the Don, they entered Asia, and finally reached the long-looked-for Astrachan on the 13th of August, where a great part of Dr. Henderson's furniture and library were awaiting his permanent residence.

Starting again from Astrachan, on the first of October, on their way towards Persia, they crossed the Caucasian mountains; but, when they had advanced as far as Tiflis, their expedition was brought to a close by a difference of opinion between them and the Bible Society, which resulted in their tendering their resignation as its accredited agents. This had respect to Ali

---

[1] Memoir, p. 239.

Bey's Turkish version of the New Testament, with which the two friends were dissatisfied on grounds the validity of which was afterwards recognized, at least in a practical way, by the managers of the Bible Society. Recrossing the Caucasus, and ordering the goods which had arrived at Astrachan to be repacked and sent to St. Petersburgh, they hastened back to the Russian capital, which they reached early in February 1822. Here they were immediately retained in the service of the Russian Bible Society. To this Dr. Henderson devoted the last three years of his residence in Russia. It was not long before symptoms of a deep-laid scheme of opposition to the Bible cause began to manifest themselves. The plot, according to Dr. Paterson, embraced not only Greek ecclesiastics, but others of high eminence, among whom he names Metternich, the great Austrian diplomatist. To trace the history of this conspiracy against the word of truth, would be out of place in the present brief notice. How successful it was in the end, we all know. The Emperor Alexander remained personally friendly to the agents; but so limited had become the operations of the society, with no prospect of any enlargement in the future, that, in the spring of 1825, Dr. Henderson sought and obtained, through Prince Galitzin, the emperor's permission to resign his office. No time was lost in making arrangements for the homeward voyage, and on the the 5th of July, 1825, he and his were safely landed in the British metropolis. Dr. Paterson tarried a little longer, but he too was compelled to withdraw; and upon the accession of the Emperor Nicholas, all operations at the Bible House were speedily suspended, at least so far as concerned the distribution of the Scriptures to Russian subjects. "It only remains to be hoped," adds the memoir, "that the day may come when the second Alexander shall emulate the Christian graces and religious benevolence of the imperial relative whose name he bears; and that the house of Romanoff may yet be linked with Russia's highest and best prosperity."[1]

It ought to be added that, during his last three years' residence in St. Petersburgh, the Ethiopic was the language to which Dr. Henderson particularly devoted himself.

"Among his papers, and dated April, 1823, is a neatly-executed collation of St. John's Gospel, in the Ethiopic, as preserved in manuscript in the Public Imperial Library. His standard of comparison was the Ethiopic of the London Polyglott, and each instance of a various reading appears to be noted down in its order."[2]

But he did not content himself with being simply a student of God's word, and an agent for its distribution. He sought opportunity to preach it also. Turning his attention to the English sailors at Cronstadt, he began to preach

[1] Memoir, pp. 299, 300.   [2] P. 276.

there regularly beneath the Bethel flag, going out on Saturday and returning on the Monday's boat. The interest which he thus felt in seamen was cherished after his return to his native land, and he was often employed in advocating their cause on the platform or from the pulpit.

With Dr. Henderson's return to England, his missionary labors, extending over a term of twenty years, were brought to a close. We are now to contemplate him in the character of a teacher and an author. The decease of Rev. Dr. Bogue, in October 1826, left vacant the Theological Tutorship of the Missionary College at Hoxton, which was under the supervision of the Directors of the London Missionary Society. On the recommendation of several friends, Dr. Henderson was invited to take provisional charge of the missionary students, until some permanent arrangement could be made. Here he so approved himself to the Directors, that, in the following spring, they agreed on inviting him to accept the permanent tutorship in that institution. Thus, by one of those easy movements which are so characteristic of God's providential government, he was quietly inducted into an office for the fulfilling of whose duties he had been for years unconsciously qualifying himself. It was not, however, without hesitation, that he consented to occupy this responsible situation. In a letter addressed to the treasurer of the society, while the question of his acceptance was still pending, he says:

"Though I can truly say that nothing would give me greater delight than to be in any way instrumental in preparing missionary candidates for the great and weighty office towards which their attention is directed, I do feel the duties and responsibilities attaching to the Theological Tutorship to be of so very serious a nature, that I should consider it the height of presumption in a mere stripling like myself to think of undertaking the task.

"Surely, my dear sir, the Directors are not aware that the course of study which I enjoyed before leaving Scotland was extremely limited; and that during the *twenty* years I have spent in foreign parts, my time has been so completely occupied with business of an altogether desultory kind, as to preclude the possibility of my giving any attention to the study of systematic theology."[1]

That the objection thus ingenuously stated by him was in itself weighty, need not be denied. The fact, however, that he so felt its weight, is the best evidence that the Directors acted wisely in disregarding it. Had he been one of those men who are always boasting of their limited advantages in early life, instead of assiduously occupying themselves, as he did, in making amends for what was then deficient by the diligent improvement of all the means at their disposal, he would not have merited the confidence of the Directors. But, understanding that he was one who could master any subject to which he gave

[1] Memoir, pp. 307, 308.

close attention, and who would spare no pains to fit himself for the conscientious discharge of any duty he might be prevailed on to undertake, they, by their deputation, overcame his scruples, and induced his consent. He brought to his work not only a true missionary spirit, but also a rich fund of experience. Hence he was able to enrich his lectures with apposite and forcible illustrations, which gave pointedness and weight to the maxims that he inculcated. First of all he sought to elevate the standard of piety among the missionary students. "The business," said he, "on which you go forth is of so unearthly a nature, — it has so immediately to do with God, the souls of men, and the eternal world, — that except you are influenced by motives drawn from these sources, you must inevitably fail of becoming efficient laborers in the missionary field. It is not to learn languages, translate books, or introduce the arts and sciences of civilized life, that you go to the heathen. Whatever of this description may engage your attention, is merely subordinate and accessory. You go to instruct, to win, to save souls. To this everything must bend; to this everything must be laid under contribution. * * * And can you possibly expect to prove successful in such an enterprise, to enter heartily into it, or prosecute it with enthusiasm, vigor, and perseverance, if your spirit be worldly, and your affections low and grovelling?"[1] While thus giving, as was meet, the foremost place to the culture of the heart, he assiduously strove to foster a taste for theological and linguistic acquirements. The following extracts, from the pen of one who had access to Dr. Henderson's class-room, will best illustrate his characteristics as a teacher:

"As a teacher, he brought nothing into the class-room which had not been carefully and even elaborately prepared. * * * It was rather his intense application and indomitable industry, than any extraordinary talent, that distinguished him. If by genius is meant the undoubted possession of the creative or inventive faculty, then genius was not the property of my friend. If anything, he was rather wanting in imagination. * * * He never indulged much in illustration, and his illustrations never partook of the daring of genius. But if, on the other hand, 'genius is the instinct of enterprise,' and if the instinct of enterprise is labor, then, in this sense, my honored friend was the possessor of this mighty gift. * * * As Dr. Henderson was not a man who lived without a purpose, so neither was he a man to spend his hours without a plan. His time was faithfully divided; and in each division he had his self-appointed round of duties and engagements, to which he devoted himself with unwearied and strenuous perseverance. His lectures were the result of extensive reading and careful investigation. * * * He excelled in weighing evidence, and impressing upon it its relative value. His discrimination was clear, and his judgment was sound. He was wholly free from

[1] Memoir, p. 319.

the date of this re-issue. Abbott's "Corner Stone" underwent revision at his hand, and the English editions of Prof. Stewart's Commentaries also passed under his eye. In 1836 appeared his well-known treatise on "Divine Inspiration," which has passed through several editions. At a later period, after his labors at Highbury had been brought to a close, he superintended the republication of five works from the pen of the Rev. Albert Barnes, prefixing prefaces of his own to two of them, viz., the Commentaries on the books of Job and Revelation. The other works were, "Notes on the Book of Daniel," "The Way of Salvation," and "Essays on Science and Theology."

Passing by other works of minor importance published or edited by him, we come to his Commentaries. The first of these, on the Prophet Isaiah, appeared in the year 1840, when the author was now fifty-six years of age. It was the result of long, patient, earnest study. This book had sometimes formed the basis of his readings with the fourth year's class at college, and he justly felt that something further was needed in the way of elucidating it. Vitringa was too prolix; Lowth far from satisfactory, and abounding in many needless and conjectural emendations of the text. The modern German commentaries were all more or less tainted with neology; and the commentaries of Barnes and Alexander, in this country, had not yet appeared. It is stated by the biographer that "some four or five years seem to have been occupied in the actual compiling of the volume."[1] This commentary, like all the succeeding, he terms, "critical, philological, and exegetical." In the first of these departments, criticism of the sacred text, he steadfastly abides by the ordinary text, where there is no overwhelming amount of manuscript evidence in favor of some other reading. In his philological remarks he makes an abundant yet sober use of the cognate languages, relying, first of all, on a collation of the several passages in which a given word occurs in the sacred text, and having recourse to the cognate tongues only as a supplementary aid. In the exegetical department it is his aim to evolve the exact scope and force of the prophetic declarations as at first uttered, and under a full view of the circumstances that attended their utterance.

The same general characteristics belong to the present commentary on the "Minor Prophets," which appeared next in order, in the year 1845. This is the most learned and elaborate of all his works. In the wonderful diversity of style and manner by which each of the twelve Minor Prophets is so clearly distinguished from all the rest, — a diversity very apparent in the English version, but displaying itself in its full beauty only to him who reads them in the original, — Dr. Henderson's pen found a fine field of exercise, which it did not fail to improve in a very thorough way. It is stated

[1] Memoir, p. 390.

by the biographer that the popularity of this work among the students of the sacred text "has been fully as great as was that of his 'Isaiah,'— among the Americans even greater."[1] This is due partly, perhaps, to its greater intrinsic merit, but still more to the paucity of commentaries on the Minor Prophets, that unite rich and varied learning with the pure evangelical spirit.

It was after his retirement from Highbury that his commentaries on Jeremiah and Ezekiel appeared — the former in 1851, the latter in 1855. These are of a less elaborate character.

"The Commentary on Jeremiah contained, as it required, a proportionately smaller number of notes than had been needful in the preceding volumes. But the notes which it did thus contain have been deemed by no means inferior to those of an earlier date, either in thought or expression. * * * The five lamentations, or elegies, of the prophet, are appropriately included in the work."[2]

Of the book of the prophet Ezekiel it can hardly be said that for its full illustration it required fewer notes than Isaiah or the Minor Prophets. The brevity of Dr. Henderson's commentary on this book is ascribed in the biography to the fact that "the tide of life was receding, and the fulness of life's labors was diminishing."[3] It must not be supposed, however, that the matter which it contains is of an inferior quality. It embodies the results mainly of his previous investigations, stated in a clear and perspicuous manner, though the biblical student could wish for fuller discussions of some points.

To the above sketch, drawn from the materials furnished by the biography, with only here and there the addition of a passing reflection, it may be proper to add, by way of independent judgment, a single general criticism on Dr. Henderson as an expounder of prophecy. In perusing his commentaries, not a few will feel that he carries to an unwarrantable extent the principle of restricting the prophetic declarations and delineations to specific events. This makes necessary the assumption of very abrupt transitions backwards and forwards, where it would seem that the principle of a progressive fulfilment — "first the blade, then the ear, after that the full corn in the ear" — would have the double advantage of being in harmony with all that we know of the plan of God's government, and also of carrying the interpreter consistently through

---

[1] Memoir, p. 417. The present is a reprint from the English edition, with the exception of some few corrections furnished by Dr. Henderson himself. With the exception of the Ethiopic, the quotations from the cognate languages with which the commentary abounds, as also those from the Greek and Latin, have been corrected by a comparison with the original sources.
[2] Memoir, pp. 433, 434.
[3] P. 454.

passages in which the near and more remote future are manifestly blended. For example, in Isa. 4: 1, the reference is undeniably to judgments near at hand ; in the verses that follow, the future glory and safety of the church are exhibited as following and effected by the mighty judgments of Jehovah coöperating with the efficacious working of his Spirit. Both passages are closely connected by the introductory words of verse 2 : *In that day*.[1] Dr. Henderson, in his commentary, makes a distinct chapter to begin with verse 2, remarking that, " having depicted the wickedness of the Jews, and the awful judgments with which it would be punished, the prophet devotes this short chapter (chap. 4 : 2—6) to an announcement of the glory and felicity of the Church in the time of the Messiah." His note on the two introductory words is the following : " 2. בַּיּוֹם הַהוּא, *at* or *after that period*. The prep. בְּ does not always strictly express what is contained within any given time or space ; it also points out nearness, society, or accompaniment, that which is in connection with, or which follows upon something else. In prophetic vision, the two states of adversity and prosperity were so closely connected, that one period might be said to comprehend them both." The meaning of the last clause, taken in connection with what precedes, seems to be that the two states of prosperity and adversity are connected to the prophet's vision, because he does not discern the wide interval of time which actually separates them. Would it not be a more exact statement to say that the prophet sees the two states of prosperity and adversity in connection, because they are thus connected in their inmost nature, being both parts of one indivisible whole, viz., the progress of God's people through severe discipline, to peace and universal victory ; that, therefore, the predicted calamities which should befall the Jews in connection with their first captivity, though having a true historic fulfilment, yet stand as the representatives of like calamities to be repeated in their history, and that of the Christian Church, which is their true heir, as often as their sins shall make it necessary ; and that the promised future glory of God's people, though having its perfect accomplishment only in the latter days of the Christian dispensation, yet includes in itself all previous deliverances and enlargements from the prophet's day onward, even as the perfect day includes in itself the morning dawn which ushers it in, and is a part of it ?

To take another example : Dr. Henderson rightly regards Ezekiel's temple-vision as a symbolic representation, the model presented being ideal, not that of an actual structure to be literally realized in all its details in the coming future. But for limiting its direct reference to the resettlement of the Jews in their own land, and the literal restoration of their sanctuary privileges

---

[1] בַּיּוֹם הַהוּא.

and sacrificial institutes in the metropolis of Canaan, he seems to have no good warrant. The resettlement of the land of Canaan, and the rebuilding of the city and temple after the captivity, were only a part, and a very small part, of the "good things to come" which the vision shadowed forth. Its fulfilment belongs to the whole history of the church from Ezekiel's day onward, and it will be completed only in that yet future day when God shall make good to the uttermost his ancient promise: "O thou afflicted, tossed with tempest, and not comforted! behold I will lay thy stones with fair colors, and lay thy foundations with sapphires. And I will make thy windows of agates, and thy gates of carbuncles, and all thy borders of precious stones. And all thy children shall be taught of the Lord; and great shall be the peace of thy children."[1] Then shall the name of that spiritual city of God be called, in the fullest sense of the words, "THE LORD IS THERE."

Such would be the general criticism which we should offer on Dr. Henderson's commentaries. At the same time we should warmly commend them to the diligent study of the Biblical scholar, as rich sources of instruction and profit.

[1] Isaiah 54: 11—13.

GENERAL PREFACE.

The Minor Prophets are first mentioned as the Twelve by Jesus the Son of Sirach.[1] Under this designation, they also occur in the Talmudic tract, entitled Baba Bathra;[2] and Jerome specifies, as the eighth in the second division of the sacred books of the Jews, The Book of the Twelve Prophets, which, he says, they call *Thereasar*.[3] Melito, who is the first of the Greek Fathers that has left us a catalogue of these books, uses precisely the same language.[4] That they were regarded as forming one collective body of writings at a still earlier period, appears from the reference made by the protomartyr Stephen to the Book of the Prophets,[5] when quoting Amos v. 27. The same style is employed by the Rabbins, who call Isaiah, Jeremiah, Ezekiel, and the Twelve, the Four Latter Prophets.[6] They are also spoken of as one book by Gregory Nazianzen, in his poem, setting forth the component parts of the sacred volume.[7]

At what time, and by whom they were collected, cannot be determined with certainty. According to Jewish tradition, the collection of the sacred books generally is attributed to the men of the Great Synagogue, a body of learned Scribes, said to have been formed by Ezra, and continuing in existence till the time of Simon the Just, who flourished early in the third century before Christ. In the opinion of many, Nehemiah completed this collection, by adding to those books which had already obtained a place in the canon, such as had been written in, or near his own times.[8] If this actually was the case, it cannot be doubted that he must have availed himself of the authority of Malachi in determining what books were really entitled to this distinction; and this Prophet, who was the last in the series of inspired writers under the ancient dispensation, may thus be considered to have given to the canon the

---

[1] Καὶ τῶν δώδεκα προφητῶν τὰ ὀστᾶ ἀναθάλοι ἐκ τοῦ τόπου αὐτῶν. Ecclus. xlix. 10.

[2] בבא בתרא.

[3] תרי עשר; or, as it is generally contracted, תריסר.

[4] τῶν δώδεκα ἐν μονοβίβλῳ.

[5] Καθὼς γέγραπται ἐν Βίβλῳ τῶν προφητῶν, Acts vii. 42.

[6] ארבעה נביאים אחרנים.

[7] Μίαν μέν εἰσιν ἐς γραφὴν οἱ Δώδεκα·
Ὡσηὲ κ' Ἀμὼς, καὶ Μιχαίας ὁ τρίτος,
Ἔπειθ' Ἰωὴλ, εἶτ' Ἰωνᾶς, Ἀβδίας,
Ναούμ τε, Ἀββακούκ τε καὶ Σοφονίας,
Ἀγγαῖος, εἶτα Ζαχαρίας, Μαλαχίας,
Μία μὲν οἶδε. *Carmen* xxx. iii.

[8] —— Καὶ ὡς καταβαλλόμενος βιβλιοθήκην, ἐπισυνήγαγε τὰ περὶ τῶν βασιλέων καὶ προφητῶν, καὶ τὰ τοῦ Δαυὶδ, καὶ ἐπιστολὰς βασιλέων περὶ ἀναθεμάτων. 2 Macc. ii. 13.

sanction of Divine approbation. Within a century and a half afterwards, they were translated into Greek, along with the rest of the sacred books, and have ever since obtained an undisputed place among the oracles of God.

To these twelve prophetical books the epithet "Minor" has been applied, simply on the ground of their size, compared with those which precede them, and not with any view of detracting from their value, or of representing them as in any respect inferior in point of authority.

The books are not arranged in the same order in the Hebrew and Septuagint texts, and in neither is the chronology exactly observed, as may be seen from the following table, in which the mean time is assumed as the basis of the calculation:

HEBREW.	LXX.	CHRONOLOGICAL ORDER.	
1. Hosea.	1. Hosea.	1. Joel	about 865 B.C.
2. Joel.	2. Amos.	2. Jonah	" 810
3. Amos.	3. Micah.	3. Amos	" 790
4. Obadiah.	4. Joel.	4. Hosea	" 750
5. Jonah.	5. Obadiah.	5. Micah	" 730
6. Micah.	6. Jonah.	6. Nahum	" 710
7. Nahum.	7. Nahum.	7. Zephaniah	" 630
8. Habakkuk.	8. Habakkuk.	8. Habakkuk	" 608
9. Zephaniah.	9. Zephaniah.	9. Obadiah	" 590
10. Haggai.	10. Haggai.	10. Haggai	" 520
11. Zechariah.	11. Zechariah.	11. Zechariah	" 520
12. Malachi.	12. Malachi.	12. Malachi	" 440

Newcome, Boothroyd, and some other translators, have adopted the order which appeared to them to be chronologically correct; but in the present work that is retained which is found in the Hebrew Bible, and followed in the Vulgate, in all the authorized European versions, and in those of Michaelis, Dathe, De Wette, and others, simply on the ground of the facility of reference, which the other arrangement does not afford, but which is practically of greater importance than any advantage derivable from the change.

The Minor Prophets have generally been considered more obscure and difficult of interpretation than any of the other prophetical books of the Old Testament. Besides the avoidance of a minute and particular style of description, and the exhibition of the more general aspects of events only, which are justly regarded as essentially characteristic of prophecy, and the exuberance of imagery, which was so admirably calculated to give effect to the oracles delivered by the inspired Seers, but which to us does not possess the vividness and perspicuity which it did to those to whom it was originally exhibited, there are peculiarities attaching more or less to each of the writers, arising either from his matter, or from the manner of its treatment, which present difficulties of no ordinary magnitude to common readers, and many that are calculated to exercise the ingenuity, and, in no small degree, to perplex the mind of the more experienced interpreter. We are frequently left to guess historical circumstances from what we otherwise know of the features of the times, and sometimes we have no other means of ascertaining their character than what are furnished by the descriptive terms employed in the predictions themselves. Though in such cases general ideas may be collected respecting the persons or things which are presented to view in the text, yet we want the historical commentary which would elucidate and give point to its various particulars. The accounts contained in the books of Kings and Chronicles are frequently too brief to furnish us with a key to many of the prophecies which were fulfilled during the period which they embrace; while the pages of profane history only slightly touch, if they touch at all, upon events which the scope and bearing of the predictions determine to periods within the range of subjects professedly treated of by its authors.

Against none of these prophets has the charge of obscurity been brought with greater appearance of justice than against Hosea, whose prophecies are obviously, for the most part, mere compendia, or condensed notes of what he publicly delivered, though preserving, to a considerable extent, the logical and verbal forms which characterized his discourses. Besides a profusion of metaphors, many of which are derived from sources little accordant with the dictates of occidental taste, we find in his book a conciseness of expression, an abruptness of transition, a paucity of connecting particles, and changes in person, number, and gender, to which nothing equal occurs in any of the other prophets. The visions of Zechariah also are not without their difficulties; but these arise, not from the language, which is remarkably simple in its character, but from the symbols which represent certain historical scenes and events.

The period of time within which the authors of the books flourished, includes the entire prophetic cycle of more than four hundred years — Isaiah, Jeremiah, Ezekiel, and Daniel, having also lived in it. It is unquestionably the most eventful in the history of the Hebrews. It embraces the introduction of image-worship, and that of Phœnician idolatry, with all its attendant evils, among the Israelites; the regicidal murders and civil wars which shook their kingdom to its centre; the corruptions of the Jewish state in consequence of its adoption of the idolatrous practices of the northern tribes; the Assyrian and Egyptian alliances; the irruption of the Syrian, Assyrian, and Chaldean armies into Palestine; the Assyrian and Babylonian captivities; the Persian conquests; the release of the Jews, and their restoration to their own land; and the state of affairs at Jerusalem during the governorship of Nehemiah. Upon all these various events and circumstances, the predictions, warnings, threatenings, promises, and moral lessons, have, in a multiplicity of aspects, a more or less pointed and important bearing. Events subsequent to this period likewise form the subjects of prophetic announcement — such as the progress of Alexander the Great; the successes of the Maccabees; the corruptions which prevailed in the last times of the Jewish state; the destruction of Jerusalem by the Romans; the dispersion, future conversion, and restoration of the Jews; and the universal establishment of true religion throughout the world. Intermingled with these topics, and giving to each a significance and interest which it could not otherwise have possessed, are some of the clearest and most illustrious predictions respecting the Messiah, in his divine and human, his sacerdotal and suffering, and his regal and all-conquering character that are to be found in the Old Testament.

It is impossible seriously to peruse this collection of prophetical writings without discovering the Omniscient Eye to which all future events, with the most minute of their attendant circumstances, are present; the Omnipotent Arm, which, in the most difficult cases, secures the accomplishment of the Divine purposes; the glorious attributes of Jehovah as the Moral Governor of the universe, and the special Friend and Protector of his people; the deep depravity of the human heart; the multiform phases of moral evil; and the just retributions which befall mankind in the present state of existence. These, and numerous subjects of a kindred nature, furnish abundance of matter "profitable for doctrine, for reproof, for correction, for instruction in righteousness," which, while it is able to make "men wise unto salvation, through faith which is in Christ Jesus," is also admirably fitted to "make the man of God perfect, thoroughly furnished unto all good works." 2 Tim. iii. 15—17.

The principles on which the Author has proceeded in preparing the present work are the same by which he was guided in composing his Commentary on the Prophet Isaiah. It has been his great aim to present to the view of his readers the mind of the Spirit as expressed in the written dictates of inspiration. With the view of determining this, he has laid under contribution all the means within his reach, in order to ascertain the original state of the Hebrew text, and the true and unsophisticated meaning of that text. He has constantly had recourse to the collection of various readings made by Kennicott and De Rossi; he has compared the renderings of the LXX., the Targum, the Syriac, the Arabic, the Vulgate, and other ancient versions: he has availed himself of the results of modern philological research; and has conducted the whole under the influence of a disposition to place himself in the times of the sacred writers — surrounded by the scenery which they exhibit, and impressed by the different associations, both of a political and a spiritual character, which they embody. In all his investigations he has endeavored to cherish a deep conviction of the inspired authority of the books which it has been his object to illustrate, and of the heavy responsibility which attaches to all who undertake the interpretation of the oracles of God.

In no instance has the theory of a double sense been permitted to exert its influence on his expositions. The Author is firmly convinced, that the more this theory is impartially examined, the more it will be found that it goes to unsettle the foundations of Divine Truth, unhinge the mind of the biblical student, invite the sneer and ridicule of unbelievers, and open the door to the extravagant vagaries of a wild and unbridled imagination. Happily the number of those who adhere to the multiform method of interpretation is rapidly diminishing; and there cannot be a doubt, that, in proportion as the principles of sacred hermeneutics come to be more severely studied, and perversions of the word of God, hereditarily kept up under the specious garb of spirituality and a more profound understanding of Scripture, are discovered and exposed, the necessity of abandoning such slippery and untenable ground will be recognized, and the plain, simple, grammatical and natural species of interpretation, adopted and followed.

CONTENTS.

	PAGE
HOSEA	1
JOEL	87
AMOS	123
OBADIAH	183
JONAH	196
MICAH	216
NAHUM	264
HABAKKUK	285
ZEPHANIAH	320
HAGGAI	340
ZECHARIAH	354
MALACHI	440

HOSEA.

PREFACE.

RESPECTING the origin of this prophet nothing is known beyond what is stated in the title, ver. 1. If, as is now generally agreed, Jeroboam II. died about the year B. C. 784, and Hezekiah began to reign about B. C. 728, it would appear from the same verse that the period of his ministry must have embraced, at the very least, fifty-six years. To some this has seemed incredible, chiefly on the ground that his prophecies are comprised within the compass of fourteen brief chapters. It must be remembered, however, that the prophets were not uninterruptedly occupied with the delivery of oracular matter. Sometimes considerable intervals elapsed between their communications, although there can be no doubt that, having once been called to the office of public teachers, they devoted much of their time to the instruction of the people among whom they lived. Besides, there is no reason for believing the contents of the book are all that he ever uttered. They constitute only such portions of his inspired communications respecting the Israelites, as the Holy Spirit saw fit to preserve for the benefit of the Jews, among whose sacred writings they were incorporated.

Hosea was contemporary with Isaiah, Micah, and Amos, and, like the last-mentioned prophet, directed his prophecies chiefly against the kingdom of the ten tribes.

From the general tenor of his book, and from the history of the times contained in the Books of Kings, he manifestly lived in a very corrupt age. Idolatry, a fondness for foreign alliances, civil distractions, and vice of every description abounded, the impending judgments on account of which he was commissioned to announce.

Though he occasionally mentions Judah, yet the entire scene is laid in the land of Israel, where, there can be little doubt, he lived and taught.

With the exception of the first and third chapters, which are in prose, the book is rhythmical, and abounds in highly figurative and metaphorical language. The diction is exceedingly concise and laconic; so much so, that Jerome justly describes him as "commaticus et quasi per sententias loquens." The sentences are in general brief and unconnected; the unexpected change of person is of frequent occurrence; number and gender are often neglected; and the similes and metaphors are frequently so intermixed, that no small degree of attention is required in order to discover their exact bearing and force. He is more scanty in his use of the particles than the other prophets, which adds not a little to the difficulty of interpreting his prophecies. In many instances he is highly animated, energetic, and sublime. Of all the prophets he is, in point of language, the most obscure and hard to be understood.

CHAPTER I.

This chapter contains the inscription, ver. 1; a representation of the idolatrous kingdom of Israel under the image of a female, whom the prophet was ordered to marry, but who should prove false to him, 2, 3; and of the punishment with which it was to be visited, by the symbolical names of the prophet's children, together with a distinct intimation that the kingdom of Judah should not be involved in the same destruction, 4-8. It concludes with a gracious promise of the joint restoration of all the tribes, and their flourishing condition in the land of their fathers, subsequent to the Babylonish captivity.

---

1 THE word of Jehovah which was communicated to Hosea, the son of Beeri, in the days of Uzziah, Jotham, Ahaz, and Hezekiah, kings of Judah; and in the days of Jeroboam, the son of Joash, king of Israel.

2 The beginning of the word of Jehovah by Hosea. Jehovah said

1. The kings here mentioned are those specified in the inscription to the prophecies of Isaiah, with the addition of Jeroboam, the son of Joash, commonly called Jeroboam the Second, to distinguish him from the son of Nebat. This monarch carried on very successful wars with his northern neighbors, and recovered out of their hands the territories of which they had taken possession; but though thus signally prospered, as an instrument in the hand of Jehovah, he was a wicked character, and greatly promoted idolatry in Israel. See 2 Kings xiv. 23-28.

By דְּבַר, *word*, is meant the prophetic matter contained in the book. Thus the Targ. נְבוּאַת פִּתְגָם.—הָיָה is commonly rendered "came" in such connection, but it seems preferable to retain its usual signification, only adding another verb, as *communicated, imparted*, or such like, to suit the English idiom.

2. דִּבֶּר is equivalent to דָּבָר and is rendered as a noun in the LXX., Targ., and Syr. It occurs in the absolute form דַּבֵּר, Jer. v. 13, with a similar reference to inspired matter. Some have attempted to show from the words תְּחִלַּת דִּבֶּר־יְהוָה בְּהוֹשֵׁעַ that Hosea was the first of the prophets employed to convey Jehovah's messages to his ancient people; but contrary to the import of the words, which merely refer to the commencement of the prophecies of Hosea. For the use of the preposition בְּ in such connection, see Numb. xii. 2; 2 Sam. xxiii. 2. Comp. ἐν προφήταις, Heb. i. 1.

The transaction here described, and that narrated chap. iii. 1, are clogged with almost insuperable difficulties; and, as may be expected, have given rise to very different modes of interpretation. By most commentators, the things specified are considered to have actually taken place in the outward history of the prophet. Others, as Abarbanel, Kimchi, Maimonides, Ruffinus, Œcolampadius, Marckius, Pococke, and recently Hengstenberg, regard the whole in the light of internal prophetic vision; while Calvin, Luther, Osiander, Rivetus, Danæus, Rosenmüller, Hitzig, and others, treat it as a species of parabolical representation, in which the prophet appropriates to himself imaginary circumstances, aptly fitted to impress the minds of those whom he addressed with a sense of their wickedness, and the punishment to which it exposed them.

To the last of these opinions it may justly be objected that the language, "And Jehovah said to Hosea, Go," etc. is identical with that used Is. vii. 3, viii. 1, xx. 2; Jer. xiii. 1-7, xviii. 1, 2, xix.;

to Hosea: Go, take thee a lewd woman, and lewd children, for the land hath committed great lewdness, in a state of separation from Jehovah.

Ezek. iv. v. xii. xxiv.; and in many other passages, which cannot without violence be understood parabolically. Not the slightest hint is given, in the present case, that the circumstances are fictitious. Besides, it has been observed, that there is no instance of any of the prophets ever making himself the subject of a parable.

The same objection lies with equal force against the assumption, that the things described were merely exhibited internally to the mind of the prophet. The Divine mandate was doubtless internal; but there is no intimation that what follows was in vision, any more than in the instances above quoted. On the contrary, it is set forth as real matter of fact. When internal scenic representations were granted, the verbs הָיָה or רָאָה, to see, are always employed to describe the experience of the person who viewed them, which is not the case here. See Is. vi.; Jer. xxiv. 1; Ezek. ii. 9 — iii. 3; Zech. i. 8, ii. iii. etc. Comp. also the phraseology of the Apocalypse.

We are, therefore, shut up to the literal interpretation, according to which the transactions, though symbolical, were real, and outward in the history of Hosea. Those, however, who adopt this view, are not agreed on the subject of the females specified: — some being of opinion that only one is intended in both passages; others, two; some, that Gomer was not a lewd character before the prophet took her, but became such afterwards; others, that she was originally unchaste; some, as Thomas Aquinas, that he did not marry her at all, but merely lived with her as a concubine! Lyra and Newcome think that nothing more is meant by "a wife of lewdness," than an Israelitess — one of those who had become guilty of spiritual fornication or idolatry. The position that Hosea was commanded to marry an impure female cannot be sustained, for two reasons. First, the children were clearly those afterwards described as born to the prophet, and are

spoken of as lewd as well as their mother. Secondly, on the supposition that Gomer had been guilty of acts of impurity previous to her connection with the prophet, there would be no congruity in constituting her a type of Israel, who is represented as lewd because she had lapsed into idolatry, in violation of the marriage contract entered into at Sinai. See Gesen. Lex. p. 306, 2. Consistency of interpretation absolutely requires the adoption of this view of the subject, as is admitted both by Hengstenberg and Hitzig. The objections otherwise produced by the former of these authors against the literal character of the transactions are more specious than real. Besides being the most obvious and natural, it has much to recommend it on the ground of the public notoriety which infidelity on the part of the wife of a prophet must have created, and its aptness to typify the conduct of the Israelites towards Jehovah. It may indeed be said, that his marrying a notoriously lewd character must have produced a much greater sensation. True, but besides the encouragement which it must have been calculated to give to the formation of unhallowed and irreligious connections, it would not, as was just observed, have been in accordance with the design of the transaction, which was, not to represent the character of the Hebrews before the period of their national reception into alliance with Jehovah, but their conduct as exhibited in the pages of their subsequent history. The phrases אֵשֶׁת זְנוּנִים, וְיַלְדֵי זְנוּנִים, *a lewd woman and lewd children*, have the same import, and are not to be interpreted as if the mother alone were guilty, and the children merely the product of her guilty conduct. Comp. the phrase יַלְדֵי פֶשַׁע, *children of transgression*, i. e. transgressors. Thus as to sense the Targ.; and the Syr. ܘܒܢܝܐ

ܕܙܢܝܢ, *and children that commit lewdness.* Thus also Rosenmüller. Both are

3 So he went and took Gomer, the daughter of Diblaim, and
4 she conceived, and bare him a son. And Jehovah said unto
him, Call his name JEZREEL; for yet a little while, and I will
avenge the blood of Jezreel upon the house of Jehu, and will
5 cause the kingdom of the house of Israel to cease. And it shall
come to pass in that day, that I will break the bow of Israel in
the valley of Jezreel.

anticipative as to the relation of the prophet, though typical of what had already taken place on the part of the ten tribes. Viewed as a kingdom they are represented as a mother; and as individual subjects of that kingdom, they are spoken of as her children. The plural זְנוּנִים is emphatic, as הַמָּה in אִישׁ הָעָם, etc. Comp. זְנוּנֵי אִשָּׁה, chap. iv. 12, and ii. 4. That they are otherwise to be identified appears from the use of קַח, take, which properly applies only to the female, but here governs both nouns, as Jerome observes, ἀπὸ κοινοῦ. The reason of the symbolic action is assigned at the close of the verse — the atrocious conduct of the Israelites in renouncing the pure worship of Jehovah, and addicting themselves to idolatry. Comp. Lev. xvii. 7; xx. 5, 6; Hos. iv. 12. הָאָרֶץ, the land, is put, by metonymy, for its inhabitants. The preposition מִן has here the force of a negative, which strongly expresses the state of separation which had taken place.

3. That the names *Gomer* and *Diblaim* are to be taken symbolically, as Hengstenberg interprets, does not appear. His exposition of them is fanciful, as is that of Jerome, who takes pretty much the same view. The use of לוֹ, *to him*, i. e. to Hosea, proves that the child was not of spurious origin. The word is wanting, indeed, in three of Kennicott's MSS., and one of De Rossi's, the Complut. edition of the LXX., the Itala, and the Arab.; but the omission in all probability originated in an attempt to render the phraseology comformable to that of verses 6 and 8.

4, 5. יִזְרְעֶאל, *Jezreel*, i. e. God will *scatter*, from זָרַע, to *scatter*, *disperse*, as in Zech. x. 9; Targ. מְבַדְּרָא. It was otherwise the proper name of a city in the tribe of Issachar, on the brow of the central valley in the great plain of the same name, and the royal residence of Ahab and his successors. It was here Jehu exercised acts of the greatest cruelty, 2 Kings x. 11, 14, 17. These acts were speedily to be avenged in the extinction of the royal family, and the entire cessation of the Israelitish state. It had been announced to Jehu that his sons should occupy the throne till the fourth generation, 2 Kings x. 30. Two of these generations had passed away by the time of the prophet — Jeroboam being the great grand-son. In the following generation, the prediction received its accomplishment. By the "bow of Israel" is meant her military prowess, which was completely subdued by the Assyrian army. The valley here mentioned, afterwards called *Esdraelon*, was famous for the battles fought there from the most ancient times. It consists of the broad elevated plain which stretches from the Jordan to the Mediterranean, near Mount Carmel, and is well adapted to military operations. Accordingly, Dr. E. D. Clarke observes, "Jews, Gentiles, Saracens, Christian Crusaders, and Anti-Christian Frenchmen, Egyptians, Persians, Druses, Turks, and Arabs, warriors out of every nation which is under heaven, have pitched their tents upon the plains of Esdraelon, and have beheld the various banners of their nations wet with the dews of Tabor and Hermon." It was, therefore, natural that the Israelites should endeavor to make a stand against the Assyrians in this valley; but being overpowered by numbers were obliged to succumb to the enemy. Of this discomfiture, and the consequent dispersion of the ten tribes, the name of the prophet's son was symbolical.

CHAP. I. HOSEA. 5

6   And she conceived again, and bare a daughter; and He said to him, Call her name LO-RUHAMAH; for I will no more have mercy upon the house of Israel, but will utterly take them
7   away. But I will have mercy upon the house of Judah, and will save them by Jehovah their God, and will not save them by bow, nor by sword, nor by battle, nor by horses, nor by horsemen.
8   And she weaned LO-RUHAMAH, and conceived, and bare a
9   son. And He said, Call his name LO-AMMI; for ye are not my
10 people, and I will not be yours. Nevertheless the number of the children of Israel shall be as the sand of the sea, which can neither be measured nor numbered; and it shall be, that instead of its having been said to them, Ye are not my people, it shall be said to them, Ye are the children of the living God.
11 Then shall the children of Judah, and the children of Israel, be

6, 7. לֹא רֻחָמָה, Lo-RUHAMAH, i. e. *unpitied.* נָשָׂא לְ elsewhere signifies *to forgive;* and were the verb preceded by the copulative וְ, it might be so rendered here, only supplying the negative לֹא from the preceding clause; but as כִּי, *but,* excludes such repetition, the phrase must be rendered as in the translation. LXX. ἀντιτασσόμενος ἀντιτάξομαι αὐτοῖς. Syr. ܡܛܥܐ ܐܛܥܐ ܐܢܘܢ. Vulg. *oblivione obliviscor* eorum — reading נָשֹׁא יַשֶּׁה, which is found in De Rossi's MS. 596, at first hand, instead of נָשֹׂא. The kingdom of Israel was never more to be restored, though, in conjunction with the Jews, the scattered Israelites were to return to Canaan after the Babylonish captivity, ver. 11. It was to be very different with the Jewish power. Though likewise attacked, and threatened with utter extinction by Sennacherib, they were mercifully delivered by a divine interposition, without all human aid. And though they were afterwards carried away to Babylon, their civil polity was restored, which was not the case with the Israelites. מִלְחָמָה, *war,* stands elliptically for אַנְשֵׁי מִלְחָמָה, *warriors.*

8. The mention here made of the weaning of Lo-Ruhamah, seems designed rather to fill up the narrative, than to describe figuratively any distinct treatment of the Israelites.

9. לֹא עַמִּי, Lo-AMMI, i. e. *not my people,* further sets forth the rejection of the ten tribes by Jehovah. Nothing could have been better calculated to make an impression upon the minds of his countrymen, than for the prophet thus to give to one child after another a name strongly significant of the disastrous circumstances to which they should be reduced. Instead of לֹא־אֶהְיֶה לָכֶם, *I will not be yours,* i. e. your God, Houbigant and Newcome would read לֹא אֱלֹהֵיכֶם, *I am not your God:* but though the antithesis is common, it admits of an ellipsis, just as in Ezek. xvi. 8, there is an ellipsis of לְאִשָּׁה. Comp. Ps. cxviii. 6. The MSS. and versions exhibit no variation.

10, 11. These verses contain a gracious promise of the recovery of the descendants of the Israelites, along with those of their brethren the Jews, at the termination of the Babylonish captivity. Though entirely and for ever broken up as a distinct kingdom, yet, during the period of their residence in the regions of the East, whither they were to be transported, they should greatly multiply, and afterwards be reinstated in the privileges of adoption, as members of the theocracy. The eleventh verse teaches the reunion of all the tribes, and their return under Zerubbabel to their own land. That this prince is meant by the רֹאשׁ אֶחָד, *one head,* must be maintained,

gathered together, and they shall appoint for themselves one
12 head, and shall come up out of the land. For great shall be the
day of Jezreel. Say ye unto your brethren, Ammi; and to
your sisters, Ruhamah.

since the Messiah, who is by many supposed to be intended, is nowhere spoken of as appointed by men, but always as the choice and appointment of God, ארץ, *land*, signifies, in this connection the country of Babylon, not excluding those other regions of the East in which the descendants of the different tribes were found. יזרעאל, *Jezreel*, is obviously used here in a different acceptation from that in which it is taken ver. 4. That of *sowing* is alone appropriate. Illustrious should be the period when the tribes should again be sown in their own country. Comp. chap. ii. 22, 23; Jer. xxxi. 27.

The principle on which part of ver. 10, and chap. ii. 23, are quoted, Rom. ix. 25, 26, and 1 Pet. ii. 10, seems to be that of analogy. As God had taken pity upon the ten tribes, who had become heathens, as it respects idolatrous and other practices, so he had pitied the Gentiles who had been in the same circumstances. What was said of the one class was equally descriptive of the other.

CHAPTER II.

The prophet proceeds in this chapter to apply the symbolical relation described in the preceding. He calls the Israelites to reform their wicked conduct, 1, 2; threatens them with a series of calamities, the effect of which should be their repentance and return to the service of Jehovah, 3-15; and promises a gracious restoration to his favor, and the enjoyment of security and prosperity in their own land, 16-23.

---

1   Contend with your mother, contend;
2   For she is not my wife,
    Neither am I her husband:
    That she may remove her lewdness from her face,
    And her adulteries from between her breasts.

1, 2. The individual members of the Israelitish state are here summoned to urge upon their nation the consideration of its wickedness in having departed from God. Of these the *nation* of the ten tribes was the אם, *mother*. Cocceius, Dathe, Kuinoel, and Rückert, render כִּי, *that*, and interpret: Argue the point with your nation, and show her that in consequence of her wicked conduct all relations between us have ceased. The casual signification of the conjunction, however, seems preferable. The words which it introduces form a parenthesis; and ותסר, which, though future, is to be rendered potentially: *that she may remove* connects with ריבו, *contend ye*. The ו is, as frequently to be taken τελικῶς. The repetition of ריבו is emphatic, as *ducite* in Virgil:—

"Ducite ab urbe domum, mea carmina, ducite Daphnin."

By זנוניה נאפופיה, *fornications and adulteries*, are meant the tokens or indications of lewd character:—boldness of

3 Lest I strip her naked,
And set her as in the day when she was born,
And make her as the desert,
And make her like a dry land,
And cause her to die with thirst.
4 Upon her children I will have no mercy,
For they are lewd children.
5 Because their mother hath committed lewdness,
Their parent hath acted shamefully;
For she said: I will follow my lovers,
That give me my bread and my water,
My wool and my flax, my oil and my wine.

countenance, and an immodest exposure of the breasts. Both forms are reduplicate, to express the enormity of the evil. What the prophet has in view is the reckless and unblushing manner in which the Israelitish nation practised idolatry. The LXX. have read מִפָּנַי, "from *my* face;" improperly in this connection, though a similar phrase occurs elsewhere.

3. A striking accumulation of synonymous denunciations for the purpose of describing the state of complete destitution to which the idolatrous Israelites would be reduced by the infliction of divine judgments. They should be placed in circumstances analogous to those in which they had originally been in Egypt. Comp. Ezek. xvi. 4; xxiii. 25, 26, 28, 29. For מִדְבָּר comp. Jer. ii. 6.

4. Individuals might expect that they would escape, and not be treated as the nation in its collective capacity; but Jehovah here declares, that he would treat them according to the demerits of their individual wickedness. For בְּנֵי זְנוּנִים, comp. יַלְדֵי זְנוּנִים, ch. i. 2. The second noun is, as frequently, used adjectively.

5. כִּי, *since* or *because*, and לָכֵן, *therefore*, ver. 8, correspond to each other, the former marking the protasis, the latter the apodosis. The second כִּי introduces parenthetically an illustration of the statement made at the beginning of the verse. הוֹרָה is the feminine participle of הָרָה *to conceive, be pregnant,* Comp. הוֹרָתִי, Song iii. 4. According to the Jewish exegesis, הוֹרָה, Gen. xlix. 26, is used of male progenitors. The Targ. and Jarchi suppose teachers to be here meant; but the term is merely a synonyme of אֵם, *mother,* in the preceding hemistich. Interpreters are not agreed respecting the rendering of הוֹבִישָׁה. In most instances in which the word occurs it certainly has the transitive signification; but here the intransitive seems more appropriate. Comp. Jer. vi. 15, where it is explained by בִּי הוֹעֵבָה עָשׂוּ. Comp. also הִתְעִיב, הֵרַע, הֵיטִיב, as Hiph. intransitives. The paragogic ה in אֵלְכָה, elongating the future, is expressive of a decided purpose, desire, or bent of mind; it is my settled determination to follow those who richly supply my wants in return for my religious services. מְאַהֲבִים *lovers,* which is here employed metaphorically to denote *idols,* is seldom used except in a bad sense. This interpretation, which is that of Joseph Kimchi and Abarbanel, is more in keeping with the symbolical character of the prophecy, than that suggested by the Targ. בְּנֵי עַמִּךְ הָרְעִים, which takes the word in the sense of idolaters, or idolatrous nations, such as Assyria, etc. Comp. as strictly parallel, Jer. xliv. 17-19. The language indicates complete alienation of heart from Jehovah, the only giver of all good, and a blind confidence in, and devotion to the service of idols. The articles specified comprehend both the necessaries and the luxuries of ancient Hebrew life. שֶׁמֶן, *oil,* is much in use among the Orientals, both in its simple

6 Therefore, behold! I will hedge up thy way with thorns,
And will raise a wall, that she may not find her paths.
7 And she shall eagerly pursue her lovers, but she shall not overtake them;
And shall seek them, but shall not find them:
Then shall she say: I will go and return to my first husband,
For it was better with me then than now.
8 Because she knew not that it was I that gave her
The corn, and the new wine, and the oil;
And furnished her abundantly with silver and gold,
Which they made into images of Baal:
9 Therefore I will take back my corn in its time,
And my new wine in its season;
And I will recover my wool and my flax,
Designed to cover her nakedness.

state, and as compounded with other ingredients. It is specially applied as ointment to the body after bathing. Comp. Psalm xxiii. 5; Prov. xxi. 17. יִצְהָר denotes here all kinds of artificial drink, being used in distinction from מַיִם. The Aldine edition of the LXX. reads ὁ οἶνός μου; but the usual reading is πάντα ὅσα μοι καθήκει, with which the Targ. and Syr. agree. The word occurs, Ps. cii. 10; Prov. iii. 8; and is evidently derived from שָׁקָה. Arab. سقى;

Eth. ስቀየ : to make to drink, to water.

6. For הִנְנִי in הִנְנִי־שָׂךְ the LXX. Arab. and Syr. read הִנֵּה, but most likely in order to produce uniformity in the use of the affix. The metaphor here employed is borrowed from the condition of a traveller whose progress is interrupted by a hedge thrown across his path, or who can no longer pass through the gap of an enclosure which used to be in his way; and who is consequently reduced to straits and difficulties. Turned out of his accustomed course, he is bewildered, and strives in vain to extricate himself. Comp. Job xix. 8; Lam. iii. 7, 9. גְּדֵרָה, a wall, is pointed גָּדֵר, in the editions of J. H. Michaelis, and Jahn, and this punctuation Hengstenberg attempts, without success, to defend. The wall means the external hindrances which the captivity interposed between the ten tribes and the objects of their idolatrous attachment.

7. Convinced by bitter experience of the folly of idolatry, the Israelites would renounce it, and return to the service of Jehovah. רִדְּפָה is intensive, and expresses the ardor of the pursuit. The Vau in וְאָמְרָה, marking the apodosis, points out the consequence or result of the failure — a resolution to turn from idols to serve the living God. It might be rendered so that, but not in order that, as Manger proposes. אָז, then, designates the period previous to the apostasy of the ten tribes, when in reward for external obedience, they enjoyed temporal blessings. Thus the Targ. אֲרֵי טָב לִי בַד הֲוֵיתִי פָלְחָא קֳדָמוֹהִי מִכְּעַן לָא אִצְלַח לְעַגְלַיָּא.

8, 9. ו and לָכֵן at the beginning of these verses stand in the same relation to each other as כִּי and לָכֵן, verses 5th and 6th. Before יָדְעָה supply אֲשֶׁר. By בַּעַל, Baal, the prophet means "images of Baal," the singular being used collectively for the plural. Comp. ch. viii. 4, where עֲצַבִּים, idols, correspond to בַּעַל in the present case. Hitzig would restrict וְזָהָב, understood, to זָהָב, gold, supposing the golden calves set up at Bethel and Dan to be meant; but, as it does not appear that the name of Baal was ever applied to them, his interpretation is groundless. See chap. viii. 4; which also clearly proves that by עָשׂוּ

10 And now I will expose her vileness before her lovers,
And none shall deliver her out of my hand.
11 And I will cause all her joy to cease;

לְבַעַל we are not to understand the consecration of the silver and gold to the service of Baal, but the actual conversion of these precious metals into images of that idol, or át least into plating with which to cover such as were made of wood. 2 Chron. xxiv. 7, to which Secker appeals in favor of the former meaning of the phrase, is also to be so understood. The rendering of Gesenius, "which *they offered* to Baal," is equally objectionable; the phrase עָשָׂה לְ, when thus used, being referred to sacrificial victims. Targ. מְנִיאָה עָבְדִי לְטַעֲוָתָא. Hengstenberg attempts to support the position that consecration is meant; but his reasons are altogether futile. The very passage which he quotes as parallel (Ezek. xvi. 17, 18,) is directly opposed to his exegesis of the phrase. *Baal* was perhaps the most ancient of all the gods worshipped in the East. He was, according to Dr. Münter, the representative of the sun, the generative power in the eastern mythology, and had associated with him Astarte, the female power, which was viewed as representing the moon. Gesenius, however, is of opinion, that under these names the planets Jupiter and Venus were worshipped. See on Isaiah xvii. 8. From the frequency with which his name occurs in compound Phœnician names, as Hannibal, Hasdrubal, etc., the worship of Baal appears to have been common among that people; and from them, especially the Tyrians, it was borrowed by the Israelites. Mention is made of this idolatry in the time of the Judges, see chap. ii. 11, 13; iii. 7; vi. 25; it became prevalent even in Judah in the days of Ahaz; and, though abolished by the pious king Josiah, was revived by Manasseh. In Israel it rapidly gained ground after the introduction of the worship of the golden calves by Jeroboam, and reached its height in the reigns of Ahab and Hosea. The verb שׁוּב, *to return, turn back,* is frequently used adverbially. So here וְלָקַחְתִּי שׁוּב, *I will again take away,* or *take back,* i. e. deprive of. The

meaning is, that instead of reaping the fruits of the earth, etc. as they expected at the usual season, they should be trodden down, consumed, or taken away by the Assyrian army under Shalmaneser. Jehovah vindicates his right to the various articles specified, because they had been bestowed by his providence; calling them *his*, with obvious reference to ver. 5, in which Israel had called them *hers*. The land and all it contained were specially his. לְבַד; Arab. نَصَل, *liberatus fuit*, expresses the idea of *rescuing* or *recovering* what was unjustly held. The לְ in לְכַסּוֹת denotes end or purpose, and is quite in its place; so that there is no necessity, with Houbigant, Dathe, Horsley, Newcome, Boothroyd, and others, to change it into מ, out of deference to the LXX. who render τοῦ μὴ καλύπτειν.

10. נַבְלֻת occurs only in this place, but is obviously equivalent to נְבָלָה, *atrocious, shameful, detestable wickedness.* Targ. קִלְקָהּ, *her shame*, LXX. τὴν ἀκαθαρσίαν αὐτῆς; Syr. ܓܠܝܘܬܗ, *nudatio in malum*, pudenda. Castel.; Arab. عورتها, *her nakedness.* Occuring in immediate connection with the preceding עֶרְיָה, *nudity*, it conveys the superadded idea of obscenity, *i. e.* by metonymy, the results or consequences of idolatrous conduct, a complete destitution of all the necessaries of life. Comp. Jer. xiii. 26; Nah. iii. 5. This exposure was to be made in the very presence of the idols which Israel had served, none of which should be able to afford deliverance. By a prosopopœia, the idols are first endowed with the faculty of vision, and then their utter imbecility is strikingly set forth. אִישׁ, not only signifies *man*, but *any one*, and is frequently used of inanimate objects. In connection with לֹא, it signifies *none*.

11, 12, explain the denouncement made ver. 10. The country was to be desolated by the invading armies, and all

2

Her festivals, her new moons, and her sabbaths,
And all her appointed assemblies.
12 I will also lay waste her vines and her fig-trees,
Of which she said: They are my hire
Which my lovers have given me:
I will turn them into a forest,
And the beasts of the field shall devour them.
13 I will avenge upon her the days of the Baals,
On which she burned incense to them;
And decked herself with nose-rings and trinkets,
And followed her lovers,
And forgat me, saith Jehovah.

the festivities and seasons of religious observance were to cease. The different terms here employed are those by which the seasons of worship, etc. appointed by Jehovah in the Mosaic law, are designated; but it is not hence to be inferred that such were observed according to his appointment. The Israelites professed to worship him, but, at the same time, served other gods. While from habit they continued to keep them as portions of time unappropriated to the ordinary occupations of life, they were doubtless converted into seasons of carnal indulgence. The nouns are those of multitude, and must be rendered in the plural. גֶּפֶן and תְּאֵנָה are likewise to be taken as collectives, or rather, as Horsley suggests, plantations of vines and fig-trees. These should be left uncultivated on the removal of the inhabitants into foreign regions. Comp. Is. v. 6; vii. 23, 24. אֶתְנָה, like אֶתְנַן, is used only of the hire of a harlot, and is peculiarly appropriate in this connection. Thus Tanchum on chap. viii. 9;—هو ما يبدل للزانية من الجعل. Comp. Is. xxiii.

17, 18. The wild beast is here to be taken literally, and not figuratively, as Abarbanel does,—supposing the heathen invaders to be meant.

13. הַבְּעָלִים, the *Baals*, i. e. the idols which they had set up to Baal in the cities and different parts of the country, as well as in their private houses. Hence the names *Baal-Gad, Baal-Hermon, Baal-meon*, etc. By אֶת־יְמֵי הַבְּעָלִים, are

meant the days specially devoted to the celebration of idolatrous rites. To cause grateful odors to ascend from the altars, was considered peculiarly acceptable to the objects of worship. It appears to have originated partly in the gratification afforded by agreeable smells, and partly in the custom of burning perfumes in rooms, etc. with a view to purify them from noxious vapors. נֶזֶם and חֶלְיָה appear to be employed here to denote female ornaments generally; though strictly taken, the former commonly signifies such rings as the oriental females wear in the nostril. See on Is. iii. 21. חֶלְיָה, from חָלָה, *to be smooth, polished;* Arab. حلي, *ornavit monilibus mundove suo (mulierem,)* حلية, *mundo ornata*, denotes a trinket, necklace, or the like. According to Firuzabad: ما يزين به من مصبوغ المعدنيات او الحجارة *quodcunque ornamentum vel e metallis conflatum, vel e lapidibus pretiosis confectum.* Rosenm.; the Syr. and Targ. have *pearls*. That courtesans decked themselves with the most costly ornaments they could command is mentioned by Juvenal, Sat. vi. :—

" Meechis foliata parantur;
    Emitur his quicquid gracilis huc mittitis Indi."

The prophet has in view the gay ornaments in which the Israelites decked

14 Nevertheless, behold! I will allure her,
And, though I lead her into the desert,
Yet I will speak soothingly to her.
15 And I will grant her her vineyards from thence,
And the valley of Achor for a door of hope:

themselves on idolatrous holidays. Their entirely abandoning themselves to the service of idols, and their dereliction of the God of their fathers, are brought forward at the conclusion of this description of their conduct, in order to heighten the aggravation of their guilt, and render the announcement of the kindly disposition of Jehovah towards them, at the beginning of the following verse, the more surprising.

14. לָכֵן cannot with any propriety be rendered "therefore" in this connection, if the following words are to be regarded as promissory of good, and not as containing a further threatening of punishment. And that they are to be so regarded, the subsequent context sufficiently shows. This particle must therefore possess the force of the Arab. لكن verumtamen, but yet, notwithstanding, nevertheless. It thus marks the unexpected transition from threats to promises, as Is. vii. 14; x. 24; xxvii. 9; xxx. 18, et freq. — פָּתָה, of which מְפַתֶּה is the Piel participle, signifies to open, be open, easily persuasible; hence in Piel, both in a good and a bad sense, to persuade, allure, prevail upon by suitable inducements. It is here necessarily to be taken in the sense of inducing or gaining over to that which is good, by the use of soothing and persuasive means, as the concluding words of the verse וְדִבַּרְתִּי עַל־לִבָּהּ abundantly prove. As the Israelites were to be forcibly removed from their land by the king of Assyria, there is a singular want of propriety in assigning to ו, in וְהֹלַכְתִּיהָ, its usual copulative power. It is obviously to be understood exceptively, or as introducing a kind of parenthetical sentence, expressive of what was to take place in the history of the ten tribes previously to their conversion from idolatry; and which, though it might seem severe, was indispensable for the attainment of that object. For this signification of ו, See Ruth ii. 13; 1 Sam. i. 5; Eccles. ix. 16; Mal. ii. 14; and other instances in Noldius, No. 46. Bauer thinks the desert between Assyria and Judea is meant, through which the Israelites were to be conducted on their release; Döderlein, Theol. Biblioth. explains it of Judea itself, at that time desolate and waste. I imagine the country of Babylon is intended. Jehovah is here said to do what he would employ the Assyrians in doing. For the phrase דִּבֶּר עַל לֵב, see Is. xl. 2. When reduced to circumstances of affliction in the countries of the East, whither they were to be carried, Jehovah declares that he would administer consolation to them; holding out to them the cheering prospect of restoration, on their repentance to their native land.

15. The Israelites had altogether forfeited their possessions; nor could they acquire a new right to them except in the way of a fresh grant from the Lord. This grant he here promises them, as he had of old promised Canaan to their fathers when in the wilderness. מִשָּׁם, thence, means, returning from the wilderness; just as שָׁמָּה indicates the homeward direction of the exiles. To take מִשָּׁם as a particle of time, which Gesenius proposes, is less suitable. "The valley of Achor" lay in the vicinity of Jericho, and was noted in the sacred history for the judgment inflicted upon Achan. From Is. lxv. 10, it appears to have been a fertile and pleasant region; and on this account alone it is thought by Calvin, Zanchius, Rivetus, and others, to be referred to by our prophet. Most of the Rabbins, however, and after them, many Christian interpreters, consider allusion to be made to the name, which signifies *trouble* or *molestation*, and to this I incline. This valley had proved very inauspicious to the Hebrews on their former entrance into Canaan. They had been forced to turn their backs before

And she shall sing there, as in the days of her youth,
Even as in the day when she came up from the land of Egypt.
16 And it shall be in that day, saith Jehovah,
That thou shalt call me, ISHI;
And shalt no more call me, BAALI.
17 For I will take away the names of the Baals from her mouth,
And they shall no more be remembered by their name.
18 And I will make a covenant for them in that day
With the beasts of the field, and with the fowls of heaven,
And with the reptiles of the ground;

the native inhabitants, and their hearts melted, and became as water, Josh. vii. 5, 8, 12, 24, 26. But on their return from the captivity, the exiles would pass through it with the undisturbed expectation of a peaceable and joyful occupation of the country. By פֶּתַח תִּקְוָה, *a door of hope*, is meant a *hopeful entrance* into the holy land. — עָנְתָה, the LXX. Syr. Arab. and Symm. take in the signification *to be humbled or afflicted;* and this idea is adhered to by Grotius, who combines it with that of singing: "Intellige autem carmen fictûs et precum;" but that of celebrating the Divine goodness in songs of gratitude and joy, better suits the connection. The ה in עֲנִיָּה, as before observed, indicates the homeward direction of the exiles — yet not without special reference to their approach to the valley of Achor. The point of comparison, as it respects the singing, seems to be the Song of Moses at the Red Sea. As the people then united in celebrating the goodness of Jehovah displayed in their deliverance, so should the returning Israelites do, on again taking possession of their native land.

16, 17. The word בַּעַל, *Baal*, had originally been used in its unexceptionable acceptation of *husband*, and is thus applied to Jehovah, Is. liv. 5; but as it had become common in its application by the Israelites to the heathen deities which they had worshipped, and besides, conveyed the idea of *possession* and *rule*, rather than that of *affection*, God here declares that in future he would be called אִישׁ, *Ish*, the name more usually employed to express the relation of husband, and which was not liable to the same objections: —

"Sic mihi servitium video, dominamque paratam,
Jam mihi libertas illa paterna vale."
Tibullus, lib. ii. Eleg. 4.

Before אִישִׁי, two MSS. the LXX. Aq. Syr. insert לִי; while two MSS., and originally seven, more, and four printed editions, omit it after תִקְרְאִי. — בְּעָלִים, is not here to be taken as a plural of excellency, but is used, according to its strict import, to denote the different images of Baal worshipped by the Israelites, such as *Baal-Gad, Baal-Ammon*, etc. Comp. Exod. xxiii. 13; Zech. xiii. 2. The prophecy was fully accomplished at the return from the Babylonish captivity.

18. Such should be the security of the returned exiles under the immediate care and protection of Jehovah, that every thing capable of injuring them should be rendered perfectly harmless. The irrational animals should be restrained, as if under the bond of an inviolable compact; and the Assyrian armies should no more attack them. Some understand the former part of the verse figuratively — the different creatures there specified denoting men corresponding to them in disposition; but the language is rather to be regarded as hyperbolical, being merely intended to heighten the effect. Comp. Job v. 23; Ezek. xxxiv. 25. Before הַיּוֹם לָהֶם, supply בַּל, or בַּאֲשֶׁר, as in chap. i. 7. Targ. אֲעֲבֵד נְיָח.—וְחֶרֶב וּקְשֶׁת is a pregnant phrase, meaning, *I will break and remove away from*. שָׁבַת is here expressive of the

The bow, and the sword, and the battle, I will break and remove
    from the land,
And will cause them to recline securely.
19 I will also betroth thee to myself forever;
I will even betroth thee to myself with righteousness and with
    justice,
And with kindness, and with tender compassion.
20 Yea, I will betroth thee to myself with faithfulness:
And thou shalt know Jehovah.
21   And it shall be in that day,
I will respond, saith Jehovah,

reclining posture in which the orientals indulge whenever they are released from active exertion. At the time predicted there would be no enemy or danger to break in upon their repose.

"Ipsæ lacte domum referent distenta capellæ
Ubera, nec magnos metuent armenta leones.
Ipsa tibi blandos fundent cunabula flores.
Occidet et serpens, et fallax herba veneni
Occidet, Assyrium vulgo nascetur amomum." *Virgil*, Eclog. iv.

19, 20. אָרַשׂ signifies to contract a matrimonial alliance, and is here specially selected in order to impress the minds of the Israelites with a sense of the distinguished character of the Divine benignity. Though they had rendered themselves totally unworthy of his regard, he declares that he would treat them as if they had never apostatized to idolatry. He would form a new conjugal relation, as with a female in her virgin state. The triple repetition of the verb expresses intensity of desire, and gives the strongest assurance to the party to which the promise is made. לְעוֹלָם, *for ever*, is to be taken as Gen. xiii. 15; Exod. xxxii. 13; Is. xxxv. 10. The several particulars here enumerated further discover, by the amplification which they form, the great kindness of Jehovah to his people. By "righteousness" and "justice," is meant every equitable obligation which God could be expected to place himself under in the new conjugal relation — all that the Israelites could possibly expect in the way of supply from their Divine protector. To these, however, are added "kindness," and "tender compassion," which express the strong internal affection from which the former should proceed, and the high degree of interest which God would take in his recovered people. To remove every doubt from their minds, he crowns the whole by a gracious assurance that his engagements should be "faithfully" performed. רַחֲמִים, τὰ σπλάγχνα, lit. *the bowels*, but commonly employed figuratively to denote tender affection or love. Horsley's interpretation of the terms in application to our Saviour, is, like most of his exegesis, in the highest degree fanciful, being totally unsupported by the scope and connection of the passage. The knowledge of Jehovah here predicated is not speculative, or a bare intellectual acquaintance with his character, but experimental, or that which results from the actual enjoyment of his love. Instead of אֶת־יְהוָֹה, twenty-six MSS., originally thirteen more, now two, and perhaps other two, two editions, supported by the Vulg., read כִּי אֲנִי יְהוָֹה, *i. e.* they shall know *that I am Jehovah*.

21, 22. One of the most beautiful instances of prosopopœia to be found in Scripture. Comp. the address to the Nile in Tibullus, lib. i. Eleg. vii. ver. 25 : —

"Te propter nullos tellus tua postulat imbres,
Arida nec pluvio supplicat herba Jovi."

While second causes have here their

> I will respond to the heavens,
> And they shall respond to the earth,
> 22 And the earth shall respond to the corn, and the new wine, and the oil,
> And they shall respond to Jezreel.
> 23 For I will sow her for myself in the land,
> And will have mercy upon Lo-Ruhamah,
> And will say to Lo-Ammi, Thou art my people;
> And they shall say, My God!

appropriate place allotted to them, as so many connected links in the chain of Divine Providence, the sovereign influence of the Great First Cause is strongly asserted by the emphatic repetition of אֶעֱנֶה, *I will respond to*, or *answer*. It must, however, be observed, that this verb does not occur the first time in one of Kennicott's MSS.; it has originally been wanting in another of De Rossi's; and is omitted in the LXX. Syr. and Arab. One of De Rossi's MSS, omits אֶעֱנֶה נְאֻם יְהוָה entirely; and another,

the second אֶעֱנֶה originally. — יִזְרְעֶאל, *Jezreel*, here means *that which God hath sown*, i. e. his people whom he had *scattered*, but whom he would again restore to their native soil. Comp. chap. i. ver. 4, and 11.

23. כ is causal, introducing a declaration which is designed to account for the appropriation of the name Jezreel at the end of the preceding verse. The metaphor is agricultural. The rest of the verse contains a repetition of what is promised, chap. i. 10.

CHAPTER III.

This chapter contains a new symbolical representation of the regard of Jehovah for his people, and of their condition at a period subsequent to their re-establishment in Canaan at the return from Babylon. The prophet is commanded to become reconciled to Gomer, though she had proved unfaithful to him, as predicted chap. i. 2, ver. 1. He obeys the command, and purchases her from the individual with whom she was living in adultery, but stipulates that she was to wait for a lengthened period before she could be restored to the enjoyment of her conjugal rights, 2, 3. In the two last verses, the symbolical proceeding is explained of a long period during which the Hebrews were to live without the celebration of their ancient rites, and at the same time be free from all idolatrous practices. The direct prediction respecting their conversion to the Messiah, ver. 5, clearly proves, that their condition during the present dispersion is intended.

1 And Jehovah said unto me: Go again, love a woman beloved

1. עוֹד, *again*, obviously refers back to chap. i. 2. The transaction here commanded, bearing so near a resemblance to what is enjoined in that chapter, has

occasioned nearly the same diversity of interpretation. To me there appears no consistent method of explaining it but that which assumes an identity of the

by a friend, yet an adulteress, according as Jehovah loveth the children of Israel, though they have turned to other gods, and 2 love grape cakes. So I bought her to myself for fifteen pieces

female here specified with Gomer, whom the prophet had previously married. For, first, such construction is absolutely required by the analogy. It was Israel that stood in the relation of wife to Jehovah from first to last. No other nation was admitted to the same relation. Secondly, the female is one already married, but who had proved unfaithful; which was precisely the case with Israel. Thirdly, except she had been the prophet's own wife, who had become unfaithful to him, there would be no point in comparing his love to her with that borne by Jehovah to idolatrous Israel. Fourthly, a command to love the wife of another man, who, notwithstanding her infidelity was still attached to her, would be totally repugnant to every idea of moral justice and propriety. Lastly, the command is not קַח, *take*, as in the former instance, chap. i. 2, the usual formula by which marriage is expressed; but אֱהַב, *love*, i. e. renew thy kindness to her; receive her back into thy house and make kind provision for her. This view of the passage is decidedly adopted by Ewald in his *Propheten des Alten Bundes*, recently published.

The words לֵךְ אֱהַב אִשָּׁה אֲהֻבַת רֵעַ וּמְנָאָפֶת, are equivalent to, "Go, love thy wife, to whom, though an adulteress, thou art attached;" but the indefinite form אִשָּׁה, *a wife*, is purposely selected, instead of אִשְׁתֶּךָ, *thy wife*, in order to intimate the state of separation in which they lived. For the same purpose רֵעַ, *a friend* or *companion*, is used, and not אִישָׁהּ, *her husband*; it being here employed not so much as a term of endearment, as indicating that, whatever might be his disposition towards her, they were not living on the same terms as formerly. Comp. for this acceptation of רֵעַ, Jer. iii. 20. The LXX. mistaking the word for רַע, *evil*, and taking אֲהֻבַת for the Benon. אֹהֶבֶת, render ἀγαπῶσαν πονηρά; for which the Syr. has ܐܳܝܶܠܳܟ݂ ܘܰܪܚܶܡ ܐܰܢ݇ܬ݁ܬ݂ܳܐ, *an adulterous woman who loveth evil things.* The words בְּאַהֲבַת יְהֹוָה וגו׳, are to be connected with אֲהֻבַת רֵעַ, and not with אֵשֶׁת. The kind feeling of the prophet towards his faithless wife corresponded, as a type, to the love of God towards the idolatrous Israelites. The sentence just quoted in part, as well as the words פֹּנִים אֶל־אֱלֹהִים אֲחֵרִים, form only two out of numerous instances in which Hosea uses the language of the Pentateuch, as Hävernick has shown in his *Handbuch der historcrit. Einleit. in das A. T.* 1 Theil. 2 Abtheil. p. 608. אֲשִׁישֵׁי עֲנָבִים, have been variously interpreted. LXX. πέμματα μετὰ σταφίδος or σταφίδων, *baked meats with raisins.* Aq. renders the former word by παλαιά, evidently reading יְשָׁנֵי. According to the Hexap. Syr. Theod. adopts the same rendering: ܥܰܬ݁ܺܝܩܶܐ. Symm. ἀκάρτους; Vulg. *vinacia uvarum*; Syr. ܘܰܓ݂ܒ݂ܺܝܢܳܐ ܕ݁ܥܶܢܒ݁ܶܐ, *placenta uvis passis condita.* Junius, Tremellius, and others, have *flagons of wine*, as in our common version. The word אֲשִׁישָׁא is employed by Jonathan in his Targ. on Exod. xvi. 31, to express the meaning of צַפִּיחִת, *a flat cake*. The most probable derivation is from אֲשַׁשׁ, *to press, compress;* and the meaning will be, pressed cakes of dried grapes. Such cakes are highly esteemed in the East, on account of their sweet taste, and doubtless formed part of the offerings presented to idols, and afterwards eaten at idolatrous feasts.

2. Because the purchase of wives was not uncommon, as it still is, in eastern countries, (See Michaelis on the Laws of Moses, Art. LXXXV. Grant's Nestorians, p. 214; Perkins's Eight Years in Persia, p. 236,) most expositors have supposed that such a transaction is intended in this place. The fact, however, that the price here specified, one half in

3 of silver, and for an homer and an half of barley. And I said unto her: Thou shalt remain for me many days; thou shalt not commit lewdness, nor become any man's; and I also will remain
4 for thee. For the children of Israel shall remain many days

money, and the other half in grain, was the exact amount of what was allowed for a female slave, Exod. xxi. 32, induces the belief that the payment was made by the prophet for the liberation of his own wife, who had become the property of the person with whom she had been living in adultery. The sum was too parsimonious to have been given as a dowery. The signification of *buying* as attaching to כרה, is sufficiently established by Deut. ii. 6, and Job xl. 30, and the use of the Arab. كرى, Conj. vi. and viii., *conduxit* rem, LXX. ἐμισθωσάμην. Hengstenberg's attempt to explain it here of *digging*, in the sense of boring the ear in token of a state of slavery, is unsuccessful. A לתך, *lethek*, according to the Rabbins, contained fifteen seahs, or half an homer. Theod. γομὸρ ἀλφίτων; Symm. θύλακος κριθῶν; but the other Greek versions, ἡμίκορον, *half a cor*, which was equal to an homer. The LXX. unaccountably have νέβελ οἴνου. The repetition of שערים is not unusual in Hebrew, but the abbreviated form of expression is better English.

3. ישב properly signifies *to sit*, but likewise *to dwell, remain*, etc. לא תזני explains its meaning here to be a refraining from all cohabitation with others. לי, and אליך, are correlates; and וגם אני forms an antithesis; "while I, on the other hand," etc. As the wife of the prophet was to continue for a long time in a state of separation equally from paramours and from her husband, and he was likewise to form no connection with any other woman, so the Israelites should long live without serving either false gods or Jehovah; while, on his part, he would enter into no national relationship to any other people. This application of the symbol is distinctly marked by כי, and by the resumption of ישבו, ver. 4. The choice of the fuller preposition אל, in אליך, in preference to ל, seems designed to express the strength of affection with which the symbolical female was still to be regarded; consequently the powerful inclination of the Lord towards his unfaithful people.

4. This verse describes a period of great length, during which the Israelites were to have no civil polity, either under regal or princely rule; no sacred sacrifice; no idolatrous statue; no mediating priest; and no images or tutelary deities. This period cannot be that of their dispersion previous to the return from Babylon; for the restoration of the wife of the prophet prefigured the restoration which took place on that return, agreeably to chap. ii. 19, 20, 23. It is true that when they were brought back along with the Jewish exiles, the Israelites had no more any civil or ecclesiastical polity of their own; neither did they relapse into idolatry: but still, as in common with their brethren, they were subject to the same political rule, and offered their sacrifices to Jehovah at Jerusalem, it follows that the days here predicted must be those which have succeeded to the times of the Asmonean dynasty, or the dispersion consequent upon the final destruction of Jerusalem. During the protracted period of more than eighteen centuries, (ימים רבים) they have been precisely in the circumstances here predicted — separated from idolaters, and professedly belonging to Jehovah, yet never acknowledged by him in a church relationship. They have neither had a civil ruler, nor any of the consecrated offices and rites of their ancient economy. Thus Kimchi on the passage, ואלה הם ימי הגלות שאנחנו בו היום ואין לנו לא מלך ולא שר מישראל כי בציור הגוים אנחנו וברשות מלכיהם ושריהם — "And these are the days of our present captivity, for we have neither king nor prince of Israel, but are under the rule of the nations, even under the rule of their kings and their princes." This interpretation, which alone suits the views furnished of the subject by the

without a king, and without a prince, and without a sacrifice, and without a statue, and without an ephod, and without images. 5 Afterwards the children of Israel shall return, and shall seek Je-

prophet, overturns the hypothesis of Dr. Grant, that the Nestorian Christians are the remains of the ten tribes. It cannot properly be said of them that they have continued יָמִים רַבִּים, in a state of separation from God, for they received the gospel in the earliest ages of Christianity. Some explain זֶבַח, both of legitimate sacrifices and of such as were offered to false gods; but the grouping of this term with מַצֵּבָה, *a statue*, as אֵפוֹד, *ephod*, following, is with תְּרָפִים, *teraphim*, clearly shows that the prophet meant the former restrictively. Kimchi briefly explains: "אֵין זבח לאל ואין מצבה לע״ז, "without sacrifice to God, and without an image for idolatrous worship." From the prohibition Lev. xxvi. 1; Deut. xvi. 22, and the history, 2 Kings iii. 2; xvii. 10; x. 26, 27, it is manifest that מַצֵּבָה does not stand for altar, as the ancient versions render it, but denotes a statue or image of some false deity. Comp. Micah v. 13. אֵפוֹד, *the ephod*, was that part of the high priest's dress which was worn above the tunic and robe. It consisted of two pieces which hung down, the one in front over the breast, and the other covering the back, and both reaching to the middle of the thigh. They were joined together on the shoulders by golden clasps, set in precious stones, and fastened round the waist by a girdle. In the breast part was the חֹשֶׁן, or pectoral, containing the Urim and Thummim, by which divine responses were vouchsafed to the Hebrews. According to the Jews, the ephod in its complete state ceased with the captivity: for they specify the Urim and Thummim among the five things with respect to which the first temple differed from the second. LXX. ἱερατεία, *priesthood*, which I doubt not the Hebrew term was intended metonymically to denote in this place. תְּרָפִים, *the teraphim*, were penates, or household gods. They were used at a very early period, as appears from the history of Rachel, Gen. xxxi. 19, 30, 32, 34, 35. Comp. 1 Sam. xix. 13; 2 Kings xxiii. 24; Ezek. xxi. 21; Zech.

x. 2. That they were not only kept as tutelary deities, but also consulted for the purpose of obtaining a knowledge of future events, appears from several of the passages just quoted. Hence the rendering of the LXX. δήλων. The etymology of the word is altogether uncertain.

5. At a period still subsequent to that of their existence in the state just described, the Israelites (now amalgamated with the Jews,) are to be converted to the true worship and service of Jehovah, under the spiritual reign of our Saviour, the promised Messiah. To him they will then submit themselves, and richly enjoy the blessings of divine grace, communicated through his mediation. That דָּוִיד, *David*, here means neither the royal house of David, nor any human monarch of that name who is yet to reign over the Jews, as some have imagined, but the great Messiah himself, appears evident from Scripture usage. See Is. lv. 3, 4; Jer. xxx. 9; Ezek. xxxiv. 23, 24; xxxvii. 24, 25. As the name properly signifies *The Beloved*, it quite accords with ὁ ἀγαπητός, Matt. iii. 17, and ὁ ἠγαπημένος, Eph. i. 6. Thus the Targ. וְיִשְׁתַּמְעוּן לִמְשִׁיחָא בַר דָוִד. "And they shall obey Messiah the Son of David." The following is the Rabbinical interpretation:— אמריך אהך מלכא משיחא אם מן חייא דוד שמיה ואם מן [הַמֵּתִיא] הוא דוד שמיה. "The Rabbins say, that He is the king Messiah; whether he be of the living, his name is David, and whether he be of the slain, his name is David." Berachoth Jerus. in Raym. Martini Pugio Fidei, Fol. 277. See also the Rabbinical Commentaries on the above passages in Ezekiel. The use of אֶל, in the phrase וּפָחֲדוּ אֶל־יְהוָה, and not מִן, or מִפְּנֵי, the usual form, is intended to show that the fear here specified is not of the kind which "hath torment," and which causes those who are under its influence *to recede from* its object, but such fear as attracts or induces them *to approach to* it. This the addition וְאֶל טוּבוֹ "and *to* his good-

hovah their God, and David their king; and they shall tremblingly hasten to Jehovah and to his goodness in the latter day.

ness," clearly shows. Comp. Micah vii. 17. As, however, the idea of fleeing or hastening from danger is also implied in verbs signifying to fear, I have rendered the words so as to include both. In this way Rabbi Tanchum: ويقزعون اليه من كل مايخاف "They shall flee to him for help from all that may be feared." Comp. Jer. xxxi. 12. LXX. ἐκστήσονται ἐπὶ τῷ Κυρίῳ καὶ ἐπὶ τοῖς ἀγαθοῖς αὐτοῦ. Ewald renders, *und werden beben zu Jahve und zu seinem Gute*, u. s. w.; and Hitzig explains, *bebend in freudiger Erwartung werden sie herbeieilen*. While on the one hand the Jews, under the influence of alarm, shall be excited to flee from the wrath to come, they shall be attracted by the display of the divine goodness in the mediation of Christ, to confide in Him for all the blessings of salvation. אַחֲרִית הַיָּמִים, *the last of the days*, i. e. the days of the Messiah, as the Rabbins interpret the phrase. See on Is. ii. 2, where Kimchi says expressly, בכל מקום שנאמר באחרית הימים הוא ימות המשיח "wherever it is said, 'In the last of the days,' it means the days of the Messiah."

CHAPTER IV.

The prophet now addresses himself more directly to the castigation of the flagrant evils which abounded in the kingdom of Israel during the interregnum which followed upon the death of Jeroboam, and the reigns of Zechariah, Shallum, Menahem, and Pekahiah. He calls the attention of his countrymen to the divine indignation, and the causes of it, 1, 2; denounces the judgments which were about to be executed upon them, 3; describes their incorrigible character, especially that of the priests, 4–11; and expatiates on the grossness of their idolatrous practices, 12-14. A solemn warning is then given to the members of the Jewish kingdom not to allow themselves to be influenced by their wicked example, 15-19.

1 Hear the word of Jehovah, ye children of Israel!
For Jehovah hath a controversy with the inhabitants of the land;
Because there is no truth, nor kindness, nor knowledge of God in the land.

1, 2. The initiatory words are those of Hosea, summoning attention to the divine message which he was commissioned to deliver. בְּנֵי יִשְׂרָאֵל is equivalent to בֵּית יִשְׂרָאֵל, ch. v. 1; שְׁבָטֵי יִשְׂרָאֵל, ch. v. 9; and frequently to יִשְׂרָאֵל and אֶפְרַיִם; and all these different epithets are used of the kingdom of the ten tribes in contradistinction to יְהוּדָה and בֵּית יְהוּדָה, which designate the tribes of Judah and Benjamin. רִיב signifies here *ground of complaint*, or *judicial proceeding*. LXX. κρίσις. The wickedness which abounded is first set forth negatively, and then positively, under certain items; and the infinitive absolute is employed with great effect, as expressing more emphatically, by its abstract form,

2 There is nothing but swearing and lying,
   And murder, and theft, and adultery;
   They have burst forth,
   And blood reacheth to blood.
3 Therefore shall the land mourn,
   And every one that dwelleth in it shall languish;
   With the beasts of the field and the fowls of heaven;
   The fishes of the sea also shall be removed.
4 Yet let no man contend with, nor reprove another;
   For thy people are like those that contend with the priest.
5 Therefore thou shalt fall by day,
   And the prophet also shall fall with thee by night;
   And I will destroy thy mother.

the heinousness of the evils described. The force of this I have given in a free translation. Ewald improperly limits the signification of the verb פָּרַץ in this place to the act of *breaking into* houses; but the metaphor seems rather to be taken from the bursting forth of a torrent, which, in its progress, spreads wider and wider, and sweeps all before it. The plural form דָּמִים, *blood*, has also a degree of emphasis, signifying much bloodshed. What the prophet means is, that murder was so common, that no space was left as it were between its acts. LXX. αἵματα ἐφ' αἵμασι μίσγουσι. Coverdale, *one bloudgiltynes foloweth another*. And Ritterhusius powerfully in his poetical metaphrase:—

" —— sic sanguine sanguis
Truditur, et scelerum nullus finisve
modusve est."

See 2 Kings xv.; Micah vii. 2.
3. Comp. Is. xix. 8; xxiv. 4; Joel i. 10, 12, אֻמְלַל, in the Pulal. Conj., is usually employed after אָבַל, in order more forcibly to describe the calamitous state of a country. בְּ here signifies *with, extending to, accompanied by*, and includes what follows in the general predicate. Comp. Gen. vii. 21. אָסַף, is cognate with סוּף, and signifies *to gather up, away, back, take away*, as well as simply to collect together, Zeph. i. 2, 3. LXX. ἐκλείψουσιν; Syr. ܘܢܣܘܦܘܢ; Targ.

יָם.—יַם, signifies not only what we call the *sea*, but any lesser collection of water, as pools, and even rivers. See Is. xix. 5.
4. אַל is here prohibitory, and not simply negative, as some have rendered it. The introduction of the sentence by אַךְ, *yet, nevertheless*, is designed to show the hopeless character of the persons spoken of. All reproof on the part of their friends or neighbors generally would prove fruitless, seeing they had reached a degree of hardihood, which was only equalled by the contumacy of those who refused to obey the priest, when he gave judgment in the name of the Lord, Deut. xvii. 12. The passage is thus quite plain, and requires no transposition or emendation of the words as adopted by Houbigant, Newcome, and Boothroyd. מְרִיבִי כֹהֵן is the same as if it were אֶת מְרִיבֵי הַכֹּהֵן. Comp. כְּמָסִיגֵי גְבוּל, chap. v. 10. All the ancient versions, except the LXX. and Aq. read עַמֶּךָ. The Hexap. Syr. has

ܟܗܢܐ ܕܡܥܨܐ.

5. By a sudden transition to the second person, the prophet addresses himself directly to his guilty people, and predicts their utter destruction. הַיּוֹם, Kimchi, Drusius, Œcolamp. Grotius, and Ewald, improperly render "to-day." As contrasted here with לַיְלָה, *night*, it is equivalent to בַּיּוֹם, *by day*. Comp. Neh. iv. 16. That the article is not repeated before לַיְלָה, may be owing to the common adverbial use of this noun without it.

6   My people is destroyed for lack of knowledge;
    Because thou hast rejected knowledge,
    I will also reject thee, so that thou shalt not be a priest to me;
    Because thou hast forgotten the law of thy God,
    I also will forget thy children.
7   According to their increase, so they sinned against me;
    I will change their glory into shame.
8   They devour the sin-offering of my people,
    And long for their iniquity.

The false prophets by whom the Israelites had been encouraged in wicked practices should render them no assistance in the season of calamity, but should be themselves involved in the same common ruin. נִדְמֵיתִי, the LXX. renders ὡμοίωσα; and several translate, "I have reduced to silence;" but the verb is obviously used in the sense of *destroying*, as נִדְמוּ is, ver. 6. Comp. Zeph. i. 11. By אִמֶּךָ, *thy mother*, the Israelitish state is meant, of which the citizens were the children. See chap. ii. 1. Thus Kimchi, Jerome, Grotius, Michaelis, Rosenmüller, and Maurer. Others, as Cornelius à Lapide, Houbigant, Capellus, Pocockc, Bauer, and Newcome, suppose the metropolis to be intended.

6. מִבְּלִי חַדָּעַת, having here the article before the noun, and occurring in connection with הַדָּעַת, immediately following, is not to be taken in the sense of *unexpectedly*, as מִבְּלִי דַעַת is, Is. v. 13, but strictly means that destitution of the true knowledge of God which was the source of the sins now about to be punished. This ignorance is principally charged upon the religious teachers of the nation, each of whom is directly addressed in אַתָּה חַכֹּהֵן מֵאֹס. Thus Pagninus, *O sacerdos;* which Dathe also inserts in his text. The persons addressed pretended to be priests of Jehovah, though they taught the people to combine with his worship that of pagan deities, or at least that of the golden calves, which, no doubt, paved the way for the universal spread of idolatry in Israel. The position adopted by Horsley, that the Jewish high-priest is intended, does not suit the connection. The third א in וְאֶמְאָסְךָ, is not found in a great number of Kenni-

cott's and De Rossi's MSS., nor in some of the earlier printed editions; in others it is marked as redundant, and some few have קְרִי. The antitheses in this verse are pointed and forcible. כִּי is understood as repeated in וַתִּשְׁכַּח, and וְ before אֶשְׁכַּח.

7. As the priests are obviously the nominative to the verbs in the three following verses, and form the subject of discourse in that which precedes, they must likewise be the persons spoken of in this. It has been queried whether the increase was in number, or in wealth, power, etc. Michaelis thinks the latter is meant? still the former may be included, in harmony with the mention made of their children, ver. 6. In proportion as they multiplied in numbers and grew in influence, they promoted the increase of idolatry: but the wealth and dignity (כְּבוֹדָם) which they acquired, and which they thus prostituted, should be destroyed by foreigners, by whom they would be carried into captivity. כְּרֻבָּם, and כְּבוֹדָם, form a slight paronomasia.

8. חַטָּאת here signifies *sin-offering,* as it frequently does in the Levitical code. So Kimchi; and it is thus rendered in Pococke's Arab. Ms. خطايا قومي ياكلون; and Castalio, *piaculo.* The priests greedily devoured what the people brought for the expiation of their sins; and instead of endeavoring to put a stop to abounding iniquity, only wished it to increase, in order that they might profit by the multitude of the victims presented for sacrifice. נָשָׂא נֶפֶשׁ, *to lift up the animal soul* for any thing, means to *lust after it,* long, or have a strong desire for it, Deut. xxiv. 15; Jer.

9 Therefore it shall be, like people, like priest;
I will punish them according to their ways,
And requite them for their deeds.
10 For they shall eat, but shall not be satisfied;
They shall commit lewdness, but shall not increase:
Because they have ceased to regard Jehovah.
11 Lewdness and wine and new wine take away the heart.
12 My people consult their stock;
Their staff announceth to them:

xxii. 27. ו in לשבט, is used distributively to express the fact that such was the character of each of the priests. The reading כעמים, found in ten MSS., originally in seven more, and perhaps in one, and supported by the LXX. Syr. Targ. Vulg. and Arab., most probably originated in emendation. Not unfrequently a proposition commences with the plural, and ends with the singular, and *vice versâ*.

9. Comp. Is. xxiv. 2. The rank and wealth of the priests would not exempt them from sharing the same fate with the rest of the nation.

10. וְאָכְלוּ is a resumption of יֹאכֵלוּ, ver. 8.— הִזְנוּ is here used intransitively as in ver. 18, v. 3, and is to be understood literally of the sensual indulgences of the Israelitish teachers, not the verb יִפְרֹצוּ shows. For the signification *to abound in children*, as attaching to this verb, see Gen. xxviii. 14. Saadius, Arnold, (Blumen althebraisch. Dichtk.) and Horsley, disjoin לִשְׁמֹר from the preceding verb, and connect it with the following nouns, thus:—

"They have forsaken Jehovah,
Giving heed to fornication," etc.

But, notwithstanding the apparent force of the bishop's remarks, there is something so repugnant to Hebrew usage in the combination לִשְׁמֹר זְנוּת וְיַיִן וְתִירוֹשׁ *to observe fornication, and wine, and new wine*, that it is altogether inadmissible. Though the verb שָׁמַר may in no other passage take זְנוּת for its object, yet it takes שָׁוְא הֶבְלֵי, *lying vanities*, i. e. idols, Ps. xxxi. 7; Jonah ii. 9; in which latter passage it is connected with עָזַב, as in

the present case. The division of the words found in our common version is that of the Hexap. Syr. ܐܘܢܘܬܐ ܠܡܛܪ, ܐܠܗܐ, and the Slavonic; and is approved by Michaelis, Tingstadius, Newcome, Dathe, Boothroyd, De Wette, Hitzig, and Ewald.

11. This verse has the appearance of a moral adage. The influence of habits of impurity and intoxication in blunting the moral feelings, and weakening the intellectual powers, is a well-established fact in the history of man.

"Nox et amor vinumque nihil moderabile suadent;
Illa pudore vacat, liber amorque metu."
Ovid.
"Nox, vinum, mulier; nihil perniciosus adolescentulo."
Plaut.

There can be little doubt that the prophet has specially in view the impure and bacchanalian orgies which were connected with the Syrian idolatry. For the prevalence of drunkenness in Ephraim see Is. xxviii. 1; Amos iv. 1.

12. The LXX., and most versions which follow them, connect עַמִּי with בְּ, at the end of the preceding verse; a mode of construction adopted by Michaelis and Dathe, but otherwise disapproved by modern translators. The Syr. Targ. and Vulg. divide properly. Hosea here adduces proofs of the mental hebetude to which the sinful practices of the Israelitish people had reduced them — their application to their wooden idols and images for oracular counsel, and their use of rhabdomancy or divination by

For a lewd spirit hath caused them to err;
They have lewdly departed from under their God.
13 They sacrifice on the tops of the mountains,
And offer incense upon the hills;
Under the oak, and the poplar, and the terebinth,
Because their shade is pleasant:
Therefore your daughters commit lewdness,
And your daughters-in-law adultery.
14 I will not punish your daughters when they commit lewdness,
Nor your daughters-in-law when they commit adultery;
For they themselves go aside with harlots,

rods. Leo Juda: "ligno suo oracula quærit." That by עֵץ, *wood*, is here meant an idol made of such material, the connection shows. Comp. Jer. ii. 27: x. 8; Hab. ii. 19. מַקֵּל is properly a *shoot* or *twig*, then a *rod, walking staff*, etc. Occurring as it does here, in reference to an idolatrous or superstitious practice, it denotes such a staff employed for purposes of divination. Some have been of opinion that it is to be taken as strictly parallel to עֵץ, and that a staff is meant which had the image of some god carved upon it; but the use of the phrase יַגִּיד לוֹ, *announceth, pointeth out*, shows that a divining rod is meant. Rhabdomancy (ῥαβδομαντεία) was very common among the ancient idolaters, as it has been in later times in different countries of the East. The ancient Arabs consulted their gods in this way, taking two rods, on one of which was inscribed *God bids*, and on the other *God forbids*, and drawing them out of the case into which they were put, acted agreeably to the direction which first came forth. See Pococke, Specimen. Hist. Arab. p. 327. Maimonides quotes an ancient book entitled Siphri, in which a diviner is defined to be one who takes his staff, and inquires, Shall I go? or, Shall I not go? The Runic wands of the Scandinavian nations, on which were inscribed mysterious characters, and which were used for magical purposes, appear to have originated in the more ancient divination of Asia. רוּחַ זְנוּנִים, lit. *a spirit of whoredoms*, i. e. a powerful impetus to commit acts of idolatry. Instead of the simple form הִתְעָם, some few MSS. the Babyl. Talmud, the Syr. Vulg. and Targ. read הִתְעָם; while the LXX. and Arab. read יָתְעוּ. For אֱלֹהֵיהֶם פָּנִים, comp. Numb. v. 19, 20; Ezek. xxiii. 5; and ὕπανδρος, Rom. vii. 2.

13. Mountains and hills were selected by idolaters on which to erect their altars, and offer their sacrifices, on account of their supposed proximity to the host of heaven, which they worshipped. That this custom was very ancient, appears from the prohibition, Deut. xii. 2. For imitating it, the Hebrews are frequently reproved, Is. lxv. 7; Jer. iii. 6; Ezek. xviii. 11. זִבֵּחוּ, being in Piel, expresses the eagerness and frequency with which the Israelites offered their idolatrous sacrifices. They also selected groves of oak, terebinth, etc., for purposes of superstition and idolatry, under whose umbraceous cover they might at once be screened from the heat of the sun, and indulge in lascivious practices. The sacrifice of female virtue which was required in the religious service of the Phœnician goddess Astarte, seems clearly to be referred to in this and the following verse. לִבְנֶה, LXX. λεύκη, *the white poplar*, from לָבַן, *to be white*.

14. Kuinoel, and others, taking לֹא, as standing for הֲלֹא, read the first part of the verse interrogatively, which is not unsupported by examples in Hebrew usage. It seems better, however, to understand it here as a simple negative, and the meaning to be that, as the parents and husbands indulged in the flagitious practices here described, Jehovah would not make examples of the females, or suffer them to be punished, as if they alone

And sacrifice with prostitutes:
And as for the undiscerning people, they shall be overthrown.
15 Though thou, O Israel, art lewd,
Yet let not Judah be found guilty;
Come ye not to Gilgal,
Neither go ye up to Beth-aven,
Nor use the oath, "Jehovah liveth."

were guilty; but would punish with condign punishment their natural protectors, who not only abandoned them to seduction, but themselves rioted in the same wickedness. Thus Munster: "Durissimè animadvertam in parentes et sponsos, ut filiæ et sponsæ eorum punitæ videantur esse extra pœnam." The transition from the second to the third person, for the purpose of more graphically exhibiting the subject of discourse, is not without examples. See Is. xxii. 16. The use of the separate pronoun הם, also adds to the emphasis of the language. פרד, in Piel, strongly marks the studied withdrawment of the Israelites from the assembled throngs, to such places as were devoted to scenes of impurity; while זבח, in the same conjugation, signifies in this connection, to commit lewdness as an act of idolatrous devotion. Between זנות, and קדשות, there seems to be this difference, that the former were ordinary females who prostituted themselves for gain, but the latter those who devoted themselves to the service of Astarte, by offering their persons to be violated in her temples at the sacred festivals. See Selden de Diis Syris, Synt. ii. cap. 2; Herodot. lib. i. cap. 199; Euseb. Vit. Constantin. lib. iii. cap. 35; Spencer de Leg. Heb. lib. ii. cap. 22 and 23; Lucian de Dea Syra. Of this latter term, the mas. קדשים, *catamites*, occurs, 1 Kings xiv. 24; xv. 12: xxii. 47; and in the ancient book of Job, chap. xxxvi. 14, which shows at how very early a period such abominations obtained. It likewise occurs in both genders in the prohibition, Deut. xxiii. 18. To these practices the LXX. doubtless had respect in rendering the word τετελεσμένων, *initiated*. Its derivation from קדש, *to be sacred, consecrated*, or destined to the service of the temple, confirms our interpretation.—לבט; Syr.

ܠܚܒ, *concitavit*; Arab. لبط, *conjecit in terram* aliquem, in Niph. *to be cast down, overthrown*, or the like. The verb occurs only here, and Prov. x. 8, 10, where see Schultens.

15. A solemn warning to the Jewish kingdom to beware of mixing itself up with that of Israel in the practice of idolatry. Here זנה, *to commit lewdness*, is again used figuratively. אשם, properly signifies *to contract guilt*, or become subject to its consequences. גלגל, *Gilgal*, was a town situated between the Jordan and Jericho, near the confines of the kingdom of Samaria. It was regarded as a holy place as early as the days of Joshua, chap. v. 15; and sacrifices were offered there to Jehovah in those of Samuel, 1 Sam. x. 8, 13; xv. 21, 33. In process of time, however, it came to be converted into a place of idolatrous worship, Amos iv. 4, 5; Hos. ix. 15; xii. 11. בית און, *Beth-aven*, i. e. *the house of vanity* or idols, a name given by the minor prophets, by way of contempt, to *Bethel*, i. e. *the house of God*, a place sacred to true religion in the time of the patriarchs, and the judges; but afterwards selected by Jeroboam as the principal seat of the worship of the golden calves, 1 Kings xii. 29, 32, 33; xiii. 1; Amos iii. 14; vii. 10, 13; Jer. xlviii. 13. It originally belonged to the tribe of Benjamin, but was taken by that of Ephraim, Judges i. 22–25. That there was a city of the name of *Beth-aven* near to Bethel, appears from Josh. vii. 2, which may have suggested the appropriation of the name to the latter. LXX. οἶκον Ὤν, reading און, the native name of Heliopolis, Aq. and Symm. οἶκον ἀνωφελῆ; Theod. οἶκον ἀδικίας; and with this the Arab. agrees بيت الظلم, *the house*

24 HOSEA. CHAP. IV.

16 Since Israel is refractory, like a refractory heifer;
   Jehovah will now feed them, like a lamb in a large place.
17 Ephraim is joined to idols;
   Leave him to himself.
18 When their carousal is over they indulge in lewdness;
   Her shields are enamored of infamy.

of iniquity. Comp. Amos iv. 4; v. 5. From the warning here given to the Jews not to participate with the Israelites in their idolatry, it is evident the prophecy was delivered at a time when they were comparatively free from that evil. The prohibition not to swear by the formula יְהוָֹה חַי, respects the combination of the divine name with those of idols, or the profession of attachment to Jehovah, if the persons addressed were guilty of idolatry. Comp. Zeph. i. 5. That it was otherwise lawful to use it, appears from Jer. iv. 2. Comp. Deut. x. 20.

16. The metaphor is here taken from a heifer that obstinately refuses to be yoked. Thus the Syr. ܣܪܪ ܬܘܪܬܐ. For the force of סָרַר, comp. Deut. xxi. 18. The latter hemistich contains the language of irony. As lambs are fond of ranging at large, but are in danger of being lost or devoured, so God threatens to remove the Israelites into a distant and large country, where they would be separated from those with whom they associated in idolatrous worship, and thus be left solitary and exposed as in a wilderness. The phrase רָעָה בַמֶּרְחָב, *to feed in a large place,* is elsewhere used in a good sense, Is. xxx. 23.

17. אֶפְרַיִם, *Ephraim,* as the most numerous and powerful of the tribes, and that in which the kingdom was established, is put for all the ten. חָבוּר, from חָבַר, *to be joined, closely united, adhere to,* to be allied to by voluntary choice, Gen. xiv. 3. In this last sense the term is here used. The Israelites had voluntarily addicted themselves to the service of idols, and thus identified themselves with their interests. While the word עֲצַבִּים, *idols,* suggests the idea of their being merely the fabrication of human labor, it also intimates the pain or sorrow resulting from idolatry. The root has both significations. הַנַּח־לוֹ strongly implies the obstinacy and incorrigible character of the ten tribes, and indignantly abandons them to their fate. They are irreclaimably devoted to the gods of the heathen: let them take their own way, and reap the consequences of their perverse choice. Their case is desperate. Comp. Jer. vii. 16; Ezek. xx, 39. Thus Tanchum, Jarchi, Kimchi, Calvin, Tarnovius, Zanchius, Coverdale, Drusius, Lively, Leo Juda, Pococke, Kuinoel, Michaelis, Tingstadius, Newcome, Stuck, and Ewald. Others, as the Targ. Jerome, Mercer, Diodati, Grotius, Rosenmüller, Maurer, etc., regard the words as simply containing a warning to the inhabitants of Judah to keep aloof from, and take no part in the idolatries of the Ephraimites. The LXX. ἔθηκεν ἑαυτῷ σκάνδαλα, reading הִנִּיחַ in the preterite, and supplying the idea of idols from the preceding part of the verse.

18. Before סָר, the particle אָז, *when,* is to be supplied, which in poetry, for the sake of conciseness and energy, is frequently omitted. For the acceptation *past, passed away, over,* etc. comp. 1 Sam. xv. 32, סָר מַר־הַמָּוֶת. Horsley, Ewald, and some others, are of opinion that סָר means *rapid, degenerated, sour,* etc., but less aptly. The meaning is, that no sooner were their compotations over than they indulged in excessive lewdness. Instead of סָבְאָם, *their drink, drinking bout,* one of De Rossi's MSS. has originally read סוֹבְאִים, *drunkards;* another סְבָאָם, *their host;* and one of Kennicott's סֹבְאִים, *Sabeans;* but none of these variations suits the entire construction of the verse. The LXX. strangely, ᾑρέτισε Χαναναίους, which the Arab, as usual, follows. The impurity in which, when inflamed with

19 The wind hath bound her up in its wings,
That they may be ashamed of their sacrifices.

liquor, they indulged, was most probably that connected with the worship of Venus. To express the excess to which it was carried, the verb is first put in the infinitive absolute, and then repeated in the finite form. זָבוּ is not separately expressed in the LXX. the Arab. or in either of the Syriac versions; though it cannot hence be inferred that it was not in the Hebrew text. It is wanting, however, in three of Kennicott's MSS. If it did not originate in some copyist having written the two last syllables of the preceding word over again, it must be regarded as having originally formed part of that word in the reduplicate form אֲהַבְהֲבוּ; in which, not only is the second syllable of the verb repeated (אֲהַבְהֲב), but the pronominal sufformative is retained in the middle of the word, and the first radical (א) rejected on that account in the reduplication. Such form is of extremely rare occurrence: עַמְּתֻמֻנִי, lit. *they destroy, destroy me*, Ps. lxxxviii. 17, being the only other instance of the kind with which I am acquainted. In this way the form is partly accounted for by the ancient Jewish grammarian Abuwalid Ibn Jannahi, as quoted by Pococke. What confirms this view of the reduplicate form is the use of הֲבָבִים, a gemination somewhat resembling it, by our prophet, chap. viii. 13. The rendering *give ye*, as if it were the imperative of יָהַב, proposed by Abenezra and Kimchi, and adopted by our translators, is not so suitable to the connection. Maurer; *mirifice amant ignominiam*: Ewald; es

lieben lieben schmach seine Schilde. Kuinoel very unjustifiably omits זָבוּ in his Heb. Text. קָלוֹן, *shame*, a collective abstract noun, expressive of the infamous acts connected with idolatrous worship. מָגִנֶּיהָ, *shields*, are tropically used for *princes*, as the natural protectors of their people, here and Ps. xlvii. 10. The feminine suffix הָ, refers to אֶרֶץ, understood; the inhabitants being meant.

19. By an expressive figure, borrowed from the sudden force with which any thing is carried off by the wind, the prophet announces the suddenness and violence with which the ten tribes should be removed from their land. The combination בְּכְנָפֶיהָ רוּחַ, *wings of the wind*, is too firmly established in Hebrew usage, see Ps. xviii. 11; civ. 3, to allow either of the acceptations *spirit* or *vanity* being given to רוּחַ, or that of *borders* to בִּכְנָפֶיהָ in this place. רוּחַ being of both genders, accounts for the masculine of the verb, and the feminine pron. affix. For אוֹתָהּ, two of De Rossi's MSS., and the Vat. and Alex. copies of the LXX. read אֹתָם, which gives no suitable sense. In the distant countries of the Medes, by whom all image-worship was held in abomination, the exiles would be brought to a due sense of the wickedness and absurdity of their conduct. ו, in וְיֵבֹשׁוּ, is used τελικῶς. Jer. xlviii. 13. *Sacrifices* are here put by synecdoche for the whole system of idolatry in which they indulged. For the reading מִזִּבְחוֹתָם, *of their altars*, adopted by Newcome, there is no authority except the Targ. and Syr.

CHAPTER V.

This chapter commences with an objurgation of the priests and the royal family, as the principal seducers of the nation to idolatry, 1, 2. Then follows a description of the unblushing wickedness of the people, interspersed with denunciations of impending punishment, 3–7. The approach of the divine judgments is ordered to be proclaimed, and their certainty declared, 8, 9. The prophet then abruptly turns to the two tribes and a half whose guilt and punishment he denounces; yet so as to show that his predictions were chiefly directed against the northern kingdom, the rulers of which, like those of Judah, instead of looking to Jehovah for deliverance from civil calamities, applied in vain for foreign assistance, 10-14. The 15th verse sets forth the certainty and the beneficial effects of the divine judgments.

---

1 HEAR this, O ye priests!
And hearken, O house of Israel!
Give ear, O house of the king!
For the sentence is against you,
Because ye are a snare at Mispah,
And a net spread upon Tabor.
2 The apostates slaughter to excess,
But I will inflict chastisement on them all.

1. בֵּית יִשְׂרָאֵל, *house of Israel*, i. e. the ten tribes. בֵּית הַמֶּלֶךְ, *house of the king*, i. e. the king and his court. From the references made to the idolatry and punishment of Judah in this and the following chapter, it would appear that the king whom Hosea had specifically in view was Pekah, the son of Remaliah; since it was in the reign of Ahaz, who was contemporary with him, that idol worship was carried to such a height in that kingdom as to call for the calamities inflicted upon it by the confederate forces of Israel and Syria, as well as by the king of Assyria. By לָכֶם הַמִּשְׁפָּט is not meant, as the Targ. interprets, followed by Abenezra, Kimchi, Abarbanel, Pagninus, Junius, Tremellius, and others, that it belonged to them to know and execute justice, but that the judgment or punishment was directed against them. They had merited it, and it was now coming upon them. LXX. πρὸς ὑμᾶς ἐστι τὸ κρίμα. Thus most Christian expositors. מִצְפָּה, *Mispah*. As there were several places of this name, some degree of uncertainty attaches to it as occurring here; but as the object of the prophet seems to be to set forth the means employed for seducing the whole of the ten tribes to idolatry, it is more probable that he had in his eye Mispah of Gilead, on the east of the Jordan, just as he specifies mount Tabor to the west of that river. See Judges x. 17; xi. 29.

On both of these elevated positions false worship had been established for the purpose of ensnaring the inhabitants of the adjacent regions. The means employed to bring them over to it are compared to the snares and nets used for catching birds and wild beasts upon the mountains. By metonymy, the leaders of the people are spoken of as such nets and snares, because of their bad example, and the influence which they otherwise exerted for evil.

2. שַׁחֲטָה, *slaughtering*, the infinitive absolute, with ה paragogic, of שָׁחַט, *to kill*, for food or sacrifice. Here, from its close connection with the preceding verse, it has the latter signification. Some think murder is meant; but this is less likely, though the verb is also used in this sense in other places. שַׁחֲטָה שֵׂטִים הֶעְמִיקוּ, lit. *they deepen to slaughter*, i. e. by a peculiar idiom, they slaughter to excess, kill an immense number of sacrificial victims. Comp. הֶעְמִיקוּ שֵׂטִים; Is. xxxi. 6. שֵׂטִים, *apostates*, the Benoni participle of שׂוּט, *to turn aside, decline from the right way, apostatize*; as לֵצִים, *scoffers*, from לוּץ, *to scoff*. Comp. Ps. xl. 5, שָׂטֵי כָזָב, *those that turn aside* to falsehood; and שֵׂטִים-חֲטָאִים, Ps. ci. 3. Two or three MSS., the edit. of Soncin., and a few others, have ס instead of שׂ, in our text.

Syr. ܐܣܛܝ, *seduxit*, ܡܣܛܝܢܘܬܐ, *declinatio, apostasia*. The idolatrous

3 I know Ephraim,
  Israel is not hid from me;
  Surely now thou committest lewdness, O Ephraim!
  Israel is defiled.
4 They frame not their deeds
  To return to their God;
  For a lewd spirit is within them,
  And they regard not Jehovah.
5   The pride of Israel testifieth to his face;
  Therefore Israel and Ephraim shall fall through their iniquity;
  Judah also shall fall with them.

Israelites multiplied their sacrifices in order that they might enjoy prosperity under the protection of the deities to whom they offered them; but Jehovah here declares that none of them should escape the punishment which he was about to inflict upon them. Before מַעַלְלֵיהֶם supply אֶתֵּן. The ancient versions are here greatly at fault, from their authors having supposed that the reference to hunters is still continued in this verse.

3. *Ephraim*, as distinguished from *Israel*, means the tribe of Ephraim, from which most of the apostate kings sprang, and in which idolatry most abounded. By Israel the other nine tribes are meant. As having incurred the more aggravated guilt, the former is here addressed in the second person. Two of Kennicott's MSS. indeed, and one of De Rossi's, originally read הִזְנֵיתָ; and one of Kennicott's has נִטְמֵאתָ for נִטְמָא, but both are, in all probability, from the hand of correctors. הִזְנֵיתָ is here used figuratively. The polluting influence of the Ephraimites was felt through the whole nation. To express an assertion more strongly the Hebrews put it first in the form of an affirmative, and then in that of a negative. עַתָּה, *now*, is not without emphasis; pointing out the undeniable fact that they had been the cause of the spread of idolatry.

4. The language now changes to the plural, to express the character of the people generally. By some מַעַלְלֵיהֶם is construed as the nominative to יִתְּנוּ, and rendered, *their deeds do not permit them*, etc. Thus the Syr. Abenezra, Drusius, etc.; and among the moderns, Horsley, Tingstadius, Manger, Kuinoel, Stuck, Maurer, and Ewald. But in order to establish this construction, we should have to read מַעַלְלֵיהֶם or אֶת מַעַלְלֵיהֶם, "permitted *them*," the accusative of the person always following the verb in such case. See Gen. xx. 6; Exod. iii. 19. In the present instance נָתַן is used in the sense of *placing, ordering, framing*, like שׂוּם and עָשָׂה, as it is given in the common version, and rendered by Tanchum, Leo Juda, Mercer, Tarnovius, Michaelis, Rosenmüller, Noyes, and Hitzig. The meaning is, that the Israelites did not reform, did not so regard their wicked practices as to abandon them and return to the pure worship of Jehovah.

5. That בְּ עָנָה means *to testify for* or *against* any person or thing, is obvious from its use, Gen. xxx. 33; Job. xvi. 8. It is properly a Judicial phrase, and refers to the testimony given by a witness, either *for* or *against* another, according to circumstances. The rendering *to be humbled*, which is that of the LXX. Syr. Targ. Jarchi, and recently of Michaelis, Newcome, Noyes, and Maurer, cannot be philologically sustained. The addition בְּפָנָיו, *to his face*, gives emphasis to the phrase, *openly, publicly*, in such a manner that he himself may see it, without the adduction of further evidence. That גָּאוֹן signifies *pride, insolence*, notwithstanding what Horsley asserts to the contrary, is sufficiently apparent from Prov. xvi. 18, and Is. xvi. 6. I should rather think, however, that by the term as here used, we are to understand the objects of which the ten tribes were proud, their

6 With their flocks and their herds,
   They may go to seek Jehovah,
   But they shall not find him:
   He hath withdrawn from them.
7 They have proved false to Jehovah;
   For they have begotten strange children:
   Now shall a month destroy them and their portions.

splendid or magnificent idols, etc. As Jehovah is spoken of as גְּאוֹן יַעֲקֹב, *the excellency*, or *boast* of Jacob, Amos vi. 7, so the idols might be called גְּאוֹן יִשְׂרָאֵל, *the excellency*, or *proud boast* of Israel. They gloried in them as the objects of their confidence and attachment. These very gods, by their utter impotence, bear open witness that they could afford no help to those who trusted in them; so that their worshippers could not but have been convinced of their folly, if their hearts had not become morally obscured by the practice of iniquity. The religion itself (עֲוֹנָם, *their iniquity*,) from which they expected safety, would prove the cause of their ruin. The words are repeated with a similar reference chap. vii. 10.

The concluding line of the verse contains an abrupt and unexpected application of the threatening to the Jews. As they had suffered themselves to be influenced by the example of the Israelites, they should also share in their punishment. The respective captivities of both are here threatened. On comparing this threatening with chap. iv. 15, it appears to have been delivered at a period considerably subsequent to that which is there spoken of, when the evils of idolatry had made some progress in the southern kingdom. To express more strongly the certainty of the event, the verb יִכָּשֵׁל is put in the preterite; whereas it had simply been used in the future יִכָּשְׁלוּ, in reference to the Israelites.

6. The idolaters are here told that though in the hour of calamity they might bring their flocks and herds as propitiatory sacrifices to Jehovah in order to avert the punishment, it would be altogether in vain. הֵלִיץ signifies *to draw* or *put off* any person or thing, *to withdraw one's self*. Comp. the Arab.

خَلَصَ, *salvus evasit, progressus est,* and خَلَعَ, *extraxit, exuit*. Pocock's Arab. MS. has اللّٰه خلع معونته منهم, *God hath withdrawn his help from them*. The Israelites and Jews could no longer reckon on the divine presence, and the effectual aid which that presence implied.

7. The prophet seems here to allude to the mention made of זְנוּנִים, and בָּנִים זְנוּנִים, *lewd children*, chap. i. 2; ii. 4. זָרִים, *strange, foreign*, is selected in order to show that the idolatry was the result of intercourse with foreigners. The verb בָּגַד, *to act unfaithfully*, is also used of the breach of the matrimonial covenant, Jer. iii. 20. This idea is expressed in the Arab. MS. of Pocock, بعهد اللّٰه غدروا, *they have broken the covenant of God*. כִּי has here the signification of *itaque*, and marks the consequence of the conjugal infidelity just specified — the production of a race of idolaters. The relation of the words is well expressed by Stuck: "quoniam Deo infideles sunt, propterea liberos peregrinos habent." עַתָּה, *now*, is here to be taken not as determining the exact point of present time, but the speedy and certain arrival of the event. The term חֹדֶשׁ, *month*, has greatly, and, in my opinion, very unnecessarily perplexed interpreters. Houbigant at once cuts the knot by an arbitrary emendation: עַתָּה אֹכֶל חָרוּם, *omnino est legendum* יֹאכֵל הֶחָרוּם יַעֲרִיצֵם, *nunc igitur absumet rubigo*. He appeals to the ἐρυσίβη of the LXX. as his authority; but ἐρυσίβη signifies *mildew*, with which חָסִיל, *a locust*, the word he proposes to substitute for חֹדֶשׁ, has no manner of affinity. That the same word which

8   Blow ye the horn in Gibeah,
    The trumpet in Ramah;
    Raise a shout at Beth-aven;
    He is behind thee, O Benjamin!
9 Ephraim shall become desolate
    In the day of punishment;
    Among the tribes of Israel
    I have made known that which is sure.

is now in the Hebrew text was found in it in the time of Aquila, is evident from his rendering it νεομηνία. Symm. and Theod. have μήν. Michaelis, Dathe, Kuinoel, and Stäudlin, give to the word the signification of the Arab. حلّ, what is *new and unexpected*, and explain it of a sudden calamity. Most moderns take it in the sense of *new-moon*, i. e. either at the feast of the new moon, when the Israelites were assembled to worship; or, at that time their calamities should commence. It seems most natural to abide by the usual meaning of the term, and consider the prophet as announcing, that within the space of one month they should be visited with merited punishment. The calamity predicted seems to have been that occasioned by the invasion of Tiglath-pileser, who ravaged the country, and carried into captivity the tribes of Reuben and Gad, the half-tribe of Manasseh, and that of Naphtali, besides the inhabitants of several cities in other parts of the country, 2 Kings xv. 29; 1 Chron. v. 26. That Judah also suffered on this occasion, see 2 Chron. xxviii. 19–21. חֶלְקֵיהֶם, *their portions,* are commonly interpreted to mean their possessions or property; but I should rather think the prophet has in view their idols, whom they regarded as the authors of their possessions and enjoyments. See Is. lvii. 6, and my Comm. on that verse.

8. An alarm is ordered to be given to the southern kingdom of the approach of the enemy. The verse intimately coheres with the foregoing, and is not to be taken for the commencement of a new prophecy, as Jerome, Abarbanel, Michaelis, Dathe, Manger, and others, suppose. The difference between the שׁוֹפָר and the

חֲצֹצְרָה seems to be, that the former was the same as the קֶרֶן, *horn,* being made of the curved horn of animals, Josh. vi. 5, 6, 8. Arab. شبور, *lituus foraminibus instructus;* whereas, the latter was made of metal, such as the two silver trumpets which were employed for convoking the congregation, Numb. x. 2; from חָצַץ, Arab. حصّ, *in angustiam redegit; angusto pectore preditus fuit.* Gesenius considers the word to be an onomatopoetic, imitating the broken pulse-like sound of the trumpet, (*hâtzotzêrâh,*) like the Latin *taratantara,* and the German *trarara.* Their shape and size may be seen in the representations of the arch of Titus. Comp. Jer. iv. 5; Joel ii. 1; Hos. viii. 1. The LXX. render גִּבְעָה, *Gibeah,* and רָמָה, *Ramah,* τοὺς βουνοὺς and τῶν ὑψηλῶν, as if heights or elevated places in general were meant; but they are to be taken as proper names, just as Beth-aven and Benjamin are. They both lay in the tribe of Benjamin, see on Is. x. 29, as did also Bethel, here called *Beth-aven.* See on chap. iv. 15. Before אַחֲרֶיךָ subaud. אֹיֵב, *the enemy* "is behind thee," i. e. close upon thee. The fifth Greek version has κατὰ νότου σοῦ, *to the south of thee;* but if the local signification were at all admissible, the *west* is the only sense in which the word could be understood.

9. Having apprised the Jews of the danger with which they were threatened, the prophet returns to describe the calamity which was to be inflicted upon the ten tribes; and in the course of the following verses directs his discourse to the two kingdoms alternately. The nominative to תִּהְיֶה is אֶפְרַיִם, implied in אֶפְרַיִם.—הוֹכֵחָה, primarily means *proof*

10 The rulers of Judah are like those who remove the boundary;
   I will pour out my wrath upon them like water.
11   Ephraim is oppressed,
   He is crushed in judgment;
   Because he consented,
   He followed the order.
12 I am as a moth to Ephraim,
   And as rottenness to the house of Judah.
13 And Ephraim saw his sickness,
   And Judah his wound;

or *demonstration,* from יָכַח, *to be before one, be clear, obvious;* in Hiph. *to place before one* in the way of evidence, convince, convict, and then *rebuke, chastise, punish.* The word is synonymous with שָׁפַט, ver. 2. The latter hemistich of the verse shows that the ten tribes were the scene of the prophet's ministry. אֶפְרַיִם, the feminine used for the neuter.

10. By the "princes" or "rulers of Judah," king Ahaz and his courtiers are intended. For כְּמַסִּיגֵי גְבוּל, comp. Deut. xxvii. 17; אָרוּר מַסִּיג גְּבוּל רֵעֵהוּ, Prov. xxii. 28; xxiii. 10; Job xxiv. 2. It was reckoned a flagrant offence to remove the marks by which the divisions of property were defined. The language seems to have become proverbial to designate unprincipled conduct. What the prophet here reprobates appears to be the means adopted by Ahaz and his supporters to introduce idolatry into Judah. See 2 Kings xvi. 10–18. If the כְּ be regarded as the *Caph veritatis,* it will strongly express the fact that these princes had actually removed the boundaries which separated the true religion from the false. Divine judgments are frequently compared to the overflowing of water from a river. שָׁפַךְ, *to pour out,* expresses the fulness of their infliction. Comp. Zeph. iii. 8. עֶבְרָה, prop. *effervescence, flowing over,* also denotes the greatness of the punishment.

11. עָשׁוּק מִשְׁפָּט, the genitive of cause, *broken in pieces* by the *judgment,* or punishment inflicted. צַו refers not to any divine commandment, but to the order issued by Jeroboam to worship the golden calves, 1 Kings xii. 28–33. Such an order his subjects were bound by higher authority to have resisted; but they readily complied with it, and thus became prepared to indulge in all the gross idolatries to which this worship proved the introduction. From the circumstance that the LXX. have rendered the passage ὀπίσω τῶν ματαίων, *after vanities,* it has been conjectured that they read שָׁוְא instead of צַו; but it is more likely they intended to give the sense of the whole, rather than the signification of this particular word. They are followed by both the Syriac versions, and in part by the Targ. Jerome, on the other hand, has read the same letters which now stand in the text; for he renders *sordes,* pointing the word צֹא, and regarding it as merely a contracted form of צֹאָה or צֵאָה, *filthiness.*

12. The reference in עָשׁ, Arab. عُثّ, *moth,* is to the consumption of garments, Ps. xxxix. 12; Is. l. 9; in רָקָב, *rottenness,* to that of wood. See Job xiii. 28, where both words occur together as here. The LXX. freely render the former by ταραχή, the latter by κέντρον. The meaning is not that God was regarded as the moth and rottenness, *i. e.* with disgust; but that he was the author of those judgments by which the idolaters should be consumed.

13. רָאָה, *to see,* has here the sense of *feeling, experiencing,* as in the phrases *to see life, death, good, evil,* etc. מָזוֹר, lit. *a bandage,* from זוּר, *to compress, bind* as a wound, see Is. i. 6; hence, as here, *a bandaged wound,* corresponding to חֳלִי, *sickness, disease,* in the other member of the parallelism. For the use of such metaphors in application to the state of

Then Ephraim went to Assyria;
He sent to the hostile king;
But he could not cure you,
Nor remove your wound from you.
14 For I will be like a lion to Ephraim,
And like a young lion to the house of Judah;
I, even I will tear the prey, and depart;
I will carry it away, and there shall be none to rescue.
15 I will depart, I will return to my place,
Till they suffer punishment;

political affairs, comp. Is. i. 5, 6, iii. 7; Hos. vi. 1, vii. 1. After מלך, supply as its nominative, ויהודה : *Judah*, from the preceding part of the verse, which forms an alternate quatrain; the third line connecting with the first, and the fourth with the second. ירב is not a proper name, but an appellative, signifying *one who contends, is contentious, hostile;* from ריב, *to strive with, quarrel, contend.* The form is the apocopated future, and is contracted for אֲשֶׁר יָרִיב, *he that acts hostilely.* Tanchum مَلِك خاصِم, *the king that contended.* Comp. יוֹיָרִיב, *Joiarib,* Neh. xi. 5. Aq. δικαζόμενον; Symm. ἔκδικον, or ἐκδικητήν; Theod. κρίτην. Jerome, *ad regem ultorem.* De Wette, *Der könig der rächen soll.* That the king of Assyria is meant there can be no doubt. See chap. x. 6. He was ever ready to mix himself up with the affairs of neighboring states, in order to extend or consolidate his gigantic empire, and was justly regarded by the Hebrews as their most powerful adversary. The application made by the northern kingdom was that which took place in the reign of Menahem, when that monarch sent to Pul a thousand talents of silver for the purpose of engaging him on his behalf, 2 Kings xv. 19. But this alliance proved of no real value; for the subsidy was raised by oppression, and in the course of the following reign, Tiglath-pileser invaded and depopulated great part of the country, ver. 29. The embassy from the kingdom of Judah was that sent by Ahaz to Tiglath-pileser, when attacked by the united kings of Syria and Israel, 2 Kings xvi. 7, 8; 2 Chron. xxviii. 21. גהה as a verb, occurs only in this place; but a noun derived from it is used Prov. vii. 22, in the sense of *healing.* If we may judge from the Syr. ܐܳܣܶܐ, *recedere, fugere,* Aph. *liberare,* it properly signifies *to remove, relieve,* and so with respect to a wound, *to heal.* LXX. οὐ μὴ διαπαύσῃ; Syr. ܠܳܐ ܢܶܬܐܣܶܐ, *neque sanabit.*

14. No effort to recover a state of prosperity while the anger of Jehovah was excited against them, could possibly succeed. שַׁחַל, *the black lion,* and כְּפִיר, *the young lion,* are frequently employed to convey the ideas of strength and ferocity, Ps. xci. 13. The reduplication אֲנִי אָנִי is, as usual, emphatic. Comp. Is. xliii. 25; xlviii. 15. טֶרֶף, *prey,* is understood after אֶשָּׂא and אֶטְרֹף.

15. As God's coming to a people, and being with them, implies their experiencing efficient protection and aid, so his withdrawment of his presence implies the deprivation of these blessings. אָשַׁם, like many other verbs, has a *sensus pregnans;* conveying not only the idea of *contracting guilt,* but of *suffering its consequences.* The latter idea seems clearly to be conveyed in this passage. The Rabbins, indeed, and after them, Glassius, and many others, attempt to attach to the verb the superadded signification of *acknowledging,* which is that adopted by our translators; but it is by no means supported by Lev. iv. 22; v. 5; Zech. xi. 5; the passages usually adduced in proof. "בַּקֵּשׁ פְּנֵי פ, *to seek the face* of any one, means to strive to obtain his favor. See 1 Kings

Then will they seek my face:
When they are in trouble, they will seek me early.

x. 24; Prov. xxix. 26. The phrase occurs very frequently in the Psalms, in reference to application to Jehovah in prayer. Comp. Dan. ix. 3. שִׁחֵר is synonymous with בִּקֵּשׁ, but is only used in poetic diction.

CHAPTER VI.

The nation, in both its divisions, is here introduced as taking up language suitable to the circumstances described in the concluding verses of the preceding chapter, 1-3; but however appropriate it was to the condition of the people, that it was not the result of sound and thorough conversion, appears from ver. 4, in which they are expostulated with on the ground of their inconstancy. Notice is then taken of the means, both of a moral and a punitive nature, that had been employed for their recovery, 5, 6; their deceitful and wicked conduct, especially that of the Israelites, is placed in a strong light, 7-10; and a special denunciation of punishment is directed against the Jews, who flattered themselves with the hope that whatever might befall the northern tribes, no calamity would happen to them.

1 COME, let us return to Jehovah,
For he hath torn, but he will heal us;
He hath smitten, but he will bind us up.
2 He will restore us to life after two days:

1, 2. It has been disputed whether these words be those of the prophet exhorting his countrymen to repent and turn to God, or whether they are to be regarded as employed by themselves to give expression to their feelings of penitence, their confidence in God for deliverance from punishment, and their resolutions of amendment for the future. The latter appears, from the bearing of ver. 5, to be the preferable interpretation. The intimate connection of the words with the preceding context, and the repetition, in part, of its language, induces to the conclusion that the same subject is here continued, viz. the castigation of the Hebrew kingdoms on account of idolatry, and the effect produced by it. This connection the ancient versions have endeavored to establish by inserting a word corresponding to לֵאמֹר; though it is not found in any Heb. MSS. From the apparent agreement of the language of ver. 2, with the circumstances of time connected with the death and resurrection of our Saviour, many interpreters, as Lactantius, Tertullian, Origen, Jerome, Augustine, Luther, Œcolampadius, Mercer, Riberus, Tarnovius, Hammond, etc., have maintained that it is to these respect is had in the prophecy. I fully concur, however, in the judicious remarks of Calvin on this interpretation, "Sed sensus ille videtur mihi nimium argutus. Et semper hoc spectandum est nobis, ne volitemus in aëre; placent argutæ speculationes primo intuitu, sed postea evanescunt. Ergo quisquis volet proficere in Scripturis, semper hanc regulam teneat, ut solidum sit quicquid colligit sive in

On the third day he will raise us up,
And we shall live before him.
3 Then we shall know, we shall strive to know Jehovah:
Like the dawn, his going forth is fixed.
Yea, he will come to us like the rain,
Like the latter rain, which watereth the earth.

prophetis, sive in Apostolis." The exegesis of Grotius, Horsley, and many others, who regard the words as primarily applicable to the Jews, and secondarily, or allusively, to the resurrection of Christ, is equally unsatisfactory. The simple meaning of the passage is, that on their conversion from the service of idols to that of Jehovah, the Hebrews should experience the removal of the national calamities with which they had been visited; the nation which had been reduced to a state of political death would be resuscitated, and enjoy a renewal of its former prosperity. From the metaphor of disease, ver. 1, there is in ver. 2, an advance to that of actual death, and a consequent resurrection, in order to place their present and also their anticipated condition in a more striking light. For the use of the latter metaphor in application to the national affairs of the Jews, see Is. xxvi. 19; Ezek. xxxvii. 1–14. בַּיּוֹם הַשְּׁלִישִׁי, *on the third day*, is expletive of מִיָּמָיִם, *after days*, i. e. two days; LXX. μετὰ δύο ἡμέρας. That a short period is meant, appears from *two* and *two three* being used to denote a few, or very few, 1 Kings xvii. 12; Is. vii. 21, xvii. 6. Comp. Luke xiii. 32, 33. The afflicted Hebrews confidently hoped that their punishment would be of brief duration, and that God would assuredly restore them to the enjoyment of his favor. Such enjoyment is expressed by *living* לְפָנָיו, *before him*, experiencing his presence and blessing. The phrase contrasts with that employed chap. v. 15, and indicates the result of בַּצַּר לָהֶם there predicted.

3. In נִרְדְּפָה לָדַעַת, there is a rise from a resolution simply to acquire a true knowledge of Jehovah, to a determination to make such knowledge the object of earnest and unwearied pursuit.

The ה of the elongated futures marks this bent or inclination of mind. To separate the verbs, and connect the former with the preceding verse, as Horsley does, would quite destroy the force of the prophet's language. At the same time the ו at the beginning of the verse is inferential, intimating that what follows would be the result of the divine interposition on behalf of the Hebrew people. Some few MSS. insert ו before נֵדְעָה. נָכוֹן, *to be fixed, established, certain.* As certain and delightful as the dawn of the morning would be the coming forth of the favor of Jehovah after the dark night of adversity. This beautiful metaphor is taken from the sunrise. See, for such application of מוֹצָא, Ps. xix. 7. The other images were peculiarly appropriate in Palestine, where rain falls seldom, except in spring and autumn. At these seasons it is heavy, and greatly contributes to the fertility of the soil, on which account its bestowment was regarded as among the most necessary of temporal blessings, and its absence a source of awful calamity. The former, commonly called יוֹרֶה, or מוֹרֶה, the *darting rain*, from the root יָרָה, *to dart, cast*, etc.; here גֶּשֶׁם, *the rain*, by way of eminence; *the heavy, violent rain*, as the word properly signifies. It falls from the middle of October till about the middle of December, and is called the early or former rain. LXX. ὑετὸς πρώϊμος, because the Jews commenced their year at that time. It prepares the ground for the reception of the seed. מַלְקוֹשׁ, the *latter rain*, LXX. ὑετὸς ὄψιμος, falls in the latter half of February and during the months of March and April, just before the harvest; from which circumstance it receives its name — לָקַשׁ, signifying *to gather* or *collect*, the late fruit. Comp. לָקַט, *to collect*, Syr.

4 What shall I do to thee, O Ephraim!
  What shall I do to thee, O Judah!
  For your goodness is like the morning cloud,
  And like the dew which early departeth.
5 For this cause I have hewed them by the prophets,
  I have slain them by the words of my mouth:
  Thy judgments went forth like the lightning.
6 For I desired mercy and not sacrifice;
  And the knowledge of God, rather than burnt offerings.

ܡܚܣܕ, *serotinus*. Before יוֹרֶה supply אֹשֶׁר.

4. That the declarations contained in the preceding verses are not to be viewed as divine promises, but express the hopes and resolutions of the afflicted Hebrews, appears from the affecting expostulations here addressed to them, and the description of the temporary and evanescent character of their boasted reformation. Like a tender parent who is anxious, if possible, to reclaim a wayward child, Jehovah asks what other means could possibly be employed for the recovery of his rebellious people. They had been tried both with mercies and judgments, but without effect. Comp. Is. v. 4–7. חֶסֶד properly means *kindness, benignity, mercy*; here *piety, religion*, as Is. xl. 6. Syr. ܛܒܘܬܟܘܢ, *your goodness*; Pocoke's Arab. MS. دينكم, *your religion*. Theodoret not inaptly gives the meaning thus: ἡ παρ' ὑμῶν γενομένη μεταμέλεια πρόσκαιρός ἐστι, καὶ οὐ διαρκής. In Palestine, and other countries of the same latitude, the dense clouds which cover the heavens during the morning are all gone by nine or ten o'clock; and the dews, however copious, early disappear. מַשְׁכִּים is here, as frequently, to be taken adverbially; *early*, in the morning. As the cognate Ethiop. ጠዐነ፡ signifies *to carry a burden*, and beasts of burden are usually loaded in the morning, the Hebrew שָׁכַם came in Hiphil to signify the doing of any thing at an early hour. הֹלֵךְ is not to be construed with הַשְׁכֵּם, but with טַל.

5. The severity of the threatenings communicated through the instrumentality of the prophets is compared to the incisions made in stone or wood with the axe, and those made in the human body with the sword. Comp. Is. xi. 4; Heb. iv. 12. After חֲצַבְתִּי supply ם or אֹתָם. To make the pronominal affixes agree, the LXX. Syr. and Targ. read מִשְׁפָּטַי, "*my* judgments," and so likewise Dathe, Kuinoel, Boeckel, Newcome, Boothroyd, and Ewald, instead of מִשְׁפָּטֶיךָ, "*thy* judgments." Vulg. judicia tua. Hexap. Syr. ܘܕܝܢܝ ܢܦܩܘ. There is no variety in the MSS., except that one of Kennicott's, and originally one of De Rossi's, have מִשְׁפָּטְךָ, "thy judgment," in the singular. The reference of the affix is to לְךָ, ver. 4; and the meaning is, the judgments which belong to *thee*, which *thou* deservedst, and which were inflicted upon *thee*. The genitive is that of object. Comp. מִשְׁפָּטֶךָ, 1 Kings xx. 40; מִשְׁפָּטָם, Jer. li. 9; and especially מִשְׁפָּטֵךְ, Zeph. iii. 15. Thus Lyranus: "pœnæ tibi inferendæ." יֵצֵא, though future, is modified by the preceding preterite, and is to be rendered accordingly. אוֹר has here the sense of *lightning*, as in Job xxxvii. 3, 15. The LXX. Syr. Targ. and Arab. supply כְּ before אוֹר. Sudden and awful as the lightning were the inflictions of merited punishment upon the idolatrous Hebrews.

6. חֶסֶד means here *true piety*, of which mercy or charity is only a branch. דַּעַת אֱלֹהִים corresponding to it in the second member of the verse, likewise means *a practical knowledge of God*, in opposition to that which is merely speculative. Comp. Jer. xxii. 16. The present is one

7 But they are like men that break a covenant:
There they proved false to me.
8 As for Gilead, it is a city of evil-doers;
Marked with footsteps of blood.

of several passages in the Old Testament, in which the comparative worthlessness of ceremonial observances is taught. See Is. i. 11–17; Ps. xl. 7–9, l. 8–23; Mic. vi. 6–8. Comp. Matt. ix. 13. xii. 7.

7. Translators and commentators have been greatly divided respecting the precise meaning of אָדָם as occurring in this passage. Some, as Jarchi, Jerome, Leo Juda, Castalio, Grotius, Clarius, Manger, Tingstadius, Newcome, Rosenmüller, Boothroyd, and Stuck, regard it as a proper name, and suppose the reference to be to the conduct of Adam in transgressing the divine commandment; while Kimchi, Munster, Vatablus, Tremellius, Beza, Drusius, Lively, Calvin, Rivetus, Piscator, Zanchius, Œcolampadius, Mercer, Lowth, De Wette, Maurer, Hitzig, Ewald, etc., take it to be an appellative, and interpret the passage of the treacherous violation of contracts among mankind. In favor of the former view, it is alleged, that it places the guilt of the Israelites in a much more aggravated light; and Job xxxi. 33, Ps. lxxxii. 7, are appealed to in proof of a similar allusion. It is, however, very doubtful whether there be any such allusion in these passages; and as to the force of the comparison, it seems sufficiently supplied by supposing men in general to be understood, who break the engagements into which they have entered with each other. The Israelites had treated God as if he had been one of themselves, and as if the sanctions of his covenant were as little to be regarded as those of ordinary contracts were by men of unprincipled character. If we except the three passages in question, it is universally admitted that there is no other, after the first chapters of Genesis, in which אָדָם is used as a proper name, or in which any reference is made to our first parent. The absolute and indefinite form too in which בְּרִית occurs, (comp. on the other hand בְּרִיתִי, "*my* covenant," chap. viii. 1,) shows, that both this noun and the preceding verb עָבְרוּ, stand in immediate relation to אָדָם, which, as very frequently, is a collective, and is thus used instead of a plural, which it nowhere exhibits. It may also be objected to the first mentioned interpretation, that nowhere in Scripture is God said to have entered into a בְּרִית, or *covenant* with Adam. The obligations under which he was placed are represented as those of a מִצְוָה, *command* or *interdict*, rather than any of a federal nature. כְּאָדָם, *like Edom*, the reading proposed by Michaelis, has found no supporters. Before עָבְרוּ, supply אֲשֶׁר, of which there is frequently an ellipsis in Hebrew poetry. See Noldius, p. 103.—שָׁם, *there*, points graphically to the northern or Israelitish kingdom as the principal scene of idolatrous defection, and anticipates the regions more specifically referred to in the two following verses.

8. גִּלְעָד, *Gilead*, is the nominative absolute, and is here the designation of a city, in all probability *Ramoth-Gilead*, the metropolis of the mountainous region beyond Jordan, and south of the river Jabbok, known by the name of Gilead, Josh. xxi. 38; 1 Kings iv. 13. It was here that Jacob and Laban entered into a solemn covenant with each other, Gen. xxxi. 21, 23, 25. Burckhardt found ruins of cities on two mountains in that region, still known by the names of Djebel, Djelaâd, and Djelaûd, one or other of which may have been that here mentioned. It was one of the cities of refuge, Deut. iv. 43; Josh. xx. 8; but appears from the present passage to have afterwards become notorious for idolatry and bloodshed. Some would restrict פֹּעֲלֵי אָוֶן to idolaters, in imitation of the LXX. who render ἐργαζομένη μάταια; but it seems better to take the phrase in its more enlarged meaning, as including all manner of wickedness. Of this, indeed, idolatry has ever been found to be the fruitful parent. Various expla-

HOSEA. CHAP. VI.

9 As troops of robbers lie in wait for a man,
So is the association of priests:
They commit murder in the way to Shechem;
Yea, they practise deliberate crime.
10 In the house of Israel I have seen what is horrifying;
There is the lewdness of Ephraim;
Israel is polluted:
11   Also for thee, O Judah! a harvest is appointed.

nations of עֲקֻבָּה have been advanced; but the simplest is that which regards it as signifying *traced*, from עָקֵב, *the heel, step, print of the foot*, and describing the marks or traces of blood left by the feet of the murderers who resided there. Syr. ܡܥܩܒܬܐ ܡܢ ܕܡܐ, *stained with blood.* Jewish Span. *immunda de sangre*. To what historical facts the prophet refers we have no information, except perhaps that contained in 2 Kings xv. 25, from which it appears that fifty of the inhabitants of Gilead were implicated in the regicidal conspiracy against Pekahiah.

9. שְׁכֶם, *Shechem*, was another city of refuge, situated between Ebal and Gerizim. It still exists under the name of نابلس, *Nabloos*, and has, from very ancient times been the seat of the religious community of the Samaritans. Having been for a time the residence of Jeroboam, 1 Kings xii. 25, its inhabitants became so corrupted, that the priests resident there banded together, waylaid, and murdered with impunity the persons who were fleeing to the asylum for refuge. The ה in שֶׁכְמָה is that of direction, and connects in sense with דֶּרֶךְ. The interposition of the verb יְרַצְּחוּ between these two nouns occasions no difficulty, since we have instances of nouns in construction being separated. See Gen. vii. 6; Is. xix. 8; Hos. xiv. 3. Our common version, and many others, following the Targ. חַד חֲדָא, שֶׁכְמָה, *one shoulder*, translate שְׁכֶמָה, *with one consent*, which well suits the connection; but is not borne out by Hebrew usage — the term occurring but once, Zeph. iii. 7, in this metaphorical acceptation, and then not שְׁכֶמָה as here, but אֶחָד שְׁכֶם. זִמָּה is generally considered to be an imitation of the Chaldee form of the Infin. in Piel, from זָמַם, *to wait, lie in wait for;* but it seems more likely to be the abbreviated form of the Piel Participle מְזַמֵּה, the מ being dropped, as in עֲשֻׁיָּה, Eccles. iv. 2, and in several instances of the Pual Participles. See Gesen. Lehrgeb. p. 316. בְּחַד־אִישׁ will thus form the genitive of object. Three MSS. substitute ה for י; and instead of the prepositive בְּ, three MSS. and three printed editions read בָּ. . Before חָדָה־בֵּית there is an ellipsis of כִּי, corresponding to בְּ in בְּמָה.—זִמָּה is used to denote presumptuous or deliberate wickedness, from זָמַם; Arab. سم, *proposuit sibi, to form a purpose, lay a deliberate plan of action;* chiefly employed in a bad sense. LXX. ἀνομία. Hitzig, *Unthat*.

10. שַׁעֲרוּרִיָּה, LXX. φρικώδη, occurs under the forms שַׁעֲרוּרָה and שַׁעֲרוּרִית, Jer. v. 30, xxiii. 14, xviii. 13. It is explained immediately after of the atrocious idolatry which, through the influence of the tribe of Ephraim, had spread itself over the whole kingdom of Israel.

11. For the various interpretations which have been given of this verse see Tarnovius or Pococke. Ewald is the only modern that adopts *branch* as the rendering of קָצִיר, as Kimchi proposed, and explains it of the introduction of idolatry into Judah. How Horsley could assert that *harvest* is used in a good sense, as an image of the ingathering of the people of God, is inconceivable. See Jer. li. 33; Joel iii. 13; Rev. xiv. 15-20. Nowhere in prophecy does it appear to be used in this sense. In all probability, the punishment predicted is that recorded, 2 Chron. xxviii. 6-8. שָׁת is here used impersonally. Instead of לָךְ, four MSS. originally two more, the Targ. and two

old editions, read חָלָה. The words בְּשׁוּבִי שְׁבוּת עַמִּי have no meaning, if connected with the preceding, which form a concise apostrophical warning to the Jewish kingdom. They must, therefore, be transferred to the following context, with which they will be found to be in harmony. Thus Moerlius, Michaelis, Jahn, Eichhorn, Kuinoel, Stuck, De Wette, and Boothroyd, divide.

CHAPTER VII.

The prophet continues his description of the wickedness of the ten tribes. Regardless of Jehovah, they persevered in falsehood and violence, 1, 2; flattered their rulers, and thereby obtained their sanction to their nefarious conduct, 3, 5; and indulged to the utmost in licentiousness, 4-7. The murder of their kings successively is predicted, and their hardihood and folly are further set forth, 7-10. The prophet next adverts to their fruitless application for assistance to Egypt and Assyria, and their equally fruitless, because false professions of return to the service of God, 11-16.

---

1 WHEN I reversed the captivity of my people,
When I healed Israel,
Then was the iniquity of Ephraim revealed,
And the wicked deeds of Samaria;
For they practised deceit;
The thief entered,
And the banditti plundered in the street.
2 And they considered not in their heart,

1. Some would render בְּשׁוּבִי שְׁבוּת עַמִּי, "When I again lead my people into captivity;" but altogether contrary to the established usage of the language. See Deut. xxx. 3; Ps. xiv. 7; Jer. xxxi. 23; Zeph. iii. 20. The words are explained by the following כְּרָפְאִי לְיִשְׂרָאֵל, *when I heal Israel*. בְּ and לְ frequently alternate with each other, when used of the time at which any thing is done. The restoration here mentioned is in all probability that of the two hundred thousand Jewish captives, to which reference is made 2 Chron. xxviii. 8-15. The conduct of the Israelitish rulers upon that occasion held out some hope of improvement in the character of the nation, and a consequent change in the Divine conduct towards it; and this expectation was confirmed by a temporary cessation of the judgments of God, during which they might be said to have been *healed*; but it was soon entirely frustrated by the open increase of wickedness among them. וְנִגְלָה has the force of *then, on the contrary*, become more manifest, etc. For *Samaria*, see on Is. xxviii. 1. Being the metropolis of the ten tribes, it was the head spring of that corruption of manners which overspread the kingdom. יָבֹא and פָּשַׁט בַּחוּץ describe the acts of violence that were committed by breaking into and plundering private houses, and those which were perpetrated on persons in the streets. The reference is not to foreign enemies, as Horsley and others expound, but to lawless Israelites.

2. For the phrase אָמַר בִּלְבָבוֹ, comp. the

That I remembered all their wickedness:
Now their deeds encompass them;
They are before my face.
3 With their wickedness they cheer the king,
And with their falsehoods the princes.
4 They are all adulterers;
They are like an oven, heated by the baker;
Who resteth from heating it,
From the time he kneadeth the dough,
Until it be leavened.
5 On the day of our king,

Arab. قَالَ فِي قَلْبِهِ, and قَالَ فِي نَفْسِهِ; and our, *say to one's self*. Ps. xiv. 1, *et freq.* Instead of לְלִבָּם, the form exhibited in the printed text, "*to their heart,*" ten MSS., originally seven more, now one, perhaps another, and the Complut. Bible, read בְּלִבָּם, "*in their heart.*" One of De Rossi's MSS. states in the margin that the latter reading is found in other copies. It is also supported by the Syr. Vulg. Targ. and Arab. versions. Both forms describe internal or mental conversation, only ל indicates an endeavor to persuade. So far were the persons spoken of from bringing themselves to act on the conviction, that God was privy to their wicked deeds, that they evinced the contrary disposition. Still, however, the phrase may best be rendered by *think*, *consider*, or the like. To the words סָבְבוּ עֲלִילֹתָם, two interpretations have been given. They either mean, that the evil practices of the Israelites crowded round them as so many causes of punishment, as enemies surround and shut up the object of their attack; or, that they crowded about them as so many witnesses to reveal the wickedness of their character. The latter would seem, from the following words, to be the true meaning.

3. Their rulers, instead of repressing, took delight in the immoral and irreligious conduct of the people.

4. In this connection, מְנָאֲפִים is to be taken in its literal signification. Comp. Jer. ix. 1, xxiii. 10. For the conjecture of Stuck, that the word was originally

מֵאֹפֶה, *baked* or *cooked*, there is no foundation. To place the violent and incontinent character of their lust in the strongest light, the prophet compares it to a baker's oven, which he raises to such a degree of heat, that he only requires to omit feeding it during the short period of the fermentation of the bread. Such was the libidinous character of the Israelites, that their impure indulgences were subject to but slight interruptions. Comp. ἀκαταπαύστους ἁμαρτίας, 2 Pet. ii. 14. בֹּעֵרָה, in the feminine agrees with תַּנּוּר, which is of common gender. The latter word Gesenius derives from the Aram. תְּנַן, *to smoke*, and נוּר, *fire*. Comp. the Arab. تنور and Syr. ܬܢܘܪܐ *fornax, clibanus*. The oven here referred to is not the pitcher-oven of the Arabs, but the larger kind, pretty much like our own, which was, as it still is, used in public bake-houses. בֹּעֵרָה מֵאֹפֶה is elliptical for *burning*, having been kindled *by the baker*. Before יִשְׁבּוֹת supply אֲפֶה. The meaning is, who *only* ceaseth from heating, etc. Most interpreters take מֵעִיר in the sense of *stirring*, *rousing up*, etc., and apply it to the stirring of the fire in the oven; but it is preferable to regard it as the part. of עִיר, Arab. عَارَ, *to be hot, burning;* hence in Hiph. *to cause to burn, heat,* etc. Thus the LXX. ἀπὸ τῆς φλογός. The interpretation *from the city*, given in the Syr. Targ. and Vulg. is altogether inappropriate. For the feminine form of the Infin. הַחְמִצָתוֹ, Comp. חֻמְצָה, Ezek. xvi. 5.

5. By יוֹם is meant *a festal day;* either that of the king's birth, or, as the

The princes are sick with the fever of wine;
He stretcheth out his hand with the scoffers.
6 For though they approach with their heart warm as an oven,
Yet it is in their plot;
Their baker sleepeth all the night;
In the morning it burneth like a blazing fire.

Targ. Jarchi and Kimchi give it, that of his inauguration. The preposition ב is understood. Michaelis thinks the reference is to the accession of a new king to the throne. Instead of מַלְכֵּנוּ, *our king*, twenty-two MSS. and the Syr. read מְלָכֵינוּ *our kings;* LXX. ἡμέραι τῶν βασιλέων ὑμῶν. הֶחֱלוּ is used intransitively. The LXX. Syr. Targ. Vulg. Abarbanel, Leo Juda, Newcome, Michaelis, and Boothroyd, refer this verb to the root חלל; but, not to insist on its requiring in such case to be read הֵחֵלּוּ, there is something so intolerably tame in the rendering, "The princes *began* to be heated with wine," that it cannot be admitted as the language of the prophet. Besides, חֲמַת would likewise require to be changed into חֵמֶת, which would produce an anomalous infinitive. חֵמֶת, *bottle*, less agrees with מִן following than חֵמָה, *heat*. Comp. Arab. حَمِىَ, حُمَّى. חֲמַת מִיָּיִן is an instance of the construct state with a preposition intervening between the nouns. Comp. מֻכֵּה בַב־ יִרְאֵי, Ezek. xiii. 2; שְׁכֻרַת וְלֹא מִיַּיִן, Is. li. 21, and see Gesen. Lehrgeb. p. 679. The words mean the heat or fever produced by intoxication. While the courtiers thus indulged to excess, the monarch, forgetting his dignity, participated in their cups, and joined in their scoffs. Because לֹצְצִים occurs nowhere else, Houbigant would have it changed into the usual form לֵצִים, most uncritically. Comp. קִיץ and קַיִץ. Aq. χλευαστῶν; LXX. less properly, λοιμῶν. The reduplicate form is intensive, and expresses the awfully profligate character of the persons described.

6. I consider the prophet to be continuing in this verse his description of the abandoned courtiers, in imagery borrowed from that introduced ver. 4. In their intercourse with the monarch,

they approached him with the warmest professions of loyalty; but in private they were scheming how to get rid of him. The ringleader waited till he could conveniently carry the plot into execution; and speedily they effected the nefarious purpose. Were it not that all the ancient versions render קֵרְבוּ as a verb, I should have been inclined to point it קִרְבָּם, and translate, "For their inward part is like an oven; their heart is in their plot." Comp. וּבְקִרְבּוֹ יָשִׂים אָרְבּוֹ, Jer. ix. 7. The rendering I have given, however, equally suits the connection. Though there is no word in the text corresponding to "warm," its insertion in the translation is fully justified by the comparison in כְתַנּוּר, *like an oven*, and the intensive force of קָרַב in Piel. That this verb ever signifies *to make ready* or *prepare*, I do not find. All attempts to justify the rendering of the LXX. and Syr. ἀνεκαίθηραν, ܠܡܐ, by the conjectural readings חָרְבוּ, צָרְבוּ, and קָדְרוּ, have proved abortive. According to the Hexapla, Symm. (ܗܡܐ ܚܡܘ), Aq. and Theod. (ܚܡܝܘ? ܠܡܚܡܐ), read as we now do; as did likewise the Targ. אֲקָרְבוּ. — אֹפֵהֶם, *their baker*, (many MSS. and various printed editions have אֹפֵיהֶם, which may be regarded as a singular form, י taking the place of the third radical ה, as in other nouns or participles derived from verbs in לה,) the Targ. and Syr. render רִהְיוֹנֵיהוֹן, ܐܦܗܘܢ, as if the reading were אַפָּם, *their anger*. Ἐφραΐμ, found in the LXX. shows that the former must have been the reading of the MS. which they used, as the latter could not have so easily been mistaken for this proper name. אָפֵיהֶם, which Dathe proposes, and Kuinoel

7 They all glow as an oven,
　　They devour their judges;
　　All their kings have fallen:
　　None among them calleth unto me.
8 　　Ephraim mixeth himself up with the nations;
　　Ephraim is a cake unturned.
9 Strangers devour his strength,
　　But he knoweth it not;
　　Yea, gray hairs are sprinkled upon him,
　　Yet he knoweth it not.

adopts into his Heb. text, nowhere occurs in the sense, *ira, furor, eorum*. By "their baker" seems to be meant the leader of the conspiracy, whom some suppose to be Menahem, others Shallum, 2 Kings xv. 10-15; but I should rather infer from what is stated ver. 7, that the prophet includes all the conspiracies which took place in Israel. Having prepared the rest of the conspirators, he, like the baker, abided his time, when, of a sudden, the plot burst forth like a flame.

7. Comp. 2 Kings xv. כֻּלָּם, *all of them*, corresponds to כֻּלָּם, ver. 4. יֵחַמּוּ is the future in Kal of חָמַם, *to be warm, hot*, etc. The prophet still continues the comparison. As the fire in the oven devours the fuel, so the persons spoken of destroyed those who were in authority. נָפַל is not to be taken in the sense of *falling off* or apostatizing from God, as Jerome, Ribera, Menochius, Tirinius, and some others interpret, but in that of falling by the hands of murderers. This, אָכְלוּ, *they devour*, in the preceding hemistitch, shows. The source of the evil, however, lay in apostasy from Jehovah, which had reached such a height, that none implored the Divine aid even when in calamity.

8. Ewald renders יִתְבּוֹלָל, *veraltet*, "hath become old," which might seem to derive some support from the latter part of ver 9; but the verb can, with no propriety, be referred to any other root than בָּלַל, Arab. بَلَّ, *madefecit, commistus fuit*, Syr. ܒܠܠ *confudit, to mix by pouring, mix, confound*. LXX.

συνεμίγνυτο. Syr. ܐܬܚܠܛ. Targ. אִתְעָרֵב. Comp. Psalm cvi. 35, where יִתְעָרְבוּ בַגּוֹיִם is similarly used of promiscuous intercourse with idolaters. That such intercourse generally, including the adoption of their idolatrous practices, and not specifically the entering into leagues with them, is meant, appears from the following clause, in which, to express the worthlessness of the Ephraimitish character, the people are compared to a cake, which, from not having been turned, is burnt, and good for nothing. The Arabs bake their bread on the ground or hearth, covering it with hot embers, and turning it every ten minutes or quarter of an hour, to prevent its being burnt. When neglected it is unfit for food, and is thrown away. Such was the state of the apostate Israelites. They had corrupted themselves, and were only fit for rejection. LXX. ἐγκρυφίας, *bread baked in hot ashes*, Cyril, τῶν ἐπὶ λίθοις ὀπτομένων ἄρτων.

9. זָרִים, *strangers, foreigners*, i. e. the Syrians, Assyrians, etc. See 2 Kings xiii. 7; xv. 19, 20; xvii. 3-6. The state, drawing to its close, without the fact being observed by its citizens, is compared to a person on whose head gray hairs begin to make their appearance, without his becoming sensible of the approach of age.

"Sparserit et nigras alba senecta comas." *Propertius.*

10-12. A repetition of part of chap. v. 5, which see. Though the apostate Israelites had abundant proof of the

10 The pride of Israel testifieth to his face,
　Yet they turn not to Jehovah their God,
　Nor seek him for all this.
11 Ephraim is like a silly dove, without understanding;
　They call in Egypt, they go to Assyria.
12 As they go, I will spread my net upon them,
　I will bring them down like the fowls of heaven:
　I will chastise them,
　As it hath been heard in their assembly.
13 Woe unto them! for they have wandered from me;
　Destruction unto them! for they have rebelled against me.
　Though it was I that redeemed them,
　Yet have they spoken lies against me.
14 They cry not to me with their heart,
　But howl upon their beds:

inefficiency of their idols, yet they returned not in the exercise of true repentance to God, who alone could deliver them in the hour of trouble, but formed alliances with foreign powers in the delusive hope of protection. The simplicity of the dove is proverbial. Thus the Arabs, ليس شي ابله من الحمام, *there is nothing more simple than the dove.* The word פותה is here, however, used in a bad sense, as אֵין לֵב, *without heart,* i. e. without understanding, shows. The point of comparison is the inconsiderate flight of the dove from one danger into another; from the alarm which makes her leave her abode for the net of the fowler. Such would be the case with the Israelites. Jehovah had distinctly announced to them, that foreign alliances would prove their ruin; yet they heedlessly rushed into destruction. אֶפְרֹשׂ stands either for אֶפְרֹשָׂה or לֶאֱפֹרשׁ. The spreading of the net refers to the taking of birds that are on the ground; the bringing down, to those that are in the air, by the use of missile weapons. Instead of the Hiphil אַיְסִרֵם, which occurs only here, the Soncin. edit. of the Prophets, and some few MSS. read אֶאְסְרֵם in Piel, which may also be interpreted causatively. כְּשֵׁמַע לַעֲדָתָם, lit. *according to the report to their assembly,* i. e. the public congregations, to which the Divine messages were delivered. God had given them sufficient warning by Moses and the prophets. The versions vary in rendering the last word, which has given rise to the conjectural readings לְבִצְרָתָם, לְעָצְתָם, and בְּרָעָתָם. Aq., however, renders, κατὰ ἀκοῆς τῆς συναγωγῆς.

13. That אִי is denunciative and not plaintive, the following שׁ plainly shows. נָדַד is often used of the flight of birds that wander from their nest, see Prov. xxvii. 8; Is. xvi. 2; Jer. iv. 25; and is here employed with reference to the silly dove, ver. 12. The redemption from Egypt, and that which, in numerous instances, they afterwards experienced, Jehovah adduces in aggravation of their guilt. Their preferring the service of idols to that of the true God, was not merely a practical denial of his all-sufficiency, but a violation of the solemn pledge which they had given of undivided obedience to his law, when, as stated, chap. vi. 1-3, they professed to return to him.

14. When pressed down by the calamities which their sins had brought upon them, they cried to God for deliverance, but without any genuine repentance or sincere resolution to obey him in future. עַל־מִשְׁכְּבוֹתָם, *upon their beds,* i. e. in the night-season, when their anxiety pre-

For the sake of corn and new wine they assemble;
They rebel against me.
15 Though I instructed them, and strengthened their arms,
Yet they devised evil against me.
16 They may turn, but it is not to the Most High;
They are like a deceitful bow;
Their rulers shall fall by the sword,

vented them from sleeping. יִתְגּוֹרָרוּ, the LXX. reading יִתְגּוֹרָדוּ, render κατετέμνοντο, *they cut themselves*, supposing that in token of grief, or like the maddened priests of Baal, 1 Kings xviii. 28, they inflicted wounds upon their bodies. This is also, in all probability, what the Syr. translator intended by ܡܬܚܒܠܝܢ. But though יִתְגּוֹדָדוּ is found in six MSS. has been in eight more originally, and is the reading of two early editions, one of which is the Soncin. of 1486, it is not sufficiently supported to warrant its adoption into the text. The Targ. Abul-walid, Jarchi, Abenezra, Kimchi, Munster, Piscator, Leo Juda, Junius, Tremellius, Boothroyd, Rosenmüller, Maurer, and Gesenius, support the textual reading, and render *congregate*. This decidedly agrees better with the following יָסוּרוּ בָּם. Instead of returning to Jehovah, the Israelites assembled before their idols to propitiate them by sacrifices, in order to obtain a fruitful harvest. Lee renders, *they become withdrawn, withdraw themselves*, i. e. for idolatrous purposes. To mark more strongly the atrociousness of their apostasy, בִּי, "*against me*," is employed, instead מִמֶּנִּי, of "*from me*," the preposition that otherwise follows סוּר, which is frequently used of apostasy from God to idolatrous practices. The whole phrase is in this case best rendered by *rebel against*, as in our common version.

15. יִסַּר does not signify *to bind*, but *to chastise* or *instruct*. The LXX. instead of rendering the last words of the preceding verse, have ἐπαιδεύθησαν. Pococke's Arab. MSS. وانا ادبت. Those whose character is here described, had been instructed not only by words, but also in a more severe manner, by the judgments which had been inflicted upon them; but that the former kind of instruction is meant, seems clear from the phrase חִזַּקְתִּי זְרוֹעֹתָם, *to strengthen the arm*, i. e. to impart strength or power for the performance of any undertaking. Comp. Ezek. xxx. 24, 25, where both the impartation and the deprivation of such power are mentioned. What the רָע, *evil*, or *wickedness* was, which they cogitated, is not specified; but it most likely consisted in some new idolatrous alliance, such as that with Egypt, referred to in the next verse. LXX. πονηρὰ; Targ. בִּישָׁן, *evil things*.

16. יָשׁוּבוּ לֹא עַל, "*convertunt se ad non-summum*, i. e. ad non-deum, collect. non-deos, i. e. ad deos fictos, vanos." Maurer. Thus also Gesen. in voc. עַל. Comp. for the use of this idiom, Is. x. 15, note. Hosea, who is fond of brevity, uses here and chap. xi. 7, עַל, instead of the longer form עֶלְיוֹן, *Most High*. Kametz is used instead of Pattach, on account of the accent. Arab. علا *altus, excelsus fuit*, to be high in dignity. عال, *altus*, Pococke's Arab. MS. in chap. xi. 7. العالي; Syr. ܐܠܗܐ, *God*; one of De Rossi's MSS. עַל. What the apostate Israelites worshipped, so far from being the Most High, was the direct opposite — wood or stone, the produce of the earth. The LXX. ἀπεστράφησαν εἰς οὐδέν, and Syr. ܐܬܗܦܟܘ ܠܠܐ ܡܕܡ to the same effect, though giving the sense rather than an exact translation. The Latin translation of the Syr. *nulla de causa*, is quite erroneous. Most moderns, less aptly, take עַל in its adverbial

On account of the insolence of their language:
This shall be their derision in the land of Egypt.

acceptation, and render, *they return not upwards;* which yields, however, nearly the same meaning. Thus Rosenmüller, Winer, Manger, Stuck, and others. Newcome's conjectural emendation, לֹא יוֹעִיל, *that which cannot profit,* has not been approved; while the translation of Dathe, *Pœnitentiam agunt, sed non sinceram,* though approved by Kuinoel, Tingstadius, and others, is not borne out by Hebrew usage. קֶשֶׁת רְמִיָּה some render *a slack bow,* supposing that its inutility, owing to the absence of elasticity, is what is intended; but *false* or *deceitful* better suits the connection, and Ps. lxxviii. 57; and the reference is to something faulty in the construction of the bow, which causes it to shoot or throw out the arrow wide of the mark. Root רָמָה, Arab. رمى, *jecit, projecit; to throw, shoot,* etc. There seems no ground for the opinion of Gesenius, that the phrase is used poetically for treacherous bowmen, who feign tight in order to deceive. The Israelites hypocritically pretended to turn to Jehovah, but their actions took a different direction. Comp. לְשׁוֹן רְמִיָּה, *a deceitful tongue,* Ps. cxx. 2, 3. The *insolence* (Aq. and Symm. *ἐμβρίμησιν,*) *of their language* doubtless consisted in their proud boast of Egypt as a source of protection from the Assyrian invasion, which God was about to bring upon them. לַעְגָּם, *their derision,* i. e. the subject of derision to the Egyptians, to whom they should in vain apply for help. Comp. 2 Kings xvii. 4; Is. xxx. 1–7, though the latter passage is immediately directed against a contemporaneous application on the part of the Jews.

CHAPTER VIII.

The prophet announces the sudden irruption of the Assyrians, 1; by whom the Israelites were to be punished, on account of their hypocrisy and apostasy, 2, 3; their illegitimate government, and their idolatry, 4. He then exposes the folly of their idolatrous confidence, and predicts their captivity, 5–10; remonstrates with them for their devotion to the worship of idols, in opposition to the express and numerous prohibitions of the evil contained in the divine law, 11, 12; and insists that their pretended service of Jehovah, while in reality they forgot him, so far from being of any avail to them, would only bring destruction upon them, 13, 14.

---

1 Put the trumpet to thy mouth;
"Like an eagle against the house of Jehovah;"

1. It is not unusual for the prophets without naming the invading foe, to announce his approach. See Is. xiii. 2. The words אֶל־חִכְּךָ שֹׁפָר, *to thy palate the trumpet!* are singularly abrupt, and indicate the suddenness of the threatened invasion. חֵךְ, *palate,* is here, as Job xxxi. 30, Prov. viii. 7, put for the mouth. Comp. chap. v. 8. The LXX. (*εἰς κόλπον αὐτῶν, ὡς γῆ*) appear to have read

For they have transgressed my covenant,
They have rebelled against my law.
2 They may cry to me: "O my God;
We — Israel — acknowledge thee."
3 Israel hath rejected what is good;
The enemy shall pursue him.
4 They made kings, but it was not from me;

אֶל חֵקִי בְּעָם, which makes no sense. The following words עַל־בֵּית יְהֹוָה — בַּעַם, which contain the announcement, are equally abrupt. The point of comparison is the rapidity of flight for which the eagle is celebrated, and which is frequently employed to denote the speedy approach of an enemy. Comp. Deut. xxviii. 49; Jer. iv. 13, xlviii. 40; Lam. iv. 19. בֵּית יְהוָֹה, *the house of Jehovah*, cannot here mean the temple at Jerusalem, which is otherwise so designated, since the threatenings are specially denounced against the kingdom of the ten tribes. It must, therefore, be taken to denote the people of Israel, the whole nation viewed as the family or church of God. Comp. chap. ix. 15; Numb. xii. 7; Heb. iii. 2; just as the christian church is called *the house of God*. 1 Tim. iii. 15, and of Christ, Heb. iii. 6. For עָבְרוּ בְרִיתִי, comp. chap. vi. 7. The nominative to עָבְרוּ *they have transgressed*, is בֵּית יְהוָֹה, *the family*, i. e. the members of the church, *of Jehovah*. The Israelites had violated the obligations of the theocracy. בְּרִית and תוֹרָה are synonymous.

2. יִזְעָקוּ is the future used potentially and not with irony. אֱלֹהַי, "O *my God*," is construed as a distributive with the plural verb — each of the persons spoken of being regarded as using the language. Inattention to this has led the Syrian translator to render, [Syriac] *O our God*.

יִשְׂרָאֵל, *Israel*, is in apposition with יְדַעֲנוּךָ, *we acknowledge thee*, and not the nominative to יִזְעָקוּ, from which it is too far removed. It is entirely omitted in the LXX. Syr. and Arab. as it is in one of Kennicott's MSS., and originally in one of De Rossi's אֵלֶיךָ יִשְׂרָאֵל, *O God* *of Israel*, the conjecture of Houbigant, is unnecessary. The present position of the word is more in keeping with the style of Hosea, and the use of it well agrees with the vain confidence which the unbelieving Israelites were ever prone to place in their relation to the patriarchs.

3. זָנַח, Arab. [Arabic], *corruptum fuit et fœtuit, to be corrupt, loathsome*, and *to reject* as such. To treat as loathsome what was truly excellent, such as the worship of God and the practice of religion, argued an awfully depraved state of moral feeling. The use of יִשְׂרָאֵל, *Israel*, finely contrasts with that made of it in the preceding verse. טוֹב, *good*, is, by Jerome, Abenezra, Kimchi, and others, taken for God himself, who is described as טוֹב וּמֵטִיב, *good and doing good*, Ps. cxix. 68. *Deum summum bonum*, Œcolampadius. It seems, however, to be used in a more general acceptation. Before אִישׂ there is an ellipsis of the illative לָכֵן. Forty-seven of De Rossi's MSS. and two more by correction; eight of the most ancient, and sixty-two other editions; the Syr. Vulg. and Targ. read יִרְדְּפוֹ instead of יִרְדְּפוֹ, exhibited in the Textus Receptus. See De Rossi's Scholia Critica.

4. Some think the kings and princes here referred to were Shallum, Menahem, Pekahiah, Pekah, Hoshea, and such of their partisans as were invested with authority; but from the allusions made in the following verses to the origination of image worship in Israel, it is more probable that the entire series of Israelitish kings and rulers is intended. Though in the providence of God, and agreeable to the declaration of Ahiah the prophet, the ten tribes revolted from the house of David, and set up a separate and inde-

They set up princes, but I acknowledge them not:
Of their silver and their gold they have made for themselves idols,
In order that they may be cut off.
5 Thy calf, O Samaria! is abominable;
Mine anger burneth against them:
How long shall they be incapable of purity?
6 For it came from Israel,

pendent kingdom, yet they were actuated merely by rebellious motives, and had no regard to a divine sanction, 1 Kings xi. 31–39, xii. 20. יָדַע, signifies not only *to know*, but also *to approve* of that which is known, *regard, allow, own.* Job. ix. 21, xxxiv. 4; Ps. i. 6, *et freq.* LXX. καὶ οὐκ ἐγνώρισαν μοι. Syr. ܘܠܐ ܐܘܕܥܘܢܝ *and did not acquaint me*, i. e. held no communications with me upon the subject. The Heb. however, will not bear this interpretation. ו in both cases before לֹא, has the force of a relative, which must either be adopted in translation, or the personal pronoun must be supplied. For their conversion of their silver and gold into idols, comp. chap. ii. 8. לְמַעַן does not appear ever to be taken in a retrospective sense, and so to be referred to what goes before, but is always used with direct reference to what follows. לְמַעַן יִכָּרֵת is, therefore, to be rendered, *in order that they may be cut off;* not *so that they shall*, etc. Comp. Jer. vii. 10, xliv. 8. In all such cases the preposition is employed to give peculiar emphasis to the subject. The Israelites could not seriously, or in reality, have intended their own destruction, but they acted as if they had; and it would assuredly overtake them. The nominative to יִכָּרֵת may either be Israel, understood; or it may have respect to the people collectively.

5. The *calf of Samaria* was not any set up in that city, but that set up at Bethel with another at Dan, or both, if we take the noun as a collective, which its inhabitants, and those of the country generally, worshipped. The metropolis appears to be used here by synecdoche for the whole land occupied by the ten tribes;

but, at the same time, there can be little doubt that its inhabitants were pre-eminent in their devotion to idolatry. זָנַח, is used in its primary acceptation, *to be loathsome, abominable*. See on ver. 3. Such construction is preferable to that which would make עֶגְלֵךְ the accusative to זָנַח, assuming זָנִיחַ understood to be the nominative, or that in our common version, which makes it the nominative, and *Samaria* in its pronominal reference the accusative. The introduction of the worship of the golden calves by Jeroboam, in imitation of Apis, at Memphis, and Mnevis, at Heliopolis, which he must have seen during his residence in Egypt, paved the way for the imitation and adoption of the gross idolatries practised by the Phœnicians, Syrians, and Chaldeans. חָרָה אַף יְהֹוָה, *the anger of Jehovah burneth*, is an anthropopathic mode of expression of frequent occurrence in the Hebrew Scriptures, denoting the unconquerable opposition of God to all moral evil, and the severity of the punishment with which it is visited. בָּם, *against them*, i. e. the Israelites who worshipped the golden calves. עַד־מָתַי לֹא יוּכְלוּ נִקָּיֹן, *how long shall they be incapable of purity?* i. e. how long shall they be obstinately attached to the impure service of idols, and reject the means by which they might be recovered from its stain and punishment.

6. The golden calf had its origin in Israel: it was not made by any of the surrounding idolaters. The ו in וְהוּא is emphatic. שְׁבָבִים יִהְיֶה, *shall be* or *become flames*, i. e. shall be burnt. שְׁבָבִים is a ἅπαξ λεγ. and has no root in Heb.; but comp. the Arab شبّ, *accendit ignem*, شبيب, *ardor, flamma*. As the calf was made by man, so it should by man be converted

The carpenter made it;
It is not God:
Surely the calf of Samaria shall become flames.
7 Because they have sown wind,
They shall reap the whirlwind.
They shall have no stalk;
The growth shall produce no grain;
Should it peradventure produce it,
Strangers shall swallow it up.
8 Israel is swallowed up;
They are now among the nations,
Like a vessel in which is no delight.
9 For they went up to Assyria,
Like a solitary wild ass:
Ephraim hath given the hire of love.

into fuel for the flames. It consisted, in all probability, of wood, thickly overlaid with gold. When taken as a present to the king of Assyria, (see chap. x. 6,) instead of being worshipped or held in respect, it would be stripped of the gold, and consigned to the flames. The LXX. followed by the Arab. Horsley, and Newcombe, improperly translate בְּ מִיְשְׂרָאֵל, ἐν τῷ Ἰσραήλ, في اسرايل in Israel, and join the words to those of the preceding verse.

7. סוּפָתָה is the emphatic form of סוּפָה, a tornado, whirlwind. Leo Juda, magnum turbinem. Comp. אֵימָתָה, Exod. xv. 16; יְשׁנָתָה, Ps. iii. 3. The nominative to לֹּו is יִשְׂרָאֵל, understood; but it is best to take it collectively, in harmony with the plural of the preceding verbs. Observe the paronomasia in צֶמַח בְּלִי יַעֲשֶׂה־קֶּמַח. The Israelites should be unsuccessful in all their undertakings; and whatever partial gains they might acquire, would be eagerly seized by the Assyrians.

8. What Hosea had just foretold is here realized in prophetic vision. He sees them in a state of exile — the objects of contempt to their oppressors. Comp. Jer. xxii. 28.

9, 10. עָלָה, to go up, is elsewhere used of foreigners coming to the land of Israel; but is here employed with singular propriety of the Israelites going to Assyria, to intimate their depressed condition, and their acknowledgment of the superiority of the Assyrian power. The reference is not to their going into captivity, but to the embassy which they sent for the purpose of obtaining aid from that quarter. אַשּׁוּר stands for אַשּׁוּרָה, the ה of direction being omitted. The point of comparison in the "wild ass" is his untractableness, and his disposition to take his own way, in consequence of which he forsakes the society of others, and loves the solitariness of the desert. See Job xxxix. 5-8. Thus it was with Israel. Despite of all the councils and warnings given them by the prophets, they persisted in entering into foreign alliances. תָּנָה, to give presents, hire, etc. is purposely chosen, to convey the idea of a violation of the marriage contract by unlawful commerce with another party — the derivatives אֶתְנַן and אֶתְנָה, properly denoting a gift or reward given to a whore. See on chap. ii. 12. The aggravation of the evil is signified by representing the female as offering these rewards to her paramours to induce them to commit lewdness, instead of her being prevailed upon by presents made by them. Comp. Ezek. xvi. 33, 34. Though in Hiphil, the verb has here the same signification as in

10 Yet though they have hired among the nations,
    I will now gather them;
    And they shall suffer in a little
    By reason of the tribute of the king of princes.
11   When Ephraim multiplied altars to sin,

Kal. אֲהָבִים, lit. *loves*, a plural not in use in English. Jerome, who renders, *numera dederunt amatoribus*, either read אֶחָבִים which is found in one of De Rossi's MSS., or he took אֲהָבִים in a concrete sense, as our translators appear to have done, for which there is no necessity. Instead of יִתְנוּ at the beginning of ver. 10, two of De Rossi's MSS. the LXX. Syr. Vulg. Targ. and Arab. read יֻתְּנוּ, as if from נָתַן; according to which, the Israelites are represented as *delivered over to*, or placed in the power of the nations. The fifth Greek version, however, has ἀλλὰ καὶ ὅταν μισθώσηται ἔθνη, which is preferable, as it is most likely that the prophet repeated the verb he had just used, and as the other rendering is less suited to the connection. מְעָט, *now*, i. e. shortly. Comp. מְעָט immediately after. The suffix in אֲקַבְּצֵם, "I will collect them," belongs to הַגּוֹיִם, *the nations*, and not to the nominative to יֻתְּנוּ, or the Israelites. קבץ is used in Piel in a bad as well as in a good sense. Comp. Ezek. xvi. 37. Thus Kimchi and Abarbanel. Instead of affording any assistance, the Assyrians would be collected against the apostate Israelites, invade their land, and carry them into captivity. Into that state of suffering, imposed upon them by the king of Assyria, they were shortly to be brought, as a punishment for their idolatrous desertion of the true worship of God. וַיָּחֵלּוּ מְעָט מִמַּשָּׂא מֶלֶךְ שָׂרִים has been variously interpreted. Gesenius renders, "*and they* (the hostile nations,) *shall presently set* them *free from the burden of the king*, i. e. from his oppressive yoke;" but without any suitable sense — the whole passage being of a comminatory nature, and not promissory of good. הֵחֵל, the Hiph. of חָלַל, has nowhere the signification of *loosing* or *setting free*. Nor is there any propriety in taking it in the usual sense of *beginning*, and so construing it with מְעָט, as if the latter word were the infinitive of the verb מָעַט, *to be diminished*. The ancient versions refer to יָחֵל, as the root, in the sense of *waiting, desisting from*, etc. LXX. κοπάσουσι. Symm. μενοῦσιν. Theod. διαλείψουσι. Syr. ܘܢܬܬܢܝܚܘܢ Vulg. *quiescent*. And in this reference I concur, especially as ten MSS. and forty-four editions, read וְיָחֵלּוּ without the Dagesh in the Lamed; only I would abide by the signification, *to be in pain, affliction*, which is that given to the verb in our common version. Such construction alone suits the connection. By some שָׂרִים מֶלֶךְ are considered to be an instance of asyndeton; and twenty-one MSS. and originally ten more, the LXX. Aq. Syr. Vulg. Targ. and Talm. Babl. supply the copulative ו before שָׂרִים. So Kimchi, Mercer, Piscator. Grotius, Houbigant, Dathe, Michaelis, Kuinoel, Newcome, Tingstadius. It has been doubted, however, whether, according to this resolution of the word, they should be referred to the native king and princes, or to those of Assyria. Some, as Maurer, take them to be the nominative to יָחֵלּוּ, and make the sense end with מַשָּׂא, *the burden or tribute*, supposing the heavy taxes imposed by the Israelitish rulers to be intended. The best sense is brought out by reading מֶלֶךְ שָׂרִים in construction, *the king of princes*, and applying the phrase to the king of Assyria, who had many kings and princes subject to his sway. Comp. Is. x. 8. Thus Pococke's Arabic MS., Leo Juda, Drusius, Jun. and Tremel., Piscator, Eichhorn, Boeckel, Goldwitzer, Hitzig, and Ewald. The מַשָּׂא, *burden*, was the tribute exacted by Menahem, and paid to Pul, amounting to a thousand talents of silver, 2 Kings xv. 19-22. Comp. מַשָּׂא מֶכֶס, *tribute money*, 2 Chron. xvii. 11.

11. By multiplying altars, in opposi-

They became to him altars to sin, •
12 I may prescribe for him the numerous things of my law;
   They are treated as a strange thing.
13 As for my sacrificial offerings,
   They sacrifice flesh and eat it;
   Jehovah accepteth them not:
   He will speedily remember their **iniquity**,
   And will punish their sin:
   They shall return to Egypt.

tion to the express prohibition, Deut. xii. 13, 14, the Ephraimites not only contracted great guilt, but paved the way for the introduction of other sins. Syr. ܟܣܝܘܬܐ ܙܒܐ, *ad crimen ingens*. There is an easy but beautiful variation in the repetition of the words. As used the second time, חטא possesses considerable emphasis. Comp. for a similar instance of varied repetition, Is. xxvii. 5. It shows how much the mind of the prophet was affected by the wickedness of his people. Some suppose that there is a play upon the double meaning of חטא as signifying *to sin*, and *to be punished for sin*, just as our Lord uses νέκροι in two senses, Matt. viii. 22; but the second signification cannot attach to the verb in this connection.

12. אֶכְתּוֹב, Keri אֶכְתָּב‎, is continuative and potential, and is equivalent to, I have prescribed, I still prescribe by my prophets, and I may go on prescribing; it will be of no avail. Keri רֻבֵּי in many MSS. רִבֵּי, the plural of רֹב, which is properly the infinitive of רָבַב, *to be great, numerous*, etc. Here the idea of number is evidently designed to express the abundant provisions God had made in his written law, and its enforcement by the prophets, against the commission of idolatry. According to the Chethiv רִבּוֹ, we should render, "I may prescribe to him my laws *by myriads;*" Ewald, *by thousands;*" Hitzig, *by ten thousands,*

The Syr. ܣܓܝܐܘܬ ܐܘܪܝܬܝ. Targ. סַגִיאָא אוֹרַיְתִי. Vulg. *multiplices leges meas*. Pococke's Arab. MS. عشر

Aq. πληθυμένους νόμους. Symm. πλῆθος νόμων μου. חֻקִּים, *statutes*, are understood. חָשַׁב signifies not only *to think, regard*, etc., but also to treat in a manner corresponding to the estimation in which a person or thing is held. Tanchum, يطرحونها كالغريب الذي لا يغوبه البد *they reject them like a strange thing to which no regard is paid.*

13. זִבְחֵי הַבְהָבַי. זִבְחֵי הַבְהָבַי form the nominative absolute. הַבְהָבַי *my gifts*, or *offerings*, i. e. such as they professedly offer to me. The word is contracted for יְהַבְהָבַי, and is derived from יְהַב, *to give*. It seems preferable to abide by this usual signification of the verb, which it has likewise in Aramaic, Arabic, and Ethiopic, than to follow Kimchi, who refers the noun to a root הָבַב, to which he assigns the signification *to burn, scorch, roast;* or Ewald, who, appealing to the Chald. הַבְהֵב, and the Arab. هب and سهب renders, *raw offerings*. הַבְהָבַי is a more choice term for מִנְחוֹת, or מַתָּנוֹת. For the reduplicate form, comp. אֲהַבְהָב, chap. iv. 18; which word the LXX. Syr. and Targ. appear to have followed in this place; of which Hitzig seems to approve. Aq., observant of the gemination, renders, θυσίας φέρε φέρε θυσιάζουσιν. Symm. θυσίας ἐπαλλήλους. Theod. θυσίαν μεταφορῶν ἐθυσίασαν. Jehovah rejected the sacrifices that were offered, not according to his own appointment, but to gratify the carnal appetite of the worshippers. Reference is had to the sacrifices offered to him, as represented by the golden calf. In רָצָה לֹא is a meiosis.

14 Because Israel hath forgotten his Maker, and built temples,
And Judah hath multiplied fortified cities;
Therefore will I send a fire into his cities;
And it shall consume the palaces of each.

עַתָּה, *now*, is here used in the sense of *speedily, shortly*. From the references made chap. ix. 3, 6, xi. 11, it is clear that the last clause of the verse predicts the actual return of a number of the Israelites to Egypt, whither, in all probability, they fled when the kingdom was broken up by the Assyrians. The threatening pointedly reminded them of the depressed condition in which their ancestors had been in that country. Comp. Deut. xxviii. 68. The LXX. add, καὶ ἐν 'Ασσυρίοις ἀκάθαρτα φάγονται; but the words are wanting in the Aldine edition, and in seven MSS. They have evidently found their way into the text from chap. ix. 3, where they stand in accordance with the reading of all the Heb. MSS.

14. וַ in וַיִּשְׁכַּח marks the protasis; in וְשִׁלַּחְתִּי the apodosis. The הֵיכָלוֹת were doubtless *idolatrous temples* erected after the models of those in use among the Syrians and Phœnicians. See, for the word, my note on Is. vi. 1. Though idolatry had not made the same progress in Judah, the inhabitants nevertheless evinced a want of confidence in Jehovah by fortifying a number of cities, to which they trusted for defence. The masculine suffix in עָרָיו refers to Judah; the feminine in אַרְמְנוֹתֶיהָ to each of the cities, taken singly. Ewald strangely asserts, that the words of this verse appear to have been inserted from some book of Amos no longer in existence! Compare, however, for the latter distich, Jer. xlix. 27; Amos i. 4, 7, 10, 12, 14, ii. 2, 5; and see note on Amos i. 4.

CHAPTER IX.

The prophet checks the propensity of the Israelites to indulge in excessive joy on account of any partial relief from their troubles, 1; predicts the failure of the crops, etc. in consequence of the Assyrian invasion, 2; their removal to Egypt and Assyria, where they should have no opportunity, even if they were inclined, to serve Jehovah according to their ancient ritual, 3–5; and the hopelessness of their returning to enjoy the property they had left behind, 6. He then announces the certain infliction of the divine judgments, and points out the true character of the false prophets, by whom the people had been led astray to their ruin, 7, 8. Illustrative references are next made to the early history of the Hebrew nation, accompanied with appropriate comminations couched in varied forms, in order to render them more affecting, 9–17.

1 CARRY not thy joy, O, Israel! to exultation, like the nations,

1. אַל־תִּשְׂמַח—אֶל־גִּיל, lit. *rejoice not to exultation*. The LXX. Syr. Targ. and Vulg. read אַל גִּיל, *exult not;* but contrary to the *usus loquendi*, which requires

For thou hast lewdly departed from thy God;
Thou hast loved the hire,
On all the corn floors.
2 Neither the floor nor the vat shall nourish them;
And the new wine shall fail therein.
3 They shall not dwell in the land of Jehovah,
But Ephraim shall return to Egypt,
And in Assyria, they shall eat what is unclean.

the verb following אֶל to be in the future tense, as Secker properly observes. Some find in the comparison "like the nations," an imitation of their idolatrous festivities; but the language is rather predictive of the joyless condition to which the Israelites were to be reduced. While those by whom they were surrounded and especially their Assyrian invaders, should indulge in unrestrained mirth, they should experience affliction and sorrow. There is most probably a reference to the joy occasioned by the league entered into with Pul, by which peace seemed to be secured. Their joy was to be of short duration, and therefore required to be moderate. Instead of בְּעַמִּים, thirteen MSS., originally five more, one by correction, and five editions, read בָּעַמִּים, "*among* the nations," of which Rosenmüller, following Abarbanel, approves. The prophet adds the reason why they should have no cause for exultation—their abounding idolatries, by which they incurred the judgments of God. These idolatries they carried to such a pitch, that they erected shrines at their threshing floors, in order to offer at them the oblations of their grain. The crops were considered to have been bestowed by the idols in compensation for the worship rendered to them, (see chap. ii. 5, 12, 13;) and are therefore spoken of as אֶתְנָן, a *meretricious reward*.

2. For בָּם, in reference to the failure of the productions of the earth, see Hab. iii. 17. The verb properly signifies *to lie, deceive*, etc.; figuratively, *to fail*. Twenty-six MSS., originally sixteen more, and perhaps two, three editions, with the support of the LXX. Syr. Targ. and Vulg. read בָּם, *in them*, i. e. *them*, the Israelites, instead of בָּהּ, *in her*, the re-

ceived reading. It is, however, too plainly an emendation to entitle it to adoption. Nothing is more common than for our prophets to use first a plural, and then a singular suffix of the same subject: according to the rule laid down by Tanchum, that when in a continued discourse a nation or people is spoken of, either in the feminine affix agreeing with עֵדָה, *congregation*, or the masculine agreeing with עַם, *people*, may be used; as also, that the singular may be used of them, viewed as a body, and the plural, when they are regarded as consisting of distinct individuals. See in Pococke. At the same time it is better in a translation to render them alike, as in the ancient versions just quoted.

3. Canaan was called אֶרֶץ יְהוָה, *the land of Jehovah*, because he had appropriated it for an inheritance to those whom he had chosen to be his peculiar people. It was his gift to Abraham and his posterity, to be enjoyed by them on condition of their fidelity in his service. For this end he attached to it his special blessing, Deut. xi. 10–12. Comp. Jer. ii. 7, xvi. 18; Ezek. xxxvi. 20. The return to Egypt being here mentioned in connection with an exile in Assyria, proves that it is to be taken literally, and that it is not designed to express a servitude similar to that of Egypt. See on chap. viii. 13. The fulfilment of this prediction in the history of the ten tribes, is nowhere mentioned in Scripture. No doubt the number that fled to Egypt was small, compared with the body of the nation carried into the Assyrian exile. By טָמֵא is meant *prohibited food*, meats pronounced unclean by the Mosaic law. Comp. Ezek. iv. 13. To such necessity should they be reduced as captives.

4 They shall not pour out wine to Jehovah,
Neither shall their sacrifices please him;
They shall be to them as the bread of mourners,
All that eat thereof shall be unclean:
For their bread shall be for themselves;
It shall not come unto the house of Jehovah.
5   What will ye do on the day of assembly?
On the day of Jehovah's festival?
6 For, behold! they go away from destruction,
But Egypt shall gather them, Memphis shall bury them;
As for their coveted treasuries of money, nettles shall possess them:
Thorns shall be in their tents.

4. נָסַךְ is used of the pouring out of wine for a libation, Gr. σπένδειν. Exod. xxx. 9. עָרַב, properly to mix, mingle, came to signify, sweet, agreeable, pleasing, from the circumstance, that what was pleasant to the taste, often consisted of mixed ingredients. לֶחֶם אוֹנִים, bread, or food of sorrows, i. e. such as was eaten by mourners for the dead, and consequently regarded as unclean, on account of the contact in which they were supposed to come with the dead body. See Numb. xix. 14, 15, 22; Jer. xvi. 7, 8; Ezek. xxiv. 17; Hagg. ii. 12, 13. Instead of feasting upon the sacrifices as their fathers had been accustomed to do, when they slew them according to the law, which was always an occasion of joy, they should be placed in circumstances in which no such sacrifices could be offered, and no such feasts enjoyed. Their food should all be common — לְנַפְשָׁם, for their soul, or life, i. e. merely for its sustenance; not fit to be presented to the Lord. Thus Schmidius, Grotius, and others.

5. In captivity they would find it impossible to observe their solemn feasts — a great aggravation of their punishment. Comp. chap. ii. 11. The exposition of Jarchi, Abenezra, Kimchi, Mercer, Capito, and others, according to which, the day of punishment, represented under the idea of sacrifice, is meant, cannot be sustained.

6. The prophet here specially describes those Israelites who should take alarm at the invasion of the country by the Assyrians, and flee for safety into Egypt. They imagined that their stay there would only be temporary; but it is predicted that they should no more return to their possessions, and be buried in their fathers' sepulchres, but should die in the land, and have their interment among the mummies of Egypt. For *Memphis* as the great necropolis of that country, see my note on Isaiah xix, 13. קָבַץ, to *gather*, is here used in reference to the removal of the soul at death, into the world of spirits, and is equivalent to אָסַף, Numb. xx. 26, or the full phrases נֶאֱסַף אֶל־עַמָּיו, and נֶאֱסַף אֶל־אֲבוֹתָיו, *to be gathered to one's people or fathers*, which is always spoken of as something different from death and burial. Comp. Jer. viii. 2; Ezek. xxix. 5, in which latter passage אָסַף, and קָבַץ, are used as synonymes. According to the signification of the cognate Arab. verb. قبض *cepit*, *apprehendit* manu rem, it conveys the idea of God's taking away the soul. Hence the phrase قبضه الله *mortuus est*, literally, *God took him;* and قبض simply, *mortuus* est (ad Dei misericordiam delatus). Freytag. When it is said that Egypt should gather and Memphis bury the Israelitish fugitives, the meaning is that they should be removed out of this world, and that their bodies should be buried there. The personification is employed, as usual, for the sake of effect. מַחְמָד, *desire, covetousness;* that which is *the object of desire, what is covetable, coveted,* from חָמַד, *to desire, covet.* As

7   The days of punishment are come,
    The days of retribution are come;
    Israel shall know it:
    The prophet is foolish,
    The man of the spirit is frantic,
    Because of the greatness of thy punishment,
    And because the provocation is great.

the verb יֵדְעוּ has a plural suffix, this noun is here to be taken as a collective, and rendered in the plural. The idea of treasury is supplied by the connection. כֶּסֶף is used generally of *money*, as in most other places, when זָהָב, *gold*, is not combined with it. Targ. בֵּית חֶמְדַּת כַּסְפְּהוֹן, *the house of their desirable money.* Symm. τὰ ἐπιϑυμήματα τοῦ ἀργυρίου αὐτῶν. Others, less aptly, explain the words of houses, palaces, etc. adorned with silver. On leaving those treasures which they could not carry with them, the Israelites would naturally bury them in the earth, which accounts for the very significant phrase, "the nettles shall inherit them." For the combination קִמּוֹשׂ or קִמּשׂ and חוֹחַ, comp. Is. xxxiv. 13. The whole verse is miserably translated by the LXX.

7. פְּקֻדָּה, *visitation, punishment*. Comp. Is. x. 3; 1 Pet. ii. 12. יֵדְעוּ, *shall know experimentally.* By the נָבִיא is obviously to be understood in this place, the false *prophet* or prophets by whom the people of the ten tribes were seduced from the right worship of Jehovah, who taught them to worship the golden calves, and otherwise encouraged them in their idolatrous practices. Thus Pococke's Arab. MS. المدعي نبوة, *he that pretends to prophesy;* and Kimchi, נְבִיאֵי שֶׁקֶר, *lying prophets.* With this, the phrase אִישׁ הָרוּחַ, *the man of the spirit,* is synonymous; one pretending to inspiration, or professing to deliver oracles under the influence of a divine efflatus. LXX. ἄνϑρωπος ὁ πνευματοφόρος. Syr. ܓܒܪܐ ܕܚܠܝܛ ܒܗ ܪܘܚܐ, *the man that is clothed, or endued with the spirit,* only adding by way of explanation, but erroneously, ܕܫܛܝܘܬܐ, *of folly.* Comp.

Mic. ii. 11. אִישׁ הֹלֵךְ רוּחַ; 1 Cor. xiv. 37. εἴ τις δοκεῖ προφήτης εἶναι ἢ πνευματικός; 2 Pet. i. 21, ὑπὸ πνεύματος ἁγίου φερόμενοι; and see my Lectures on Divine Inspiration, p. 25. מְשֻׁגָּע *insane, frantic;* Arab. شجم, *locutus fuit rhythmice,* to speak in an impassioned manner, like an inspired poet; hence, from the violence of the gesticulations, tones. etc., *to act like a madman, to be mad, insane.* Comp. Jer. xxix. 26, where אִישׁ מְשֻׁגָּע and מִתְנַבֵּא are synonymous. The meaning is, that the pretenders to inspiration, by whose false predictions of uninterrupted prosperity the people had been deluded, should be convicted of *folly*, and reduced to a state of absolute frenzy by the infliction of the divine judgments upon the nation. Hosea introduces this declaration respecting the Israelitish prophets parenthetically, thereby giving force to his own prediction of impending calamity. The affix in עֲוֹנְךָ refers to יִשְׂרָאֵל, to whom the prophet turns in the way of direct address. עָוֹן means here, not the *crime*, but its punishment. Comp. for this signification of the term, Is. v. 18, and my note there. In מַשְׂטֵמָה subaud. כִּי, *because.* The adjective רַבָּה, is here placed before its substantive for the sake of emphasis. See on Is. liii. 11. From the use of שָׂטַם in the sense of *hating, evincing hostility,* etc., there can be little doubt that the derivative מַשְׂטֵמָה, which occurs only in this and the following verse, has the signification of *hostility, provoking conduct, provocation.* That of *snare* or *trap*, which Gesenius assigns to it, is not borne out, even by the Syriac ܫܠܡ which signifies *vinxit, compedivit,* but not to *ensnare.* Comp. the Arab. سلم, *acies gladii; acutiores et*

8   Ephraim expecteth help from my God;
    The prophet is a fowler's snare in all his ways:
    The cause of provocation in the house of his god.
9   They have deeply corrupted themselves,
    As in the days of Gibeah;
    He will remember their iniquity,
    He will punish their sins.
10 I found Israel, like grapes in the desert;
    Like the first early fruit of the fig tree, at its commencement,

fervidiores hominum. LXX. μανία; Aq. ἐγκόσησις; ΑΛΛ ἔκστασις; all of which convey the idea of great excitement, and yield support to the interpretation I have given. The idolatrous practices of the Israelites are meant, by which they provoked the righteous indignation of Jehovah.

8. צֹפֶה אֶפְרַיִם, are not in construction, and to be rendered as in most versions, "the watchman of Ephraim," to justify which construction various modes of exegesis have been resorted to; among others that of Horsley, who would have the watchman to be Elijah. Nor can the rendering of Ewald be sustained, who gives the passage, *Ein Späher ist Ephraim gegen mein Gott.* "Ephraim is a spy against my God." When עִם signifies *against*, it follows verbs of more active import. *E. schaut nach Weissagungen aus neben meinem Gott;* "Ephraim looks for prophecies besides my God," — the rendering of Hitzig, is equally objectionable. I quite agree with Gesenius and Lee, in assigning to צפה in this place the signification of *looking out, expecting,* as in Ps. v. 4; Lam. iv. 17, in Piel. עִם, *with,* is used elliptically for מֵעִם, *from with,* i. e. *from.* A similar ellipsis undeniably occurs Job xxvii. 13. זֶה חֵלֶק־אָדָם רָשָׁע עִם־אֵל, *this is the portion of the wicked man from* (עִם, *with,*) *God,* as appears, not only from the synonymous phrase מִשַּׁדַּי, "FROM *the Almighty,"* in the corresponding hemistich, but from the actual use of מִן, *from,* in the parallel passage, chap. xx. 29. What the prophet asserts is, that the Ephraimites indulged in expectations of good from Jehovah, notwithstanding their dereliction of his worship in its pure and legitimate forms, and their adoption of the idolatrous practices of the heathen around them. In this they were encouraged by the false prophets, who caught them by their ensnaring doctrines, as is declared immediately after. בֵּית אֱלֹהָיו is here used in the same acceptation as in the preceding verse, only there is a metonymy of the effect for the cause. By בֵּית אֱלֹהָיו, "the house of his god," is not meant the temple or people of the true God, but the temple or temples in which the false worship was performed, which the prophets here reprobated were specially active in promoting.

9. הֶעְמִיקוּ שִׁחֵתוּ, an instance of the *constructio asyndeta.* The former of the two verbs is to be rendered adverbially. For its use before infinitives, see on chap. v. 2. Mercer, "Quam corruptissimi sunt." שִׁחֵתוּ may either be taken intransitively, or דַּרְכֵּיהֶם, עֲלִילֹתֵיהֶם, or the like, must be supplied. So great was the depravity evinced by those whose conduct the prophet here describes, that it could only be paralleled by the atrocity of the inhabitants of Gibeah, specified Judges xix. 22-30.

10. יִשְׂרָאֵל, *Israel,* here means the ancestors of the Hebrew nation. It has been asked, "How could God be said to find the Hebrews in the wilderness, since he conducted them into it from Egypt?" To remove the difficulty, some very unwarrantably explain the wilderness of Egypt itself; but others connect כַּעֲנָבִים בַּמִּדְבָּר, *like grapes in the desert,* and explain מָצָא of *finding by experience, trial,* etc. Such they were, proved themselves to be, in my judgment. And this seems to be the proper division and interpretation of the words At the same

I regarded your fathers;
But they came to Baal-peor,
And separated themselves to the object of shame;
They became abominable, like the object of their love.

11 As for Ephraim, their glory shall fly away, like a bird;
There shall be no birth, no womb, no conception.

12 Yea, though they should rear their children,
I would take them away from among men;
But woe to them! when I depart from them.

---

time בָּאֵת מְצָא אֶצָּא occurs in reference to the same subject, Deut. xxxii. 10, where the verb must be taken in the sense of *reaching* with sufficient aid. Comp. the Eth. ወፅአ፡ *venit*; Arab. ڡضى, *perduxit, tractavit*, negotium; and chap. xiii. 5; Jer. xxxi. 2. The point of comparison in the verse is the delight with which a traveller enjoys grapes found in a desert, in which they were unexpected, and where they served most opportunely to quench his thirst; or the early fig, which is accounted a great delicacy in the East. When Jehovah entered into covenant with the people of Israel at Sinai, they were regarded by him with delight, being free from idolatry, and engaging to adhere to his service. Comp. chap. xi. 1; Jer. xxxi. 3. The scene, however, was soon changed. הֵמָּה, *illi, these* very persons. At Baal-peor, they proved faithless, and indulged in the very atrocities of which their posterity were guilty in the days of the prophet. For the transactions referred to, see Numb. xxv. 1-5. Priapism, which Hosea justly characterizes as in the highest degree abominable, was the worship peculiarly acceptable to the god of Peor. See Calmet and Winer in voc. — נָזַר signifies *to separate one's self* from any person or thing, and also, followed by לְ, to separate or *devote one's self* to some religious object. Hence the substantive נָזִיר, a *Nazarite*, נֵזֶר *consecration*. בֹּשֶׁת is the abstract for the concrete, and denotes the obscene or shameful idol which the Moabites worshipped. שִׁקּוּצִים, lit. *abominations*, but used here adjectively, *loathsome, abominable*. אֶבֶץ is properly the substantive, אָהַב — the points being changed on account of the suffix. Vulg. facti sunt abominabiles sicut ea, quae dilexerunt. The Hebrews became as abominable as the impure idol whose rites they celebrated. הַתּוֹעֵב הוּא שִׁקּוּץ שֹׁקֵץ, *he that serveth an abomination, is himself an abomination*. Kimchi's MS. note in Pocoeke.

11, 12. אֶפְרַיִם, *Ephraim*, is of the nominative absolute, which gives prominence to the name, and its signification. As for *Ephraim*, (אֶפְרַיִם, from פָּרָה, *to be fruitful* Gen. xli. 52,) such may be his name, but, etc. כְּבוֹדָם, *glory*, is in contrast with בֹּשֶׁת, *shame*, in the preceding verse. The lewd and idolatrous conduct of the Israelites should meet with a fit retribution. Instead of having an increase of children, that might grow up and become the *glory* of the land, those who might now be accounted such should speedily be removed into Assyria, and there would be nothing but sterility to characterize the nation. The preposition מִן, prefixed to the three last substantives, is privative in signification. בֶּטֶן, *womb*, stands here for *pregnancy*, or for the *foetus* in the womb. The order of the words presents an instance of the gradatio inversa. בָאָדָם, *among men*, as אִשָּׁה תִשַׁכֵּל מִנָּשִׁים, "thy mother shall be childless *among women*," 1 Sam. xv. 33. Ewald and Hitzig translate בְּשׂוּרִי, *when I look away from them*, contending that we should read שׁ instead of בְּ; but no MS. is thus pointed, and the present punctuation is so far supported by the LXX. (ἡ σάρξ μου, i. e בְּשָׂרִי), Aq. Vulg. and Targ. Three MSS. and one edit. have בְּשָׂרִי, to which בְּשׂוּרִי is doubtless here equivalent. Many instances occur of the substitution of שׂ for ס, and *vice versâ*.

13 I see Ephraim, like Tyre, planted in a pleasant place;
    But Ephraim shall bring out his children to the murderer.
14   Give them, O Jehovah! — what wilt thou give?
    Give them a miscarrying womb, and dry breasts.
15 All their wickedness is in Gilgal;
    Surely I have hated them there:
    On account of the wickedness of their deeds,
    I have driven them out of my house;
    I will love them no more:
    All their princes are rebels.
16 Ephraim is smitten, their root is dried up;
    They shall produce no fruit :

The meaning is, when I withdraw my protection from them; no longer showing them any favor, but delivering them over to their enemies. For the abortive attempt of Lyra to prove a corruption of the passage by the Jews, and to palm upon the rendering of the LXX. ἡ σάρξ μοῦ ἐξ αὐτῶν, the doctrine of the incarnation of the Messiah, see Pococke.

13. After אֶפְרַיִם supply רָאִיתִי, from the following רָאִיתִי לְצוּר בְּאָבֶן. Though רָאָה commonly governs the accusative, yet, in Ps. lxiv. 6, it is followed as here by the dative, without any difference of signification. LXX. εἰς θήραν, reading, לָצַיִד, instead of לְצוּר. Aq. Symm. ἀκρότομον ; Theod. πέτραν ; Arnoldi, and after him Hitzig, would derive צוּר from the Arab. صور, as signifying the Palm ; but it only signifies the root of that tree, or describes it as small in size, an acceptation which would ill suit the present connection. Ewald renders, Bild, image or likeness. The point of comparison is the beautiful situation of Tyre. See Ezek. xxvii. 3, xxviii. 12, 13. The notion of planting seems to have been suggested by the name of Ephraim. See on the preceding verse. The territory occupied by that tribe, and several of the other nine, was distinguished for its beauty and fertility; and the prosperity of its inhabitants, who traded extensively with the Phœnician ports, was only surpassed by Tyre herself. Yet the fruit of this lovely region was only to be produced in order to its being destroyed. The inhabitants were to be slain in great numbers with the sword. The ל before the infinitive in לְהוֹצִיא, is future in signification, indicating what was about to be, or would be done.

14. These words strongly mark the effect produced upon the mind of the prophet by the contemplation of the wickedness of his people. In holy ardor of soul, he feels himself excited to imprecate what he had predicted ver. 11. Some, less appropriately, render מַה, not as an interrogative, but as signifying *that which*, i. e. give them whatever thou wilt. Barrenness was accounted a great misfortune among the Jews.

15. For *Gilgal*, see on chap. iv. 15. Being one of the chief places of idolatrous worship, the wickedness of the nation might be said to be concentrated in it. When God is represented as *hating* the wicked, it must be understood in regard to the odiousness of their moral character, and his infliction of positive punishment upon them on account of it. Hitzig considers שָׂנֵא to be here used inchoatively. For the sense in which בֵּיתִי, *house*, is to be taken, see on chap. viii. 1. Hatred and love are contrasted as here, Mal. i. 2, 3. In שָׂרֵיהֶם סוֹרְרִים is a paronomasia.

16. The figurative language here employed is suggested by the meaning of the name Ephraim, as in verses, 11, 13. יַעֲשׂוּן is in the future, while הֻכָּה and יָבֵשׁ are in the preterite, to mark the state of unfruitfulness as following upon

Yea, though they should beget children,
I will kill the beloved of their womb.
17 My God will abhor them,
Because they have not listened to him:
They shall be wanderers among the nations.

the injury done to the tree. The resolution of the figure in the latter half of the verse possesses much force. Most of the MSS. and some few editions read, with the Keri, בָּל instead of בְּלִי, which occurs, however, before a verb, Job xli. 18. For בְּסֹרְרִים, comp. on סֹרֵרָה, ver. 6.

17. Though the pronominal affix in אֱלֹהַי is omitted by the LXX. and Arab. and one of Kennicott's MSS., it is, in such connection, more in the style of Hosea than אֱלֹהִים. The dispersion of the ten tribes is here expressly predicted.

CHAPTER X.

In this chapter the prophet continues to charge the Israelites with idolatry, anarchy, and want of fidelity, 1–4. He expatiates with great variety on the judgments that were to come upon them in punishment for these crimes, 5–11; and then abruptly turns to them in a direct hortatory address, couched in metaphorical language, borrowed from the mode of representation which he had just employed, 12. The section concludes with an appeal to the experience which they had already had of the disastrous consequences of their wicked conduct.

1 ISRAEL is a luxuriant vine;
He putteth forth his fruit;
According to the increase of his fruit,
He increased altars;
According to the excellence of his land,
They prepared goodly statues.

1. The wickedness which manifested itself in idolatry, etc. is here traced to the abuse of the prosperity which God had conferred on the Israelites. Instead of spending the bounties of providence for the glory of God, they appropriated them to idolatrous uses, and that in proportion to the abundance of their bestowment. בּוֹקֵק, ‏ﻏﺰﺭ‎, multus fudit, fœcundus fuit,

multum pluviam demisit, florere cœpit planta, is here used to express the luxuriance of the vine, and not, as in our common version and some others, its unfruitfulness. The idea of emptying, which the verb also has, derived from that of pouring out entirely or abundantly the contents of a vessel, does not suit the present connection. LXX. εὐκληματοῦσα,

2 Their heart is divided, they shall now be punished:
He will cut off their altars, he will destroy their statues.
3 Surely now shall they say: We have no king;
For we fear not Jehovah:
As for the king then, what can he do for us?
4   They utter empty speeches;
Swearing falsely, making covenants;
Therefore judgment blossoms like the poppy
On the ridges of the field.

or, as in other copies, ἐγκληματοῦσα. Aq. ἄνυδρος. Symm. ὑλομανοῦσα. Vulg. *frondoso.* Comp. Gen. xlix. 22; Ps. lxxx. 9-11; Ezek. xvii. 6. In every other instance יֶפֶן is construed as a feminine; but here the masculine name יִשְׂרָאֵל, Israel, required it to be taken as of that gender. שָׁוָה, *to resemble, be equal to, sufficient;* in Piel, like the Eth. ቀደመ, *to bring to maturity, produce fruit.* לֹו, in the phrase יְשַׁוֶּה־לֹּו, is pleonastic, as in הָלַךְ־לֹו, etc., but may here be rendered as a possessive pronoun.

2. חָלַק is here to be taken intransitively, as in our common version, and refers, not to any difference of opinion among the Israelites respecting the claims of their numerous idols, but to their insincerity in the service of Jehovah, — professing to worship him, while they likewise addicted themselves to the worship of idols. Thus Tanchum: —

تقسم بالهم وعقلهم ورايهم ان اشركوا بالله غيره, "their mind and their understanding, and their opinion are divided, while they associate others with God." The acceptation *to be smooth,* which some propose, is to be rejected, on the ground that, though the verb is used in this signification of the tongue, it nowhere is of the *heart.* For the meaning of אָשֵׁם, see on chap. v. 15. The nominative to הוּא, *He,* is אֱלֹהִים, *God,* in אֱלֹהָי, chap. ix. 17. Jehovah is here said to do, what he would effect by means of the Assyrians. עָרַף is properly a sacrificial term, signifying *to cut off the head of a victim, by striking it on the neck;* hence, *to drop as blood* from the place thus struck; and *to drop* generally. It is here, with much force, used metonymically, in application to the destruction of the altars on which the animals were offered. Ewald renders, *Er wird ihre altäre enthaupten;* "he will decapitate their altars." For the distinction between מִזְבְּחוֹת and מַצֵּבוֹת, see on chap. iii. 4. עַתָּה, *now,* in this and the following verse, has the signification of *soon, speedily.*

3. The language of desperation is here put into the mouth of the apostate Israelites, at the time of the infliction of divine judgment. Their king, to whom they had naturally looked for protection, was removed; they had forfeited the favor of God, who was now become their enemy; and, therefore, it was vain to expect help from an earthly monarch. Some think the prophet refers to the time of anarchy during the interregnum, between the murder of Pekah and the accession of Hoshea.

4. דָּבַר דָּבָר, lit. *to speak a word,* or *speech,* i. e. what is merely such; empty, false pretences. Comp. the Lat. *verba dare.* The prophet begins with the finite form of the verb, and then, for the sake of more specific description, changes it for the infinitive. Comp. Is. lix. 13. For אָלוֹת, as an absolute infinitive, instead of אָלֹה, comp. שָׁתוֹת, Is. xxii. 13; רָאוֹ, chap. xlii. 20. בְּרִית, *covenant,* is here used as a collective noun, and is to be rendered in the plural. Whether the false swearing and the entering into covenants refer to the conduct of the Israelites in regard to each other, or whether they respect their conduct in reference to foreign powers, has been disputed. The latter would seem to be the more probable, since it is the making of

5 For the calves of Beth-aven,
  The inhabitants of Samaria shall be in fear;
  The people thereof shall mourn on account of it;
  The priests thereof shall leap about on account of it —
  On account of its glory,
  Because it hath departed from it.
5 It shall itself also be carried to Assyria,
  A present to the hostile king:
  Ephraim shall take disgrace,
  And Israel shall blush for his own counsel,

covenants and not the breaking of them, of which the prophet speaks as something criminal. He seems to have in his eye the historical circumstances narrated 2 Kings xvii. 4. By מִשְׁפָּט is meant the divine judgment which was to be inflicted upon the people of Israel. So Jarchi, משפטי יסורין ופורענית. This he compares to the rapid and luxuriant growth of the poppy, which overruns the fields, and is destructive as a poison. Celsius, in his Hierobot. supports the common rendering *hemlock*, as the signification of ראש; but that of *poppy*, proposed by Gesenius, is preferable, both to such construction of the term, and to that of *colocynth* advanced by Œdmann, or that of *lolium* or *darnel* suggested by Michaelis. The term is usually rendered *poison* in our common version; sometimes *gall*. LXX. ἄγρωστις. תַּלְמֵי שָׂדַי rather signify the ridges between the furrows than the furrows themselves. See Pocockc.

5, 6. In these verses the object of idolatrous worship is spoken of, now in the plural, and now in the singular number, which Hitzig accounts for on the ground, that though the Israelites might have multiplied golden calves, that set up by Jeroboam would still be held in peculiar honor. Four MSS. have עֶגְלַת, *calf*, in the singular, which is also the rendering of the LXX. Syr. and an anonymous Greek version in the Hexapla. This reading is very uncritically adopted by Kuinoel, Dathe, Newcome, and some other moderns. For בֵּית אָוֶן, *Beth-aven*, see on chap. iv. 15. שָׁכֵן is a collective. The nominative to the pronominal affixes in כְּלָיו, עַם, כְּמָרָיו, etc. is the עֵגֶל, *calf* of Jeroboam, singled out from the rest.. עַם, *its people*, those devoted to its worship. Comp. Numb. xxi. 29. כְּמָרִים is only used in Hebrew to designate *idolatrous priests*, and occurs but twice besides, viz. 2 Kings xxiii. 5; Zeph. i. 4; but in the Syriac ܟܘܡܪܐ, *kumro*, signifies a priest of the true God, as well as one engaged in the service of idols. Gesenius derives the noun from כָּמַר, *to burn, be scorched, black*, supposing the reference to be to the black dress of monks or ecclesiastics; but this seems too modern to be entitled to adoption. The derivation of Iken, in his Dissert. de *Cemarim*, who refers the word to the Persic کمر *sacrum magorum ignicolarum cingulum*, of which frequent mention is made in the Sadder of Zoroaster, is much more natural. Comp. the Chald. קְמוֹרָא, כְּמָר, *a belt* or *girdle*. Some think the Lat. *camillus*, an inferior order of priests, who attended upon and assisted the flamens, is derived from this root. Ewald renders the word by *Pfaffen*, which is used of priests by way of contempt, in German. Those who render יָגִילוּ, *they rejoiced*, which is the usual signification of the verb, supply אֲשֶׁר before it; but the Vau conversive connects it so closely with עַל, as to render such supplement inconsistent with the construction. It is, therefore, better to revert to the primary signification of גִּיל, *to move about, leap, dance*, or the like. Comp. the Arab. جال, *circumivit*. Such would be the excitement of the idolatrous priests at the capture of their God, that they would leap about in a state of desperation, like those of Baal, 1 Kings xviii. 26. The

7 As for Samaria, her king is cut off;
    He is like a chip upon the surface of the water.
8 The high places of Aven, the sin of Israel, are destroyed;
    Thorns and thistles shall grow upon their altars:
    They shall say to the mountains, Cover us;
    And to the hills, Fall upon us.
9 Since the days of Gilead, thou hast sinned, O Israel!
    There they remain:
    Shall not the war against the unjust overtake them in Gilead?

glory of the idol consisted in its ornaments, wealth, etc. בם אוֹתוֹ is emphatic: *itself also*, i. e. the idol or golden calf. For the meaning of יָרֵב, *Jareb*, see on chap. v. 13. The worshippers of the golden calf would be ashamed of him, when they found that, instead of protecting them, he was himself carried into captivity. That נִשְׁבָּה is not to be changed into בִּשְׁבָה, and rendered *in a sound sleep*, as Horsley does, nor into בִּשְׁבָה, *in this year*, with Michaelis, the parallelism sufficiently shows.

7. For the sake of emphasis, שֹׁמְרוֹן is put absolutely. The whole phrase is equivalent to *the king of Samaria*, etc. That נִדְמֶה agrees with מַלְכָּהּ, and not with שֹׁמְרוֹן, the gender shows. קֶצֶף has nowhere the signification of *foam* or *scum*. It is derived from קָצַף, Arab. قَصَفَ, *fregit, to cut, cut off*, and signifies any *chip* or small fragment of wood. Comp. קְצָפָה, a fragment, Joel i. 7. Arab. قَضِيبٌ, *fractus aboris ramus*, قَصَفَة, *tenuitas arboris*. LXX. φρύγανον. Syr. ܩܝܣܐ, *festucam*. The comparison of the king to a small chip of wood, which cannot resist the force of the current, is very beautiful and forcible. *Spuma*, which is the rendering of the Targ. Jerome, Symm. Abulwalid, Tanchum, and many moderns, is less apt, even if it could be philologically sustained.

8, אָוֶן, *Aven*, is an abbreviation of the full form, בֵּית־אָוֶן, *Beth-aven*, or Bethel. חַטַּאת, *the occasion of sin* to Israel. See ver. 10. In the midst of the calamities that should come upon the people, death

would be preferable to life. Comp. Rev. vi. 15, 16.

9. That reference is here made to the transactions recorded Jud. xix. xx., there can be no doubt. The prophet declares that as a nation his people had all along, from the period referred to, evinced a disposition to act in the same rebellious and unjust manner as the Gibeonites had done. Comp. chap. ix. 9. The words שָׁם עָמָדוּ, *there they remain*, continue, persist, graphically express the character of the inhabitants in his day. The Gibeonites are still, what they have ever been, a wicked and abandoned people. They are here singled out as a fit specimen of the whole nation; and are called בְּנֵי־עַלְוָה, *sons of wickedness*, to mark the enormity of their conduct. Instead of עַלְוָה, the Brixian edition, thirty-nine MSS. originally seventeen, and perhaps a few more, have עַוְלָה, the common form, which is supposed to have been changed by a simple transposition of the letters. Albert Schultens, however, in his notes ad Harir. i. p. 15, justifies the present reading by deriving it from the Arab. علا, *modum excessit, extulit se;* and Michaelis, in his Suplem. by referring it to the Syriac, ܥܠܐ, and the Eth. ዐለወ ፡ *fidem fefellit, perfidus fuit*. Comp. ሠርጉ ፡ ዐለዉ ፡ *Rex tyrannus, scelestus*. ዐለቱ ፡ *transgressio æqui et boni, scelus, perversitas*. That the Targumist read the text as it now stands is clear from his rendering of the word עָלוּ, *they went up*. The words לֹא תַשִּׂיגֵם בַּגִּבְעָה מִלְחָמָה עַל־בְּנֵי עַלְוָה are somewhat

10 My desire is to punish them;
The nations shall be collected against them,
When they are bound for their two iniquities.
11 •Ephraim is a well-trained heifer, loving to thresh;
But I will pass on beside her fair neck;
I will place a rider on Ephraim:
Judah shall plough,
And Jacob shall break the clods.

involved, but the meaning is obvious. Destruction should assuredly overtake the wicked Israelites. ב, the verbal suffix in בְּעֵינָם, is anticipative of בִּכְבשָׁ ב. לֹא stands for הֲלֹא, the interrogatory negative.

10. בְּאַוָּתִי, the LXX. have read בְּאתִי; rendering it ἦλθε; or, according to the Alexandrian MS. and the editions of Aldus and Breitinger, ἦλθεν. Of this Houbigant, Dimock, Newcome, Tingstadius, and Boothroyd, approve, and adopt it as an emendation; but contrary to all other authority, ancient or modern, and without necessity. ב prefixed is the *Beth Essentiæ*, indicating the substantive character of the affection. See my note on Is. xxvi. 4. אָוָה, *to be strongly propense, desire greatly,* expresses the irresistible inclination of infinite purity to punish sin. אֶאֱסֹרֵם is the future in Kal of יָסַר, *to chastise, punish,* compensation having been made for the first radical י, by inserting Dagesh in the ס. בְּאָסְרָם, the infinitive of אָסַר, *to bind, bind as a prisoner* or *captive,* which is the sense in which the word is here to be taken. לִשְׁתֵּי עֵינֹתָם has occasioned great variety of interpretation. Michaelis translates it *plough-shares,* attempting to derive it from the Arabic. Jarchi, Lively, and, among the moderns, Ewald, render *eyes,* "before their *two eyes,*" i. e. openly; but the word is always written עֵינַיִם when applied to real eyes, and only עֲיָנוֹת when applied to fountains or artificial eyes. Some translate *habitations;* but most, *furrows,* which is the rendering adopted by Abenezra, Kimchi, Abulwalid, Tanchum, Munster, Vatablus, Zanchius, etc., after the Targum — some expounding the passage one way, and some another. The only satisfactory exegesis is that founded on the Keri, לִשְׁתֵּי עֲוֹנֹתָם, *for their two iniquities,* i. e. the two golden calves which Jeroboam had erected, and which proved the source of all the evils which they had afterwards committed. They had many other idols, but these were the principal; and they are called *iniquities* by a metonymy of the cause for the effect. Comp. ver. 8, where חַטַּאת, *sin,* is similarly applied. This reading is in the text of a great many MSS. and is expressed in all the ancient versions.

11. The general meaning of this verse seems to be, that the Ephraimites had been accustomed in the plenitude of their power to crush and oppress others, especially their brethren of the two tribes; but they were now themselves to be brought into subjection to the king of Assyria, by whom they should be placed in circumstances of great hardship in foreign countries. The metaphors are agricultural. For דּוּשׁ, *to tread* or *beat out the corn,* partly by the feet of oxen, and partly by sledges with instruments adapted to the purpose, see on Is. xxviii. 27, 28. The י in אֹהַבְתִּי, is paragogic, as מַלְאֲתִי and רַבָּתִי, Jer. xxii. 23; יֹשַׁבְתִּי, chap. li. 13, though in these passages it has been left unpointed by the Masoretes. See Ewald, § 406. The form is otherwise the participle אֹהֶבֶת. עָבַר עַל signifies here *to pass on beside* one, as the driver does beside an ox in the yoke. Thus Jehovah would, in his providence, lead forth the Israelites, from the midst of their prosperity, to the toils and hardships of captivity. אַרְכִּיב אֶפְרַיִם lit. *I will cause to ride Ephraim,* meaning I will place a rider upon him — a conqueror, who shall lead him forth from his land. Thus Calvin, Zanchius, Lyra Tarnovius,

12 Sow to yourselves for righteousness:
Reap according to piety;
Break up for yourselves the fallow ground:
For it is time to seek Jehovah,
Till he come, and teach you righteousness.
13 Ye have ploughed wickedness, ye have reaped iniquity;
Ye have eaten the fruit of falsehood:
Because thou trustedst in thy way —
In the multitude of thy mighty ones.

Rosenmüller, and Ewald. The judgments of God were not, however, to be confined to the northern kingdom: the southern should also be involved in them. In short, they should overtake the whole posterity of Jacob. The prediction was fulfilled during the two captivities. לֹא, in יְשֶׁדְּךָ לֹא, is pleonastic.

12. Continuing his agricultural metaphors, the prophet here abruptly calls upon the nation to reform its manners. לָכֶם is the Dat. commodi. ל in לִצְדָקָה points out the end or object to be obtained by sowing. Sow what will produce the fruits of righteousness. The second imperative is here equivalent to the future: "Sow, and ye shall reap;" or the subjunctive, "Sow, so that ye may reap." That חֶסֶד, *piety* or *goodness*, is to be referred, not to God, but to man, its being parallel with צְדָקָה, *righteousness*, manifestly proves. To change רְעוּ into רִבְעוּ, and join this word with פִּי־, preceding, as Newcome, following the LXX. and Arab., does, is unauthorized and inept. The Israelites had long neglected Jehovah: it was now high time to return to his fear; and though they might not meet with immediate tokens of his favor, they were to persevere in seeking him, in the assurance that he would be gracious to them. Such is the force of עַד, *until*. This favor was to be manifested by his coming and communicating to them instruction respecting the only righteousness which could avail the guilty at his bar. That the words וְיֹרֶה צֶדֶק לָכֶם are not to be rendered *he will grant you suitable rain*, but, *he will teach you righteousness*, and that they contain a prophecy of the advent and prophetical office of the Messiah, has been maintained by Jerome, and many other interpreters. In support of the rendering, *He will teach you righteousness*, may be adduced the Syr. ܟܺܐܦ

ܐܳܡܶܣ݂ܕ݂ܶܐ ܠܟܽܘܢ ܘܰܢܚܰܘܶܐ, *till he come and show to you his righteousness;* Pococke's Arab. MS. الي ان يجي ويرشدكم العدل, *till he come and guide you to righteousness.* The Targ. to the same effect, וְיִתְגְּלֵי וְיֵיתֵי זָכוּ לְכוֹן, *now he shall be revealed, and shall bring righteousness to you;* Vulg. *cum venerit qui docebit vos justitiam.* Thus also Dathe, Hitzig, Winer, and others. Kimchi remarks, וילמד את תדרשו אם לדעת תורתו ומשיחתו הוא יבא ויורה אדרכי בצע, *there are those* (of the Rabbins) *who expound, If ye seek the Lord, to know his law and his commandments, he will come and teach you righteousness.* And Abenezra asserts the same, in nearly the same words. Such construction of the passage seems, from the preceding use of לִצְדָקָה, to be more apt, than to take צֶדֶק absolutely for לִצְדָקָה, *in due proportion, adequately, fully*, according to the claims or necessities of your condition. See on Joel ii. 23.

13. Instead of following such a course as that to which they had just been exhorted, the Israelites had pursued one directly opposite, and now reaped the disastrous consequences. The same metaphors are here continued. חֲרַשְׁתֶּם־רֶשַׁע, *fruit of falsehood*, seems rather to mean *the effects of their false and hypocritical conduct* in professing attachment to the true God, while they addicted themselves to the worship of other deities, than *fal-*

14 Therefore a tumult shall arise among thy people,
And all thy fortresses shall be destroyed,
As Shalman destroyed Beth-arbel in the day of battle:
When the mother was dashed in pieces with her children.

lacious and disappointing results. Seeker would read בְּרִכְבֶּךָ, *in thy chariots*, instead of בִּדְרָכֶיךָ, *in thy way*, on the LXX. ἐν ἅρμασί σου, which reading is found in Compl. Ald. Barb. Reg. Laud. Cyrill. Ital. Ambros. Arab. Slav. Hexap. Syr. and a Copt. MS.; and Kuinoel has actually adopted it into his Hebrew text. It is, however, unsupported by any Heb. MSS., or any of the ancient versions, and is justly to be rejected. Four MSS. originally two, the Syr. and Targ. read בִּדְרָכֶיךָ, *in thy ways*. The *way* of the Israelites was the wicked course of conduct which they had adopted in opposition to the will of God. Kimchi: דרך הרעה והמעשה הרע, *the way of wickedness and bad religion.* The Vat. copy of the LXX. has ἐν ἁμαρτήμασί σου. Comp. Is. lvii. 10; Jer. ii. 23.

14. The prophet now denounces a severe threatening against his rebellious countrymen, foreshowing that they should be involved in all the horrors of war. קָאם, with א epenthetic, after the manner of the Arab. قَامَ; or it may be regarded as merely a *mater lectionis*. Some few MSS. and some others in the margin, read קָם וּ. Twenty-four MSS., one originally, four of the early editions, and all the ancient versions, read בְּעַמֶּךָ, *thy people*, instead of בְּעַמֶּיךָ, *thy peoples*. For minor varieties in the readings, see Kennicott and 'De Rossi. The nominative to יָקוּם is כֹּל, taken as a collective, comprehending the whole. That שַׁלְמַן, *Shalman*, and בֵּית אַרְבֵּאל, *Beth-Arbel*, are proper names, is now universally admitted. The best interpretation of them is that given by Tanchum: שלמנאא אבי ואמא ملكب אבו السلامنאא فهو امم وقيل انه مركب من שלמנאא فاختصر ولعل اسمعین فاسقط احدهما للعرف اسم بلد ويقول انها التي يقال لها اليوم اربאל אربאל. "As for *Shalman*, it is a proper name, and is said to stand for *Shalmanassar*, king of Assyria, only it is abbreviated; and perhaps *Shalmanssar* is compounded of two names, one of which is omitted because it was well known: and *Arbel* is the name of a city, and is said to be that which is called *Arbel* at the present day." The abbreviation of proper names is not uncommon in Scripture, as כָּנְיָהוּ, *Coniah*, for יְהוֹיָכִין, *Jehoiachin*, etc. It was this monarch that besieged Samaria for the space of three years, and took it in the ninth of Hoshea, B. C. 722, carrying the king and most of his subjects into exile. 2 Kings xvii. 1-6. To this interpretation it has been objected that our prophet wrote before the time of Shalmaneser, and therefore could not speak of his destroying Arbel as something that had already happened. It must, however, be recollected, that though Hosea prophesied before the time of that king, he continued to deliver his predictions as far down as the time of his successor Sennacherib, and must, therefore, have been well acquainted with the previous Assyrian invasions. With respect to בֵּית אַרְבֵּאל, or, as some MSS. read, בֵּית אַרְבֵּל, *Beth-Arbel*, commentators are divided in opinion. Some think that the Assyrian city *Arbela*, situated between the Lycus and the Tigris, celebrated for the victory obtained there by Alexander the Great over Darius, is meant; but it is far more probable that the prophet refers to the Ἀρβήλα of 1 Macc. ix. 2, which Josephus places near Sephoris in Galilee; Eusebius, in the plain of Esdraelon. Of the battle here mentioned, no account indeed is given either in sacred or profane history; but as the contemporaries of Hosea are supposed to have been acquainted with it, there is reason to believe that it took place on the invasion of the kingdom of Israel by the Assyrian army. The ancient

15 Thus shall he act towards you at Bethel,
On account of your flagrant wickedness:
In the morning shall the king of Israel be utterly cut off.

versions of this clause of the verse are more or less at fault; but have afforded abundant scope for the exercise of emendatorial criticism. See Newcome, who renders, *Like the destruction of Zalmunna by the hand of Jerubbaal;* and supposes the reference to be to Jud. viii. עַל here signifies *with*, in the sense of being super-added. See Gen. xxviii. 9. xxxi. 50.

15. The nominative to עָשָׂה is Shalman in the preceding verse, or perhaps יְהֹוָה, Jehovah, understood, but not בֵּית־אֵל, Bethel, as in our common version, since this does not so well agree with what follows. The words contain a special prediction against Bethel, where the wickedness of the Israelites had been most conspicuously exhibited. רָעַת רָעַתְכֶם lit. *the wickedness of your wickedness*, i. e. your excessive, or most flagrant wickedness. A rare example of a noun put in construction with itself repeated *in the singular*, in order to form the superlative degree. There is no necessity with Newcome, to resort to emendation. Instead of בַּשַּׁחַר, "*in* the morning," fifteen MSS., and perhaps one more, six originally, the Proph. of Soncin. 1486, the Venet. edit..of 1818, in the margin, and the Vulg. read כַּשַּׁחַר, "*like* the morning." Were the following verb דָּמָה to be taken in the sense of *resembling, being like*, etc., the latter reading might possess some claim on our attention; but as the idea of *being destroyed* best comports with the connection, that of the Textus Receptus is preferable. The difference of reading has arisen from the similarity of the letters ב and כ. The reference is to the suddenness with which Hoshea was to be seized by the king of Assyria, and an entire end put to the regal dignity. See 2 Kings xvii. 4. The doing of anything early or soon is frequently expressed by its being done in the morning.

CHAPTER XI.

To aggravate his representations of the guilt of the Israelites, the prophet adduces the divine benefits conferred upon them from the earliest period of their history, 1—4. He then threatens them with unavoidable punishment on account of their obstinacy, 5, 6; but, all of a sudden, introduces Jehovah, compassionating his rebellious children, and promising them a restoration from their captivity in foreign lands, 7—11.

---

1 WHEN Israel was a child, I loved him,
And called my son out of Egypt.

1. That these words relate to the nation of Israel — being a description of what Jehovah had done for it ages before the prophet wrote, and not a prophecy of any future event, is so evident, that no person who impartially examines the preceding and following context, can for a moment call it in question. Nor but for their having been applied by the Evangelist Matthew (ch. ii. 15.) to our Lord's

2 According as they called them, they went from their presence,
 They sacrificed unto Baals,
 And burned incense to graven images.
3 Though I taught Ephraim to walk,
 Taking them by their arms,
 Yet they knew not that I healed them.

return from Egypt, would it ever have been imagined that they had or could have had any other reference. It is only, therefore, with respect to such application that any difficulty can exist respecting their exegesis; and, in my judgment, there appears to be nothing in the N. T. application beyond the mere appropriation of the language of the prophet, for the purpose of giving to Jewish readers a more vivid impression of the strikingly analogous circumstances of the sojourn of our Saviour in Egypt, and his return from it, to those of the ancient Israelites. The Evangelist does not affirm, that the words as used by Hosea were a prophecy of Christ; he only adduces them, to show how aptly they described the historical event which he was narrating, just as he does Jer. xxxi. 15, in application to the murder of the infants at Bethlehem, and Ps. lxxviii. 2, in application to our Lord's teaching in parables. "He must be a stranger to the *Hebrew* writers, that does not know, that nothing is more common among *them* than such accommodations of the text upon all occasions. They abound in such applications; I may say their Midrashim do very much *exceed* in them." Kidder's Demon. of the Messiah, Pt. II. p. 216. "Parodiarum in N. T. omnia sunt plena, e. g. *Matt.* ii. 15 and 23, ubi *impleta* dicuntur *Scripturæ* tum etiam, cum nulla historica aut typica est impletio, sed analogica tantum." Hottinger in Primit. Heidelberg, p. 80. See Surenhusii. βίβλος καταλλης, p. 338. Horne's Introd. vol. ii. pp. 341, 342. Robinson's Greek Lex. in ἵνα, C. 2, d. Instead of בְּנִי, the LXX. appears to have read בָּנָיו; but instead of τὰ τέκνα αὐτοῦ, *his children*, which is their reading, that of Aq. Symm. Theod. the Slavon. and Matthew, agree with the Hebrew text. The Hebrew people are also called the son of God in the same figurative sense, Exod. iv. 22, 23. The early period of their existence is frequently represented as their youth. See Is. liv. 13; Jer. ii. 2, iii. 24, 25, xxii. 21; Hos. ii. 15.

2. The use of the verb קָרָא, *to call*, in the preceding verse, suggested the idea of the subsequent messages which had been delivered to the Israelites by the prophets, to which Hosea now appeals, in order to contrast with the means which had been employed for their reformation, the obstinate character of their rebellion. Before קָרְאוּ subaud. בָּאֲשֶׁר, to correspond to כֵּן. Thus the LXX. καθ᾿ ὡς. The nominative is the prophets, understood. The very presence of the prophets being an annoyance to them, they withdrew from it, that, unmolested, they might indulge in idolatry.

3. תִרְגַּלְתִּי, an instance of the *Tiphil* conjugation, equivalent to Hiphil in signification, and, in all probability, formed by hardening the preformative ה into ת. Indeed, one of De Rossi's MSS. reads הִרְגַּלְתִּי, instead of תִרְגַּלְתִּי. There exist only two other instances in the Hebrew Bible, viz. תִּתְחָרֶה, Jer. xii. 5, and מְתֻרְתָּה, xxii. 15, if תַּחֲרוּתְךָ, xxv. 34, is not to be so taken. Compare the Shaphel Conjugation in Syriac, in which language this very verb occurs in the form ܫܰܪܓܶܠ. See Knös Chrest. Syr. p. 112. It is a denominive from רֶגֶל, *the foot*, and signifies to *cause*, or *teach to use the feet*, or *walk*. Syr. and Targ. רַבֵּרִית, *I led*, only the latter paraphrases, וַאֲנָא בְמַלְאֲכָא שָׁלִיחַ מִן קֳדָמַי דַּבָּרִית, *and I led*, etc. *by an angel sent from my presence*. The use of the personal pronoun אָנֹכִי before the verb gives additional force to the language. לָה in קָחָם is the infinitive used as a gerund, as in Ezek. xvii. 5. Both

4 I drew them with the bands of man,
With the cords of love;
I was also to them as those who lift up the yoke from their neck,
I held out meat to them, I made them eat.
5   They shall not return to the land of Egypt;
Assyria shall be their king:
Because they would not be converted.
6· The sword shall be whirled in their cities,
It shall destroy their barriers, and devour,
Because of their devices.

the suffixes ם and י refer to Ephraim. See on chap. ix. 2. Four MSS. for זְרֹעֹתָיו, "*his* arms," read זְרֹעֹתַי, "*my* arms," which is also in another originally, and now in another, and in the Soncin. edition of 1486. It is also supported by the LXX. Syr. Vulg. Another MS. reads זְרוֹעֹתָם, but they are all corrections of the original, and are only to be tolerated in translation. The metaphor taken from teaching children to walk is continued, as those who do so take hold of their arms to keep them from falling while they move their feet. It beautifully expresses the condescension of God to the circumstances of his people, and the kind care which he exercised over them. Comp. Deut. i. 31, xxxii. 11. His *healing them*, refers to his recovering them from the calamities which they had brought upon themselves by their sins.

4. בְּחַבְלֵי אָדָם, *the bands of man*, are explained by the parallel phrase בַּעֲבֹתוֹת אַהֲבָה, *cords of love*, i. e. humane, gentle, persuasive methods, such as men generally employ when they would induce to action. There seems to be still a reference to the case of children, who, when taught to walk, are not only held by the arms but also by soft cords or leading-strings, are led about, or drawn in a gentle manner by those who have the care of them. The terms, however, naturally suggesting the idea of the ropes by which oxen are bound and led about, the metaphor is immediately changed into one borrowed from agricultural life. כִּמְרִימֵי עֹל וגו does not mean to *remove* the yoke entirely, but to raise it from the neck and checks of the animal, so as to allow it freely to eat its food. This better suits the following connection than the idea of taking the yoke off any place that may have been galled by it, in order to afford relief. The עֹל, *yoke*, not only included the piece of wood upon the neck, by which the animal was fastened to the pole, but also the whole of the harness about the head, which was connected with it. The yokes used in the East are very heavy, and press so much upon the animals, that they are unable to bend their necks. וְאַט אֵלָיו. Ewald renders, *und sanft gegen ihn*, "and gently towards him," etc.; but it is preferable to take אַט as the apocopated future in Hiph. of נָטָה, *to stretch out, extend, reach any thing* to another. The verse sets forth the kind relief afforded to the Hebrew nation in Egypt, and the provision with which they were miraculously supplied in the wilderness.

5. שׁוּב, *to turn, return*, which is used at the beginning of the verse in its proper acceptation, is employed at the close metaphorically to express *conversion to God*. The Israelites seem to have been very generally inclined to migrate for a time to Egypt, in order to enjoy the protection of its monarch; the prophet assures them that they should not carry their purpose into effect, but that they should be subject to the Assyrian rule, as a punishment for refusing to listen to the calls given them to repent and turn from their idolatries.

6. Most of the Rabbins take חוּל in the sense of *resting, remaining;* but it seems preferable to adopt the signification *to turn, be turned*, or *whirled about*, as a sword when it is brandished or when it is employed in cutting down the enemy.

7 For my people are bent upon defection from me;
Though they call them to the Most High,
Yet none of them will exalt him.
8 How shall I give thee up, O Ephraim?
How shall I deliver thee over, O Israel?
How shall I make thee as Admah?
How shall I make thee as Zeboim?
My heart is turned within me;
All my feelings of compassion are kindled.
9 I will not execute the fierceness of my anger;
I will no more destroy Ephraim;

Comp. the Arab. حَالَ, *conversa fuit res. V. se convertit; versus mutatusque fuit.* בָּרִים, *barriers*, Gesenius and Lee take metaphorically, as denoting *chiefs* or *princes*.

7. תְּלוּאִים = תְּלָאִים, which one of De Rossi's MSS. reads originally, the Pahul Par? of תָּלָה, *to hang*, used here metaphorically in the sense of *bending*, or *being propense* to anything. The idea of *doubt* or *suspense*, which some attach to the word in this connection, ill agrees with the character of the Israelites as otherwise depicted in this book. מְשׁוּבָה is always used in a bad sense, *defection*, *apostasy*, etc. Comp. chap. xiv. 5. The suffix in מְשׁוּבָתִי is to be taken passively; defection which has me for its object, and cannot with any propriety be rendered as by Horsley, "my returning." For אֶל־עַל, *ad summum*, see on chap. vii. 16; and for יִקְרָאֻהוּ, on ver. 2. After קֹרְאִים, supply אֹתָם, *him*, from עַל, *the Supreme*, preceding. Jehovah had been degraded by his being worshipped through the medium of images, and having idols associated with him; yet none of his apostate people were inclined to raise him from this degradation, by rejecting them and celebrating His praise, as the sole and glorious object of adoration. Pococke's Arab. MS. لم يكن احد منهم يشرف اسم الله, *there was not one of them that glorified the name of God.* יַחַד with a negative is to be rendered *not one;* without it, *altogether, wholly*, as in the following verse.

8, 9. Now follows one of the most affecting instances of the infinite tenderness of the divine compassion to be found in Scripture; the point of which is enhanced by its being introduced immediately after a description of the odious conduct of the Israelites. It is, as Bishop Lowth characterizes it, exquisitely pathetic. The repetitions and synonymous features of the parallelism greatly add to the effect. The words belong to the period after the subjugation of Samaria, and the carrying away of the Israelites by Shalmaneser, 2 Kings xvii. 5, 6, xviii. 9–12. They were designed to inspire the captives with hope in the mercy of God, and thus lead them to true repentance. אֲמַגֶּנְךָ, the LXX. render ὑπερασπιῶ σου; Aq. ὅπλῳ κυκλώσω σε; Vulg. *protegam te;* deriving the idea from the signification of the substantive מָגֵן, *a shield;* but it is used of *delivering over enemies*, Gen. xiv. 20. Symm. ἐκδώσω σε. Before אֶתֶּנְךָ is an ellipsis of אֵיךְ, which had already been twice repeated. The destruction of Admah and Zeboim is only referred to as an example in one other case, viz. Deut. xxix. 23, and then in connection with Sodom and Gomorrah. To the awful catastrophe recorded Gen. xix. the sacred writers frequently appeal, in order to produce a sense of the evil of sin, and the severity with which it deserves to be punished; or when they would convey the idea of complete and irretrievable ruin. Comp. Is. i. 9, xiii. 19; Jer. xlix. 18; Lam. iv. 6; Amos. iv. 11, Matt. x. 15; 2 Pet. ii. 6; Jude 7. Some would render עַל־לֵב נֶהְפַּךְ,

For I am God and not man,
The Holy One in the midst of thee;
I will not come in wrath.
10 They shall follow Jehovah, when he roareth like a lion;
When he roareth, the children shall hasten from the sea.

"my heart is turned *against* me," i. e. my pity rises in overpowering opposition to the determination to which I had come to inflict punishments; but the phraseology will scarcely bear such construction, though it cannot be questioned, that it is designed to express a powerful, inward revolution. Comp. מַה־תֶּהֱמִי עָלַי, Ps. xlii. 6, 12, xliii. 5; הִתְעַשְּׁשָׁה עָלַי רוּחִי, cxlii. 4; עָלַי לְבַד דַּוָּי, Jer. viii. 18; in all which passages the preposition conveys the idea of mental *contiguity, nearness, in, within,* as נֶהְפַּךְ לִבִּי בְּקִרְבִּי, *my heart is turned* WITHIN *me,* Lam. i. 20, incontestably shows. From the connection in which it occurs, in the last cited passage, it is obvious the phrase is there designed to express great mental distress. כָּמַר is used in Niphal, of *the stirrings of natural affection,* Gen. xliii. 30; 1 Kings iii. 26. The idea seems to be derived from the commotion produced by the kindling of a fire, and the heat or warmth in which it results. Tanchum explains the word by سما *concitatus fuit.* LXX. συνεταράχϑη, or, as in the Complut. διεταράχϑη. נְחוּמִים, the same in effect as רַחֲמִים, *compassion, feelings of tender pity and affection.* Targ. רַחֲמַי, *my compassions.* It is derived from נָהַם, *to be inwardly affected,* whether with grief, pity, consolation, or anger. In the idea of displeasure with one's self, has originated the signification, *to repent,* which accounts for the renderings, μεταμέλεια, *pœnitudo, repentings,* etc. See my note on Is. i. 24. The language is in the highest degree anthropopathical. The 9th verse contains a declaration of the purpose of God founded upon his compassion, and quite in keeping with the manner in which expression had just been given to it. שׁוּב in לֹא אָשׁוּב לְשַׁחֵת is, as frequently to be taken adverbially. The captivity was the last judgment that was to come upon the ten tribes as a punishment for their idolatry. The rendering, "I will not enter into the city," affords no suitable sense, and would require the article בָּעִיר, as indeed, one of De Rossi's MSS. reads. Bishop Lowth's translation, "though I inhabit not thy cities," (Lectures, vol. ii. p. 38.) is equally unsatisfactory with the interpretation of Jerome and Castalio: I am not like those who dwell in cities; living after human laws, and deeming cruelty to be justice. Such construction Maurer states to be in his opinion "artificiosior quam elegantior. I, therefore, adopt the interpretation hinted at by Jarchi, and since approved by Schroeder, Secker, Dathe, Manger, Tingstadius, Eichhorn, De Wette, Noyes, Boothroyd, Gesenius, Maurer, and Ewald, which takes עִיר not in the sense of *city,* but of *anger* or *wrath;* comparing the Arab. غَلَ, *ferbuit æstu* dies. Comp. Jer. xv. 8; Hos. vii. 7; and עַר, *an enemy,* 1 Sam. xxviii. 16; Ps. cxxxix. 20. The words are thus strictly parallel, and synonymous to לֹא אִישׁ, *and not man.* The derivation from بَعِي, to which Michaelis assigns the signification *angry.* بَعِي, *ira in Deo,* Orient. Bib. Pt. XIX. p. 9, is less appropriate, though the sense which he gives is the same.

10, 11. These verses contain gracious promises of the return of the Israelites to the true worship and service of God, and their restoration to their own land from the different places in which they had been scattered during the captivity. יֵלֵךְ אַחֲרֵי יְהוָה, *to walk after Jehovah,* is always used in the religious sense of addicting one's self to his worship, and keeping his commandments, and is not to be interpreted, as Hitzig does, of a mere following of providence by taking advantage of the opportunity that would be afforded of returning from Babylon. So the Targ. בָּתַר פּוּלְחָנָא דַיָי, *after the*

11 They shall hasten, like a sparrow, from Egypt,
And like a dove, from the land of Assyria;
And I will cause them to dwell in their own houses,
Saith Jehovah.

worship of Jehovah. For the contrary, see ver. 2. As צָאַג, *to roar,* like the lion, always conveys the idea of terror or awe, it cannot be here applied either to any invitation to the Jews as a people, or to the preaching of the gospel generally; but must be referred to the awful judgments which God executed upon Babylon, Egypt, etc. through the instrumentality of Cyrus and his successors; thereby opening the way for the liberation of the Israelites who were found in these countries. Comp. Is. xxxi. 4; Jer. xxv. 30; Joel iv. 16; Amos i. 2, iii. 8. By בָּנִים, *sons,* or *children,* are meant the Israelites, who had been for a time rejected, but were again acknowledged in that character, because they were to be reinstated in the privileges of adoption. Comp. chap. i. 10. חָרַד is here pregnant with meaning — signifying to come or hasten under the influence of great agitation. The idea of trepidation, though implied, and connecting well with that of the roaring previously mentioned, is not so prominent as that of quick or nimble motion. Excited to the utmost by the revolutions of empires, which allowed them to take possession of their native country, they would use all haste in repairing thither. LXX. ἐκστήσονται; but in the following verse ἐκπέτεσονται. Syr. ܢܬܬܙܝܥܘܢ, *they shall move* or *be moved.*

"Sic Lat. *trepidare* etiam sumitur pro*festinare,* observantibus Bocharto in Hieroz, et Schultensio in Animadverss. philol. ad. Is. xix. 17." Winer, *in voc.* The same idea of velocity is further carried out by comparing the return of the Israelites to the flight of birds remarkable for their swiftness. צִפּוֹר is here used not in its generic sense of *bird,* but specifically of the *sparrow,* as the use of יוֹנָה, *dove,* immediately after, shows. The יָם, *sea,* is the Mediterranean, or the islands and other maritime regions in the west. Kimchi, הַמַּעֲרָב, *the west;* Pococke's Arab. MS. من جزاير البحر, *from the isles of the sea.* Comp. Is. xi. 11–16; a passage strictly parallel, only including the Jews as well as the Israelites. The three quarters of the globe here specified embrace all the countries mentioned by Isaiah; and as the ten tribes form the subject of Hosea's discourse, the present prophecy furnishes an additional proof of their return also, after the Babylonish captivity. To argue, therefore, from this passage, that they are still in existence, and are yet to be restored in their tribal capacity, is hermeneutically unwarranted. עַל in the phrase עַל־בָּתֵּיהֶם, instead of בְּ, seems to have special reference to the custom of the Orientals, who enjoy their time *upon,* rather than *in* their houses.

CHAPTER XII.

This chapter commences with renewed complaints against both Ephraim and Judah, more especially against the former, 1, 2. The conduct of their progenitor Jacob is then adduced in order to excite them to apply, as he did, for the blessings which they required, 3, 4; to copy which they are further encouraged by the unchangeable character of Jehovah, 5, 6. The prophet next reverts to the deceitful and hypocritical character of the ten tribes, notwithstanding the numerous means that had been employed to promote true piety, 7—10; renews his castigation of their idolatrous practices, 11; again appeals to the kindness of

God to the nation in its obscure origin in the person of Jacob, 12, 13; and denounces anew the judgments that were to be inflicted upon it, 14.

1 EPHRAIM hath encompassed me with falsehood,
And the house of Israel with deceit;
And as for Judah, he is still inconstant with God,
Even with the Holy Ones.

1. The LXX. Vulg. Targ. and our common version join this verse to the preceding chapter; but improperly—there being no connection whatever with the previous verses, whereas it is manifest from the renewed reference to Judah, ver. 3, that the three verses intimately cohere. The proper exegesis of this verse depends upon the signification assigned to רָד, and the consequent application of נֶאֱמָן. That the former cannot grammatically be referred either to רָדַד or רָדָה, *to subdue, bear rule*, or to יָרַד, *to descend*, as Jerome renders it, is now agreed on all hands; and there is no alternative left but to derive it from רוּד, which occurs only in three other passages, viz. one in Kal, Jer. ii. 31, and twice in Hiph. Gen. xxvii. 40, and Ps. lv. 3. In the two first, the ideas of becoming or being *unfaithful, rebelling, wandering at large*, are obviously conveyed. In the third, the verb is applied figuratively to an agitated or unsettled state of mind, to which the notion of *wandering* seems much more natural, than that of mourning, which is that expressed by our translators. Thus also the derivative מָרוּד may best be rendered *circumvagatio, erratio,* Lam. i. 7, iii. 19. Compare the Arabic رَادَ, رَادَ, *quæsivit pabulum; ultro citroque ivit; mobile fuit; discurrit huc illuc mulier apud vicinas suas.* مَرَدَ, *locus, quo in pascuis cameli modo prodeunt modo retrocedunt.* Eth. ሐደደ ፡ *persequi, insurrexit*, etc. The signification *dominatur*, which has been given to רוּד, is altogether gratuitous. The meaning of the prophet will, therefore, be, that Judah or the inhabitants of the southern kingdom acted with vacillancy in regard to Jehovah. So far were they from adhering steadfastly to his covenant, and seeking their happiness in obedience to his will, that they resembled animals that are dissatisfied with their pasture, break loose, and run wildly up and down in search of what is more agreeable to their appetite; or like a female who, discontent at home, seeks for satisfaction by gadding about among her neighbors. The description applies to the state of things among the Jews towards the end of the reign of Jotham, and during that of Ahaz, who introduced a Syrian altar, and other idolatrous objects, by which the people were tempted to infidelity towards Jehovah, but had not yet altogether renounced his service. Hence the force of עוֹד, *yet, still.* Though the idea of hostility implied in the verb would not justify the use of the preposition, עִם, *with,* taken as in the phrases עִם נִלְחַם, רִיב עִם, *to fight with, contend with;* yet it well agrees with its use after verbs of acting *towards*, or *in reference to* any one, such as עָשָׂה עִם, עָשָׂה טוֹב עִם, רָצָה עִם, etc. Thus Schroeder, Dathe, Eichhorn, De Wette, Boothroyd, Kuinoel, Gesenius, Noyes, Hitzig, Maurer, and Ewald. Such construction of the passage is fully borne out by ver. 3, which cannot be consistently interpreted, if Judah were here represented as faithfully maintaining the principles of the theocracy. But if the signification which has been given to רוּד be alone justifiable, then it is evident נֶאֱמָן, *faithful* cannot apply to Judah, but must be taken as qualifying קְדוֹשִׁים, the adjective noun immediately preceding. To this it cannot be objected, that the one is in the plural, while the other is in the singular; for we find a precisely similar combination in צַדִּיק אֱלֹהִים, *tho*

2 Ephraim feedeth upon wind,
He pursueth the east wind;
Every day he multiplieth falsehood and violence;
Yea, he maketh a covenant with Assyria,
And oil is carried into Egypt.
3 Jehovah hath also a controversy with Judah,
And he will punish Jacob, according to his ways;
According to his deeds, he will recompense him.
4 In the womb he took his brother by the heel,
And by his strength he strove with God;

righteous God, Ps. vii. 10. That קְדֹשִׁים, *the Holy Ones*, cannot here be applied either to human saints, or to angels, but must be interpreted of God himself, the law of parallelism clearly requires. Comp. Josh xxiv. 19, אֱלֹהִים קְדֹשִׁים ; Prov. ix. 10, בִּינָה קְדֹשִׁים דַּעַת; xxx. 3ודעת קדשים. Kimchi himself allows that קְדֹשִׁים must be so understood in this place. Between the inconstancy of the Jews, and the faithfulness of God, the contrast was placed in a very striking point of view. They had never known him to fail in giving effect to any of his promises; while they, on the contrary, had all along shown more or less of a fickle and roving disposition. The ancient versions exhibit considerable diversity of rendering in this place; but none of them suggests a meaning preferable to that just given, or warrants any alteration in the reading of the Hebrew.

2. By "the wind," and "the east wind," are meant empty, unsatisfying and pernicious objects. Such were the idolatrous confidence and foreign alliances of the Israelites. קָדִים, the LXX. render καύσων, the Arab. السَمُوم, the *Samoom*, or scorching wind, called the "east wind," because it blows from the desert to the east of Palestine. See on Is. xxvii. 8. In proportion to the insincerity and faithless conduct of the nation was the destruction which it brought upon itself. Such conduct was specially exhibited in the leagues that were formed, and the friendships that were entered into with the two most powerful of the ancient monarchies. שֶׁמֶן, *oil*, was one of the most valuable productions of Canaan,

and formed a profitable article of exportation. It is here spoken of as a present sent to the king of Egypt, doubtless among other costly articles, with a view to obtain a favorable hearing to the embassy which was despatched to secure his aid against the Assyrians.

3. "Judah" and "Jacob" stand for the two kingdoms respectively, the latter name denoting the ten tribes, as Is. xvii. 4. The declaration here made manifestly shows, that in ver. 1 the conduct of Judah is to be viewed in an unfavorable light. At the same time the language of both verses in reference to that power is not so strong as that which is employed respecting Israel.

4, 5. Having introduced the name of Jacob in reference to his posterity, Hosea adverts to three interesting incidents in his personal history, with the view of encouraging his countrymen to apply themselves with all assiduity to the service of God, who alone could, and would extricate them from the calamitous circumstances into which their sins had brought them. Though יַעֲקֹב, from which the name יַעֲקֹב, *Jacob*, is derived, Arab. عَقِبَ, *e vestigio secuutus fuit, a calce renit*, etc. signifies *to come behind any one, take him by the heel, trip, circumvent,* etc., it is obviously used here in a good sense, to denote the supernatural indication which his taking his brother Esau by the heel afforded of the superiority, which, in the course of divine providence, he and his posterity were to obtain. Gen. xxv. 22, 23, 26. To this effect the Targ. הֲלָא יַעֲקֹב עַד דְּלָא אִתְיְלִיד אֲמִיר דְּיֶהֱוֵי רַב מֵאֲחוּהִי, *was it not said of Jacob before*

5 Yea, he strove with the Angel and prevailed;
He wept and made supplication to him;
He found him at Bethel, and there he spake with us;

he was born, that he should be greater than his brother? The Israelites were reminded of the promise, "The one people shall be greater than the other people;" and had they acted on the faith of it, they would have found that, with Jehovah on their side, they were not only stronger than the Edomites, but even than the Assyrian power itself. The idea of *power* having thus been suggested to the mind of the prophet, he was reminded of the remarkable occurrence which took place at Peniel, when Jacob wrestled with the divine messenger of the covenant, and prevailed. שָׂרָה, *to put forth power, exercise rule as a prince,* or *commander,* the verb from which יִשְׂרָאֵל, *Israel,* the other name of Jacob, is derived, is that employed Gen. xxxii. 29, where the language is nearly identical with that used in these two verses. In the resumption of the subject, ver. 5. יָשַׂר is employed, which, though equivalent to שָׂרָה in signification, must be referred to the root שׁוּר. Comp. Jud. ix. 22, and Hos. viii. 4. אוֹן properly signifies *manly vigor.* Here הַמַּלְאָךְ, *the Angel,* corresponds to אֱלֹהִים, *God,* ver. 4, and designates the UNCREATED ANGEL, of whom we read so frequently in the Old Testament, to whom, as here, names distinctive of Deity are ascribed, and who is represented as possessing the divine attributes. See on Is. lxiii. 9, and Dr. M'Caul's Observations appended to his translation of Kimchi on Zechariah, chap. i. אֶל specially points to the Angel as the object towards whom the conflicting efforts of the patriarch were directed. Of the circumstances of his weeping and making supplication, no particular mention is made in Genesis, but they may be regarded as implied in the words, "I will not let thee go, except thou bless me." The struggle was not merely corporeal, it was also mental. The outward conflict was only a sign of that which was internal and spiritual. The prophet, as in the former reference, leaves the Israelites to make the application. If they would only now redeem their character as descendants of Israel, and show that they were entitled to the name, by sincerely and earnestly engaging in supplication to the God of their ancestor, they too should prevail, and obtain every necessary blessing. The third reference is to the narrative Gen. xxviii. 11-22, which contains an account of the scene at Bethel, and the promises which God then made, not to the patriarch only, but also to his posterity. The nominative to יִמְצָא, *he found,* is God, and not Jacob, as Abenezra, Tanchum, and several others have attempted to maintain. The meaning is, that Jehovah afforded to the solitary traveller the gracious aid which his exposed situation rendered desirable. בֵּית־אֵל, *Bethel,* is here the accusative of place, and is used with singular effect, in reference to the contrasted appropriation of it by the patriarch, and by his apostate posterity. The LXX. not perceiving this, have rendered it οἶκος Ὤν, *the house of On,* as elsewhere in this book. עִמָּנוּ, "*with us,*" Aq. Symm. Theod. Syr. Tanchum, Abulwalid, and several moderns, render as if it were עִמּוֹ, "*with him;*" but there is no variety of reading in the MSS., and נוּ is nowhere used of the third person singular. The LXX. have πρὸς αὐτούς, *to them,* as if they had read עִמָּם, which so far as pronunciation is concerned, goes to confirm the Masoretic punctuation. That the prophet here speaks per κοινώσιν, identifying himself and his contemporaries with their progenitor, in whose loins they may be said to have been, when he received the gracious promises which related not to himself only, but also to his posterity, is the interpretation advocated by Manger, Horsley, Hitzig, Maurer, and Rosenmüller. Comp. Ps. lxvi. 6; Heb. vii. 9, 10. On the other hand, Ewald, following Jarchi and Joseph Kimchi, renders the words יְדַבֵּר עִמָּנוּ, *he will speak with us,* in the future, and considers the prophet to be announcing, that God would renew his communications at Bethel, provided the Israelites returned to obedience.

6 Even Jehovah the God of hosts:
Jehovah is his memorial.

But though this seems less entitled to adoption, it cannot be denied that his design in the adduction of this instance was to lead his people to repentance, in order that they might inherit the promised blessings.

6. ו in וְיהוה is expletive. Ewald strangely gives to the combination the form of an oath: "bei Jahve," explaining it in his note, "wahr ist das bei Jahve," By Jehovah it is true! The incommunicable name is here introduced for the express purpose of showing that He who had made promises respecting the posterity of Jacob, would not prove unfaithful to his word. While אֱלֹהֵי הַצְּבָאוֹת, *the God of hosts*, LXX. Παντοκράτωρ, conveys the idea of supreme and infinite power by which he is able to carry all his purposes into effect, his peculiarly distinctive name יהוה, conveys that *of immutable constancy*, and, by implication, fidelity to his promises. Some refer the word to the root הָוָה, *to exist, be;* but that it is to be derived from the cognate and more ordinary verb of existence הָיָה, appears evident from Exod. iii. 14, where, in the explanation of the name, the form of the future is not אֶהְיֶה, but יִהְיֶה. But as י is nevertheless inserted in יהוה, which also retains ו, preformant of the third person singular, it is impossible not to acquiesce in the opinion, that the noun is made up of הָיָה, *He was*, הֹוֶה, *He is*, and יִהְיֶה, *He will be.* What confirms this hypothesis, is the peculiar designation of God, Rev. i. 4, 8. Ὁ ὢν καὶ ὁ ἦν καὶ ὁ ἐρχόμενος, *He that is, and that was, and that is to come*, which is merely a translation into Greek of these different forms of the verb. See Pococke on Joel i. 19. In this derivation Abenezra and other Rabbins concur; and, accordingly the second article of the Jewish creed concludes with the words והוא לבדו אלהינו חיה הוה ויהיה, "And he alone is our God; He was, He is, and He shall be." It is a coincidence in no small degree remarkable, that this threefold description of the divine existence obtained both among the ancient Egyptians and Brahmins. On the Saïtic temple of Isis was the inscription, Ἐγώ εἰμι πᾶν τὸ γεγονὸς καὶ ὂν καὶ ἐσόμενον, καὶ τὸν ἐμὸν πέπλον οὐδείς πω θνητὸς ἀνεκάλυψε, "I am all THAT WAS, AND IS, AND SHALL BE, and no mortal hath ever uncovered my veil." Plutarch de Iside. In the Bhagavat the Supreme Being thus addresses Brahma: — "Even I WAS at first, not any other being; THAT WHICH EXISTS unperceived; Supreme: afterwards I AM THAT WHICH IS; and HE WHO MUST REMAIN am I." Asiat. Researches, vol. i. p. 245. Comp. Ζεὺς ἦν, Ζεὺς ἐστί· Ζεὺς ἔσσεται· ὦ μεγάλε Ζεῦ. "Zeus was; Zeus is; Zeus shall be; O great Zeus!" Pausan. Phoc. x. 12. Whether the name יהוה was in use before the time of Moses, has been, and still is matter of dispute. That the patriarchs were unacquainted with it, has been concluded from Exod. vi. 3, where God declares, that the name under which he revealed himself to them was אֵל שַׁדַּי, GOD ALMIGHTY, but that he was not known to them by his name יְהוָה, JEHOVAH. Since, however, we meet with this name not only in the history of the patriarchs, but also expressly employed by themselves, as in Gen. xv. 2, xvi. 2, xxii. 14, xxiv. 3, xxvii. 7, xxiii. 20, 21, etc. it seems undeniable that they were acquainted with it; so that what is meant by the words וּשְׁמִי יְהוָה לֹא נוֹדַעְתִּי לָהֶם, is, that God had not caused them *to experience the import* of his name יְהוָה, JEHOVAH. For this signification of the phrase יָדַע שֵׁם, *to know a name*, or, *to know*, comp. Is. lii. 6, lxiv. 1; "Jer. xvi. 21. It had special reference to something future — the fulfilment of the promises which he had given them; and as these promises began to be fulfilled when he interposed for their deliverance from Egypt, there was singular propriety in its being selected as the name by which Moses was to announce him to his people, on opening his commission to them. The same futurity of reference may be said to have continued to attach to it all along till the advent of Messiah, in whom all the promises are

7 Thou, therefore, return to thy God;
Observe mercy and judgment,
And wait continually on thy God.
8 As for Canaan, deceitful balances are in his hand;
He loveth to oppress.
9 Ephraim saith, Surely I am rich,
I have acquired wealth;
In none of my labors am I chargeable with guilt.

yea and amen, 2 Cor. i. 20 ; just as it is still prominently exhibited in ‛Ο ἐρχόμενος, THE COMING ONE, of the Apocalypse, which obviously respects the revelation of the Lord from heaven to fulfil the mystery of God. Such interpretation alone goes to fully justify the emphatic statement made in the text of our prophet, יְהֹוָה דְּבָרִי, compared with Exod. iii. 15, זֶה־דְּבָרִי לְדֹר דֹּר, in which the Most High declares, that this name was to be employed for the purpose of perpetuating the knowledge of his character with respect to promised blessings. Comp. also Ps. cxxxv. 13. That it should have come into oral disuse among the Jews, could only have originated in a feeling of superstitious veneration, which led them to regard it as too sacred to be pronounced without profanation. The earliest trace of such superstition is thought to be found in the words, Ecclesiasticus xxiii. 9, ὀνομασίᾳ τοῦ ἁγίου μὴ συνεθισθῇς, "use not thyself to the naming of the Holy One;" but Philo de Nomin. mutat. makes express mention of it. Whenever the Jews meet with it in the text, they read אֲדֹנָי, LORD, instead of it, except when it follows אֲדֹנָי, in which case they point it יְהוִֹה, and read אֱלֹהִים, GOD. Some are of opinion, that the present punctuation יְהוָֹה is merely that of אֲדֹנָי, the simple Shěva taking the place of Hateph-Patach, which only occurs in connection with gutturals; but the employment of the two first syllables with precisely the same points in the formation of compound proper names manifestly goes to show that our present pronunciation is correct. Compare יְהִישַׁע, יְהֹואָחָז, יְהֹונָתָן, etc. The change of the Segol into Kametz may be accounted for on the ground of the grave manner

in which the final syllable required to be accented, if it was not intended to stand for the second vowel of the preterite הָיָה.

7. An exhortation to duty derived from what God had been, and would still, in accordance with the significant aspect of his name, in continuance be, to those who served him in sincerity.

8. כְּנַעַן, Canaan, is the nominative absolute, introduced abruptly for the purpose of graphically describing the real character of the Ephraimites. The word may, indeed, be rendered *merchant*, but then אִישׁ, *man*, must be supplied; אִישׁ כְּנַעַן, *a man of Canaan*, meaning *a merchant* — the inhabitants of that country being the celebrated merchants of antiquity. The prophet seems rather to place the names of *Canaan* and *Israel* in antithesis; in which there is great point, as the Israelites were accustomed to hold the Canaanites in the utmost contempt. Comp. Ezek. xvi. 3. Horsley renders *a trafficker of Canaan*, which weakens rather than strengthens the antithesis. The fraudulent practices of merchants were quite proverbial among the Jews. "As a nail sticketh fast in the joinings of the stones, so doth sin stick close between buying and selling." Ecclesiasticus xxvii. 2.

9. The character assumed in the preceding verse is here directly applied, only the ten tribes are represented as flattering themselves that they had employed no illegal means in acquiring their affluence. יִמְצְאוּ, *they shall find*, is used impersonally. עָוֹן is employed to denote the *act of distortion* or iniquity, חֵטְא its *guilt* or *culpability*. The words literally rendered are, *with respect to all my efforts, they shall not find attaching to me iniquity which is sin;* and the meaning is,

10 Yet I, Jehovah, am thy God from the land of Egypt;
I will still cause thee to dwell in tents as on feast days.
11 I have spoken to the prophets,
I have multiplied visions;
And through the prophets I have used similitudes.

might be punished. "The merchant imagines that it is not possible to get through business without some deceit; but he takes care not to commit any gross or deadly act of delinquency, hoping that God will not be strict in regard to the rest." — *Michaelis*.

10. Commentators have been greatly divided in opinion as to whether these words are to be taken as a promise, or as a threatening. Those who take the latter view interpret the living in tabernacles of such a life as those lead who have no settled habitations, like the Israelites in the wilderness, or like those who assembled at the annual festivals, and who could only be accommodated in tents without the city. But, though such exegesis might at first sight seem to suit the connection, yet there is something so forced in comparing a state of captivity to that of the Hebrew nation during the celebration of the most joyful of all their festivals, that I am compelled to regard the verse as containing a promise of what God would still do for the Israelites on their repentance and reformation. Those who are familiar with the sudden and abrupt transitions which abound in Hosea, and the frequency with which he intermingles promises with threatenings, will not be surprised at this unexpected assurance of the divine clemency. The argument is this: the Israelites have indeed acted a most wicked and deceitful part, and justly deserve to be forever cast off from all participation in my favor; but I am still, what I have been from the beginning of their history, their covenant-God, and will yet cause them to renew their joy before me. That they were not to enjoy any such privilege in their apostate condition is taken for granted. The promise was fulfilled on the return from the captivity.

11. Jehovah adduces a further proof of the kindness of his disposition towards the nation — the abundant means of instruction which he had afforded them; while at the same time, the language is so worded as to draw their attention to the messages which the prophets had delivered. These messages contained the most powerful dissuasives from idolatry, and the greatest encouragements to cleave unto the Lord. עַל in דִּבַּרְתִּי־עַל, following a verb of announcement, is equivalent to אֶל, *to*, and is not to be pressed so as to make it signify the *coming down* or *resting* of inspiration upon the prophets. Comp. Job xxxvi. 33. LXX. πρὸς προφήτας. If Hosea was one of the earliest of the Hebrew prophets, whose books are now in our hands, reference must here be had to those who had flourished before his time, such as Ahijah the Shilonite, Shemaiah, Iddo, Azariah, Hanani, Jehu, Jahaziel, Eliezer, Elijah, Elisha, Micaiah, Joel, and Amoz, not to include the hundred prophets of the Lord whom Obadiah hid in a cave, after Jezebel had put a number to death. Not only had Jehovah made numerous communications of his will through the instrumentality of these messengers, but he had employed such modes in making these communications as were calculated at once to gain and secure attention. For הִרְבֵּיתִי, see on Is. i. 1. אֲדַמֶּה from דָּמָה, *to be like, resemble;* in Piel, to *liken, employ, similes,* or *comparisons;* or, in general, to use figurative language. In such language, including metaphor, allegory, comparison, prosopopœia, apostrophe, hyperbole, etc., the prophets abound. They accommodated themselves to the capacity and understanding of their hearers by couching the high and important subjects of which they treated under the imagery of sensible objects, and invested them with a degree of life and energy which could only be resisted by an obstinate determination not to listen to religious instruction. Though אֲדַמֶּה is in the future, it borrows its temporal signification from

12 Verily Gilead is iniquitous,
   Surely they are false:
   In Gilgal they sacrifice oxen;
   Their altars are like the heaps
   On the ridges of the field.
13 Jacob fled to the country of Syria;
   Israel served for a wife;
   And for a wife he kept the flocks.
14 By a prophet Jehovah brought Israel up from Egypt,
   And by a prophet he was kept.

the two preceding verbs, רִבְּתִי and הִרְבֵּיתִי, which are in the preterite.

12. אִם is not used here as a particle expressing doubt; it rather expresses the certainty of what is affirmed, as אַךְ following, evidently shows. The two places here mentioned were celebrated in the history of the Hebrews: — *Gilead*, on account of the solemn agreement which Laban and Jacob entered into there with each other; and *Gilgal*, on account of the general circumcision of the people, and the solemn observance of the passover when they had passed over Jordan. They are adduced by the prophet to remind the Israelites of the sacred obligations under which they lay, and the sacred character which, as the peculiar people of God, they ought ever to sustain. Pointing, as it were, to the heap of stones which Jacob had erected in testimony of the transaction between him and Laban, Hosea asks, Is Gilead the scene of iniquity? Are its inhabitants actually worshippers of idols? And then he fearlessly charges them with idolatry. Both אָוֶן and שָׁוְא are specially used of idols, in order to express their nothingness and vanity. The abstract stands for the concrete. By גִּלְעָד, *Gilead*, is meant not merely the place, but its inhabitants. Comp. for the wickedness of the Gileadites, chap. vi. 8. גִּלְגָּל, *Gilgal*, had also become desecrated by idolatrous practices, chap. iv. 15, ix. 15, which abounded to such an extent, that the number of the altars was like that of the heaps of stones which have been collected and left in various parts of the ridges of a field. In גַּלִּים, *heaps*, comp. Josh. vii. 26, there is an obvious reference to the name גִּלְגָּל.

Both are derived from גָּלַל, *to roll, roll stones*, etc. For שָׂדָי, תַּלְמֵי שָׂדָי, comp. chap. x. 4.

13, 14. The argument of both these verses is the same, though it is only in the latter that it is expressly stated, viz. the divine goodness in preserving Jacob and his posterity. God was with the patriarch, according to his promise, and protected and prospered him all the time he was in servitude in Padan-aram; and he likewise delivered his descendants from Egyptian bondage, and conducted them safely to the land of Canaan. אֲרָם, *Aramæa*, Syria, *the high country*, from רוּם, *to be high*; here specially the region between the Euphrates and the Tigris, called on this account, אֲרַם נַהֲרַיִם, *Aram of the two rivers*, LXX. Μεσοποταμία, *Mesopotamia*. Being lower than the rest of Syria on the west, it is here called שָׂדֶה, *field*, which corresponds to אֶרֶץ, a *level* or *plain*, Gen. xlviii. 7; hence *Padan-aram*. שָׁמַר, *to keep*, is used without צֹאן, *sheep*, in the sense of *keeping a flock*. See Gen. xxx. 31; 1 Sam. xvii. 20. To the verb as thus employed in its literal acceptation, ver. 13, the figurative use in נִשְׁמָר, ver. 14, corresponds. The church of God is frequently compared to a flock. The נָבִיא, *prophet*, here referred to was Moses, who was so κατ' ἐξοχήν. See Exod. iv. 15, 16; Numb. xii. 6-8; Is. lxiii. 11, 12, The repeated reference to the Hebrew legislator in this character, was evidently intended to impress the minds of the Israelites with a conviction of the necessity of attending to the messages which the Lord sent to them by his prophets.

15 Ephraim hath given most bitter provocation,
   Therefore will his Lord leave his blood upon him;
   And bring back upon him his reproach.

15. הַמְרֵרִים, lit. *bitterness*, i. e. *most bitter*, or *bitterly*. The object of provocation is not expressed, but that it is Jehovah is clear from the following clause. The blood of Ephraim was, in all probability, that of human victims which had been shed in the service of Moloch. אֲדֹנָיו, *his Lord*, is improperly applied by Horsley to the king of Assyria. By חֶרְפָּתוֹ,

his reproach, is meant the disgraceful conduct of the ten tribes in abandoning the true God, as unworthy of their service, and transferring it to idols. אֲדֹנָיו is the nominative to יִטּוֹשׁ as well as to יָשִׁיב, and in our language the corresponding term *Lord* requires to be used before the former, and understood before the latter of the two verbs.

CHAPTER XIII.

After contrasting the prosperity of the tribe of Ephraim, during the period of its obedience to the divine laws, with the adversity which it had suffered in consequence of idolatry, 1, the prophet proceeds in the same manner. as in the preceding chapter, to intermingle brief descriptions of sin and guilt, 2, 6, 9, 12; denouncements of punishment, 3, 7, 8, 13, 15, 16; and promises of mercy, 4, 9, 14.

---

1 WHEN Ephraim spake, there was tremor;
   He was exalted in Israel;
   But he offended through Baal, and died.

1. *Ephraim* means here the tribe properly so called, in distinction from the other tribes of *Israel*, mentioned immediately after. Such was the power and influence which it originally exercised over the rest, that they showed it the utmost deference. רְתֵת, a ἅπαξ λεγόμενον, but obviously cognate with רַעַד, Jer. xlix. 24, Syr. ܪܬܝܬܐ, Targ. רְתִיתָא, *fear, trembling*. In Pocoeke's Arab. MS. the words are rendered عند خطاب اغرايم الرعدة تقع علي الناس, *when Ephraim spake, trembling fell upon men*. And so Tanchum, المعني ان الناس يهابوه, وبرعدون من كلامه, *the meaning is, that men revered him, and trembled at his word*. The same construction is adopted by Jerome, Kimchi, Abarbanel, Munster, Vatablus, Clarius, Drusius, Lively, Grotius, Rivetus, Tingstadius, Dathe, Kuinoel, Horsley, De Wette, Maurer, Noyes, and Hitzig. It is impossible to approve the translation of Ewald: "Wie Efraim redete Empörung, es aufruhr machte in Israel," *When Ephraim gave utterance to sedition, it produced rebellion in Israel.* Neither רְתֵת nor נָשָׂא admit of being so translated. To take רְתֵת adverbially, and render it *tremblingly*, or *trembling*, as in our common version, though it affords an apt sense in itself, is less suited

2 And now they continue to sin,
And make for themselves molten images,
Idols of their silver according to their skill;
All of them the work of artificers;
The men that sacrifice, say of them,
Let them kiss the calves.

to the connection. נִשָּׂא occurs in the sense of *elevating one's self*, Ps. lxxxix. 10; Nah. i. 5, or *being exalted*. Hence נָשִׂיא, *a prince*. בְּ in בָּבַד, has the force of, *in union with*, *in the matter of*, and marks the participation of the Ephraimites in the service of Baal. מוּת, *to die*, is here to be taken in a civil or political sense; to lose one's influence, become subject to misery, punishment, etc. It forms an antithesis to נִשָּׂא, *to be exalted*. No sooner did the Ephraimites forsake the true God and take up with idols than he inflicted judgments upon them, by which their power was weakened, and at last became entirely extinct — "ex quo peccavit, nulla jam est autoritate in populo Dei." Œcolampadius. "Vita ærumnosa et tristis pro morte censetur; ideirco exules mortui dicuntur, et exilium sepulchri nomine notatur, Ezech. cap. 37." Rivetus.

2. This verse sets forth their perseverance in idolatrous practices, notwithstanding the chastisements with which they had been visited. זֹבְחֵי אָדָם, the LXX. Vulg. Jarchi, Abenezra, Abarbanel, Tanchum, Calvin, Piscator, Leo Juda, and among the moderns, Schmid, J. H. Michaelis, Horsley, Hitzig, Stuck, and J. Fr. Schröder, render *sacrifice*, or *sacrificers of men*, on the principle, that the presentation of human sacrifices is meant. This, however, was called in question by Kimchi, who explains, בְּנֵי אָדָם הַבָּאִים לִזְבֹּחַ, *the men who come to sacrifice*. To the same effect Munster, Piscator, Junius and Tremelius, Rivetus, Mercer, Glassius, Lively, Drusius, Bochart, our own and most of the authorized versions, Lowth, Newcome, Boothroyd, Noyes, De Wette, Gesenius, Maurer, and Ewald. The rule of syntax laid down by Gesenius respecting this mode of construction, Lehrgeb. p. 678, is, that when a genitive following an adjective is a noun of multitude, or of the plural number, such adjective is particularly used in poetry for the purpose of designating those of the multitude to which the specified quality belongs. Instances are Isaiah xxix. 19, אֶבְיוֹנֵי אָדָם, *the poor of men*, i. e. those of men who are poor; Micah v. 5, נְסִיכֵי אָדָם, *the anointed of men*, i. e. such of men as are anointed. So in the present case, זֹבְחֵי אָדָם, *sacrificers of men*, i. e. those of, or among men that sacrifice, which is merely a periphrasis for *priests*. Although, therefore, it is a fact, that the ten tribes did sacrifice their children to Moloch, 2 Kings xvii. 17, it would be more than precarious to draw any such inference from the present passage, especially as the prophet mentions the *calves*, of whose worship human sacrifices, so far as we know, formed no part. עֲגָלִים יִשָּׁקוּן, *let them kiss the calves*. It was customary for idolaters to give the kiss of adoration to the objects of their worship. This was sometimes done by merely touching the lips with the hand, to which reference is made Job xxxi. 27. Comp. Lucian περὶ Ὀρχήσεως i. p. 918, edit. Bened. Minutius Felix, cap. 2, *ad fin.* Apuleius Apol. p. 496. At other times the idol itself was kissed by the worshippers. Comp. 1 Kings xix. 18. Thus Cicero tells us, that at Agrigentum in Sicily there was a brazen image of the Tyrian Hercules whose mouth and chin were worn by the kisses of his worshippers — "non solum id venerari, verum etiam osculari solebant." Act. ii. in Verrem, lib. iv. cap. 43. Nothing is more common in the Russian churches than for the devotees to kiss the picture of the virgin, or of St. Nicholas. The construction of the words זֹבְחֵי אָדָם עֲגָלִים יִשָּׁקוּן is somewhat difficult. As usually divided they are interpreted thus: they, *i. e.* the Ephraimites, say of them, the images, let the sacrificers kiss the calves; but it is better to take זֹבְחֵי אָדָם, *the sacrificers*, as in

3 Therefore shall they be like the morning cloud,
   And like the dew which early departeth,
   Like chaff blown by a whirlwind from the threshing-floor,
   And like smoke from the window.
4 Yet I, Jehovah, have been thy God from the land of Egypt,
   Thou knewest no God besides me;
   Nor was there any Saviour besides me.
5 I regarded thee in the wilderness,
   In the land of burning thirst.
6 As they were fed, so were they satiated;
   They were satiated, and their heart was lifted up;
   Therefore they forgat me:
7 So that I became to them as a lion,
   I watched for them as a leopard by the way.
8 I met them as a bear bereaved of her cubs,

apposition with and exegetical of הֵם אֹמְרִים, *they say*, i. e. they, the men that sacrifice, say to the people, let them kiss the calves. While the priests presented the sacrifices, they encouraged the worshippers to come forward and kiss the objects of their adoration.

3. Comp. chap. vi. 4. גֹּרֶן, *the threshing floor*, being an open area, generally on an eminence, was peculiarly exposed to the wind, which carried off the chaff, on its being trodden out, or separated from the grain. מֹץ, Aq. ἀπὸ καταῤῥάκτου, which Jerome explains, "foramen in pariete fabricatum per quod fumas egreditur;" Symm. ὀπῆς, ὀπὴ, *an orifice*; Theod. καπνοδόχην, *a hole for the passage of smoke.* It is very common in the East for the light to be admitted, and the smoke to make its escape by the same passage or orifice in the wall. The idea of a speedy removal is that conveyed by all the images here employed.

4. Comp. chap. xii. 10. The long addition in the LXX. is totally unsupported, and was most probably inserted in that version by some scholiast.

5. Here יְדַעְתִּיךָ, *I knew*, contrasts with יֵדַע in the preceding verse, only it is to be taken in the sense of *knowing effectively, taking notice of, caring for.* Comp. Amos iii. 2. תַּלְאֻבוֹת, lit. *thirstiness, great thirst, extreme drought*, from לָאַב, Arab. لاب, *sitivit*, Comp. לָהַב, *to burn*, Arab. لهب, *arsit, sitivit, siti, arsit.* Munster renders, "terra siti ardente." Comp. Deut. viii. 15.

6. כְּמַרְעִיתָם, *according to their feeding*, i. e. in proportion to their enjoyment of the provision which I made for them, feeding them with manna from heaven, and afterwards abundantly supplying their wants. It is equivalent to, "as they were fed." For the rest of the verse comp. Deut. xxxii. 13-15.

7, 8. ו in וָאֱהִי is inferential, showing that what follows was the result of what is stated in the preceding verse. The context requires the verb to be taken in the past time. The images here employed are of frequent occurrence. Comp. Job x. 16; Ps. vii. 2; Is. xxxviii. 13; Lam. iii. 10. נָמֵר, *the leopard*, so called from his *spots* or *streaks*. Arab. نمر, *maculosus fuit, maculis punctisve respersus fuit; pardus.* See Jer. xiii. 23, הֲיַהֲפֹךְ כוּשִׁי עוֹרוֹ וְנָמֵר חֲבַרְבֻּרֹתָיו. The leopard is noted for his swiftness, ferocity, and especially his cruelty to man. He lurks in the dense thicket of the wood, and springs with great velocity on his victim. With respect to the bear, Jerome remarks, "Aiunt, qui, de bestiarum scripsere naturis, inter omnes feras nihil esse ursa saevius, quum perdiderit catulos vel indignerit cibis." דֹּב being of common gender, the participle שַׁכּוּל is put in the

And rent the caul of their heart;
I devoured them there, as a lioness;
The wild beast rent them in pieces.
9 O Israel! Thou hast destroyed thyself,
Nevertheless in me truly is thine help.
10 Where is thy king now?
That he may save thee in all thy cities;
And thy judges, of whom thou saidst,
Give me a king and princes,
11 I gave thee a king in mine anger,
And took him away in my wrath.

---

masculine, though the female bear is meant. Comp. אֱלִיפְּנוּ מְסֻבָּלִים, Ps. cxliv. 14. סְגוֹר is the pericardium, or membrane which contains the heart in its cavity, and is thus fitly called its *enclosure*. For אָשׁוּר, *I watched*, sixteen of De Rossi's MSS. and one in the margin, three ancient editions, and twenty-four others, the LXX. Syr. Vulg. and Arab. read אַשּׁוּר, *Assyria*, which some prefer, on account of the number of lions, panthers, tigers, etc. with which the regions of southern Asia abound. The text would then read, *as a leopard, in the way to Assyria;* but the common reading is more in accordance with the spirit of the passage.

9. שִׁחֶתְךָ, I take to be a noun with the suffix, *thy destruction!* i. e. the destruction is thine own; thou hast brought it upon thyself by thy sins. It is, therefore, equivalent to "thou hast destroyed thyself," and cannot be better rendered. Thus the Vulg. *Perditio tua, Israel.* Dathe, *Ipsi estis o Israelitæ! exitii vestri causa.* Some, however, as Kimchi, supply הָעֵגֶל, *the calf*; others, מַלְכְּךָ, *thy king,* from the following verse; others, some other noun; and take שִׁחֵת to be the third person singular of Piel. Comp. for the form שַׁלֵּם, Deut. xxxii. 35; דִּבֶּר, Jer. v. 13; קִצֵּר, Hos. i. 2; דִּבֶּר, Jer. xliv. 21. Newcome unwarrantably adopts the rendering of the Syriac, "I have destroyed thee." Most of the moderns give a hostile sense to the בְּ in the following בִּי בְעֶזְרֶךָ, *against me, against thy help;* but, considering how frequently declarations of kindness are mixed up with charges of evil, and that some verb

denoting rebellion would be required to support such construction, it seems preferable to give to כִּי the common adversative signification of *yet*, *nevertheless*, and to regard the בְּ in בְעֶזְרֶךָ as the *Beth Essentiæ*, which renders the phrase much more emphatic than the pronoun, or the substantive verb would have done. It is equivalent to, In me is thy real help. Other sources may be applied to, and they may promise thee assistance; but from me alone efficient aid is to be expected, and in me it is to be found. So our translators. See on Is. xxvi. 4. This exegesis is strongly supported, if not rendered absolutely necessary, by the pointed interrogations in the following verse. The LXX. τίς βοηθήσει; turning בְּ into מִי, and omitting the second בְּ altogether. Thus also the Syr.

10, 11. אֱהִי is in all probability a metathesis for אַיֵּה, *where!* It is thus rendered by the LXX. Syr. Vulg. Targ. Abulwalid, Tanchum, Luther, Drusius, Mercer, Osiander, Rivetus, Castalio, and by most modern expositors. It is also so taken by Gesenius, Lee, Winer, and Fürst; and alone suits the connection. Comp. in support of this interpretation, the combination אַיֵּה אֵפוֹא, Jud. ix. 38; Job xvii. 15; Is. xix 12. One of Kennicott's MSS. and perhaps another, one of De Rossi's in the margin, read אַיֵּה instead of אֱהִי, though probably by correction. Another of De Rossi's has a note in the margin, stating that the word is so explained. The וִיהוֹשִׁיעֲךָ is pleonastic, except it be regarded as introducing the apodosis. אֶרֶץ is so intimately connected with the past transactions im-

12   The guilt of Ephraim is bound up,
    His punishment is laid up in store.
13 The pangs of a woman in labor shall come upon him;
    He is an unwise son,
    Otherwise he would not remain long
    In the place of the breaking forth of children.
14 I will deliver them from the power of Sheol;
    I will redeem them from death:

plied in לִי־תְּנָה אָמְרִתָּ, *thou saidst, give me,* that, though future in form, it cannot with any propriety be rendered otherwise than in the preterite. Some refer the circumstances here mentioned to the selection and removal of Saul; but it is more in keeping with the specialty of the prophet's address to consider the king to be Jeroboam and his successors in the regal dignity; and that the removal regards the frequent changes which took place in the history of the Israelitish kings, which proved a source of great calamity to the nation. See 2 Kings xv.

12. The metaphors are here borrowed from the custom of tying up money in bags, and depositing it in some secret place, in order that it might be preserved. The certainty of punishment is the idea conveyed by them. Comp. for the former, Job xiv. 17; and for the latter Deut. xxxii. 34, Job xxi. 19.

13. Another instance of two metaphors closely connected, the transition from the one to the other of which is, in the manner of the Orientals, rapid and unexpected. See Dathe's very judicious note. It is not unusual in Scripture to compare the calamities of a people to the sorrows of childbirth. In addition to this the danger and folly of Ephraim in protracting repentance, in the midst of the afflictive circumstances in which he was placed, is fitly compared to the extremely critical condition of a child on the point of being born, but, owing to the want of strength on the part of the mother, or other causes, is detained in its passage from the womb. The LXX. οὗτος ὁ υἱός σου ὁ φρόνιμος has doubtless originally been οὗτος ὁ υἱός οὐ φρόνιμος. כִּי introduces the contrary of the preceding proposition, and is used elliptically for the sentence, "*For if it*

were not so,*" etc. It may best be rendered into English by *otherwise, else,* or the like. עֵת, *time,* is here to be taken adverbially, in the sense of *for a time, long,* etc. Winer, *aliquod tempus, aliquamdiu.* Comp. the Arab. زَمَنٌ, when used in opposition to وَقْتٌ. מִשְׁבֵּר, the *os uteri.* Comp. 2 Kings xix. 3; Is. xxxvi. 3, lxvi. 9. Without a national παλιγγενεσία, no prosperity could be expected. It was for the Israelites by true repentance to accelerate and ensure their deliverance from threatened destruction, and their enjoyment of a new period of peace and happiness.

14. The ideas of Sheol and Death were naturally suggested by the perilous circumstances described in the preceding verse. Extinction as a people is there apprehended. Here it is viewed as having already taken place; and a gracious promise is given of the restoration of the Israelites, and the complete destruction of the enemies by whom they had been carried into captivity. מִיַּד, *from the hand,* a common Hebraism for *from the power.* פָּדָה properly signifies to *redeem,* or *buy loose,* by the payment of a price; גָּאַל, *to avenge* the murder of a relative, and also to *recover* or *redeem* property by repayment. Both verbs, however, are used in a more extended signification, and especially in reference to the deliverance of the Hebrews from Egypt, and from the captivity in Babylon. That שְׁאוֹל, *Sheol,* and מָוֶת, *Death,* are here to be taken in a figurative sense, with application to the state of the Israelites in the Assyrian and Babylonish captivity, deprived as they were of all political existence, and subject to the most grievous

Where is thy destruction, O Death?
Where is thine excision, O Sheol?
Repentance is hid from mine eyes.

calamities, the exigency of the passage imperatively demands. Comp. Is. xxvi. 19. Respecting אֱהִי interpreters are far from being agreed. Symm. the Vulg. Coverdale, Drusius, Tingstadius, Horsley, Dathe, Kuinoel, De Wette, Noyes, Rosenmüller, Hesselberg, and Maurer, take it to be the first person future of the substantive verb הָיָה, to be; whereas the LXX. Aq. the fifth edition, (Paul, 1 Cor. xv. 55,) Syr. Arab. Abulwalid, Tanchum, Junius and Tremellius, Mercer, Newcome, Boothroyd, Ewald, and Hitzig, consider it to be used as in ver. 10, for אַיֵּה ποῦ, where? With the latter authorities I concur, partly on the ground that it is not likely the prophet would employ the same word in the same form in two different acceptations in verses 10 and 14; and partly because I find אֱהִי nowhere used absolutely as an apocopated future; but always with the Vau conversive prefixed. See for the full form אֶהְיֶה, chap. xiv. 6. To which add, that the interrogation is more in keeping with the animated style of the passage. Instead of the plural דְּבָרֶיךָ, thy destructions, one hundred and twenty-two MSS. originally five more, now two, and four of the early editions read דְּבָרְךָ, thy destruction in the singular. דֶּבֶר, Arab. ردب, death; specially the plague, pestilence; the awful destruction of human life effected by it. Hence the LXX. mostly render it θάνατος; here δίκη, but in all probability originally νίκη, for which Paul reads νίκος, only transposing νίκος and κέντρον, by which latter term the LXX. render קֶטֶב, excision, cutting off, destruction. The cause of this transposition is obvious. The apostle had just quoted the passage in Isaiah, agreeably to the version of Theodotion, in which νίκος occurs, whereby he was reminded of the same words as occurring in Hosea, and, under the influence of strong emotion, he commences his quotation with νίκος prominently in his mind. Olshausen thinks νίκος is a later form for νίκη.

Root קָטַב, Arab. قطب, to cut, cut off, destroy. That דֶּבֶר is the genuine reading, and that דָּרְבָן, a goad, which some would substitute for it, in order to make the Hebrew correspond to κέντρον, is to be rejected, may very conclusively be gathered from the similar occurrence of the words דֶּבֶר and קֶטֶב together, Ps. xci. 6. Comp. Deut. xxxii. 24. The import of this animated apostrophe, as used both by Jehovah in the prophet, and by the apostle, is, Where are now the effects of the destructive influence which you have exerted? Your victims are recovered from your dominion: they are alive again, and shall no more be subject to your power. The speakers place themselves as it were in the period after the resurrection: the former in that after the restoration from Babylon; the other in that after the literal restoration of the dead to life at the last day. Both look back, and triumphantly exult over the conquerors. With respect to the appropriation of the words by the apostle in reference to the doctrine of the final resurrection, it appears to be made, not in the way of proof, but merely to give expression, in the triumphant language of the prophet, to the animated feelings which had taken possession of his breast. His direct quotation in the way of argument is made from Is. xxv. 8, and consists of the words κατεπόθη ὁ θάνατος εἰς νίκος. It would, therefore, be improper to identify the subject of which he treats with that treated of by our prophet. "Neque enim ex professo semper locos adducunt apostoli, qui toto contextu ad institutum quod tractant pertineant: sed interdum alludunt ad unum verbum duntaxat, aliquando aptant locum ad sententiam per similitudinem, aliquando abhibent testimonia.—Atqui satis constat, Paulum illo 15 cap. 1 ad Corinth. non citasse prophetæ testimoniam ad confirmandum illam doctrinam de qua disserit." Calvin in loc. See also Horsley's critical note. טָנָה, LXX. παράκλησις,

15 Though he be fruitful among his brethren,
    Yet an east wind, a wind of Jehovah,
    Shall come up from the desert,
    And dry up his fountain;
    And his spring shall become dry:
    He shall spoil the treasure of all pleasant vessels.
16 Samaria shall be punished,
    Because she hath rebelled against her God:
    They shall fall by the sword;
    Their infants shall be dashed in pieces,
    And their pregnant women shall be ripped up.

Syr. ܢܶܚܳܡܳܐ, Vulg. *consolatio;* but *repentance* better suits the connection. It expresses the immutability of the divine purpose, which had the deliverance of his people for its object. Comp. Rom. xi. 29. Horsley strangely refers the repentance to man, and not to God.

15. This and the following verse set forth the devastation and destruction of the kingdom of the ten tribes, which was to precede the deliverance promised in that which precedes. While the promise was designed to afford consolation to the pious, and encouragement to the penitent, the threatening was equally necessary for the refractory and profane. הוּא, *he,* refers to Ephraim, ver. 12. יַפְרִיא an ἅπαξ λεγ. but obviously equivalent to יִפְרֶה, the Hiphil of פָּרָה, *to be fruitful.* It is here used with special reference to the name of אֶפְרַיִם, being the root whence it is derived, and not improbably exhibits א instead of ה, because it forms the first letter of the noun. The tribe of Ephraim was the most numerous in regard to population, and was for a time in the most flourishing circumstances. That such is the signification of the verb, and that it is not to be rendered *divide* or *separate,* as in the ancient and several of the modern versions, nor *act like a wild ass,* which others exhibit, appears from the mention of a *spring* and a *fountain,* which naturally suggests the idea of a tree, the roots of which are plentifully supplied by their water. For קָדִים, see on chap. xii. 2, and Is. xxvii. 8. רוּחַ יְהוָֹה, like אֵשׁ אֱלֹהִים, Job. i. 19, is the genitive of cause, a wind caused, sent by or proceeding from Jehovah; not "a great wind," as some interpret. The Assyrian army is meant. הוּא יָבֹא, *He,* i. e. the Assyrian, couched under the metaphor of the destructive wind, shall plunder every valuable article belonging to the Israelites.

16. [Chap. xiv. 1.] This verse begins the following chapter in the Hebrew Bible, but it more intimately coheres with the preceding context. תֶּאְשַׁם, LXX. ἀφανισθήσεται, Vulg. *pereat.* The word signifies *to be guilty of crime,* and *to be treated as guilty, to suffer punishment, be punished.* Samaria as the metropolis, and the source of all the calamities which were coming upon the Israelites, is put as representing the whole nation; but not to the exclusion of the peculiarly severe punishment which the inhabitants of that city had to expect. מָרְתָה, some render *to embitter, provoke bitterly;* but *rebelling, resisting, striking against* any one, are the ideas more properly conveyed by the verb. Thus the LXX. ἀντέστη πρὸς τὸν θεὸν αὐτῆς. The addition of the affix in אֱלֹהֶיהָ, "*her* God," gives great emphasis in such connection. Comp. chap. xii. 10, xiii. 4. The aggravations of sin are increased by the relations sustained by the sinner. For the concluding portion of the verse, comp. 2 Kings viii. 12, xv. 16; Amos i. 13. That such cruelties were not unknown among other nations, see Iliad vi. 58;—

—— μηδ' ὅντινα γαστέρι μήτηρ
Κοῦρον ἐόντα φέροι, μηδ' ὃς φύγοι ;—

and Horace, Carm. iv. Ode 6. The construction הֲרִיוֹתָיו יְבַקֵּעַ is *ad sensum*, though not according to the strict rule of grammar, and may have been occasioned by the form of יְרֻשְּׁעוּ immediately preceding.

CHAPTER XIV.

This chapter contains an urgent call to repentance, the supplication and confession expressive of which are put in a set form of words into the mouths of the penitents, 1—3. To encourage them thus to return to God, he makes the most gracious promises to them, 4—7; their entire abandonment of idolatry is then predicted, and the divine condescension and goodness are announced, 8; and the whole concludes with a solemn declaration, on the part of the prophet, respecting the opposite consequences that would result from attention or inattention to his message.

RETURN, O Israel! to Jehovah thy God:
For thou hast fallen by thine iniquity.
2 Take with you words, and return to Jehovah;
Say to him,
Forgive all iniquity, and graciously receive us,
Then we will render to thee the calves of our lips.

1, 2. The ה of direction in the imperative שׁוּבָה is, as usual, intensive, marking a strong desire on the part of the speaker that the action expressed by the verb might take place. For the emphasis attaching to the affix in אֱלֹהֶיךָ, "*thy* God," see on chap. xii. 16. נָשָׂא עָוֹן is a phrase of such frequent occurrence with the meaning *to pardon iniquity*, that it is surprising how Horsley could insist upon its meaning to " take away the sinful principle within us — the carnal heart of the old Adam." His construction of קַח טוֹב, " accept as good, what, so regenerate, we shall be enabled to perform," though sound divinity, is equally indefensible on the ground of philology. טוֹב is used adverbially, *benigne, in bonam partem;* and the meaning is, graciously receive us back into thy favor. With respect to the interposition of the verb תִשָּׂא, between בֹּל and עָוֹן, it may be observed, that it is not a solitary instance of such construction. See on Is. xix. 8, and comp. Job xv. 10.

פָּרִים, *calves* or *bullocks*, used here metaphorically for *victims, sacrifices*. The word occurring in the absolute form, some render פָּרִים שְׂפָתֵינוּ, *bullocks our lips,* as if the two nouns were in apposition; but there are instances of nouns thus put, which cannot be explained otherwise than in the construct, as to sense. Thus Deut. xxxiii. 11, מָתְנַיִם קָמָיו, *the loins of those who oppose him;* Jud. v. 13, אַדִּירִים עָם, *the princes of the people;* Prov. xxii. 21, אִמְרִים אֱמֶת, *words of truth.* Gesenius supposes the governing noun to be mentally repeated, and that the full form would be פָּרִים, פָּרֵי שְׂפָתֵינוּ, *bullocks, the bullocks of our lips.* Such construction in full he adduces in the instance Exod. xxxviii. 21, הַמִּשְׁכָּן מִשְׁכַּן הָעֵדֻת, *the tabernacle, the tabernacle of testimony.* Some would change פָּרִים into פְּרִי, *fruit,* on the ground of the reading found in the LXX. ἀνταποδώσομεν καρπὸν χειλέων ἡμῶν, which is followed by the Syr. and Arab. and is supposed to have been borrowed by the apostle,

3 Assyria shall not save us;
We will not ride upon horses;
Neither will we say any more, " Our gods,"
To the work of our hands:
For by thee the destitute is pitied.
4 I will heal their apostasy;
I will love them freely;
For my anger is turned away from them.
5 I will be as the dew to Israel;

Heb. xiii. 15. There is, however, no variety in the Hebrew MSS.; while the Targum and all the other authorities support the textual reading. The LXX. have committed a similar mistake in rendering פָּרֶיהָ, her bullocks, τοὺς καρποὺς αὐτῆς, her fruits, Jer. l. 27. The conjecture of Pococke, that they used καρπὸς in the sense of κάρπωμα, which they employ to express SACRIFICE, oblation, etc., is less probable. See the important note of Horsley. The prophet's meaning is, We will render, in grateful return for thy forgiving and restoring mercy, the only sacrifices worthy of it — our tribute of thanksgiving and praise. For such use of שָׁלֵם, to requite, render back, comp. Ps. lvi. 12, אֲשַׁלֵּם תּוֹדֹת לָךְ, I will render thanks unto thee: so that the construction proposed by some, "we will offer the sacrifices which our lips have vowed," cannot be regarded as unexceptionable, even if it were in keeping with the spirit of the passage. The only parallels fully corresponding to it are Ps. li. 15-17, lxix. 31, 32.

3. Three of the sins to which the ten tribes were specially prone are here implied: dependence upon the aid of the Assyrians; application to Egypt for horses in direct violation of the divine command, Deut. xvii. 16; Is. xxxi. 1; and idolatry. These they now forever renounce, and avow their determination henceforth to trust in Jehovah alone; adding as the reason of such determination, the experience which they had had of the divine favor in time of need. אֲשֶׁר is here used in a causal sense, because for, forasmuch as. Comp. Gen. xxxi. 29; Eccles. iv. 9. יָתוֹם, orphan is applied in this place metaphorically to the unprotected and destitute circumstances in which the Israelites had been, while in a state of separation from the Lord.

4. מְשׁוּבָתָם is not, with Horsley, to be rendered "their conversion," but their apostasy. See on chap. xi. 7. נְדָבָה, lit. spontaneousness, willingness, is used adverbially for willingly, liberally, freely. It is derived from נָדַב, Arab. ندب, instigavit, impulit, ad aliquid; agilis in conficienda re promptusque vir; generosus; and is expressive of the free, unmerited, and abundant love of God towards repentant sinners. מִמֶּנּוּ, "from him," i. e. Israel, the collective noun, ver. 2, resolved by the Syr. Lat. and other translators into a plural.

5, 6. The love of God to his people, and its effects in their happy experience, are here couched in similes borrowed from the vegetable kingdom. The dew is very copious in the East, and, by its refreshing and quickening virtue, supplies the place of more frequent rains in other countries. Kimchi thinks that the constancy with which the dew falls is the point here more specially referred to, and to which the divine blessing is compared. שׁוֹשַׁנִּים, lilies, abound in Palestine, even apart from cultivation. There are two kinds; the common lily, which is perfectly white, consisting of six leaves, opening like bells; and what the Syrians call ܫܘܫܢܐ ܡܠܟܝܐ, the royal lily, the stem of which is about the size of a finger in thickness, and which grows to the height of three and four feet, spreading its flowers in the most beautiful and engaging manner. Comp. Matt. vi. 29. To these productions the moral beauty of regenerated Israel is very aptly com-

He shall blossom as the lily,
And strike his roots like Lebanon.
6 His suckers shall spread forth,
And his beauty shall be as the olive tree,
And his fragrance as Lebanon.
7 They that dwell under his shade shall revive as the corn,
And shoot forth as the vine:
Their fame shall be as the wine of Lebanon.
8 Ephraim shall say,
What have I any more to do with idols?

pared. For *Lebanon*, see on Is. x. 34. The mountain stands here by metonymy for the trees which grow upon it, such as the celebrated cedars, whose roots striking far in depth and length into the ground, give them a firmness which no storms can shake. The ideas of strength and stability are those conveyed by the simile, whether we refer the roots to the trees, or, metaphorically, to the mountain itself; but the amplification in the following verse renders the former the preferable construction. הָלַךְ is often used, not merely of continued, but of increased action, and here denotes *to spread out* as the suckers or small branches of trees. The olive is frequently referred to, on account of its beautiful green, and the pleasing ideas associated with its produce. Though the former only is expressed, yet the idea of fragrance is implied, only it is with the strictest propriety extended in the following clause to the whole of Lebanon, on account of the number of odoriferous trees and plants with which it abounds. In these verses, the rendering *frankincense*, which Newcome prefers to *Lebanon*, is not to be admitted. The stability, extension, glory, and loveliness of the church of God are forcibly set forth.

7. The Israelites are represented as again enjoying the protection of the Most High, and affording the most convincing proofs of prosperity. שׁוּב is used as auxiliary to חָיָה; both verbs, in such connection, signifying nothing more than *revive, thrive again*, or the like. The pronominal affix in צִלּוֹ, *his shade*, refers to Jehovah; but in וְרֵיחוֹ, *his celebrity, fame*, to Israel, understood, as before, collec-

tively, but best rendered in the plural. יֹשְׁבֵי בְצִלּוֹ, the construct with the preposition, as in חוֹסֵי בוֹ, Ps. ii. 12. Modern travellers concur in their high commendations of the excellence of the wines of Lebanon. Von Troil, in particular, says, "On this mountain are very valuable vineyards, in which the most excellent wine is produced; such as I have never drunk in any country, though in the course of fourteen years I have travelled through many, and tasted many good wines."

8. Several interpreters take אֶפְרַיִם to be in the vocative sense, but, as it seems harsh to refer the words immediately following to Jehovah, it is better to regard it as a nominative absolute, and to supply יֹאמַר thus:—As for Ephraim—the tribe distinguished above all the rest for its addictedness to idolatry, and the fit representative of the whole people—his language in future shall be, etc. For לִי, *to me*, the LXX. read לוֹ, *to him*, which facilitates the construction, and is adopted by Ewald, but without sufficient authority. אֲנִי, *I*, is not without emphasis in this connection, in which mention is made of idols. שׁוּרִי signifies to *view with regard and care, care for, watch over*. Every provision should henceforth be made for the protection and prosperity of restored Israel. בְּרוֹשׁ, *the cypress*, with all its tall and fair ever-green appearance, not being a fruit-bearing tree, it is added with singular effect, that in this respect there existed a difference between the object and the subject of the metaphor. The children of Israel should not only enjoy protection and refreshment as the result of the divine favor, but rich

I have answered him, and will regard him;
I am like a green cypress;
From me thy fruit is found.
9   Who is wise, that he may understand these things;
Prudent, that he may know them?
For the ways of Jehovah are right;
The righteous shall walk in them;
But the rebellious shall stumble in them.

supplies of spiritual provision for their support. Such supplies were to be found in God alone. Manger thinks there is here a dialogistic parallelism, which he exhibits thus:—

EPHRAIM. What have I further to do with idols?
GOD. I have answered him, and will regard him.
EPHRAIM. I am like a green cypress.
GOD. From me is thy fruit found.

9. These words form an epilogue or conclusion to the whole book. The interrogation is employed for the purpose of excitement and to give energy to the truths conveyed. It is worthy of remark that this is the only verse in which the prophet uses צַדִּיקִים, *the righteous*, or any synonymous term, in the course of his recorded prophecies. So awfully depraved were the times in which he lived, that the very character had disappeared. The contrasted characters and states of the godly and the wicked are pointed and affecting. הָלַךְ, *to walk*, signifies here *to go forward prosperously*; כָּשַׁל, *to stumble*, so as to fall to one's injury and utter ruin.

"—— anfractu et liberam ab omni
Hanc justus teret, hoc semper se in calle
    tenebit,
Felicique gradu ad requiem contendat
    amicam.
At defectores videas impingere in iis-
    dem,
Exitiumque sibi factis properare scelestis."
                                —*Rittershusius*.

JOEL.

PREFACE.

WE possess no further knowledge of Joel than what is furnished by the title of his book, or may be gathered from circumstances incidentally mentioned in it. That he lived in Judah, and, in all probability, at Jerusalem, we may infer from his not making the most distant reference to the kingdom of Israel; while, on the other hand, he speaks of Jerusalem, the temple, priests, ceremonies, etc. with a familiarity which proves them to have been before his eyes.

With respect to the age in which he flourished, opinions have differed. Bauer places him in the reign of Jehoshaphat; Credner, Winer, Krahmer, and Ewald, think he lived in that of Joash; Vitringa, Carpzov, Moldenhauer, Eichhorn, Holzhausen, Theiner, Rosenmüller, Knobel, Hengstenberg, Gesenius, and De Wette, in that of Uzziah; Steudel and Bertholdt in that of Hezekiah; Tarnovius and Eckermann assign the period of his activity to the days of Josiah; while the author of Sedar Olam, Jarchi, Drusius, Newcome, and Jahn, are of opinion that he prophesied in the reign of Manasseh. The most probable hypothesis is, that his predictions were delivered in the early days of Joash; that is, according to Credner, B. C. 870 — 865. No reference being made to the Babylonian, the Assyrian, or even the Syrian invasion, and the only enemies of whom mention is made being the Phœnicians, Philistines, Edomites, and Egyptians, it seems evident that Joel was unacquainted with any but the latter. Had he lived after the death of Joash, he could scarcely have omitted to notice the Syrians when speaking of hostile powers, since they not only invaded the land, but took Jerusalem, destroyed the princes, and carried away immense spoil to Damascus, 2 Chron. xxiv. 23, 24. The state of religious affairs as presented to view in the book is altogether in favor of this position. No mention is made of idolatrous practices; while, on the contrary, notwithstanding the guilt which attached to the Jews, on account of which Jehovah brought judgments upon the land, the principles of the theocracy are supposed to be maintained; the priests and people are represented as being harmoniously occupied with the services of religion; and Jerusalem, the temple and its worship, appear in a flourishing condition. Now this was precisely the state of things during the high-priesthood of Jehoiada, through whose influence Joash had been placed upon the throne. See 2 Kings xi. 17, 18, xii. 2-16; 2 Chron. xxiv. 4-14. It will follow that Joel is the oldest of all the Hebrew prophets whose predictions have come down to us.

The delivery of his prophecy was occasioned by the devastations produced by successive swarms of locusts, and by an excessive drought which pervaded the country, and threatened the inhabitants with utter destruction. This calamity, however, was merely symbolical of another, and a more dreadful scourge — the invasion of the land by foreign enemies, on which the prophet expatiates in the second chapter. In order that such calamity might be removed, he is commissioned to order an universal fast, and call all to repentance and humiliation before God; to announce as consequent upon such repentance and humiliation, a period of great temporal prosperity; to predict the effusion of the Holy Spirit at a future period of the history of his people; to denounce judgments against their enemies; and to foretell their restoration from the final dispersion.

In point of style Joel stands preëminent among the Hebrew prophets. He not only possesses a singular degree of purity, but is distinguished by his smoothness and fluency; the animated and rapid character of his rhythmus; the perfect regularity of his parallelisms; and the degree of roundness which he gives to his sentences. He has no abrupt transitions, is everywhere connected, and finishes whatever he takes up. In description he is graphic and perspicuous; in arrangement lucid; in imagery original, copious, and varied. In the judgment of Knobel, he most resembles Amos in regularity, Nahum in animation, and in both respects Habakkuk; but is surpassed by none of them. That what we now possess is all he ever wrote, is in the highest degree improbable: on the contrary, we should conclude from the cultivated character of his language, that he had been accustomed to composition long before he penned these discourses. Whatever degree of obscurity attaches to his book, is attributable to our ignorance of the subjects of which it treats, not to the language which he employs.

CHAPTER I.

After summoning attention to the unexampled plague of locusts with which the country had been visited, 2—4, the prophet excites to repentance by a description of these insects, 5—7, and of the damage which they had done to the fields and trees, 8—12; calls the priests to institute a solemn season for fasting and prayer, 13, 14; and bewails, by anticipation, a more awful visitation from Jehovah, 15, while he further describes the tremendous effects of the calamity under which the country was suffering, 16—20.

1 THE word of Jehovah which was communicated to Joel, the son
   of Pethuel:
2 Hear this, ye aged men!
   Give ear, all ye inhabitants of the land!
   Did such as this happen in your days,
   Or, in the days of your fathers?
3 Tell your children of it,
   And let your children tell their children,
   And their children another generation.

1. דְּבַר יְהוָה אֲשֶׁר הָיָה אֶל, the usual introductory formula employed to express the communication of divine revelations to the prophets, or the divinely inspired matter which they were commissioned to teach. Comp. Hos. i. 1; Mic. i. 1; Zeph. i. 1; Mal. i. 1. The name יוֹאֵל, *Joel*, Jerome interprets ἀρχόμενος, id est incipiens, referring it to the verb יָאַל, which signifies to *begin;* but that he was not ignorant of another derivation is evident from his commentary, in which, after giving *incipiens*, he adds, vel *est Deus*. It is, however, beyond all doubt compounded of יְהוָֹה, in one of its more contracted forms, and אֵל, and signifies, *Jehovah is God*. Who בְּתוּאֵל, LXX. Βαθουήλ, *Pethuel*, the father of our prophet was, we are not informed. The introduction of his name was necessary in order to distinguish the present Joel from others of the same name, and cannot be admitted in proof of his having been a prophet or some person of eminence. It was common among the Hebrews, as it still is among the Orientals, to add the name of the father to that of the son.

2, 3. These verses contain an animated introduction to the following subject. זֹאת, properly *this*, the feminine according to the Hebrew idiom being used for the neuter, but it occurs here elliptically for כָּזֹאת, *like this, such, the like,* and refers to the astounding calamity of the locusts about to be described. שִׁמְעוּ and הַאֲזִינוּ frequently occur as parallel initiatives in Hebrew poetry. See Gen. iv. 23; Deut. xxxii. 1; Is. i. 2. For the latter verb, הַקְשִׁיבוּ is sometimes used. See Is. xxviii. 23; Mic. i. 2. זְקֵנִים is here to be understood, not in the official sense of *elders*, but in that of *aged men*, as the connection shows. Those who were most advanced in years, and might be expected to have their memories stored with ancient occurrences, are appealed to for a parallel to the case referred to. Comp. Deut. xxxii. 7; Job. xxxii. 7. אָבוֹת is often used in the sense of *ancestors, forefathers*. ה in הֶהָיְתָה, like זֹאת, refers to the plague of locusts. בְּנֵי בְנֵיכֶם, *children's children*, is not unfrequent, but the language here employed by Joel is cumulative beyond example.

" Et nati natorum, et qui nascentur

4 That which the gnawing locust hath left,
The swarming locust hath devoured:
And that which the swarming locust hath left,

ab illis." *Æneid* iii. 98. καὶ παῖδες παίδων, τοί κεν μετόπισθε γένωνται. *Iliad*, xx. 308.

4. The plague, which occasioned the following discourses of the prophet, is now described in terse, though repetitious terms. This verse may be considered as the text on which he afterwards expatiates. Interpreters have found great difficulty both in determining the precise signification of the several terms employed to describe the scourge, and the light in which it was designed to be understood. While some are of opinion that different kinds of insects are meant, most are agreed in considering locusts to be intended. Yet here again discordant views obtain: some insisting on different species of locusts, and others on different states of the same species. Credner, for instance, in a work on our prophet, full of erudition, considers גָּזָם to be the migratory locust; אַרְבֶּה the young brood; יֶלֶק the young locust in the last state of transformation; and חָסִיל the perfect locust. The locust belongs to the genus of insects known among entomologists by the name of *grylli*, which includes the different species, from the common grasshopper to the devouring locust of the East. The largest of the latter is about three inches in length; has two antennæ, or horns, about an inch long, and two wings, which, with their cases, are applied obliquely to the sides of the body when in repose. The feet have only three joints, but are six in number. The two hind ones are much larger than the rest, and are formed for leaping. The locusts are of different colors, brown, gray and spotted. In all stages, from the larvæ to the perfect insect, the locusts are herbivorous, and do immense injury to vegetation. The subject so far as it occurs in Scripture, may be said to have been almost exhausted by the learned Bochart, in his Hierozoicon, Pars Post. Lib. iv. cap. i. — viii. The fourth chapter he specially devotes to the explanation of the passages in

Joel. See also Œdmann's Vermischte Sammlungen, and Credner's Joel. The first name, גָּזָם, occurs only here and Amos iv. 9, and is rendered by the LXX. κάμπη; and by the Vulg. *eruca, caterpillar*. This interpretation is supported by the Targ. זַחֲלָא, *the crawling insect*, by which, however, may be meant the locust in its wingless state. The Syr. renders the word by ܩܡܨܐ, *locusta non alata*. It is evidently derived from the same root with the Arab. جَرَم, *resecuit, amputavit*, جَازَم, *secans;* Eth. ጐዘመ *: excidit, abscidit;* Syr. ܓܙܡ *incidit;* Talmud. גָּזַם, *amputavit;* and expresses the knawing or cutting action of the sharp teeth of the locusts on the leaves, and even the bark of trees. Comp. Plin. Nat. Hist. lib. ii. cap. 29: *omnia vero morsu erodentes*. אַרְבֶּה is the generic name of the locust, so called from the almost incredible numbers which breed in different parts of the East; being derived from רָבָה, *to multiply, be numerous*, etc. Comp. Jer. xlvi. 23, רַבּוּ מֵאַרְבֶּה, *more numerous than the locusts*. From its migrating in swarms it is called by Forskål *gryllus gregarius*, and by Linnæus, gryllus *migratorius*. By the LXX. the word is rendered seventeen times by ἀκρίς, *the common locust;* thrice by βροῦχος, *the unwinged locust*, which browses on the grass; once by ἐρυσίβη, *mildew;* and once by ἀττέλαβος, *the young* or *small locust*. That אַרְבֶּה is generic, appears from Lev. xi. 22, where we read, הָאַרְבֶּה לְמִינוֹ, *the locust according to its species*. The third name, יֶלֶק, from לָקַק, equivalent to לָקַק, *to lick*, designates the locust as *licking off* the leaves, and whatever is green on the trees, grass, etc. This derivation is preferable to that proposed by Michaelis, who refers the word to the Arab. ولق, *properavit, volubilis*

The licking locust hath devoured;
And that which the licking locust hath left,
The consuming locust hath devoured.

fuit, or يَلِق, *albus fuit*, and thinks that the chafer is meant. In Nah. iii. 16, it is represented as *winged*, and in Jer. li. 27, it is described as סָמָר, *rough, bristly, terrific*. LXX. βροῦχος four times; ἀκρίς thrice. חָסִיל, the remaining term comes from חָסַל, *to consume, devour*. LXX. βροῦχος, or βροῦκος. Vulg. *rubigo*, mildew. Syr. ܙܚܠܐ, which Risius, the Archbishop of Damascus, describes as resembling the locust, only differing from it, inasmuch as it never migrates, and confines its ravages to the fruits and herbs, but leaves the trees untouched. It is also noted for the noise which it makes at night. A comparison of the different passages in which these names occur, renders it more than probable that they are here employed by the prophet, not with any reference to the species into which the locusts may be scientifically divided, but to designate four successive swarms, according to certain destructive qualities, by which, as a genus of insects, they are distinguished, and thereby to heighten the terror which his description was intended to produce. Just as Job accumulates the terms לָבִיא, שַׁחַל, כְּפִירִים, לַיִשׁ and אַרְיֵה, chap. iv. 10, 11, with a similar view. They are rather poetical synonymes, than distinctive of different species. At all events, that locusts are meant, may be inferred from the facts, that wherever יֶלֶק occurs, with the exception of a single passage, it occurs along with אַרְבֶּה; and that אַרְבֶּה, which Moses uses in describing one of the plagues of Egypt, Exod. x. 10-20, is not only employed by the Psalmist, lxxviii. 46, cv. 34, but also חָסִיל and יֶלֶק, as synonymous terms, for the sake of variety. Add to which that the verb חָסַל from which חָסִיל is derived, is employed to express the action of the אַרְבֶּה, Deut. xxviii. 38, יְחַסְלֶנּוּ הָאַרְבֶּה, "the locust shall consume it." In the translation I have given the meaning of the several names in terms expressive of the qualities suggested by each. The passage might otherwise be rendered with Noyes:—

"That which one swarm of locusts left, a second swarm hath eaten;
And that which the second left, a third swarm hath eaten;
And that which the third left, a fourth swarm hath eaten."

It is a question of greater importance: Are the statements of Joel in the first and second chapters to be understood literally of those insects, or figuratively of enemies that were to invade and lay waste the Holy Land? The latter is the more ancient opinion. It is that of the Targum, the Jews whom Jerome consulted, and Abarbanel; and is, with various modifications, adopted by the following christian interpreters: Jerome, Ephraim Syrus, Theodoret, Cyril of Alexandria, Hugo de St. Vincent, Ribera, Sanchez, a Lapide, Luther, Grotius, Markius, Bertholdt, Theiner, Steudel, and Hengstenberg. On the other hand, Abenezra, Jarchi, Kimchi, Lyranus, Vatablus, Joh. Schmidius, Jahn, Eichhorn, Rosenmüller, von Coelln, Justi, Credner, and Hitzig, maintain that the language is to be understood literally of locusts. This interpretation has certainly much in its favor, and if it could without violence be applied throughout, might fairly be adopted. But the announcement of a second and more awful judgment, chap. i. 15, ii. 1, 2; the distinct recognition of a foreign rule, ii. 17; and the assignment of the *North* as the native country of the enemy, ii. 20; present insuperable obstacles to its adoption. See on these verses. There seems no possibility of effecting a consistent interpretation on any other principle than that laid down and defended by Cramer, Eckermann, and Holzhausen, *viz*: that in the first chapter, Joel describes a devastation of the country which had been effected by natural locusts; but predicts in the second its devastation by

5   Awake, ye drunkards! and weep;
    Howl, all ye drinkers of wine!
    On account of the sweet wine,
    For it is made to cease from your mouth.
6   For a nation hath come up upon my land,
    Mighty and innumerable;
    Their teeth are the teeth of a lion;
    They have the grinders of a lioness.

political enemies, in highly-wrought metaphorical language, borrowed from the scene which he had just depicted.

5. הָקִיצוּ the Hiph. of קוּץ, is here used, like the cognate root יָקַץ, Gen. ix. 24, in the sense of awaking from a sleep occasioned by wine. Since, however, the persons addressed had been deprived of the means of intoxication, the prophet is rather to be understood as borrowing the term from the state in which they had too often been found. שֹׁתֵי־יָיִן being parallel with שֹׁתֵי יָיִן, *drinkers of wine*, does not here mean persons actually *intoxicated*, but such as were in the habit of using intoxicating liquors, and by implication, to excess. Thus Kimchi: אדם הרגילים להשתכר ביין, *ye who are accustomed to make yourselves drunk with wine*. It is derived from סָבָא, *to drink to the full*. Arab. سبا, *implevit, vas, ebrius fuit*. Hence סֹבֵא, *strong, or intoxicating drink*, whether wine itself, or, more commonly, liquor resembling wine, which is distilled from barley, honey, or dates, and sometimes mingled with spices. By עָסִיס, is meant the *fresh wine*, or juice of the grape, or other fruit, which has just been *pressed out*, and is remarkable for its sweet flavor, and its freedom from intoxicating qualities. R. עָסַס, *to tread, tread down, or out*. Targ. חֲמַר מְרַת, *pure wine*. It differs from תִּירוֹשׁ, inasmuch as the latter term is confined to the juice of the grape; and being derived from יָרַשׁ, *to take possession of*, indicates that however new, it had already obtained an inebriating quality. The locusts are here represented as specially attacking and destroying the vines and other fruit-trees, from the produce of which these wines were prepared. To such they are known to be very destructive. Comp. Theocrit. Idyll. 5, 108, in which a shepherd beseeches them not to injure his vines:

'Ακρίδες, ἃς τὸν φραγμὸν ὑπερπεδῆτε τὸν ἀμόν,
Μή μευ λωβάσεσθε τὰς ἀμπέλας· ἐντὶ γὰρ ἅβαι.

כרת properly signifies to *cut, cut off*, but here, as wine is the subject spoken of, it must be taken in the sense of *destroying*, or *causing to cease*.

6. גּוֹי, *nation*, especially used of foreign, barbarous and profane nations, and here selected on purpose to express the number and hostility of the locusts, and at the same time to prepare the minds of the Jews for the allegorical use made of these insects in chap. ii. If it had not been for some such end, the prophet might have adopted the term עַם, *people*, which Solomon applies to the ants, Prov. xxx. 25, 26, and which would equally have conveyed the idea of multitude. Comp. chap. ii. 2. This metaphorical use of the term is common in the classics. See instances in Bochart and Gesen. Heb. Lex. *in voc*. גּוֹי. The Arabs employ قوم in a similar way. עָלָה עַל is used in a hostile sense of an army, Is. vii. 1; but here figuratively of the locusts. In אַרְצִי, "*my land*," the pronominal affix belongs to Jehovah, not to the prophet. Comp. Is. xiv. 25; Jer. xvi. 18; Ezek. xxxvi. 5, xxxviii. 16. Joel ii. 18. עָצוּם, *strong, powerful*. The strength of the locust consists in the immense numbers, which, forming themselves into compact bodies, darken the air, and advance forward, one swarm after another, attacking whatever comes in their way. They may well be described as אֵין מִסְפָּר, *innu-*

CHAP. I.   JOEL.   93

7 They have laid waste my vine,
And broken down my fig-tree;
They have completely stripped it, and thrown it down;
Its branches they have left white.

merable. All who refer to them, both in ancient and modern times, speak of them in the same language.

'Ακρίδων πλῆθος ἀμύθητον.
Agatharc. v. 27.

"Immensæ locustarum multitudines." Orosius, v. 11. Shaw speaks of "infinite swarms following each other," Barrow states that those which he saw in South Africa, might literally be said to cover the ground for an area of 2000 square miles. A later writer in the Cape Town Gazette, describes a cloud of them as passing before him in a train of many millions thick, and about an hour in length; and mentions further that, though millions perished in consequence of attempts made to destroy them, their number appeared nothing decreased. And Dr. Bowring states in his Report, that some years ago the army of Ibrahim Pasha, in the attempt to extirpate an immense swarm, gathered up no less than 65,000 ardebs, equal to 325,000 bushels of English measure! How appropriate the name אַרְבֶּה! What is innumerable is frequently compared to them by the sacred writers. See Jud. vi. 5, vii. 12; Ps. cv. 34; Jer. xlvi. 23; Nah. iii. 15. מְתַלְּעוֹת, *teeth,* Gesenius considers as standing by transposition for מַלְתְּעוֹת, and derives the noun from an obsolete root לָתַע, *to bite;* but it may more properly be referred to the Arab. لَثَغَ, *longum fuit,* and denotes the grinders or jawteeth of animals. The metaphor, however, has no respect to the size of the teeth of lions, but only to the terrible and complete destruction which they effect. Pliny, speaking of the locust, says:— "Omnia morsu erodentes et fores quoque tectorum." According to Fabricius, in his Genera Insectorum, p. 96, the teeth of the locust are three-forked and sharp. The same metaphor is used Rev. ix. 8, ὀδόντες αὐτῶν ὡς λεόντων ἦσαν.

7. For the pronominal reference in גַּפְנִי and תְּאֵנָתִי, see on אַרְצִי in the preceding verse. The vines and fig-trees might be called Jehovah's, because, in a special sense, the land on which they grew was his. The *vine* has, from time immemorial, abounded in Palestine. It often grows to a great size, and produces grapes of corresponding bulk. Schulz describes one at Beitshin, near Ptolemais, the stem of which was about a foot and a half in diameter, its height was about thirty feet, and by its branches and branchlets, which had to be supported, it formed a hut upwards of thirty feet broad and long. The clusters of these vines are so large, that they weigh ten or twelve pounds, and the berries may be compared with our small plums. When such a cluster is cut off, it is laid upon a board about an ell and a half broad, and three or four ells long, and several persons seat themselves about it to eat the grapes. Rosenmüller, In Bib. Cab. vol. xxvii. p. 223. Comp. Numb. xiii. 23, 24. Palestine was equally celebrated for its *fig-trees,* which are not reared in gardens, as with us, but grow spontaneously in the open country. The figs were not only eaten fresh, but also preserved for food. שׂוּם, *to put,* is often used with nouns instead of the simple forms of the verbs to which the nouns are related. קְצָפָה, *breakage,* Arab. قَصْف *fregit.* قَصِيف, *a branch broken off* from a tree. See on Hos. x. 7. LXX. συγκλασμός, *Compl.* κλασμός. Syr. ܩܠܳܣܳܐ, *concissio, divulsio.* The locusts not only consume the fruit and leaves of the trees, but strip them of the very bark.—"Nec culmus, nec gramen ullum remanent, et arbores frontibus et cortice tanquam vestibus nudatæ, instar truncorum alborum conspiciantur." Ludolf, Comment. p. 178. הִלְבִּין is here taken in its proper causative signification. What they do not

8 Lament, as a virgin girded with sackcloth,
   On account of the husband of her youth.
9 The offering and the libation,
   Are cut off from the house of Jehovah:
   The priests howl, the ministers of Jehovah.
10 The field is laid waste,
   The ground mourneth;
   For the corn is laid waste,

devour, they so injure that it falls off the tree. שָׂרִיגִים, *branches*, properly the *intertwining tendrils* of the vine, from שָׂרַג, *to interweave*. The vine, being the more valuable of the two kinds of trees, the suffix refers back to it; and the fig-tree is treated as subordinate. הִלְבִּינוּ, *they have made* or *left white*.

8. The land, under the metaphor of a female, is here addressed. אֱלִי is the second person feminine of the Imperative in Kal of אָלָה, which usually means *to swear*, call on God as witness; but here it takes the signification of the Syriac ܐܶܠܺܝ *ululavit, deploravit.* ܐܶܠܝܳܐ *ululatus, lamentum.* The derivation from אֵל, *God*, in the sense *God have mercy*, is less natural. One of Kennicott's MSS. reads אֲבְלִי. LXX. θρήνησον. A country is frequently said to mourn, when it is subject to devastation. See Is. xxiv. 3; Jer. iv. 28, xii. 4; Hos. iv. 3. בְּתוּלָה, *a virgin*, a young woman, affianced to a husband, and, in this sense, viewed as married to him. The idea of the strength of youthful affection, that is designed to be conveyed by the passage. In proportion to the force of such affection, would be the excessive degree of grief for his loss. Holzhausen thinks that she would also grieve עַל בְּתוּלֶיהָ, *on account of her virginity*, and compares Jud. xi. 38; but this the text does not suggest. LXX. νύμφη. Compl. παρθένος. Wrapping oneself in sackcloth was a token of deep mourning. בַּעַל, properly *lord, master, possessor;* and secondarily *husband*, because in the East, wives were, and still are, considered as the property rather than the companions of their husbands. Comp. the Greek κύριος γυναι-

κός; and for the application of ἀνήρ to one only betrothed, Matt. i. 19. According to the Roman law, *consensus facit nuptias*.

9. To a pious mind the gloomiest view of external calamities will be taken from their influence upon the cause of God. The cessation of the usual solemnities of the temple worship, occasioned by the destruction of the fruits of the earth, must have occasioned great grief to the religious Jew. Jerome and others think that as the priests would be deprived of their regular support, by the cessation of the offerings, they mourned on that account; but of this I should say with Maurer, " Vates hic non videtur cogitasse." מִנְחָה, stands here for *offerings* in general, whether bloody or unbloody, — comp. Gen. iv. 4; LXX. θυσία, — even when restricted in its signification to *meat offering*, such as consisted of meal, salt, oil, and incense, the proper sacrifices. זְבָחִים, are understood, as they were always connected with them, except in the case of the sin and trespass-offerings. The libation, or drink-offering, was called נֶסֶךְ, on account of its being *poured out*, from the root נָסַךְ, *to pour*. From the circumstance that Joel prefixes the article to הַכֹּהֲנִים, *priests*, but not to אִכָּרִים, *husbandmen*, and כֹּרְמִים, *vine-dressers*, Credner argues that he must either have been personally related to them, or that prophets and priests must have been more closely united at the time he wrote than afterwards. Comp. הַכֹּהֲנִים, ver. 13, ii. 17. מְשָׁרְתִים, *ministers*, is a more dignified official term than עֲבָדִים, *servants*, which is employed to denote common slaves, as well as persons in more elevated situations about a king.

10–12. The prophet enters here more minutely into a description of the devas-

The new wine is dried up,
The oil languisheth.
11 Be ashamed, ye husbandmen!
Howl, ye vine-dressers!
On account of the wheat and the barley;
For the harvest of the field hath perished.
12 The vine is dried up,
And the fig-tree languisheth;

tation occasioned by the locusts. תִּירוֹשׁ, *new wine*, which is already in a state of fermentation, and so intoxicating; from יָרַשׁ, *to take possession* of anything. See on ver. 5, where it is distinguished from עָסִיס. " Syr. ܚܰܙܺܝܢ, sic dictum, quod *se possessorem* hominis *facit*, ejus cerebrum *occupando*, ut ille non amplius sui compos sit. Sic Arab. *vinum* dicitur سُبِيَة, a *captivando*, et عَقَل, a *tenendo et vinctum habendo.*" Winer *in voc.* שָׂדֶה, *field*, and אֲדָמָה, *ground*, are synonymes; but differ in this respect, that the former denotes the open, free, unin-closed part of a country, Arab. سِلْ, *extendit, dilatavit;* the latter, the rich red soil which is particularly fit for cultivation. Hence אִישׁ הַשָּׂדֶה, *a man of the field*, means a hunter, Gen. xxv. 27; אִישׁ הָאֲדָמָה, *a man of the ground*, an agriculturist. Root אָדַם, *to be red.* The land is here, as frequently in the Hebrew prophets, made the subject of personification. Some would render הוֹבִישׁ, as applied to the new wine, *to be ashamed:* but occurring as it does in parallelism with אֻמְלַל, *to droop, languish* like plants, it is better to retain the primary motion of יָבֵשׁ, *to become dry, dry up.* Both תִּירוֹשׁ and יִצְהָר stand for the *vine* and the *olive tree*, from which the wine and oil are obtained. In the second instance הוֹבִישׁ takes the signification of בּוֹשׁ, *to be ashamed*, being another form of the Hiphil for הֵבִישׁ. Both are used intransitively. The LXX. retaining the signification of יָבֵשׁ, improperly render ἐξηράνθησαν γεωργοί.

רִמּוֹן, *the pomegranate tree,* is indigenous in Palestine in Syria, and is reckoned one of its noblest botanical productions. It grows to the height of twenty feet, has a straight stem, spreading branches, lancet-formed leaves, with large and beautiful red blossoms. The fruit is of the size of an orange, brown in color, and affording a highly delicious and cooling juice. It is also planted in gardens, and in the courts of the houses; and its fruit is greatly improved by cultivation. It is still one of the trees most frequently seen in those countries. So celebrated were the dates of Palestine, that Pliny, speaking of the תָּמָר, *date,* or *palm-tree,* says, "Judæa vero inclyta est vel magis palmis." It was adopted as a symbol of the country in coins struck under Vespasian and Domitian; and is frequently referred to in the Old Testament. It sometimes reaches the height of an hundred feet, is remarkable for its straight, upright growth, and forms one of the most beautiful trees in the vegetable kingdom. The fruit, which grows in clusters under the large leaves, is of an exceedingly sweet and agreeable taste, and, as an article both of sustenance and traffic, is of great value to the inhabitants. In Abyssinia, the natives extract a juice from it which they manufacture into a spirituous liquor resembling champagne. Its importance is here significantly expressed by the particle גַּם being used intensively before it. תַּפּוּחַ Arab. تُفَّاح, the *apple-tree.* Rosen-müller derives the word from נָפַח, *to breathe,* and in this Gesenius concurs, supposing the fragrant *breath,* i. e. smell

The pomegranate, the palm-tree also, and the apple-tree,
All the trees of the field are withered;
Yea, joy is withered away from the children of men.
13   Gird ye, and mourn, O ye priests!
Howl, ye ministers of the altar!
Enter, spend the night in sackcloth,
Ye ministers of my God!
For the offering and the libation
Are withholden from the house of your God.
14 Appoint a sacred fast, proclaim a day of restraint;
Assemble the elders — all the inhabitants of the land,

or scent, to have originated the name. The former of these writers adopts the opinion of Celsius, that the quince tree is specially intended; but as the Arabs include under تُفَّاح, oranges, lemons, peaches, apricots, etc., the Hebrew term is likewise in all probability generic in its signification. To give to his description the utmost latitude, Joel adds, כָּל־עֲצֵי הַשָּׂדֶה, *all the trees of the field*, i. e. as Jerome explains "omnia ligna, vel infructuosa, vel fructifera;" and, to bring it more home to the feelings of his countrymen, he represents the consequence to be, the entire removal of their joy. Some improperly limit שָׂשׂוֹן to the joy of harvest. The construction הוֹבִישׁ מִן, *to dry away from*, is what is usually termed pregnant, and more forcibly expresses the removal of the object on which the verb terminates.

13. The prophet now addresses himself to the priests, and calls them first to personal mourning, and then, in the following verse, to institute a sacred fast, in order that such mourning might be general. After חִגְרוּ supply with the Syr. עַל, as in one of Kennicott's MSS., or שַׂקִּים, as in one of De Rossi's. Both forms occur in connection with the verb, which is not here to be restricted to mere girding, but rather signifies to *wrap round* one. Comp. Jer. iv. 8; Is. xxii. 12. סָפַד, primarily *to smite, strike*, then *to strike the breast*, in token of mourning. See on Is. xxxii. 12. The LXX. always render it by κόπτεσθαι, except in two instances, in which they give it by κλαίειν, *to weep*. For מְשָׁרְתֵי מִזְבֵּחַ, comp. οἱ νῷ θυσιαστηρίῳ παρεδρύοντες, 1 Cor. ix. 13. Some think that בֹּאוּ, *come*, is to be taken idiomatically as a particle of exhortation, like לְכוּ before another verb, and appeal to chap. iii. 13, for another instance in our prophet. As however, the verb is, to say the least, not necessarily to be so understood in that passage, and as mention is made of the altar, immediately before, it appears more proper to take it in the sense of *entering*, i. e. into the court of the temple, where, in the more immediate presence of Jehovah, the priests were to bewail their sins, and those of the people. Thus the LXX. εἰσέλθετε, and Kimchi, בֹּאוּ בֵית יְיָ וְשִׁימוּ שָׂקִים, *enter ye the house of God, and there mourn*. לִין or לוּן, signifies *to spend, or remain over the night*, and retains this signification in the present passage, though, from the connection, it is obvious not one night only, but many nights are meant. The priests were not only to wear the habit of mourning during the day, they were also to remain in it all night. Ahab is said to have lain in sackcloth, when he humbled himself before God, 1 Kings xxi. 27. LXX. ὑπνώσατε.

14. קַדֵּשׁ, *to hallow, consecrate; to keep holy; to appoint sacred or religious services;* here, to *institute a sacred* fast by fixing the time and circumstances, and preparing the people for its proper

To the house of Jehovah your God,
And cry unto Jehovah.
15 Alas for the day!
For the day of Jehovah is near,
And cometh as a mighty destruction
From the Almighty.
16 Is not the food cut off before our eyes?
Are not joy and gladness from the house of our God?
17 The seeds are become dry beneath their clods;

observance. The Pual participle is used even of warriors; see on Is. xiii. 3. The interpretations of the Rabbins, Jarchi and Kimchi, חזמינו, and Abenezra, חבינו, are defective, by leaving out the idea of sacredness, which the verb always conveys. עֲצָרָה, restraint, or being held back or prevented from labor: יוֹם, day, or period, understood. See on Is. i. 13. The Jews were to abstain from their worldly avocations, and spend the portion of their time thus consecrated to the immediate and solemn duties of humiliation, confession, and prayer. זְקֵנִים, elders, in this connection, might be taken in an official sense, denoting those holding office among the people, who were expected to take the lead, and, by their example, to excite others to engage in the religious solemnities; but a comparison of this verse with chap. ii. 15, in which "children" and "sucklings are mentioned, would rather require us to understand the term as referring to age. The central point of convocation was the temple — the special theocratic residence of Him whose wrath was to be deprecated, and his mercy implored.

זָעַק, Arab. عَقَّ, نَعَقَ, to cry out, cry earnestly for help. LXX. κεκράξετε ἐκτενῶς. "Ardentissimas fundite preces." Rosenmüller.

15. Joel now exclaims, אֲהָהּ לַיּוֹם, alas! for the day! "O infaustum et tristissimum illum diem!" Rosenmüller. To give intensity to the exclamation, the LXX. have the triple οἴμοι, οἴμοι, οἴμοι. That the יוֹם יְהוָה, day of Jehovah, i. e. the period of pun-

ishment, does not mean that of the plague of the locusts, but a more awful period still future, the term קָרוֹב, near, at hand, which is never used to denote the actual presence of anything, but its speedy approach, sufficiently proves. What the Jews were then suffering was only a prelude to still more dreadful calamities. For מִשֹּׁדֵי כְּשֹׁד, which forms an elegant paronomasia, see on Is. xiii. 6, where the same form occurs. The כְּ is, as there, the *Caph veritatis*, and expresses the greatness of the evil.

16. The verb כָּרַת is understood in the latter hemistich. The annual festivals were occasions of great rejoicing. See Lev. xxiii. 40; Deut. xii. 12, 18.

17. This, and the three following verses, describe the drought which was simultaneous with the judgment of the locusts. It exhibits the singular phenomenon of four ἅπαξ λεγόμενα within the short space which it occupies. For the elucidation of עָבַשׁ, some compare the Chaldee עֲבַשׁ, *to rot*, but it is with more propriety referred to the Arab.

عبس, *siccus fuit*; and so is of the same signification with יָבֵשׁ, *to be dry, dried up*. Thus Abulwalid. By the desiccating influence of the heat, the seeds that had been sown in the ground would lose all their moisture, and perish. That פְּרֻדוֹת mean *seeds* or *grains* of corn, etc. seems satisfactorily determined by the use of the Syr. ܦܪܕܐ, *granum*, Matt. xiii. 31; John xii. 24; 1 Cor. xv.

The granaries are desolate, the store-houses are destroyed,
Because the corn is withered.
18 How the cattle mourn!
How the herds of oxen are perplexed!
Because they have no pasture;
Yea, the flocks of sheep are destroyed.
19 To thee, O Jehovah! I cry,
For fire hath consumed the pastures of the desert,
And a flame hath burnt all the trees of the field.

37, in the Peshito; and the signification of גָּרַד, *to separate*, an action which takes place when, in sowing, the husbandman scatters the seed in distinct grains. To the same effect Tanchum, الحبوب المعدودة للزراعة ,لانها تفرق في الارض *grains prepared for sowing, so called because they are scattered in the ground*. מֶגְרְפֹת, *clods*, or lumps of earth. Comp. the Arab. جرف *gleba terræ;* ارض ,جرفة *terra diversa varia*. Thus also جروف, signifies a mark on the body, occasioned by the contracting or drying up of the skin, and resembling a round lump of earth or dung. מְגֻרוֹת is synonymous with אֲגֻרוֹת, *granaries;* and, according to the force of the local מ prefixed, signifies *places* or *houses containing store rooms*, or granaries, in which grain was deposited. The Dagesh in the second מ is euphonic. The simpler form מְגֻרָה, occurs Hag. ii. 19; and both are to be referred to the root גרר, *to gather, collect*. For the diversified and unsatisfactory renderings of the ancient versions, see Pococke *in loc*. The verbs שָׁמֵם and חָרַס are here to be taken in the sense of being left or neglected like places that have been laid waste or destroyed.

18. בוך, in Niphal, expresses the *perplexity* to which any one is reduced who does not know how to extricate himself from difficulty. The brute creation are graphically represented as being in this condition from the total failure of pasturage. The גַּם before עֶדְרֵי־בָקָר is intensive; *even* the sheep, which subsist on herbage unsuitable for the oxen, are deprived of food. As the idea of *punishment* is conveyed by the verb אָשַׁם, it was in all probability used by the prophet, in order to teach the Jews that innocent creatures are involved in the consequences of guilt incurred by transgressors. Comp. Exod. xii. 29; Jonah iii. 7.

19. It is not unusual for the Hebrew prophets to give expression to their own feelings, while describing the judgments that were brought upon their country. Comp. Is. xv. 5, xvi. 11, xxi. 3, 4, xxii. 4; Jer. xxiii. 9. It has been questioned whether the "fire" and "flame" are here to be taken literally of the actual burning of the grass, which often happens in extreme heat, or whether they are used figuratively of the heat itself. The former is more probably the meaning. נְאוֹת, Kimchi explains, מְקוֹמוֹת דֶּשֶׁא, *grassy places*, places of pasturage; hence pasturage itself. It is derived from נָוָה, *to be pleasant*, (comp. נָאָה) *to dwell*: but signifying in this connection the green, grassy spots, so eagerly desired by the cattle, and pleasant both to man and beast. From the circumstance that such places would naturally be selected for occupancy by tents, dwellings, etc. the word came also to signify *habitations*. Comp. the Arab. ,اوي *diversatus fuit, hospitio excipit:* ,ماوي *mansio, sedes commorationis.*

20 The very beasts of the field look up to thee,
Because the streams of water are dried up,
And fire hath devoured the pastures of the desert.

20. עָרַג, Arab. عرج, Eth. ዐረገ: *ascendit : to look up with panting or earnest desire.* Arab. عجرج, *inclinatio, propensio* in rem. The word beautifully expresses the natural action of animals parched with thirst, and deprived of all supply of water. They hold up their heads, as if their only expectation were from the God of heaven. LXX. ἀνέβλεψαν. Comp. Ps. xlii. 2, where the force of עֲרֹג־אֵלֶיךָ מַיִם is lost by the rendering of our common version, "*after* the water-brooks." It should be *at* or *beside*, as the Psalmist evidently intended to represent the deer standing on the brink of the channels in which water usually flowed, but which had become dry. To their pitiable condition he compares his own circumstances when deprived of the usual means of spiritual refreshment. The idea of their crying to God, which the Syr. ܠ, and the Rabbins attach to the word, is derived from such passages as Job. xxxviii. 41; Ps. civ. 21, cxlvii. 9, rather than from anything expressed by the word itself.

CHAPTER II.

THE prophet reiterates his announcement of the approach of a divine judgment more terrific in its nature than that of the locusts, but employs language borrowed from the appearance and movements of these insects, in order to make a deeper impression upon his hearers, whose minds were full of ideas derived from them as instruments of the calamity under which they were suffering, 1–11. He then summons anew to humiliation and repentance, 12–17; giving assurance that on these taking place, Jehovah would show them pity, destroy their enemy, and restore them to circumstances of great temporal and religious prosperity, 18–27; and the chapter concludes with a glorious promise of the abundant effusion of the influences of the Holy Spirit in the apostolic age, 28, 29, and a prediction of the Jewish war, and the final subversion of the Jewish state, 30, 31, in the midst of which such as embraced the worship and service of the Messiah should experience deliverance, 32.

1   BLOW ye the trumpet in Zion!
    And sound the alarm in my holy mountain!

1. To give the greater effect to the alarm here commanded to be sounded, Jehovah himself is introduced as speaking. The persons addressed are the priests, on whom it devolved to blow with trumpets. ἡ σάλπιγξ ὄργανον ἐστι

Let all the inhabitants of the land tremble;
For the day of Jehovah cometh; it is near.
2 A day of darkness and gloom,
A day of clouds and dense obscurity;
Like the dawn spread over the mountains
A numerous and mighty people:
None such have ever been,
Neither shall there ever be after them,
During the years of successive generations.

πολέμου. Philo de Septenario. They were to warn all of the threatened judgment. Comp. chap. i. 15, where the prophet anticipates what is now about to be the subject of a special description.

2. Synonymes are here accumulated to give intensity to the expression of the thought. The awful calamity which was to come upon the Jews is set forth under the metaphor of darkness, which is of frequent occurrence in the Hebrew Scriptures, when sufferings and misery are the subjects of discourse. Comp. Is. viii. 22, lx. 2; Jer. xiii. 16; Amos v. 18; Zeph. i. 15. In the present instance, however, there was a singular propriety in adopting the language, since the prophet was just going to introduce an allegory founded upon the fact, that swarms of locusts had come over the land, and intercepting, by their density, the light of the sun, had occasioned an universal darkness. See on ver. 10. Some interpreters have stumbled at the apparent incongruity of comparing the coming affliction with the שחר, *aurora*, since the idea usually suggested by the figurative use of that term is *joy*, or *prosperity;* but as this idea is not exclusively conveyed by the use of it, as it is also employed to express the *certainty*, Hos. vi. 3, and *suddenness* of anything, Hos. x. 15, so here the obvious points of comparison are merely the *suddenness* and *extent* of the change produced by the diffusion of the rays of light, without any reference to the nature of the change itself.

Joel now proceeds to introduce and describe the hostile army of the Assyrians in the same terms in which he had metaphorically described the locusts, chap. i. 6; only exchanging גוי, *nation*, for עם, *people*, which is also used of foreign and idolatrous nations, Numb. xxi. 29; 1 Chron. xvi. 20; Jer. xlviii. 42. In this description, he not only transfers the metaphor back to the proper subject from which it was taken, but converts it into an allegory, and at considerable length, and in the most minute manner, exhibits the invasion, the formidable character, and the ravages of the barbarian foe. So perfectly is the allegorical veil woven throughout, that most commentators have been able to discover nothing more than natural locusts in the passage. At the time in which the prophet delivered his message the locusts covered the land; they were before his eyes; the idea of them had so taken possession of his mind, that, considering the striking resemblance which they bore to an invading army, nothing was more natural than to exhibit the latter in sensible images taken from the scene by which both he and his hearers were surrounded. And, accustomed as they had been to the parabolic style of prophecy, they could have been at no loss to discover, that when in this part of his discourse he appeared to speak of locusts, it was not natural but political locusts he had in view. While the decidedly future aspect of the calamity, chap. i. 15, ii. 1, proves that it had not taken place at the time the words were delivered, a comparison of the language in the concluding part of verse 2, with

3 Before them fire devoureth,
And behind them a flame burneth;
Before them the land is like the garden of Eden,
But behind them a desolate wilderness:
And there is no escape from them.
4 Their appearance is like the appearance of horses,
And they run like horsemen.

that employed chap. i. 2, equally proves that a plague of locusts could not have been intended. We must, therefore, with the alteration of a single word, adopt the language of Jerome, "*dum locustas legimus, Assyrios cogitamus.*" That the Assyrian invasion under Sennacherib, and not that of the Chaldeans under Nebuchadnezzar, is meant, appears from the emmense number of the army, its entire destruction in the land of Palestine, and there being no reference whatever to the captivity in Babylon, the omission of which is unimaginable, on the supposition that the latter of the two invasions was intended. The army of Sennacherib must have been the largest that ever entered Palestine, since only that division of it which invested Jerusalem, amounted to nearly 200,000 men, Is. xxxvii. 36. It was marching forward to the conquest of Egypt, and, like a swarm of locusts, covered the whole land. All the fortified cities of Judah were taken, Is. xxxvi. 1; the cultivated fields and vineyards were trodden down or consumed, xxxvii. 30; and nothing short of utter destruction seemed to await the inhabitants. The design of the Divine Spirit, to whose infinite mind the future event was present, in dictating the prediction in the language here employed, appears to have been, to deepen the impressions produced by the plague of locusts, and thereby to excite to that repentance and amendment of life, which alone could secure to the Jews the continuance of their national blessings.

3. A description of the desolate state to which Judea was to be reduced, in language borrowed from that given of the drought, chap. i. 19. לְפָנָיו, *before* him, and אַחֲרָיו, *behind him*, are used to express universality; *ubicunque.* Comp. 1 Chron. xix. 10. This construction is confirmed by what follows: פְּלֵיטָה בָּם לֹא־הָיְתָה, *and there is no escape from them,* or, more literally, *in reference to them.* פְּלֵיטָה properly signifies those who have escaped in the war; who have not been killed, or taken prisoners; but it is also used of fruits of the earth which have not been destroyed, Exod. x. 5. The contrast between the beauty of Paradise and the desolation of a desert, is exquisitely forcible and affecting.

4. The allegory now becomes special and minute in its features, which are selected from the phenomena and operations of an invading army, the subject of which it is to be understood; but having the invasion by the locusts as its basis, and therefore presenting these prominently to view, and comparing them to the army, which is thus studiously concealed. On this principle there is no difficulty in accounting for the particle of comparison, so liberally used in this and the following verses. So strong is the resemblance of the head of the locust to that of a horse, that they are on this account called *cavalettes* by the Italians. This feature Theodoret thus notices: εἴ τις ἀκριβῶς κατίδοι τὴν κεφαλὴν τῆς ἀκρίδος, σφόδρα τῇ τοῦ ἵππου ἐοικυῖαν εὑρήσει. In Rev. ix. 7, the locusts are compared to horses harnessed for battle: τὰ ὁμοιώματα τῶν ἀκρίδων ὅμοια ἵπποις ἡτοιμασμένοις εἰς πόλεμον. Such comparison is very common among the Arabs. The point of comparison in the second member of the parallelism, is the swiftness with which cavalry advance to the attack.

5 They bound like the rattle of chariots on the tops of the mountains;
    Like the crackling of the flame of fire devouring the stubble;
    Like a mighty people arranged for battle.
6 Before them the people tremble;
    All faces withdraw their color.
7 They run like mighty men;
    They scale the wall like warriors;
    They all march in their courses,
    They break not their ranks.
8 They press not each other:
    They march on, each in his path;
    Though they fall among the missiles,
    They break not up.
9 They run eagerly through the city;
    They run upon the wall;

5. רָקַד is used of the rapid and bounding course of chariots over a rough surface, Nah. iii. 2. See also Rev. ix. 9.

" — per purum tonantes
Egit equos volucremque currum."
                    Horace, Carm. i. 34, 7.

" ——— vacuos dat in aëra saltus
Succubiturque alte, similisque est currus inani."
                    Ovid. Metam. ii. 165.

Speaking of the noise made by a swarm of locusts, Forskäl says: "Transeuntes grylli super verticem nostrum sono magnæ cataractæ ferebant." To the same effect Morier: "On the 11th of June, while seated in our tents about noon, we heard a very unusual noise, that sounded like the rustling of a great wind at a distance. On looking up, we perceived an immense cloud, here and there transparent, in other parts quite black, that spread itself all over the sky, and at intervals shadowed the sun." It is however, not improbable, that the sound here referred to is that produced by the large hind legs of the locust in leaping. The comparison at the end of the verse, is to the clashing of arms, and the shouting of an army on the point of engaging in battle.

6. יְחִילוּ, *they tremble*, from חוּל, *to turn round, twist one's self, writhe with pain;* then *to tremble.* Arab. حَالَ, med. Wau, *to be turned.* פָּארוּר, *warmth, ruddiness* of countenance. Arab. فَارَ, *æstuavit, efferbuit.* קָבְצוּ פָארוּר, *to withdraw their ruddiness,* or *color,* i. e. to change color, grow pale with terror. Nah. ii. 11. Comp. קָבַץ, *to turn pale.* The ancient versions concur in rendering the words, *every face like the blackness of a pot;* deriving the last word from פָּרוּר; hence פָּארוּר, *pot,* without א. Of the terror inspired by locusts, we cannot have a better proof than the Arabic proverb: اجرد من الجراد, *more terrible than the locusts.*

7-9. Here the description quite excels in the graphic. The comparison to warriors is admirably carried out. First, their rapid advance upon the city is specified; next, their scaling the walls in the most regular order; then their consentaneous encounter with the troops of defence, their invulnerability, their progress through the streets, their climbing the walls, and entering the windows of the houses, are set forth in terms

They go up into the houses;
They enter the windows like a thief.

of singular and appropriate beauty. עָקַב, Arab. عقب, *fidit, vulneravit,* عقب, *fissus,* has here the signification of *breaking up* the order or regularity with which a body of troops proceed when marching to the attack. Abenezra and Kimchi compare עָוָה, to *to pervert, turn aside* which comes nearly to the same thing. LXX. ἐκκλίνωσι. Syr. ܢܣܛܘܢ. Gesenius thinks the verb is here used in a sense cognate with the significations in Kal and Hiphil, *to give* or *take a pledge;* but the idea of *exchange, change,* is not clearly brought out. The regular military order with which the locusts advance, has been frequently described. 'Αβασίλευτον γὰρ ἡ ἀκρὶς, ἐστρατεύει μὲν γὰρ ἐξ ἑνὸς εὐτάκτως κελεύσματος· φασὶ δὲ αὐτὰς στοιχηδὸν ἰέναι, καὶ ὡς ἐν τάξει διιπτάσθαι, καὶ ἥκιστα μὲν ἀπονοσφίζεσθαι, περιέπει δὲ οὕτως ἀλλήλας, ὡσανεὶ καὶ ἀδελφαὶ, φύσεως αὐτῆς βραβευούσης τὸ φιλάλληλον. Cyril. The testimony of Jerome, as an eye-witness in Palestine, is peculiarly valuable: "Hoc nuper in hac provincia vidimus. Quum enim locustarum agmina venirent, et aerem, quo inter cœlum et terram est, occuparent tanto ordine ex dispositione jubentis Dei volitant, ut instar tesserularum, quæ in pavimentis artificis figuntur manu, *suum locum teneant, et ne puncto quidem, ut ita dicam, ungueve transverso declinent ad alteram.*" Morier also remarks on those which he saw: "They seemed to be impelled by one common instinct, and moved in one body, which had the appearance of being organized by a leader." Comp. Prov. xxx. 27, מֶלֶךְ אֵין לָאַרְבֶּה וַיֵּצֵא חֹצֵץ כֻּלּוֹ, *there is no king to the locusts, yet they go forth, all of them dividing,* i. e. themselves into regular companies or swarms, with all the discipline of a well-ordered army. דָּחַק signifies so to *press upon* one as to compel him to move from his place. Not-

withstanding the immense crowds of the locusts, not only does none of them break the ranks by deviating from the straight course which they pursue, but none forces his fellow from his rank. Their watchword may be said to be *onward ;* for they never turn back. If they enter houses, they go straight through them, and out at the opposite side. Thus Abulphargius relates in his Chron. Syr. p. 134 : "postquam a latere meridionale domos intraverant, a latere septentrionale egrediebantur. שֶׁלַח, properly means any missile weapon thrown at an enemy, from שָׁלַח, *to send* or *cast forth ;* but it is also frequently used of the sword. Comp. the Arab. سلاح, *arma.*

בְּעַד, is of somewhat difficult determination. The ground idea seems to be that of *mediation, a being,* or *doing anything between two ;* hence הִתְפַּלֵּל בְּעַד, *to make supplication for* any one, i. e. by interposing *between* him and the party to whom the supplication is addressed. To this the signification derived from the Arab. بعد, *post,* nearly approximates, as occurring in the Hebrew. *Between,* or *among,* will suit most of the passages in which the word occurs. See Winer and Credner. Taking שֶׁלַח as a collective noun, the meaning of נָפַל בְּעַד הַשֶּׁלַח, will be *to fall among the missiles,* i. e. to light, or come down among them; and referring בְּעַד to the whole swarm, what it expresses is, that they are not *broken up,* or *interrupted* in their course. Compare a similar use of בָּצַע, *to break,* Dan. xi. 22, בָּעִיר, *in the city,* i. e. any city or town that may lie in their way. Credner's appeal to chap. iv. [iii.] 17, in proof that Jerusalem is specifically meant, cannot be sustained, since that part of the prophecy relates to a totally different subject. The scene is rather the land of Judah, with its fortified cities, which were overrun and plundered by the Assyrian troops.

10 Before them the earth trembleth,
   The heavens shake,
   The sun and the moon are darkened,
   And the stars withdraw their shine.
11 Jehovah uttereth his voice before his army;
   Surely his camp is very large;
   Surely it is mighty, executing his order;
   Surely the day of Jehovah is great, and very terrible:
   Who can endure it?
12 Now, therefore, saith Jehovah,
   Turn ye to me with all your heart,
   And with fasting and weeping and mourning;
13 And rend your heart, and not your garments,
   And turn to Jehovah your God;
   For he is pitiful and compassionate,

10, 11. Though the language here employed may in part admit of a literal application to the obscuration of the air by the locusts, yet it is, as a whole, to be regarded as a specimen of the highly wrought hyperbolical, which forms one of the more distinguishing features of Hebrew poetry. קוֹל יְהֹוָה, *the voice of Jehovah*, is here, as frequently, *thunder*, and not any word of command, as some have imagined. Com. Exod. ix. 23, 29, 33; Ps. xviii. 14; Ps. lxxvii. 18, 19. The locusts are called the חֵיל, *army of Jehovah*, with further reference to the numbers and power of an army. One of the laws of Mohammed is thus expressed:

لا تَنْتِلُوا الجَرادَ فَانَّها جُنْدُ اللهِ الأَعْظَم, *Ye shall not kill the locusts, for they are the army of God Almighty*. Damir. And رَبُّ الجَرادِ, *Lord of the locusts*, is one of the names of God among the Mohammedans. The entire description closes with the brief but pointed interrogation, מִי יְכִילֶנּוּ, *Who can endure it?* to which the implied answer is, None. Comp. Mal. iii. 2, וּמִי מְכַלְכֵּל אֶת־יוֹם בֹּאוֹ, and Jer. x. 10, לֹא יָכִלוּ גוֹיִם זַעֲמוֹ.

12. Jehovah himself is here intro- duced, urging the necessity of immediate humiliation. וְגַם־עַתָּה, is intensive. The ו is that of consequence, deducing an argument from what had preceded; גַּם is augmentative and emphatic, as usually in Joel; and עַתָּה has special reference to the existing circumstances of the persons addressed, and the instant attention which the divine message required. The combination marks strong feeling in the speaker, and the urgent nature of the subject to which it is introductory. It is to be connected with עָדַי שֻׁבוּ, and not with נְאֻם יְהֹוָה.

13. The prophet resumes his address, and founds upon the call of Jehovah, contained in the preceding verse, an exhortation to sincere inward repentance, which he supports by encouragements deduced from the benignity of the divine character. Rending the garments was usual on occasions of great mourning, see Gen. xxxvii. 29, 34; 1 Sam. iv. 12; 1 Kings xxi. 27; Ezra ix. 3, 5; Is. xxxvii. 1. This custom obtained not only among the Hebrews, but also among the Babylonians, Persians, Egyptians, Greeks and Romans. חָרְפָה, is neither the plague of locusts, nor the invasion of the Assyrians, but the calamities in general which God brings upon mankind. This interpretation the preceding context requires.

Long-suffering, and of great mercy,
And repenteth of the evil.
14 Who knoweth? He may turn and repent,
And leave a blessing behind him —
An offering and a libation,
For Jehovah your God.
15 Blow ye the trumpet in Zion,
Appoint a sacred fast;
Proclaim a day of restraint.
16 Assemble the people: convene a sacred assembly;
Collect the aged; gather the children,
And those that suck the breasts;
Let the bridegroom come forth from his chamber,
And the bride from her nuptial bed.
17 Between the porch and the altar,
Let the priests, the ministers of Jehovah, weep;
And let them say, Have pity, O Jehovah! upon thy people,

14. The question מִי יוֹדֵעַ, *who knoweth*, while it suggests the idea of the greatness of the sin to be pardoned, also conveys that of the possibility of such pardon,

"——— ἀλλ' ἔτι καὶ νῦν,
Ταῦτ' εἴποις 'Αχιλῆϊ δαΐφρονι, αἴκε πίθηται.
Τίς δ' οἶδ' εἴ κέν οἱ, σὺν δαίμονι, θυμὸν ὀρίναις,
Παρειπών;"
Iliad. xi. 789.

God's leaving a blessing behind him, presupposes his return to visit his people in mercy. The first-fruits of prosperity are due to Him through whose blessing it is conferred.

15, 16. Comp. ver. i. and chap. i. 14. Here the distribution into classes is more minute than in the latter of these passages. The mourning was to be universal. The חֻפָּה, was the bridal couch, richly provided with a canopy, curtains, etc. Root חָפַף, *to cover, protect.* See for the force of the reference to the last class mentioned, Deut. xxiv. 5.

17. אוּלָם, Arab. اوّل, *prior, anterior;* the πρόναος, or *porch*, before the temple, more strictly taken. It was an hundred and twenty cubits high, twenty broad from north to south, and ten long from east to west. The מִזְבֵּחַ, *altar*, was that of burnt-offering in the court of the priests. Here, with their backs toward the altar, on which they had nothing to offer, and their faces directed towards the residence of the Shekinah, they were to weep, and make supplication on behalf of the people. לִמְשָׁל־בָּם גּוֹיִם, Jarchi, Secker, Michælis, Rosenmüller, Justi, Crednor, Winer, Gesenius, Maurer, Noyes, Hitzig, and Ewald, render, *that the nations should make a proverb of them;* but such construction is totally unauthorized by Hebrew usage. In upwards of fifty instances, in which בְּ מָשַׁל occurs in the Hebrew Bible, it is never once used in the sense of employing *derision*, or *satirical language*, but uniformly in that of *likening*, or of *exercising rule* or *dominion*. In fact, the verb is nowhere used either with or without the preposition in the signification of deriding. It is the noun alone that is thus employed in the forms הָיָה לְמָשָׁל, נָתַן, שִׂים, הֱיֵה, to *be, set, give*, etc. *to a derision.* Ezek. xvi. 44, forms no exception. The ancient versions all agree in the translation, *that the heathen should rule over them.* LXX. τοῦ κατάρξαι αὐτῶν ἔθνη. Targ. לְמִשְׁלַט בְּ

And deliver not thine heritage to reproach,
That the nations should rule over them.
Why should they say among the people,
Where is their God?
18   Then Jehovah will be jealous for his land,
And take compassion upon his people:
19   Yea, Jehovah will answer, and say unto his people,
Behold! I will send you the corn,
And the new wine, and the oil,
And ye shall have abundance thereof:
And I will no more deliver you to reproach among the nations.
20   I will also remove the Northern from you,
And drive him into a dry and barren land;

עַמְּךָ ׃ בְּהוֹן . Syr. ܡܚܣܕܠܝܢ, Vulg. *ut dominentur eis* nationes. Hexap. Syr. ܘܫܘܠ, ܘܫܠܛܘ ܒܗܘܢ ܥܡܡܐ Thus also Kimchi, Abenezra, Leo Juda, Junius and Tremellius, Jewish-Spanish, Lyranus, Drusius, Calvin, Newcome, Dathe, Boothroyd, and Hengstenberg; and there does not appear to be any reason why it could ever have been rendered otherwise, but for the influence of the hypothesis, that the preceding part of the prophecy relates to locusts, and not to political enemies. "Ideo ridiculum est quod multi putant contexti sermonem de locustis: illud prorsus alienum est a Prophetæ mente." Calvin, *in loc.*

18. קָנָא, Arab. كَنَأَ, *valde rubuit*; in Piel קִנֵּא, *to be jealous*, from the redness or flush by which the face is suffused, when a person is under the influence of passion.

19, 20. In the former of these verses, respect is had to the removal of the calamity, from which the Jews were suffering at the time the prophecy was delivered; in the latter, that of the foreign enemy by whom the country was to be invaded. The article is placed before תִּירוֹשׁ דָּגָן, and יִצְהָר, to give them prominence, as the principal objects which had suffered from the locusts, and which were now to be restored. The term הַצְּפוֹנִי, *the Northern, Northlander*, or, as Coverdale renders, *Him of the North*, is of prime importance in the interpretation of the prophecy. It has been urged against its having any reference to the locusts, that they visit Palestine from the south, and not from the north; but this objection can scarcely be regarded as valid, since, though they do not usually come from that quarter, yet they may be carried by a south wind across Arabia Deserta, and then, when to the north of Palestine, be driven south, or south-west into that country. That, however, which determines the question, is the addition of the patronymic to צְפוֹנִי, indicating that the North was not merely the quarter whence the subject of discourse came, but that its *native country* lay to the north of Palestine: just as הַתֵּימָנִי, *the Temanite*, means *the Southern*, or he who dwells to the right of Palestine; מִצְרִי, *a native Egyptian;* in Arabic مكي, *a Meccite*, مديني, a *Medinite*, i. e. a native or inhabitant of Mecca and Medina. Now it is agreed on all hands, that the native country of the locusts is the regions of Arabia, the Lybian deserts, and the Sahara of Egypt; so that according to the *usus loquendi*, they cannot be meant by the term here employed. Indeed, so much has this

His van towards the Eastern sea,
And his rear towards the Western sea;
And his odor shall come up,
And his stench ascend,
Because he hath done great things.

been felt by some of those who have advocated the hypothesis, that locusts are intended, that they have been under the necessity of having recourse to far-fetched expedients, in order to support it. Justi, contrary to all analogy, proposes to render, "the locusts that march *northwards*." or to explain the term *north* of what is dark, hostile, or barbarous; which construction of the meaning is, in part, adopted by Hitzig. Maurer, on the other hand, setting aside these and other methods, has recourse to the Arab. ضفن *deposuit excrementum*, and thence deduces for צְפוֹנִי, the signification of *stercoreus*, or, in case this derivation should not be approved, to سفو, *decorticare radendo*, and considers the reference to be either to the injurious influence of their dung on the trees, herbage, etc., or to their stripping them of their verdure.

On the supposition that by הַצְּפוֹנִי, *the Northern*, the Assyrians are meant, every difficulty vanishes. And that they may with the strictest propriety be so termed, is proved by Zeph. ii. 13: "And he will stretch out his hand עַל־צָפוֹן, upon *the North*, and destroy *Assyria*, and will make *Nineveh* a desolation, and dry as a wilderness." The Jews were accustomed to call Assyria and Babylonia *the North*, and the North country, because they lay in that direction from Palestine. "Quæres, quisnam hic Aquilonaris? S. Hieron. Theodor. Remigius, Albertus et Hugo accipiunt Sennacherib, quem Dominus, longè fecit à Jerusalem: quia dum eam obsideret, angelus Domini una nocte percussit centum octuaginta quinque millia militum, itaque eam fugere compulit. 4 Reg. xix. 35." — *A Lapide*.

The geographical specification which follows in the verse is designed to express the universality of the destruction of the Assyrians. They were to be dispersed in every other direction but that from which they had come. By חַיָּם הַקַּדְמֹנִי, *the Eastern Sea*, is meant the Asphaltic lake; by הַיָּם הָאַחֲרוֹן, *the Western Sea*, the Mediterranean; and by אֶרֶץ צִיָּה וּשְׁמָמָה, *a dry and desolate land*, the deserts of Arabia. Literally the words הַקַּדְמֹנִי, and הָאַחֲרוֹן, signify what is *before* and *behind*, and are applied geographically in reference to the Orientals reckoning the different quarters according to the positions of front and rear, right and left, while they face the east, which is with them the principal point of the compass. The language of the prophet is figurative, the metaphor being still borrowed from the locusts, which perish when blown by a storm into the sea, or the sandy desert. Jerome refers to a similar scene, which literally happened when he was in Palestine. "Etiam nostris temporibus," he says, "vidimus agmina locustarum terram texisse Judæam, quæ postea vento surgente in mare primum et novissimum precipitata sunt." And he immediately adds, what illustrates the statement of Joel relative to the ascending of the stench: "Cumque littora utriusque maris acervis mortuorum locustarum quas aquæ evomucrant, implerentur, putredo earum et fœtor in tantum noxius fuit, ut acram quoque corrumperet, et pestilentia tam jumentorum, quam hominum gigneretur. פָּנִים and סוֹף, *face* and *end* are here used in the military sense of *van* and *rear*, and cannot, without violence, be interpreted of the swarm of locusts, and a brood which succeeded them. צַחֲנָה, is a ἅπαξ λεγ. comp. צָחַן, *to be foul, putrid, to stink*. Arab. ضَنَخَ, *sordes*. Giving an account of the locusts, Thevenot says, "They live not above six months, and, when dead, the stench of them so

JOEL. CHAP. II.

21 Fear not, O land! rejoice and be glad,
   For Jehovah doeth great things!
22 Fear not, ye beasts of the field!
   For the pastures of the desert spring up,
   For the tree beareth its fruit;
   The fig-tree and the vine yield their strength.
23 Rejoice, ye sons of Zion! and be glad in Jehovah your God;

corrupts and infects the air, that it often occasions dreadful pestilences." The concluding words of the verse convey the idea of moral agency, and can with no propriety be interpreted of the locusts. הִגְדִּיל לַעֲשׂוֹת. LXX. ἐμεγάλυνε τὰ ἔργα αὐτοῦ. Syr. ܐܬܪܘܪܒ ܒܥܒܕܘܗܝ. *he exalted himself in acting.* The phrase is obviously used here in a bad sense, and indicates the pride of the Assyrians; comp. 2 Kings xxi. 6, where הִרְבָּה לַעֲשׂוֹת, a similar idiom, occurs. As employed in the following verse of our prophet, it is placed in antithesis with the sense in which it is here used, and is to be differently understood: *viz.* of the great things that God would do for his people, comp. Ps. cxxvi. 2, 3.

21–23. In these verses there is a beautiful gradation. First, the land, which had been destroyed by the enemy, is addressed in a prosopopœia; then the irrational animals which had suffered from the famine; and lastly, the inhabitants themselves. All are called upon to cast off their fears, and rejoice in the happy change which Jehovah would effect. Desolation, barrenness, and famine, would disappear, and times of prosperity and happiness return. בְּנֵי צִיּוֹן, *Sons of Zion,* properly the inhabitants of Jerusalem, but here evidently used to denote those of the land generally, of which Jerusalem was the metropolis, and Zion the centre of religious influence. מוֹרֶה לִצְדָקָה, is rendered in the Targ. מַלְפְּכוֹן בְּזָכוּ, *your teacher in righteousness;* which Abarbanel explains, הוא מלך המשיח שיורה את בני לבב בה. זאת המצוה אשר יעשון. *And he is the king Messiah, who shall teach them the way in which they shall walk, and*

the works that they should do. The same, or a similar construction of the words is found in the Vulg. Rufinus, Jarchi, Pagninus, Munster, Leo Juda, Castalio, the Jewish-Spanish, Remigius, Rupertus, Vatablus, Ribera, Mercer, Œcolamp., Luther, and most of the early Lutheran interpreters; and, among the modern, Pick and Hengstenberg, the latter of whom contends for it at considerable length, and decidedly considers the passage to be one of the Messianic prophecies. That מוֹרֶה signifies *teacher,* is beyond all doubt, see 2 Chron. xv. 3; Job xxxvi. 22; Is. ix. 15, xxx. 20; and from the occurrence of the word in this place in connection with צְדָקָה, *righteousness,* which is so frequently referred to the Messiah both in the Old and New Testaments, there is something very plausible in the application of the term to him who is specially called by Malachi שֶׁמֶשׁ צְדָקָה, THE SUN OF RIGHTEOUSNESS, chap. iv. 4, *i. e.* the author of that illumination of knowledge which has righteousness for its object. To such interpretation, however, there appear to me to be the following insuperable objections:—First, it is repugnant to the circumstances of the context; "non videtur tamen ferre hunc sensum circumstantia loci." Calvin; who says of the reason adduced in support of it, that it would be out of place to give such prominence to merely temporal blessings: "sed ratio illa est nimis frigida;" and goes on to show that, in accordance with the custom of the prophets, Joel begins with these inferior blessings, and afterwards, in ver. 28, proceeds to treat of those which are spiritual. Secondly, the repetition of the same term, מוֹרֶה, immediately after, where, as all allow, it must be taken in the acceptation of *rain.* And thirdly, the pecul-

For he giveth you the former rain in due measure;
Yea, he causeth the heavy rain to descend for you —
The former and the latter rain as before:
24 So that the floors shall be full of grain,

iar force and coherence of the words, אֶת־הַמּוֹרֶה, and וּמַלְקוֹשׁ גֶּשֶׁם. The emphasis given to מוֹרֶה, by prefixing not only the article ה, but also the determinating particle אֶת, shows that the prophet had some immediate and definite object in view, which we cannot imagine to have been any other than the autumnal rain, which was indispensable any year, and more especially after such a season of drought, to prepare the ground for nourishing the seed. It must have been an object of universal and anxious desire, and has, in consequence, a high degree of importance and prominence allotted to it in the text. See on the force of אֶת the Lexicons of Lee and Gesenius. The same consideration will account for the form, and the particular signification of לִצְדָקָה in this place. The ל is to be taken adverbially, as pointing out the rule or measure according to which the rain was to be צְדָקָה, so that the meaning will be, *in just quantity, adequately*, in the proportion suitable to the exigency of the case. צָדַק, the root from which this noun is derived, signifies to be *just, right ;* to come up to certain claims, *to be what a person or thing ought to be.* Comp. Lev. xix. 36, where צֶדֶק is used of weights and measures that were exact, or came up to the demands of the law. Some propose to render לִצְדָקָה, *bountifully*, but this would give the Chaldee rather than the Hebrew signification. Ewald translates, *the early rain for justification,* and explains it of the Jews being again accounted righteous by God. To the objection of Hengstenburg, that if מוֹרֶה in the first half of the verse does not designate a different divine benefit from מוֹרֶה in the second, an idle tautology will ensue, it is only necessary to reply, that the words occur in parallelism, and that in the second instance מוֹרֶה is merely a resumption for the sake of dividing the גֶּשֶׁם mentioned

immediately before into its two regular divisions, the *former* and the *latter*. The term elsewhere used for the *former* or autumnal *rain*, which falls from the middle of October until the middle of December, is יוֹרֶה, lit. *waterer*, being the Benoni Participle of יָרָה, *to dart, cast*, or scatter, as drops of water. מוֹרֶה, however, which is the Hiph. Participle of the same verb, does occur in the same acceptation, Ps. lxxxiv. 7. Comp. my note on Hosea vi. 3, where מַלְקוֹשׁ, the *latter* or vernal rain is also explained.

The reading יוֹרֶה, which is found instead of the former מוֹרֶה, in twenty-three MSS., originally in eleven more, now in three, in the Jerusalem Talmud, and as Keri in the margin of two of De Rossi's Codices, is in favor of the rendering *rain*, which is that of all the early versions, but may possibly have originated in emendation. With respect to the latter occurrence of the word, there is no variety of reading. גֶּשֶׁם, Arab. جسم

corpus, et omne id quod longum, largum et profundum est; Chald. *the body :* applied to such rain as is *heavy,* or violent, and pours down as it were in a body. The verbs נָתַן, and וַיּוֹרֶד, are prophetic futures. To render בָּרִאשׁוֹן, *in the first month*, would involve a contradiction, since only one of the two rains could happen in that month. It seems, therefore, necessary to suppose an ellipsis of כְּ, the particle of comparison, and read כְּבָרִאשׁוֹן, *as formerly*, or *as in former times.* Comp. Jer. i. 22 ; Jer. xxxiii. 11, where כְּבָרִאשׁוֹן is similarly used; and for רִאשׁוֹן, in the sense of *former*, 1 Sam. xvii. 30; Hagg. ii. 3. Thus the LXX. Syr. Vulg. Arab. One of Kennicott's MSS. and perhaps another, reads כְּבָרִאשׁוֹן. The ellipsis of כְּ is not infrequent in the Hebrew Scriptures.

24. Here the happy results of the plentiful and seasonable rains are set

And the vats shall run over with new wine and oil.
25 Thus he will make good to you the years
Which the swarming locusts hath devoured,
The licking locust, the consuming locust, and the gnawing locust,
My great army which I sent against you.
26 And ye shall eat plentifully and be satisfied,
And praise the name of Jehovah your God,
Who hath dealt wondrously with you:
And my people shall never be ashamed.
27 Then shall ye know, that I am in the midst of Israel,
And that I, Jehovah, am your God, and none else;
And my people shall never be ashamed.
28 And it shall come to pass, afterwards,
That I will pour out my Spirit upon all flesh;

forth. The ן in וְגָאֲלוּ, is consequential. הֵשִׁיק, comp. the Arab. سوق, *propulit,* vii. Conj. *impulsus fuit, fluxit,* to *cause to flow,* or *run over.* For רָקַב, see on Is. v. 2.

25. That the prophet has here in view the plague of locusts described in chap. i. cannot well be doubted. The names, though placed in a different order, are identical with those there specified. They are called God's great *army,* a name still given to them by the Arabs. See on ver. 11. Though the scourge lasted only one year, yet as they not only destroyed the whole produce of that year, but also what was laid up in store for future years, there is no impropriety in the plural form of שָׁנִים, *years.* The term is used metonymically for the produce and supply of years. The loss of these Jehovah promises to recompense or make good by not only furnishing the Jews with an abundance of temporal enjoyments, but affording them the delightful experience of his presence and favor as their covenant God. This promise is amplified in verses —

26, 27, In which the future prosperity of the Jewish church is described in terms, which obviously characterize the period which succeeded that of the Babylonish captivity. The divine recompense was not merely to cover the evils sustained by the ravages of the locusts; it was to extend to those which both the Assyrians and the Chaldeans were to inflict upon the nation. This interpretation is confirmed by what immediately follows respecting the outpouring of the Holy Spirit. By God's being in the midst of his people, is meant the special manifestation of his presence in the communications of his favor. The resumption of אֲנִי in וַאֲנִי, forms a beautiful anadiplosis.

28, 29. The prophet now proceeds to predict the impartation of richer gifts in future times than those temporal blessings which had just been promised to the Jews. אַחֲרֵי־כֵן, *afterward,* LXX. μετὰ ταῦτα, Hengstenberg would place in antithesis with בָּרִאשׁוֹן, ver. 23, which he renders *first;* but the latter phrase has reference to what had already taken place, and was not future to the time of the prophet. אַחֲרֵי־כֵן, though indefinite, is nearly equivalent in force to אַחֲרִית הַיָּמִים, Is. ii. 2, as appears from its having been rendered by the apostle Peter ἐν ταῖς ἐσχάταις ἡμέραις, *in the last days.* Jarchi, לְעָתִיד לָבֹא, *in futurity;* Abenezra, אמר ר' ישוע כל זאת הנבואה היא לעתיד ור' משה הכהן אמר אם כן למה אמר אחרי כן רק והיה באחרית הימים. "Rabbi Jeshua saith, All this is a prophecy of the future; and Rabbi Moses the priest saith, If so, why does he say *after this?* but it is the same as,

And your sons and your daughters shall prophesy,
Your old men shall dream dreams,
Your young men shall see visions;
29 And even upon the male and the female servants
I will pour out my Spirit in those days.

and it shall come to pass in the latter days;" in which interpretation Kimchi concurs, adding, לפי שאמר וידעתם כי בקרב ישראל אני. אמר עתה תדעו ולא ודיעה שלמה כי עוד תשובו ותחטאו לפני אבל אחרי זאת הידיעה יבא זמן שתדעו אותי ידיעה שלמה ולא תחטאו עוד והוא לימות המשיח שנאמר כי מלאה הארץ דעה את יהוה, "Because it is said, And ye shall know that I am in the midst of you. What he says is, Now ye know, but not with a perfect knowledge, for ye will again commit sin before me; but after this knowledge there shall come a time when ye shall know me with a perfect knowledge, and shall sin no more, namely, in the days of the Messiah." That the two phrases are identical in meaning, clearly appears from a comparison of Jer. xlviii. 47, with xlix. 6. See on Is. ii. 2. שָׁפַךְ signifies to *pour out, to communicate in a plentiful and abundant manner,* and is here used with the greatest propriety to denote the larger and richer supplies of divine influence, which were to be afforded to the church under the gospel dispensation. רוּחַ, *spirit,* means here the *influences* and *gifts* of the Holy Spirit, as in numerous other passages, in which the Spirit is said to be *put, given,* etc.; and these communications are described in language which shows that they were both to be more general and more special in their character. In a more general point of view, they were to be bestowed upon כָּל־בָּשָׂר, *all flesh,* i. e. mankind generally, without distinction of nation or country. To restrict this phrase to the Jews, as is done by Abenezra, Kimchi, Albo, Hitzig, and others, is irreconcilable with Scripture usage, according to which it constantly signifies mankind generally, or the whole human race; just as in Arabic, بشر and إبشار signify *homo, humanum genus,* and Adam is called أبو البشر, *the father of flesh,* i. e. of mankind. Credner would have the phrase to include the animal creation, than which no construction could be more preposterous in such connection, or more at variance with other passages in which the communication of the influences of the Spirit are limited to the human family. The influence, of which universality is here predicated, is the saving energy which is exerted by the Holy Spirit, in commencing, carrying on, and consummating the work of grace in the souls of men. It accompanies the presentation of divine truth to the mind, and removes the obstacles which the force of innate depravity opposes to the reception of the gospel. See my Lectures on Divine Inspiration. pp. 525–530. Besides the influence which was thus to be vouchsafed for the purposes of salvation, the prophet specifies that which should be more limited in its communication, consisting in the miraculous endowment of a certain number of Jews, of different classes and conditions, with the knowledge of divine things, and the ability infallibly to communicate them to others. The persons on whom these gifts were to be conferred are their "sons and daughters;" their "aged men," and their "youths;" their "male" and "female servants;" terms which are manifestly designed to teach that their bestowment was to embrace persons of different classes, ranks, and conditions of life. נָבָא, Arab. نبأ, *indicavit, annunciavit,* Eth. ነገረ፡ *locutus est,* ተናገረ፡ *vaticinatus est, prædixit,* is used not merely to denote the foretelling

112   JOEL.   Chap. II.

30 And I will show prodigies in the heavens and in the earth,
  Blood and fire, and columns of smoke.
31 The sun shall be turned into darkness,
  And the moon into blood,

of the future events, but to express the giving of utterance to divine truth under a miraculous impulse, or the pretending to such impulse, whether the utterance was made in the way of direct communication, as was the case when the prophets addressed their hearers, or by the rehearsal or singing of sacred hymns under extraordinary divine impulse, as when Miriam sung at the Red Sea, Exod. xv. 20, 21; or when the sons of the prophets and Saul prophesied, 1 Sam. x. 5, 6, xix. 20-24. Comp. Acts xix. 6, xxi. 9; 1 Cor. xi. 4, 5, xiv. 1, 5, 6, 22, 24, 31, 39; which passages furnish striking illustrative examples of the fulfilment of the prophecy of Joel. See also 1 Chron. xxv. 1-3; and Mede's works, Book I. Discourse xvi. That we are fully warranted to interpret it of the extraordinary supernatural gifts which were vouchsafed in the apostolic age, is placed beyond doubt by its allegation by Peter, in justification of the phenomenon which took place on the day of Pentecost. τοῦτό ἐστι, *this is the fact* predicted by Joel, Acts ii. 16. The quotation was the more apt, since the words of the prophet had just been read in the pentecostal service of the Synagogue. See my Biblical Researches and Travels in Russia, p. 326. חֲלֹמוֹת, *dreams*, and חֶזְיֹנוֹת, *visions*, belonged to the different modes in which God revealed his will to the prophets. Numb. xii. 6; 1 Sam. xxviii. 6, 15; Jer. xxiii. 25-28; Dan. vii. 1, 2. See my Lectures on Inspiration, pp. 147-165. Though no express mention is made of dreams in the apostolic writings, yet repeated reference is to *visions*. See acts ix. 10, 12, x. 3, 17, xi. 5, xvi. 9, xviii. 9, xxvi. 19; 2 Cor. xii. 1; Rev. ix. 17. גַּם, *and even*, indicates a rise in the prophecy, which was intended to exclude none, not even the lowest and most despised "servants," from a participation in the large bestowment of divine influence. In beautiful harmony with this feature of the prophecy is the special recognition of οἱ πτωχοί, *the poor*, in the New Testament. The repetition אֶשְׁפּוֹךְ אֶת רוּחִי *I will pour out my Spirit*, shows, that the influence of which, in general, they were to be partakers, was not merely that which consisted in the miraculous gifts, but also that ordinary and saving influence which is experienced by all believers. What incontrovertibly proves that the prophecy includes both a more ordinary, and a more extraordinary or miraculous divine agency, is the extension given to it by the apostle Peter, Acts ii. 38, 39; where he teaches that it was to comprehend "all that are afar off," *i. e.* the Gentiles, "even as many as the Lord our God shall call."

30, 31. In connection with this period of the rich enjoyment of divine influence, Joel introduces one of awful judgment, called as usual יוֹם יְהֹוָה, *the day of Jehovah*, the precursors of which he describes in very alarming language. That the destruction of Jerusalem and the Jewish polity is intended, most interpreters are agreed; but there exists a diversity of opinion respecting the character of the language, some taking it literally, as setting forth physical prodigies, such as those which Josephus relates to have taken place before the destruction of Jerusalem, and tremendous massacres and conflagrations in different parts of the country; while others maintain that it is symbolical, and consequently is to be figuratively explained. The latter position is more in accordance with the style of prophecy, in which we not only find a fixed set of symbols, but also, very frequently, an accumulation of images is introduced for the purpose of producing a more powerful effect on the mind. See on Is. xiii. 10, xxxiv. 3--5. The heavens and the earth,

Chap. II.   JOEL.   113

Before the great and terrible day of Jehovah come.
32   And it shall come to pass,
     That whosoever shall call upon the name of Jehovah shall be
       delivered:
     For in Mount Zion and in Jerusalem shall be the escaped,

therefore, mean the political world, with its civil and religious establishments; the sun and moon, the higher and superior ruling powers; while the other images are employed to denote the disastrous prognosticatory changes that were to happen in relation to both. Comp. Matt. xxiv. 29; Mark xiii. 24, 25; Luke xx. 25–27, where the subject is the same as that exhibited by Joel, and the symbolical language in a great measure parallel. Similar images are used by pagan writers, when describing the forerunners of civil wars, as, for instance, Lucanus, Pharsal. lib. ver. 529:—

"——— Super igne minaces
Prodigiis terras impleruntt, æthera, pontum.
Ignota obscuræ viderunt sidera noctes,
Ardentemque polum flammis, cœloque volantes,
Obliquas per inane faces, crinemque timendi.
Sideris, et terris mutantem regna cometen.
Fulgura fallaci micuerunt crebra sereno,
Et varias ignis denso dedit aëre formas."

מוֹפְתִים, *prodigies*, whatever objects are *unusual*, *portentous*, or *miraculous*, in their character. The word is most probably a derivative from יָפָה, Arab. Conj. iii. وفي, *eminuit*, to be *conspicuous*, *admirable*, *wonderful*. LXX. τέρατα. It frequently occurs in combination with אוֹתוֹת σημεῖα, *signs*. תִּימָרוֹת, only occurs once besides, and, as here, in construction with עָשָׁן, viz. Song iii. 6; where, however, nineteen MSS. and originally another read תַּמְרוֹת, without the Yod, which is doubtless the more correct orthography, the Yod having been inserted as a help to the pronunciation. There can be little doubt that it is derived from תָּמַר, *to be erect*, whence תָּמָר the palm-tree, from its tall and erect growth. Comp. the Chaldee תִּמְרָה, *a column of smoke*; תִּימוּר, Arab. تاصور and تاصورة, *turris*; and تَمَر, *to rise like a column*. The phrase will, therefore, be equivalent to עַמּוּדֵי עָשָׁן, of which we have the singular עַמּוּד עָשָׁן, Jud. xx. 40. LXX. ἀτμίδα καπνοῦ; but in Song iii. 6, στελέχη καπνοῦ. Vulg. *vaporem fumi*. Targ. יְתוּרִין דִּתְנָן, *columns of smoke*, the singular of which is used Jud. xx. 40. Tanc.: اعمدة الدخان المرتفعة, *pillars of smoke ascending up*. Those who are familiar with the account given by Josephus of the disorders, convulsions, excesses, and rebellions, which preceded the subversion of the Jewish state, will readily admit, that the figurative language here employed most appropriately sets forth the awful circumstances of the inhabitants of Palestine at that period. To render more prominent the tremendous nature of the final judgment of the Jews, when their city and polity were destroyed, it is not merely called יוֹם יְהֹוָה, but יוֹם יְהֹוָה הַגָּדוֹל וְהַנּוֹרָא, *the great and fearful day of Jehovah*; terms which are employed by the prophet Malachi, iv. 5, (Heb. iii. 23,) in reference to the same event.

32. The phrase קָרָא בְּשֵׁם יְהֹוָה, usually means *to evoke Jehovah according to his true character*, and designates such as he would regard in the light of acceptable worshippers; but on comparing the quotation of the words with direct reference to our Saviour, Rom. x. 13, with Acts ix. 14, 1 Cor. i. 2, it appears

15

According as Jehovah hath promised,
Together with those that are left,
Whom Jehovah shall call.

to be here employed as a periphrasis for those Jews who should embrace the faith of the Messiah, and render to him as יְהוָה, *Jehovah,* the same supreme worship which had been rendered to God by their pious ancestors. From the passage just quoted from the Acts, it is clear that the disciples of Christ were characterized as *invokers of his name,* i. e. as his worshippers, before they were called Christians. The prophecy contains a gracious promise, that, however terrible might be the final catastrophe in which the unbelievers should perish, provision would be made for the safety of those who believed in the Messiah. And church history records its fulfilment; for, on the approach of the Roman army, the christian inhabitants of Jerusalem took to flight, in compliance with the Saviour's warning, and retiring to Pella, on the eastern side of the river Jordan, found there a safe asylum, while the devoted city was being besieged and destroyed. — οὐ μὲν ἀλλὰ καὶ τοῦ λαοῦ τῆς ἐν Ἱεροσολύμοις ἐκκλησίας, κατά τινα χρησμὸν τοῖς αὐτόθι δοκίμοις δι᾽ ἀποκαλύψεως δοθέντα πρὸ τοῦ πολέμου, μεταναστῆναι τῆς πόλεως, καί τινα τῆς περαίας πόλιν οἰκεῖν κεκελευσμένον. Πέλλαν αὐτὴν ὀνομάζουσιν· ἐν ᾗ τῶν εἰς Χριστὸν πεπιστευκότων ἀπὸ τῆς Ἱερουσαλὴμ μετῳκισμένων, κ. τ. λ. Euseb. lib. iii. cap. v. פְּלֵיטָה, is a collective noun, signifying *those who have escaped;* in other words, ἡ ἐν Ἱεροσολύμοις ἐκκλησία, " the church in Jerusalem," as Eusebius phrases it in the above quotation, who not only made their escape from the impending calamity, but from the " untoward generation " to which they had belonged, Acts ii. 40; Is. iv. 3; so that the meaning is, not that there should continue to be deliverance for those who remained in Zion and Jerusalem during the infliction of the punishment, but that those who resided there should make their escape from it, having previously been delivered from the condition of those on whom it was inflicted. The words בַּאֲשֶׁר אָמַר יְהוָה, refer to the promise just made. וּבַשְּׂרִידִים, *together with those that have been left,*

from שָׂרַד, Arab. شرد, *aufugit, vagatusque fuit,* شارد, and شرود, *aufugiens,* to flee, make one's escape, survive a slaughter, or any other calamity. The reference seems not to be to converted Gentiles, as Schmidius, Michaelis, Holzhausen, and others interpret, but to those Jews who did not perish in the national judgments, but were called into the church of Christ. קָרָא, as employed in the last clause of the verse, signifies *to call,* in the sense of effectually prevailing upon any one to choose and participate in the blessings of the divine kingdom. Comp. Καλέω, as used by Paul, Rom. viii. 28, 30, ix. 24; 1 Thess. ii. 12. קֹרֵא, the Participle here denotes the future.

CHAPTER III.

IN this chapter the prophet returns from the parenthetic view which he had exhibited of the commencement of the Christian dispensation, and the overthrow of the Jewish polity, to deliver predictions respecting events that were to transpire subsequent to the Babylonish captivity, and fill up the space which should intervene between the restoration of the Jews, and the first advent of Christ. He announces the judgment to be holden on their enemies after the return to Judea, 1, 2; specifies the reasons why they were to be punished, and expressly mentions by name the neighboring nations of Tyre, Sidon and Philistia, 3-6; promises the restoration of those Jews whom these states had sold into slavery, while they are threatened with slavery in return, 7, 8; summons the nations to engage in the wars in which they were to be destroyed, 9-15; shows, that since these convulsions were brought about by the providence of Jehovah, whose earthly throne was at Jerusalem, his people had no ground for alarm, and would experience his protection, 16, 17; predicts times of great prosperity to them, 18; and concludes with special denunciations against Egypt and Idumea, with whose fate is placed in striking contrast the protracted existence of the Jewish polity, 19-21.

1 FOR, behold! in those days, and at that time,
When I shall reverse the captivity of Judah and Jerusalem,
2 I will gather all the nations,
And bring them down into the valley of Jehoshaphat,
And will plead with them there,

1, 2. בַּיָּמִים הָהֵמָּה וּבָעֵת הַהִיא, is a double mode of expression, employed to give greater prominence to the period. That the "days and time" here specified, are not identical with the period spoken of in the last five verses of the preceding chapter, is evident from their being connected by the relative conjunction אֲשֶׁר, with the following words, which relate to the restoration of the Jewish state. כִּי, at the beginning of the verse, is properly rendered *for*, and refers back to chap. ii. 21-27, in which verses times of great temporal prosperity are promised to the Jews. With this prosperity was intimately connected the punishment of the nations by which they had been afflicted; and, accordingly, such punishment forms the subject of the present chapter. Instead of אָשׁוּב, the Keri substitutes אָשִׁיב, in which it is supported by twenty-five of Kennicott's MSS.; but the frequent occurrence of שׁוּב שְׁבוּת, in which the Kal form is to be taken causatively, shows that there was no necessity for the emendation. See Ps. xiv. 7, liii. 7, cxxvi. 7; Is. lii. 8. Some interpret the phrase of a general restoration to circumstances of prosperity, without any reference to previous circumstances of actual captivity, as in the case of Job xlii. 10; but considering its common application to the return from Babylon, and the express mention of the scattering of the nation among the heathen, ver. 2, it seems more natural to refer it to the same event in this place. That the restoration of the Jews from their present dispersion is meant, and that the judgments to be inflicted on the nations are those which are predicted, Rev. xvi. 14, 16, is rendered impossible

On account of my people, and Israel mine inheritance,
Whom they have scattered among the nations,
And have divided my land;
3 And have cast lots for my people,
And given a boy for an harlot,
And sold a girl for wine,
That they might drink.
4 And truly, what are ye to me, O Tyre and Zidon!

by the introduction of the Tyrians, Sidonians, Philistines, etc. verses 4 and 19, since these states all received their punishment prior to the advent of Christ. By עֵמֶק יְהוֹשָׁפָט, *the valley of Jehoshaphat,* some understand the narrow valley through which the brook Kedron flows, between the city of Jerusalem and the mount of Olives. To this valley or glen, in which is the celebrated burying-place of the Jews, the Rabbins have appropriated the name, and maintain, that in it the final judgment of the world is to be held; — a conceit in which they have been followed by many Christian writers, as well as by the Mohammedans. Others suppose it to be a designation of the valley, otherwise called עֵמֶק בְּרָכָה, *the valley of blessing,* 2 Chron. xx. 26; but as neither of these localities at all comport with the magnitude of the subject treated of by the prophet, we have no alternative but that of considering the words, not as constituting a proper name, or the name of any specific locality, but as symbolical in their import, and designed to characterize the theatre of the bloody wars that took place after the Babylonish captivity, by which the hostile nations contiguous to Judea had signal vengeance inflicted upon them. They literally signify, *the valley where Jehovah judgeth,* and mean the scene of divine judgments. The term *valley* appears to have been selected on account of such locality being mentioned in Scripture as the usual theatre of military conflict. This view of the subject is supported by the Targ. in which the words are not retained, but translated מֵישַׁר פְּלֻג דִּינָא, *the plain of the distribution of judgment,* and by the translation of Theodot. τὴν

χώραν τῆς κρίσεως. The nations to be punished are restricted, ver. 2, to such as should have scattered the Jews, and occupied their land. Comp. chap. ii. 17.

3. The Jews were frequently treated in the most ignominious manner by their enemies. Such conduct is here affectingly set forth. That it was customary to cast lots for those who were taken captive, see Obad. ver. 11; Nah. iii. 10. The giving of a boy for a whore, does not mean the exchange of the one for the other, but the payment of the captive for an act of sensual indulgence; just as the selling of a girl for wine, means giving her in compensation for a draught of it. Comp. Gen. xxxviii. 17; comp. also Deut. xxii. 18, where אֶתְנַן זוֹנָה, *the hire of a whore,* is coupled with מְחִיר כֶּלֶב, *the price of a dog;* and the Arabic proverb, ابن زانية بزيت, *the son of a whore hired with oil.* Meid. xciv. Charden mentions that when the Tartars came into Poland, they carried off all the children they could, and, finding at length that they were not redeemed, sold them at the low price of a crown. In Mingrelia, he adds, they sell them for provisions, and for wine.

4. Among the nations bordering on the country of the Jews, which had rendered themselves particularly obnoxious to the divine wrath, were those on the west, for which see on Is. xxiii. and xiv. 28. וְגַם מָה אַתֶּם לִי, *and truly what are ye to me?* Think ye that I make any account of you? or that ye can successfully oppose yourselves to me? The interrogation is altogether different in meaning, as it is in form, from the idiom

And all the coasts of Philistia?
Will ye retaliate upon me?
If, indeed, ye retaliate upon me,
Speedily and swiftly I will bring your retaliation
Back upon your own head.

5 Because ye have taken away my silver and my gold;
And my goodly objects of delight
Ye have carried into your temples;

6 And have sold the sons of Judah and the sons of Jerusalem
To the sons of the Javanites,
That they might be removed far from their own border.

7 Behold! I will arouse them from the place
Whither ye have sold them;

מַה־לִּי וָלָכֶם, *what have we in common?* with which Kimchi compares it. גְּלִילוֹת, *circuits, districts.* Comp. Josh. xiii. 2, where the word is rendered *coasts* in our version. They were properly provinces, of which there were five in number, each governed by a סֶרֶן, *prince,* or *lord.* כֹּל, *all,* before גְּלִילוֹת, expresses contempt. אִם, is not here correlate with ה, in הַגְּמוּל, but puts a fresh case for the sake of argument. The case supposed, however, was true in fact. The interrogative ה assumes here the form of the article, as in several other places. See on Amos v. 25. גָּמַל, signifies to *do good* or *evil* to any one; then to *recompense* him, either with good or evil; to *reward, retaliate.* The meaning here seems to be, that if these bordering states, taking advantage of certain untoward circumstances in the history of the Jews, attempted to revenge the victories gained over them by the latter, they should be dealt with in the way of divine retaliation. Jehovah here speaks of what was done to his people as done to himself. Comp. Zech. ii. 8; Matt. xxv. 40. קַל מְהֵרָה, is an asyndeton. Comp. Is. v. 26, where the order of the words is reversed.

5. As in the preceding verse God had identified himself with his people, so here he speaks of their property as his. Some suppose the precious vessels belonging to the temple to be intended by מַחֲמַדַּי הַטֹּבִים, but the articles of private property most highly esteemed by the Jews are more probably meant; since it does not appear that ever the enemies specified by Joel plundered the temple at Jerusalem, though express mention is made of the plunder of the royal palace by the Philistines, etc., 2 Chron. xxi. 17. Comp. Hos. xiii. 15; 2 Chron. xxxvi. 19. It was customary to hang up or deposit in the idolatrous temples, as presents dedicated to the gods, certain portions of the spoils taken in war. Arrian, ii. 24. Curtius, iv. 2.

6. בְּנֵי הַיְּוָנִים, *the sons of the Javanites,* i. e. the Grecians. Comp. υἷες Ἀχαιῶν, of Homer; and see on Is. lxvi. 19. Credner, Hitzig, and some others, think that the prophet refers to Javanites of Arabia Felix, mentioned Ezek. xxvii. 19; but the reasons they adduce in favor of their opinion are insufficient to establish the point. In Ezek. xxvii. 13, Javan is mentioned, along with Tubal and Meshech, as trading in the persons of men with the merchants of Tyre. Slavery formed an important article of Phoenician commerce, and equally so of that carried on by the Greeks, to whom the former might easily convey the Jewish captives. So famous did the island of Delos become as a slave mart, that sometimes 10,000 were bought and sold in a single day.

7, 8. שְׁבָאִים, *Sabeans;* Pococke's Arab. MSS. اهل اليمن, *the people of Jemen.*

And bring back your retaliation
Upon your own head;
8 I will sell your sons and your daughters
Into the hand of the sons of Judah,
And they shall sell them to the Sabeans, to a distant nation;
For Jehovah hath spoken it.
9 Proclaim ye this among the nations;
Prepare war; rouse the mighty;
Let all the warriors approach; let them come up.
10 Beat your coulters into swords,
And your pruning-hooks into spears;
Let the feeble say, I am mighty.
11 Hasten and come, all ye nations around,

See on Is. lx. 6. As the Sabeans traded with India, it is not improbable that רָחוֹק, *distant*, may be designed to include that part of the East; though it is said of the Queen of Sheba, that she came ἐκ τῶν περάτων τῆς γῆς, Matt. xi. 42. This prophecy was fulfilled before and during the rule of the Maccabees, when the Jewish affairs were in so flourishing a state, and the Phœnician and Philistine powers were reduced by the Persian arms under Artaxerxes Mnemon, Darius Ochus, and especially Alexander and his successors. On the capture of Tyre by the Grecian monarch, 13,000 of the inhabitants were sold into slavery. When he took Gaza also, he put 10,000 of the citizens to death, and sold the rest, with the women and children, for slaves. Favorable, on the other hand, as he was to the Jews, there can be no doubt that he ordered the liberation of such of them as were captives in Greece.

9. זֹאת, *this*, refers to what immediately follows: the assembling of the different nations, in order to engage in the wars in which, in succession, they were, as political states, to be subdued and perish. קַדְּשׁוּ, is not simply to *prepare*, as Kimchi explains it, but to prepare by the use of religious rites and ceremonies, such as the heathen employed when they undertook a military enterprise.

10. Here a state of things is presented to view, directly the opposite of what was to exist in the days of the Messiah, Is. ii. 4; Micah iv. 3. Such was to be the extent of the conflict, that, in the lack of a sufficient number of arms, the ordinary implements of husbandry would be converted into weapons.

"—— squalent abductis arva colonis,
Et curvæ rigidum falces conflantur in ensem."
Virgil. Georg. i. 507.

"Sarcula cessabant, versique in pila ligones,
Factaque de rastri pondere cassis erat."
Ovid. Fast. i. 699.

11. עושו, a ἅπαξ λεγ. in all probability the same in signification with חושו, *to hasten*. The ancient versions follow the LXX., who render, συναθροίζεσθε. Arab. عَاشَ, *vitam duxit, vixit*; hence the idea of *liveliness, activity, agility*, etc. נְחַת, is the Imperative in Hiphil of נָחַת, *to descend*, go or come down. The place whither, is the scene of warfare, the valley of Jehoshaphat, implied in יְהוָה, which with the ה is frequently the same in signification with שָׁם. The abrupt transition to Jehovah has a powerful effect. Whatever might be the individual views of those engaged in the conflict, they were the instruments of Divine

And gather yourselves together;
Thither cause thy mighty ones to come down, O Jehovah!
12 Let the nations be roused, let them come up
To the valley of Jehoshaphat;
For there I will sit to judge all the nations around.
13 Put ye in the sickle, for the harvest is ripe:
Come, descend, for the wine-press is full,
The vats run over;
For their wickedness is great.
14 Multitudes! multitudes
In the valley of decision!
For the day of Jehovah is near,

wrath, and are on this account called the "mighty ones" of Jehovah. Comp. Is. x. 5–7.

12. To give prominence to the interest which God had in what was to take place, the metaphor is here changed into that of a judicial process, in which he acts as judge, and gives a just decision against the enemies of his people. For עֵמֶק יְהוֹשָׁפָט, see on ver. 2. Here, as in that verse, the nations to be punished were those מִסָּבִיב, *circumjacent* to Judea.

13. The prophet now employs metaphors taken from the harvest and the vintage, which strikingly express the havoc and destruction effected by war: the one denoting the slaughter or cutting down of armies, and the other the effusion of their blood. The same images are similarly employed, Is. xvii. 5, 6, lxiii. 2; Lam. i. 15; and especially Rev. xiv. 14–20. מַגָּל, *a sickle*, Arab. مِنْجَل, Syr. ܡܓܠܐ. In Arab. the root, نَجَلَ signifies *to cut*. The sickles of the East, as represented on Egyptian monuments, pretty much resembled ours, only some of them were smaller, and had more the appearance of a knife hooked at the end. רְדוּ, from יָרַד, *to descend*, some take to be used here in the acceptation of the Arab. رَدَى, *calcavit*. Thus the LXX. πατεῖτε. But as in

order to tread the grapes it was necessary to *go down* into the wine-press, it seems better to abide by the ordinary signification of the Hebrew verb, and to consider the action of treading to be implied, rather than expressed. At the close of the verse the metaphor is dropped, and the cause of the thing signified is boldly presented to view.

14. הֲמוֹנִים הֲמוֹנִים, *multitudes, multitudes*, a Hebraism for *immense multitudes*. This rendering is preferable to that of *tumults*. In the preceding verses, the nations are called upon to assemble, and here the prophet, beholding them congregated in obedience to the summons, breaks out into an appropriate exclamation in regard to their number. חָרוּץ, Piscator, the Geneva English, Calvin, Leo Juda, Michaelis, Justi, Holzhausen, and Credner, take in the sense of *threshing*. Kimchi, Tanchum, Abulwalid, Newcome, and some others, render *excision;* but the LXX. Theodot. Syr. Targ. Theodoret, Dathe, Rosenmüller, Gesenius, Hitzig, Maurer, Ewald, and Fürst, translate the word by *decision* or *judgment*, which seems more in keeping with the name of the valley, and the idea of a judicial process, set forth ver. 12. Comp. for the acceptation *to determine, decide,* as attaching to the verb חָרַץ, 1 Kings xx. 40; Is. x. 22. The meaning is the decision or doom of the nations to which the prophecy refers. The repetition of עֵמֶק הֶחָרוּץ, heightens the effect.

In the valley of decision.
15 The sun and the moon shall be darkened,
And the stars shall withdraw their shine.
16 For Jehovah shall roar out of Zion,
And utter his voice from Jerusalem,
And the heavens and the earth shall shake;
But Jehovah is a refuge for his people,
A stronghold for the sons of Israel.
17 And ye shall know that I Jehovah am your God,
Dwelling in Zion, my holy mountain;
Then shall Jerusalem be holy;
Foreigners shall invade her no more.
18 And it shall come to pass in that day,
That the mountains shall drop new wine,
And the hills shall flow with milk,

15. A figurative mode of representing the removal of the political rulers of the world. Comp. chap. ii. 10, 31.

16. These words, as Chandler properly remarks, seem to intimate very plainly, that at least part of the judgments here threatened to be exerted upon the neighboring nations, should be executed by the Jews themselves. They doubtless refer to the victories obtained by Mattathias, and his sons the Maccabeans. As king of the Jewish nation, Jehovah had his residence in Jerusalem, whence he caused his power to be exerted to the discomfiture of his enemies, and the deliverance and protection of his people. Comp. Ps. xviii. 13; Hab. iii. 10, 11. שָׁאַג, to roar, is properly used of the lion, but is metaphorically applied to God, to express the terrible majesty with which he encounters his foes. Comp. Jer. xxv. 30; Amos i. 2. iii. 8.

17. יָדַע, is here, as in Is. lii. 6. lx. 16; Hos. ii. 20, to be taken in the acceptation of *experiencing*, knowing by experimental proofs of the divine kindness. This the Jews did in the deliverances effected on their behalf, after the return from the captivity, especially on the death of Antiochus Epiphanes, and in the enjoyment of their national and religious privileges, till the termination of their polity. That the strong language at the close of the verse does not imply a state of immunity from invasion, to which there was absolutely to be no end, will appear on comparing Is. lii. 1, and Nah. i. 15. See my note on the former of these passages. From the death of Antiochus till the coming of the Messiah, no hostile power should take possession of the holy city. To express the perfect immunity from idolatry, by which Jerusalem should be characterized, קֹדֶשׁ, *holiness* in the abstract, is used. Comp. Obad. 17. By זָרִים, *strangers*, or *barbarians*, foreign enemies are meant.

18. A splendid figurative representation of the extraordinary prosperity to be accorded to the Jewish people after the destruction of their enemies.

Thus Tanchum in Pococke, استعارة, لكثرة الخصب والبركات, "metaphorical language, denoting abundance of plenty and blessings." Comp. Is. xxx. 23-25, xliv. 3, and especially Amos ix. 13.

" Flumina jam lactis, jam flumina nectaris ibant,
Flavaque de viridi stillabant ilice mella."
Ovid. Metam. i. 111.

And all the channels of Judah shall flow with water,
And a fountain shall go forth from the house of Jehovah,
And water the valley of Acacias.
19 Egypt shall become desolate,
And Edom a desolate wilderness,
For the violence done to the sons of Judah,
Because they shed innocent blood in their land.
20 But Judah shall be inhabited for ever,
And Jerusalem to successive generations.
21 And I will regard their blood as innocent,

Καὶ τότε δὴ χαρὰν μεγάλην θεὸς ἀν-
δράσι δώσει
Καὶ γὰρ γῆ καὶ δένδρα καὶ ἄσπετα
θρέμματα γαίης
Δώσουσιν καρπὸν τὸν ἀληθινὸν ἀνθρώ-
ποισι
Οἴνου καὶ μέλιτος γλυκέως, λευκοῦ τε
γάλακτος
Καὶ σίτου, ὅπερ ἔστι βροτοῖς κάλλιστον
ἁπάντων.
　　　　　　　　　　　　Sibyl. Orac.

הַשִּׁטִּים נַחַל, *the valley of Shittim*, i. e.
Acacias. There was a place of this name
in the country of Moab, Num. xxv. 1,
xxxiii. 49; Josh. ii. 1; but most interpreters think that the valley is meant
through which the Kidron flows to the
Dead Sea. Consistency of interpretation
requires us to understand this part of
the verse figuratively of the most desert
and arid spots, such as the acacia is fond
of. Fertility was to go forth from the
presence of Jehovah into the whole land.
Viewed in this light, there is no incongruity in representing the water as extending even across the Jordan, however
impossible it might be as a physical phenomenon. Comp. Ezek. xlvii. 1–12;
Zech. xiv. 8.

19. The wrongs done to the Jews
by the Egyptians and Idumeans, which
the prophet here declares were to be
avenged, were those committed at different times after the captivity. Palestine suffered greatly during the wars
between the Syrian and Egyptian kings,
especially in the reign of Ptolemy Epiphanes, when they exposed themselves

to the indignation of that king by
siding with Antiochus the Great. In
the time of Cleopatra also, her son Lathyrus gained a victory over the army
of Alexander Janneus, in which the Jews
lost upwards of thirty thousand men;
and who, to increase the terror of his
name, massacred the women and children,
cut their bodies in pieces, and boiled the
flesh. The Idumeans, though less formidable, never omitted any favorable
opportunity that offered of showing their
hostility to the Jews. The condition to
which both these countries were speedily
reduced, and in which they have remained to the present day, verifies the
prediction here delivered. Instead of
לִשְׁמָמָה, a number of MSS. exhibit the
synonymous לְשַׁמָּה. — יְהוּדָה בְּנֵי חֲמַס,
the violence of the sons of Judah, is the
Genitive of object, meaning the violence
done *to* them. Comp. Obad. 10. בָּקִיא is
spelt נָקִיא here and Jonah i. 14; but in
the present text, nine of Kennicott's
MSS. and four of De Rossi's, with eight
more originally, read נָקִי. Among these
are four Spanish MSS., two of which
De Rossi characterizes as *accuratissimi*.
The pronominal affix in אַרְצָם, refers to
the Jews spoken of immediately before.
20. תֵּשֵׁב, is used passively, as in Is.
xiii. 20. עוֹלָם and וָדוֹר דּוֹר, are to be
limited by the subject to which they are
predicated. Thus the state of desolation
during the seventy years' captivity in
Babylon, is said to be עוֹלָם, *for ever*,
Jer. xviii. 16.
21. In the words דָּמָם נִקֵּיתִי לֹא וְנִקֵּיתִי,

Which I have not regarded as innocent;
And Jehovah shall dwell in Zion.

there is an ellipsis of אֶת, after דָּמָם, the affix in which refers to the Jews, not to their enemies. Almost all the interpreters have stumbled at נִקֵּתִי, the verb here employed, but they have generally got over the difficulty, by giving to it the signification of נָקַמְתִּי, *I have avenged* — a signification which nowhere attaches to it in the Hebrew Bible. For the different explanations see Pocoke. נקה, Arab. نقى, *purus, mundus fuit*, ii. and iv. *mundavit*. Syr. in Pael, *sacrificavit, libavit*. In Niph. the Heb. verb. signifies to be morally pure, to be free from punishment; in Piel, as here, *to regard, pronounce*, or *treat as innocent, to pardon*. The words were doubtless suggested by דָּם נָקִיא in the preceding verse, and are to be rendered, *I will regard their blood as innocent, which I have not regarded as innocent*; i. e. I will pardon those whom I have treated as guilty. My people, whom I have punished on account of their apostasies, I will henceforth regard with favor and love. The affix ם in דָּמָם, corresponds to the same in אֶרֶץ, ver. 19. — יֹשֵׁב, the Participle used with futurity of signification.

AMOS.

PREFACE.

Amos, (Heb. עָמוֹס, *burden*, a word purely Hebrew, and not of Egyptian origin, and the same as Amasis or Amosis, as Gesenius conjectures,) was, as we learn from the inscription, a native of Tekoah, a small town in the tribe of Judah, at the distance of about twelve miles south-east of Jerusalem. The country round being sandy and barren, was destitute of cultivation, and fit only to be occupied by those addicted to pastoral life. Among these our prophet was originally found; and, though it was counted no disgrace in ancient times, any more than it is at the present day in Arabia, to follow this occupation, kings themselves being found in it, (2 Kings iii. 4,) yet there is no reason to suppose that Amos belonged to a family of rank or influence, but the contrary. No mention is made of his father; but too much stress is not to be laid upon this circumstance. That he had been in poor circumstances, however, appears from the statement made chap. vii. 14; from which also it is incontrovertible, that no change of circumstances intervened, which may be supposed to have been more favorable to mental culture, but that he was called at once to exchange the life of a shepherd for that of a prophet.

Though a native of the kingdom of Judah, he discharged the functions of his office in that of Israel — a fact which is to be accounted for, not, as Bertholdt conjectures, on the ground of some personal relations, but by an express Divine commission to occupy it as the scene of his labors. Eichhorn ingeniously supposes the reasons of his selection to have been, that the appearance of a foreign prophet was much more calculated to excite attention than that of a native, and that such a prophet was more likely to command respect than any belonging to a kingdom in which impostors and fanatics abounded.

The time at which he prophesied is stated in general terms, chap. i. 1, to have been in the reigns of Uzziah, king of Judah, and Jeroboam II., king of Israel, the former of whom reigned B. C. 811–759, and the latter B. C. 825–784, but in which of these years he was called to the office, and how long he continued to exercise it, we are not told. Even if any dependence could be placed upon the Jewish tradition, Joseph. Antiq. ix. 10, 4, and Jerome on Amos i. 1, that the earthquake mentioned here, and Zech. xiv. 5, took place when Uzziah attempted to usurp the sacerdotal functions, we should still be unable to fix the exact date, since it is uncertain in what year the attempt was made.

That he was contemporary with Hosea, appears not only from the dates assigned in both their books, but from the identical state of affairs in the kingdom of the ten tribes, which they so graphically describe. Whether he flourished also in the days of Isaiah and Micah cannot be determined.

As we have already found, from the prophecy of Hosea, idolatry, with its concomitant evils, effeminacy, dissoluteness, and immoralities of every description, reigned with uncontrolled sway among the Israelites in the reign of Jeroboam the son of Joash. It is chiefly against these evils that the denunciations of Amos are directed.

The book may properly be divided into three parts: First, sentences pronounced against the Syrians, the Philistines, the Phœnicians, the Edomites, the Ammonites, the Moabites, the Jews, and the Israelites, chapters i. and ii. Second, special discourses delivered against Israel, chapters iii.–vi. Third, visions, partly of a consolatory, and partly of a comminatory nature, in which reference is had both to the times that were to pass over the ten tribes, previous to the coming of the Messiah, and to what was to take place under his reign, chapters vii.–ix.

In point of style, Amos holds no mean place among the prophets. The declaration of Jerome, that he was *imperitus sermonie*, has not been justified by modern critics. On the contrary, it is universally allowed that, though destitute of sublimity, he is distinguished for perspicuity and regularity, embellishment and elegance, energy and fulness. His images are mostly original, and taken from the natural scenery with which he was familiar; his rhythmus is smooth and flowing; And his parallelisms are in a high degree natural and complete. In description, he is for the most part special and local; he excels in the minuteness of his groupings, while the general vividness of his manner imparts a more intense interest to all that he delivers. In some few instances, as in chapters iv. vi. and vii. the language approaches more to the prose style, or is entirely that of narrative.

From chap. vii. 10–13, it appears that the scene of his ministry was Bethel. Whether he left that place in consequence of the interdict of Amaziah, the priest, we know not. According to Pseudo-Epiphanius, he afterwards returned to his native place, where he died, and was buried with his fathers; but no dependence can be placed on the statement.

CHAPTER I.

AFTER a chronological and general introduction, ver. 1, 2, this chapter contains a heavy charge, accompanied with denunciations, against the Syrians of Damascus, 3–5; the Philistines, 6–8; the Phœnicians, 9, 10; the Idumeans, 11, 12; and the Ammonites, 13–15.

---

1 THE words of Amos, who was among the shepherds of Tekoah, which he saw concerning Israel, in the days of Uzziah, king of Judah, and in the days of Jeroboam, the son of Joash, king of Israel, two years before the earthquake.

1. With the exception of the book of Jeremiah, that of Amos is the only one of the prophets commencing with דִּבְרֵי־, "The words of —." Comp. however, Hag. i. 12. The meaning is, the subjects or matters of oracular communication which he was employed by the prophetic Spirit to deliver, and which were now, under the influence of the same Spirit, committed to writing. Their divine origin is clearly determined by what is added, אֲשֶׁר חָזָה, "which he saw," *i. e.* which were supernaturally presented to his mental vision. See on Is. i. 1. The preposition בְּ in בַּנֹּקְדִים, does not denote distinction, intimating that Amos was greater in point of wealth or respectability than the rest of the shepherds, as Kimchi would have it, but simply that he was of their number; he belonged to their condition of life, and followed their occupation. The phrase הָיָה בְּרֹעִים expresses, in fact, nothing more than הָיָה רֹעֶה. Comp. for similar usage 1 Sam. xix. 24; Ps. cxviii. 7; and the Arabic وَمَا نَحْنُ بِعَالِينَ. נֹקֵד occurs only here, and 2 Kings iii. 4. By some it is supposed to denote the shepherd or keeper of a species of sheep and goats, distinguished by certain marks, and to be derived from נָקַד, *to prick*, or *mark with punctures*, and so to distinguish by such marks. By others, it is more properly referred for illustration to the Arab. نَقَدٌ, *genus ovium deforme et brevipes,* نَقَادٌ, *ovium,* نَنَلٌ, *appellatarum pastor*. From the disesteem in which such animals were held, arose the proverb, أَذَلَّ مِنَ النَّقَدِ, *more vile than the* NYKAD. At the same time, as their wool was valuable, they were kept in great numbers. In both instances in which the term occurs, it seems to be used in a more general acceptation. Aq. ἐν ποιμνοτρόφοις; Symm. and the fifth edit. ἐν τοῖς ποιμέσιν. The explanation of Cyril is not inept: Ἀμῶς γέγονεν αἰπόλος ἀνὴρ καὶ ποιμενικοῖς ἔθεσί τε δὲ νόμοις ἐντεθραμμένος. The LXX. ἐν Ἀκκαρείμ, mistaking it for the name of a place where they supposed the prophet to have been when he received his Divine

2 And he said:
Jehovah roareth from Zion,
And uttereth his voice from Jerusalem;
The pastures of the shepherds mourn,
And the summit of Carmel withereth.
3 Thus saith Jehovah:
For three transgressions of Damascus,

communications. The ruins of תְּקוֹעַ Arab. تَقُوع, Tekú' a, Dr. Robinson found covering an extent of four or five acres on an elevated hill, not steep, but broad at the top, about two hours distant from Bethlehem. On approaching it, he describes the landscape as rocky and sterile, yet rich in pasturage, as was testified by the multitude of the flocks. (Palestine, ii. pp. 181, 182.) The surrounding region, especially that in the direction of the Dead Sea, is called מִדְבַּר תְּקוֹעַ, 2 Chron. xx. 20, and ἡ ἔρημος Θεκωέ, 1 Macc. ix. 33. In this pasturing district, our prophet originally tended his flocks, and collected the sycamore figs. For the dates here specified, see the Introduction. The prophecy is specially directed against Israel, or the kingdom of the ten tribes, though that of Judah, and likewise several foreign states, are also expressly denounced. We possess no data by which to fix the year in which the earthquake, here mentioned, occurred. Zechariah, chap. xiv. 5, refers to it as having happened in the days of Uzziah, but he does not specify the year. According to Josephus, it took place on occasion of the invasion of the sacerdotal office by that monarch, Antiq. ix. 10, 4. As earthquakes are by no means uncommon at Palestine, it must have been unusually severe to entitle it to the speciality of reference here employed. Some interpret רעשׁ of a civil commotion, but without sufficient ground, as the connection Zech. xiv. 4, 5, shows.

2. Zion, or Jerusalem, being the central point of the theocracy, was the special residence of Jehovah, to whom the judgments afterwards denounced, are, in highly figurative language, immediately referred. שָׁאַג, commonly employed to express the roaring of the lion, is here used to set forth the awful character of those judgments. Dathe, stumbling at the boldness of the figure, renders, Jova ex Zione dira pronunciat; thereby destroying the poetical force of the language. Comp. Jer. xxv. 30; Job xxxvii. 4. י in אָבְלוּ, marks the apodosis. For נְאוֹת הָרֹעִים, comp. נְאוֹת דֶּשֶׁא, Ps. xxiii. 2. כַּרְמֶל, Michaelis, Justi, and others take to be the Carmel, now called by the Arabs كَرْمُل, Kurmul, which lies near Yutta, or Juttah, between two and three hours to the south of Hebron; but though the mountainous region about that place was more in the proximity of the prophet, yet the established scripture reference to the fertility of the celebrated Mount Carmel in the tribe of Asher seems to entitle the latter to the preference. In fact, there does not appear to be any mountain deserving the name in the hill country of Judah. The hill of Maon, which is close by, is not less than two hundred feet higher than the site of the ruins of the castle of Kurmul. See Robinson, ut sup. pp. 193-200. Besides the identical phrase, רֹאשׁ הַכַּרְמֶל, the summit of Carmel, which again occurs chap. ix. 3, in immediate connection with the sea, is employed in application to the western Carmel, 1 Kings xviii. 42.

3. Here begins a series of minatory predictions against different states, which extends to chap. ii. 8, where it merges in a continued denunciation of judgments directed almost exclusively against the Israelites. Instead of proceeding at once to charge the ten tribes with the flagrant evils of which they had been guilty, Amos commences with the Syrians, and after exposing their wicked-

And for four, I will not reverse it ;
Because they threshed Gilead with sledges of iron ;
4 But I will send a fire into the house of Hazael,
And it shall devour the palaces of Benhadad.

ness, and that of the Philistines, the Phœnicians, the Edomites, the Ammonites, the Moabites, and the Jews, he comes to his proper subject, on which he dwells throughout the rest of the book. Having roused the indignation of those among whom he prophesied against sin as exhibited in others, he charges it home upon themselves. Each of the eight predictions is ushered in by the solemn אָמַר יְהֹוָה כֹּה, *thus saith Jehovah ;* and consists in part, in a repetition of the same symmetrical stanzas, with an intermixture of matter, varying according to the nature of the subjects treated of. Interpreters differ in regard to the precise meaning of the use made by our prophet of the numerals *three* and *four.* Similar formulæ are frequent in Hebrew. See Exod. xx. 5 ; Job v. 19, xxxiii. 14, 29 ; Prov. xxx. 15, 18, 21; Eccles. xi. 2 ; Is. xvii. 6 ; Mic. v. 4. Comp. the τρὶς καὶ τετράκις of Homer ; the *terque quaterque* of Virgil ; and the *ter et quater* of Horace. The notion, that the two numbers are to be added, so as to bring out the perfect number *seven*, and thus to express the completeness or full measure of the iniquity, is not borne out by Hebrew usage. That the numbers are to be taken literally, as in Prov. xxx. where there is an enumeration of each of the particulars, is equally out of the question ; the specification of the prophet being, in each case, limited to a single act of wickedness. Nor can the construction be admitted, I have not punished Damascus, etc. on account of three transgressions, but on account of a fourth I will punish her ; since לֹא אֲשִׁיבֶנּוּ, obviously connects with both numerals. The only satisfactory mode of explication is, to regard the phrase as intensively proverbial, and designed to express multiplied or repeated delinquencies, of which the last, as the most atrocious, is uniformly described. The noun to which the suffix in אֲשִׁיבֶנּוּ relates, is not expressed, either before or after the verb, on the principle, that the subject referred to would naturally suggest itself to the mind of the reader. It is anticipative of the sentence of punishment delivered in the following verses. Comp. Num. xxiii. 20, in which is an ellipsis of the noun בְּרָכָה, the idea of which is expressed by the verb. Bp. Lowth proposes to render, "I will not restore it ; " but without sufficient authority. שׁוּב שְׁבוּת, "to reverse the captivity," is the phrase employed in such case. In the phrase, " I will not reverse," is a litotes — the meaning being, "I will certainly execute." For Damascus, which, as the metropolis, is put for the kingdom of Syria, see on Is. xvii. 1. The cruel treatment of the inhabitants of Gilead here referred to, is that to which they were subjected by Hazael and Benhadad, 2 Kings x. 32, 33. xiii. 3-7, both of which princes Amos mentions by name, ver. 4. It consisted in their being thrown before the threshing sledges, the sharp teeth of iron in the rollers of which tore and mangled their bodies. See on Is. xxviii. 27, and comp. 2 Sam. xii. 31, where we find the same punishment inflicted by David, by the law of retaliation. פְּרִיצִים, the LXX. render πρίοσι σιδηροῖς, and add unwarrantably, τὰς ἐν γαστρὶ ἐχούσας ; Symm. and Theod. τροχοῖς σιδηροῖς. דּוּשׁ, to *thresh*, is the very term used in the history of the transaction, 2 Kings xiii. 7. Gilead comprehended the whole of the territory beyond the Jordan, belonging to the tribes of Reuben and Gad, and the half tribe of Manasseh ; and as it bordered on the kingdom of the Syrians, was particularly exposed to their attacks.

4. The Benhadad here mentioned was the son and successor of Hazael, and not the king of that name whom Hazael succeeded. Comp. 2 Kings viii. 7, 15,

5 I will also break the barrier of Damascus,
   And cut off the ruler from the valley of Aven,
   And the sceptre-holder from Beth-Eden,
   And the people of Syria shall go captive to Kir,
   Saith Jehovah.
6 Thus saith Jehovah;
   For three transgressions of Gaza,
   And for four I will not reverse it;
   Because they effected a complete captivity
   To deliver it up to Edom,

with xiii. 3, 24. A similar prediction was afterwards delivered by Jeremiah, chap. xlix. 27, from which and from Hos. viii. 14, it is evident that the phraseology employed by Amos here, and verses 7, 10, 12, 14, chap. ii. 2, 5, is not peculiar to that prophet.

5. According to the testimony of a native, whom Michaelis consulted, there is a most delightful valley called *Oon*, about four hours distant from Damascus, towards the desert, which has given rise to a proverb, "Have you ever been in the valley of Oon?" meaning, Have you ever been in a place of delight? As, however, this has not been confirmed by any traveller, most expositors are inclined to refer the place to what is otherwise called בִּקְעַת הַלְּבָנוֹן, "the valley of Lebanon," or البقاع, *el Buká'a*, between the ridges of Lebanon and Anti-Lebanon. Here are the celebrated ruins of the temple of Baalbec, the Syrian Heliopolis, to which the LXX. have expressly referred אָוֶן, *Aven*, only pronouncing it אוֹן, *On* — ἐκ πεδίου Ὤν; just as they have rendered the latter word when it is employed to denote the city of the same name in Egypt, which was dedicated to the sun. The Hebrews in Palestine, to express their abhorrence of the idolatrous worship practised at both places, pronounced the word אָוֶן, *Aven*, which properly signifies *nothingness, vanity*, and hence an *idol*, on account of its inutility. Comp. with the present passage Ezek. xxx. 17. יֹשֵׁב does not here denote inhabitant, or inhabitants generally, but as the parallel תּוֹמֵךְ שֵׁבֶט, *sceptre-holder*, shows, one who *sits* upon, or occupies a throne — a judge, prince, or king — the person exercising authority in the district specified. For the latter phrase, the σκηπτοῦχος of Homer may be compared. בֵּית עֶדֶן, *Beth-Eden* was, in all probability, the locality in the mountains of Lebanon, which Ptolemy, v. 15, calls Παράδεισος; where the royal family had a palace, and where one of its members usually resided. The name is still given to a delectable valley to the west of Damascus. The *Aram*, or Syria, here referred to, is that of which Damascus was the capital. By קִיר, *Kir*, is meant the river and region of the Cyrus in Iberia, now called *Kur*. See on Is. xxii. 6; and for the accomplishment of the prediction in the successful expedition of Tiglathpileser, king of Assyria, 2 Kings xvi. 9. The version of the LXX. is here extremely faulty, as the slightest compariso with the original will show.

6. עַזָּה, Arab. غزّة, *Ghuzzeh, Gaza*, was the southernmost of the five principal cities of the Philistines, which formed the capitals of so many satrapies of the same names. It was situated at the distance of about an hour's journey from the south-east coast of the Mediterranean, from which it was separated by low hills and tracts of sand. It was built upon a hill, and strongly fortified, as the name imports. The modern city is built partly on the hill, but mostly on the plain below; and according to Dr. Robinson, contains a population of about 15,000 souls.

7 But I will send a fire into the wall of Gaza,
  And it shall devour her palaces;
8 And I will cut off the ruler from Ashdod,
  And the sceptre-holder from Ashkelon:
  And will turn back my hand upon Ekron,
  And the residue of the Philistines shall perish,
  Saith the Lord Jehovah.
9   Thus saith Jehovah :
  For three transgressions of Tyre,

It must have been a place of high antiquity, for its name occurs in the genealogical table, Gen. x.; and it occupied so commanding a position, that it formed the key to Palestine on the south. It stands here by synecdoche for the whole of Philistia. By גָּלוּת שְׁלֵמָה, we are neither to understand, with the LXX. αἰχμαλωσίαν τοῦ Σαλωμών; nor with Justi, "a holy or pious captivity;" nor with Grotius and Michaelis, *captivitatem pacificam ;* but the *immense number* of captives which were carried away from Judea in the reign of Ahaz, 2 Chron. xxviii. 18. The capture was indiscriminate and universal; none escaped. Comp. for the phrase Jer. xiii. 19. What aggravated the guilt of the Philistines, was that they did not treat the Jews as prisoners of war, but sold them as slaves to the Edomites, who were their bitterest enemies, and would treat them with the utmost cruelty. They were doubtless conveyed to Petra, the great emporium of commerce, and there sold to such as might purchase them. Comp. Joel iii. 4-6.

7. אֵשׁ, *fire*, is here metaphorically used for *war*, in carrying on which, however, it is often employed as one of the most destructive elements. Comp. Num. xxi. 28 ; Is. xxvi. 11.

8. For the meaning of יוֹשֵׁב, see on ver. 5. Three others of the principal cities of the Philistines are now threatened, אַשְׁדּוֹד, *Ashdod*, for which see on Is. xx. 1 ; אַשְׁקְלוֹן, Arab. عسقلان,

Askelon, occupying a strong position on the top of a ridge of rock, which encircles it, and terminates at each end in the

sea, and distant from Gaza about five hours in the direction of NN. E.; and עֶקְרוֹן, *Ekron*, now called by the natives عاقر, *Akir*, the most northerly of the five, and at some distance inland from the line of hills which run along the coast of the Mediterranean. See Dr. Robinson's Palestine, III. 21-26. The reason why *Gath*, the remaining city of the five, is not mentioned, is assigned by Kimchi to be, its having been already subdued by David ; but as it was afterwards occupied both by the Syrians, 2 Kings xii. 17, and the Philistines, 2 Chron. xxvi. 6, it seems more natural to refer its omission to the fact of its reduction by Uzziah, in the days of our prophet, as narrated in the latter of the above passages. It is also omitted Zeph. ii. 4, 5. הֲשִׁיבֹתִי יָדִי עַל, *to turn the hand upon*, means to exert one's power anew, whether in the way of favor or of hostility. Here it is obviously to be taken in the hostile sense. No part of Philistia was to remain unvisited by Divine judgments. Comp. Jer. xlvii. 4; Ezek. xxv. 16. In which of the reductions of the Philistines, the prediction received its fulfilment, we cannot determine. One of these took place during the reign of Uzziah, 2 Chron. xxvi. 6, 7; another in that of Hezekiah, 2 Kings xviii. 8 ; they were afterwards successively reduced by Psammeticus, king of Egypt, by Nebuchadnezzar, by the Persians, by Alexander, and ultimately by the Asmoneans.

9. A similar charge is here brought against the Phœnicians, with the superadded aggravation of a breach of an-

And for four, I will not reverse it;
Because they delivered up a complete captivity to Edom,
And remembered not the covenant of the brethren.
10 But I will send a fire into the wall of Tyre,
And it shall devour her palaces.
11   Thus saith Jehovah:
For three transgressions of Edom,
And for four, I will not reverse it;
Because he pursued his brother with the sword,
And did violence to his pity,
And his anger tore continually,
And he retained his wrath for ever.
12 But I will send a fire into Teman,
And it shall devour the palaces of Bozrah,

cient faith. Comp. Joel iii. 4–6. The בְּרִית אַחִים, *covenant of brethren*, includes the terms of friendship and mutual assistance which were agreed upon between David and Hiram, 2 Sam. v. 11; and afterwards between Solomon and the same monarch, 1 Kings v. See especially ver. 12, (Heb. ver. 26,) where it is expressly stated, that וַיִּכְרְתוּ בְרִית שְׁנֵיהֶם, "they two made a league," or *covenant*.

10. For *Tyre*, and the accomplishment of this prediction, see on Is. xxiii.

11. For *Edom*, and the fulfilment of the prophecy here pronounced against it, see on Is. xxxiv. 5. The guilt of the cruelties exercised by the Idumeans upon the Jews was greatly aggravated by the circumstance of their original relationship, Obad. 10, and the unrelenting perpetual character of their hatred. שִׁחֵת רַחֲמָיו, lit. *to spoil*, or *destroy compassions*; i. e. so to repress all the tender feelings of pity, as to become hardened against objects of distress. Comp. the phrase, שִׁחֵת חָכְמָה, *to destroy wisdom*, Ezek. xxviii. 17. The LXX. Ital. Arab. Döderlein, Dathe, Vater, Justi, and some others, take רַחֲמִים, in the sense of רֶחֶם, *the womb*, and explain it either of pregnant females, or of the fruit of the womb, i. e. children; but the plural is never used in this acceptation. Aq. σπλάγχνα αὐτοῦ; Symm. σπλάγχνα ἴδια. The root

רָחַם, Arab. رحم, Syr. ܪܚܡ, signifies *to love*, in Piel, *to regard with tender affection, to cherish feelings of compassion* towards any one. The ה in שְׁמָרָה, is generally considered to be an instance of a paragogic in the third person, but it is preferable to construe it as the pronominal feminine affix, agreeing with עֶבְרָה in the nominative absolute. The absence of the Mappic forms no objection, as there are several instances of its omission where we might have expected it. The accent on the penultimate favors this construction, being occasioned solely by the absence of the Mappic. The verb, to be taken as a feminine, must be pointed שָׁמְרָה, but this would require עֶבְרָה to be the subject instead of the object, which would be intolerably harsh. Comp. for the sentiment, and an elliptical form of the phraseology, Jer. iii. 5. The Hebrews speak of *keeping* a quality, whether good or bad, when they would express its prolonged or continued exercise. See Neh. ix. 32; Dan. ix. 4.

12. That תֵּימָן, *Teman*, was a city, seems evident from its being mentioned along with בָּצְרָה, *Bozrah*, for which see on Is. xxxiv. 6. Though Jerome speaks of it as a region, he mentions, in his Onomasticon, a town of this name, at the distance of five miles from Petra. On

13 Thus saith Jehovah:
For three transgressions of the sons of Ammon,
And for four, I will not reverse it;
Because they ripped up those who were pregnant in Gilead,
That they might enlarge their border.
14 But I will kindle a fire on the wall of Rabbah,
And it shall devour the palaces thereof;
With a shout in the day of battle,
With a tempest in the day of the storm.

the map of Burckhardt and Grimm, it is placed to the south of Wady Mûsa. It was doubtless the principal place in the district inhabited by the descendants of Teman, one of the grandsons of Esau, Gen. xxxvi. 11, 15, who were celebrated on account of their superior wisdom, Jer. xlix. 7. Comp. Obad. 8, 9, and Baruch iii. 22. Eliphaz, one of Job's friends, was a Temanite. The reason why no mention is made of Sela, or Petra, Credner thinks is to be found in the fact, that it had already been captured by Amaziah, 2 Kings xiv. 7, of whose conquests in that direction advantage was taken by his son Uzziah, ver. 22; 2 Chron. xxvi. 2.

13. בְּנֵי עַמּוֹן, the Ammonites, descendants of Lot, Gen. xix. 3, occupied the territory on the east of the Jordan, between the rivers Jabbok and Arnon, but more in the direction of the Arabian desert. That portion of country which lay along the Jordan, of which they had possessed themselves, originally belonged to the Amorites, which accounts for its being given to the tribe of Gad, Josh. xiii. 25. They frequently annoyed the Hebrews, but were repelled by David and several of his successors. For the sake of plunder, they joined the Chaldeans on their invasion of Judea; and, even after the captivity, they evinced the same hostile disposition. They were severely chastised by Judas Maccabeus, 1 Macc. v. 6, 7. Justin Martyr speaks of them as still a numerous people in his day, 'Ἀμμανιτῶν ἔστι νῦν πολὺ πλῆθος. Dial. cum Tryph. p. 347. Ed. Paris, 1615. The atrocious cruelty here charged upon the Ammonites, appears to have formed no unusual part of the barbarities practised by the ancients in war. Comp. 2 Kings viii. 12, xv. 16; Hos. xiii. 16, (Heb. xiv. 1;) and my note on the last passage. See also 1 Sam. xi. 2. The object of the Ammonites was to effect an utter extermination of the Israelites inhabiting the mountainous regions of Gilead, in order that they might extend their own territory in that direction.

14. רַבָּה, Rabbah, i. e. "the Great," was the metropolis of the country of the Ammonites, the extensive ruins of which have recently been discovered by Seetzen and Burckhardt on the banks of the river Moiet Amman, which empties itself into the Jabbok. The full form of the name was רַבַּת בְּנֵי עַמּוֹן, Deut. iii. 11, by which it was distinguished from Rabbah of Moab, and a city of the same name in the tribe of Judah. It is called Ῥαβαθάμανα by Polybius and Stephen of Byzantium; but it otherwise went among the Greeks by the name of Φιλαδέλφια, which it derived from Ptolemy Philadelphus. It is now known by that of عمان, Amman, the same given to it by Abulfeda in his Tab. Syr. p. 91. By תְּרוּעָה, is meant the tremendous shout which eastern armies give at the commencement of battle, partly to excite their courage, and partly to strike terror into the enemy. Comp. Exod. xxxii. 17; Josh. vi. 5, 20. Thus the Iliad, iii. 1, etc. —

Αὐτὰρ ἐπεὶ κόσμηθεν ἅμ' ἡγεμόνεσσιν ἕκαστοι,
Τρῶες μὲν κλαγγῇ τ', ἐνοπῇ τ' ἴσαν, ὄρνιθες ὥς·
Ἠΰτε περ κλαγγὴ γεράνων, κ. τ. λ.

15 Their king shall go into captivity,
He and his princes together,
Saith Jehovah.

סַ֫עַר, *hurricane*, and סוּפָה, *storm* or *tempest*, mark the resistless force of the onset, and the utterly destructive consequences resulting from it. That they are poetically applied to the warlike operations against Rabbah, is clear from יוֹם סוּפָה, *the day of storm*, being parallel with יוֹם מִלְחָמָה, *the day of battle*.

15. מַלְכָּם, *their king*, the Syr. and Vulg. have understood of *Malcam* or *Milcom*, i. e. Moloch, an idol of the Ammonites and Moabites; but the LXX. and Targ. support the common rendering, which שָׂרָיו, *his princes*, following, would seem absolutely to require. It is true, this term might be taken figuratively to signify priests, as in Is. xliii. 28; and such interpretation might appear to be countenanced by the occurrence of כֹּהֲנָיו

his priests, in the parallel prophecy of Jeremiah, chap. xlix. 3; but the use of שָׂרָיו, *his princes*, immediately after by that prophet, shows that, if the former term be not an interpolation, it denotes the idolatrous priests who were in attendance upon the king, just as the princes were the chiefs and civil officers about the court. Οἱ ἱερεῖς αὐτῶν, which the LXX. have added in Amos, and which is copied in the Syr. and Arab., was probably borrowed from the passage in Jeremiah; or it may have been inserted in the Greek text by some copyist before these other versions were made. The combination of שָׂרִים, *princes*, with שֹׁפֵט, *judge*, chap. ii. 3, confirms the above interpretation.

CHAPTER II.

In this chapter we have the continuation of charges and denunciations against different nations, as the Moabites, 1-3; the Jews, 4, 5; and finally, the Israelites, who were to form the principal objects of the prophet's ministry, 6-8. Amos then proceeds to insist on their ungrateful conduct, notwithstanding the experience which they had had of distinguished favors at the hand of God, 9-13; and the futility of all hopes of escape which they might be led to entertain, 14-16.

---

1 Thus saith Jehovah:
For three transgressions of Moab,
And for four, I will not reverse it;

1 For *Moab*, see on Is. xv. The particular act here charged against the Moabites is nowhere recorded. Michaelis is of opinion, that reference is had to 2 Kings iii. 27; but the prince there spoken of was the son of the king of Moab, and not the future heir to the Idumean throne. The wickedness appears to have consisted in a wanton violation of the sanctity of the tomb, by the disinterment and burning of the royal remains. It was indicative of an enmity which was not satisfied with inflicting every possible injury upon its

Because they calcined the bones of the King of Edom.
2 But I will send a fire into Moab,
And it shall devour the palaces of Kerioth;
And Moab shall die in the tumult,
At the shout, at the sound of the trumpet,
3 I will cut off the judge from the midst thereof,
And kill all the princes thereof with him,
Saith Jehovah.
4 Thus saith Jehovah:
For three transgressions of Judah,
And for four, I will not reverse it;
Because they have despised the law of Jehovah,
And have not kept his statutes;
And their false deities have caused them to err,
After which their fathers walked.
5 But I will send a fire into Judah,
And it shall devour the palaces of Jerusalem.

victim while living, but pursued him even into the regions of the dead. Comp. Is. xxxiii. 12.

2. קְרִיּוֹת, *Kerioth;* LXX. τῶν πόλεων αὐτῶν; Targ. בָּרְכָּא, *the fortress* or *citadel;* in all probability, the chief city, elsewhere called קִיר מוֹאָב, *Kir-Moab,* and here put in the plural, to describe its size, or appearance, as comprehending more than one. Comp. Jer. xlviii. 24, and on Is. xv. 1. שָׁאוֹן, here means the *tumult* of battle. Is. xiii. 4; xvii. 12.

3. From the circumstance that שֹׁפֵט, *judge,* and not מֶלֶךְ, *king,* is selected to describe the chief magistrate of Moab, it has not without reason, been supposed, that, at the time the prophet wrote, or, at least, at the time to which his prophecy refers, a change had taken place in the government of that country; but whether it was occasioned by the extinction of the royal house, or the appointment of a ruler by a foreign power, it is impossible to decide. The reference which some have made to Ps. ii. 10, in proof that judge and king are identical, is not in point; for, though the terms as there used are so far synonymous, that they both designate persons high in office, yet there is an obvious distinction both as it respects the degree of their rank, and the nature of the offices with which they were invested. The connecting of the princes with Moab (שָׂרֶיהָ) and not with the judge (שֹׁפְטוֹ) as in chap. i. 15, goes to confirm the view just given.

4, 5. The charges brought against the Jews differ from any of the preceding, in the crimes which they involve having been committed directly against God, and not against man. They had become weary of his service, abandoned his worship, and addicted themselves to idolatrous practices. Between the synonymes here employed there is this difference of meaning: תּוֹרָה, *law,* stands for the institute of Moses generally, of which the moral code formed the basis; חֻקִּים, *statutes,* for the ceremonial and judicial enactments. By כְּזָבִים, *lies,* idols are meant, and the word is so rendered here in the Vulg. The LXX. have taken the same view of it, rendering it μάταια, *vanities.* Comp. for this acceptation Ps. xl. 5. Idols were so called because their pretensions and oracles were founded on falsehood, and because they deluded with false hopes those who worshipped them. Instead of being weaned from

6   Thus saith Jehovah:
For three transgressions of Israel,
And for four, I will not reverse it;
Because they sold the righteous for money,
And the poor for a pair of sandals:
7 Who pant for the dust of the earth on the head of the poor,
And turn aside the way of the afflicted;
A man and his father go in to the same damsel,
In order to profane my holy name.
8 They stretch themselves upon pledged garments,
Close to every altar;

their attachment to the gods which their ancestors had, at different times, served, the Jews became increasingly addicted to them, and thereby brought upon themselves the punishment inflicted by Nebuchadnezzar.

6. The prophet, having secured the attention of the Israelites by his predictions against those communities which they regarded with feelings of hostility, comes now to his proper subject, which was to charge upon themselves the guilt which, in various ways, they, as a people, had contracted. ישראל, *Israel,* i. e. the Israelites, consisted, after the revolt in the time of Rehoboam, of the ten tribes, whose capital was Samaria, and whose worship, originally that of Jehovah, under the visible image of the golden calves, speedily merged in the basest and most licentious idolatry. מכר, *to sell,* has no reference, as some have thought, to the conduct of a corrupt judge, who for money gives a verdict against the innocent, the term never being used to express any such act; but describes the selling of a person into slavery. They even deprived the poor of their liberty for the most paltry consideration. Comp. chap. viii. 6. נעלים, *sandals,* are greatly inferior in value to shoes, consisting merely of soles of leather or wood, fastened by two straps to the feet, one of which passes over the forepart of the foot, near the great toe, and the other round the ankle.

7. שאף, signifies *to breathe hard, to pant, eagerly to desire,* which well suits the connection, so that there is no necessity, with Houbigant, Newcome, and others, to change the verb into שוף, *to attack, bruise,* etc. The meaning of the prophet is, that the persons whom he describes were so avaricious, that, after having robbed others of their property, and reduced them to a state of poverty, they even begrudged them the small quantity of dust which they had cast on their heads in token of mourning. Comp. 2 Sam. i. 2; Job ii. 12. ב, as in בראש, is elsewhere used in the acceptation of *on* or *upon,* and is here the more appropriately adopted, on account of the more usual preposition על having just been employed. Comp. chap. viii. 4. הטה דרך, *to turn,* or *thrust aside* as *to the way;* i. e. to turn any one out of his right course, into a trackless region, where he can expect nothing but inconvenience, perplexity and danger; here, to render the afflicted still more miserable. From the reference made in the following verse to idolatrous deities and altars, it is most probable that הנערה, *the damsel* here spoken of, was not an ordinary or common strumpet, but one who prostituted herself in honor of Astarte, at one of her shrines. LXX. τὴν αὐτὴν παιδίσκην. Such an act of daring profligacy was the more atrocious from its having been committed in a heathen temple, with the express design, as the prophet states, of doing indignity to Jehovah. See Gesenius, Lex. in נער, A) 2.

8. To retain pledged raiment over night was expressly prohibited by the

And drink the wine of the amerced
In the house of their gods.
9 Yet it was I that destroyed the Amorite before them,
Whose height was as the height of cedars,
And who was strong as the oaks;
I destroyed his fruit above,
And his roots beneath.
10 It was I also that brought you up from the land of Egypt,
And led you in the desert forty years,
To inherit the land of the Amorite.
11 And I raised up of your sons to be prophets,

Mosaic law, Exod. xxii. 26, 27, as it deprived the owner of his covering: to stretch one's self upon it in an idol's temple was a great aggravation of the crime. חֲבֻלִים, *pledged*, lit. *bound*, held in bondage, from חָבַל, *to bind*. Arab. خبل, Syr. ܚܒܠ, *debitum*. It was not unusual for the heathen to sleep near the altars of their gods, that they might obtain communications in dreams; but as it was customary to eat in a recumbent posture, the stretching here referred to would rather seem to have respect to participation in idolatrous feasts, especially as the drinking of wine in the temples is specified in the following line. יֵין עֲנוּשִׁים *the wine of the amerced*, means wine purchased with money exacted by the imposition of fines. בְּבֵית, for בְּבֵית, as frequently. Regardless of the sufferings of those whom they oppressed, the apostate Israelites revelled in sensual indulgences.

9. ו in וְאָנֹכִי, is strongly adversative, and introduces the contrast between the Divine conduct and that of the Israelites. The signal benefits which, as a nation, they had received from Jehovah, ought to have attached them for ever to his service. The conjunction and pronoun are repeated for like effect, verse 10. הָאֱמֹרִי, *the Amorites*, are here taken in a wide sense, as including all the inhabitants of Canaan, on account of their being the largest and most powerful of the nations which occupied that country. Comp. Gen. xv. 16, xlviii. 22. In a more special point of view, they inhabited both sides of the Jordan, and particularly the mountains afterwards possessed by the tribe of Judah. Their gigantic height and extraordinary strength, to which reference is frequently made in the history of the Hebrews, are here beautifully compared to cedars and oaks, the most majestic and sturdy trees of the forest. The Hebrew as well as the profane poets, often compare men to trees. Comp. Ps. xxxvii. 35, xcii. 12–15; Isa. x. 33, 34; Ezek. xvii. 3, xxxi. Sixteen MSS., originally twelve more, and now five; five of the oldest editions, and the Rabboth read מִפְּנֵיכֶם, "before *you*," instead of מִפְּנֵיהֶם, "before *them*," but these authorities, under all the circumstances of the text, are insufficient to warrant an alteration.

10. Jehovah goes back to still earlier, but no less remarkable displays of his kindness to the nation, showing that from the commencement of its history he had been its benefactor. Comp. Jer. ii. 6. עָלָה, *to come* or *go up*, is always used in Hebrew in reference to local or political elevation, and not, as Rosenmüller asserts, to the North. The circumstance that many of the regions or places to which persons are said to have gone up, lay to the north of those from which they came, is purely accidental; whereas the propriety of the use of the term lies in the fact of the mountainous character of the land of Canaan, while Egypt and the intervening regions were low and flat.

11. The prepositive מ in מִבְּנֵיכֶם, and מִבְּחוּרֵיכֶם, is partitive, indicating that

And of your young men to be Nazarites.
Is it not even so, O ye sons of Israel?
Saith Jehovah.

12 But ye made the Nazarites drink wine,
And ye charged the prophets,
Saying, Prophesy not.

13 Behold, I will press you down,
As the cart presseth which is full of sheaves.

14 And refuge shall fail the swift,
The strong man shall not exert his strength,

some or certain persons out of the number were selected. The Divine condescension in the selection of any of their race to fill the offices here specified, laid them under additional obligations to devote themselves to the service of the true God; and not only was thereby a distinguished honor conferred upon them, but such institutions furnished them with the means of religious instruction, and examples of holy living. For נְבִיאִים, the *prophets*, see on Hos. xii. 11. נְזִרִים, *Nazarites*, LXX. ἡγιασμένος, εἰς ἁγιασμόν, from נזר, *to separate, set one's self apart, abstain*, were a class of persons among the Hebrews who ordinarily bound themselves by a voluntary vow to abstain either for a time, or for the whole period of life, from wine and all intoxicating liquors, and everything made of the produce of the vine; and not to shave their head nor touch any dead body. Sometimes persons were, before their birth, devoted by their parents to this abstinence; as in the cases of Samson, Samuel, and John the Baptist. For the law of the Nazarite, see Num. vi. and Winer's Realwörterb. The object of the institute appears to have been, to exhibit to the view of the nation the power of religious principle operating in the way of self-control, indifference to sensual gratification, and an entire consecration to the service of God. The importance which was attached to it in a moral point of view, is evident from those who thus exercised themselves in self-denial being classed along with the prophets. Respecting the undeniableness of the fact a pointed appeal is made at the close of the verse.

12. What could have been more flagrant than to tempt the pious to break their solemn vow, and attempt to induce the inspired ambassadors of Jehovah to withhold the communications of his will?

13. Here commence the denunciations against the apostate Israelites. The Participle מֵעִיק, after הִנֵּה, is future in signification. See on Is. vii. 14. עוק occurs only here as a verb; but that it signifies *to press, oppress*. etc., is clear from the signification of the derivatives צָקָה, Ps. lv. 4, and מוּצָקָה, Ps. lvi. 2, as well as from the connection in which it here occurs. Comp. צוק, and the Syr. ܐ݂ܠ݂ܨ, *angustiatus est*. ܐܘܠܨܢܐ, *angustia, pressura*. Comp. also the Arab. عاق, *retinuit, impedivit:* عوائق, *accidentia fortunæ, quæ impediunt hominem*. The verb is used transitively in both instances, according to the ordinary signification of Hiphil. There is more force in speaking of a fully laden cart pressing the ground under it, than its being itself pressed by its contents. תַּחַת is to be taken in the sense of *down*, as in Job xl. 12. לָהּ is pleonastic. The renderings of the LXX. and Vulg. ἐγὼ κυλίω ὑποκάτω ὑμῶν; *ego stridebo subter vos*, though advocated by some, are less appropriate. Newcome translates the latter hemistich thus: "As a loaded corn-wain presseth its sheaves;" but עָמִיר is the objective case to הָעֲגָלָה, and not to תָּעִיק. As the object of the verb, supply אֶת־הָאָרֶץ.

14–16. Every attempt to resist or escape from the evils that were coming upon the nation, would prove utterly

15 Neither shall the mighty deliver himself;
He that handleth the bow shall not stand,
And the swift-footed shall not escape:
Neither shall he that rideth the horse deliver himself.
16 And he that is courageous among the heroes,
Shall flee away naked in that day,
Saith Jehovah.

fruitless. This sentiment is expressed under various forms, which are obviously accumulated for the sake of effect. ו at the beginning of ver. 14, is not merely conjunctive, but marks the consequence or result. Verse 15th is wanting in some of Kennicott and De Rossi's MSS. and in the Arab.; but the omission is no doubt owing to the homoioteleuton of this and the preceding verse; just as, for the same reason, the words corresponding to לֹא־יְמַלֵּט נַפְשׁוֹ at the end of ver. 14 are omitted in the Alexandrian copy of the LXX. The preposition בּ in בַּגִּבּוֹרִים, gives to אַמִּיץ לִבּוֹ, the force of the superlative. Comp. גִּבּוֹר בַּבְּהֵמָה, *the strongest of beasts*, Prov. xxx. 30; הַיָּפָה בַּנָּשִׁים, *the most beautiful of women*, Song i. 8, v. 9, vi. 1; εὐλογημένη ἐν γυναιξίν, Luke i. 28.

CHAPTER III.

THE prophet resumes the subject of the Divine goodness towards the Hebrew people, and grounds upon their misimprovement of it, the certainty of their punishment, ver. 1; he then, in a series of pointed and appropriate interrogations, illustrates this certainty, 3-6; which he follows up by a vindication of his commission, 7, 8. Foreign nations are then summoned to witness the execution of judgment upon the kingdom of Israel, which would be signally severe, 9-15.

1 HEAR ye this word, which Jehovah speaketh against you, O sons of Israel,
Against all the family which I brought up out of the land of Egypt;
Saying:

1 Instead of בְּנֵי יִשְׂרָאֵל, "*sons of Israel*," forty-three MSS., one in the margin, originally seven, and five by correction, read בֵּית יִשְׂרָאֵל, "*house of Israel*;" which reading is supported by the LXX. and Arab. versions. Both forms are employed in the book of Amos, but the former is the less frequent; which awakens the suspicion that the latter has been introduced here by way of correction. That the phrase is intended to include the whole Hebrew people, is evident from the words which follow in apposition, and describe the distinguished favor conferred upon the entire race of Jacob.

מִשְׁפָּחָה, Eth. ፩ሐ, *to spread out* a *tribe*, or *clan*; but here obviously used in a national sense, as in Jer. viii. 3, xxv. 9; Micah ii. 3.

2 Only you have I known of all the families of the earth,
Therefore I will punish you for all your iniquities.
3 Will two walk together
Except they be agreed?
4 Will the lion roar in the forest
When he has no prey?
Will the young lion cry out from his den,

2. ידע, *to know*, is here employed in the sense of knowing with the idea of volition, or goodwill; to *acknowledge, regard, care for*, and by implication, *to show favor to*. Comp. Ps. i. 6, cxliv. 3; and γινώσκω, John x. 14, xv. 17; 2 Tim. ii. 19. The Israelites alone were acknowledged by Jehovah as his people, and as such treated with peculiar favor; but in proportion to the distinction which they enjoyed, was the degree of punishment which their ungrateful and rebellious conduct merited.

3. In this and the three following verses, a series of parabolic interrogations are employed, highly calculated to produce conviction in the minds of those to whom they were addressed. They are familiar indeed, but so much the more appropriate and forcible. Instead of נועדו, the LXX. Arab. and Vulg. read יודעו, with apparent reference to the signification of ידע in the preceding verse. The primary signification of יעד, Syr.

ܝܥܕ *condixit, constituit*, Arab. وَعَدَ, *significavit affecturum alicui quid*, is *to point, point out, appoint* a time or place, hence in Niphal, *to meet by appointment; to do anything by common consent; to be agreed*. This last seems to be the acceptation in which the verb is to be taken in this place: for to render, How can two set out upon a journey, except they meet by appointment? would express that to be impossible, which is very often true in fact. Interpreters are divided in opinion respecting the persons to whom the number שנים, *two*, refers. Munster and some others think, that the prophets generally, or Joel and Amos in particular, are meant; Vatablus, Drusius, Lively, Newcome, Bauer, Rosenmüller, Ackermann, and Maurer, explain it of God and the prophet; while Clarius, Grotius, Danæus, Marckius, Lowth, Harenberg, and Dahl, are of opinion that God and Israel are intended. The last construction of the passage best agrees with the bearing of the other interrogations. Between Jehovah and his apostate people there could no longer be any fellowship; and instead of the blessings which accrued to them from such fellowship, they had now nothing to expect but punishment. As they had walked contrary to him, so he would now walk contrary to them. They had broken his covenant, and must take the consequences.

4. The lion is quiet till he sees his prey, but roars at the sight of it, and thereby inspires it with such terror, that it is deprived of the power of escape. In like manner the young lion, which has been weaned, and is just beginning to hunt for prey, will lie silent in his den, till it is brought near, when the smell of it will rouse him from his quiet. Poiret, in his Travels in Barbary, Strasb. 1789, vol. i. p. 283, states, that the lion has two different modes of hunting his prey. When not very hungry, he contents himself with watching behind a bush for the animal which is the object of his attack, till it approaches, when, by a sudden leap, he attacks it, and seldom misses his aim; but if he is famished he does not proceed so quietly, but, impatient and full of rage, he leaves his den, and fills, with his terrific roar, the echoing forest. His voice inspires all living beings with fear and dread; no creature deems itself safe in its retreat; all flee, they know not whither, and by this means, fall into his fangs. אריה, *the lion*, and not כפיר, *the young lion*, is the nominative to the verb לפני. The certainty of destruction is the point at

Except he have taken it?
5 Will the bird fall into an earth-snare,
And there is no gin for it?
Will the snare spring from the ground,
When nothing whatever is caught;
6 Shall the trumpet be blown in a city,
And the people not tremble?
Shall there be evil in a city,
And Jehovah hath not inflicted it?
7 Surely the Lord Jehovah inflicteth nothing,
Except he reveal his purpose
To his servants the prophets.
8 The lion hath roared, who will not fear?

which the prophet aims in the similitude.

5. Between פַּח and מוֹקֵשׁ there is no essential difference. The sense would have been the same had the latter word been omitted, and we had simply read, וְאֵין לָהּ; but the insertion of the synonyme gives more force to the sentence. כִּי connects with צִפּוֹר, as its antecedent. יַעֲלֶה is to be taken as the future of Kal, and regarded as expressing the sudden spring of an elastic snare, or net, which, on the bird's touching it, suddenly rises and incloses it. Instruments were prepared by the providence of God for the capture of the Israelites, which would certainly do their work: there would be no escape.

6. The prophet here closes his interrogatory appeals;—first by a reference to the effect produced upon the inhabitants of a city by the sounding of the trumpet, as a signal of war; and then, by directly ascribing the infliction of temporal calamities to Jehovah, as the punisher of sin. For רָעָה in the sense of temporal evil, or calamity, see Gen. xix. 19, xliv. 34, Exod. xxxii. 14; Ezek. vii. 5. Arab. ﺟﻼ, experimentum, *calamitas afflictio.*

7. Though the infliction of punishment of his guilty people was determined in his holy and righteous counsel, yet Jehovah would not proceed to execute it until he had given them full warning, and afforded such of them an opportunity of escaping as should repent and return to his service. He thus mixed mercy with judgment. סוֹד, Theod. Βουλή, *counsel, purpose, decree;* from יָסַד, Arab. ﺟﺴﺪ, *posuit, firmiter statuit; to found,* lay a foundation, *establish a plan, ordain.* It is rather, I imagine, on this acceptation of the verb that the idea of *purpose* or *decree* is based, than upon that of a divan, or an assembly of persons, sitting and deliberating on couches: but see Gesenius in סוֹד. As the Divine plan or purpose is necessarily secret till it be revealed, hence the acceptation *secret* came to be attached to the word. In this verse a high honor is vindicated to the prophetical office. The holy men of God were, by inspiration, entrusted with a knowledge of the Divine purposes, in so far as it was necessary for them to divulge them to the world. יַעֲשֶׂה, is the frequentative future, indicating what God is accustomed to do, and is best rendered by our present. For the sentiment, comp. Gen. xviii. 17.

8. With reference to what he had expressed ver. 4. and in keeping with the mode of representation which he had employed chap. i. 2, Amos formally announces the awful character of the message he had heard from the Lord, and the impossibility of withholding the communication. The roar of the lion is loud and terrific, especially in the solitary forests which form his proper domain. See on ver. 4.

The Lord Jehovah hath spoken, who will not prophesy?
9 Proclaim ye in the palaces of Ashdod,
And in the palaces in the land of Egypt,
And say:
Assemble yourselves on the mountains of Samaria,
And behold the great commotions within her,
And the oppressions in the midst of her.
10 For they regard not the practice of rectitude,
Saith Jehovah,
That amass rapine and spoil in their palaces.
11 Therefore thus saith the Lord Jehovah:

9. הַשְׁמִיעוּ, *cause it to be heard, publish ye!* those are addressed who had intercourse with the places here specified, and had thus an opportunity of conveying the message. Comp. ὁ ἀκούων εἰπάτω· Ἔρχου! Rev. xxii. 17. For *Ashdod*, see on chap. i. 8. It is here used synecdochically for the whole of Philistia. Instead of בְּאַשְׁדּוֹד, the LXX. have read בְּאַשּׁוּר, ἐν Ἀσσυρίοις, which Seeker attempts to justify! For הָשָּׁמְעוּ עַל אַרְמְנוֹת, comp. κηρύξατε ἐπὶ τῶν δωμάτων, Matt. x. 27. It was, and is still, customary in the East to assemble on the flat roofs of the houses. To the princes and courtiers thus assembled on their palaces, as well as to all within hearing, the invitation was to be conveyed. There is something exceedingly forcible in these heathen rulers, etc. being called to witness the enormities that were practised in Samaria. If their judgment, pagans as they were, could not but be unfavorable, what must be the judgment of the holy and righteous God? What the punishment which he must inflict? Nothing can be more graphic than the description of the position which these foreigners were to occupy. They were to assemble עַל הָרֵי שֹׁמְרוֹן, *upon the mountains of Samaria.* שֹׁמְרוֹן, *Samaria,* the metropolis of the kingdom of Israel, was built on a round hill, near the middle of a large valley, surrounded by mountains on every side, by which it was completely overlooked. From these elevations persons might distinctly see what was done in the city. That מְהוּמֹת רַבּוֹת

and עֲשׁוּקִים are intimately connected, and are both to be referred to the rich and powerful inhabitants of Samaria, appears evident from what is stated in the following verse. The latter term is properly the Pahul Participle, *oppressed*, but is here used as a noun, as in Job xxxv. 9; Eccles. iv. i. Comp. the forms זְבוּל, *dwelling* מַמְלָכָה, *kingdom.*

10. וְלֹא יָדְעוּ, *they know not*, is not intended to express simple ignorance, but that state of mind which is hostile to the entertainment of knowledge. The magnates of Samaria had no regard for the practice of what was just and right, but the contrary. נְכֹחָה, *rectitude*, that which is straight, in opposition to what is crooked, distorted, or morally wrong. Comp Is. xxvi. 10, xxx. 10, lix. 14. חָמָס וָשֹׁד, *violence and desolation*, mean, by a metonymy of the cause for the effect, what has been obtained by violating the rights and desolating the property of others. Such spoils they accumulated in their palaces, but they should not enjoy them. On the contrary, as the prophet shows in the following verses, they should be plundered and carried away by the enemy. Dathe well expresses the meaning of the verse: "Recte factis nequaquam delectantur, inquit Jova, sed thesauros in aedes suas congerunt vi atque injuria partos."

11. צָר, the LXX., who are followed by Aq. and the Arab., preposterously render Τύρος, *Tyre;* one of De Rossi's MSS. reads צֹר, and one of Kennicott's, -צֹר. The Syr. Chald. *tribulation,* which

There shall be an enemy, and that around the land;
And he shall bring down thy strength from thee,
And thy palaces shall be plundered.
12 Thus saith Jehovah:
As the shepherd rescueth from the mouth of the lion
Two legs, or the portion of an ear,
So shall the sons of Israel be rescued,
Who sit in Samaria on the corner of a bed,
And in Damascus on that of a couch.

has been adopted in many modern versions. Thus Dathe, Hesselberg, Dahl, Justi, and Hitzig. But Calvin, Newcome, Michaelis, Struensee, Bauer, Rosenmüller, Vater, and Noyes, translate *enemy*, which better suits the connection, as it supplies a proper nominative to the verb הוֹרִיד, immediately following. Com. as to derivation, the Arab. ضَرّ, *noeuit, noxa affecit, læsit*. The words, צַר וּסְבִיב הָאָרֶץ are abrupt and elliptical, but, for this very reason, possess more point. At צַר, supply יָבֹא הִנֵּה, or the like. ו in וּסְבִיב has the force of *et quidem*, or *isque*. The reading יַסְבִּיב, suggested by Houbigant, considered probable by Newcome, and adopted by Bauer, is altogether unsustained by any example of a similar case in verbs whose second and third radicals are the same. סָבִיב הָאָרֶץ is equivalent to בְּכָל־הָאָרֶץ, 2 Kings xvii. 5. where the invasion by Shalmaneser is described. עֹז, *strength*, denotes whatever Samaria confided in, or made her boast of, such as her treasures, fortifications, warriors, etc. All was to be brought down into the valley, and what was capable of being removed, carried away by the enemy: *i. e.* Shalmaneser, the king of Assyria. A just retribution for the spoliations which her inhabitants had committed.

12. A very appropriate image is here borrowed from a scene in pastoral life, such as the prophet himself may have witnessed. Nothing but a mere remnant of the Israelites should with difficulty escape from the enemy. Although a lion may not be induced to quit his prey, if he is hungry and has but just seized it,

Is. xxxi. 4; yet if he has almost devoured it, leaving nothing but what is here specified, no difficulty would be found in effecting a rescue. For כַּאֲשֶׁר יַצִּיל הָרֹעֶה, comp. ἐῤῥύσθην ἐκ στόματος λέοντος, 2 Tim. iv. 17; 1 Sam. xvii. 34, 35. בְּדַל occurs only this once, but signifies a *part* or *piece;* from בָּדַל, *to separate*. There is a species of goat in the East, the ears of which are often a foot in length, and broad in proportion; so that more importance would be attached to them by the shepherd, than would be the case with us in the West. The concluding words of the verse have greatly perplexed interpreters. Most of the moderns explain דַּמֶּשֶׂק of the silk manufactured at Damascus, which from the name of the place, is called *damask*, and render בְּדַמֶּשֶׂק עָרֶשׂ, *in damask couches*. What has been supposed to confirm this explanation of the term is the occurrence of the same word in Arabic, only with the letters, or similar letters transposed, as

دمقس دمقاس دمقص, etc.,

all signifying *silk*. Gesenius has a long article on the word in his Thesaurus, p. 346; but fails in establishing the point of identity. Instead of דַּמֶּשֶׂק with *Shin*, upwards of twenty of De Rossi's MSS. read, or have read, דַּמֶּשֶׂק with *Sin;* which reading is also that of eighteen printed editions, and is the proper orthography of the name of Damascus. What appears to have originated the above view of the word was the idea, that as the wealthy and voluptuous inhabitants of Samaria are supposed to be intended, there was a special propriety in adverting to the sumptuousness of the couches or

13 Hear ye, and testify against the house of Jacob,
Saith the Lord, Jehovah, the God of hosts,
14 Surely in the day when I punish the transgressions of Israel,
I will punish the altars of Bethel;
The horns of the altar shall be cut down,
And they shall fall to the ground.
15 I will also smite the winter-house with the summer-house,
The ivory mansions shall perish,

sofas on which they reclined. But this idea is totally alien from the bearing of the passage, which requires something to correspond to what had been expressed in the comparison of the fragments left by the lion. Besides, פָּאָה signifies the *outer* or *extreme* corner, and not the inner, which is regarded as the seat of honor, so that the observations of Harmer, chap. vi. Obs. xxx., are totally inapplicable, even if there were much point in them. The words are elliptical, and the parallelism, expressed in full, would stand thus:

הַיֹּשְׁבִים בְּשֹׁמְרוֹן בִּפְאַת מִטָּה
הַיֹּשְׁבִים בְּדַמֶּשֶׂק בְּעֶרֶשׂ׃

The persons referred to are the sick and infirm poor, who had nothing left but the side or part of a couch, and whom the king of Assyria would not think it worth his while to be at the trouble of removing. All the rest, the robust and active, the opulent and powerful, should be carried into captivity. For the fulfilment see 2 Kings xvii. 5, 6, xviii. 9–12. The reason why Damascus is mentioned along with Samaria, is, that, at the time of the Assyrian invasion, that city was in the power of the Israelites, having been conquered by Jeroboam II. See 2 Kings xiv. 28. On the conquest, no doubt many belonging to the ten tribes went there to reside.

13. The same persons are here addressed, who were summoned from Philistia and Egypt to witness the enormities practised in Samaria, ver. 9. They were now to testify to the facts of the case, that the punishment to be inflicted upon the inhabitants might be seen to have been richly deserved. הָעֵד בְּ, as frequently means to *testify against any* one. אֲדֹנָי יְהוִֹה אֱלֹהֵי הַצְּבָאוֹת. LXX. Κύριος ὁ Θεὸς ὁ Παντοκράτωρ: an accumulation of Divine appellatives for the purpose of striking awe into the minds of the guilty.

14. Signal vengeance was to be taken upon the place whence all the evils which spread through the ten tribes originated. For *Bethel*, see on Hos. iv. 15. From the term הַמִּזְבֵּחַ having the determinative article, rendering it emphatic, while מִזְבְּחוֹת in the plural also occurs, it may be inferred that at Bethel, besides the great altar erected by Jeroboam, there was a number of lesser ones at which sacrifices were offered. Comp. Hos. viii. 11, x. 5. The קַרְנֹת, *horns*, were four projecting points in the shape of horns at the corners of ancient altars. They may be seen in the representations of those dug up by Belzoni in Egypt. As they were ornamental, the action here described was designed to express the contempt in which the altar would be held by the Assyrians.

15. Eastern monarchs and princes, as well as others of the great, have summer as well as winter residences. The latter are in cities and sheltered situations; the former in forests, or upon mountains. שֵׁן, properly *tooth*, but used specially of the tusk of the elephant; *ivory*. LXX. οἶκοι ἐλεφάντινοι. By ivory houses are not meant houses or palaces composed of that material, but richly ornamented with it. The ancients used it for decorating the ceilings, panels, doors, etc., of their rooms, by inlaying it with other costly articles. See 1 Kings xxii. 39; Ps. xlv. 9. Odys. iv. 73. Diod. Sic. iii. 47. Pausan. i. 12. 4. Od. ii. 18. 1. All these sumptuous palaces in which the leaders of the people rioted, and

And the great houses shall come to an end,
Saith Jehovah.

indulged in all manner of profaneness, were to be completely destroyed. סוּף, *to come to an end, cease.* The rendering of בָּתִּים רַבִּים, by "*large* houses," is more agreeable to the connection than that of "*many* houses," though this is equally expressed by the phrase.

CHAPTER IV.

THIS chapter contains a continuation of the denunciation pronounced against the Israelites, at the close of the preceding, 1-3; an ironical call to them to persevere in their will-worship, which was the primary cause of their calamities, 4. 5; an enumeration of the different judgments with which they had been visited, but which had effected no reformation, 6-11; and a summous to them to prepare for the last and most awful judgment, which the omnipotent Jehovah was about to inflict upon them, 12, 13.

---

1 HEAR ye this word, ye kine of Bashan !
That are in the mountain of Samaria;
That oppress the poor; that crush the needy;
That say to their master,
Bring now, that we may drink.

1. בָּשָׁן, *Bashan,* was celebrated for the richness of the pasturage, and its excellent breed both of large and small cattle. Deut. xxxii. 14; Ps. xxii. 12; Ezek. xxxix. 18. It lay on the east of the Jordan, between Hermon and the mountains of Gilead, and extended eastward as far as the cities of Salchah and Edrei, which it included. Some are of opinion, that by פָּרוֹת הַבָּשָׁן, *the kine,* or *cows of Bashan,* the proud and luxurious females of Samaria are intended ; and that they are introduced on account of the corrupting influence which, through their husbands, they exerted on the state of public affairs. Of these may be mentioned, most of the Rabbins, Theodoret, Liveley, Grotius, Michaelis, Vater, Dahl, Justi, Gesenius and Winer. Others, as the Targ. Jerome, Munster, Calvin, Vatablus, Clarius, Drusius, Danæus, Mercer, Marckius, Harenberg, Dathe, Rosenmüller, and Maurer, maintain that the prophet has the princes and rulers in view, whom he describes in this debasing language, in order to set forth the effeminacy, wantonness, and obstinacy of their character. At first view the former exposition might appear to recommend itself for adoption ; but I am induced to give my adhesion to the latter, chiefly on the ground, that it is scarcely possible, otherwise, to account for the repeated intermixture of masculine forms with the feminine. Thus we have שִׁמְעוּ, אֲדֹנֵיהֶם, הֲבִיאָה, אֶתְכֶם, אַחֲרִיתְכֶן, all occurring very closely together. Now, though it must be admitted that there are instances in which the gender is neglected, as in Ruth i., yet none of them will bear comparison with the present case. On the principle, that males are the real, and females the fig-

2   The Lord Jehovah hath sworn by his holiness:
Behold, the days are coming upon you,
When ye shall be taken away with hooks,
And your posterity with fish-hooks.
3   And ye shall go out through the breaches,
Each one right before her;
Ye shall even be thrown out of the palace,
Saith Jehovah.

urative subjects of discourse, it is easy to perceive how the genders would be used just as the one or the other were prominently in the mind of the prophet. Some translators suppress the figurative language altogether, as Dathe: *Audite hoc, vos divites et potentes Samariæ;* but such practice is quite unwarrantable, as it destroys the effect of the prophetic mode of representation. צִבֹּאת, one of those onomatopoetic verbs, the very sound of which strongly expresses the character of the action which they are intended to describe. It signifies to *break, crush, dash in pieces.* Comp. the Arab. رَضَ, *conduit, fregit.* אֲדוֹן in אֲדֹנֵיהֶם, though plural in form, is singular in signification, and means the king of Israel, whom his courtiers and others, indulging in their compotations, importune for fresh supplies of wine, reckless of the oppression and rapine by which it might be procured. Comp. Hos. vii. 5. ה suffixed in הֲבִיאָה, is the ה directive, or optative.

2, 3. כִּי is pleonastic. It is surprising that so judicious an interpreter as Calvin should attempt to vindicate the rendering of קָדְשׁוֹ, *his sanctuary,* when that of *his holiness* is so natural and proper. Comp. Ps. lxxxix. 36, and lx. 8. Jehovah appeals to all that is involved in the infinite excellence of his moral character for the certainty of his punishing sin. The Nominative to בָּאִים is the enemy, understood; but as the verb is put in the impersonal form, it is best rendered passively. Döderlein and some others object to the adoption, in this place, of *hooks* and *fish hooks,* as the signification of צִנּוֹת and סִירוֹת דּוּגָה, as too violent a change of the figure; and propose that we should retain the primary acceptation of *thorns,* which they think is more in keeping with the idea of cows. They accordingly render the passage: "Ye shall be driven into thorny districts, and among the gloomy thorn bushes." There is, however, no necessity for supposing that the prophet had the alleged idea in his mind when he delivered the words, but the contrary; and as *fishing* and *hooks* are elsewhere employed figuratively in reference to human beings, there can be no real ground for rejecting such tropical application of the disputed terms in this place. See 2 Chron. xxxiii. 11; Is. xxxii. 29; Jer. xvi. 16; Ezek. xxix.

4. אִשָּׁה נֶגְדָּהּ *each one right before her,* means, in a captive state, not being permitted by the enemy to turn to the right or the left. הִשְׁלַכְתֶּנָה is pointed הִשְׁלַכְתְּנָה in De Rossi's Spanish MS. marked 23, which punctuation has been adopted in Hahn's small printed edition. Comp. הִשְׁלְכָה, Dan. viii. 11. It is supported by the LXX. Syr. Symm. Vulg. and Arab. all of which versions exhibit the passive. ה at the end of the verb is that of the fuller form of the pronoun אַתֶּנָה, the fragment of which is used as a suffix. It occurs but seldom in the preterite. Of הַהַרְמוֹנָה almost every possible interpretation has been given. LXX. τὸ ὄρος τὸ 'Ρεμμάν; Cod. Vat. 'Ρομμάν; in many of the MSS. of Flamin. Nob. 'Αρμανά. Syr. ܐܘܪܡܝܢܝ; Chald. טוּרֵי חַרְמִינִי, *the mountains of Armenia.* Vulg. Armon. Arab. after the LXX. جبل الرامة Aq. 'Αρμανὰ ὄρος. Symm. 'Ερμηνίαν, doubtless for 'Αρμενίαν.

4 Come ye to Bethel, and transgress;
   At Gilgal, multiply transgression;
   Bring your sacrifices every morning,
   Your tithes every third year.
5 Offer incense of the leavened thank-offering;
   Proclaim the voluntary offerings: publish them abroad;
   For ye love to have it so, O ye sons of Israel,
   Saith Jehovah.
6 And though I have given you cleanness of teeth in all your cities,

Theod. ὅρος Μονά. Edit quint. ὑψηλὸν ὅρος. Luther and Vater, *Hermon*. Michaelis, Strœnsee, Dathe, Bauer, De Wette, *Armenia*. Justi and Hezel, *Harem*. Volborth, *Net*. Hitzig takes it to be a corruption of הֲדַדְרִמּוֹן, *Hadadrimmon*, which he explains of a place near Samaria where Adonis was worshipped. Newcome cuts the knot and renders "will utterly destroy it." The only satisfactory solution of the difficulty presented by this ἅπαξ λεγ. is that of Kimchi, which is approved by Gesenius, Winer, and Lee, *viz.* that אַרְמוֹן stands for אַרְמוֹן, *a palace*, or *citadel*. Comp. the Arab. ܐܪܡ, *a lofty edifice, a pyramid*. Changes in letters of the same organ are not unfrequent in Hebrew, as אֵיךְ, חָבַר־אָךְ; חָמוֹץ־אָמוּץ; לָקַח־לָתַח; וְנֵיד־נוּד etc. The ה at the end is not the feminine termination, but simply paragogic, as in אַרְצָה, Job xxxiv. 13, xxxvii. 12; Is. viii. 23; and תַּחְרַסָה, Judges xiv. 18. The noun will thus be the accusative absolute, and the construction will be "cast down *as to the palace*," i. e. from it, over its walls, or the like. The place in which the princes had rioted, and in the strength of which they confided, should afford them no safety.

4, 5. The language of these verses is that of the keenest irony. The Israelites were addicted to the worship of the golden calf, and to that of idols, whereby they contracted guilt before Jehovah, and exposed themselves to his judgments; at the same time they hypocritically professed to keep up the observance of certain feasts which had been appointed by Moses. For *Gilgal*,

as a place of idolatrous worship, see on Hos. iv. 15. The opinion of Abenezra, approved by Rosenmüller and Maurer, that by לִשְׁלֹשֶׁת יָמִים, we are to understand *every third day*, seems forced and unnatural. That the words by themselves might have this meaning is unquestionable: but the idea of *tithes* being brought every third day is inadmissible, even into a passage so strongly ironical as the present. I cannot doubt that the prophet has in view the enactment recorded Deut. xiv. 29, xxvi. 12. יָמִים, *days*, mean, here, as Lev. xxv. 29; Judges xvii. 10, the fullest complement of days, i. e. *a year*. קַטֵּר is most probably the infinitive, used for the second plural of the imperative; or it may be the second singular of the same. There is no necessity for attaching to חָמֵץ, the meaning of *violence*, though Gesenius would justify it, on the ground of חָמוֹץ being used, Ps. lxxi. 4, to designate an oppressor; and because the rendering of the Chald. in this place is אֲנִיס, *rapine* or *oppression*. It is not impossible that the translator mistook חָמֵץ for חָמָס, which has this signification. The point of reference is doubtless the ordinance, Lev. vii. 13, that, besides the unleavened cakes, the Hebrews were to offer "*leavened* bread" with the sacrifice of thanksgiving. What the Israelites, therefore, are supposed to be in the habit of doing was, so far as the material of the thing was concerned, not contrary to the law, but in strict accordance with its requirement. For אֲהַבְתֶּם כֵּן, comp. אָמְרוּ כֵן, Jer. v. 31.

6. From this verse to the 11th inclusive, Jehovah describes the different

And want of bread in all your places,
Yet ye have not returned unto me,
Saith Jehovah.

7   And though I have withholden the rain,
Three months before the harvest;
And have caused it to rain upon one city,
But upon another city I have not caused it to rain;
One portion was rained upon,
And the portion upon which it rained not, withered:

8   And two or three cities wandered to one city,
To drink water, but have not been satisfied,
Yet ye returned not to me,
Saith Jehovah.

9   I have smitten you with mildew and much blight;
Your gardens, your vineyards, and your figs, and your olives,
The locusts hath devoured;
Yet ye have not returned unto me,
Saith Jehovah.

10   I have sent among you the plague, such as that of Egypt;
I have slain your young men with the sword,

---

corrective measures which he had employed for the purpose of effecting a change in the Israelites, and at the close of each mentioned in the series, the obstinate impenitence, under the influence of which they persisted in their wicked courses, is emphatically marked by the declaration, לֹא־שַׁבְתֶּם עָדַי נְאֻם יְהוָה׃ *yet ye returned not unto me,* saith Jehovah. Such repetition gives great force to the reprehension. נִקְיוֹן שִׁנַּיִם, *cleanness of teeth,* and חֹסֶר לֶחֶם, *lack of bread,* are synonymous; both expressing the famine with which the nation has been visited. עָדַי, *to me,* the Chald. paraphrases, לְדֶחְלָתִי, *to my worship,* or *service.*

7, 8. The famine was followed by the judgment of drought, which at once produced sterility, and cut off the necessary supply of drink for man and beast. The rain that had been withheld, was the מַלְקוֹשׁ, *vernal,* or latter rain, which falls in the latter half of February, the whole of March and April, and thus precedes the harvest, as here stated. See on Hos. vi. 3. Whatever rain fell was exceed-ingly partial and insufficient. Instead of הִמְטִיר, the reading אַמְטִיר is found in two MSS. and is supported by the renderings of the LXX. Arab. and Vulg. The textual reading must be taken impersonally. עָרִים, *cities,* stands for their inhabitants. Comp. for a lengthened and graphic description of the judgment here specified, Jer. xiv. 1–6.

9. A bad harvest, arising from the destruction of the corn by the *blighting* influence of the east wind (שִׁדָּפוֹן, *scorching, blasting,* from שָׁדַף, *to scorch;* Chald. שְׁדַף, *to burn;* Arab. اسلى, *niger,* LXX. πύρωσις. Arab. Ver. السموم, *the Simoom,*) and the *mildew,* or smut. יֵרָקוֹן, Arab. يرقان, *rubigo.* הִרְבּוֹת, the infinitive absolute of רָבָה in Hiphil, with the force of an adjective or an adverb. This word some improperly connect, as a construct noun, with the following substantives. גָזָם, a name given to the *locust.* See on Joel i. 4.

10. Though the plague has from time

Together with your captive horses:
And I have made the stench of your camps to come up into
  your nostrils;
Yet ye have not returned unto me,
Saith Jehovah.

11 I have overthrown some among you,
As God overthrew Sodom and Gomorrah;
And ye have been as a brand snatched from the burning;
Yet ye have not returned unto me,
Saith Jehovah.

12 Therefore, thus will I deal with thee, O Israel!
Forasmuch as I will do this to thee,
Prepare to meet thy God, O Israel!

immemorial been endemic in Egypt, and might so far be described as דֶּרֶךְ מִצְרָיִם, *the way of Egypt;* yet comparing Is. x. 26, in which the same phrase is used as here, it obviously means, *as the Egyptians were treated,* or as God punished them with the plague. See Exod. ix. 3, etc. שְׁבִי סוּסֵיכֶם, lit. *the captivity of your horses:* i. e. those taken and destroyed by the enemy. See 2 Kings xiii. 7. בְּאֵשׁ the LXX. render ἐν πυρί, having read בָּאֵשׁ, which is the pointing of three of De Rossi's MSS., and of three others originally; as also of the Brixian edition. Aq. σαπρίαν. The ו in בְּאַפְּכֶם, Houbigant, Dahl, and some others would cancel, on the ground of its harshness, and its not having been expressed by the LXX. Arab. Syr. and Vulg. It is translated in the Targ., and is to be retained, as an intensive particle, adding force to the preceding verb. Comp. the somewhat similar use of the Greek καί.

11. בְּ in בָּכֶם is used partitively: *inter,* among, or the like; indicating that the subverting was not total. כְּמַהְפֵּכַת אֱלֹהִים, *like God's overthrowing:* proper'y Hiphil participle, but construed as a.. infinite. Comp. Deut. xxix. 22; Is. xiii. 19; Jer. l. 40; 2 Pet. ii. 6; Jude 7. אֱלֹהִים, which stands for the affix of the first personal pronoun, Newcome improperly converts into a superlative, and renders, "the great overthrow!" His remark on את, as sometimes the sign of the genitive case, is likewise totally inapplicable, as in the present case it can only mark the accusative. To what physical phenomena reference is here specifically made, it is impossible to determine, owing to the absence of all historical data. Some think the earthquake, mentioned chap. i. 2, is intended; but this is altogether out of the question, since the prophecy was delivered two years before that event. From the allusion to fire, it has been deemed probable that some of the cities of the Israelites had been burnt, either by lightning from heaven, or by the army of the king of Syria. At all events, that the language is not to be understood figuratively is evident from the close connection of the verse with those preceding, each of which describes a separate physical calamity, and closes, as this one does, with a reprehension of the impenitence by which the nation continued to be characterized. אוּד מֻצָּל מִשְּׂרֵפָה, *a brand snatched from the burning,* is proverbial, and expresses the narrow escape from utter extinction which had been experienced. Comp. Zech. iii. 2; and 1 Cor. ii. 15: αὐτὸς δὲ σωθήσεται, οὕτως δὲ ὡς διὰ πυρός.

12. All the means that had been employed to reform the Israelites having proved ineffectual, they are here summoned to prepare for the final judgment, which was to put an end to their national existence. To this judgment re-

13 For, behold! it is He that formed the mountains;
And created the wind;
And declareth to man what is his thought;
That maketh the morning darkness,
And walketh upon the heights of the earth:
Jehovah, God of hosts, is his name.

ference is emphatically made in the terms כֹּה, *thus*, and זֹאת, *this*. There is a brief resumption of the sentence delivered verses 2 and 3. That by הָכוֹן any such *preparation* is intended as would involve genuine and universal repentance, by which the threatened judgment might have been averted, cannot be admitted in consistency with the bearing both of the preceding and the following context. The removal of the Israelites, as a nation, is denounced as certain, and inevitable. It is rather to be understood as הָכֵן לְךָ, *prepare thee*, Jer. xlvi. 14. God is now coming against you as the avenger of your wickedness. Consider how you shall meet, or endure the infliction. Comp. Ezek. xxii. 14; Heb. x. 31. Individuals might by repentance obtain the forgiveness of their personal transgressions, and thus have their minds brought into a state in which they would enjoy support and comfort in the midst of national calamity; but this was all that could now be expected.

13. To give full effect to the preceding call, one of the most sublime and magnificent descriptions of Jehovah, to be met with in Scripture, is here introduced. The participial form of the five verbs employed by the prophet greatly enhances the beauty of the passage; but it cannot be successfully imitated in a translation. Some have doubted whether רוּחַ does not here signify *spirit*, rather than *wind*; but it seems more natural to take the term in the latter acceptation, on account of the close coherence of this clause of the verse with that immediately preceding. The rendering of the LXX. ἀπαγγέλλων εἰς ἀνθρώπους τὸν χριστὸν αὐτοῦ, announcing to men his anointed, has originated in their mistaking מַה־שֵּׂחוֹ for מְשִׁיחוֹ. Theodoret, in commenting upon the version, thinks Cyrus is intended, and not Christ, as we may otherwise imagine the fathers would expound it. By שֵׂחוֹ is not meant God's thought, or his purposes, as some have taken it, but the thoughts or meditations of man, of which alone the verb שִׂיחַ and its derivatives, when applied to intelligent beings, is used. שִׂיחַ is followed by a double accusative: that of the material out of which the thing is made, and that of the matter into which it is converted. It must, however, be observed, that upwards of twenty of Kennicott's MSS. read, or have read, וְעֵיפָה, which is the reading of the LXX. and Arab. According to this construction, the passage must be translated thus: "He that maketh the aurora and the darkness."

CHAPTER V.

AFTER giving utterance to a brief elegy over the prostrate and helpless condition of the kingdom, which had just been predicted, 1-3, the prophet introduces Jehovah still addressing himself to the inhabitants; calling upon them to relinquish their superstitious and idolatrous practices, and return to his service, 4-9. He then adverts the picture of wickedness which the nation exhibited, 10-13; repeats the call to cultivate habits of piety and righteousness, 14, 15; describes, in plaintive strains, the destruction that was coming upon the land, 16-20; exposes the inutility of ceremonial rites when substituted for moral rectitude, or combined with unauthorized worship, 21-26; and expressly threatens the Israelites with transportation into the East, 27.

1 HEAR ye this word, which I utter concerning you —
A lamentation, O house of Israel!
2 The virgin of Israel is fallen;
She shall rise no more;
Prostrate upon her own land,
There is none to raise her up.
3 For thus saith the Lord Jehovah,
The city that went out by a thousand,
Shall have an hundred left;
And she that went out by an hundred,
Shall have ten left
To the house of Israel.

1. קִינָה is properly an *elegy*, or song of mourning and lamentation, from קוּן, in Piel, to compose or chant such a song. It consisted of plaintive effusions poured forth by mourning relatives, or by persons hired for the purpose, at funerals; and was distinguished for the tender, pathetic, broken and exclamatory nature of the expressions of which it was composed, as well as the touching features of the subject which they were designed to embody. Of this mode of composition the Hebrew prophets frequently avail themselves, especially Jeremiah, who, besides introducing it into several of his prophecies, has left us a whole book of קִינוֹת, elegies, or lamentations. See Lowth, Lect. xxii. For the introduction of the present subject, comp. שָׂא קִינָה עַל or עֲלֵי, Ezek. xix. 1, xxvii. 2, xxxii. 2, and the common oracular forms מַשָּׂא, מַשָּׂא, etc. Some are of opinion that the elegy thus introduced extends to the end of the chapter, but it is far more likely that it consists merely of the plaintive exclamations contained in verse 2. Compare the beautiful lament of David on the death of Jonathan, 2 Sam. i. 17-27.

2. The Israelitish state is called בְּתוּלָה, *a virgin*, because it had never been subdued by any foreign prince. See on Is. xxiii. 12. The passages, Jer. xviii. 13, and Lam. ii. 13, which Rosenmüller adduces against this interpretation of the term, are not in point, since both refer to the character which Jerusalem sustained previous to the deplorable condition to which she had been reduced by the violence of the enemy. It cannot, therefore, be regarded as merely synonymous with בַּת, *daughter*, as idiomatically applied to describe the inhabitants of a city or state. This brief, but touching elegy describes the utterly prostrate and helpless condition to which the Assyrians were to reduce the kingdom of the ten tribes.

3. The depopulated state of the country is here affectingly depicted. עִיר, *the city*, stands by metonymy for its inhabitants. The LXX. ἡ πόλις ἐξ ἧς ἐξεπορεύοντο χίλιοι, and so the other ancient versions. הַיֹּצֵאת, *that went out*, is used elliptically for הַיֹּצְאָה לִצְבָא, *that went forth to war*. The population or size of a city was estimated according to the number of warriors it could furnish. Thus the Scholiast on Iliad ix. 383, 384: οὐ τὸ πλάτος τῶν πυλῶν θέλει σημαίνειν, οὐδὲ γὰρ ἅμα πάντας ἐξιέναι φησίν ἀλλὰ τὸ μέγεθος τῆς πόλεως, καὶ τὸ πλῆθος τῶν ἀνδρῶν.

150   AMOS.   CHAP. V.

4   For thus saith Jehovah to the house of Israel,
    Seek ye me, and live.
5   And seek not Bethel;
    And go not to Gilgal;
    Neither pass through to Beersheba;
    For Gilgal shall surely go into captivity,
    And Bethel shall come to nought.
6   Seek ye Jehovah, and live,
    Lest he rush down, like fire, upon the house of Joseph;

4. While the divine judgments are not executed, there is still room for repentance and reformation. דָּרַשׁ, *to seek*, is very often used as a religious term, implying application to God, or to a false deity, for assistance, direction, etc. and then generally to worship him, and have respect to his will. Ps. xxiv. 6; Is. viii. 19, lv. 6. Comp. Heb. xi. 6, ἐκζητεῖν τὸν Θεόν. בָּקַשׁ is similarly used. חְיוּ, *live ye*, is employed as a second imperative, in order emphatically to express the certainty of the result that would ensue from compliance with the command given by the first.

5. A strong dissuasive from idolatry, derived from the predicted fall of the objects and places of false worship. בְּאֵר שֶׁבַע, *Beersheba*, lit. "the Well of the Oath;" LXX. τὸ φρέαρ τοῦ ὅρκου; see Gen. xxi. 22–31. It was situated about twenty-five geographical miles south of Hebron, on the frontier of the Holy Land towards Idumea, and is still called by the Arabs بير السبع, *Bir-es-seba'*. Dr. Robinson fell in with its ruins on the north side of a Wady of the same name, but found nothing bearing the marks of high antiquity, except two wells, one of which he ascertained to be forty-four feet and a half in depth to the surface of the water, and the other forty-two feet. As it lay in the extreme south of Palestine, the verb עָבַר, *to pass over* or *through*, is most appropriate. From this verse, and from chap. viii. 14, it appears to have been a place of idolatrous resort, but wherein the idolatry consisted we are not told. In הַגִּלְגָּל גָּלֹה יִגְלֶה is a forcible paronomasia,

though the words are from different roots. "Gilgal gallando gallabitur, si posset fingi aliquod tale verbum; hoc est, vertetur volubili versione." Calvin, *in loc.* There is likewise a play upon the word אָוֶן, which is used to denote *wickedness, idolatry, idol, nothing*, etc. What had originally been בֵּית־אֵל, *Bethel, a house of God*, but had by the Israelites been converted into בֵּית־אָוֶן, *Beth-aven, a house of idolatry*, see Hos. iv. 15, x. 5; should be reduced to אָוֶן, *aven nothing*.

6. The prophet here repeats, for the sake of effect, the call which he had introduced, ver. 4. צָלַח, which more commonly has the significations attaching to the Arab. صلح, *recte se habet res, aptus fuit*, etc. has here that of the Syriac ܨܠܚ, *descendit, perrupit*. The general idea of motion, either forward or downward, seems to be conveyed by it, only, in certain cases, with the superadded notion of violence or force. Thus וַתִּצְלַח עָלָיו רוּחַ יְהוָה, is not improperly rendered in our common version, "And the Spirit of the Lord came *mightily* upon him." Dahl prefers the rendering *perdidit*, which he derives from the Arab. صولح, *exitiale malum*; but the form صلحم, مصلحم, *penetrans, vehemens*, might rather be compared. Jehovah is often compared to fire. See Is. x. 17; Lam. ii. 3. אֵשׁ, being of common gender, is the nominative to תִּצְלַח, so that the object of

And it devour, and there be none in Bethel to quench it.
7 Ye who turn justice into wormwood,
  And cast righteousness to the ground,
8 Seek Him that made the Pleiades and Orion;
  That turned deathshade into morning;
  That maketh day dark as night;
  That calleth the waters of the sea,
  And poureth them forth upon the earth;
  Jehovah is his name.

comparison takes the place of וַיְהִי, who is the subject, and the proper nominative. בֵּית יוֹסֵף, *the house of Joseph*, is a less frequent designation of the ten tribes, the principal of which was that of Ephraim, the son of Joseph. It occurs several times in the historical books, but only twice besides in the prophets, viz. Obad. 18; Zech. x. 6. The name יוֹסֵף, *Joseph*, by itself, is similarly employed, Amos v. 15, vi. 6. Comp. Ezek. xxxvii. 16. For בֵּית־אֵל, *Bethel*, the LXX. Arab. and one of De Rossi's MSS. read בֵּית יִשְׂרָאֵל, *Beth Yisrael*, which reading is adopted by Newcome. One of Kennicott's MSS. has יִשְׂרָאֵל, *Israel*, which Houbigant, Dathe, and Bauer, approve. Jerome, Rosenmüller, Dahl, Justi, Struensee, and others, retain the received reading, which is supported by the Targ., Syr., and Vulg. Some would connect בֵּית־אֵל with מְכַבֶּה, and render, "there shall be none to quench Bethel;" but the verb כָּבָה is never constructed with ל, which marks here the Dative of possession. The true construction is, וְאֵין לְבֵית־אֵל מְכַבֶּה. The people of Israel put their trust in the idols which they worshipped at Bethel, but none of them could remove the Divine judgments from the land.

7. הַהֹפְכִים, *ye that turn*, is to be referred to רָשָׁע and בֵּית יוֹסֵף in the preceding verse. This construction is more natural than that which would take בֵּית יוֹסֵף alone as the nominative, in the third person. Such changes of person as that presented in וַיְהִי, are too frequent to occasion any difficulty; nor is it always necessary to express them in a translation. Ewald takes an effectual method of removing the supposed difficulty, by striking out the verse, and inserting it at the beginning of verse 10. Of course, the whole will then read very smoothly; but the question still remains, Did Amos so connect the words? לְלַעֲנָה, Arab. اعبج, *abegit, execratus est*, is the Hebrew name of *wormwood*, and is given to it on account of its disgustingly bitter and injurious quality. The LXX. now read ὁ ποιῶν εἰς ὕψος κρίμα; but there can be little doubt that the original reading was ἄψινθος. The meaning is, that the persons spoken of so perverted their judicial proceedings, as to render them both obnoxious and injurious to those whom they affected. For הִנִּיחַ לָאָרֶץ, see on Is. xxviii. 2.

8. Another sublime description of the Most High, almost verbally identical with that furnished Job ix. 9. The participles are to be referred to יְהוָה, *Jehovah*, ver. 6, as their antecedent. Newcome, following the Targ. and Syr., inserts " that have forsaken " at the commencement of the verse, but these authorities are not sufficient to warrant the addition, which, indeed, the text does not require. The article, used as a relative in הַיּוֹצְרִי and יְבַלֵּל, is omitted before עֹשֵׂה and הֹפֵךְ, because they are in construction. Two of the principal constellations as selected from the heavenly bodies as specimens of the effects of Omnipotence. כִּימָה, *the Pleiades*, or *Seven Stars*. This word occurs only here and Job ix. 9, xxxviii. 31. The derivation from a supposititious root בָּמַם, cognate with הוּם. חָמַם, חָמַם, *to be warm, hot*, adopted by Castellus, Schultens,

9 That bringeth destruction suddenly upon the mighty,
   And destruction cometh upon the fortress.

Parkhurst, and others, is to be rejected for that preserved in the Arab. كوم, Conj. II. *cumulum fecit;* hence, كومة *cumulus;* with which may be compared كيم, *socius,* according to which the name expresses what is brought or bound together, especially *in abundance.* The name given to this constellation by the Arabs is ثريا, *an abundance* or *multitude,* from ثر, *multus ac numerosus evasit, numerosus reddidit.* For the same reason it was called by the Greeks Πλειάδες, according to one of the derivations of Eustathius on Homer, Iliad. xviii. 446: Αἱ δὲ πλειάδες ἤτοι ἀπὸ τῆς μητρὸς αὐτῶν Πληϊόνης ἢ ὅτι πλείους ὁμοῦ κατὰ μίαν συναγωγὴν εἰσι, κ. τ. λ. And most of the ancients express the same idea; as Seneca, *densi pleiadum greges;* Propertius, *pleiadum chorus,* etc. According to the Greek mythology, the Pleiades were seven daughters of Atlas, who, being pursued by Orion, were changed by Jupiter into doves, and having been transplanted to the heavens, form the assemblage of the Seven Stars in the neck of Taurus. In the passage in the Iliad just referred to, they are portrayed on the shield of Achilles along with Orion, in the same order as in our prophet:

Πληϊάδας, ϑ' Ὑάδας τε, τό τε σϑένος Ὠρίωνος.

In the mythology of the Sabians or Mendaites ܡܣܚܒܐ, *the Seven,* and ܟܘܟܒܐ ܫܒܥܐ, *the Seven Stars,* cut no inconsiderable figure. See Norberg's Liber Adami. For כִּימָה, see on Is xiii. 10. Both terms have been entirely mistaken by the LXX. who render ὁ ποιῶν πάντα καὶ μετασκευάζων, which is faithfully copied by the Arab. الصانع كلا ومهيئه —צַלְמָוֶת, *the shadow of death,* one of the very few Hebrew compounds. See on Is. ix. 1. לְ is to be supplied before לְבֹקֶר, as, indeed, it is in fourteen MSS., primarily in three more, and now by correction in one; in both the Soncin. editions; in both of Bomberg, 1518 in the margin, and in the appendix to Munster's, 1536. In הַמַּשְׁחִיר, there is a transition from the participial to the finite form of the verb. To render the clause uniform, the construction would be, מַבְשִׁיר יוֹם לְלַיְלָה. The passage quoted from Pindar, by Clemens Alexandrinus, is beautifully parallel:—

Θεῷ δὲ δυνατὸν ἐκ μελαίνας
Νυκτὸς ἀμίαντον ὦρσαι φῶς·
Κελαινῷ νέφει δὲ σκότου καλύψαι
Καθαρὸν ἁμέρας σέλας.

The following words are descriptive, not of rain, as Jerome, Theodoret, Kimchi, Drusius, Lively, Marckius, Dahl, and Rosenmüller maintain, but of a deluge or inundation, the waters of which may emphatically be said to be poured over the earth. Thus Grotius, Clarius, Bauer, and likewise Lowth, though he admits the possibility of the other view being right. The Alex. reading of the LXX. ὁ Θεὸς ὁ παντοκράτωρ is found in the Arab., in a Copt. MS., and in the Slavon. Bible, has the support of three MSS., yet it is more likely an addition from chap. iv. 13, than otherwise.

9. After the prophet had apparently completed his magnificent description of the Divine character, with the words יְהֹוָה שְׁמוֹ, he appends in this verse an additional view of it, in order to make it tell more practically on the fears of those who boasted of the strength of Samaria. בָּלַג, Arab. بلج, *nituit, fulgit* aurora, not only conveys the idea of *shining, being bright, cheerful,* etc. but also that of *suddenness,* suggested by the rapidity with which the dawning light is diffused over the horizon. The Hebrews applied such terms figuratively to the sudden production of misery, as well as to that

10   They hate him that reproveth in the gate,
   And abhor him that speaketh uprightly.
11 Wherefore, because ye trample upon the poor,
   And take from him the tribute of corn:
   Though ye have built houses of hewn stone,
   Ye shall not dwell in them;
   Though ye have planted pleasant vineyards,
   Ye shall not drink of their wine.
12 For I know that your transgressions are many,
   And that your sins are great:
   Oppressing the righteous,
   Taking a bribe,
   And turning aside the poor in the gate.
13 Therefore the prudent shall be silent at that time;
   For it is an evil time.

of happiness. See on Joel ii. 2. Winer, *oriri faciens, inducens super potentes vastationem.* The ancient versions are all at fault here.

10. Ewald thinks that by בַּשַּׁעַר מוֹכִיחַ, *the reprover in the gate*, Amos himself is meant; but, from the recurrence of שֹׁפֵט, and בַּשַּׁעַר, in connection with מִשְׁפָּט, ver. 15, it is far more natural to interpret the phrase of a magistrate, senator, or judge. Comp. also ver. 12, and see on Is. xxix. 21. In הָעֵת בָּ, which is to be taken adverbially, as Judges ix. 9, is an ellipsis of בְּ.

11–13. בּוֹשַׁסְכֶם is, in all probability, a faulty orthography of בּוֹסַסְכֶם, the Polal. of בּוּס, Arab. ݣݫ, *vilipendit rem, to tread down, trample upon,* etc. De Rossi's codex 380, reads בְּבוֹסַסְכֶם with *Sin.* מַשְׂאַת, *what is raised,* as a *tax, tribute,* etc. from נָשָׂא, *to raise.* Instead of remitting to the poor the tax which they were unable to pay, the rulers and proprietors rigidly exacted it, that they might consume it upon their lusts. But in whatever state and luxury they might have lived, and whatever preparations they might be making for further indulgences, Jehovah declares that they should not continue to enjoy them. The enemy would speedily remove them from all the objects on which they proudly doated, or from which they expected gratification.

For the contrary of the threatening, see Is. lxv. 21, 22; Amos ix. 14. The adjectives רַבִּים and עֲצֻמִים, are placed before their substantives, because they are predicatives, and not qualificatives. Before both, the conjunction כִּי is to be supplied. The ellipsis was probably occasioned by its having been used at the beginning of the verse. כֹּפֶר is most commonly used in the sense of λύτρον, ἀντίλυτρον, *ransom,* or *price of redemption,* on which account Ewald and some others render it so here; but the close connection in which the whole phrase stands with the perversion of justice, specified in the last clause of the verse, decides in favor of the signification *bribe, bribery,* which the word unquestionably has, 1 Sam. xii. 3. Targ. מָמוֹן דִּשְׁקַר, *the mammon of falsehood.* Syr. ܫܘܚܕܐ, *a bribe.* LXX. ἀλλάγματα. The other Greek versions, ἐξίλασμα. If כֹּפֶר צַדִּיק could be taken to mean, "*shutting up,* or *imprisoning* the righteous," then כֹּפֶר might mean ransom; but such usage does not obtain. The only course left for the pious to pursue in the midst of such atrocious perversion of order and justice, was that of quietly submitting to the hand of God, which they were taught to recognize in the permission of these evils, and patiently to abide the issue of

14 Seek good, and not evil, that ye may live;
   And it shall be so; Jehovah, God of hosts, shall be with you,
   According as ye say.
15 Hate evil and love good,
   And establish justice in the gate;
   Perhaps Jehovah, God of hosts, may pity
   The residue of Joseph.
16 Therefore thus saith Jehovah, God of hosts, the Lord:
   In all the broad places there shall be wailing;
   And in all the streets, they shall say, Oh! Oh!
   They shall call the husbandman to mourning;
   And all who are skilled in elegy to wailing.

events. Any attempt, under these circumstances, to stem the current, or effect a reformation, or even to plead for private or public rights, would only aggravate their calamities. הַמַּשְׂכִּיל, *the intelligent, prudent*, is to be understood, in the best sense, of one who acts upon the principles of enlightened piety.

14, 15. Reiterated calls to reformation, in order to ensure the return of Divine favor. Both the style and the sentiments have their parallel in Is. i. 16, 17. Notwithstanding the sad apostasies of the Israelitish people, they still had their profession of the religion of Jehovah to fall back upon, in case of necessity. They boasted that he was with them, but it was an empty pretence while their profession was insincere, being combined with the worship of idols. For the force of the conditional particle אוּלַי, *perhaps*, in such connection, compare Gen. xvi. 2, and εἰ ἄρα, Acts viii. 22. Comp. also Joel ii. 13, where the same idea is expressed in מִי יוֹדֵעַ, *who knoweth?* שְׁאֵרִית יוֹסֵף, *the remainder of Joseph*. For this use of the patronymic, see on ver. 6. Numerous as the Israelites still were, they might well be called a *remainder*, in consideration of the havoc made by Hazael, who, when "the Lord began to cut" them "short, smote them in all the coasts of Israel; from Jordan eastward, all the land of Gilead, the Gadites, and the Reubenites, and the Manassites, from Aroer, which is by the river Arnon, even Gilead and Bashan." 2 King x. 32, 33.

16. לָכֵן, *therefore*, refers not to the contents of verses 14, 15, but to verses 7, 10, and 12. We may suppose a considerable pause to intervene before ver. 16. Foreseeing that the people would not repent, Jehovah here declares that the threatened punishment was inevitable. The slaughter involved in this punishment would be general. Samaria, however, and its vicinity, seem specially intended. The position in which אָמַר is here placed, is altogether unusual. Indeed, I am not aware that it is so found in any other passage. Yet I would not, with Newcome, cancel it, on the slender authority of seven MSS. the LXX. Arab. and Syr. It seems rather to have been purposely added, in order to give greater solemnity to the sentence which was to be pronounced. רְחֹבוֹת, *broad*, or *open places*, or *wide streets* in a city; and distinguished from חוּצוֹת, which signify ordinary or narrow streets, such as are common in the East. Gr. πλατεῖα. מִסְפֵּד, strictly means a *smiting of the breast*, (LXX. κοπετὸς,) from סָפַד, *to beat, smite;* see on Is. xxxii. 12. Here, however, it is used to denote wailing or mourning in general. הוֹ הוֹ, *Oh! Oh!* This onomatopoetic I have rendered by the corresponding English interjection, which, when prolonged and swelled in the pronunciation, as it is by persons giving utterance to excessive grief, is much more appropriate than *Alas! Alas! Alas!* Syr. ܘܳܝ ܘܳܝ; Chald. וַי וַי; Vulg. *væ! væ!* in other

17 In all the vineyards there shall be wailing,
For I will pass through the midst of thee,
Saith Jehovah.
18 Wo unto you that desire the day of Jehovah!
What is the day of Jehovah unto you?
It shall be darkness and not light.
19 As when one fleeth from a lion,
And a bear meeteth him;
Or he entereth the house, and leaneth his hand on the wall,
And a serpent biteth him.
20 Shall not the day of Jehovah be darkness and not light;
Even thick darkness, without any brightness?

Latin versions, *eheu! eheu!* The אִכָּר, *husbandmen*, were to be called to participate in the mourning, not as Newcome, Rosenmüller, and some others have thought, on account of the desolation of the fields, but either on account of the loudness of their rustic voices, or because the slaughter of the citizens of Samaria would be so great, that a sufficient number would not be left to perform the funeral rites. Such construction of the meaning is required by the following parallelism: וּמִסְפֵּד אֶל־יוֹדְעֵי נֶהִי. There is no necessity for supposing that the words of this sentence have been transposed, and that they originally stood thus: וְקָרְאוּ אִכָּר אֶל־מִסְפֵּד. The preposition אֶל is understood before מִסְפֵּד, and קָרְאוּ, as repeated to govern אֶל, which it often does, as well as the accusative. נֶהִי, *wailing, lamentation*, from' נָהָה, Syr. ܢܗܐ, *to utter lamentable cries.* The persons here spoken of as "skilled in wailing," were mourners by profession, who were hired for the occasion, and sung doleful tunes around the corpse of a deceased person, which they preceded when it was carried to the grave, giving utterance to dismal cries and howlings, beating their breasts, throwing ashes on their heads, and showing every artificial token of excessive grief. These were the mourners whom Solomon describes as going about the streets, Eccles. xii. 5. That females were especially employed on such occasions, appears from Jer. ix. 17–19, where נֶהִי is twice used as here by Amos. The same custom obtained among the Greeks and Romans. Thus Homer speaking of the funeral of Hector, says:

——— τὸν μὲν ἔπειτα
Τρητοῖς ἐν λεχέεσσι θέσαν, παρὰ δὲ εἷσαν
ἀοιδούς,
Θρήνων ἐξάρχους, οἵ τε στονόεσσαν ἀοιδὴν
Οἱ μὲν ἄρ' ἐθρήνεον, ἐπὶ δὲ στενάχοντο
γυναῖκες.
Iliad. xxiv. 720, etc.

See also Horace de Arte Poet. ver. 433. In his edition of Harmer's Observations, vol. iii. p. 42. Dr. A. Clarke gives a description of the ancient funeral solemnities of the Irish, and the translation of a song of wailing prepared for the occasion, which bears a strong resemblance to those used by the Orientals. Comp. Wilkinson's Ancient Egyptians, second series, vol. ii. pp. 402–407.

17. The vineyards, which usually exhibited scenes of rejoicing, should now be frequented by disconsolate mourners. For Jehovah's passing through the land, comp. Exod. xii. 12, 23 ; only in the latter case the punishment was miraculously inflicted ; in the former, the king of Assyria, as an instrument in the hand of God.

18–20. These verses intimately cohere with the preceding. *The day of Jehovah* means the time when his judgments should be inflicted. The Israelites could only have given expression sarcastically

21 I hate, I loathe your festivals;
    Neither do I delight in your days of restraint,
22 When ye offer to me holocausts and bloodless sacrifices,
    I will take no pleasure in them;
    Neither will I regard the thank-offerings of your fatlings.
23 Take away from me the noise of the songs;
    I will not hear the music of thy harps.

to the wish that this day might soon reach them. It was an impious daring of Jehovah to do his worst. Comp. Is. v. 19: Jer. xvii. 15. The prophet tells them plainly that it would be to them a day of unmitigated affliction. The fallacy of every hope of escape is illustrated by two simple, but forcible comparisons, borrowed from the pastoral life. Bochart regards the language as proverbial, and supports his opinion by two Arabic stories: the one beginning, اسد قصد ابسانا وهرب والتجا الي سجرة وانا علي بعض اغصنها دب يقطق ثمرها "A lion, pursuing a man, he took refuge in a tree, in the branches of which a bear having fixed himself, was plucking its fruit," etc.; and the other, هرب رجل من الاسد فوقع في بير ووقع الاسد خلفه فانا في البير دب, "A man fled from a lion, and fell into a well, into which the lion went down after him. And there was a bear in the well," etc. Hierozo. lib. iii. cap. ix. pp. 810, 811. Kimchi tersely expresses the meaning thus, תצא מצרה אל יָעה, Ye shall go out of calamity into calamity. Comp. Job xx. 24; Is. xxiv. 18. The adjective אפל is explained by the following words. It occurs only in this place; but the substantives אֹפֶל, אֲפֵלָה dense obscurity, are used in several passages of Job, the Psalms, and the prophets. אֲפֵלוֹת, however, in the sense of concealed, occurs Exod. ix. 32. Comp. the Arab. أفل, occidit sol, etc. Thus in Hariri, Consess. xv. the noun أفول is employed

انقراض العلم ودروسه واڤول اتباره وشهسه, "Extirpatio cruditionis et obliteratio ejus: Lunarumque ac Solium ejusdem occasus." נָגַהּ, on the contrary, signifies to shine, be light; and its derivative נֹגַהּ is used of the rising of the sun, Prov. iv. 18, and is contrasted with אֲפֵלָה, ver. 19.

21–23. The same aversion from the ceremonial observances of the insincere and rebellious Israelites which Jehovah here expresses, he afterwards employed Isaiah to declare to the Jews, chap. i. 10–15. The two passages are strikingly parallel; only the latter prophet amplifies what is set forth in a more condensed form by Amos. It is also to be observed, that where Amos introduces the musical accompaniments of the sacrifices, Isaiah substitutes the prayers; both concluding with the divine words, לֹא אֶשְׁמָע=אַיִן, שֹׁמֵעַ, I will not hear. The verbs שָׂנֵאתִי, מָאַסְתִּי follow each other immediately, for the sake of more emphatically expressing the Divine abhorrence. Com. תוֹעֵבָה היא לֹא and אָרְחָה in Isaiah. לֹא אָרִיחַ, lit. I will not smell; but meaning here, I will take no delight in. עֲצָרוֹת, restraints, periods, days of restraint, or assemblies collected on such days. See on Is. i. 13. חַג, used here collectively for the plural חַגִּים. — מִעֲלַי הָסֵר, lit. remove from upon me; conveying the idea of a burden which vexes and annoys the bearer. Isaiah expresses it in full: הָיוּ עָלַי לָטֹרַח, "They are a burden upon me." Comp. further for the force of the compound preposition, Exod. x. 28. The music here referred to was that performed at the Hebrew festivals by the Levites, before and during the

24 Let justice roll on like water,
And righteousness like a mighty stream.
25 Did ye not present sacrifices and offerings to me,

offering of the sacrifices, and on other public occasions.

24. While no direction is given respecting the regulation of the sacrifices, in order that they might be presented in an acceptable manner, a special injunction is imparted in regard to justice and rectitude, on the principle that to obey is better than sacrifice, and to hearken than the fat of rams," 1 Sam. xv. 22. "Nec in victimis, licet optimæ sint, auroque præfulgeant, Deorum est honos, sed pia ac recte mente venerantium." Seneca de Beneficiis, i. 6. That אֵיתָן, Arab. وثن, *perennis fuit,* is to be here rendered *perennial,* or overflowing, and not *mighty*, has been maintained by some interpreters; but a comparison of the several passages in which it occurs, goes to show that it is rather to be referred to اوثن, *valida, fuit, multus fuit,* and is to be rendered *great* or *mighty*. It thus better corresponds with גָּלַל, *roll, to roll on*, used in the former hemistich. LXX. ὡς χειμάρροις ἄβατος. Syr. ܐܡܪ ܓܠܝܕܐ ܚܡܝܕܐ Vulg. *quasi torrens fortis,* Arab. مثل الوادي الذي لا يسلك *like a Wady that cannot be passed.* The ideas of abundance and moral power are those conveyed by the prophet. I must differ from Prof. Lee, who (Heb. Lex. in voc. אֵיתָן) renders, "for judgment rolleth (away) as the waters (roll away), and righteousness (disappears) like the mighty torrent." The verse as thus rendered ill suits the context, and is not in keeping with parallel passages in which, after a reprehension of hypocritical observances, the moral qualities of truth and righteousness are required. The construction put upon it by Theodoret, Kimchi, Munster, Veil, and Hitzig, that the coming of the Divine judgments is intended, is, for the same reasons, to be rejected.

25-27. These verses have not a little perplexed expositors, both ancient and modern. The first difficulty lies in what is said respecting the presentation of sacrifices. Greve, Dahl, and Maurer, take the ה in הַזְּבָחִים to be the article, and not the particle of interrogation, and render, *the sacrifices and offerings ye presented to me,* etc., viz. those prescribed in the law: *but now ye bear the shrine,* etc. According to this mode of construction, the present idolatrous course of the Israelites is contrasted with their former obedience to the Divine will. In order, however, to justify this interpretation, the article must have been repeated before מִנְחָה, which it is not. The insertion of the compensative Dagesh in the letter Zain cannot be pleaded in its favor, since there are several instances in which the interrogative ה takes the form of the article, before words beginning with Sheva, as הַלְבֵן, Gen. xvii. 17; הַדֶּרֶךְ, Ezek. xviii. 29; הַגְּמוּל, Joel iv. 4, etc. The ancient translators have all read interrogatively. LXX. Μὴ σφάγια καὶ θυσίας προσηνέγκατέ μοι, κ. τ. λ.; Syr. ܕܒܚܐ ܘܩܘܪܒܢܐ ܩܪܒܬܘܢ ܠܝ. Vulg. *Numquid hostias et sacrificia obtulistis mihi,* etc. Targ. הֲזִבְחִין וְקוּרְבָּנִין קְרֵיבְתּוּן קֳדָמַי אַרְבְּעִין שְׁנִין בְּמַדְבְּרָא. And so almost all the moderns, some of whom suppose the force of the question to lie in לִי, *to me,* taken emphatically, "Was it to ME," etc. while others think that an absolute denial of the presentation of sacrifices in the wilderness is implied in the words. In support of the latter opinion, it has been attempted to prove, that the Israelites could not have offered any sacrifices for want of cattle. Such a position, however, is contrary to the express declarations found in Exod. xii. 38, xvii. 3. xxxiv. 3; Lev. xvii. 1–9. Num. vii. *passim*, xx. 4, 19. The life which they led in the desert was that of Nomades, so that there could have been

During forty years in the desert, O house of Israel?
26 And yet ye bare the shrine of your king,

no lack of animals for sacrifice. The true construction of the passage is founded on the principle, that not unfrequently in Hebrew the interrogation implies, and calls for an emphatic affirmative, either expressed or understood; and is thus equivalent to a negative interrogation in our language, and indeed to הֲלוֹא in Hebrew. See 1 Sam. ii. 27, 28; Job xx. 4; Jer. xxxi. 20; Ezek. xx. 4. In the present case, as in these just cited, the persons addressed are supposed to admit' the fact couched in the appeal; but the question is so put in order the more forcibly to introduce the adversative sentence which follows in the 26th verse. The connection of the two verses is this: " Did ye not present sacrifices and offerings to me in the wilderness forty years, O house of Israel? Yes; and yet ye bare the shrine," etc. That the conjunction ו is frequently to be rendered *and yet, but yet*, or the like, see Gen. xvii. 21; Judges xvi. 15: Ps. l. 17; Is. liii. 7. What is here charged upon the ancient Israelites was their indulging in idolatrous practices while they professedly attended to the ritual observances of the Mosaic law — the very sin which Amos was commissioned to charge upon their descendants in his day, and on account of which they were to be carried into captivity. The opinion of Forsayeth (quoted by Newcome), Dahl, and others, that the sin reproved in ver. 26 was exclusively that of those who lived in the time of the prophet, is less admissible than that which refers to their ancestors, yet so that the reproof was intended to be applied on their own case by those whom the prophet addressed. — The 26th verse has been very differently rendered, as well as variously interpreted. The translation of the LXX. is as follows: Καὶ ἀνελάβετε τὴν σκηνὴν τοῦ Μολὸχ, καὶ τὸ ἄστρον τοῦ θεοῦ ὑμῶν ' Ραιφάν, τοὺς τύπους αὐτῶν, οὓς ἐποιήσατε ἑαυτοῖς; as if the Hebrew had read, אֵת סִכּוּת וְאֵת כִּיּוּן אֱלֹהֵיכֶם כּוֹכַב אֱלֹהֵיכֶם אֲשֶׁר עֲשִׂיתֶם לָכֶם׃ No vestige, however, of any such order of the words is found in any Hebrew MS., or in any other monument of antiquity, except the speech of Stephen, as recorded by Luke, Acts vii. 43, which is an almost verbal quotation from the LXX. Theod. renders thus: Καὶ ἤρατε τὴν ὅρασιν τοῦ βασιλέως ὑμῶν, ἀμαύρωσιν εἰδώλων ὑμῶν, ἄστρον τοῦ θεοῦ ὑμῶν; so that he must have read the words as they now stand in the Hebrew text. The same may be said of the Syr., Vulg., and Targ., though their renderings differ from each other in one or two minor particulars. The remark of Jerome on the discrepancies between the Hebrew text and the ancient Greek versions deserves to be quoted here: " Observandum est, apostolos et apostolicos viros in ponendis testimoniis de Veteri Testamento, non verba considerare sed sensum, nec eadem sermonum calcare vestigia, dummodo a sententiis non recedant." Comment. *in loc.* Most interpreters follow the LXX. in giving סִכּוּת by σκηνή, *a tent ;* deriving it, like סֻכָּה, and סֹךְ, of the same signification, from סָכַךְ, *to intertwine*, as branches, so as to form a booth or hut. Others, such as Jarchi, Calvin, Mercer, and Rosenmüller, take it to mean an image or idol, and render, *Siccuth your king*. They explain it by referring to the Chald. סִכְּתָא, a *wooden post*, which they suppose formed the pedestal on which the idol stood, and so the word might be transferred to the idol itself. Ewald takes much the same view. The former derivation is alone admissible. The text appears to have had something of the texture, as it had the design of the σκηνῆς ἱερᾶς, *sacred tent*, in the Carthaginian camp, mentioned by Diodorus Siculus, lib. xx. cap. 25, and described as consisting ἐκ καλάμου καὶ χόρτου, of reeds and grass. Comp. Wilkinson's Ancient Egypt, second series, vol. ii. pp. 270-275. Only, as it is certain Moses would not have tolerated anything of the kind if its size had been such as to bring it to his cognizance, it may be inferred, that it was only a small temple or shrine, which might easily be concealed in the interior

And Chiun of your images, the star of your god,
Which ye made for yourselves.

of a tent. Such diminutive temples were in use among the Egyptians, from whom no doubt the Hebrews took the idea. Herodotus, describing an idol worshipped at Papremis, says, τὸ δὲ ἄγαλμα ἐὸν ἐν ΝΗΩι ΜΙΚΡΩι ξυλίνῳ κατακεχρυσωμένῳ προεκκομίζουσι τῇ προτεραίῃ ἐς ἄλλο οἴκημα ἱρόν, "The image, being in a *small temple* of gilt wood, they carry out on the previous day to another sacred habitation." Compare the ναοὶ ἀργυροῖ, shrines, or small temples of Diana, mentioned Acts xix. 24. That any connection is to be traced between סֻכּוֹת, *Siccuth*, and סֻכּוֹת בְּנוֹת, *Succoth-benoth*, 2 Kings xvii. 30, the tents in which the daughters of the Babylonians prostituted themselves in worship of Venus, does not appear. מַלְכְּכֶם, *your king*, thus Symm. Theodot. and Leo Juda, and most moderns; but the LXX. Μολὸχ, Syr. ܡܠܟܘܡ, *Malcum*, Aq. Μέλχεμ, Vulg. *Moloch*, exhibit the word as the proper name of the god of the Ammonites, *i. e.* מֶלֶךְ, also called מִלְכֹּם, *Milcom*, 1 Kings xi. 5, and מַלְכָּם, *Malcam*, Zeph. i. 5; and this construction some moderns have adopted; but as מֶלֶךְ, *king*, is also employed by the Hebrews in application to idols, Is. xxxvii. 13, Zeph. i. 5, it is better to retain its usual signification. The Phœnicians gave the title of מֶלֶךְ עֹלָם, *king of the world*, to the sun, and מַלְךְ־קַרְת=מִלְקַרְת, *king of the city*, to Hercules Comp. Ζεῦ ἄνα. Iliad. iii. 351, xvi. 233; and *Ω 'ναξ ἦλθε παρ' ἡμέας ἱκέτης, Herod. I. 159. In Ethiopic አምላክ, *Amlak*, the proper name for God, is derived from መለከ, *imperavit, rexit*, and is applied in the plural to idols. The learned are generally agreed, that the Moloch of Scripture was the image of the planet *Saturn*, and thus identical with *Chiun*, mentioned by Amos in the following clause of the verse. The Phœnicians were in the habit of offering to him human sacrifices, especially children, to which horrible custom repeated reference is made in the historical books of the Old Testament. See Michaelis on the laws of Moses, Art. ccxlvii. Suppl. No. 1115; Selden de Diis Syris, cap. vi.; Spencer de Legibus Hebræor. lib. ii. cap. 10; Gesenius, in his Thesaurus, *sub voc.*; Winer, Realwörter-buch. כִּיּוּן צַלְמֵיכֶם, *Chiun of your images*, i. e. represented by them; the model after which they were made. While the idol so called, which the Hebrews carried about in a sacred shrine, was itself a symbol or representative of one of the heavenly bodies, it was in its turn represented by a number of copies, or smaller images, which they used as penates or household gods in the practice of astrology. Such appears to me to be the meaning of the words. To this construction, however, C. B. Michaelis, Vitringa, Rosenmüller, Hesselberg, Hengstenberg, and others object, that it makes כִּיּוּן a proper name, which, with the older grammarians, they allege cannot be put in regimen. But to this rule, it must be admitted, there are many exceptions, as רִמּוֹן חֲרֵמוֹן, בַּעַל גָּד, בְּרִית יְהֹוָה, כֹּהֲנוֹת צְבָאוֹת אֱלֹהֵי אֲדָמָה, בְּגָדִים, etc. Nor can it justly be objected that as סִכּוּת is an appellative, כִּיּוּן being parallel to it, must necessarily be the same. The necessity of the case is not obvious. Both are mentioned as objects which the Hebrews carried about for idolatrous purposes, — the one, the portable temple of the idol; the other the idol itself placed in this temple, of which numerous miniature resemblances were privately distributed throughout the camp. The LXX. unquestionably regarded the word as a proper name, whatever they may thereby have intended to designate. And this view of the subject is confirmed by כּוֹכָב, *a star*, being put in apposition with כִּיּוּן, in order to explain it, an explanation which cannot apply, if by the latter term we understand merely the *pedestal* or *stand* on which the idol was placed. It is now

AMOS. CHAP. V.

27 Therefore, I will carry you away captive beyond Damascus,

almost a settled point, that by כִּיוּן, *Chiun*, the planet *Saturn* is meant. If we except the Syr., which reads ܟܹܐܘܿܢ, *Kevon*, the earliest authorities which we have for this interpretation of the passage are the rabbins Abenezra and Kimchi; but their testimony as relating to a matter of fact is irrefragable, however slightingly Hengstenberg seems to treat it, Authen. des Pentat. p. 113. The former thus comments upon the passage: ומלח כיון ידוע בלשון ישמעאל גם פרס כי הוא כיאן והוא שבתי כי עשו לו צלם, "And as for the term *Chiun*, it is known in the Arabic and Persic languages by the name *Kivan*, which is Saturn, to which they made an image." And the latter, in nearly the same words: הוא כוכב שבתי וכן נקרא בלשון ישמעאל ופרס כיאן, "It is the star Saturn, and thus he is called *Kivan* in the Arabic and Persic."

كيوان, *Keivan*, seems to have been adopted from the latter into the former of these languages, in the Lexicons of which, as a foreign word, it is explained by زحل, the usual name for Saturn in Arabic. It occurs in the Persian work entitled Dabistan, the author of which, describing the temples which the ancient Persians dedicated to the planets says:

پیکر شت کیوان را از سنگ سیاه, that "the image of *Keivan* was of black stone." Lee's Hebrew Lex. *in voc.* אֶרֶץ. He speaks, in fact, of the خانه, *shrine*, and پیکر, *image*, of the planet, just as Amos does of סִכּוּת and כִּיוּן. According to the Zendavesta the seven planets are Tir, Behram, Achuma, Anahid, *Keivan*, Gurtsher, and Dodidom Mushewer. Bundehesh. V. In the codex Nasareus, containing the doctrines of the Sabæans, which was published by Norberg, we find a list of the demons which rule these planets, among whom ܟܹܐܘܿܢ ܫܡܗ, the fifth is *Kivan*, p. 54. It is afterwards

added in the same page: ܘܗܘܿ ܪܥܡܐ ܡܢܐ ܘܕܡܥܬܐ ܐܡܣܪ ܘܐܘܪܡܐܠ ܠܓܒܪܐ ܟܠܗܘܢ ܚܣܢܐ ܐܢܐ ܡܢ ܠܒܘܬܐ ܟܠܗܘܢ, "The demons of *Kivan* inject lamentation, weeping and mourning into the hearts of men, and rob them of happiness." And we farther read, p. 212, ܠܟܝܘܢ ܡܚܣܟ ܣܠܣܪܐ ܘܩܠܠܐ ܡܢ ܣܩܡܬܐ ܘܚܣܪܢܐ, "To *Kivan* is attributed malice, because from it come diminution and want." Ascribing the same evil influence to Saturn, the Arabs likewise give to it the name of النحس الاكبر, *the great disaster*; and the idea frequently occurs in the Latin classics. See Lucan i. 650; Juven. vi. 569; Macrob. Saturn. i. 19. If the Hebrew כִּיוּן be pointed כֵּיוָן, the exact pronunciation of the name of the planet in the other Oriental dialects will be brought out, and thus the evidence of identity be complete. With respect to 'Ραιφὰν, the rendering of the LXX., or 'Ρέφαν, as it is to be spelt, on the authority of the best MSS., Acts vii. 43, there is every reason to believe that they mistook ב for ר, as they have done in other instances; and so have given *Rephan*, instead of *Kephan*. That PHΦAN should occur in the Arabico-Coptic table of the planets exhibited by Kircher in his Ling. Ægypt. Restit. p. 49, by no means proves that this was the ancient Egyptian name of Saturn; for as that table is of no great antiquity, and as the other names are chiefly derived from the Greek, we may reasonably infer that the one in question was copied from the Coptic version of this very passage of the LXX. At all events, no such name of a deity has yet been found in the Egyptian pantheon. סִכּוּת, the

Saith Jehovah: God of hosts is his name.

star, is expletive of כִּיוּן, in so far as it informs us that the figure of the idol was that of a star, and thus proves the idolatrous worship to have been the Sabæan, with which the Hebrews became acquainted during their stay in the Arabian desert.

27. Instead of מֵהַלְאָה לְדַמֶּשֶׂק, LXX. ἐπέκεινα Δαμασκοῦ, "beyond Damascus," with which all the other authorities agree, Stephen has ἐπέκεινα Βαβυλῶνος, "beyond *Babylon*," Acts vii. 43, obviously by way of interpretation. הָלְאָה naturally suggests the idea of *remoteness*, though it is sometimes used in reference to what is at no great distance.

Root הָלַךְ, Arab. هَلَكَ, *recessit*, Syr. ܗܠܟ, *removit, elongavit*. The ה added is paragogic. While what Amos states is included in the statement made by the proto-martyr, the latter embraces what was known from fact to be the fulfilment of the prophecy: the Israelites having been carried, not merely beyond Damascus, but beyond Babylon, into the country of the Medes. The chapter closes with a vindication of the supremacy of Jehovah above all the objects of Sabæan worship: יְהוָה צְבָאוֹת שְׁמוֹ, *God of Sabaoth is his name!*

CHAPTER VI.

THIS chapter embraces the character and punishment of the whole Hebrew nation. The inhabitants of the two capitals are directly addressed in the language of denunciation, and charged to take warning from the fate of other nations, 1, 2. Their carnal security, injustice, self indulgence, sensuality, and total disregard of the divine threatenings, are next described, 3–6; after which the prophet announces the captivity, and the calamitous circumstances connected with the siege of Samaria, by which it was to be preceded, 7–11. He then exposes the absurdity of their conduct, and threatens them with the irruption of an enemy, that should pervade the whole country, 12–14.

1 Wo to them that are at ease in Zion,
And to them that are secure in the mountain of Samaria;
The distinguished men of the first nations,

1. Though chiefly directed against the northern of the two kingdoms, the language of this prophecy is so constructed as to apply to both: and in the present verse express mention is made of the inhabitants of Jerusalem, who resembled those of Samaria in carelessness and carnal security. בָּטַח and שָׁאַן are similarly connected and applied, Is. xxx. 9, 11; so that the rendering of the LXX. τοῖς ἐξουθενοῦσι Σιών, adopted by Dathe, cannot be justified. For the primary meaning of שַׁאֲנָן, compare the cognate שָׁעַן, in Niphal, *to lean, lean upon, trust*. The reduplicate *Nun* expresses intensity. נָקַב has here the acceptation of the Arab. نَقَبَ, *rerum gentis administrator, princeps gentis*: from نَقَبَ, *perfodit, creatus est*; *creatus fuit dux*. Whence also نِقَابَة, *prefectura*. The Hebrew phrase נְקֻבֵי בְּרֵאשִׁית, *to be marked*,

21

To whom the house of Israel come!
2 Pass over to Calneh, and see;
And go thence to Hamath the great;
Go down also to Gath of the Philistines:
Were they better than these kingdoms?
Were their boundaries more ample than yours?
3 Wo to them that put off the day of evil,

distinguished by name, is always used in reference to persons who had been chosen or designated for some special service. Num. i. 17; 1 Chron. xii. 31, xvi. 41; 2 Chron. xxviii. 15, xxxi. 19. The term is here employed for the purpose of specifying more particularly the leading men in the two kingdoms, whose profligacy and irreligion preëminently aggravated the national guilt. By רֵאשִׁית הַגּוֹיִם we are not, with Newcome, to understand "the chief of the idolatrous nations," and that the persons spoken of were called after them, but the Hebrew nation, which is so called because it was the *principal*, or most distinguished of all the nations of the earth; having been constituted the peculiar people of God, and possessing laws and privileges unknown to any other. It might well be said to occupy the *first* rank. Comp. רֵאשִׁית גּוֹיִם עֲמָלֵק, Num. xxiv. 20, where the reference is to the distinguished place which the Amalekites held among the nations of Canaan. לָכֶם is to be construed with הַרְבִּים, and not with גּוֹיִם, or with צִיּוֹן and שֹׁמְרוֹן. The people of Israel were in the habit of going up to their princes and leaders for the decision of differences, etc. They exerted an influence over the entire people. Both the LXX. and the Syr. are greatly at fault in the translation of this verse.

2. Three heathen cities are here selected as specimens of the greatness and prosperity of the nations to which they belonged, and the Israelites are challenged to institute a comparison of the circumstances of these nations and the extent of their territory, with those of their own, as also, to reflect on the present prostrate condition of the cities mentioned, in order that they might become sensible of the superiority with

which Jehovah had distinguished them, and the greater punishment to which they had exposed themselves by their ungrateful returns. For כַּלְנֵה, *Calneh*, and חֲמָת, *Hamath*, see on Is. x. 9. Hitzig attempts to prove that by the latter name, אַחְמְתָא, *Ecbatana* or *Hamedan* is meant; but there is no reason to believe that the Hebrews had any knowledge of this city in the days of Amos. It is here called רַבָּה, *great*, not to distinguish it from other cities of the same name, but to express its size and magnificence. Comp. צִידוֹן רַבָּה, *Sidon the great*, Josh. xi. 8. גַּת, *Gath*, was the chief city of one of the five satrapies of the Philistines, with whose name it is here associated, to distinguish it from Gath-Hepher, and Gath-Rimmon. It had more than once been reduced before the time of Amos, and disappeared at an early period from the annals of geography. No trace of it has been discovered by any modern traveller. The ה in הַטֹּבִים has been regarded as the Article by the LXX., Syr., and Vulg. translators, and is thus found in twelve of De Rossi's MSS.; but the more natural construction is that of the Targ. and most modern versions, which makes it interrogative. Before the מִן of comparison is an ellipsis of הֵמָּה; and הָאָרֶץ, הַמַּמְלָכוֹת, *these kingdoms*, must be understood as designating those of Israel and Judah, with which the prophet had immediately to do, and to which he thus emphatically points. In this way only can an appropriate reference be found for the distinctive affixes in גְּבוּלְכֶם and גְּבוּלָם.

3. Supply הוֹי, *wo to*, from ver. 1. הַמְנַדִּים, the Targ. not inappropriately explains by מַרְחִיקִין, *remove to a distance*. The root is נָדָה, which in the other dia-

And bring near the seat of oppression;
4 That lie upon beds of ivory,
And are stretched upon their couches;
That eat lambs from the flock,
And calves from the midst of the stall;
5 That strike up songs to the sound of the lyre;
Like David they invent for themselves instruments of music;
6 That drink in bowls of wine,
And anoint with the first of oils;
But are not grieved for the destruction of Joseph!

lects signifies *to separate, remove* as an object of disgust. Aq. οἱ ἀποκεχωρισμένοι, Symm. ἀφωρισμένοι. The persons addressed could not bear the idea that the period of threatened punishment was impending; they endeavored as much as possible to keep it out of view. Comp. Ezek. xii. 21-28. In striking antithesis to this, they are represented in the following hemistich, as acting in such a manner as speedily to bring it upon them.

"Sed quam cœcus inest vitiis amor ?
omne futurum
Despicitur, suadentque brevem præsentia fructum;
Et ruit in vetitum damni secura libido,
Dum mora supplicii lucro, serumque quod instat
Creditur."
    Claud. Eutrop. lib. ii.

I cannot agree with Jerome, Grotius, Newcome, Justi, and some others, in referring שֶׁבֶת חָמָס, *the seat* or *throne of oppression*, to the rule of the king of Assyria: it is much more natural to regard the prophet as describing the wickedness of the people themselves in yielding support to a system of flagrant injustice and oppression, on the part of their own rulers and judges. Thus most expositors. שֶׁבֶת occurs nowhere else in the sense of *throne*; but יָשַׁב, of which it is properly the infinitive, is used in application both to kings and judges, as is also the participle יֹשֵׁב. The term is synonymous with כִּסֵּא, which is also used both of the throne and the bench. הִגִּישׁ is here taken by most interpreters to have the same signification as in Kal, *to approach;*

but as in every other instance in which the verb is used in Hiphil it vindicates to itself the causative acceptation, and in the present case is obviously intended to form a contrast to מְנַדִּים, which conveys the idea of *removing to a distance*, I must retain the rendering of our common version. Thus Hitzig and Ewald. The meaning is, that instead of putting away from them all illegal and oppressive judgment, they encouraged those who were guilty of them, by assisting in carrying them into execution.

4. For מִטּוֹת שֵׁן, *beds of ivory*, see on chap. iii. 15; and comp. *lecti eburnei* of Horace, and *lecti eborati* of Plautus. סְרֻחִים, from פָּרַח, Arab. ﺳﺮح, *libere dismisit, to be thrown negligently along*, is descriptive of the self-indulgent mode in which the Orientals recline upon their sofas or couches, being stretched upon them at full length. The whole verse sets forth in well chosen expressions the luxurious habits of the opulent. LXX. κατασπαταλῶντες.

5, 6. פָּרַט is a ἅπαξ λεγ., and has been thought by Gesenius, Hitzig, and Ewald, to have been selected on purpose, instead of שִׁיר, *to sing*, in order to express the contempt in which the music deserved to be held. Such interpretation, however, does not appear to be philologically sustained, and ill suits the corresponding hemistich. According to the LXX. ἐπικρατοῦντες, *presiding over*, or *at*, the verb is synonymous with נָצַח, in Piel, *superintend, lead in music.* Hence מְנַצֵּחַ, the *chief musician.* Comp. the Arab. ﻓﺮط, *prævertit, præcessit.* The

7 Therefore now they shall go captive at the head of the captives,
And the shouting company of those that recline shall depart.
8 The Lord Jehovah hath sworn by himself,
Thus saith Jehovah, God of hosts,
I abhor the splendor of Jacob,
And I hate his palaces:
Therefore will I deliver up the city, and all that is in it.
9 It shall be, that if ten men should be left in one house,

persons reprobated were so passionately fond of song, that they could not be content to listen to the performances of professed musicians, but took the lead in striking up songs to the sound of the lyre. The reference to David, who was the sweet singer of Israel, and of whose musical instruments express mention is made Neh. xii. 36, is manifestly ironical; implying that, while that monarch devoted his musical talent to the glory of God, the dissipated grandees of Israel consulted only their personal gratification, and that of those who joined their giddy circle. מִזְרָקִים were properly *basins*, or *bowls*, of a larger size, used for sacrificial purposes, Exod. xxxviii. 3; Num. vii. 13, 19. The persons referred to, indulged to such excess, that ordinary cups were unsuited to their compotations. They likewise anointed themselves with the most precious oils, and evinced a total apathy in regard to the calamities to which their people had already been subject, or the still more serious evils which threatened them. For the meaning of יוֹסֵף, *Joseph*, see on chap. v. 6.

7. מִרְזַח, Arab. مِرْزَح, *vox, the shout* or *cry*, in which the merrymakers indulged over their cups. The persons giving the shout seem to be intended, and, as the term is also used in reference to a cry of lamentation, Jer. xvi. 5, it may be implied that their joy would be turned into sorrow. They are spoken of collectively. Symm. ἑταιρεία τρυφητῶν. Those who had taken the lead in revelry and all manner of wickedness, were to be first in the procession of captives. In such a position, their disgrace would be more conspicuous.

8. The double form of asseveration here employed is unusual, and is strongly emphatic. מְתָאֵב, the Piel participle of תָּאַב, a root of the same signification with תָּעַב. Compare for a similar interchange of these letters נָגַב and גָּנַב, נָשָׂא and גָּשָׂא. Though the phrase גְּאוֹן יַעֲקֹב, *the excellency of Jacob*, cannot be otherwise understood than of God himself, as the only legitimate object of glorying on the part of his people, chap. viii. 7, yet, in the present instance, it is to be taken in application to the country and peculiar privileges of the Hebrews. It was once a country piously celebrated in song as *the excellency of Jacob*, Ps. xlvii. 5, and the peculiar object of divine regard; but now defiled by the wickedness of its inhabitants, it had become the object of his abhorrence. By עִיר, the *city*, Amos had most probably Samaria in his eye. Hitzig attaches to הִשְׁבַּעְתִּי, the signification of Kal, *to besiege, shut up*, but the usual Hiphil signification better agrees with the following connection. מְלֹא, *fulness*, conveys the idea of multitude, or great abundance, and comprehends here both the numerous inhabitants themselves, and the wealth and means of gratification in which they abounded. Comp. Ps. xxiv. 1. For the accomplishment of the prediction, see 2 Kings xvii. 5, 6.

9, 10. The scene is not necessarily laid in the city; it might also have been realized in any of the towns or villages in the country that had been depopulated by the Assyrians. It depicts, in the most affecting manner, the deplorable condition of the few that had escaped the enemy, and had now been attacked by the plague — a usual attendant on

They also shall die.
10 And one's relative, even he that burneth him shall take him up,
To remove his bones out of the house;
And shall say to him that is in the innermost part of the house,
Is there yet any with thee;
And he shall say, None!
Then shall he say, Hush!
For we must not mention the name of Jehovah.
11 For behold! Jehovah hath commanded,
And he will smite the great house with breaches,
And the small house with fissures.

war in the East. The prophet declares, that if as many as ten had been left in one house, which might be regarded as a rare instance, they should die, one after another, of this fatal disease. דוד is not here to be taken in the special sense of *uncle*, but denotes any near relative on whom it devolved to attend to the funeral rites. Targ. קְרִיבֵיהּ. Vulg. *propinquus*. In the present case, such would be the paucity of hands, that he would have to perform the whole himself. The copulative ו, prefixed to מְשָׂרְפוֹ, is epexegetical, and is to be rendered *even*, as in Zech. ix. 9. Instead of מְשָׂרְפוֹ, many both of Kennicott's and De Rossi's MSS. read correctly מְשָׂרְפוֹ. But comp. the Syr. ܡܣܶܦ. Some have attempted to prove from this, and some other passages, that it was the practice of the Hebrews to burn their dead. But what is said 2 Chron. xvi. 14, xxi. 19; Jer. xxxiv. 5, obviously refers to the burning of spices, and not of dead bodies. 1 Sam. xxxi. 12, and our present text, exhibit special cases. In the former of these, the object was so to dispose of the corpses that it might not be in the power of the Philistines further to dishonor them; while in the latter, it was either, as Grotius supposes, to prevent contagion, or to dispose of the body in the only way of which the circumstances of the time would allow. That by עֲצָמִים, not mere *bones* are meant, nor bodies so emaciated as to be nothing but skin and bone, which is Winer's opinion, but *dead bodies*, seems established beyond all doubt by a reference to Gen. 1. 25; Exod. xiii. 19; 2 Kings xiii. 21; Jer. viii. 1, 2. בְּיַרְכְּתֵי הַבַּיִת, is well rendered in the Vulg. *in penetralibus domus*. See on Is. xiv. 13. Having burnt and removed one body after another, the relative, discovering a patient in one of the innermost rooms or corners of the house, inquires whether he is the only survivor? and on receiving for answer that he is, he suddenly enjoins silence upon him. There is some difficulty in dertermining what occasioned this injunction, and for what reason the Divine name was not to be mentioned. Most probably the patient had begun to give vent to his feelings in expressions of praise to Jehovah, for sparing his life in the midst of such prevailing mortality; when the other, from some superstitious notion, or from the supposed incongruity of praising God in such circumstances, interrupted his pious effusions. הַזְכִּיר בְּשֵׁם, means to *mention*, or *record with approbation*, as an object of trust. Comp. Josh. xxiii. 7; Ps. xx. 8. The phrase cannot, therefore, be construed into the language of despair — as if the person who gave utterance to the words besought God to take him away likewise, and thus terminate the melancholy scene. Nor, for the same reason, can it imply, as Michaelis interprets, that he had confirmed what he had stated with an oath.

11. Grotius, Dahl, Justi, and Ewald, adopt the interpretation of the Targ., Jerome, and Cyril, that by the "*great house*" is meant the kingdom of Israel,

12 Shall horses run upon a rock?
    Will one plough there with oxen?
    Yet we have converted justice into poison,
    And the fruit of righteousness into wormwood.
13 Ye that rejoice in a thing of nought,
    That say,
    Have we not by our own strength,
    Taken to ourselves horns?
14 But behold! I will raise up against you, O house of Israel!
    A nation, saith Jehovah, God of hosts;
    And they shall oppress you,
    From the entrance of Hamath,
    To the river of the desert.

and by the "small house" that of Judah; and comp. chap. ix. 8, 9, where the same participial form נִגָּזָה is employed as here before another verb. רְסִיסִים, mean *atoms*, or the minute parts to which the materials of a building are reduced, when it is utterly destroyed. The word otherwise signifies the small drops of any liquid that is sprinkled, and is derived from רָסַס, *to sprinkle*. בְּקָעִים, are *fissures*, or rents in an edifice, which threaten its fall. There was to be a marked difference in the treatment of the two kingdoms; the one was to be utterly destroyed, while the other, though greatly injured, was still to stand. Rosenmüller, however, regards the interpretation as "arguta magis, quam vera." Calvin, Vatablus, Marckius, Coccejus, Lowth, Michaelis, and Maurer, likewise take the words literally, as applying to the houses both of the rich and the poor. The destruction, more or less, was to be universal.

"Regum turres ac pauperum tabernas."
                                Horace.

This construction of the verse is confirmed by a comparison with chap. iii. 15.

12. The folly of expecting real prosperity while committing acts of injustice, is forcibly represented by comparing it to the absurdity of attempting to run horses upon a rock, or to plough it with oxen. To add to the strength of the representation, it is put in the interrogative form. חֲיֻרַשׁ is to be taken impersonally.

13. The participles, with the הַ demonstrative, are again employed as in verses 3, 4, 5, 6. לֹא דָבָר, *non-re*, what is so perishable and evanescent, that it may well be said to have no existence. *Horns* are the symbol of power and dominion.

14. Few instances will be found in Hebrew, in which the object of a verb is so far removed from it as ־כִי here is from מָקוֹם. Some have referred נַחַל הָעֲרָבָה, *the river of the Desert*, to the Rhinocorura, otherwise called the river of Egypt; and others to "the brook of the willows," נַחַל הָעֲרָבִים, or the *Wady el-Ahsa*, which flows into the Dead Sea, near Zoar; but it is obvious from 2 Kings xiv. 25, in which the limits here specified are described as constituting those of the kingdom of the ten tribes, that it must mean the brook Kidron, which falls into the Dead Sea to the south of Jericho. One of the names given to this sea is יָם הָעֲרָבָה, *the Sea of the Desert*; הָעֲרָבָה, *the desert*, forming what is now commonly called الغور,

El-Ghor, or the low sterile region in which the valley of the Jordan terminates, and which extends as far as the Elanitic Gulf.

VII.—VIII. 3.

This portion of the book contains four symbolical visions respecting successive judgments that were to be inflicted on the kingdom of Israel. They were delivered at Bethel, and in all probability at the commencement of the prophet's ministry. Each of them, as they follow in the series, is more severe than the preceding. The first presented to the mental eye of the prophet a swarm of young locusts, which threatened to cut off all hope of the harvest, 1-3; the second, a fire, which effected an universal conflagration, 4-6; the third, a plumb-line, ready to be applied to mark out the edifices that were to be destroyed, 7-9; and the fourth, a basket of ripe fruit, denoting the near and certain destruction of the kingdom, viii. 1-3. The intervening eight verses, which conclude the seventh chapter, contain an account of the interruption of Amos by Amaziah, the priest of Bethel, whose punishment is specially predicted. In point of style, this portion differs from that of the rest of the book, being almost exclusively historical and dialogistic.

---

1 Thus the Lord Jehovah showed me, and, behold, he formed locusts at the beginning of the shooting up of the latter grass: and, behold, it was the latter grass after the king's mowings.
2 And it came to pass, when they had entirely devoured the grass of the land, I said:

1. All the four visions are introduced in nearly the same language: כֹּה הִרְאַנִי אֲדֹנָי יְהוִה וְהִנֵּה. The repetition of הִנֵּה, *behold*, is peculiar to this verse. In the latter of the two instances, it is employed for the sake of emphasis, instead of the substantive verb, גֹּבַי, a name of the locust. occurring only here, and Nah. iii. 17, and synonymous with אַרְבֶּה, Is. xxxiii. 4, Comp. the Arab. جَابٌ and جَابِي, *locusta*, from جَبَى, *egressus fuit*, in reference to its coming forth out of the egg, which had been deposited in the earth to be hatched. The term is, therefore, strictly descriptive of the locust in its caterpillar state, and thus agrees with the use of the verb יָצַר, *to form*, which is here used. Prof. Lee derives it from جُوبٌ, *secuit*. Credner on Joel, pp. 299-302, elaborately attempts to set aside the above derivation of Bochart, yet allows that the word denotes the insect in the first stage of its existence. The plural termination ־ִי, is found in several masculine nouns, as דָּבָר, חֲלָלִי, לְבוּשׁ, etc.; but the anomaly has not yet been satisfactorily accounted for. See, however, Gesen. Lehrgeb. p. 523. Lee's Heb. Gram. Art. 139, 4, 2d edit. לֶקֶשׁ, an *after-math*, or second crop, which comes up immediately after the mowing of grass. לֶקֶשׁ, cognate with לָקַשׁ, Arab. لَقَشَ, *legit, collegit*, signifies in Piel *to gather the late fruit*. Comp. the Syr. ܠܩܫ, *serotinus*, and מַלְקוֹשׁ, *the latter rain*. The phrase גִּזֵּי הַמֶּלֶךְ may either mean the mowings of the grass which grew on the royal domains, or the first mowings of that belonging to the people, to which the king tyrannically laid claim. Considering the character of the times, there can be little doubt that the latter are meant.

2. That the locusts here referred to are not intended to represent a literal swarm of these insects, but are to be taken figuratively, as denoting a hostile army, just as the fire in the second vision is to be regarded as symbolical of war, may be inferred from the figurative

O Lord Jehovah! forgive, I be[seech thee!]
Who is Jacob, that he should st[and?]
For he is small.

3 Jehovah repented of this:
It shall not be, saith Jehovah.

4 Thus the Lord Jehovah showed me, [and behold], the Lord Jehovah called to contend by fire; and [it c]onsumed the great abyss, and devoured the portion.

5 Then I said:
O Lord Jehovah! desist, I beseech thee!
Who is Jacob, that he should stand?
For he is small.

6 Jehovah repented of this:
It also shall not be, saith the Lord Jehovah.

7 Thus he showed me, and behold the Lord stood upon a per-

---

character of the two visions, ver. 7, and chap. viii. 1. Most probably the army of Pul, king of Assyria, is meant. The Israelites had been greatly reduced by repeated invasions on the part of the Syrian kings, and were on the point of being attacked by the Assyrians, but purchased their retreat with the sum of one thousand talents of silver. See 2 Kings xv. 19, 20. מִי יָקוּם יַעֲקֹב, concisely for מִי יָקוּם בְּיַעֲקֹב, *who is Jacob, that he should stand?* meaning, how can he possibly sustain the threatened attack, reduced and weak as he is in resources. קוּם signifies *to stand fast, continue, endure*, as well as *to rise*. One of De Rossi's MSS., and another originally, read יָקִים, and another יָקִם, and thus the LXX. Syr. Symm. and Vulg.; but less appropriately in such context.

3. נִחַם, Piek renders, *gave consolation*, which is not so suitable here as the signification, *to repent*. Such repentance is to be understood θεοπρεπῶς, appearing, as Veil observes, "in effectu, citra mutationem in effectu." Comp. 1 Sam. xv. 11; Jer. xlii. 10. Targ. אֲתִיב יְיָ, *the Lord turned away his wrath*. זֹאת, the feminine pronoun, stands for the neuter of other languages.

4. קֹרֵא corresponds in form to קֹרֵא ver. 1. לָרִב, an abbreviated form of the Hiphil infinitive, לְהָרִיב. Comp. Is. iii. 13. The verb signifies to *contend judicially*, to treat according to one's deserts, to punish. By the fire here spoken of we are not to understand a great heat which produced a drought in the land, but *war*, of which it is an appropriate symbol. See Num. xxi. 28; Judges ix. 15, 20; Is. lxvi. 16. To express the extent of the threatened calamity, the fire, by a bold figure, is represented as drying up the *ocean* (תְּהוֹם רַבָּה), and consuming whatever was found on the *dry land*. This acceptation of חֵלֶק, a *division, portion*, or *allotment* of land, the antithesis requires; still, however, the term is chosen with special application to the land of Canaan, which was divided to the children of Israel as their portion. The definite form of the noun אֶת־הַחֵלֶק, indicates as much. The invasion of the land of Israel by Tiglath-Pileser, and the first captivity of that people seem to be the subjects of the vision. See 2 Kings xv. 29; 1 Chron. v. 26. That in the former vision, the calamity had not been inflicted, the use of the verb סָלַח, *forgive*, intimates. In this, it had in part, as the use of חָדַל, *desist*, obviously implies.

5, 6. In these verses, as in vers. 2 and 3, we have a beautiful instance of the influence of prayer in averting or mitigating the judgments of God.

8 pendicular wall; and in his hand was a plumb-line. And Jehovah said to me, What seest thou, Amos? And I said, A plumb-line. And the Lord saith:
Behold, I will set a plumb-line
In the midst of my people Israel;
I will pass by them no more.
9 The high-places of Isaac shall be desolated,
And the sanctuaries of Israel laid waste;
And I will rise against the house of Jeroboam with the sword.
10 Then Amaziah, the priest of Bethel, sent to Jeroboam, the

7, 8. This vision, and that described chap. viii. 1–3, differ from the two preceding, in the distinct and express application of the symbols to the punishment of the Israelites. The Divine patience is exhausted. Jehovah takes active measures for executing his threatenings, and at last inflicts the exterminating judgment on a people ripe for destruction. The prophet, in consequence, intercedes no more. חוֹמַת אֲנָךְ, a perpendicular wall, lit. a wall of the plummet, so called from the plumb-line being applied in order to secure its perpendicularity. אֲנָךְ, which occurs only in these verses, properly signifies lead or tin. Arab. اَنَكٌ, Syr. ܐܰܢܟܳܐ, plumbum. Aq. γάνωσις, stannatura. The line and plummet were used not only when houses were building, but also when they were to be destroyed. See 2 Kings xxi. 13; Is. xxviii. 17, xxxiv. 11; Lam. ii 8. The LXX. and Symm. ἀδάμαντα, which the Syr. also exhibits. In the explanation of the vision, it is expressly stated, that the plummet was to be applied to the people of Israel in order to mark them out for destruction; and its being placed in *the midst* of them denoted, that this destruction was not to be confined to a part only of the kingdom, as it had been in the case of Tiglath-Pileser's invasion, but that it should reach the very centre. This took place when Shalmaneser, the successor of that king, after a siege of three years, took Samaria, put an end to the kingdom of the ten tribes, and carried them away captive into Assyria, 2 Kings xvii. 3, 5, 6, 23. עָבַר, to pass, pass on or away, means, in application to sin, to pass it by, to forgive, not to punish it. Prov. xix. 11; Micah vii. 18. See on this latter passage.

9. A definite prediction of the destruction which was to overtake the places of idolatrous worship, and the royal house by which that worship had been established and supported. These are specially mentioned, because to them, as the procuring causes, the destruction was to be traced. For the meaning of בָּמוֹת, *high places*, see on Is. lxv. 7. מִקְדְּשֵׁי, the parallel term, denotes the temples, or structures, consecrated to the worship of idols. Comp. מִקְדָּשׁ, ver. 13. יִשְׂחָק, instead of יִצְחָק, is not peculiar to our prophet; the same orthography is found Ps. cv. 9; Jer. xxxiii. 26. There is no reason whatever to suppose that the word was purposely so written, or that it was intended to be taken otherwise than as a proper name; yet the LXX. have βωμοὶ τοῦ γέλωτος; and so the Syr. Michaelis finds a paronomasia in it; Dahl, an instance of irony; and even Calvin thinks that the name was used by Amos μιμητικῶς. It is here, and ver. 16, parallel with יִשְׂרָאֵל, and denotes the ten tribes.

10, 11. Verses 10–17 contain an interesting historical episode. As there was doubtless a number of priests who conducted the idolatrous services at Bethel, כֹּהֵן must here be understood κατ' ἐξοχὴν of the chief or high priest, attached to the royal temple. In the spirit which has characterized a false

170   AMOS.   CHAP. VII.

king of Israel, saying: Amos hath formed a conspiracy against thee, in the midst of the house of Israel: the land cannot con-
11 tain all his words. For thus hath Amos said:
Jeroboam shall die by the sword;
And Israel shall surely be led away captive from his land.
12   And Amaziah said to Amos: Seer! Go, flee to the land of
13 Judah, and eat there bread, and prophesy there. But pro-
14 phesy no more at Bethel, for it is the king's sanctuary, and a royal residence. And Amos answered and said to Amaziah: I am no prophet; neither am I the son of a prophet; but I am
15 an herdsman, and a cultivator of sycamores. And Jehovah

priesthood in every age, Amaziah brings against the prophet the groundless charge of treason. That לְהָכִיל is to be rendered *contain*, and refers to number and not to atrocity, appears from כָּל, *all*, being employed before the following noun. Com. for this signification of the verb in Hiphil, 1 Kings vii. 26, 37; Ezek. xxiii. 32. In the Syr. in which a verb signifying *to endure* is used, כָּל is omitted, as not suiting the Oriental idiom.

12, 13. It does not appear that the king took any notice of the message that was sent him, so that Amaziah was left to try what the interposition of his own authority would effect. He addressed the prophet by the title חֹזֶה, *seer*, most probably with contemptuous reference to his visions; though it was adopted in the later Hebrew, as equivalent to נָבִיא, and corresponds in signification to רֹאֶה, which was anciently used, 1 Sam. ix. 9. Not imagining that Amos could be actuated by any higher principle than that of selfishness, which reigned in his own heart, the priest advised him to consult his safety by fleeing across the frontier into the kingdom of Judah, where he might obtain his livelihood by the unrestrained exercise of his prophetical gifts. The words לֵךְ בְּרַח־לְךָ, though pleonastic are emphatic. At all events, he could not be permitted any longer to prophesy in the city of Bethel, which was distinguished not only as the principal seat of the king's religion, but also as being one of his royal residences. Though the ordinary residence of the Israelitish monarchs was at Samaria, yet as they went at certain stated seasons to Bethel to worship the golden calf, they had had a palace built there for their accommodation.

14. Amos modestly but firmly repels the charge of selfishness, by declaring, that he was not a prophet by profession; that he had not been educated with a view to such profession; that he was a person of rustic habits; and that his Divine mission was altogether of an extraordinary character. בֶּן־נָבִיא, *the son*, i. e. pupil or disciple *of a prophet*. In all probability some of the schools of the prophets, of which we read in the first book of Samuel, were still in existence, in which young men were educated, who devoted themselves to the service of the theocracy in the capacity of public instructors, and to these or to more private studies, under the guidance of some prophet, Amos may be supposed to refer. בּוֹקֵר, strictly taken, means an *ox-herd*; but as בָּקָר came, in a larger acceptation, to denote cattle in general, it might signify a keeper of any kind of cattle. There is, therefore no occasion, with some, to suppose that the word was originally נוֹקֵד, as in chap. i. 1. בּוֹלֵס occurs nowhere else in the Hebrew Scriptures; but the Arab. بَلَس, signifies a *white fig*, and the Eth. ባላስ: both the *fig-tree* and its fruit. As, however, the participial form of the word is that which denotes agency, it must mean one who is occupied with, or cultivates figs. The particular mode in which the an-

(15) took me from following the flock; and Jehovah said to me:
16 Go, prophesy to my people Israel. And now, hear the word of Jehovah. Thou sayest, Prophesy not against Israel; and,
17 Drop nothing against the house of Isaac. Therefore thus saith Jehovah:
Thy wife shall commit lewdness in the city,
And thy sons and thy daughters shall fall by the sword;
Thy land, also, shall be divided by line,
And thou shalt die in a polluted land;
And Israel shall surely be taken away captive from his land.

cients cultivated fig-trees, the LXX. appear to have had in their eye, when they rendered it by κνίζων, a *nipper* or *scratcher*; for we are informed by Theophrastus, that iron nails or prongs were employed to make incisions or scratches in the tree, that by letting out some of the sap, the fruit might be ripened: πέπτειν οὐ δύναται ἂν μὴ ἐπικνισθῇ· ἀλλ' ἔχοντες ὄνυχας σιδηρᾶς ἐπικνίζουσιν· ἃ δ' ἂν ἐπικνισθῇ, τεταρταῖα πέπτεται, iv. 2. See also Plin. Hist. Nat. xiii. 14; Forskal, Flor. Egypt. p. 182. שִׁקְמִים, *sycamores*, a species of tree, abounding in the East, pretty much resembling the mulberry tree, the fruit of which is similar to the fig. It is, however, very inferior in quality, and is only eaten by the poorest class of the people. From this circumstance it may be inferred that Amos occupied a humble station in life previous to his being called to prophesy in Israel.

15. נִבָּא אֶל is used both in a good and in a bad sense, and is here to be rendered indefinitely, *to prophesy to*. The pronominal suffix in עַמִּי, " *my* people," is not without emphasis. The Israelites were Jehovah's by right; he still claimed his propriety in them; and, by the ministry of his prophet, would have recovered them to his service.

16. Instead of listening to the prohibition of Amaziah, and retiring from his sphere of duty, Amos continued to discharge the duties of his office at Bethel; but before proceeding to give an account of another vision which he had had, he directs a pointed prediction against the idolatrous priest by whom he had been interrupted. הַטִּיף, *to distil*, to cause to come down in pleasing and flowing discourse; here parallel with נָבָא, *to prophesy*. Comp. Ezek. xxi. 2, 7; Micah ii 6, 11. Syr. ܐܰܛܶܦ, Arab. طفل, Eth. ዘነመ: *stillavit*, ዘነጸ: *percolavit*.

17. Between אָמַר יְהוָה in this verse, and אָמַר אַתָּה in ver. 16, is a marked antithesis. תִּזְנֶה is not to be understood of voluntary acts of infidelity on the part of the wife of Amaziah, but of the violence to which she would have to submit on the part of the enemy. This being done בָּעִיר, *in the city*, i. e. openly and publicly, was a great aggravation of the evil.

Ὧδέ σφι ἐγκέφαλος χαμάδις ῥέοι, ὡς ὅδε οἶνος
Αὐτῶν, καὶ τεκέων, ἄλοχοι δ' ἄλλοισι
μιγεῖεν.   *Iliad*. b. iii. 300, 301.

Every country, except Canaan, was regarded by the Hebrews as אֶרֶץ טְמֵאָה, a *polluted land*, though, at this time, their own land had become such. Is. xxiv. 5, where חנף is similarly used; Jer. ii. 7. The land of Assyria is that to which Amos points.

CHAPTER VIII.

AFTER giving an account of a fourth vision, in which was represented the ripeness for destruction at which the Israelites had arrived, and the certainty of such destruction, 1-3, the prophet resumes his denunciatory addresses to the avaricious oppressors of the people, 4-7; predicts the overthrow of the nation, 8-10; and concludes with threatening a destitution of the means of religious instruction, 11-14.

---

1 Thus the Lord Jehovah showed me, and, behold, a basket of
2 ripe fruit! And he said, What seest thou, Amos? And I said,
   A basket of ripe fruit.
   Then said Jehovah to me:
   The end is come to my people Israel;
   I will pass by them no more.
3 And the songs of the palace shall howl,
   In that day, saith the Lord Jehovah;
   The carcasses are many!
   Throw them out anywhere!
   Hush!
4 Hear this! ye that pant after the needy,

1. This vision may be regarded as a continuation of the subject with which the last concluded, in the development of which the prophet had been interrupted by Amaziah. בְּלוּב, Syr. ‍‍ܟܠܘܒܐ, a *cage*, or *basket*; Arab. كلّ, *inseruit loro inter duas corii partes;* كلّة, *lorum vel filamentum lignosum palmæ, quo consuitur:* what is braided from twigs, such as wicker work. קַיִץ is used both of *summer*, and of the *fruit* which is gathered in *summer*. It is to the *ripeness* of the fruit at this season that prominence is here designed to be given. The verb occurs but once in Heb. viz. Is. xviii. 6. Arab. قبظ, *media æstas:* قاظ, *admodum ferbuit, æstiva habuit.*

2. The paronomasia in קַיִץ and קֵץ is marked and forcible. Comp. Ezek. vii. 6: קֵץ בָּא בָּא הַקֵּץ הֵקִיץ אֵלָיִךְ הִנֵּה בָּאָה.

3. Instead of the pathetic elegies loudly and continuously poured forth at the princely funerals, nothing was to be heard but the frantic howl, announcing, but instantly checked in announcing, the greatness of the disaster. Into such howling the joyous songs of the palace were to be converted. Symm. ὀλολύξουσιν αἱ ᾠδαί. The dead bodies were to be cast forth indiscriminately, without any regard to the places where they might lie; and even this was not to be effected without exposing those who performed it to the attacks of the enemy. Hence silence was to be enjoined. Some improperly render הֵיכָל, *temple.* For הָס, comp. chap. vi. 10.

4. The prophet resumes his usual style of direct comminatory address. Comp. chapters iv. v. and vi. For שֹׁאֲפִים, see on chap. ii. 7. לְהַשְׁבִּית=לְהַשְׁבִּית, *to cause to cease, bring to an end, annihilate, destroy.* The ו in לְהַשְׁבִּית is to be taken τελικῶς, as denoting the end or aim of

That ye may destroy the poor of the land,
5 Saying, When will the new moon be over,
That we may sell corn?
And the Sabbath,
That we may open out grain?
Making the ephah small,
And the shekel great,
And falsifying the balances for deceit.
6 That we may purchase the poor for money,
And the needy for a pair of sandals;
And sell the refuse of the grain.
7 Jehovah hath sworn by the excellency of Jacob:
I will never forget any of their deeds.

the oppressions practised by the avaricious Israelites.

5. From this and other passages it is obvious that the Israelites, notwithstanding their idolatrous practices, still kept up the observance of the times and seasons appointed in the law of Moses. שַׁבָּת and הַשְׁבִּיר שֶׁבֶר, lit. *to break a breaking*, but meaning *to sell grain*, is supposed to be so named from its being broken to pieces when ground at the mill. Some, however, think the name is derived from its being broken up or separated by a measure into portions, with a view to sale; while others are of opinion that it is so called because it breaks or puts an end to hunger, comparing Ps. civ. 11. By פָּתַח בָּר, *opening the corn*, is meant opening the *sacks* or *granaries* in which it was kept, and bringing it out for sale. Thus the LXX. Syr. and Targ. The אֵיפָה, *ephah*, was a corn measure, containing three seahs, and according to Josephus, equal to the Attic *medimnus*, or somewhat above three English pecks. It is uncertain whether the word be originally Hebrew, or whether it be Egyptian. שֶׁקֶל, from שָׁקַל, *to weigh*, Arab. قَلَسَ, *ponderosus fuit, gravitatem et pondus exploravit*, is here used of weights in general. It was originally any piece of metal weighed as an equivalent for what was bought; but came afterwards to signify standard money, and differed in value, according as it was of silver or gold, and as it was estimated by the sacred or the royal standard, Exod. xxx. 13; 2 Sam. xiv. 26. For the sake of greater emphasis, instead of saying, *to make* or *to use* deceitful balances, the verb עָוָה, *to bend, twist, pervert*, is employed, which, in point of meaning, is pleonastic. LXX. ποιῆσαι ζυγὸν ἄδικμον.

6. See chap. ii. 6. מַפָּל, from נָפַל, *to fall;* what has fallen off, *refuse*, chaff, etc.

7. The iniquitous conduct of the Israelites having been minutely described, the severe punishment which they had merited is now threatened. בִּגְאוֹן יַעֲקֹב, *the excellency of Jacob*, has been variously interpreted. The Targ. Grotius, Dahl, Newcome, and Bauer, understand the excellence conferred upon Jacob; Justi and Ewald, very preposterously, the pride or haughtiness of the people; the Rabbins and some others, the temple; but the only appropriate construction of the phrase, in this connection, is that which refers it to Jehovah *himself*, in whom alone the Hebrews gloried while they adhered to the purity of his worship, and in whom they still ought to glory. Thus the Syr. ܥܦܐ ܚܝܠܬܢܐ ܕܝܥܩܘܒ, *the Lord, the Mighty One of Jacob;* Munster, Vatablus, Mercer, Drusius, Lively, Gesenius, Hitzig, Maurer. Com. chap. vi. 8, where בְּנַפְשׁוֹ יְהוָה occurs instead of the present phrase, which, however, is also there used in a bad

8   Shall not the land tremble for this,
    And every one that dwelleth therein mourn?
    Shall not all of it rise like the river?
    Shall it not be driven, and subside,
    Like the river of Egypt?
9   It shall come to pass in that day,
    Saith the Lord Jehovah,
    That I will cause the sun to go down at noon,
    And will darken the land in the clear day.
10 I will turn your festivals into mourning,
    And all your songs into lamentation:
    I will bring sackcloth upon all loins,
    And baldness upon every head;
    I will make it as the mourning for an only son,
    And the end of it a bitter day.

sense. אִם־אֶשְׁכָּחֵךְ, *if I forget*, is the usual formula of swearing, implying that it should not take place. כֹּל, in this connection, implies both totality, and the single items of which that totality is made up. Comp. Ps. ciii. 2.

8. The guilt of the people was so enormous, that it was sufficient to induce an entire subversion of the existing state of things. To express this more strongly, the land is metaphorically represented as rising and swelling like the Nile, and again falling like the same river. Of course, the idea of the heaving and subsiding of the ground during an earthquake is what is intended, as the beginning of the verse shows. For the sake of energy and impression, the interrogative form is, as frequently, employed. That כָאֹר, by an elision of the letter Yod, is a defective form of כַיְאֹר, is evident from the parallel passage, chap. ix 5. Fifteen MSS. originally two more, and perhaps other three, and one of the early editions, read כַיְאֹר in full. For the origin and meaning of the word, see on Is. xix. 6. גָרַשׁ is used in Niphal, to express the violent agitation of the sea when raised by the wind, Is. lvii. 20. It here denotes the rise of the Nile, which is generally above twenty feet. For נִשְׁקְעָה, the Keri and a great many MSS. in the text, read וְנִשְׁקְעָה, which is undoubtedly genuine. The root שָׁקַע occurs in a similar connection, chap. ix. 5. It signifies to *sink down*, or *subside*.

9. Some think the prophet here predicts the total eclipse of the sun, which took place at one of the great festivals in the year that Jeroboam died, (see Usher's Annals, A. M. 3213); but whatever there may be in the language borrowed from such an event, consistency of interpretation requires it to be taken metaphorically, as descriptive of a change from circumstances of prosperity to those of adversity. Comp. Jer. xv. 9; Ezek. xxxii. 7-10.

10. The Hebrew festivals were occasions of great joy, and were no doubt on this very account kept up among the ten tribes after they had lost their religious importance. The calamitous result of the Assyrian invasion under Shalmaneser is here most graphically depicted. Comp. Is. xv. 2; Jer. xlviii. 37; Ezek. vii. 18. The death of an only son was regarded by the Hebrews as the most mournful of events. Comp. Jer. vi. 26; Zech. xii. 10. The pronominal reference in הֲפַכְתִּיהָ and שַׂמְתִּיהָ is אֶרֶץ understood. כְּ in כְּאֵבֶל יָחִיד, is the *Caph veritatis*.

11 Behold, the days come, saith the Lord Jehovah,
When I will send a famine into the land;
Not a famine of bread, nor a thirst for water,
But of hearing the words of Jehovah.
12 And men shall wander from sea to sea,
And shall run up and down, from the North even to the East,
Seeking the word of Jehovah,
But they shall not find it.
13 In that day the fair virgins shall faint,
And the young men also, for thirst;
14 That swear by the sin of Samaria,
And say, By the life of thy God, O Dan!

" Nunc et amara dies, et noctis amarior umbra est;
Omnia jam tristi tempora felle madens."
Tibullus, Eleg. lib. ii. Eleg. iv. 11.

11, 12. The Israelites now despised the messages of the prophets, and by a just retribution, in addition to all their other calamities, they should experience a total withdrawal of all prophetic communications. Comp. Ezek. vii. 26; Micah iii. 7. In whatever direction they might proceed, and whatever efforts they might make to obtain information relative to the issue of their trouble, they should meet with nothing but disappointment. מִזְרָח, *sun-rise*, is used, where geographically we should have expected יָמִין, or נֶגֶב, *the south;* but the term may have been chosen in order to intimate the complete alienation of Israel from Judah, in consequence of which no one would think of repairing to Jerusalem for oracular information. That any transposition of the words has taken place, I cannot, with Houbigant and Newcome, suppose. It is, however, just as probable that the cardinal points were not intended to be strictly marked, but that the object was to indicate generally the hopelessness of the attempts mentioned. The Athnach is improperly placed under מִזְרָח, instead of under יְשׁוֹטְטוּ, as the Vau prefixed to יָצֻף and the form of the verb show.

13. אָפָה in this verse, is to be understood of the natural *thirst* to be experienced by the inhabitants of Samaria during the siege predicted in the preceding verses; הִתְעַלֵּף, properly means, *they shall feel themselves involved in darkness*, which is physically true of those who are seized with syncope. The root עָלַף, Arab. غلف, signifies *to cover, envelop;* here, *with darkness*, understood. After הַבְּתוּלוֹת subaud. יִתְעַלָּפְנָה.

14. אַשְׁמַת שֹׁמְרוֹן, *the sin* or *crime of Samaria;* i. e. the golden calf and other objects of unlawful worship which were the occasion of sin and guilt to the Israelites. Hitzig thinks that Astarte is specifically meant; but the term was doubtless intended to comprehend the calf at Bethel, the religious veneration of which led to the grosser forms of idolatry. At the same time, אֲשֵׁרָה, *Astarte*, is spoken of, 2 Kings xiii. 6, in distinction from the worship specially instituted by Jeroboam. See on Is. xvii. 8. The *god of Dan* was the other golden calf, erected by Jeroboam in Dan, 1 Kings xii. 26–28. By דֶּרֶךְ בְּאֵר־שָׁבַע, Kimchi, Michaelis, and Bauer, understand literally the *way* or *pilgrimage* to Beersheba; but the phrase being parallel with the two former instances, in which objects of false worship are meant, it must here be taken in the same sense. Hence the LXX. render ὁ θεός σου. Strictly speaking, it denotes the *way* or *mode* of worship, or the *worship* itself, that was performed at Beersheba. Com. Ps. cxxxix. 24; Acts ix. 2, xix. 9, 23. See on chap. v. 5. חֵי is a formula of

And, By the life of the way of Beersheba!
They shall fall, and rise no more.

swearing: *By the life of* ——, or, *As sure as such an one lives*, and was peculiarly absurd and sinful when applied to inanimate objects.

CHAPTER IX.

THIS chapter commences with an account of the fifth and last vision of the prophet, in which the final ruin of the kingdom of Israel is represented. This ruin was to be complete and irreparable; and no quarter to which the inhabitants might flee for refuge, would afford them any shelter from the wrath of the Omnipresent and Almighty Jehovah, 1-6. As a sinful nation, it was to be treated as if it had never stood in any covenant relation to him; yet, in their individual capacity, as the descendants of Abraham, how much soever they might be scattered and afflicted among the heathen, they should still be preserved, 7-10. The concluding part of the chapter contains a distinct prophecy of the restoration of the Jewish church after the Babylonish captivity, 11; the incorporation of the heathen which was to be consequent upon that restoration, 12; and the final establishment of the Jews in their own land in the latter day, 13-15.

---

1   I saw the Lord standing beside the altar, and he said:
Smite the capital, that the thresholds may shake;
And break them in pieces, on the heads of them all;
Their posterity I will slay with the sword;
None of their fugitives shall make his escape,
Nor shall any that slip away be delivered.

1. By the Targ., Calvin, Drusius, Grotius, Justi, Rosenmüller, and Hengstenberg, the scene of this vision is laid at the temple of Jerusalem; by Cyril, Munster, Tarnovius, Schmidius, Lowth, Michaelis, Dahl, Bauer, Hitzig, and Ewald, at the idolatrous temple at Bethel, and, in my opinion, rightly. Calvin does not show his usual tact in objecting to this interpretation, on the ground that it represents Jehovah as indirectly approving of superstition; for, though the true God was seen beside the idolatrous altar, it was not for the purpose of receiving homage, but of commanding that the whole of the erection and worship at Bethel should be destroyed. No argument in favor of Jerusalem can be built on the use of the article in הַכַּפְתּוֹר "*the* altar," but the contrary. The idolatrous object to which sacrifices were offered at Bethel, having been mentioned in the preceding verse, nothing is more natural than a reference here to the altar on which they were presented. כַּפְתּוֹר, an ornamented *head* or *capital* of a column, in the shape of a sphere, or bowl surrounded by flowers. It is usually derived from כָּפַר, *to cover*, and כָּתַר, *to crown*. LXX. ἱλαστήριον, mistaking the word for כַּפֹּרֶת. When used of the ornamental part of the golden can-

2 Though they break through into Sheol,
 Thence shall my hand take them;
 Though they climb up to heaven,
 Thence will I bring them down.
3 Though they hide themselves on the summit of Carmel,
 There I will search them out and take them;
 Though they conceal themselves from mine eyes in the bottom
     of the sea,
 There I will command the serpent, and he shall bite them.
4 Though they go into captivity before their enemies,
 There I will command the sword, and it shall kill them:
 I will set mine eyes upon them for evil,
 And not for good.
5   For it is the Lord Jehovah of hosts,
 That toucheth the earth and it melteth;

dlestick, they render it σφαιρωτήρ. For כפתר, see on Is. vi. 4; the similarity, in some respects, between which passage and the present, appears to have suggested the idea that the temple at Jerusalem is here meant. The temple was to be smitten both above and below, to indicate its entire destruction. בצעם, break them, i. e. the capitals, etc., upon the head of all the worshippers. It does not appear that ראש and אחרית are here used antithetically. The latter denotes the children of those who perished in the attack upon the idolatrous temple. When threatened by the Assyrians, they would flock in crowds to Bethel, to implore protection from the golden calf, and, while thus assembled, they should perish, along with the vain object of their trust; they should, in fact, be buried in the ruins.

2–4. These verses exhibit a beautiful series of supposed cases of attempt at escape from the judgments of God, and the utter futility of every attempt of the kind. שאול and השמים, are, as usual, employed as extreme points of opposition. Comp. Job xi. 8; Ps. cxxxix. 8; Is. xiv. 13, 14; Matt. xi. 23. אם־יחבאו. Not only was Mount Carmel celebrated on account of its general fertility, but also on account of the dense forests and large caverns with which it abounded. These, together with its height, which is about twelve hundred feet, afforded the fittest possible places of concealment. Richter, in his Pilgrimage, p. 65, says: "Mount Carmel is entirely covered with green; on its *summits* are pines and oaks, and further down, olive and laurel trees, etc. These forests would furnish safe hiding places, equally with the caves, which are chiefly on the west side facing the sea." קרקע הים, *the bottom of the* Mediterranean Sea, forms a striking contrast to the summit of Carmel, which beetles above it. קרקע, Arab. قرقر,

terra æquabilis; when spoken of a house, the *foundation* or *floor;* here the *bottom* or *basis,* on which the sea rests. For נחש, *sea-serpent,* see on Is. xxvii. 1.

" ——— Immensis orbibus angues
Incumbant pelago, pariterque ad littora
    tendunt."
                    Æneid. ii. 204.

The מ in מהם, in verses 3 and 4, loses its proper prepositive signification, as in מצרים, מימין, etc. and merely denotes position or place.

5, 6. A sublime description of the almighty and uncontrollable power of Jehovah. For the reference to the Nile, see on chap. viii. 8. Instead of ותבגע, the Keri and not a few MSS. read ועלתה in full. Comp. ועליתיה Ps. civ. 3, 13.

And all that dwell in it mourn;
It riseth, all of it, like the river,
And subsideth like the river of Egypt.
6 He that buildeth his upper chambers in the heavens,
And foundeth his vaults upon the earth;
That calleth to the waters of the sea,
And poureth them out on the surface of the earth;
Jehovah is his name.
7   Are ye not as the Cushites to me,
O sons of Israel? saith Jehovah.
Did I not bring Israel from the land of Egypt?
The Philistines from Caphtor?
And the Syrians from Kir?
8 Behold, the eyes of the Lord Jehovah are upon the sinful kingdom,

Αἰθέρος οἶκον ὑπέρτατον ναιετάεις.
Oppian. Halieut. i. 490.
Θεοῦ οἰκητήριον τοῦ κόσμου τὸ ἄνω.
Aristot.

אֲגֻדָּה, a body or mass, the parts of which are firmly compacted; Arab. اجان, *forniz firma compaginis et structuræ;* an *arch* or *vault;* obviously used of the רָקִיעַ, or hemispheric expanse or vault of heaven; which, from its appearing to the eye to rest upon the earth, is here said to be founded upon it. To render it, with the Targ., *congregation*, and apply it to the Church, as a body of believers, firmly united together, is altogether unsuitable to the connection. The rendering of the LXX., Syr., and Arab. would seem to indicate that וִיהִי צְבָאָם originally stood in the text, at the end of ver. 8; but only one of De Rossi's MSS. has this reading at first hand.

7. By appealing to the fact, that, in his providence, he had removed different nations from their original abodes, and settled them elsewhere, Jehovah repels the idea, which the Israelites were so prone to entertain, that, because he had brought them out of Egypt, and given them the land of Canaan, they were peculiarly the objects of his regard, and could never be subdued or destroyed. He now regarded, and would treat them as the Cushites, who had been transplanted from their primary location in Arabia, into the midst of the barbarous nations of Africa. כֻּשִׁיִּים, *Cushites*, are here the inhabitants of the African Cush, or Ethiopia. See on Is. xviii. 2. Arab. بني الحبش, *Abyssinians.* Αἰθίοπας, τοὶ διχθὰ δεδαίαται, ἔσχατοι ἀνδρῶν, Οἱ μὲν δυσομένου ὑπερίονος, οἱ δ᾽ ἀνιόντος.
Odyss. i. 23, 24.

For פְּלִשְׁתִּים, see on Is. xiv. 28. Gesenius hesitates between Crete and Cappadocia, as designated by the Hebrew *Caphtor,* but inclines to the former. Thesaurus, p. 709. LXX. Καππαδοκία. אֲרָם, *Aram*, or Syria, put for the *Syrians,* i. e. the inhabitants of the countries about Damascus. They are here represented as having migrated from קִיר. *Kir,* the country lying on the river *Kur,* or Cyrus. See on Is. xxii. 6.

8, 9. עֵינֵי בְּ, the eyes of a person are said to be *in* any one, when he keeps him steadily in view, in order either to do him good, or to punish him. In the present instance, the phrase conveys the idea of hostility. Though the kingdom of the ten tribes was to be utterly and forever destroyed, yet, as descendants of their patriarchal ancestors, they should not become extinct. In the midst

And I will destroy it from the face of the earth;
Yet I will not utterly destroy the house of Jacob,
Saith Jehovah.

9 For, behold, I will command,
And will sift the house of Israel among all the nations,
As one sifteth corn in a sieve,
And not a grain falleth to the ground.

10 But all the sinners of my people shall die by the sword,
That say, The evil shall not reach nor overtake us.

11 In that day I will raise up the booth of David that is falling,
And will close up its breaches;

of the wrath which their sinfulness should bring upon them, God would remember mercy. כִּי אֶפֶס is strongly adversative. כְּבָרָה, *a sieve*, which is used to separate the chaff and other refuse from the pure grain, is most probably derived from רָבַב, *to be many*, from the number of small holes in it. LXX. λικμὸς. Aq. and Symm. Κόσκινον. צְרוֹר is used as a diminutive of צֹר, *the smallest stone*, 2 Sam. xvii. 13; here it signifies the smallest *grain* or *particle* of corn. While the figurative language here employed expresses the violence of the sifting process to which the Israelites should be subjected in order that their idolatry and other sins might be removed from them; it likewise sets forth the great care that would be exercised for their preservation. The universal character of their dispersion is likewise strongly marked.

10. Those are here specially intended, who scoffingly denied the possibility of the Assyrian conquest, namely, the dissipated magnates of Samaria. Such should perish in the war. הַקְדִּים בַּעַד is unusual. Perhaps the meaning is, Shall not come forward, or advance in our rear, so as to cut off our retreat.

11. The Israelites now disappear from the scene, in order to give place to a brief but prominent exhibition of the restoration of the Jews from their depressed condition, during the anticipated captivity in Babylon, and the great design of that restoration — the introduction of the Messianic dispensation, during which the blessings of the covenant of mercy was to be extended to the Gentile world. With this reference in view, the apostle James expressly quotes the prophecy, Acts xv. 15-17. The quotation is made from the version of the LXX.; but as regards verbality, differs fully as much from it, as the latter does from the Hebrew text; his object being to give the general sense of the passage, and not the identical phraseology. It must further be observed that, though he quotes the entire passage, consisting of the 11th and 12th verses, his obvious design was to give prominence to what is contained in the latter, viz. the conversion of the Gentiles, the very point required by his argument; so that all attempts to apply what is said respecting the booth of David to the Christian church, are unwarranted and futile. דָּוִד, *David*, is used by the prophet, not in its figurative, but in its proper meaning, as denoting the Hebrew monarch of that name. By בַּיּוֹם הַהוּא, *that day*, for which James has, quite indefinitely, μετὰ ταῦτα, we are to understand the period of the dispersion of the Israelites among the nations, subsequent to the fall of their kingdom. Though that kingdom would never be restored, yet the Jewish polity would be re-established at Jerusalem. This polity is here called סֻכַּת דָּוִיד, *the booth*, or *hut of David*, to denote the reduced state of his family, and the affairs of the people. Comp. Is. xi. 1, and my note there. When the prosperity of that family is spoken of, the more

And I will raise up its ruins,
And build it as in the days of old.
12 That the remnant of Edom may be possessed,
And all the nations upon which my name shall be called,
Saith Jehovah that doeth this.

dignified phrase, בֵּית דָּוִיד, *the house of David*, is employed. See 2 Sam. iii. 1; 1 Kings xi. 38; Is. vii. 2, 13. אֹהֶל דָּוִיד, *the tent*, or *tabernacle of David*, Is. xvi. 5, would seem to express an intermediate state of things. That דָּוִיד, *David*, is here to be understood of the Messiah, I cannot find. סֻכָּה, *tugurium*, *a hut*, or booth, so called from its being constructed by interweaving the boughs and branches of trees with each other, and its thus forming a rude shelter from the storm. It was in such booths the Hebrews were to dwell during the seven days of חַג הַסֻּכּוֹת, *the feast of booths*, commonly called "the feast of tabernacles." See Levit. xxiii. 40–43. Root סָכַךְ, *to weave, interweave, protect*. Still more definitely to mark the depressed condition of the Jewish kingdom, is described as נֹפֶלֶת, *falling*. The present participle is here, as frequently, used to denote an action which was happening at the time of narration, and which would be continued. About the time of Amos the Jewish affairs had begun to decline; and, though they occasionally and partially revived, yet, taken as a whole, they continued to deteriorate till the Babylonish invasion, when they were reduced to the deplorably fallen state in which they continued till the return from the captivity, when the restoration here predicted took place. From the phraseology employed by the prophet, the Rabbins derived one of the names which they give to the Messiah: בַּר נַפְלִי *the son of the fallen*. Thus in the Talmud, Sanhed. fol. 96, 2: "R. Nachman said to R. Isaac: Hast thou heard when *Bar-naphli* comes? To whom he said, Who is *Bar-naphli*. He replied, The Messiah: you may call the Messiah *Bar-naphli*; for is it not written, In that day I will raise up, etc.?" quoting the present verse of Amos. For other passages to the same effect, see Schoet-

genii Horæ Hebraicæ et Talmud. The feminine suffix in פִּרְצֵיהֶן is to be referred to the different parts or cities of the kingdom, understood. The masculine in הֲרִסֹתָיו, has דָּוִיד for its antecedent, and the feminine in בְּנִיתִיהָ refers to סֻכָּה.

12. The grand end of the restoration from the captivity in Babylon is now stated, viz. the introduction of the universal economy of the gospel. The church of God had formerly consisted of persons belonging to a particular nation: henceforth it was to comprehend those of all nations, even such as had been most hostile to its interests, whom God would call to be his people. יָרַשׁ, *to take possession of, inherit*, is here used figuratively of the influence for good which the church should exert over the Gentiles, bringing them within her pale, and using them for her holy and benevolent purposes. In the words, וְיִרַשׁ גִּירֶשׁ זַרְעֲךָ, "thy seed shall possess," or "inherit the nations," Is. liv. 3, we have a strictly parallel prophecy, couched in the same language. Comp. also Is. xlix. 8, and Rom. iv. 13, where, in reference to the blessing of the Gentiles with faithful Abraham, that patriarch is called "*the heir of the world.*" Among the first of the foreign nations that were to experience his beneficent influence, the Idumeans are expressly mentioned. Owing to the enmity which had existed between them and the Jews, they had mutually harassed and wasted each other, in consequence of which, and of invasions and wars on the part of other powers, nothing but שְׁאֵרִית, *a remnant*, of the former was left. Of this remnant, a portion was proselytized to the Jewish faith in the time of John Hyrcanus, and the remainder amalgamated with the tribes of Arabia, which embraced the Christian faith. It is to these last that specific reference

13 Behold, the days are coming, saith Jehovah,
That the ploughman shall overtake the reaper,
And the treader of grapes him that soweth the seed;
And the mountains shall drop with new wine,
And all the hills shall melt.

is here made. וְיָרַשׁ is to be taken impersonally, and rendered passively; and the power of its future must be carried forward to יִקְרָא. The calling of a name upon any person or thing, denotes the assertion of the claims of the individual whose name is mentioned upon the person or thing specified. כָּל־הַגּוֹיִם is the accusative, אֵת being understood as repeated. לְמַעַן יִירְשׁוּ אֵת־שְׁאֵרִית אֱדוֹם the LXX. have rendered ὅπως ἐκζητήσωσιν οἱ κατάλοιποι τῶν ἀνθρώπων, or, as some MSS. read, ἐκζητήσωσί με, as if their Hebrew text had been לְמַעַן יִדְרְשׁוּ אֹתִי שְׁאֵרִית אָדָם, that the residue of men may seek me. Newcome supposes that the reading אֹתִי is a contraction for אֶת יְהֹוָה; but though τὸν Κύριον, which we find in the quotation, Acts xv. 17, might seem to favor this supposition, there is no evidence to prove that the contraction אֶת יְ, so common in Rabbinical writings, is of such antiquity. Τὸν Κύριον I consider to be merely an interpretation of με. No Hebrew MSS. afford any countenance to the Greek translation, nor do any of the versions, except the Arabic, which, as usual, follows the LXX. For this reason, and regarding the latitude used by the writers of the New Testament when quoting from the Old, I cannot perceive how the passage can justly be charged with corruption. To which add, that the words as they stand in the Hebrew text, admirably suit the connection, as they equally do the argument of the apostle; though quoting, according to custom, from the Greek version, he adopted in the main the construction which it exhibits as sufficiently expressive of the fact which he had in view.

13. Comp. Levit. xxvi. 5. The language imports the greatest abundance; and this verse, with the two following, refer to a period subsequent to that of the calling of the Gentiles. This the introductory phrase הִנֵּה יָמִים בָּאִים, *Behold, the days are coming,* distinguished as it is from בַּיּוֹם הַהוּא, *In that day,* ver. 11, the position of the prophecy, and other features which characterize it, sufficiently show. The verses are parallel with Is. lxi. 4, lxii. 8, 9, lxv. 21-23; and are to be interpreted of the future restoration of the Jews to their own land, and their abundant prosperity in the latter day. For מֹשֵׁךְ הַזֶּרַע, *to draw out the seed,* comp. מֶשֶׁךְ הַזֶּרַע, Ps. cxxvi. 6. The idea seems to be that of conveying the seed with the hand from the sack or vessel in which it was carried, yet not to the exclusion of the act of sowing. Comp. the Eth. ቀስት: *jaculatus est sagittas.* For עָסִיס, *fresh* or *sweet wine,* see on Joel i. 5. The metaphorical language here employed is at once, in the highest degree, bold and pleasing. The Hebrews were accustomed to construct terraces on the sides of the mountains and other elevations, on which they planted vines. Of this fact the prophet avails himself, and represents the immense abundance of the produce to be such, that the eminences themselves would appear to be converted into the juice of the grape.

" ———— Subitis messor gaudebit aristis:
Rorabunt querceta favis, stagnantia passim
Vina fluent, olcique lacus."

Claudian, in Rufin. lib. i. 382.

How striking the contrast between the scene here depicted, and that which the face of Palestine has presented during the long period of the dispersion!

14 I will reverse the captivity of my people Israel,
 And they shall build the desolate cities, and inhabit them;
 And they shall plant vineyards, and drink the wine of them;
 They shall also make gardens, and eat the fruit of them.
15 For I will plant them in their own land,
 And they shall no more be plucked up from their land
 Which I have given them,
 Saith Jehovah thy God.

14, 15. It is impossible to conceive of prophecy more distinctly or positively asserting the future and final restoration of the Jews to Canaan than that contained in these verses. Once and again they have been removed from that favored land, on account of their wickedness; but still it is theirs by Divine donation to their great progenitor. And when they return to the faith of Abraham, beholding in retrospection the day of the Messiah, which he saw and was glad, but deeply bewailing their guilt in having crucified him, and persevered for so many centuries in the rejection of his gospel, they shall regain possession of it, and remain its happy occupants till the end of time.

OBADIAH.

PREFACE.

THE prophecy of Obadiah, consisting only of twenty-one verses, is the shortest book of the Old Testament. Jerome calls him, *parvus propheta, versuum supputatione, non sensum.* Of his origin, life, and circumstances, we know nothing; but, as usual, various conjectures have been broached by the Rabbins and Fathers: — some identifying him with the pious Obadiah who lived at the court of Ahab; some, with the overseer of the workmen, mentioned 2 Chron. xxxiv. 12; and some, with others of the same name; while there is no lack of legendary notices respecting the place of his birth, sepulchre, etc. See Carpzovii Introd. tom. iii. pp. 332, 333.

That he flourished after the capture of Jerusalem by the Chaldeans, may be inferred from his obvious reference to that event, verses 11–14; for it is more natural to regard these verses as descriptive of the past, than as prophetical anticipations of the future. He must, therefore, have lived after, or been contemporary with Jeremiah, and not with Hosea, Joel, and Amos, as Grotius, Huet, and Lightfoot, maintain. Sufficient proof of his having lived in or after the time of that prophet, has been supposed to be found in the almost verbal agreement between verses 1–8, and certain verses inserted in the parallel prophecy, Jeremiah xlix.; it being assumed that he must have borrowed from him. This opinion, however, though held by Luther, Bertholdt, Von Coelln, Credner, Hitzig, and Von Knobel, is less probable than the contrary hypothesis, which has been advocated by Tarnovius, Schmidius, Du Veil, Drusius, Newcome, Eichhorn, Jahn, Schnurrer, Rosenmüller, Holzapfel, Hendewerk, Hävernick, and Maurer. Indeed, a comparison of the structure of the parallel prophecies goes satisfactorily to show the priority of our prophet, as has been ably done by Schnurrer, in his Disputatio philologica in Obadiam, Tubing. 1787, 4to. Add to which, that Jeremiah appears to have been in the habit of partially quoting from preceding prophets. Comp. Is. xv. xvi. with Jerem. xlviii. This view is confirmed by the opinion of Ewald, that both these writers copied from some earlier prophet, since he admits that Obadiah has preserved, in a less altered condition, the more energetic and unusual manner of the original than Jeremiah. In brief, the portion in question is so entirely in keeping with the remainder of the book, that they must be considered as having been originally delivered by the same individual; whereas Jeremiah presents it in the form of *disjecta membra poetæ.*

In all probability the prophecy was delivered between the year B. c. 588, when Jerusalem was taken by the Chaldeans, and the termination of the siege of Tyre by Nebuchadnezzar. During this interval, that monarch subdued the Idumeans, and other neighboring nations.

Of the composition of Obadiah, little, as Bishop Lowth observes, can be said, owing to its extreme brevity. Its principal features are animation, regularity, and perspicuity.

The subjects of the prophecy are the judgments to be inflicted upon the Idumeans on account of their wanton and cruel conduct towards the Jews at the time of the Chaldean invasion; and the restoration of the latter from captivity. The book may, therefore, be fitly divided into two parts: the first comprising verses 1–16, which contain a reprehension of the pride, self-confidence, and unfeeling cruelty of the former people, and definite predictions of their destruction; the latter, verses 17–21, in which it is promised that the Jews should not only be restored to their own land, but possess the territories of the surrounding nations, especially Idumea.

The reason why the book occupies its present unchronological position in the Hebrew Bible, is supposed to be the connection between the subject of which it treats, and the mention made of " the residue of Edom," at the conclusion of the preceding book of Amos.

OBADIAH.

THE prophecy commences by announcing the message sent in the providence of God to the Chaldeans, to come and attack the Idumeans, ver 1; and describes the humiliation of their pride, 2, 3; the impossibility of their escape by means of their boasted fastnesses, 4; and the completeness of their devastation, 5. It then proceeds with a sarcastic plaint over their deserted and fallen condition, 6-9; specifies its cause — their unnatural cruelty towards the Jews, 10-14; and denounces a righteous retribution, 15, 16. The remaining portion foretells the restoration of the Jews, their peaceful settlement in their own land, and the establishment of the kingdom of Messiah, 17-21.

1 THE Vision of Obadiah.
Thus saith the Lord Jehovah concerning Edom:
We have heard a report from Jehovah,
And a messenger is sent among the nations:
" Up ! let us rise against her to battle ! "
2 Behold, I have made thee small among the nations ;

1. Eichhorn, Rosenmüller, Jaeger, and Hendewerk, have raised unnecessary doubt respecting the genuineness of the title and introduction contained in this verse, which have been fully obviated by Schnurrer, Maurer, and Hitzig. For חֲזוֹן, see on Is. i. 1. עֹבַדְיָה, Obadiah, " the servant of Jehovah," equivalent to עַבְדְּאֵל, Abdeel, Jer. xxxvi. 26; Arab. عبد الله, Abd-allah; Ger. Gottschalck. For אֱדוֹם, Edom, see on Is. xxxiv. 5. The words שְׁמוּעָה שָׁמַעְנוּ מֵאֵת יְהֹוָה, we have heard a report from Jehovah, are not to be regarded as designed to describe the reception of the Divine message by the prophet, but express the communication made to the nations by the ambassador sent to summon them to the attack upon Idumea, as the following clause shows. The שְׁמוּעָה, report, or communication itself, is contained in the last line of the verse. The plural form שָׁמַעְנוּ, " we have heard," for which Jeremiah has שָׁמַעְתִּי, " I have heard," is so qualified by the passive verb שֻׁלַּח in the second member of the parallelism, that it is equivalent to the passive form נִשְׁמְעָה, hath been heard.

There is, therefore, no necessity to inquire whether Obadiah meant himself and other prophets, or whether he identified himself with his countrymen. All that is intended is the circulation of the hostile message in regard to Idumea; and the tracing of the movement to the overruling providence of God, by which Nebuchadnezzar and his allies were led to turn their arms against that country. See Calvin, in loc. צִיר, a messenger, or ambassador; Arab. صار, صير, ivit, profectus est. LXX. περιοχὴν, but in Jer. ἀγγέλους ; Symm. here ἀγγελίαν. Com. Is. xviii. 2, and my note there. קוּמוּ, arise! up! like לֵךְ, come! go! etc., is frequently used as a term of excitement. With it the address of the herald commences ; who, identifying himself with the nations which he summons, proceeds to employ the plural of the same verb in its strictly hostile sense, followed by the preposition עַל. עָלֶיהָ, though properly masculine, is here viewed as אֶרֶץ, a country ; hence the feminine suffix in עָלֶיהָ.

2. Here the masculine gender is adopted, which is continued through. t

24

Thou art exceedingly despised.
3 The pride of thine heart hath deceived thee,
  Thou that dwellest in the clefts of the rock,
  Whose habitation is high!
  That saith in his heart,
  Who shall bring me down to the ground?
4 Though thou shouldest soar like the eagle,
  And shouldest set thy nest among the stars,
  Thence I will bring thee down, saith Jehovah.

the prophecy — עַם, *people*, being understood. The past time of the verbs expresses the certainty of the events; and קָטֹן, *small*, and בָּזוּי, *despised*, are not designed to mark the comparatively limited and despicable character of Idumea, geographically considered, as Newcome interprets, but describe the miserable condition to which it was to be reduced by its enemies.

3. The Idumeans are taunted with the proud confidence which they placed in their lofty and precipitous mountain fastnesses, and the insolence with which they scouted every attempt to subdue them. These positions, strong by nature, and many of them rendered still more so by art, they deemed absolutely impregnable. Such inaccessible places are appropriately called חַגְוֵי־סֶלַע, *cliffs of the rock*, Syr. ܟ̈ܐܦܐ, *rupes*; the Arab. ܚܒܐ, *confugit*; and hence the idea of *refuge*, which is secondary, and less proper to be adopted here. LXX. ἐν ταῖς ὀπαῖς τῶν πετρῶν. Syr. ܒܢܩܥܐ ܒܢܩܥܐ *in fortissima rupe*. Some interpreters are of opinion that by סֶלַע, *Sela*, we are to understand the city of that name, otherwise called *Petra*, situated in Wady Mûsa, and celebrated as the capital of Idumea. See on Is. xvi. 1. The חַגְוֵי, *cliffs*, would, on this interpretation, be the high and inaccessible rocks which beetled over that metropolis. I prefer taking the word in its literal acceptation, and view it as a collective, equivalent to the plural of the LXX. and other ancient versions, and thus describing the rocky character of the country generally, as well as that about Petra in particular. Instead of הִשִּׁיאֶךָ, *hath deceived thee*, four of De Rossi's MSS. and originally two more, read הִשִּׂיאֶךָ; but though this reading is supported by the LXX., Arab., Vulg., and Hexaplar Syr. it is inferior to that of the Textus Receptus, which has the suffrages of the Syr. and the Targ., especially as there are no other instances in which נָשָׂא is used in the sense of *raising*, or *elevating*. The י in שֹׁכְנִי is simply a poetic paragogic, of which several examples occur in the Benoni participle. See Gen. xlix. 11; Deut. xxxiii. 16; Is. xxii. 16; Micah vii. 14. In יְבִיאֶנּוּ there is a transition from the second person to the third, for the sake of more graphically pointing out the proud position of Edom. Comp. Is. xxii. 16.

4. By a bold but beautiful hyperbole, the Idumeans are told, that, to what height soever they might remove, and how entirely they might imagine themselves to be beyond the reach of their enemies, Jehovah would dislodge them, and deliver them into their power. For the soaring of the eagle, and his building his nest on the inaccessible crags of the rock, comp. Job xxxix. 27, 28:

אִם־עַל־פִּיךָ יַגְבִּיהַּ נָשֶׁר
וְכִי יָרִים קִנּוֹ׃
סֶלַע יִשְׁכֹּן וְיִתְלֹנָן
עַל־שֶׁן־סֶלַע וּמְצוּדָה׃

"Is it at thy command the eagle soars,
And erects his nest on high?
The rock he inhabits, and makes his abode
On the point of the rock, and the fastness."

5 If thieves had come to thee,
  Or robbers by night (how art thou destroyed!)
  Would they not have stolen what was sufficient for them?
  If vintagers had come to thee,
  Would they not have left some gleanings?
6 How is Esau explored!

עלו Ewald and Hitzig take to be a passive participle; but that it is the infinitive construct, is rendered certain by its having the preposition עד before it, Job xx. 4. In the present instance, and in Num. xxv. 21, in which, as here, it is followed by קָמָה, it stands elliptically for עם הקמה; which sufficiently accounts for the rendering of the LXX., Syr., Targ., and Vulg., which exhibit the second person singular of the verb. The term כוכבים is to be understood literally of the *stars*, as the highest objects which present themselves to the eye, and not of the tops of the highest rocks, or even heaven itself, as some have maintained. אורידך is a direct reply to the vaunting question, מי יורידני, ver. 3. Theodoret well expresses the sense thus: Ἐπειδὴ τοίνυν, φησὶ ταύταις θαρρῶν ἀλαζονεύῃ καὶ μέγα φρονεῖς ὡς ἀχείρωτος, εὐάλωτόν σε καταστήσω καὶ εὐχείρωτον τοῖς ἐχθροῖς, καὶ τῶν πολεμίων οὐ διαφεύξῃ τὰς χεῖρας, οὐδὲ εἰ δίκην ἀετοῦ μετέωρος ἀρθείης, κ. τ. λ.

5. The Idumeans are here taught, that their devastation would be complete. This prophetic intelligence is communicated in the form of interrogative illustrations, derived from customs with which they were familiar. The manner in which they should be treated would be very different from that adopted by private thieves, or by a party of marauding nomades, who usually seize as much as they can, and especially what they have set their minds on, in the hurry of the moment, leaving the rest of the property to its possessors. They should even fare worse than the vines, on which the vintages, though they cut down the bunches generally, still left some that might be gleaned afterwards. In Jeremiah the order of the illustrations is reversed, the vintagers being taken first. שדדי לילה, *night-robbers*. In such a country as Idumea, a predatory attack could only have been attempted in the night, especially on such places as were most strongly fortified by nature, and commanded a view of the immediately surrounding regions. Hitzig thinks the prophet has Petra specially in his eye, on account of its having been the great emporium of that part of the world. Instead of אם־גנבים באו לך אם־שודדי לילה, Jeremiah has only אם־בצרים באו לך, which is less forcible. He also substitutes הִשְׁחִיתוּ for גנבו. The position of the words אֵיךְ נִדְמֵיתָה, *How thou art destroyed*, has offended some fastidious critics, some of whom would remove them to the beginning of the verse, and others to the commencement of the following. What might be accounted their natural place would be the end of the present verse; but the prophet, struggling to give expression to the feeling which agitated his mind, breaks in upon his illustrations with the interjected exclamation, and then carries them on to a close. The words are omitted by Jeremiah. נִדְמָה has two leading significations: *to be like*; and, according with the Arab. دمى, *vulneravit, perdidit, to cause to cease, destroy,* etc. LXX. ποῦ ἂν ἀπερρίφης; having read נִדְמֵיתָ, a verb, which nowhere occurs in Niphal. דַּיָּם, *their sufficiency*, i. e. what was requisite for supplying their present wants, or such a quantity as they had sufficient strength to remove. LXX. τὰ ἱκανὰ ἑαυτοῖς. Syr. ܣܦܩܗܘܢ, *sufficentia eorum*. The apodosis is omitted; but there is a beautiful propriety in leaving it to be supplied by those to whom the appeal was made.

6. The prophet here resumes his strain of sarcastic plaint over the fall of Idumea, which he had abruptly adopted in the

And his hidden places searched!
7 All thine allies have driven thee to the frontier;
Those who were at peace with thee have deceived thee;
They have prevailed against thee:
They that ate thy bread have laid a snare under thee;
There is no understanding in him!

preceding verse, repeating the אֵין there employed, which is again understood before עָבָיו. The patronymic עֵשָׂו is construed as a collective noun with the plural of the verb, and, at the same time, with the singular pronominal affix. In the translation I have been obliged to employ the singular in both cases. מַצְפֻּנָיו, like מַטְמֹנִים, may either signify places where treasures are *hidden*, or the treasures themselves; or the term may be explained of *hiding places*, to which men resort in order to elude an enemy. I prefer the last of these significations, as better agreeing with the persons of the Edomites, mentioned in the former hemistich; though the hiding of their treasures is also naturally implied. The form is that of the Arabic passive مَقْطُول. Such places abound in Idumea. "Revera," says Jerome, "ut dicamus aliquid de natura loci, omnis australis regio Idumæorum de Eleutheropoli usque Petram et Ailam (hæc est enim possessio Esau) in specubus habitatiunculas habet. Et propter nimios calores solis, quia meridiana provincia est, subterraneis tuguriis utitur." Instead of the exclamatory form here employed, Jeremiah adopts that of direct personal assertion: כִּי־אֲנִי חָשַׂפְתִּי אֶת־עֵשָׂו גִּלֵּיתִי אֶת־מִסְתָּרָיו; changing, at the same time, חפשׂ into חשׂף, and מַצְפֻּנָיו into מִסְתָּרָיו.

7. שָׁלַח, which in Kal has the signification *to send, send away*, signifies in Piel, *to dismiss, eject, expel*, conveying the superadded idea of compulsion or violence. Connected, as here, with עַד, the verb implies expulsion beyond the frontier specified; and the whole sentence is descriptive of transportation into a state of captivity. Thus the Targ. מִן חוּמֵי תְחוּמָא יַגְלוּן יָתָךְ, *they shall lead thee captive from the border*. By אַנְשֵׁי בְרִיתֶךָ, the men of thy covenant, are meant those who had formally pledged assistance to the Edomites; *confederates*, *allies*; by אַנְשֵׁי שְׁלֹמֶךָ, the men of thy peace, neighboring states, which were on terms of peace and friendship with them. LXX. ἄνδρες εἰρηνικοί, those who were peaceably inclined towards them. Before לַחְמְךָ supply אַנְשֵׁי from the preceding — *the men of thy bread*; or אֹכְלֵי, may be understood, *those who eat thy bread*; and thus the phrase will be descriptive of dependents;' some of the poorer tribes of the desert, who subsisted on the bounty of the Edomites, and whose aid they might reasonably expect in case of any emergency. Comp. Ps. xli. 10, where a similar combination of אוֹכֵל לַחְמִי with אִישׁ שְׁלוֹמִי occurs; though there the idea of familiarity, rather than that of dependence, seems intended to be expressed. Five of De Rossi's MSS. and originally two more, read לַחְמְךָ אַף, instead of לַחְמְךָ יָשִׂימוּ, as also one of the early editions, the LXX. and Arab.; but the common reading is to be preferred. To לַחְמְךָ, thirty MSS., originally eleven more, four by emendation, the Soncin. and Complut. editions, the Soncin. Prophets, and the Syr., prefix the copulative, which the difference of sense in the two verbs requires. There is some difficulty in determining the meaning of מָזוֹר. LXX. ἔνεδρα; Syr. ܟܡܐܢܐ, *insidiæ*, Vulg. *insidiæ*; Targ. תַּקְלָא, *offendiculum* — all agreeing in the idea of treachery, or the employment of means by which one might be subverted or ensnared. This seems to be the only suitable meaning in this place, as the signification of *wound*, which attaches to the word, Jer. xxx. 13, Hos. v. 13, the other pas-

8   Shall I not in that day, saith Jehovah,
    Cause the wise men to perish from Edom?
    And the men of understanding from Mount Esau?

sages in which it occurs, will not, with any tolerable degree of propriety, apply. Two derivations have been proposed, the Arab. مرج, *distendit, equaliter, distendit*, to which Tingstadius appeals in Supplement. ad Lexx. Hebrr. p. 23 ; but which is far-fetched, as there is no proof that the verb is used in the sense of spreading out a net, or the like; and زور, *mentitus fuit,* زور, *fallum, mendacium,* with which the Hebrew זוּר, *to decline* from the way of truth, has been compared. The use of תַחְתֶּךָ יָשִׂימוּ, *they place under thee,* most naturally suggests the idea of a *gin* or *trap,* which may be said to deceive or act falsely by those who tread upon it; so that the notions of *treachery, plot, net, snare,* may be combined in furnishing the true signification. Fürst, who derives the word from זֵר, gives the significations thus: " circumligare, obligatio vulneris, fascia, hinc medicina ; moraliter : *laqueorum connexio, perfidia fallax, insidiosa, fraudulenta.*" To no quarter could the Idumeans look for aid. Their allies, their neighbors, their very dependents, so far from assisting them, would act treacherously towards them, and employ every means, both of an open and covert nature, to effect their ruin. At the close of the verse, the prophet turns off again from the direct mode of address, and employs the third person, for the purpose of more emphatically exposing their folly in placing confidence in those who were totally unworthy of it. It would be highly uncritical, with the Targ., Hougibant, and Newcome, to change בֹּו, *in him,* into בָּךְ, *in thee.*

8. The Idumeans confided, not only in the natural strength of their country, but in the superiority of their intellectual talent. That they excelled in the arts and sciences, is abundantly proved by the numerous traces of them in the book of Job, which was undoubtedly written in their country. They were, indeed, proverbial for their חָכְמָה, philosophy, for the cultivation of which, their intercourse with Babylon and Egypt was exceedingly favorable, as were likewise their means of acquiring information from the numerous caravans whose route lay through their country, thus forming a chain of communication between Europe and India. Speaking of wisdom, the author of the book of Baruch says, in reference to their celebrity as sages of antiquity, chap. iii. 22, 23 :

" It hath not been heard of in Canaan,
Neither hath it been seen in Teman.
The Hagarenes that seek wisdom upon earth,
The merchants of Meran and of Teman,
The mythologists, and investigators of intelligence,
None of these have known the ways of wisdom,
Nor remembered her paths."

These sages are here called חֲכָמִים, and their accumulated stores of wisdom are expressed by תְּבוּנָה, *intelligence,* the term which had just been employed at the close of the preceding verse. The interrogative הֲלֹא is here strongly affirmative ; and ו in וְהַאֲבַדְתִּי is merely conversive. הַר עֵשָׂו, *the mount of Esau,* is the mountainous region of Seir, to the south of Palestine, now called جبل شراء, *Jebel Sherah,* and الشراء, *esh-Sherah,* extending as far south as Akabah. It was originally inhabited by the Horites, or Troglodytæ, so called because they dwelt in the caves of the mountains, whom the posterity of Esau expelled, and taking possession of the country, spread themselves as far towards the north as the borders of Moab. It was particularly to the more northerly portion of this region that the name of جبل, *Jebel,* or Gebalene, was given. הַר, *mountain.*

9 Thy mighty men, O Teman! shall be dismayed,
That every one may be cut off from mount Esau.
10 For the slaughter, for the injury of thy brother Jacob,
Shame shall cover thee, and thou shalt be cut off for ever.
11 In the day when thou didst take a hostile position,
In the day when foreigners took captive his forces,
And strangers entered his gates, and cast lots upon Jerusalem,
Even thou wast as one of them.

being here, and verse 9th, obviously used in a collective sense I have translated it in the plural.

9. For תֵּימָן, *Teman*, see on Amos i. 12. מֵרָצַח has been variously construed. Ewald unnaturally renders it, *without battle*. Schnurrer treats it as a participle in Pael or Poel, pointing it מְרֻצָּח or מְרֻצַּח, and regarding it as equivalent to the Arab. مُقَاتِل, *vir prœlio aptus*. He would thus make it parallel with גִבּוֹרִים, *mighty men*, in the preceding hemistich. Rosenmüller, De Wette, and some others, translate, *by slaughter*. Leo Juda, most of the older modern translators, followed by Jæger, Hesselberg, Hendewerk, and Maurer, render, *propter cædem*, and suppose the prophet to be here assigning the cause of the destruction of the Idumeans which he had just predicted, intending more fully to dilate on the subject in the following verse. To this construction, however, it must be objected, that it clogs the parallelism, which properly ends with חַתְּ־שָׁי, as in the verse preceding; and also that the words מִקֶּטֶל גְּדָבִים are too closely allied, both in form and reference, to admit of such a pause as that which is introduced by the Soph-Pasuk. I, therefore, do not hesitate to follow the division of the verses adopted by the LXX., Syr., Hexaplar Syr., Vulg., Dathe, Lively, Newcome, and Boothroyd, by which מִקֶּטֶל is removed from verse 9th, and placed at the beginning of verse 10th.

10. מִקֶּטֶל מֵחֲמַס אָחִיךָ. Both nouns are in construction with אָחִיךָ, and the genitive thus formed is that of object: *the slaughter of, and the violence done to, thy brother*. The Edomites had not only slain the Hebrews, but injured them in every possible way; and their cruelties were highly aggravated by the consideration, that those who were the objects of them were descended from the same common parent. Comp. Amos i. 11. *Jacob* is used as a patronymic to denote the Jews. Two distinct periods in the future history of the Idumeans are here pointed out: that during which they should be the subjects of ignominy as a conquered people: and that during which they were to be entirely extinct. From the former they recovered about a century before the Christian era; but they were reduced by John Hyrcanus, and afterwards lost every vestige of their separate existence.

11. This and the three following verses contain a series of pointed expostulations, which, while they inculpate the Idumeans, describe the various modes in which they had manifested their malice towards the Jews. Some have thought that עֲמָדְךָ מִנֶּגֶד means here to stand aloof, to assume a neutral position, whence one may observe the movements of two opposing parties; but the declaration at the end of the verse, as well as what is stated in verses 13th and 14th, clearly shows that the phrase is to be taken in a hostile sense, as in 2 Sam. xviii. 13; Dan. x. 13. That חֵילוֹ is not to be rendered *wealth* or *riches* in this passage, but *forces*, *army*, or the like may be inferred from reference being made to the division of the substance of the citizens of Jerusalem by lot in the following hemistich. נָכְרִים and זָרִים describe the Chaldeans, by whom Jerusalem was taken. שְׁבוֹת is in Piel, contracted for שְׁבוֹת. Comp. יַדּוּ, Lam. iii. 53. Instead of שְׁעָרָיו, the read-

12 Thou shouldest not have looked on in the day of thy brother,
    In the day of his being treated as an alien;
    Thou shouldest not have rejoiced over the sons of Judah,
    In the day of their destruction:
    Neither shouldest thou have spoken insolently
    In the day of distress.
13 Thou shouldest not have entered the gate of my people,
    In the day of their calamity;
    Thou, even thou, shouldest not have looked on their affliction,
    In the day of their calamity;
    Nor stretched forth thy hand to their wealth,
    In the day of their calamity.

ing of the text, many MSS., four of the earliest printed editions, and some more recent ones, exhibit שְׂעִירוּ, the full form, as proposed by the Keri. That the word may originally have been read as the singular, is clear from its occurrence in this number, ver. 13; but then, in both cases, it is to be taken as a collective.

12. The future forms אַל־תֵּרֶא, אַל־תִּשְׂמַח, אַל־תָּבוֹא, אַל־תַּגְדֵּל, אַל־תִּשְׁלַחְנָה, אַל־תַּגֵּר, and אַל־תָּסְגֵּר, are all qualified in signification, by the circumstance, that the speaker has a past event prominently in view, in reference to which he places himself and those whom he addresses in the time of its passing, and points out what was their duty in reference to it. They are properly subjunctives of negation, expressive of what *should not* have been done, and therefore have the usual force of the imperative. " Verba Hebræorum sæpe non actum, sed debitum vel officium significat." Glassii Philolog. Sacr. lib. iii. tract. 3, can. 6. Nicholson's Ewald, § 264. רָאָה בְּ, means here *to look upon with malignant pleasure*, to feast one's eyes with the calamity of another. יוֹם אָחִיךָ, *the day of thy brother*, is afterward explained by יוֹם־נָכְרוֹ, יוֹם אָבְדָם, יוֹם צָרָה, יוֹם אֵידָם, which describe the calamitous circumstances in which the Jews were placed. יוֹם, *day*, is often used to express a *disastrous* or *calamitous period.* נָכְרוֹ, which is taken actively to denote

severe treatment, punishment, Job xxxi. 3, is here used passively of the experience of such treatment. Comp. the Arab. نَكَرَ, *difficilis ac durus fuit; gravis ac difficilis; improbavit.* The idea radically inherent in the term is that of treating any one as a stranger, *i. e.* an alien or enemy. הִגְדִּיל פֶּה, *to enlarge*, or *make great the mouth*, Ger. *den Mund voll nehmen:* to use insolent or contumelious language, such as those employ who exult over a fallen foe. Comp. Ezek. xxxv. 13.

13. גַּם in גַּם־אַתָּה is emphatic. תִּשְׁלַחְנָה, some take to be the third plural feminine, having for its object יָדַיִם; but the entire construction of the passage requires the second person singular masculine, תִּשְׁלַח. The syllable נָה is added with a view to give intensity to the verb, as in Jud. v. 26; thus expressing the eagerness with which the Idumeans seized upon the spoil. Rosenmüller is of opinion that the ה is paragogic, and the נ epenthetic; but Gesenius is rather inclined to compare it with the energetic Future of the Arabs. Lehrgeb. p. 801. LXX. μὴ συνεπιθῇ; Syr. ܠܐ ܬܘܣܦ; Vulg. *non emitteris;* Targ. וְלָא תוֹשִׁיט. See for more instances of this intensive form Job xvii. 16; Is. xxviii. 3; Exod. i. 10. For the omission of יָד, *hand*, see 2 Sam. vi. 6: Ps. xviii. 17.

14 Neither shouldest thou have stood at the pass,
   To cut off those of his that escaped;
   Neither shouldest thou have delivered up those of his
   That were left in the day of distress.
15 For the day of Jehovah is near against all the nations;
   As thou hast done, it shall be done unto thee;
   Thy deed shall come back upon thine own head,
16 For as ye have drunk upon my holy mountain,
   So shall all the nations drink continually;
   Yea, they shall drink and swallow greedily,
   And shall be as though they had not been.

14. פֶּרֶק is commonly rendered *biviam*, a parting of a way, or a place where a road breaks off into two. I should rather think, from the idea of violence implied in פֶּרֶק, that it signifies a *break* or *disruption* in a rock or mountain, through which a passage might be effected into the region beyond. Comp. מִפְרֶצֶת הָרִים, 1 Kings xix. 11. LXX. διεκβολαί. Syr. ܦܳܠܫܳܐ, a narrow passage between two mountains. In all probability, the reference is to the means employed to cut off the retreat of those Jews who attempted to pass through Idumea on their way to Egypt, whither they fled from the Chaldeans. עֲמֹד עַל הַפֶּרֶק, *to stand at the ravine* or *pass*, graphically describes the attitude of those who are watching in order to intercept a caravan, or a body of travellers, especially in the rugged mountainous regions to the south of Judea. The Idumeans not only in this way prevented the escape of the fugitives; they carried them back as prisoners, and delivered them up to the enemy.

15. In this verse, the conquest of Idumea and all the neighboring nations by Nebuchadnezzar is declared to be at hand. In the war which he was to carry on against them, due retribution would be rendered to the Edomites. Comp. Ps. cxxxvii. 7, 8. For the phrase יוֹם יְהֹוָה, *the day of Jehovah*, see on Is. ii. 12.

16. The Targ., Kimchi, Munster, Vatablus, Calvin, Michaelis, Hendewerk, and Hitzig, consider the Idumeans to be still addressed, and most of them explain their drinking on Mount Zion of the festivities with which they celebrated the victory gained over the Jews. Grotius refers the words to the same people, only he takes the verb שָׁתָה in the bad sense, as denoting the drinking of the cup of divine wrath, and renders עַל־הַר קָדְשִׁי, *on account of my holy mountain*, which he explains thus: "propter Judæam a vobis lacessitam." But it seems more natural to regard the words as directed, by a sudden apostrophe, to the Jews, assuring them, that, though the sufferings to which they had been subjected were great, still greater punishment would be inflicted upon the hostile nations by which they had been attacked. The punishment which they suffered was only temporary; that of their enemies would be perpetual. The structure of the passage requires the verb to be taken in the same sense in both parts of the verse. Such, in effect, is the construction put upon the words, Jer. xlix. 12. Compare also chap. xxv. 15-29. In this manner the verse is interpreted by Abenezra, Mercer, Tremellius, Drusius, Lively, Rosenmüller, Schnurrer, De Wette, Hesselberg, and Maurer. Instead of תָּמִיד, *continually*, the reading סָבִיב, *around*, is exhibited in not fewer than seventy-eight MSS.; in seventeen more originally; in three others in the margin; in seven of the earliest printed editions; and a few other authorities: but all the ancient versions support that of the Textus Receptus, which, according

17 But in Mount Zion shall be the escaped,
And it shall be holy:
And the house of Jacob shall enjoy their possessions.
18 And the house of Jacob shall be a fire,
And the house of Joseph a flame;
And the house of Esau shall become stubble,
And they shall set them on fire, and devour them;
So that there shall not be a relic of the house of Esau;
For Jehovah hath spoken it.
19 And they of the south shall possess Mount Esau,
And they of the plain, the Philistines;
They shall also possess the country of Ephraim,

to De Rossi, is found in all the most accurate and best MSS., both Spanish and German. In all probability מוֹרָשֵׁיהֶם, was substituted by some copyist from Jer. xxv. 9. What proves that the LXX. had the word מוֹרָשָׁם in their Hebrew text, is their having mistaken it for תִּירָשָׁם, rendering it οἶνον, *wine*. לוּעַ, *to swallow* or *suck down with greediness*. Arab. لَعَو and لَعِي, *avidus*; لَغَا, لَغِي, *multum aquœ bibit*. Comp. לֹעַ *the throat*; בָּלַע, *to swallow*, etc. The idea intended to be conveyed by the use of the verb here is that of drinking *completely off* the cup of wrath, as a thirsty person would a vessel of water.

17. Obadiah here commences his predictions respecting the restoration of the Jews from the Babylonish captivity; their re-occupancy of Canaan; and the reign of the Messiah. While the surrounding nations were to disappear, the Jews should regain possession of their holy city, and the land of their fathers. פְלֵיטָה means such as had survived the captivity. קֹדֶשׁ, *holiness*, i. e. holy, refers to Mount Zion, which had been polluted by the idolatrous Chaldeans. See on Joel iv. 17. Jæger and Hesselberg refer the suffix in מוֹרָשֵׁיהֶם, *their possessions*, to the hostile nations spoken of in the preceding verse; but less naturally.

18. Though the houses of Jacob and Joseph are here spoken of separately, it was not the intention of the prophet to teach that the two kingdoms of Judah and Israel would be re-established; yet the special mention of Joseph clearly shows that the ten tribes were to return at the same time, and, jointly with Judah and Benjamin, to possess the land of Palestine and the neighboring regions. See Is. xi. 12-14; Hos. i. 11. The restored Hebrews would unitedly subdue the Idumeans, which they did in the time of John Hyrcanus, who compelled them to be circumcised, and so incorporated them with the Jews, that they henceforward formed part of the nation. See Joseph. Antiquities, book xiii. chap. ix. 1. For the metaphorical language, comp. Num. xxi. 28; Is. x. 17; and, for the ground of it, Is. v. 24.

·19. By נֶגֶב, *the south*, or the southern part of Palestine, is meant those who should occupy it; and by הַשְּׁפֵלָה, *the plain*, those who should occupy the low country along the shore of the Mediterranean. LXX. Οἱ ἐν Ναγέβ; οἱ ἐν τῇ Σεφαλά. According to the relative positions of those who should take possession of the different parts of the holy land, was to be the enlargement of their territory by the annexation of the adjoining regions, which had formerly been occupied by alien or hostile powers. As there is no subject specified before אֶת שְׂדֵה אֶפְרַיִם וְאֵת שְׂדֵה שֹׁמְרוֹן, it would seem to be intimated that the regions of Ephraim and Samaria were to be occupied by the Jews and Israelites jointly,

And the country of Samaria;
And Benjamin, Gilead.
20 And the captives of this host of the sons of Israel,
That are among the Canaanites,
As far as Zarephath,
And the captives of Jerusalem,
That are in Sepharad,
Shall possess the cities of the south.

without any regard to tribal distinctions: and the reason why the tribe of Benjamin is mentioned, is merely on account of the proximity of Gilead to the territory which it originally possessed. That עַם is here employed to denote, not a plain or level country, but a region or district in general, is obvious from the nature of the territory to which reference is made. The mountainous country of Idumea is called שְׂדֵה אֱדוֹם, Gen. xxxii. 1.

20. חֵיל, i. e. בְּנֵי חֵיל, an army, host, etc., is here used to express the number of Israelitish captives which were found in Phœnicia, into which they had been sold at different times as slaves, and thence into Greece. See Joel iii. 6, 7. בְּנֵי יִשְׂרָאֵל is elliptical for בְּנֵי יִשְׂרָאֵל, which is the reading of three MSS. Before אֲשֶׁר כְּנַעֲנִים, supply יֵשׁ from the following. צָרְפַת, Zarephath, or Sarepta, now called سُرَفَند, Surafend, a town belonging to Sidon, and situated between that city and Tyre, close to the shore of the Mediterranean. According to the etymology of its name, it must have been a place for smelting metals. In the rocks along the foot of the hills, Dr. Robinson found many excavated tombs, which he makes no doubt once belonged to this ancient city. Palestine, vol. iii. p. 414. The name is still given to a large village on a hill at some little distance. What city or country is meant by סְפָרַד, it has been hitherto found impossible to determine. The LXX. Ἐφραθά, which in all probability is a corruption of Σέφραδά. Aq., Symm. and Theod. σαφαράδ. Hexap. Syr. ܐܣܦܢܝܐ; but the Peshito ܐܣܦܢܝܐ Spain, with which agrees אִסְפַּמְיָא of the Targ.: an interpretation unanimously adopted by the Rabbins, who in like manner concur in interpreting צָרְפַת of France. Jerome, as instructed by his Jewish teacher, renders it the Bosphorus. Some refer it to Sipphara in Mesopotamia, some to Sparta, in support of which hypothesis they appeal to 1 Macc. xii. 21; while others propose סְפָרָה, Sephara, Gen. x. 30, or the town of Σαπφάρ,. mentioned by Ptolemy, as lying between the territory of the Homerites and Sabæans. To judge from the other geographical relations stated in this and the preceding verse, we should conjecture, that some place to the south or east of Judea is intended. The following list of cities and places in the possession of the Jews in the time of Alexander Jannæus is given by Josephus: κατὰ τοῦτον τὸν καιρὸν ἤδη τῶν Σύρων καὶ Ἰδουμαίων καὶ Φοινίκων πόλεις εἶχον Ἰουδαῖοι· πρὸς θαλάσσῃ μὲν Στράτωνος πύργον, Ἀπολλωνίαν, Ἰόππην, Ἰάμνειαν, Ἄζωταν, Γάζαν, Ἀνθηδόνα, Ῥαφίαν, Ῥινοκόλουραν· ἐν δὲ τῇ μεσογείᾳ κατὰ τὴν Ἰδουμαίαν, Ἄδωρα, καὶ Μάρισσαν, καὶ Σαμάρειαν, Καρμήλιον ὄρος, καὶ τὸ Ἰταβύριον ὄρος, Σκυθόπολιν, Γάδαρα, Γαυλανίτιδα, Σελεύκειαν, Γάβαλα, Μωαβίτιδας, Ἐσσεβῶν, Μήδαβα, Λεμβᾶ, Ὀρώνος, Γελίθωνα, Ζύρα, Κιλίκιον Αὐλῶνα, Πέλλαν — ἄλλας τε πόλεις πρωτευούσας τῆς Συρίας, αἱ ἦσαν κατεσραμμέναι. — Antiq. book. xiv. ch. iv. 4.

21. Though forty-four MSS., besides several others at second hand, and eight printed editions, read מוֹשִׁיעִים instead of מוּשָׁעִים, there is no difference in the meaning, the former reading being

OBADIAH.

21 And deliverers shall come up in Mount Zion.
 To judge Mount Esau;
 And the kingdom shall be Jehovah's.

merely defective in orthography. The LXX., Aq., Theod., Syr., and Arab., appear to have read מוֹשִׁעִים or מְגִּיעִים in the passive, which is unsuitable to the connection. Jerome observes that the word is active. Such *saviors*, or *deliverers* are meant, as those who were raised up in the time of the Judges. There can be little doubt that the celebrated family of the Maccabees are intended, whose valiant princes governed the Jews for the period of an hundred and twenty-six years, during which time signal victories were gained over the Idumeans, as narrated 2 Macc. x.

15–23. Joseph. Antiq. book. xiii. chap. ix. 1. שָׁפַט is here used in the sense of *punishing*, as in 1 Sam. iii. 13; and שָׁפַט in the phrase בְּ שָׁפְטִים אֹתָם, Exod. xii. 12; Num. xxxiii. 4. Comp. κρίνω, Acts vii. 7. The concluding words of the prophecy, וְהָיְתָה לַיהוָֹה הַמְּלוּכָה, refer to he reign of the Messiah, called so frequently in the N. T. ἡ βασιλεία τοῦ Θεοῦ. Comp. Dan. ii. 44, vii. 27. But for the introduction of this kingdom, no restoration of the Jews would have taken place; the temple would have remained in ruins, and the land a scene of desolation.

JONAH.

PREFACE.

AGAINST no book of Scripture have the shafts of infidelity and the sapping arts of anti-supernaturalism been more strenuously directed than against that of the Prophet Jonah. As early as the days of Julian and Porphyry it was made the subject of banter and ridicule by the pagans, who accused the Christians of credulity for believing the story of the deliverance by means of a fish; and, in modern times, while the enemies of revelation have evinced the same spirit, many of its pretended friends have had recourse to methods of interpretation, which would not only remove the book from the category of inspired writings, but, if applied to these writings generally, would annihilate much that is strictly historical in its import, and leave us to wander in the regions of conjecture and fable. Blasche, Grimm, and some others, suppose the whole to have been transacted in a dream; but, as Eichhorn justly observes,* there is not a single circumstance in the narrative that would suggest such an idea; and, besides, whenever any account is given of a dream in Scripture, the fact that such is the case, is always intimated by the writer. The manner in which the book commences and closes, is also objected to this hypothesis, which J. G. A. Müller † scruples not to assert we are on no ground whatever (durch gar nichts,) warranted to adopt. The theory of an historical allegory was advanced and maintained with great learning, but, at the same time, with the most extravagant license of imagination, by the eccentric Herman von der Hardt, Professor of the Oriental languages at the university of Helmstedt.‡ According to this author, Jonah was an historical person, but is here symbolical partly of Manasseh, and partly of Josiah, kings of Judah; the ship was the Jewish state; the storm, the political convulsions which threatened its safety; the master of the ship, Zadok the high-priest; the great fish, the city of Lybon on the Orontes, where Manasseh was detained as a prisoner, etc. Semler Michaelis, Herder, Hezel, Stäudlin, Paulus, Meyer, Eichhorn, Niemeyer, etc. have attempted to vindicate to the book the character of a parable, a fable, an apologue, or a moral fiction; while Dereser, Nachtigal, Ammon, Bauer, Goldhorn, Knobel, and others, consider it to have had historical basis, and that it has been invested with its present costume in order that it might answer didactic purposes. On the other hand, Rosenmüller, Ge-

* Einleit. Band iv. § 575. † Palus Memorabilien. Stuck vl. p. 154.
‡ Ænigmata prisci Orbis. Jonas in Luce, etc. Helmstedt. 1723, fol. For the full title of this remarkable book, see Rosenmüller's Prolegom.

senius, De Wette, Maurer, and Winer, derived it from popular tradition; some tracing it to the fable of the deliverance of Andromeda from a sea monster, by Perseus, Apollod. ii. 4, 3; Ovid, Metamorph. iv. 662, etc.; and some, to that of Hercules, who sprang into the jaws of an immense fish, and was three days in its belly, when he undertook to save Hesione, Iliad, xx. 145, xxi. 442; Diod. Sic. iv. 42; Tzetz. ad Lycophr. Cassand. 33; Cyrill Alex. in Jon. ii.

Much as some of these writers may have in common with each other, there are some essential points on which they are totally at variance; while all frankly acknowledge the difficulties which clog the subject.

The opinion which has been most generally entertained, is that which accords to the book a strictly historical character; in other words, which affirms that it is a relation of facts which actually took place in the life and experience of the prophet. Nor can I view it in any other light, while I hold fast an enlightened belief in the divine authority of the books composing the canon of the Old Testament, and place implicit reliance on the authority of the Son of God. Into the fixed and definite character of the canon, I need not here enter, having fully discussed the subject elsewhere;* but assuming that all the books contained in it possess the Divine sanction, the test to which I would bring the question, and by which, in my opinion, our decision must mainly be formed, is the unqualified manner in which the personal existence, miraculous fate, and public ministry of Jonah, are spoken of by our Lord. He not only explicitly recognizes the prophetical office of the son of Amittai ('Ιωνᾶ τοῦ προφήτου), just as he does that of Elisha, Isaiah, and Daniel, but represents his being in the belly of the fish as a real miracle (τὸ σημεῖον); grounds upon it, as a fact, the certainty of the future analogous fact in his own history; assumes the actual execution of the commission of the prophet at Nineveh; positively asserts that the inhabitants of that city repented at his preaching; and concludes by declaring respecting himself, "Behold! a greater than Jonah is here." Matt. xii. 39–41, xvi. 4. Now, is it conceivable, that all these historical circumstances would have been placed in this prominent light, if the person of the prophet, and the brief details of his narrative, had been purely fictitious? On the same principle that the historical bearing of the reference in this case is rejected, may not that to the Queen of Sheba, which follows in the connection, be set aside, and the portion of the first book of Kings, in which the circumstances of her visit to Solomon are recorded, be converted into an allegory, a moral fiction, or a popular tradition? The two cases, as adduced by our Lord, are altogether parallel; and the same may be affirmed of the allusion to Tyre and Sidon, and that to Sodom in the preceding chapter.

It may be said, indeed, that a fictitious narrative of the moral kind would answer the purpose of our Saviour equally well with one which contained a statement of real transactions; just as it has been maintained, that the reference made by the Apostle James to the patience of Job, suited his pur-

---

* Divine Inspiration, pp. 450–488.

pose, irrespective of the actual existence of that patriarch; but, as in the one case, a fictitious example of patience would prove only a tame and frigid motive to induce to the endurance of actual suffering, so, in the other, a merely imaginary repentance must be regarded as little calculated to enforce the duties of genuine contrition and amendment of life.

Certainly in no other instance in which our Saviour adduces passages out of the Old Testament for the purpose of illustrating or confirming his doctrines, can it be shown, that any point or circumstance is thus employed which is not historically true. He uniformly quotes and reasons upon them as containing accounts of universally admitted facts; stamps them as such with the high sanction of his divine authority; and transmits them for the confident belief of mankind in all future ages.

It is only necessary further to add, that if the book had contained a parable, the name of some unknown person would have been selected, and not that of a prophet to whom a definite historical existence is assigned in the Old Testament. On perusing the first sentence, every unprejudiced reader must conclude that there had existed such a prophet, and that what follows is a simple narrative of facts. The formula וַיְהִי דְבַר־יְהֹוָה־אֶל is so appropriated, as the usual introduction to real prophetical communication, that to put any other construction upon it would be a gross violation of one of the first principles of interpretation. Comp. 2 Chron. xi. 2; Is. xxxviii. 4; Jer. i. 4, 11, ii. 1, xiv. 1, xvi. 1, xxviii. 12, xxix. 30; Ezek. iii. 16; Hag. i. 1, 3, ii. 20; Zech. iv. 8.

Against the plenary historical character of the book, the miraculous nature of some of the transactions has been objected; but, referring for an investigation of these transactions to the commentary, and taking for granted an interposition of miraculous agency in the deliverance of the prophet, when cast into the sea, may it not be fairly asked whether there is nothing in the circumstances of the case to justify such interposition? The commission was most important in its own nature, but likewise most unusual, and confessedly most hazardous in its execution; one from which it was extremely natural for Jonah to shrink, and which required the most confirmatory evidence of its divine origin to induce him to act upon it. The miracle selected for the purpose of furnishing him with this evidence, however extraordinary in itself, was in exact keeping with the circumstances in which he was placed; and, in so far, was parallel with those wrought in connection with the mission of Moses, Exod. iii. iv.; of Elijah, 1 Kings xvii.; and of Christ and his apostles. And it is undeniable, that most of the writers who have called it in question, have either flatly denied the existence of all Scripture miracles, or attempted, in some way or other, to account for them on mere natural principles. The same mode of reasoning which goes to set aside one, will, if fully carried out, go to set aside all.

That our prophet is the same who predicted the restoration of the ancient boundaries of the kingdom of the ten tribes, 2 Kings xiv. 25, is rendered certain by identity of name, parentage and office; and as that prediction received its accomplishment in the reign of Jeroboam II., it is obvious he must at least have been contemporary with the monarch, if he did not flourish at a still more early period. He is justly considered to have been one of the most ancient of all the Hebrew prophets whose writings are contained in the canon.

Whether Jonah composed the book himself, or whether it was written at a more recent period, has been matter of dispute. Of the circumstance, that he is spoken of in the third person, no account is to be made, since it is a style of writing frequently adopted by the sacred penmen, as it also is by profane authors. Nor can the occurrence of two or three Chaldee words, as סְפִינָה, *a ship*, עָשַׁת *to think*, טַעַם, *command*, be justly objected against the early authorship; for the prophet must have had considerable intercourse with persons who spoke foreign languages, which could not but exert some influence on his style. With respect to סְפִינָה, as it is also the Syriac ܣܦܝܢܬܐ, and Arabic سفينة, there is every reason to conclude that it was the nautical term in use among the Phœnicians, and so might have been adopted at an early period into all the cognate dialects, though they had other words by which to express the same thing. The use of the compound particles שֶׁלְּמִי and בְּשֶׁלִּי does not necessarily argue a late date, since there was nothing to prevent their being appropriated under the circumstances of the prophet, just as they came to be adopted, under somewhat similar circumstances, by other writers. The employment of שׁ, the abbreviated form of אֲשֶׁר, in Judges v. 7, is an undeniable example of its adoption at an early period; and it is indeed very doubtful whether it be proper to regard it as a Chaldaism at all, though it is found in some portions of the Hebrew Scriptures and not in others!* It has also been alleged against the antiquity of the book, that the writer uses the substantive verb in the past tense, when describing the size of Nineveh, וְנִינְוֵה הָיְתָה עִיר־גְּדוֹלָה, chap. iii. 3 ; as if the city had been destroyed before his time; but the past tense is evidently employed for the simple purpose of preserving uniformity in the style of the narrative, and, as De Wette acknowledges, *bedeutet nichts*.†

In point of style, the book is remarkable for the simplicity of its prose: the only portion of poetry is chap. ii. 3–10, which possesses considerable spirit and force, though some parts of it are evidently a repetition of certain sentences in the Psalms of David, with which the prophet appears to have been familiar.

Of the numerous traditions, both Jewish and Christian, which profess to give us information respecting Jonah, I would say with Luther, *Das glaube wer da will, ich glaube es nicht*. All that we learn from Scripture is, that his father's name was Amittai, and that his birth-place was Gath-hepher (בֶּן־אֲמִתַּי, 2 Kings xiv. 25; גִּתָּה חֵפֶר, Josh. xix. 13), a city in the tribe of Zebulon, from which latter circumstance it appears that he was an Israelite, and not a Jew.

In this book the patience and clemency of God are strikingly contrasted

---

* See Holden on Ecclesiastes, Introd. Dissert. pp. 10–13.   † Lehrbuch, § 237.

with the selfishness and unbelief of man; and, as inserted in the canon of Scripture, it was no doubt primarily designed to teach the Jews the moral lessons, that the Divine regard was not confined to them alone, but was extended to other subjects of the general government of God; that wickedness, if persisted in, will meet with condign punishment; that God has no pleasure in inflicting such punishment, but delights in the repentance of the guilty; and that if pagans yielded so prompt a compliance with a single prophetic message, it behooved those who were continually instructed by the servants of Jehovah, seriously to reflect on the guilt which they contracted by refusing to listen to their admonitions. It has been usual to speak of Jonah as a type of our Saviour, and numerous points of resemblance have been attempted to be established between them, to the no small injury of the blessed character of the latter: whereas, there is nothing more in the passage of our Lord's discourse (Matt. xii.), from which the notion has been borrowed, than a comparison of his own consignment to the tomb for *the same space of time* which the prophet spent in the belly of the fish.* The record of the event in the Jewish Scriptures could never have suggested to its readers, before Christ made the reference, the subject in the anticipative illustration of which he applies it.

* See the excellent remarks of the Rev. W. Lindsay Alexander, M. A. on types, in his Congregational Lectures, Lect. VIII.

CHAPTER I.

WE have here an account of the prophet's commission to preach at Nineveh, and his attempt to evade it by embarking for Spain, 1-3; an extraordinary storm by which he was baffled in his purpose; the alarm of the sailors, and the means which they adopted for their safety; the detection of Jonah; his being thrown into the sea; and his preservation in the belly of a fish, 4-17.

1   THE word of Jehovah was communicated to Jonah, the son of
2 Amittai, saying: Arise, go to Nineveh, that great city, and proclaim against it; for their wickedness is come up before me.

1. From the circumstance that the book commences with the conjunction ו, commonly rendered *and*, some have inferred that it is merely the fragment of a larger work, written by the same hand; but though this particle is most commonly used to connect the following sentence with something which precedes it, and is placed at the beginning of historical books to mark their connection with a foregoing narrative, as Exod. i. 1; 1 Kings i. 1; Ezra i. 1; yet it is also employed inchoatively where there is no connection whatever, as Ruth i. 1; Esth. i. 1; and, as specially parallel, Ezek. i. 1. It serves no other purpose in such cases than merely to qualify the apocopated future, so as to make it represent the historical past tense. The proper names יוֹנָה, *Jonah*, and אֲמִתַּי, *Amittai*, signify *a dove*, and *veracious* or *truthful*, but why they were given to the prophet and his father we are not informed.

2. By an emphatic idiom, קוּם, *arise*, is used before another verb, as a term of excitement. נִינְוֵה NINEVEH, the ancient capital of the Assyrian empire, was situated on the eastern bank of the Tigris, opposite to the modern town of Mosul. The name is generally allowed to signify " the residence of Ninus," from נִין, *Ninus*, and נָוֶה, *a dwelling;* but, according to Hebrew usage, the words should be reversed in order to bring out this meaning. By the Greek and Roman writers, it is called Νῖνος, *Ninus*, after its founder, who must have been indentical with Nimrod, to whom the foundation of the city is ascribed, Gen. x. 11. For, that אַשּׁוּר, *Ashur*, is there to be understood of the country so called, or Assyria, and not of a person of that name, is evident from ver. 22, where Ashur is mentioned as a descendant of Shem, and not of Ham. The omission of the local ה, which might have been expected to form אַשּׁוּרָה, cannot be brought as an objection, since it is frequently omitted. See Num. xxxiv. 4; Deut. iii. 1. In point of size, it might well be designated הָעִיר הַגְּדוֹלָה, *that great city*, having been as stated chap. iii. 3, " three days' journey " in circumference. If we reckon a day's journey at about twenty miles, which is the average rate of travelling in the East, it will give us sixty miles; which, how immense soever it may appear, quite agrees with the estimate stated by Diodorus Siculus, ii. 3 : viz. 480 stadia in circuit, 150 stadia in length, and 90 stadia in breadth. He further calls it Νῖνος μεγάλη, and adds, τηλικαύτην δὲ πόλιν οὐδεὶς ὕστερον ἔκτισε κατά τε τὸ μέγεθος τοῦ περιβολοῦ, καὶ τὴν περὶ τὸ τεῖχος μεγαλοπρέπειαν. Making every allowance for the large spaces occupied by gardens, etc., it must, according to the computation specified, chap. iv. 11, have contained a population of upwards of six hundred thousand souls, which is nearly equal to that of

3 But Jonah rose up to flee unto Tarshish, from the presence of Jehovah; and he went down to Joppa, and found a ship going to Tarshish, and paid the fare thereof, and went down into her, to go with them unto Tarshish from the presence of Jehovah.

Paris. As it had long been the mistress of the East, and its situation was favorable for commerce, it possessed immense wealth, but was, at the same time, notorious for the most flagrant corruption of manners. After a siege of three years, it was taken by Arbaces the Mede, about the seventh year of Uzziah; and a second time by the united forces of Cyaxares the Mede, and Nabopolassar, viceroy of Babylon, B. C. 626. קְרָא עָלֶיהָ, *make a proclamation against it.* This proclamation consisted in the announcement, that, within the space of forty days, the city should be destroyed. עַל the LXX. and Vulg. render *in*; and some would assign to the word the signification *to*, which אֶל has, chap. iii. 3; but it better agrees with the flight of Jonah to retain that of *against*. The idea of his going to so great a city for the purpose of denouncing punishment against its wicked population so appalled him that he shrunk from the task. It is also more in keeping with the reason assigned in the following clause of the verse. The phrase עָלָה לִפְנֵי יְהוָה, *to go, or come up before Jehovah*, is expressive of whatever is supposed specially to attract his notice, and require his interference. Comp. בֹּא בָב, Gen. vi. 13; בָּאָה אֵלַי, xix. 21. Βαβυλὼν ἡ μεγάλη ἐμνήσθη ἐνώπιον τοῦ Θεοῦ, Rev. xvi. 19. Αἱ ἐλεημοσύναι σου ἀνέβησαν εἰς μνημόσυνον ἔμπροσθεν τοῦ Θεοῦ, Acts x. 4.

3. For תַּרְשִׁישָׁה, *Tarshish*, see on Is. xxiii. 10. The Rabbins vacillate between Tarsus and Tunis. Jonathan has יַמָּא, *the sea*. Jonah resolved to make his escape into the most distant regions of the West. Com. Ps. cxxxix. 7. מִפְּנֵי יְהוָה, which strictly means the *face, person, or presence of Jehovah*, is sometimes employed to denote the special manifestation of his presence, or certain outward and visible tokens by which he made himself locally known. Thus God promised that *his presence* (פָּנַי), *i. e.* the sensible tokens of his presence, should accompany the Hebrews on their march to Canaan. Exod. xxxiii. 14. Comp. Ps. ix. 3, lxviii. 2, 8. It is also employed in reference to the *place* or *region* where such manifestations were vouchsafed, as Gen. iv. 14; where it obviously signifies the spot where the primitive worship was celebrated, and sensible proofs of the Divine favor were manifested to the worshippers. 1 Sam. i. 22, ii. 18; Ps. xlii. 3. In like manner, the place where Jacob had intimate communion with God, was called by that patriarch פְּנִיאֵל, *the face*, or *manifestation of God*, Gen. xxxii. 31. The interpretation, therefore, of David Kimchi, כי חשב שאם יצא מא״י ישראל לחוצה לארץ לא תשרה עליו רוח נבואה, *he imagined that if he went out of the land of Israel, the spirit of prophecy would not rest upon him*, is perhaps not wide of the mark. Jarchi to the same effect, באיך שכינה שורה בחוצה לא״ץ, *The Shekinah does not dwell out of the land*. Though, as Theodoret observes, he well knew that the Lord of the universe was everywhere present, yet he supposed that it was only at Jerusalem he became apparent to men; ὑπολαμβάνων δὲ ὅμως ἐν μόνῃ Ἱερουσαλὴμ αὐτὸν ποιεῖσθαι τὴν ἐπιφάνειαν. For the reason of Jonah's flight, see on chap. iv. 2. יָרַד is used of *going down* to the sea-coast from any inland place, so that it cannot be inferred from the use of the term that it was at Jerusalem Jonah received his commission. יָפוֹ, *Iapho*, LXX. Ἰόππη, Arab. يَافَا, *Yapha, Jaffa, Joppa*, a celebrated harbor on the east coast of the Mediterranean, at the distance of ten hours from Jerusalem, of which it is properly the seaport. However insecure, it was used as a harbor as early as the days of Solomon. 2 Chron. ii. 16. It was likewise thus appropriated in the Persian period, Ezra iii. 7; and was deemed so

CHAP. I.   JONAH.   203

4 But Jehovah caused a great wind to come down upon the sea, and there was a great tempest in the sea, and it was appre-
5 hended the ship would be wrecked. Then the mariners were afraid, and cried, each to his god, and threw out the wares that were in the ship into the sea, to lighten her of them; but as for Jonah, he had gone down into the innermost part of the vessel, and lay fast asleep.

important in the time of the Maccabees, that, when recovered from the Syrians, it was fortified, and afterwards underwent various fates. Its present population amounts to about 7000 souls. בֹּא, which usually signifies to *come, come into, enter*, is obviously here used in the acceptation *go, go out*. Com. Num. xxxii. 6. שְׂכָרָהּ, *her hire*, i. e. of the vessel, the fare which Jonah had to pay for a passage in her; not, that he engaged the vessel, as Benjoin, after Jarchi, would have it. רק מה שהוא חייב ליתן בחלקו, *only what he was obliged to pay as his share*. Abenezra. This fare, it has been thought, he paid beforehand, that he might secure his flight from the land of Judea; but it may have been owing to a prudential condition on the part of the captain. The affix in שְׂכָרֶיהָ refers to the ship's crew, understood.

4. The force of הֵטִיל, *to cause to come down at full length*, on application to the storm, will appear on consulting Josephus, who, speaking of the dangerous navigation of Joppa, says: κατὰ τοῦτον σαλευούσι τοῖς ἀπὸ τῆς Ἰόππης ὑπὸ τὸν ἕω πνεῦμα βίαιον ἐπιπίπτει· μελαμβόρειον ὑπὸ τῶν ταύτῃ πλωϊζομένων καλεῖται. "As they were driven about here, a violent wind fell upon them, which is called by those that sail there, the *black north wind*." De Bello Jud. iii. ix. 3. The whole section deserves to be read. Coverdale renders, "But the Lord hurled a greate wynde into the see." חָשְׁבָה, *the ship*, i. e., by metonymy, the persons on board, thought she would founder. Thus Kimchi; but Jarchi, היא נדמית כאלו נשברה, *she appeared as if she should be broken*. Syriac ܘܗܝ ܡܣܬܒܪܐ ܕܡܬܬܒܪܐ, *was going to be broken,* or *was tossed, etc.* LXX. ἐκινδύνευε. It is best to render the verb impersonally.

5. מַלָּחִים, *mariners*, from מֶלַח, *salt*, the quality of the water which they navigate. Syr. and Arab. the same. Comp. Ezek. xxvii. 9, 27, 29. Kimchi, תפשי המשוטים, *those who handle the oars*, with reference to the ancient mode of propelling vessels at sea. Being in all probability Phœnicians, they had each his tutelary deity, whose interposition he invoked in the hour of danger. From the circumstance that כֵּלִים signifies *vessels*, Benjoin infers, that the ship had not taken in a regular cargo, Jonah having paid the entire freight; but כְּלִי is used with such latitude of signification in the Hebrew Scriptures, that it may be understood of any kind of manufactured articles, such as those enumerated Ezek. xxvii. which formed the merchandise of Tyre. These the Phœnicians conveyed to Spain, whence they brought back cargoes of silver, iron, tin, and lead. That something more ponderous than a few vessels on the deck is meant, is evident from what follows in the verse, ἐκβολὴν ἐποιήσαντο, the words employed by the LXX. in translating what are the same which are used by Luke, Acts xxvii. 18. The dual form in יַרְכְּתֵי הַסְּפִינָה; the *sides* or *two sides* of the vessel, is not to be pressed; the word in this number being adopted in Hebrew usage to express a recess or remote part of any place. Comp. Ps. cxxviii. 3; 1 Sam. xxiv. 4; Is. xiv. 15; *the innermost part*, best expresses the meaning. Kimchi otherwise explains it, אל אחת מן הירכתים, *to one of the sides*, and appeals to Judges xii. 7, and Zech. ix. 9, in proof of the plural being used instead of the singular. See Gesenius, Lehrgeb. p. 665. It has been ob-

6   And the captain went close up to him, and said to him: How is it, thou art fast asleep? Arise, call to thy God; perhaps God will think upon us, that we perish not.

7   And they said to each other: Come, and let us cast lots, that we may know on whose account this calamity hath happened to

8   us: and they cast lots, and the lot fell upon Jonah. And they said to him: Tell us now on what account this calamity hath happened to us? What is thine occupation? And whence com-

9   est thou? What is thy country? And of what people art thou? And he said to them: I am an Hebrew, and I fear Jehovah, the

jected to the historical character of the book, that it is not to be supposed that the prophet could possibly have composed himself to sleep in the circumstances here described; but nothing was more natural than for a person after the fatigues of a journey, with a mind worn out by excessive anxiety, to be thrown in spite of himself, into such a condition. נִרְדָּם, which the LXX. render καὶ ἔρεγχε, is designed to qualify the preceding verb, by expressing the profound stupor into which Jonah had sunk. There is a singular beauty in putting יוֹנָה, the name of the prophet, in the nominative absolute. "But as for Jonah" — while all were full of consternation, expecting every moment to become a prey to the raging elements, he lay perfectly unconscious of what was transpiring. For סְפִינָה, *ship*, which occurs only in this place, see the Preface.

6. הַחֹבֵל lit. *the master of the ropemen* — חֶבֶל being used as a collective. Com. רַב הַטַּבָּחִים, *chief of the body-guard*, 2 Kings xxv. 8; רַב סָרִיסִים, *chief of the eunuchs*. Dan. i. 3. Kimchi explains thus: הספנים נקראים חובלי לב שמושכין וממהרין חבלי התורן כפי המוצא, "*the ship-men are called ropemen, because they draw and loosen the ropes, of the mast, according to their skill.*" LXX. πρωρεύς. Vulg. gubernator. עַשְׁתֵּר, *to show oneself considerate, to think of, set one's mind upon*; in Kal, *to invent, fabricate, produce splendid work*; hence the noun עֶשֶׁת, *artificial work*, Song v. 14. The idea of *shining* seems to be a secondary meaning; see Jer. v. 28. Comp. עַשְׁתֹּנוֹת

thoughts, Ps. cxlvi. 4. The verb has the signification of *thinking, purposing,* etc. both in Chaldee and Syriac. LXX. διασώσῃ. Targ. יִתְרָעַם, Syr. ܦܶܣ, *to deliver*. Hitzig prefers the idea of *shining, being friendly, gracious,* and the like. Having found that their heathen deities rendered them no assistance, the crew were anxious to try the effect of supplication on the part of Jonah to the God of the Hebrews, either from the supposition that he was stronger than their own gods, or that he might be displeased with the prophet, and required to be placated. It deserves to be noticed, that the word for God is here used with the article הָאֱלֹהִים, which is certainly designed to give emphasis to it; God — the true God. Comp. Deut. iv. 35, יְהוָה הוּא הָאֱלֹהִים, and 1 Kings xviii. 39, יְהוָה הוּא הָאֱלֹהִים יְהוָה הוּא הָאֱלֹהִים. Are we to infer from this circumstance, that the captain was a worshipper of Jehovah?

7-9. The casting of lots was common among the nations of antiquity, not only when they wished to know some future event, but also when they would determine cases of difficulty, and especially criminal causes, in which no witnesses could be obtained. The mode of using them is not described in Scripture, but from the verb נָפַל, הִפִּיל, *to fall, cause to fall,* being commonly employed, it is probable it was by shaking the lots in some box or vase, and then causing them to fall on the ground. Comp. Prov. xvi. 33, where יוּטַל, *to throw down*, is used, in connection with חֵיק, the *bosom*,

10 God of heaven, who made the sea, and the dry land. And the men were greatly afraid, and said to him: What is this thou hast done? For the men knew that he was fleeing from the
11 presence of Jehovah, because he had told them. They further said to him: What shall we do to thee, that the sea may cease from raging against us? for the sea groweth more and more
12 tempestuous. And he said to them: Take me up, and throw me into the sea, and the sea shall cease from raging against you; for I know it is on my account this great tempest is upon you.
13 And the men rowed hard to regain the land; but they

or large fold of the garment in front of the body; intimating, that lots were also mixed there for the sake of secrecy. בְּשֶׁלְּמִי, lit. *for that which is to whom*, i. e. בְּשֶׁל מִי, *for whose guilt.* The words in ver. 8, בַּאֲשֶׁר לְמִי הָרָעָה הַזֹּאת לָנוּ, are omitted in two of Kennicott's MSS., in the Soncin. edition of the Prophets, and in the Vatican copy of the LXX.; and Kennicott's MS. 154, omits לְמִי, most probably both by emendation, in order to avoid the repetition of what had been said in ver. 7. We should rather have expected בַּאֲשֶׁר לְמִי, "on account of what;" but מִי may be taken in a neuter sense, like the corresponding ܡܰܢ in Ethiopic, as indeed, it is in the phrase מִי שְׁמֶךָ, "*What is thy name?*" Jud. xiii. 16. Comp. also 1 Sam. xviii. 17, מִי חַיָּי, "*What is my life?*" Micah i. 5, מִי־פֶּשַׁע יַעֲקֹב מִי בָּמוֹת יְהוּדָה, "*What is the sin of Jacob?*"—"*What are the high places of Judah?*" Hexaplar Syr. ܡܛܠ ܡܢܐ, *on account of what.* Leo Juda: "*unde sit nobis hoc malum.*" The seamen were anxious to learn every particular connected with the history of Jonah, in order that they might discover the real cause of the storm. יָרֵא, *to fear*, followed by the accusative, signifies to cherish feelings of reverence, to *reverence, honor*, etc., and is not here to be interpreted in the sense of being afraid, which would have required the preposition מִן before the object in such a case as the present.

10. מַה־זֹּאת עָשִׂיתָ, *what is this thou hast done?* is not put for the purpose of obtaining information respecting his flight, for it is immediately added, that he had previously informed them of it, but is a formula which is intended to produce a strong feeling of disapprobation in the breast of him to whom it is addressed, conveying, at the same time, the idea of surprise that he could have been guilty of such conduct. Comp. Gen. iii. 13, xii. 18, xx. 9. The question shows that what Jonah had said respecting the character of the true God, had made a deep impression upon the minds of the sailors.
11. They had clearly the conviction, that as the prophet was the cause of the storm, some step must be taken in order to get rid of him; but how to dispose of him they knew not. That they wished, if possible, to save his life, is clear from the sequel. יִשְׁתֹּק מֵעָלֵינוּ conveys the idea of subsiding, so as no longer to bear down upon with violence, and graphically describes the threatening attitude of a tempestuous sea, rising above the ships that are exposed to it. שָׁתַק properly signifies *to settle down, be still, cease from raging.* הוֹלֵךְ וְסֹעֵר, lit. *going and storming*, meaning, to go on, increase, become more and more tempestuous; a common idiom in Hebrew. Comp. Exod. xix. 19; 1 Sam. ii. 26, xvii. 41; Esth. ix. 4; Prov. iv. 18.
13. חָתַר, *to dig*, or *break forcibly through anything*, is strongly expressive of the great effort made by the seamen

could not, for the sea grew more and more tempestuous against
14 them. And they cried to Jehovah, and said: O now Jehovah!
let us not perish, we beseech thee, for this man's life; and lay
not innocent blood to our charge: for thou, O Jehovah! hast
15 done as it pleased thee. And they took up Jonah, and threw
16 him into the sea, and the sea ceased from its raging. Then the
men feared Jehovah greatly, and offered a sacrifice to Jehovah,
and made vows.

14. An affecting prayer for pagans to present to the true God! The words, אָנָּה יְהוָה אַל־נָא נֹאבְדָה, are peculiarly earnest and tender. אָנָּה, the same as אָנָּא, which Gesenius takes to be compounded of אָח, *oh!* and נָא, the usual particle of entreaty. Comp. the Arab. اون, *obsecro*. The Keri marks נ in נָקְאָ as redundant, and a great number MSS. read נָקִי. נֶפֶשׁ, *life*, means here life that is taken away, having דָּם נָקִי, *innocent blood*, corresponding to it in the following clause. Comp. Deut. xix. 21; 2 Sam. xiv. 7. Coverdale, well as to the sense, "this man's *death*." The reference is not to anything that Jonah had done, but to what they were about to do to him. נָתַן דָּם עַל, *to give blood upon*, means to charge with murder. Syr. ܠܐ ܬܣܝܡ, *impute not*. The sense is, let us not be found guilty of killing an innocent person. In the concluding words of the verse, they refer the whole affair to the mysterious providence of God. They had not been brought into their present circumstances by any conduct of their own; nor could they account for the guilt of Jonah, since he was chargeable with no act of immorality. Yet he was the object of Divine displeasure.

to avoid sacrificing the life of Jonah. LXX. παρεβιάζοντο. At לָשִׁיב supply הָאֳנִיָּה אֶל.

15, 16. They now proceed calmly, though with great reluctance, to act in accordance with what they had been led to regard as the will of the Most High. The calm appears to have taken place instantaneously. According to the Rabbins, Grotius, and some others, they did not actually offer a sacrifice, but only purposed to do it before Jehovah, *i. e.* at Jerusalem; but it is more natural to conclude that they sacrificed some animal that was on board, and vowed that they would present greater proofs of their gratitude when they returned from their voyage. Michaelis thinks they intended to perform their vows when they reached Spain.

"Quin; ubi transmissæ steterint trans
  æquora classes,
Et positis aris jam vota in litore solves."
  Æneid. iii. 403.

CHAPTER II.

With the exception of the first and last verses, which give an historical account of the fate of Jonah as preserved by a great fish, this chapter contains a brief but beautiful hymn of deliverance. It was in all probability composed immediately after his reaching the dry land, but embodies some of the leading topics in reference to which he called upon Jehovah during his stay in the deep.

1 (Chap. i. 17.) Now Jehovah had appointed a great fish to

swallow Jonah. And Jonah was in the bowels of the fish three days and three nights.

1. (Chap. i. 17, in our common version.) It has been supposed by some that the fish here spoken of was created at the moment for the purpose of swallowing the prophet, though, according to Rabbi Tarphon, it was משונה משיח בראשית יגי, prepared for the purpose at the creation of the world; but there is nothing in the original word מָנָה which at all suggests the idea of creation or production. Like the Arab. ﺻﻠﻮ, *certa quanitate certoque modo definivit aliqui rem ; decretus fuit*, it properly signifies to *appoint, order, arrange,* and the like, so that all that can be legitimately inferred from its use in this place, is, that, in the providence of God, the animal was brought to the spot at the precise time when Jonah was thrown into the sea, and its instrumentality was wanted for his deliverance. In other words, it was the result of a special pre-arrangement in the Divine plan, according to which the movements of all creatures are regulated, and rendered subservient to the purposes of God's universal government. LXX. προσέταξε. Comp. chap. iv 6–8. On the subject of the fish itself various opinions have been broached. Mutianus, and after him Hermann von der Hardt, would have it to be nothing more than an inn, with the sign of "The Whale," into which Jonah was received after having been cast on shore ! Less proposed the theory of a ship with this name, which happened to be close by and rescued the prophet; while Thaddæus supposed that, on being thrown out of the vessel, he lighted upon a large fish, on which he rode for the time specified, and was at last cast on shore ! Till the time of Bochart it was commonly supposed to have been the *balæna*, or whale properly so called, owing to a misinterpretation of κῆτος, Matt. xii. 40, which signifies any great fish in general. With much ingenuity that learned author endeavors to prove, that it must have been the *carcharias*, or dog-fish, which, though not the size of a whale, yet has so large a gullet, and so capacious a stomach, that one of them has been found to contain a warrior, clad in all his armor. Bochart, Hierozo. p. ii. lib. v. cap. xii. Others have supposed that it was a shark, a species of fish abounding in the Mediterranean, exceedingly voracious, and in the belly of which whole men have been found. See Parkhurst's Greek Lexicon, *sub. voc.* Κῆτος. But we may well acquiesce in the decision of Rosenmüller : "Tota hæc de pisce Jonæ disquisitio vana videtur atque inutilis." The Scriptures leave it entirely undecided to what species of marine animals the fish belonged ; merely stating that it was דָּג גָּדוֹל, *a great fish*, one sufficiently large for the occasion. Much has been written to relieve the transaction of the miraculous ; but that it is physically possible for a human subject, which has been accustomed for years to breathe the vital air, to exist without respiration, or upon the foul air in a fish, for the length of time here specified, has never been proved. The position of Abenezra is the only one that can, with any consistency, be maintained : אין כח באדם לחיות במעי הדגה כפי שעה ואף כי זה השמשה כך במעשת נס, "No man has the power of living in the bowels of a fish for a single hour : how much less for such a number of hours, except by the operation of a miracle." The transaction was, as Kimchi observes, אחד מן הנסים, *one of the miracles.* As such it is unequivocally recognized by our Lord, when he calls it a σημεῖον, a *sign* or *token* of divine interposition, a supernatural event, manifestive of the power of God, Matt. xii. 39 ; and it behooves all his disciples implicitly and cordially to receive his decision. For the period of "three days and three nights," see Whitby on Matt. xii. 40.

2. For יִּתְפַּלֵּל, comp. יִּתְפַּלֵּל, 1 Sam. ii. 1. Some of the Rabbins, Hezel, and others, would argue from the use of מִן, *from, out of,* and not בְּ, *in,* before מְעֵי, that the prayer of Jonah was not pre-

2 And Jonah prayed to Jehovah his God from the bowels of the fish, and said :
3 I cried because of my distress to Jehovah,
   And he answered me ;
   From the interior of Sheol I cried out :
   Thou heardest my voice.
4 Thou didst cast me into the deep,
   Into the midst of the seas ;
   So that the current surrounded me ;

sented while he was in the belly of the fish, but after his deliverance; but this interpretation is justly rejected both by Abenezra and Kimchi. The preposition marks the place from which he directed his thoughts to the Most High. Comp. מִבֶּטֶן שְׁאוֹל, ver. 3 ; מִמַּעֲמַקִּים, Ps. cxxx. 1; בְּוֹר־תַּחְתִּי, Ps. cxviii. 5. The final ה in הַדָּגָה is not feminine, as has been supposed, and upon which assumption certain Rabbins have built the theory, that a still larger female fish swallowed that in which Jonah was preserved ; but the ה paragogic, which corresponds to the status emphaticus of the Aramaic, and is designed to strengthen the termination. For other instances in which it is added, at the same time that the noun takes the article, comp. הַחִידָה, Judges xiv. 18 ; הַמָּוֶתָה, Ps. cxvi. 15. The position of the accent is of no account.

3, 4. The hymn which commences here is partly descriptive, partly precatory, and partly eucharistical. These two verses are introductory, as is clear from the use of וָאֲנִי אָמַרְתִּי, and give expression to the feelings and pious sentiments of the prophet in the awful circumstances into which he had been brought. That the language, not only of the prayer, but also of the introduction, is in part borrowed from the Psalms, appears from the following comparison :

Psalm cxx. 1.	Jonah ii. 3.
אֶל־יְהוָה בַּצָּרָתָה לִּי	קָרָאתִי מִצָּרָה לִי
קָרָאתִי וַיַּעֲנֵנִי׃	אֶל־יְהוָה וַיַּעֲנֵנִי׃
xlii. 8.	ver. 4.
כָּל־מִשְׁבָּרֶיךָ וְגַלֶּיךָ	כָּל־מִשְׁבָּרֶיךָ וְגַלֶּיךָ
עָלַי עָבָרוּ׃	עָלַי עָבְרוּ׃

xxxi. 23.	ver. 5.
וַאֲנִי אָמַרְתִּי	וַאֲנִי אָמַרְתִּי
נִגְרַזְתִּי מִנֶּגֶד עֵינֶיךָ׃	נִגְרַשְׁתִּי מִנֶּגֶד עֵינֶיךָ׃
lxix. 2.	ver. 6.
בָּאוּ מַיִם עַד־נָפֶשׁ׃	אֲפָפוּנִי מַיִם עַד־נֶפֶשׁ׃
cxlii. 4.	ver. 8.
בְּהִתְעַטֵּף עָלַי נַפְשִׁי׃	בְּהִתְעַטֵּף עָלַי נַפְשִׁי׃
xxxi. 7.	ver. 9.
הַשֹּׁמְרִים	מְשַׁמְּרִים
הַבְלֵי־שָׁוְא׃	הַבְלֵי־שָׁוְא׃
iii. 9.	ver. 10.
לַיהוָה הַיְשׁוּעָה׃	יְשׁוּעָתָה לַיהוָה׃

On the supposition that Jonah was familiar with the Psalms, it was very natural for him to incorporate sentences taken from them with his own language, just as we frequently do in extempore prayer, without thinking of the portion of Scripture from which they are derived. בְּבֶטֶן שְׁאוֹל, lit. *the belly of Sheol*, i. e. the vast and hidden receptacle of the departed. Targ. מֵאֲרָעִית תְּהוֹמָא, *from the lowest part of the abyss*, but less properly. The remark of Jerome is : " Ventrum inferi alvum ceti intelligamus, quæ tantæ fuit magnitudinis, ut instar obtineret inferni." Before מְצוּלָה, ver. 4, supply בְּ. נָהָר, commonly used of a *river*, but here it is to be understood of the strong *current* or *stream* of the sea, which flows like a river. There is no foundation for the opinion of Abenezra and Kimchi, that it was intended to describe the confluence of the waters of a river with those of the sea.

————καὶ ἂν ποταμοῖο ῥέεθρα
'Ωκεανοῦ, ὅσπερ γένεσις πάντεσσι τέτυκ-
ται.   *Iliad.* xiv. 245.

All thy breakers and thy billows passed over me.
5 Then I said:
I am cast out from before thine eyes,
Yet I will look again towards thy holy temple.
6 The waters press around me to the very life;
The abyss encompasseth me;
The weed is bound to my head.
7 I go down to the clefts of the mountains;
As for the earth, her bars are shut upon me for ever.
But thou wilt bring up my life from destruction,
O Jehovah my God!

Μέσσῳ γὰρ μεγάλοι ποταμοὶ καὶ δεινὰ ῥέεθρα,
'Ωκεανὸς μέν πρῶτα.   *Odyss.* xi. 156.
Τὴν δὲ κατ' 'Ωκεανὸν ποταμὸν φέρε κῦμα ῥόοιο.   *Ibid.* 638.

5. Having described his condition, the prophet now proceeds to give the words of his prayer. נֶגֶד עֵינֶי יְהוָֹה, *to be before the eyes of Jehovah*, means to be the object of his special notice and care. Jonah had fled from the Divine presence in Canaan, but now he feels that he is expelled even from the abodes of life, and cut off, as it were, from the regard of that Providence which watches over the children of men. Still he does not abandon himself to despair. He confidently expects to be restored to the enjoyment of his privileges in the temple at Jerusalem, and there to render thanks to God for his deliverance. Green would supply the negative לֹא before אוֹסִיף, and Hitzig would point אַךְ, אַךְ הֲ for אַךְ, *how;* but both without any authority. Such sudden transitions from fear to hope are frequently expressed in Scripture.

6. עַד־נֶפֶשׁ, *even to*, or *to the very soul*, i. e. the animal life; meaning, to the extinction of life. סוּף, is the *alga*, or *weed*, which abounds at the bottom of the sea, and from which the Arabian Gulf takes the name of יַם־סוּף, *the sea of weeds.* Kimchi explains it by גֹּמֶא, the papyrus, or bulrush. Gesenius refines too much when he attaches to חָבוּשׁ in this place the idea of binding round the head like a turban. Assuredly Jonah

had no such idea in his mind. He rather describes how he felt, as if entangled by the sedge or weeds through which he was dragged.

7. קִצְבֵי, *sections, cuttings, clefts*, from קָצַב, *to cut;* Arab. قضب, *abscidit, resecuit.* Thus the LXX. σχισμὰς ὀρέων. Vulg. *extrema montium.* Targ. עִקְרֵי טוּרַיָּא, *the roots of the mountains.* The word describes the deep indentations or clefts made in the roots of mountains which project into the sea, or those divisions which are found in the rocks at its bottom. הָאָרֶץ, *the earth*, is emphatically put in the nominative absolute, as the object to which the affections of the prophet still clung. He was expelled from it, as from a habitation, and its bars had been shut upon him, so that he could not return. Gesenius takes the bars to be those of Sheol; but, as we have שַׁעֲרֵי־שְׁאוֹל, *the gates of Sheol,* Is. xxxviii. 10, the phrase here must have been שְׁאוֹל בְּרִחֶיהָ, and not הָאָרֶץ בְּרִחֶיהָ, if such had been the meaning. בַּעֲדִי is put elliptically for סָגְרוּ בַעֲדִי, the verb, סָגַר being obviously implied. Jonah adds, לְעוֹלָם, *for ever*, to express the impossibility of his ever again reaching the dry land, by any effort of his own. Yet, exposed as he momentarily was to death in the region of corruption (שַׁחַת, *the pit*, or *grave*,) he confidently expresses his hope that God would restore him. He asserts his interest in Jehovah by calling him "*his God.*"

8 When my soul was overwhelmed within me,
    I remembered Jehovah;
    And my prayer came in unto thee,
    Into thy holy temple.
9 They that regard lying vanities
    Forsake their Benefactor.
10 But as for me, I will sacrifice to thee with the voice of thanksgiving;
    What I have vowed I will perform:
    Salvation belongeth to Jehovah.
11 And Jehovah commanded the fish, and it vomited forth Jonah upon the dry land.

8. The prophet here resumes his description of the circumstances of distress to which he was reduced, his application to Jehovah, and the answer which he received to his prayer. The composition of this and the following verses, like that of verses 3 and 4, belongs to a period subsequent to his deliverance; yet while describing his condition, he occasionally directs his language to Jehovah, towards whom, as his deliverer, his thoughts naturally rose. הִתְעַטֵּף, to be in a state of *faintness, swoon*, from עטף, to *cover*, to involve in darkness, *overwhelm*. LXX. well, as it respects the sense: Ἐν τῷ ἐκλείπειν ἀπ' ἐμοῦ τὴν ψυχήν μου.

9. A striking description of idolaters, but which may also be extended to all who prefer created objects, in any shape, to God. חַסְדָּם, lit. *their mercy* or *goodness;* by metonymy for their Benefactor: i. e. *God*, the author and source of all goodness: the Supreme Good. Comp. Ps. cxliv. 2, where David calls God his חַסְדִּי. The word properly signifies *kindness* or *benignity*, and most appropriately designates Him who is good to all, and whose tender mercies are over all his works..

The Syriac reads, ܝܟܪܢܘܬܟ, *thy mercy*, which Green, on this authority alone, admits into the text!

10. Deeply sensible of the merciful interposition of Jehovah on his behalf, Jonah now solemnly engages to give expression to his feelings of gratitude by accompanying his presentation of sacrifice with a song of praise, and faithfully performing his vows, of which we may conclude, the execution of his commission to go to Nineveh formed none of the least. The paragogic ה in אֲשַׁלֵּמָה is intensive. Comp. Ps. iii. 3. In both passages, the deliverance is ascribed to Jehovah as its author, as the לְ in לַיהוָה imports.

On reviewing this prayer, and weighing the import of its several terms, it is obvious, that though Jonah was in a state of consciousness while in the belly of the fish, he had no idea that such was his situation. On the contrary, he appears to have been under the impression that he was engulfed in the sea, now forcibly carried along by its current, now entangled among its weeds, and now sinking into the profound ravines of its rocks.

11. Green and Boothroyd, on mere conjecture, remove this verse from its present position, and insert it before the hymn. Such a transposition Hitzig pronounces to be violent, unnecessary, and in short, a perversion of the passage. It is not stated where the prophet was cast on shore, but in all probability it was somewhere on the coast of Palestine. According to some, the fish carried him, during the three days and three nights, down the Mediterranean, and through the Archipelago, and the Propontis, into the Euxine sea, and deposited him on the south coast, at the nearest point to Nineveh! Not to mention how the Rabbins make him reach that city by the Tigris!!

CHAPTER III.

This chapt. contains an account of the renewal of the prophet's commission, 1, 2; his preaching to the Ninevites, 3, 4; the universal humiliation and reformation effected by it, 5-9; and the reversal of the Divine sentence by which the city had been doomed to destruction, 10.

1 AND the word of Jehovah was communicated to Jonah a second
2 time, saying: Arise, go to Nineveh, that great city, and make the
3 proclamation to it which I order thee. And Jonah arose, and went to Nineveh, according to the word of Jehovah. Now Nineveh was a great city even to God, of three days' journey.
4 And Jonah began to enter the city, a journey of one day; and he proclaimed, and said: Yet forty days, and Nineveh shall be overthrown.
5 And the men of Nineveh believed in God, and proclaimed a fast, and put on sackcloth, from the greatest of them, even to the
6 least of them. And the subject reached the king of Nineveh, and he arose from his throne, and put off his robe, and covered
7 himself with sackcloth, and sat in the ashes. And a proclama-

3. עִיר גְּדוֹלָה לֵאלֹהִים, *a city great to God.* This phrase has been variously explained. Some, with Kimchi, deem it merely a superlative form; Gesenius construes the ל instrumentally, *great through God,* i. e. through his favor. Others consider it to be equivalent to לִפְנֵי אֱלֹהִים, *before God,* Gen. x. 9. Thus the Targ. קֳדָם יְיָ. Of this last interpretation I approve, as it was most natural to refer the size of a city, to which the Hebrews could form no adequate conception, to the Divine estimation. I have accordingly rendered the words literally, as our preposition *to* is often used to note opinion or estimate. For the dimensions of Nineveh, as here given, see on chap. i. 2. The opinion of Abarbanel, that the diameter of the city is intended, is justly exploded.

4. It is impossible to determine how far Jonah penetrated into Nineveh, since it is probable that in making his announcement he would stop at different places, as the crowds might collect around him.

5. When בֵּאלֹהִים הֶאֱמִין, *believing in God,* is spoken of in reference to such as had previously been ignorant of him, it must be taken as involving the recognition of his being and character as the true God, and not simply their giving credit to the announcements of his messengers. To express the latter, הֶאֱמִין לְ is employed. See Gen. xlv. 26; Is. liii. 1. All, without distinction of age or rank, put on sackcloth, the usual attire of deep mourning.

6-8. Who the king of Assyria was at the time, is not certain. Pul, the first monarch of that empire mentioned by name in Scripture, did not begin to reign till B. C. 769. Some are of opinion that it was Sardanapalus; if so, his repentance was the more remarkable, for according to the ancients he was pro-

tion was made through Nineveh, by order of the king and his grandees, saying, Let neither man nor beast, ox nor sheep, taste anything; let them not feed, neither let them drink water.
8 But let man and beast be covered with sackcloth, and cry mightily unto God; and let them turn every one from his wicked way, and from the violence which is in their hands.
9 Who knoweth but that God may turn and repent, and turn away from the fierceness of his anger, that we perish not?
10 And God saw their works, that they turned from their wicked way, and God repented of the evil which he had said he would inflict upon them, and he inflicted it not.

verbially notorious on account of his profligacy.
"Et venere, et coenis, et plumis Sardanapali." *Juvenal. Sat.* iii.
It is said that he composed for his epitaph, "*Eat, drink, play; after death there is no pleasure.*" The description of the mourning here given is very affecting. That the irrational animals should be represented as partaking in it, is far from unnatural.
"Non ulli pastos illis egere diebus
Frigida, Daphni, boves ad flumina: nulla
  neque amnem
Libavit quadrupes, nec graminis attigit
  herbam." *Virg. Ecl.* v. 24.
"Post bellator equus, positis insignibus,
  Æthon
It lacrymans, guttisque humectat grandibus ora." *Æneid.* xi. 89.
Plutarch informs us that when Masistias, a Persian general, was slain, the horses and mules were shorn, as well as the Persians themselves.

9. The Jewish interpreters follow the construction put upon the words מִי יוֹדֵעַ, *who knoweth*, in the Targum: בָּן יָדַע דְּאִית בִּידֵיהּ חוֹבִין, *whoever is conscious that there are crimes in his hands;* only Kimchi proposes another, מִי שֶׁיוֹדֵעַ דַרְכֵי הַתְּשׁוּבָה, *He who knoweth the ways of repentance;* but it is obviously a formula expressive of great guilt, yet involving the hope of pardon. Comp. Joel ii. 14.

10. God is anthropopathically said to repent, when he changes his mode of procedure, or acts differently from what his promises or threatenings had given reason to expect. The threatening in the present case having been conditional, was repealed on the performance of the implied condition. To what extent the repentance of the Ninevites was genuine in its character, and how long the reformation of manners here specified lasted, we are not informed; but there is reason to fear it was of short continuance, for after their city had been besieged for three years by Arbaces the Mede, it was taken and destroyed. Diod. Sic. ii. 26, etc. Thus fell the ancient Assyrian dynasty, and gave place to that of the Medes, which continued till the time of Cyaxares, when Nineveh, which had been rebuilt, was again destroyed, and finally ceased to be an imperial residence. See Preface to the Book of Nahum.

CHAPTER IV.

THE selfish and repining spirit of the prophet, and the means employed by Jehovah to reprove and instruct him, are here set forth.

1 BUT Jonah was exceedingly displeased and vexed. And he
2 prayed to Jehovah, and said: Ah! now, Jehovah! was not this my word while I was yet in my own country? Wherefore I anticipated it by fleeing to Tarshish; for I knew that thou art a gracious and merciful God, long-suffering, and of great kindness,
3 and repentant of the evil. And now, O Jehovah! take, I pray thee, my life from me; for my death were better than my life.
4 And Jehovah said to him: Art thou much vexed?

1. Unwarrantable attempts have been made to soften down the character of Jonah, as exhibited in this chapter. The utmost that can be advanced in extenuation of his conduct, is, the strong tincture of national prejudice with which his spirit appears to have been imbued. Com. Luke ix. 54. ל חרה, however seems to be here used, not in the sense of being *enraged* or *angry*, but in that of being the subject of *grief* or *sorrow*. Comp. 1 Sam. xv. 11; 2 Sam. vi. 8. Grief and anger are passions nearly related; and in illustration of this application of חרה, *to burn*, the following instances may be adduced:

Τίς σκανδαλίζεται, καὶ οὐκ ἐγὼ πυροῦμαι; 2 Cor. xi. 29.

'Αλλ' ὦ Καλονίκη κάομαι τὴν καρδίαν,
Καὶ πολλ' ὑπὲρ ἡμῶν τῶν γυναικῶν ἄχθομαι. *Aristoph. Lysist.* v. 9.

" Eheu disperii! voltus neutiquam hujus placet.
Tristis incedit, pectus *ardet*."
Plaut. Mercat. Act iii. Sc. 4, v. 14.
" Tum vero *exarsit* Juveni *dolor* ossibus ingens." *Æneid.* v. 172.

And the declaration of Cicero: " Non angro, sed *ardeo dolore*." — *Epist. ad Attic.* vi. 9.

2. דברי, *my word*, i. e. what I spake within myself, my cogitation. עשׂה is here taken in the sense of doing anything in order to anticipate another. Jonah acknowledges that he used all despatch in his attempt to leave Palestine. The description of the Divine goodness here given agrees verbally with that exhibited Joel ii. 13. He recollected the numerous instances in which, instead of executing his threatenings, Jehovah had, in the exercise of his patience, borne with the guilty, and even interposed with illustrious acts of pardon; and he was afraid of compromising his character by announcing what he had reason to expect might never take place.

4 הֲהֵיטֵב חָרָה לָךְ most modern versions improperly render, " dost thou well," or, " is it right in thee to be angry?" their authors not adverting to the fact that the Hiph. Infinitive of יטב is often used adverbially in the acceptation, *greatly*, *exceedingly*, *thoroughly*, or the like. See Deut. ix. 21, xiii. 15; 2 Kings xi. 18. In like manner the finite form הֵיטַבְתָּ לִקְרֹאת Jer. i. 12. Thus the LXX. εἰ σφόδρα λελύπησαι σύ; the Syr. ܛܒ ܟܪܝܐ ܠܟ; and the Targ. הֲתָקִיף לָךְ לַחֲדָא. Kimchi explains, אם חרה לך מאד, Art thou *much* grieved? and adds, היטב

5   And Jonah went out of the city, and sat to the east of the
city, and there made a booth for himself, and sat under it in the
6 shade, till he should see what would happen in the city. And
Jehovah God had appointed a ricinus plant, and he caused it to
rise up over Jonah, to be a shade over his head, to deliver him
from his affliction: and Jonah rejoiced exceedingly on account of
the ricinus.
7   But God appointed a worm, at the rising of the dawn, on the
8 morrow, and it injured the ricinus, so that it withered. And it
came to pass at the sun-rise, that God appointed a sultry east
wind, and the sun beat upon the head of Jonah, and he fainted,
and requested that he might die; for he said, My death were bet-

רָעָה רוּחַ עָשָׂה, *As for* טוֹב, *it
imports the strengthening of a subject.*
The renderings, Will grieving do thee
any good? and, Does beneficence offend
thee? are totally to be rejected.
   5. We cannot determine on what day
Jonah abandoned his labors among the
Ninevites; but it is evident from the
conclusion of this verse, that it must
have been before the lapse of the forty
days specified in his announcements.
   6. וַיַּעַל I take to be the apocopated
Future of Hiphil, having אֱלֹהִים יְהוָה
for its nominative. קִיקָיוֹן, *the kikaion* or
ricinus plant (Ricinus communis, Linn.),
commonly known by the name of *Palma
Christi*. The word is the same as the
Egyptian KIKI, and the Talmudic *Kik*,
with the Hebrew termination. In Arabic
it is called الخِرْوَع, *El-Kheroa*, which
is not to be confounded with القَرْع,
El-Karra, the *cucurbita*. LXX. Κολο-
κύνθη. Our English rendering *gourd* is
equally inappropriate. This plant is indigenous in India, Palestine, Arabia, Africa, and the east of Europe, and on account of its singular beauty is cultivated
in gardens. It is a biannual, and usually
grows to the height of from eight to ten
feet. It is chiefly remarkable on account
of its leaves, which are broad, palmate,
and serrated, and divided into six or
seven lobes. Only one leaf grows on
a branch, but being large, sometimes
measuring more than a foot, and spread

out in the shape of an open hand with
the fingers extended, their collective
shade affords an excellent shelter from
the heat of the sun. It is of exceedingly
quick growth, and has been known in
America to reach the height even of
thirteen feet in less than three months.
When injured it fades with great rapidity.
See on ver. 10, Celsii Hierobot. pt. ii.
p. 273; Michaelis, Supplem. No. 2263;
Rosenmüller, in the Biblical Cabinet,
vol. xxvii. p. 125; Michaelis, Bibel
Ubersetz., note on the passage, where
there is a plate with an excellent representation of a ricinus. How much such
a shrub, throwing its palmy branches
over the small hut which the prophet
had erected, must have contributed to
his relief in the sultry environs of Nine-
vah, may easily be imagined. His joy
is emphatically described in the last
clause of the verse.
   8. The רוּחַ קָדִים, or *east wind*, is the
sultry and oppressive wind which blows
in the summer months across the vast
Arabian desert, and produces universal
languor and relaxation. It resembles
the Sirocco, only is free from its damp-
ness, and consequently more destructive
to vegetation. Superadded, as in the
present instance, to the heat of the
morning sun, it is exceedingly oppressive. According to the versions, חֲרִישִׁית
signifies *withering;* otherwise, as derived
from חרשׁ, it signifies to be *quiet*, *silent*,
etc., which better agrees with the idea of
sultriness.

9 ter than my life. And God said unto Jonah: Art thou much
10 vexed on account of the ricinus? And he said: I am much
vexed, even to death. And Jehovah said: Thou art affected on
account of the ricinus, with which thou hadst no trouble, and
which thou didst not rear, which came in a night, and perished
11 in a night; and I, should not I be affected on account of Nineveh, that great city, in which are more than twelve times ten
thousand human beings who cannot distinguish between their
right hand and their left, and much cattle!

9. The words הֵיטֵב חָרָה־לִי עַד־מָוֶת, the LXX. translate, Σφόδρα λελύπημαι ἐγὼ ἕως θανάτου, which nearly agree with those of our Lord, Mark xiv. 34.

10. חוּס, properly signifies *to be affected* by the sight of anything; hence to *feel concern* on account of it, to take pity or compassion. I have employed the passive form of our verb *to affect*, in order to present in the translation a word equivalent to that which is here used in the original. There seems to be necessity for taking the Hebrew verb in two acceptations. The formula, שֶׁבִּן־לַיְלָה הָיָה וּבִן־לַיְלָה אָבָד, lit. *which was the son of a night, and perished the son of a night*, is obviously intended to express the extraordinary rapidity with which the ricinus put forth its leaves and afterwards withered. That the tree itself was instantaneously produced, cannot be proved from this mode of speech, any more than from the use of the verb מָנָה, ver. 6; otherwise we should be obliged, for the sake of consistency, to maintain, that the whole tree was miraculously destroyed, and had entirely disappeared during the night. הָיָה and אָבָד are strictly antithetical. But, as all that was required in the one case, was that the broad spreading leaves should wither, so as no longer to afford protection to Jonah, though the trunk remained; so all that was necessary in the other was to give to the tree which had been previously produced, such an extraordinary accelerated power of germination, that the leaves which would otherwise have required some longer time to come to maturity, were brought to perfection in the course of a night. בֵּן, *a son*, is used idiomatically to express what is produced, or exists, during the time predicated of it. Thus it is resolved in the Targ. דִּי, בְּלֵילְיָא הֲוָה דֵּין וּבְלֵילְיָא אוֹחֲרָנָא אֲבַד *which this night was, and in another night perished.*

11. The peculiar force of the appeal lies in the immense number of rational creatures which must have perished had Nineveh been destroyed. Estimating the age of the children at about three years, and assuming them to have formed a fifth part of the population, which is the allowance generally made, we shall have six hundred thousand as the number of inhabitants. In order to enhance this number, and render it more affecting, that of the irresponsible children is estimated; and if this did not produce a suitable impression upon the mind of the prophet, the number even of irrational animals is adverted to, the latter being far superior in point of mechanism and utility to the shrub for which he was so much concerned.

There is something in the abrupt manner in which the book closes which is highly calculated to produce its effect on the mind of a reflecting reader.

MICAH.

PREFACE.

ACCORDING to the introductory statement, chap. i. 1, Micah was a native of Moresheth, which some take to be the same as Mareshah, ver. 15; but it is rather the town called Moresheth-Gath, ver. 14, which, according to Jerome, lay in the vicinity of the city of Eleutheropolis, to the west of Jerusalem, and not far from the border of the country of the Philistines.

His name, מִיכָה, *Micah*, or, as it is given in full in the Chethib, Jer. xxvi. 18, מִיכָיָה, *Micaiah*, signifies, *who is like Jehovah?*

The time at which he flourished is stated in the introduction to have been that of the reigns of Jotham, Ahaz, and Hezekiah; *i. e.* somewhere between B. C. 757 and B. C. 699; in addition to which statement, we have a positive testimony to his having prophesied in the days of Hezekiah, Jer. xxvi. 18, where chap. iii. 12 is verbally quoted. He must, therefore, have been a contemporary of Isaiah and Hosea, and is not to be confounded with Micaiah the son of Imlah, 1 Kings xxii. 8, who flourished upwards of a hundred years before the reign of Jotham.

Hartmann and Eichhorn would refer the period of his ministry to the region of Manasseh; but their hypothesis is justly rejected by Jahn, Rosenmüller, De Wette, and Knobel, on the ground, that all the circumstances brought to view in his prophecies, perfectly harmonize with the state of things in the days of the kings whose names are here specified. The unrestrained license given to idolatry in the reign of Ahaz, will sufficiently account for the numerous gross and crying evils for which Micah reproves the Jews, without our having recourse to the atrocities perpetrated in that of Manasseh. It is true, Hezekiah issued orders, that idolatry should be put down, and the worship of the true God re-established; but there is no reason to believe that the reformation was carried out to the full extent of his wishes. The relations also of the Hebrews to the powerful empires of Assyria and Egypt, are in exact accordance with the history of the same times.

The prophecies of Micah are directed partly against Judah, and partly against Israel; but by far the greater number are of the former description. He predicts the destruction of the kingdom of Israel, and of Samaria its capital; the desolation of Jerusalem by the Chaldeans, and the consequent captivity of the Jews; the restoration of the Jewish state; the successes of the Maccabees; and the advent and reign of the Messiah. He also administers reproof to different ranks and conditions of men, and furnishes some striking representations of the Divine character.

His style is concise, yet perspicuous, nervous, vehement, and energetic; and in many instances, equals that of Isaiah in boldness and sublimity. He is rich and beautiful in the varied use of tropical language; indulges in paronomasias; preserves a pure and classical diction; is regular in the formation of his parallelisms; and exhibits a roundness in the construction of his periods which is not surpassed by his more celebrated contemporary. Both in administering threatenings and communicating promises, he evinces great tenderness, and shows that his mind was deeply affected by the subjects of which he treats. In his appeals he is lofty and energetic. His description of the character of Jehovah, chap. vii. 18 — 20, is unrivalled by any contained elsewhere in Scripture.

Several prophecies in Micah and Isaiah are remarkably parallel with each other; and there is frequently an identity of expression, which can only be fairly accounted for on the ground of their having been contemporaneous writers, who were not strangers to each other's prophecies, and their having, in a great measure, had the same subjects for the themes of their ministry. See on Isaiah ii. 2–4.

The book may be divided into two parts; the first consisting of chapters i.—v.; and the second, the two remaining chapters, which are more general and didactic in their character.

CHAPTER I.

THE prophet commences by summoning universal attention, while, in sublime language, he describes the descent of Jehovah to punish the nation, 1–5; he predicts the destruction of Samaria by the Assyrians, which he pathetically laments, 6–8; and then the advance of Sennacherib against Jerusalem, 9–12; concluding with an enumeration of certain towns of Judah, the inhabitants of which had more especially enjoyed his ministry, but were to share in the desolating effects of the Assyrian invasion, and ultimately, with the whole land, those of the Babylonian captivity.

---

1   THE word of Jehovah which was communicated to Micah the Morashthite, in the days of Jotham, Ahaz, and Hezekiah, kings of Judah, which he saw concerning Samaria and Jerusalem.
2   Hear, all ye people!
Attend, O Earth! and its fulness!
And let the Lord Jehovah testify to you,
The Lord from his holy temple.
3   For, behold! Jehovah is coming forth from his place;

1. מֹרַשְׁתִּי, contracted מֹרַשְׁתִּי־גַת, a gentilic, and not a patronymic, as some have imagined. See the introduction, and on ver. 14.

2. It is not a little remarkable, that Micah should adopt as the first sentence of his prophecy, that with which his namesake concluded his denouncement against Ahab, 1 Kings xxii. 28. Hengstenberg is of opinion that he quoted the words designedly, in order to show that his prophetic agency was to be considered as a continuation of that of his predecessor, who was so zealous for God, and that he had more in common with him than the bare name. The words עַמִּים, *peoples*, and אֶרֶץ, *earth*, are by many, and recently by Hitzig, confined to the *tribes* and *land* of the Hebrews; but the sublimity of the style, and the parallel passages, Deut. xxxii. 28, xxxii. 1; and Is. i. 2, induce to the conclusion, that the prophet had all the inhabitants of the globe in his eye. Thus Justi, Maurer, and Ewald. כֻּלָּם, *all of them*, is an instance of irregular construction, in which the third person is put for the second, כֻּלְּכֶם, *all of you*. The same construction is repeated in מְלֹאָהּ, which the LXX. render according to the sense, καὶ πάντες οἱ ἐν αὐτῇ. Comp. Amos vi. 8; Is. xlii. 10. Instead of אֲדֹנָי יְהוִה, four of Kennicott's MSS. read יְהוָה אֱלֹהִים; and, instead of אֲדֹנָי repeated, upwards of fifty of his and De Rossi's read יְהוָה; but as the former cannot be altered on the slight authority by which it is supported, so it would be unwarrantable to adopt the latter reading, since the second אֲדֹנָי is manifestly a repetition of the first. LXX. Κύριος κύριος. Syr. ܡܳܪܝܳܐ ܡܳܪܶܐ, *the Lord of lords.* It has been doubted whether by הֵיכַל קָדְשׁוֹ, *his holy temple*, in this place, the temple at Jerusalem or heaven be meant; but the language expressive of descent, which is employed in the following verse, would seem to determine the correctness of the latter interpretation. Comp. 1 Kings viii. 30; Ps. xi. 4. Jehovah would bear testimony against the Hebrews, not any longer by his prophets, as he now did, but by the judgments which he would inflict upon them.

3, 4. These verses are explanatory of

Chap. I. MICAH. 219

He will descend, and tread upon the heights of the earth.
4 The mountains shall be molten under him,
And the valleys shall cleave asunder,
Like wax before the fire,
Like water poured down a precipice.
5 By the transgression of Jacob is all this,
And by the sin of the house of Israel.
What is the transgression of Jacob?
Is it not Samaria?
And what are the high places of Judah?
Are they not Jerusalem?
6 Therefore I will make Samaria a heap in the field,

that which precedes them, and set forth, in highly figurative language, the course of the Divine judgment, and the tremendous consequences that would follow. The terrible majesty and resistless power of Jehovah are expressed in images chiefly borrowed from earthquakes and volcanic eruptions. Comp. Amos iv. 13; Ps. l. 3, xcvii. 5; Is. lxiii. 19, lxiv. 2; Hab. iii. 5. For a striking image of the same nature, see Jer. l. 25, 26, which cannot properly be explained, except on the principle of reference to a volcano. That of wax occurs Ps. lxviii. 3, xcvii. 5. Comp.

" Quasi igni
Cera super calido tabescens multa liquescat." Lucr. vi. 512.
Some MSS. read הַגְּבָעֹת, the hills, instead of הָעֲמָקִים, the valleys; but obviously as an emendation: the latter being the more difficult reading. מוֹרָד, a descent or precipice, from יָרַד, to go, or come down. The events referred to were the destruction of the kingdom of Israel by Shalmaneser, and the invasion of Judah by the armies of Sennacherib and Nebuchadnezzar, by the latter of whom the Jews were carried away captive. The form הִגַּד נָא marks the futurity of the event, and transmits a future significance to the following verbs.

5. Jacob and Israel are applied to both kingdoms in common, and are merely used as synonymes for the sake of variety. After explicitly declaring, that the awful punishment which was about to be inflicted was on account of the sins of the people generally, the prophet, by the forcible employment of double interrogatives, the latter of which, being in the negative, greatly strengthens the appeal, traces these sins to their respective sources — metropolitan corruption. By metonymy the effect is put for the cause. For מִי used as a neuter, see on Jonah i. 8. For רִאשִׁית the LXX., Targ., a considerable number of MSS., and four of the earliest printed editions, have the singular. The Syr. and Vulg. agree with the Textus Receptus. בָּמוֹת יְהוּדָה, the high places of Judah, were the elevated spots on mountains and hills on which the Jews erected chapels and altars for unlawful, and very often for idolatrous sacrifice, etc. 1 Kings xii. 3, xiv. 4; Ezek. vi. 6. That these existed at Jerusalem, see Jer. xxxii. 35; and for the length to which the practice was carried in the time of Ahaz, see 2 Kings xvi. 4. Instead of בָּמוֹת, the LXX., Syr., and Targ. translate, as if חַטֹּאת, sin, were the true reading: What is the sin of Judah? but though the latter word is found in one of Kennicott's MSS., and in the margin of another, it most probably originated in a desire to render the parallelism complete, and cannot be allowed to encroach upon the present text.

6. Both in this and the preceding verse Samaria is taken up first, because its destruction was to precede that of Jerusalem, and also, perhaps, to afford the prophet an opportunity of afterwards

The plantations of a vineyard :
I will hurl her stones into the valley,
And lay bare her foundations.
7 All her images shall be broken to pieces,
All her rewards shall be burnt with fire,
And all her idols will I lay waste ;
For with the reward of a harlot she collected them,
And to the reward of a harlot they shall return.

expatiating more at large on the state of things in Judah during the approaching invasion. So complete should be the overthrow of the northern capital, that its site would resemble a heap of stones or rubbish that had been gathered out of a field ; it would even be reduced to what we may suppose it originally to have been, a place for the cultivation of the vine. Vineyards were most commonly planted on the south sides of hills or mountains, on account of their exposure to the sun ; and in all probability that of Samaria had been appropriated to this purpose before it was purchased by Omri, 1 Kings xvi. 24. The stones of the city are graphically said to be hurled down into the deep valley below ; and that such was actually the case, the present phenomena of the ruins strongly attest. "The whole face of this part of the hill suggests the idea that the buildings of the ancient city had been thrown down from the brow of the hill. Ascending to the top, we went round the whole summit, and found marks of the same process everywhere." — *Narrative of the Scottish Mission of Inquiry*, pp. 293, 294. חִגְרַתִּי, מַגְּרִים, and ver. 4, are from the root גָּג, *to flow, pour*, or *hurl down*. For יִסְדֶּה צִגְּלָה comp. Ezek. xiii. 14. The very foundations of the edifices were to be laid bare, great and ponderous as the stones might be.

7. The prophet now delivers a special prediction against the objects and accompaniments of the idolatrous worship, which drew down the judgment of God upon the devoted city. The פְּסִילִים were the *images* or *idols*, whether carved, graven or molten, which were erected in the temples, for the purpose of receiving religious adoration. LXX. τὰ γλυπτά. אֶתְנָן, properly means the *wages* or *reward of prostitution ;* from נָתַן, *to give a present* or *reward*. The word is here, as elsewhere, employed in application to idolatry, viewed as spiritual adultery or fornication. Comp. Is. xxiii. 17, 18 ; Ezek. xvi. 31, 34 ; Hos. ix. 1. Kimchi, Abarbanel, Michaelis, Maurer, and others, are of opinion that the riches, etc., of Samaria are thus spoken of, because her idolatrous inhabitants imagined, that they were rewards bestowed upon them by their gods for their zeal and devotedness to their service. It is more likely, however, that the rich gifts or presents are meant, which the apostate Israelites dedicated to their idols, and with which they adorned their temples. Comp. Ezek. xvi. 33, 34. Newcome seems to incline to the idea, that the rewards of harlotry, literally taken, are intended, because these were appropriated to the support of idolatry. עֲצַבִּים is synonymous with פְּסִילִים ; only Hitzig thinks, that a more costly kind of idols is meant by the term, such as were made of silver, and were of sufficient value to be carried away as spoil. The entire establishment of idolatry was to be broken up ; the idols were to be cut in pieces ; such as were of wood, to be burnt in the fire ; and whatever was costly was to be removed by the enemy to Assyria, there to be again devoted to idols. Instead of אֲקַבֵּץ, three of De Rossi's MSS., three more originally, and perhaps one more, the Brixian and another ancient edition, without place or date, read אֲקַבֵּץ in Pual, which two of Kennicott's exhibit with Vau Shurek instead of the Kibbutz. The Syr., Targ., and Vulg., likewise have the passive, but

8 Therefore will I wail and howl;
   I will go stripped and naked;
   I will set up a wailing like the wolves,
   And a mourning like the ostriches.
9 For her wounds are desperate;
   Surely it hath come to Judah;
   He reacheth to the gate of my people,
   Even to Jerusalem.
10 Tell it not in Gath;

in the plural. The LXX. render, συνήγαγε; which agrees with the common punctuation.

8. So terrible should be the destruction with which the northern kingdom would be visited, that it called for the most marked tones and signs of sorrow. In these the prophet declares he would indulge, that he might thereby affect the minds of his countrymen. אֵילְכָה, with Yod, may have been occasioned by the preceding form אֵילִילָה; but there are other verbs which do not reject it in the future, as יֵרְקָם, Ps. lxxii. 14. שֵׁילָל, or, as the Keri has it, שׁוֹלָל, some interpret of *mental bereavement*, a state in which the mind is *despoiled* of its reasoning powers; but, combined as it here is with עָרוֹם, *naked*, it must be referred to the body, and was in all probability designed to describe the feet as stripped of shoes. Thus the LXX. ἀνυπόδετος. The Syr. ܚܦܝܐ, for which compare יָחֵף, Is. xx.
2. For זְאֵב, *wolves*, and בְּנוֹת יַעֲנָה, *ostriches*, see on Is. xiii. 22, and Pococke's very elaborate note on the present verse. The Arab. has here, مثل التنانين, *like the wolves*, and مثل بنات اوى, *like the jackals*. The former Michaelis renders *crocodiles*, but less properly, on account of the combination. The ancient rendering, *dragons*, is altogether to be rejected. Both kinds are selected on account of the piteously howling noice which they make, especially in the night.

9. אֲנוּשָׁה, the Pahul Participle of אָנַשׁ, *to be desperately sick;* spoken of a wound, *to be incurable.* There is no necessity,

with Michaelis, to have recourse to בּוֹא, and so to regard the form as the elongated future of the first person singular. The following noun, מַכּוֹתֶיהָ, being in the plural, the same number might be expected in the Participle; but it is a rule of Hebrew syntax, that when, as in this instance the predicate precedes the noun, the number of feminine plurals is frequently neglected. Comp. Jer. iv. 14. What the prophet has in view is the irretrievable ruin in which the Israelites as a nation would be involved. But he not only beholds, in prophetic vision, the devastation of Samaria and its dependencies by the Assyrians; he sees their invasion of Judah under Sennacherib, and their investment of Jerusalem. Com. Is. x. 28-32. The nominative to בָּאָה is the calamity implied in מַכּוֹתֶיהָ: that to נָגַע is אֹיֵב, *the enemy*, understood. There is the utmost propriety in the distinctive use of the genders in this place; for though the inhabitants of Judah suffered from the Assyrian invasion, the calamity did not reach those of the capital: it was merely invested by the troops of Rabshakeh, and was relieved by their miraculous destruction. See Is. xxxvi. xxxvii.

10. Comp. 2 Sam. i. 20, where the words בְּגַת אַל־תַּגִּידוּ occur, though not in the same order of arrangement. The Philistines would hail with joy tidings of any disaster that might befall the Hebrews, and especially that occasioned by the Assyrian attack. Deeply, therefore, as the Jews might be afflicted, they are cautioned by Micah not to give such public expression to their grief as would reach the ears of their natural

Weep not in Acco:
At Beth-aphrah roll thyself in the dust.
11 Pass on, thou inhabitant of Shaphir, naked and ashamed;

enemies, but to repair to Beth-Aphrah, a city in the tribe of Benjamin, and there deplore in secret the calamity which had overtaken the land. Reland, Harenberg, Hitzig, Maurer, and Ewald, take בְעַכּוֹ to be a contraction of בְּעַכּוֹ, which Gesenius (Lex. sub. voc. עַכּוֹ) is inclined to adopt. According to this construction, the rendering will be, *weep not in Acco*, i. e. Ptolemais, a maritime city in the tribe of Asher. Other instances of ע being dropped, we have in בְּ for בַּעַי, בְּלִ for בְּעַל, etc.; and certainly the parallelism with עָפַר, the continued list of the names of cities, and the regularity of the paronomasias בְּבֵרִית—בְּבוּ; הַבְבוּ—תַּגִּידוּ; לְבֵית עַפְרָה, are all in favor of this interpretation. Though Acco was allotted to the Asherites, they never took possession of it, Jud. i. 31, and its inhabitants are, therefore, appositely classed along with those of Gath, as taking pleasure in the reverses of the Israelites. The reading of the LXX. οἱ Ἐνακείμ μή, is in all probability a corruption of οἱ ἐν Ἄκει μή, which quite accords with the preceding of ἐν Γὲθ μή. The Arabic has

والذين في اكيم, And those who are in Akim. The name Ἄκη occurs in Strabo, xvi. 2, 25. The town is still called عكا, Akka, by the Arabs, and is known to Europeans by the name of St. Jean d' Acre, which it obtained in the time of the crusades, and is celebrated in later times by its holding out a siege of sixty-one days by the French army, and its destruction by the explosion of a magazine during the bombardment in 1840. It is situated on the north angle of a bay of the same name near the foot of Mount Carmel. בֵּית לְעַפְרָה, lit. the *House of Aphrah*, or simply עַפְרָה, *Ophrah*, Josh. xviii. 23; 1 Sam. xiii. 17, a city in the tribe of Benjamin. The ל is here merely the sign of the genitive. The verb פָלַשׁ which occurs only in Hithpael, signifies to *wallow* or *roll*, as in dust,

ashes, or the like. See Jer. vi. 26, xxv. 34; Ezek. xxvii. 30. While the Hebrews were not to expose the wretchedness of their condition to the contempt of foreigners, it became them to bewail it within their own borders. הִתְפַּלָּשִׁי, *roll thyself*, is to be preferred to הִתְפַּלָּשְׁתִּי, *I roll myself*. It is the reading of the Keri, and many MSS. have it in the text. The Syr., Targ., and Vulg., have the third person plural, which is more easily traceable to הִתְפַּלָּשִׁי than to הִתְפַּלָּשְׁתִּי. Besides, it seems more natural to connect this verb with עִבְרִי in the following verse, than to suppose that the prophet resumes his lamentation ver. 8. Some take the verb to be the second feminine of the preterite, with the Yod paragogic; but every difficulty is removed by adopting the imperative.

11. In עִבְרִי לָכֶם, the second singular feminine of the verb is followed by the second plural masculine of the pronoun, on the principle that though the collective participial noun יוֹשֶׁבֶת is feminine, it was designed to include the inhabitants of both sexes. לָכֶם is not redundant, as Justi asserts, but emphatic, as the *Dativus incommodi*. שָׁפִיר, *Shaphir*, means *fair* or *beautiful*. Dr. Robinson states that there are still three villages of the name of Sawâfir, which are noted on the map as lying nearly halfway between Ashdod and Eleutheropolis, a position not much differing from that assigned by Eusebius and Jerome to *Saphir*. Palestine, vol. ii p. 370. Hitzig and Ewald think that שָׁמִיר, *Shamir*, is meant, which is enumerated among the cities of Judah, Josh. xv. 48, which Eusebius calls Σαφείρ. The Chald. of the Targ. עָבְרִי לָךְ יָפָה בְהַדְרָה is very improperly rendered in the Latin, "Transite vobis qui habitatis *in pulchritudine*," though the LXX. had translated the word by καλῶς. The Syr. has

ܥܳܒܽܘܪܬܳܐ ؟ ܫܰܦܺܝܪ, *inhabitress of Shaphir*. To Samaria there seems no good reason to refer it, since all the other

The inhabitant of Zaanan goeth not forth;
The wailing of Beth-ezel will take away continuance from you.
12 Surely the inhabitant of Maroth pineth for her goods.
Because evil hath come down from Jehovah,
To the gate of Jerusalem.
13 Bind the chariot to the swift steed, O inhabitant of Lachish !

places specified in the connection were in Judah. עֶרְיָה־בֹשֶׁת, lit. *nakedness, shame,* for shamefully naked, *i. e.* entirely so. Comp. as to form, עֵירֹם־וְעֶרְיָה, Ps. xlv. 5. What is here predicted is, that the inhabitants of Shaphir were to be led away as captives by the Assyrians; only for the sake of effect the Imperative is used. See on Is. vi. 10. For the naked condition in which captives were removed, see on Is. xx. 4. צַאֲנָן, *Zaanan,* in all probability the same as צְנָן, *Zenan,* a city in the tribe of Judah, Josh. xv. 37. It properly signifies *the place of flocks;* but to form a paronomasia with it, the prophet employs the verb יָצָא; or the peculiar orthography of the noun may have been adopted in order to make it correspond in appearance and sound with the verb. Comp. צֹאן, גְּנֵי, and צִי, which are only different modes of expressing *sheep* or *flocks.* The inhabitants of this city, under the influence of fear, did not venture forth from their retirement to condole with their neighbors who had been taken prisoners by the enemy, or they did not come forth to their rescue. LXX. Σενναάρ. Aq. Σεναάν. בֵּית הָאֵצֶל, *Beth-ezel,* in all probability the same as אָצֵל, *Azel,* Zech. xiv. 5, but where the town so called was situated, we are not informed. To judge from the connection, it must have been in the vicinity of Shaphir and Zaanan, and not near Samaria, as Ephraim Syrus conjectured. The words מִסְפַּד בֵּית הָאֵצֶל יִקַּח מִכֶּם עֶמְדָּתוֹ have greatly perplexed interpreters. Some regard מִסְפַּד as the Aramaic Infinitive, and connect it with the preceding יָצְאָה; and, supposing אוֹיֵב, *the enemy,* understood, to be the nominative to יִקַּח, explain עֶמְדָּה of a military post. But this construction affords no tolerable sense. Others render עֶמְדָּה, *measure,* conjecture, and the like, contrary to all

usage. For other interpretations, see Pocockc, *in loc.* It seems best to abide by the idea suggested by the root עָמַד, to *remain, continue, endure,* and interpret, *As for the wailing of Beth-ezel, it taketh away its continuance from you;* i. e. the inhabitants of that city cease to mourn on your account. The Shaphirites are addressed, as having gone at once into captivity and oblivion. Most likely their city was larger and more populous, and on this account was attacked by the Assyrians, while the smaller towns in the neighborhood escaped. Gesenius thinks that in אָצֵל there is an allusion to the Arabic etymology اصل, *firmly,* or *deeply rooted* in the earth, as what was so might be expected to *continue;* but this is very doubtful.

12. Of מָרוֹת, *Maroth,* (bitternesses,) we have nowhere any account. מַעֲרָת, *Maarath,* Josh. xv. 50, to which Newcome refers, appears to have been a different place. From the relation in which it is here put to Jerusalem, it probably lay between the afore-mentioned towns and the capital, against which a great army under Rabshakeh proceeded from Lachish, and doubtless plundered all that came in their way. חָלָה לְטוֹב, Newcome, after Houbigant, changes into חָלָה לְמָוֶת, and renders, *is sick unto death;* but altogether without authority. The meaning is, that the inhabitants were pained or grieved on account of the property of which they had been robbed by the enemy. Thus Rosenmüller, Gesenius, De Wette, and Hesselberg. The former כִּי is not causative, but is used, as frequently at the beginning of a verse, to express certainty. For the last clause, compare ver. 9.

13. For *Lachish,* see on Is. xxxvi. 2. רֶכֶשׁ and לָכִישׁ, form a paronomasia. רֶכֶשׁ,

224   MICAH.   CHAP. I.

(She was the beginning of sin to the daughter of Zion)
Surely in thee were found the transgressions of Israel.
14 Therefore thou shalt give a divorce to Moresheth-Gath;
    The houses of Achzib shall prove false to the kings of Israel.
15 Farther, I will bring the possessor to thee, O inhabitant of
    Mareshah!
    He shall come to Adullam, the glory of Israel.

signifies a *fleet courser.* Arab. ركض,
cucurrit. רֹתֵם is in the musculine, though
connecting with יֹשֶׁבֶת in the feminine,
because placed first in the order of the
words. The word occurs only here, but
obviously has the signification of the Arab.
رتم, *ligavit.* As a noun רֹתֶם signifies
broom, because this shrub was used
for binding. In the middle clause of
the verse there is a change of person
from the second to the third, but in the
last clause the second is resumed. For
a similar instance, in which, for the sake
of graphic effect the third person is
thus abruptly introduced, see Is. xxii. 16.
Lachish appears to have formed the link
of idolatry between Israel and Judah.
Lying on the frontier of the former
kingdom, she was the first city in Judah
that was led away by the sin of Jeroboam,
and from her the infection spread, till at
length it reached Jerusalem itself. In
the prospect of a sudden attack, it behooved the inhabitants to use all despatch
in removing their families, and what
property they could take with them, to a
distance. Lachish was besieged by Sennacherib before the threatened attack on
Jerusalem, 2 Kings xviii. 14.

14. שִׁלּוּחִים is used of the presents or
dowry *sent* with a wife, 1 Kings ix. 16,
and of letters of divorce *sent* with her
when she is dismissed by her husband.
In the acceptation ἐξαποστελλομένους,
messengers, as given by the LXX., it
nowhere occurs. The term appears to
be here employed metaphorically to denote the breaking up, or dissolution of all
connection between Lachish and Moresheth-Gath; the former city having
been taken by the Assyrians, was no

longer able to afford protection or support
to the latter. The nominative to תִּתְּנִי,
is יוֹשֶׁבֶת in the preceding verse. עַל is
equivalent, in this connection, to אֶל.
מוֹרֶשֶׁת, *Moresheth,* the birth-place of
Micah, (see Preface) is here said to belong
to *Gath,* most probably because it was
in its vicinity, and under its jurisdiction,
when in possession of the Philistines.
אַכְזִיב, *Achzib.* There were two cities of
this name, one on the sea-coast, between
Acco and Tyre, now called by the Arabs
الزيب, *Ez-Zib.* Josh. xix. 29; Jud. i.
31; and the other in the tribe of Judah,
between Keilah and Mareshah, Josh. xv.
44. That the latter is here intended, is
evident from the connection; for though,
at first view, the mention of *the kings of
Israel* might lead us to suppose that a
city bordering on the northern kingdom
is meant, yet the fact that Israel is
sometimes put for the whole people of
the Hebrews, and sometimes even for
the kingdom of Judah, as 2 Chron.
xxviii. 19, proves, that the mere use of
the term can form no objection to this
construction of the passage. It was most
probably the same place that is called
כְּזִיב, *Chezib,* Gen. xxxviii. 5. By an
elegant paronomasia, בָּתֵּי אַכְזִיב, *the
houses of Achzib,* are said to become
אַכְזָב, *deceitful.* Comp. נַחַל אַכְזָב, a *deceitful torrent,* i. e. one which, having
dried up, disappoints the hope of the traveller. Job vi. 17-19; Jer. xv. 18. Arab.
كذب, *fefellit, irritus vanusque fecit.*
The expectations of further aid from the
families, or inhabitants of that place,
should prove fruitless.

15. אֲבִי is a defective reading of אָבִיא,
which many MSS. have in the text. In

MICAH.   225

16 Make bald thy head, and shave it because of thy darling children;
Enlarge thy baldness like that of the eagle;
For they are gone into captivity from thee.

יוֹרִשׁ and מָרֵשָׁה is another paronomasia. *Mareshah* lay in the plains of Judah, Josh. xv. 44. It was fortified by Rehoboam, 2 Chron. xi. 8, and was famous for the victory obtained over the Ethiopians by Asa, 2 Chron. xiv. 9, 10. According to Josephus, Antiq. xii. 8, 6, it had been in the power of the Idumeans, but was retaken by Alexander the son of Aristobulus, Antiq. xiii. 15, 4, xiv. 1, 4. The *possessor* or *occupier* here predicted is Sennacherib, who took Mareshah and the other fortified cities of Judah, 2 Kings xviii. 14. To point him out with greater emphasis the article is used : הַיֹּרֵשׁ, "*The* possessor." עֲדֻלָּם, *Adullam*, was another city of Judah in the same direction, and near the former, Josh. xv. 35. It was a royal residence in the time of the Canaanites, Josh. xii. 15 ; was fortified by Rehoboam, 2 Chron. xi. 7 ; and had villages dependent upon it, Neh. xi. 30. Of כְּבוֹד יִשְׂרָאֵל various interpretations have been given ; such as the wealth or riches of Israel, their multitude, their nobility, their *weight* of calamity, etc. Some take the words to be in the nominative, some in the accusative, and some in the vocative case. The most natural construction is that of our common version, according to which they are in apposition with עֲדֻלָּם, *Adullam*, and express the superior situation of the place and its neighborhood. Thus also Schmidius, Rosenmüller, and Hesselberg.

16. The prophet concludes this geographical part of his denunciations by addressing himself to the land of Judah, and calling upon her to put on signs of deep-felt grief on account of the removal of her inhabitants. אֶרֶץ, *land*, is to be supplied, rather than בַּת צִיּוֹן, *daughter of Zion*. Baldness, and cutting off the beard, are tokens of mourning in the East, as they were among the nations of antiquity. Ezra ix. 3 ; Job i. 20; Jer. vii. 21, xvi. 6, xlviii. 37. "Regulos quosdam barbam posuisse et uxorem capita rasisse, *ad indicium maximi luctus.*" Suetonius, in his Life of Caligula, chap. v. "When Khaled ben Walid ben Mogaïrah died, there was not a female of the house of Mogaïrah, either matron or maiden, who caused not her hair to be cut off at his funeral." Harmer's Observ. iii. p. 5. One species of eagle is called the bald eagle, from the circumstance of its having its head almost entirely bald ; but they all more or less exhibit baldness during the moulting season. תַּעֲנוּגִים, *delights*, from עָנַג, Arab. غَنِج, *amatorius, fœminæ gestus*, to *delight, be delighted, live delicately*. It is in the former of these acceptations that the noun is here used.

As but few of the inhabitants of Judah could have been carried away by Sennacherib, it is obvious the prophet must have a much more desolating calamity in view in this verse, viz., the Babylonish captivity.

CHAPTER II.

HAVING announced the punishments which were to be inflicted upon his people for the evils in which they indulged, Micah now proceeds to specify some of these evils, 1, 2; and renews his denunciations, 3–5. He then censures those who could not endure to hear the truth, but wished for predictions of good, and shows that no such predictions could reasonably be expected by them, 6–11; concluding, however, with gracious promises of restoration after the captivity, 12, 13.

---

1   Wo to those who devise wickedness,
   And fabricate evil upon their beds;
   In the morning light they effect it,
   Because it is in the power of their hand.
2 They covet fields, and take them by force,
   And houses, and take them away:
   They oppress a man and his house,
   A man and his possession.
3 Wherefore thus saith Jehovah:
   Behold! I devise an evil against this family,

---

1. Comp. Is. x. 1, 2. In the verbs חָשַׁב, פָּעַל, and עָשָׂה, is evidently a gradation. The first describes the conception of the evil purpose in the mind; the second, the preparation or maturing of the scheme; and the third, the carrying of it into effect. Comp. Ps. lviii. 3; Is. xli. 4; Hos. xi. 9. The ה in יַעֲשׂוּהָ is the feminine used as a neuter, to agree with the nouns אָוֶן and רַע, as forming a neuter plural accusative. The phrase אֶל־אֵל יָד occurs also Gen. xxxi. 29; Prov. iii. 27; and with the negative, Deut. xxviii. 32; Neh. v. 5. It is rendered by the LXX. οὐκ ἦραν πρὸς τὸν θεὸν χεῖρας αὐτῶν, which the Syr. gives without the negative: ܘܐܪܝܡܘ ܐܝܕܝܗܘܢ ܠܐܠܗܐ, and lift up their hands to God. Vulg. quoniam contra Deum est manus eorum. Some consider the words to be equivalent to the Dextra mihi Deus of Virgil, and appeal to Job xii. 6, and Hab. i. 11, where, however, the phraseology is different; while others take אֵל to be the shorter form of the demonstrative pronoun אֵלֶּה. But the true meaning seems to be that given in our common version, according to which אֵל is to be taken in its literal signification of power, strength, etc. Thus Pococke, Rosenmüller, Bauer, Dathe, De Wette, Gesenius, Hitzig, and Ewald, after the Targ. אֲרֵי אִית חֵילָא בִּידֵיהוֹן, and Kimchi, כי ־ יש כח בידם לעשוק העניים, because there is power in their hand to oppress the poor. Just as the LXX. render, ἰσχύει ἡ χείρ, Gen. xxxi. 29, and Deut. xxviii. 32. That כִּי is to be taken causatively, and not conditionally, is evident from the connection.

2. Before בָּתִּים repeat יַחְמֹדוּ. Fifty-two MSS., six by correction, two originally; four ancient and nineteen other printed editions; the Alex. MS. of the LXX., the Targ., Vulg., and Arab., omit ו before אִישׁ. The parallelisms in this verse are very elegant.

3. חָשַׁב and רָעָה correspond here to חֹשְׁבֵי and רַע in ver. 1. הַמִּשְׁפָּחָה Rosenmüller and Maurer understand to signify " certum genus hominum nequam et perversum;" as if the prophet intended to single out such of the people as committed the atrocious acts specified ver. 2; but it is more likely that the whole people, viewed as rebellious and corrupt, is meant. See on Amos iii. 1. The figure of a yoke is here employed for the purpose of expressing the heavy and oppressive nature of the bondage to which the Hebrews were to be subjected. מִשָּׁם, thence, has the force of a pronoun in this place. LXX. ἐξ ὧν. Syr. ܡܢܗܘܢ. Comp. Gen. iii. 23; 1 Kings xvii. 13;

From which ye shall not withdraw your necks,
Neither shall ye walk haughtily;
For it shall be an evil time.
4 In that day shall one sing a ditty respecting you,
And employ a doleful lamentation,
And say : We are utterly destroyed.
He hath changed the portion of my people,
How hath he withdrawn it from me!
To an apostate he hath divided our fields!
5 Therefore thou shalt not have one to cast the line by lot,
In the congregation of Jehovah.

Ezek. v. 3. So oppressive should be the yoke, that it would be impossible for them to hold themselves erect. LXX. ὀρθοί. Targ. בְּקוֹמָה זְקוּפָה. The term רָמָה is selected with special reference to the elated and haughty manner in which they had conducted themselves. It is properly a substantive, from רוּם, *to be high*, but is here used adverbially.

4. For נָשָׂא מָשָׁל, see on Is. xiv. 4. The verb is here used impersonally. That this Mashal was to be employed by the Jews themselves, and not by their enemies, is evident from its tenor, as it follows in the verse. עֲלֵיכֶם, therefore, is not to be rendered *against you*, but *on your account*. נָהָה נְהִי נִהְיָה, *náhâ, nehi, nihyâh*, form an elegant paronomasia. There can be no doubt that נְהִי, *lamentation*, is derived from נָהָה, *to lament;* but whether נִהְיָה be likewise derived from it, and consequently merely the feminine of נְהִי, or whether it be the Niphal of the substantive verb הָיָה, *to be*, is disputed. The harshness that would arise from rendering the words, *One shall lament with a lamentation, it is done!* militates against the latter derivation ; whereas, by taking all the three words as cognates, having the same signification, the sentence is at once easy and forcible. The relative position of the verbs אָמַר, נָהָה, and נָשָׂא, confirms this construction. Thus the LXX. and Vulg. καὶ θρηνηθήσεται θρῆνος ἐν μέλει, *et cantabitur canticum cum suavitate*. And the Arab., employing for the two first words terms cognate with

the Hebrew, وَيُنَاحُ نَوْحٌ بِتَلَحُّنٍ.

נִהְיָה is the feminine of נְהִי, just as צְבִיָּה is of צְבִי, and עִבְרִיָּה of עִבְרִי. The feminine is added to the masculine for the sake of emphasis. Comp. Is. iii. 1, only there the nouns are joined by the copulative וְ. The three verbs above specified are used impersonally. The nominative to the following verbs, אָמַר, יָמִיר, and חָלַק, is Jehovah, understood.

מוּר, Syr. ܡܳܪ, *to buy;* in Aphel أَمَارَ, *to sell*, or *deliver* an article into the hand of the purchaser; Arab. رَامَ, *huc illuc mota fuit res, transivit*. The verb is here employed to convey the idea of a change of masters, or the passing of the land of the Hebrews into the power of their enemies. שׁוֹבֵב is a verbal noun, from the Pilel of שׁוּב, *to turn, turn back;* here used in a bad sense, one who has turned back, or away from God; *apostate, rebel, idolater*. Comp. Is. xlvii. 10, lvii. 17; Jer. xlix. 4. The idolatrous king of Babylon is meant.

5. לָכֵן is a repetition of that used at the beginning of ver. 3, and for the same purpose. The nominative to לְךָ, *thee*, is עַם, *people*, occurring in the preceding verse; and the denunciation relates to their being completely at the disposal of their enemies: none of themselves being permitted to allot to them portions of the land for inheritance. According to Hitzig the words are addressed by the ungodly Jews to Micah himself, and

228   MICAH.   CHAP. II.

6   Prophesy not; those shall prophesy
    Who will not prophesy of these things:
    Reproaches are incessant.
7   What language, O house of Jacob!
    Is the Spirit of Jehovah shortened?
    Are these his operations?
    Do not my words benefit him that walketh uprightly?

intimate that they would put him and his family to death for prophesying against them.

6. The words אַל־תַּטִּפוּ יַטִּיפוּן לֹא־יַטִּפוּ לָאֵלֶּה, which contain a smooth and elegant paronomasia, are very enigmatical, but must neither be rendered, "Prophesy not, they say to those who should prophesy: they shall not prophesy to such." Or: "Prophesy not; they shall prophesy who will not prophesy of such things." In the former case the interdicting language of the rebellious to the prophets is simply given, and then we have the Divine declaration, that it should be as they desired. They should be judicially abandoned to their own ways; and, as they would not hearken to the prophets when they predicted evil, they should be deprived of their ministry altogether, and not receive from them any predictions of good. In the latter, the language is entirely that of the people, by which they not merely stop the mouths of the true prophets, but declare that those only should be permitted to prophesy to them who abstained from denunciations of evil. The former requires אֹמְרִים to be supplied before יַטִּיפוּן; the latter, אֲשֶׁר before לֹא־יַטִּפוּ. The formula לְ הִטִּיף is used ver. 11, both in reference to the persons to whom the prediction is addressed, and to that which is the subject of the prophecy: אַטִּף לְךָ לַיַּיִן, "I will prophesy to thee of wine." Though contrary to the Masoretic division of the words, I prefer the second of the above modes of construction, as being the easier of the two. The use of the paragogic ן in יַטִּיפוּן forms no objection; for though it is most commonly found at the end of a sentence, yet there are many instances in which it occurs at the beginning, or in the middle. See Gen.

xviii. 28–31; Exod. xviii. 26; Deut. viii. 3; 1 Sam. ii. 22; Ps. xi. 2, lxviii. 13; Is. viii. 12. For הִטִּיף, see on Amos vii. 16. In the concluding words of the verse, לֹא יִסַּג כְּלִמּוֹת, literally, *calumnies depart not*, the Jews indignantly tax the prophets with exposing them to contempt by incessant castigation and reproof. Of this interpretation Maurer observes, "ut facillima et simplissima per se est, ita ad nexum est aptissima." The verb occurring first, is in the masculine singular, though the noun is a feminine plural. See Gesen. § 144. Ward's edit.

7. The prophet boldly meets the charge expressed in the concluding clause of the preceding verse by asking, Whether the absence of auspicious predictions could possibly be ascribed to any deficiency on the part of the Spirit of prophecy? whether the judgments denounced were operations in which Jehovah delighted, and were not rather procured by the wickedness of those on whom they were to be inflicted? and whether it was not a fact which experience had ever verified, that the Divine communications were productive of good to men of science and consistent piety? In הַאִמְרוּ the ה is used as a qualifying demonstrative with all the force of an indignant exclamation, in order to point out the flagrant character of the language employed by the Israelites. אָמוּר is the Pahul Part. signifying *what is said* or *spoken*, and with the ה prefixed, *O dictum!* Almost all the versions and Lexicons assign to this participle the signification of *being called* or *named;* but this notion attaches to the verb only in Niphal, which, in such case, is uniformly followed by the preposition לְ. See Is. iv. 3, xix. 18; Hos. ii. 1. The LXX., Aq., Vulg., and

8 But of old my people hath risen up as an enemy;
Ye strip off the vestment as well as the robe
From those who walk along securely,
From those who are returning from battle.
9 The women of my people ye thrust out from their darling home;
From their children ye take away my glory for ever.

Targ., have read הֲקֵאנִי, which is found in four of Kennicott's MSS. Ewald: "O des Wortes!" As רוּחַ קְצַר, *short of breath* or *spirit*, is contrasted with אֶרֶךְ אַפַּיִם, *long-suffering*, Prov. xiv. 29, and is obviously equivalent to אַפַּיִם קְצַר, ver. 17, (comp. קְצַר רוּחַ, Exod. vi. 9,) most of the moderns render in the present instance, *Is Jehovah prone to anger?* but prophecy being the subject to which reference had just been made, it is more natural to understand רוּחַ יְהוָה, *the Spirit of Jehovah*, in its appropriated meaning, as designating the Divine Author of prophetic communications; and to take the verb in the sense of *weakness* or *inability*. Comp. יָד קְצַר, *short of hand*, Is. xxxvii. 27. אֵלֶּה, *these*, like אֵלֶּה, ver. 6, refers to the judgments which the Lord had threatened to inflict. The interrogative form, as frequently, requires a decided negative; such judgments are not Jehovah's usual operations. Comp. Is. xxviii. 21; Lam. iii. 33; Mic. vii. 18. In הַהֹלֵךְ יָשָׁר, the substantive, which is used adverbially, is placed first, for the sake of emphasis, and on this account also it takes the article, which properly belongs to הַהֹלֵךְ. A similar instance of transposition occurs in יָקָר הֹלֵךְ, Job xxxi. 26, where the substantive is likewise used adverbially. For the meaning of the phrase, comp. תֹּם הֹלֵךְ, Prov. ii. 7; בְּתֹם הֹלֵךְ, Is. lvii. 2.

8. וְ at the beginning of this verse is strongly adversative. Very different was the character of those whom the prophet was now reproving. אֶתְמוּל, properly *yesterday*, is taken by some to signify *lately*; but it is more in keeping with the spirit of the passage to render it *anciently, of old*, or the like. See on Is. xxx. 33. The rebellious conduct of the Hebrew nation was no new thing. It had characterized every period of its history. LXX. ἔμπροσθεν. Abulwalid, contrary to the usage of the language, divides the word into אֵת and מוּל, and renders, *on the contrary*. Thus also the Vulg. The ל in לְאֹיֵב is expressive of manner; comp. לְנָגִיד, Is. xxxii. 1. שַׂלְמָה is selected to correspond in alliteration with שִׂמְלָה, and is here equivalent to מֵעַל מִבֶּגֶד, or מֵעַל. It refers, not to עֹבְרִים immediately following, but to the persons of those who were plundered. Though divided by the accent, שַׂלְמָה and אֶדֶר are to be regarded as asyndeta; the former, signifying the large loose garment which was worn immediately over the tunic, and which being indispensable to the Orientals, is placed first, for the sake of emphasis; the latter, the costly robe of fur, or other rich stuff, the robbery of which, under the circumstances described, was a matter of course. So great was the rapacity of the lawless characters spoken of, that they were not satisfied with the more valuable part of the dress, but likewise possessed themselves of what was less costly. Comp. Matt. v. 40. For שַׂלְמָה (by transposition of the first two letters of שִׂמְלָה, which is much more frequently in use,) comp. the Arab. شَلْمَة, *vestimentum*, pec. *totum corpus involvens*, from شَمَلَ, *circumdedit*. Before שׁוּבֵי repeat the preposition מִ. The passive participle is here used intransitively to describe those who were returning after having defeated their enemy in battle, and who might therefore be considered perfectly secure. Even then they were waylaid by their countrymen and neighbors, and robbed of the spoils which they had taken in war.

9. In נְשֵׁי עַמִּי and עֹלָלֶיהָ, there is, as

10 Arise! depart! for this is not the place of your rest;
Because of pollution it will destroy,
And the destruction shall be grievous.
11 If any one, conversant with wind and falsehood, lie, saying:
I will prophesy to thee of wine and strong drink,
Even he shall be the prophet of this people.

frequently, a transition from the plural to the singular pronoun. As the prophet refers to war, it is most likely he intended by the " women," the widows of those who had fallen in battle, and who ought to have been objects of special sympathy and care. Instead of which, both they and their fatherless children were expelled from their homes, and robbed of their property. הֲדָרִי, my ornament, collectively for the ornamental clothes which they wore, and with which they had been provided by Jehovah. The Holy Land, and everything connected with it, was his, so that whatever was enjoyed by its inhabitants, was to be regarded as peculiarly a Divine gift. Comp. Hos. ii. 8. לְעוֹלָם, for ever, i. e. never to make restitution. Some think there is reference to the command to restore the pledge before sun-set, Exod. xxii. 25, but this is doubtful.

10. As the Imperative is frequently used by the prophets to express more strongly the certainty of a prediction than a simple future would have done, קוּמוּ לְכוּ are to be so understood here. See on Is. vi. 10. Hitzig preposterously considers the words to be addressed by the pitiless Jews to the persons whom they oppressed by expelling them from their homes. They are obviously to be viewed as the language of Jehovah, threatening them with a removal from their own country, which they had polluted by their crimes, to a foreign and heathen land. Canaan was conferred upon the Hebrews as a *rest*, or place of quiet enjoyment, after their fatigues and troubles in the wilderness, Num. x. 33; Deut. xii. 9; Ps. xcv. 11. Before זֹאת, supply אֶרֶץ. The definite article in הַמְּנוּחָה is equivalent to the pronominal affix כֶם, and is to be rendered accordingly. A land may be said to destroy its inhabitants, when it withholds from them the means of subsistence, and forces them to leave it. With such reference it is described as devouring them and spewing them out of it, Lev. xviii. 28, xx. 22, xxvi. 38; Ezek. xxxvi. 12–14. The comparison of these passages shows the propriety of the Piel תְחַבֵּל, and renders unnecessary the passive forms תְחֻבַּל and תְחָבֵל, which some have proposed. For נִמְרָץ, comp. the Arab. مرض *morbus fuit*, only its signfications would seem to be taken from the idea of a violent or deadly disease. Thus קְלָלָה נִמְרֶצֶת, a *grievous curse*, 1 Kings ii. 8. Gesenius renders חֶבֶל נִמְרָץ, *corruptio vehementissima*.

11. Micah reverts to the subject of smooth and flattering predictions, which he had spoken of ver. 6, and shows that so corrupt had the people become, that no prophet might expect to be acceptable to them who did not sanction their sinful indulgences. To those who did, they would give a ready ear. As רוּחַ signifies both *wind* and *spirit*, there is great force in representing those who pretended to inspiration as walking or being familiar with the wind: so utterly worthless was the instruction which they communicated. הֹלֵךְ רוּחַ is otherwise equivalent to אִישׁ רוּחַ, Hos. ix. 7, and הֹלֵךְ שֶׁקֶר to בָּא בְמִרְמָה, Jer. v. 31. Dathe thinks this verse would better fit in after ver. 6, but there is no authority for the transposition; and, besides, there is a singular propriety in bringing forward the crowning sin of the Jews, viz. their preferring false prophets to the faithful messengers of Jehovah, just before introducing the glorious prediction of their restoration from captivity in the following verse.

12 I will surely gather thee entirely, O Jacob!
I will surely collect the remainder of Israel;
I will put them together like the sheep of Bozrah,
Like a flock in the midst of their pasture;
They shall be in commotion,
Because of the multitude of men.
13 The Breaker is gone up before them;
They break through and pass to the gate;

12, 13. Theodoret, Kimchi, Calvin, Drusius, De Dieu, Grotius, Tarnovius, and others, consider these verses to be a denunciation of punishment, and not a promise of deliverance; while Struensee, Hezel, Michaelis, and Forsayeth (in Newcome) regard them as the language of the false prophets, continued from ver. 11. Ewald, who takes the same view, thinks they were originally written by Micah on the margin of his manuscript, and has printed them in Italics, within brackets. Most modern interpreters, however, and among them Rosenmüller, Dathe, Justi, Hartmann, Maurer, and even Hitzig, are unanimous in viewing them as predictive of the restoration of the Jews after their dispersion. The manner in which the prophet concludes the preceding verse, proves that he had finished what he had to deliver respecting the favor shown to false prophets; and his sudden and abrupt transition to better times is so entirely in accordance with the manner of the prophets, that the last-mentioned interpretation at once recommends itself as the true. The point most difficult to determine is the point to which the prophecy has respect. Most Christian expositors explain it of the appearance of Christ, and his collecting of believers into his church; but this construction is altogether arbitrary, resting on no other foundation than the principle of giving a spiritual interpretation to whatever may, by possibility, be so interpreted. So far is there from being anything in the phraseology of the text to warrant such appropriation of it, that the very terms compel to an adoption of the literal sense. Kimchi, Jarchi, and the Jews generally, as also several modern Christian writers, maintain, that the prophecy relates to the future literal restoration of the Jews under the Messiah. For my part, I cannot but regard the more immediate restoration from the literal Babylon as the theme of the inspired announcement. The deliverance predicted is the same to which reference is made chap. iv. 10, the scene of which is there expressly declared to be Babylon. "Jacob" stands here for the ten tribes, as in Is. xvii. 4; Hos. xii. 2; and "Israel" for the kingdom of Judah, as in Obad. 18, 2 Chron. xii. 1, xix. 8, xxi. 2, 4. The two tribes and a half being few compared with the ten, might well be described as שְׁאֵרִית, the *remainder*, which had been left in the land at the time of the Assyrian invasion. To express the great extent of the population after the return, it is compared to the large collections of sheep in the folds of Bozrah; a region celebrated for the abundance of its flocks. The Targ., Vulg., Gesenius, Winer, Hitzig, and Ewald, render בָּצְרָה, *sheep-fold*, but this signification of the word is totally unsupported by usage, and is not allowed by Lee. The LXX., mistaking ב for the preposition, translate, ἐν θλίψει. It is seldom we meet with the article prefixed to a noun taking the pronominal affix, as in בְּתוֹכָהּ; yet see Josh. vii. 21, viii. 33. By הַפֹּרֵץ, *the Breaker*, some understand Cyrus; but the identity of structure between this sentence and the two with which the verse closes, compels us to interpret the term of Jehovah himself, who, through the instrumentality of that monarch, removed every obstacle which prevented the return of the Hebrews to their own land. When his providence so visibly interposed, it was easy for them to break

They go out at it;
Their King passeth on before them,
Even Jehovah at their head.

down the minor barriers which had confined them in Babylonia, and triumphantly to march out through the gates of the hostile city. To intimate that they should suffer molestation from no enemy by the way, God is represented as going before them, like a monarch at the head of his army; just as he was said to go before his people when they went up from Egypt, Deut. i. 30. In the illustrious Deliverer here exhibited, Rosenmüller recognizes the Messiah: "*Perruptor*, δεικτικῶς, est enim cum ה demonstrativo. Loquitur ergo de certa quadam persona, et antonomastice sic dicta, quæ mox vocabitur מַלְכָּם, *rex illorum* et יְהֹוָה, ut non sit dubium, Nostrum de Messia cogitasse, seu divino illo heroe, quo auspice, devictis omnibus Judæorum hostibus, aureum seculum orbem beabit." And to his interpretation I accede, only restricting the work of the Messiah, as here predicted, to his leading forth the Jews from Babylon. Comp. Exod. xxxiii. 14; Is. lxiii. 9, in which we are taught that the Divine Logos delivered, and conducted the Israelites through the wilderness.

CHAPTER III.

HAVING inserted in the two preceding verses a gracious prediction for the comfort of the few pious who might be living in the midst of the ungodly, the prophet proceeds to expatiate at greater length against the latter, directing his discourse especially to the civil and ecclesiastical officers, who, by their example, exerted so baneful an influence upon the nation. The chapter may be divided into three parts. Ver. 1-4, an objurgation of the princes; 5-7, that of the prophets; and 8-11, that of princes, prophets, and priests together. The chapter closes with a prophecy of the destruction of Jerusalem by the Babylonians.

1 AND I said: Hear, I pray you, O heads of Jacob!
   And ye judges of the house of Israel!
   Is it not yours to know justice?
2 Who hate good and love evil;
   Who strip their skin from off them,
   And their flesh from off their bones.
3 Who devour the flesh of my people,
   And flay their skin from off them;
   Who break their bones in pieces,

1—3. The לְ in לָכֶם is expressive of duty or obligation; what the persons spoken of were bound to do, and what might naturally be expected from them in the station which they filled. דַּעַת is here used, not of merely speculative knowledge, but of that which is practical. It was the province of the magistrates to exercise their judicial authority for the protection of the innocent,

And separate them as in the pot,
And as flesh in the midst of the kettle.
4 Then they may cry to Jehovah,
But he will not answer them,
But will hide his face from them at that time;
Because they have corrupted their doings.
5 Thus saith Jehovah respecting the prophets,
Who cause my people to err;
Who bite with their teeth, and cry, Peace;
But against him that putteth not into their mouth
They prepare war.
6 Surely ye shall have night without vision;
Ye shall have darkness without divination;
Yea, the sun shall go down upon the prophets,
And the day shall become black over them.

and the punishment of evil-doers. But instead of thus discharging the duties of their office, they were themselves perpetrators of the most flagrant acts of oppression and cruelty. Their inhuman conduct is very forcibly described by the prophet, in language borrowed from the process of slaying and preparing animals for food, and the feasting consequent thereon. Comp. Ps. xiv. 4; Prov. xxx. 14. The pronominal affixes in ver. 2, refer to the people, understood, and not to טוב and רעה, immediately preceding, which are obviously employed as abstract neuters. Though many MSS. read רע with the Keri, yet there are others which exhibit רעה, the proper pointing of the Chethib. No codex supports the emendation כְּשֵׁאֵר instead of בָּשָׂר. The LXX. may, or may not, have so read. The etymology of קַלַּחַת is uncertain, but that it signifies a vessel for boiling in is clear from its being here parallel with סִיר, and in 1 Sam. ii. 14 with דּוּד, כִּיּוֹר, and פָּרוּר.

4. אָז, then, and בָּעֵת הַהִיא, at that time, are anticipative of the period of divine judgment. The infliction of such judgment is implied, not expressed. The more emphatically to convey an impression of its certainty, the prophet takes it for granted. God is said to hear or answer prayer, when he grants what is sup-

plicated; and to hide his face, when he disregards or affords no relief to the suppliant. בַּאֲשֶׁר, with the LXX., Syr., Justi, Dathe, and others, I take to be causal, as in Num. xxvii. 14; 1 Sam. xxviii. 18; 2 Kings xvii. 26.

5. הַנֹּשְׁכִים בְּשִׁנֵּיהֶם, who bite with their teeth, the antithesis requires to be understood in the sense of eating the food supplied by the people. While such supplies were granted, the false prophets predicted prosperity; but if they withheld them, measures of a hostile nature, under a religious pretext, were adopted against them. Thus the Targ. דְעָזְנִין מוֹכְרֵי, לְחִוּוֹן שְׁיָן דְּבַּר מִתְגָבָן עֲלוֹיְהִי שָׁלְמָא, They prophesy peace to him who feeds them with dinners of flesh. The phrase is purposely selected in order satirically to expose the selfishness of the deceivers. For the meaning of קִדֵּשׁ, to sanctify, as here used, see on Is. xiii. 3; Joel i. 14; and comp. Jer. vi. 4.

6, 7. So completely should the predictions of the false prophets be disproved by the judgments that were to be brought on the nation, and so painfully should they themselves experience these judgments, that they could no longer have the effrontery to practise their deceptions. Under such circumstances they could not pretend to deliver any divine oracle to the people. The words

7 Then shall the seers be ashamed,
   And the diviners confounded;
   They shall all cover their beard;
   For there shall be no response from God.
8 But truly I am full of power by the Spirit of Jehovah,
   And of judgment and might;
   To declare unto Jacob his transgression,
   And to Israel his sin.
9   Hear this, I beseech you, ye heads of the house of Jacob!
   And judges of the house of Israel!
   Who abhor justice,
   And pervert all equity;
10 Building Zion with blood,

do not imply that they ever had really received any such oracles: they merely professed to have received them. מ is here to be taken privatively, and not in the signification of *ob, propter*, etc., as interpreted by some. The obscuration of the heavenly bodies, or of the light of day, is frequently employed by the prophets, as it is by oriental writers generally, to denote affliction or calamity. Amos viii. 9. שָׂפָם, LXX., in 2 Sam. xix. 25, μύσταξ, the *mustache* or *beard*, which is held in high estimation in the East, and in exhibiting which, properly grown and trimmed, the Orientals greatly pride themselves. To hide it, therefore, by covering it, was regarded as a striking mark of shame or sorrow. See Lev. xiii. 45; 2 Sam. xix. 25; Ezek. xxiv. 17, 22.

8. Full of conscious sincerity, and of his divine commission, in the execution of which he was sustained by the supernatural influence of the Holy Spirit, and zealous for the glory of God, and the recovery of his people, Micah avows his readiness, with all boldness, to announce to them his inspired message respecting their sins. His character and conduct formed a perfect contrast to those of the false prophets. The compound particle וְאוּלָם, and the pronoun אָנֹכִי, are here emphatic. כֹּחַ, means the *supernatural power* necessary for the general discharge of the prophetic office; comp. δύναμις, Luke i. 17, xxiv. 49;

Acts i. 8; מִשְׁפָּט, *a sense of moral rectitude*, distinguishing clearly between right and wrong, and impelling to the advocacy and maintenance of such actions, as are conformable to the Divine law; and גְּבוּרָה, *moral courage*, or a bold and intrepid spirit, inciting its possessor to throw aside all timidity in defending the cause of God and truth. Comp. 2 Tim. i. 7.

9. The prophet now proceeds to deliver in full the message which he had commenced, ver. 1, employing the same formula, שִׁמְעוּ־נָא, as he also does chap. vi. 1. The remaining verses of the chapter furnish a noble specimen of that bold and uncompromising fidelity which characterized his ministry.

10. בֹּנֶה, the LXX., Syr., Targ., and Vulg., render in the plural, but no Hebrew codex exhibits the variation. The authors of these versions doubtless regarded the participle as a collective, which mode of construction we must adopt, or, with Michaelis, we must suppose that the prophet had Shebna, Is. xxii. 16–18, Jehoiakim, or some other particular prince in his eye; the former interpretation is preferable. בְּדָמִים, *blood*, used for the *wealth* obtained by shedding the blood of its owners. Comp. Jer. xxii. 13; Ezek. xxii. 27; Hab. ii. 12, in the latter of which passages בְּדָמִים and בְּעַוְלָה are used as parallels, with the same particle, בְּ.

Chap. III.   MICAH.   235

And Jerusalem with wickedness.
11 Her heads judge for reward,
And her priests teach for hire;
Her prophets also divine for money;
Yet they lean upon Jehovah, saying:
Is not Jehovah in the midst of us?
No calamity shall come upon us.
12 Surely on your account
Sion shall be ploughed as a field,

11. שֹׁחַד, is a gift or bribe given to a judge to obtain freedom from punishment. Receiving bribes was strictly prohibited by the Mosaic law, Exod. xxiii. 8; Deut. xvi. 19. That the כֹּהֲנִים, *priests*, were authorized by that law to act in the capacity of ordinary religious teachers, does not appear. Their being thus employed by Jehoshaphat is narrated as something altogether extraordinary, 2 Chron. xvii. 7-9. Besides attending to the ceremonial observances, they had devolved upon them the decision of controversies, Deut. xvii. 8-11, xxi. 5; Ezek. xliv. 24; cases of leprosy, divorce, etc. Lev. x. 11. They were to lay down the law in such cases, and pronounce the final sentence. Comp. Mal. ii. 7; Deut. xxxiii. 10; and see Michaelis on the Laws of Moses, Art. lii. They are here associated with the judges, because in certain cases they gave a joint verdict; and in the time of the prophet were equally avaricious and corruptible. The verb קָסַם, to *divine*, being only used of false prophets, shows that those reproved by Micah were of that description. Comp. Jude 11. With all their wicked perversion of right, they hypocritically claimed an interest in the favor of God, and scouted the idea that the calamities denounced by his true prophets could ever overtake them. Comp. Jer. vii. 4, 8-11, where the same presumptuous confidence in the Divine presence in the temple, is exposed and condemned.

12. We have here at last an awful epiphonema, in which the destruction of the metropolis is expressly and particularly predicted. The wicked leaders of the people were now building and beautifying it, by expending upon it their unrighteous gains, ver. 10; but the time was coming when it should be completely desolated. "Zion" designates the site of the city of David on the south; "Jerusalem," the houses occupied by the inhabitants generally in the centre and the north; and "the mountain of the house," Moriah on the east. Instead of צִיּוֹן, the Chaldee termination, five MSS., five others originally, and the Babylonian Talmud, read צִיּ֑וֹן. הַבַּיִת, *the house*, i. e. κατ' ἐξοχήν, the temple. That which was their boast and confidence, was to be converted into a wilderness. יַעַר signifies not only a forest, but also a thicket of shrubs, a rough or rugged locality, from the Arab.

وَعْرٌ, *asper, salebrosus fuit; difficilis incessu, asper* locus. The whole verse contains a description of utter ruin and desolation. The enunciation of such a prophecy evinced the greatest intrepidity on the part of Micah, and is quoted as an instance of prophetic boldness, Jer. xxvi. 18, 19. The ploughing of the city by the enemy, which has its parallel in Horace, lib. i. Od. 16,

"Imprimeretque muris
Hostile aratrum exercitus insolens,"

has by some interpreters been referred to what is recorded in the Talmud, noticed by Jerome, and repeated by Maimonides, that Titus Annius Rufus, an officer in the Roman army, tore up with a ploughshare the foundations of the temple; but little or no credit is to be given to the story. See Deylingii

Jerusalem shall become heaps,
And the mountain of the house woody heights.

Observationes Sacr. pt. v. pp. 448, 450. Robinson's Palestine, vol. ii. pp. 2, 8. The circumstance, however, that what Micah predicts, relates to the city as distinguished from the temple, clearly militates against the application of his language. Equally inapposite as to the fulfilment of the prophecy are the appeals to the present partially cultivated state of Mount Zion, since the destruction to which it points was not the more distant devastations under Titus and Adrian, but the more proximate under Nebuchadnezzar. For the accomplishment, see Nch. ii. 17, iv. 2 ; Lam. v. 18.

CHAPTER IV.

BY a sudden transition, as at chap. ii. 13, the prophet passes from his denunciation of punishment, to a description of the glorious state of the church subsequent to the restoration from the captivity in Babylon. He predicts the establishment of the kingdom of Christ upon the ruins of idolatry, and the accession of the Gentiles, 1, 2; the peaceful nature of his reign, 3, and the security of his subjects, 4. He then abruptly introduces his captive countrymen, who, having been recovered to the worship of the true God, declare, that, however the idolaters around them might adhere to their several systems of creature-worship, they would never renounce the service of Jehovah, 5. The Most High promises to gather even the weakest of them from their dispersions, restore their national existence, and reign over them for ever, 6-8. The intermediate invasion of Judea, the captivity in Babylon, and the liberation of the Jews, are next depicted, 9--11. Upon which follows a prediction of the victories which they should gain over their enemies in the time of the Maccabees, and of the reverse which took place on the establishment of Herod by the Roman power.

1 AND it shall come to pass in the last of the days,
That the mountain of Jehovah's house
Shall be established on the summit of the mountains,
And be elevated above the hills,
And the people shall flow to it.
2 Yea, many nations shall go, and say:
Come let us go up to the mountain of Jehovah,

1-3. On the general identity of this prophecy with Is. ii. 2-4, see the note on that passage, to which the reader is also referred for the interpretation. The verbal discrepancies, which are few and trivial, will be best seen on consulting Newcome, who exhibits the Hebrew text of both prophets in parallel columns. The sense is the same throughout. Twenty MSS., originally ten more, one by correction, and the Complut. edition, read יֵלְכוּ instead of יֵלֵכוּ. For יֵצֵא לֹא, thirty-six MSS., probably another, seven originally, and six by correction, together

To the house of the God of Jacob,
That he may teach us his ways,
And that we may walk in his paths;
For out of Zion shall go forth the law,
And the word of Jehovah from Jerusalem.

3 And he shall arbitrate among many people,
And give decision to many distant nations,
So that they shall beat their swords into coulters,
And their spears into pruning-knives;
Nation shall not raise a sword against nation,
Neither shall they learn war any more.

4 And they shall sit each under his vine, and under his fig-tree,
And none shall make him afraid;
For the mouth of Jehovah of hosts hath spoken it.

5 Though all the people should walk
Each in the name of his god,
Yet we will walk in the name of Jehovah our God,
For ever and ever.

6 In that day, saith Jehovah,
I will gather the halting,

with four of the early editions, read לֹא; and for יִשָּׂא five MSS., four originally, and now one, read נָשָׂא.

4. This beautiful addition, which is not in Isaiah, appears to have been a common adage among the Hebrews to express a state of complete outward security. 1 Kings iv. 25; Zech. iii. 10. For a state of things precisely the reverse see my Biblical Researches and Travels in Russia, etc. p. 436.

5. Many interpreters have been puzzled how to reconcile the statement made in the beginning of this verse with the prediction contained in verse 2; and Hartmann goes so far as to assert, that it was originally a marginal gloss, written by a different pen, and afterwards inserted in the text. The difficulty will be removed, if we consider the words to be those of the Jews during their dispersion. "Hic spectanda est diversitas temporis." Calvin, *in loc.* They witnessed the eagerness with which the idolaters around them devoted themselves to the service of their gods — an eagerness which led them to despair of their ever being reclaimed; and they nobly resolved that nothing should ever again move them to abandon the service of Jehovah; but that, with equal earnestness, they would addict themselves to his worship, and the observance of his laws. כִּי is here a formula of concession: *be it so that*, *although*, or the like. Comp. for this use of the particle, Gen. viii. 21; Exod. xiii. 17; Josh. xvii. 18; Deut. xxix. 18. "הָלַךְ בְּשֵׁם בּ, *to walk in the name of any one*, means to frame one's conduct according to his will, to act by his authority, and in accordance with his character. שֵׁם, *name*, is often used for the person himself. Com. the phrases הָלַךְ בְּדֶרֶךְ יְהֹוָה; הָלַךְ אַחֲרֵי יְהֹוָה, *to walk in the way of*, *to follow Jehovah*. It seems here to be specially employed in reference to religious worship. Comp. Zech. x. 12.

6–8. That the subject of these verses is the restoration from Babylon, and the reëstablishment of the Jewish state, and not any spiritual gathering of men generally to the church of God, is placed beyond dispute by the prediction that the scattered and afflicted remnant of Israel

And collect the outcasts,
And those whom I have afflicted.
7 And I will make the halting a remnant,
And those that had been far removed a strong nation;
And Jehovah shall reign over them in Mount Zion,
From henceforth, and for ever.
8 And thou, O tower of the flock!
O hill of the daughter of Zion!
To thee it shall come,
Even the former rule shall come,
The kingdom of the daughter of Jerusalem.

was again to become a *strong nation*, ver. 7, and by the use of the phrase הַמֶּמְשָׁלָה הָרִאשֹׁנָה, *the former rule*, ver. 8, which can only be interpreted of the theocratic government at Jerusalem. When the Hebrews first returned to their own land, they were few in number, amounting only to 42,360; but they rapidly increased, and in the time of the Maccabees not only became an independent state, but acquired such power that they vanquished the formidable Syro-Grecian armies. The Asmonæan family possessed supreme authority from Mattathias to Herod the Great. To the above interpretation no valid objection can be taken on the ground that Jehovah is said, ver. 7, to reign *for ever* over those who were to be assembled. עוֹלָם, *eternity*, or long indefinite duration, whether applied to the past or the future, must always be determined by the nature of the subject. It is very often used of the Mosaic institutes, Exod. xii. 14, 17, xxvii. 21, xxviii. 43; Lev. iii. 17. It is even employed to denote the period of the seventy years' captivity, Jer. xviii. 16. For הַצֹּלֵעָה and הַנִּדָּחָה, comp. Ezek. xxxiv. 16; Zeph. iii. 19. הַנַּהֲלָאָה is the Niphal participle of הָלָא, *to be removed*. Syr. ܢܰܣܺܝܓܳܐ, *elongavit, removit.* Arabic لها II., *recessit, abstessit.* Having employed metaphors taken from the treatment of sheep, Micah calls the Jewish people, in their collective capacity, עֵדֶר, *a flock.* Comp. עֵדֶר יְהוָֹה, *the flock of Jehovah,* Jer. xiii. 17; and in

reference to the strength of Jerusalem, and the watchful care exercised by the government, he characterizes her as מִגְדַּל עֵדֶר, *the tower of the flock.* Some, indeed, think with Jerome, that a place of this name, to which reference is made Gen. xxxv. 21, and which that father says lay about a mile distant from Bethlehem, is intended; but, from its being in apposition with עֹפֶל בַּת־צִיּוֹן, *mound of the daughter of Zion,* a fortified hill or elevation on the eastern part of Mount Zion, and here put for the whole, such interpretation is inadmissible. For עֹפֶל, comp. Is. xxxii. 14; 2 Chron. xxvii. 3, xxxiii. 14; Neh. iii. 26, 27, in which last passage הַמִּגְדָּל, *the tower,* is mentioned along with it, which is doubtless identical with בַּחַן, Is. xxxii. 14. The word is derived from עָפַל, *to swell, become tumid.* Arab. عفل, *tumore laboravit, pinguendo circa perinæum capri,* etc. Τὸν Ὀφλᾶν καλούμενον ὑψηλάν. Joseph. de Bell. Jud. lib. vi. cap. 6, § 3. The LXX., Aquil. Symm., Syr., and Vulg, confound the word with עֲפֵלָה, *thick darkness.* The Targum applies the passage to the Messiah: וְאַתְּ מְשִׁיחָא דְיִשְׂרָאֵל דִּטְמִיר מִן קֳדָם חוֹבֵי כְּנִשְׁתָּא דְצִיּוֹן לָךְ עֲתִידָא לְמֵיתַיָא, "*And thou, O Messiah of Israel, who art hid on account of the sins of the congregation of Zion, to thee the kingdom will come;*" but there is no more foundation for this interpretation, than for that of Jonathan on מִגְדַּל־עֵדֶר, Gen. xxxv. 21: אֲתַר דַּעֲתִיד מִתַּמָּן לְאִתְגְּלָאָה מַלְכָּא מְשִׁיחָא, "the

9 Why, now, dost thou cry aloud?
   Is there no king in thee?
   Have thy counsellors perished?
   That pains should have seized thee
   Like a woman in travail?
10 Be in pain, and bring forth, O daughter of Zion!
   Like a woman in travail;
   For now thou shalt go forth from the city,
   And shalt dwell in the field,
   Thou shalt even go to Babylon;
   There thou shalt be delivered,
   There Jehovah shall redeem thee,
   From the hand of thine enemies.
11 And now many nations are gathered against thee,

place from which King Messiah is to be revealed at the end of the days," whatever use may be made of it in the way of *argumentum an hominem* in reasoning with the Jews. ל in לבּין is a periphrasis of the genitive.

9. עתּה is not here used in its temporal signification, but merely as a particle designed emphatically to draw attention to what follows. Five MSS. and another originally, supported by the LXX. and Targ., read ועתּה, which is the usual form. The prophet plunges at once into the circumstances of consternation in which the inhabitants of Jerusalem would be placed on the approach of the Chaldean army. The questions relative to a king and his council are put ironically, and provoke the answer, "Yes, we have, but they are nothing worth: they cannot protect us, nor contrive any means of escape." יעצך the LXX. treat as a collective: ἡ βουλή σου.

10. גחי, instead of גוחי, for the sake of euphony. Comp. in reference to childbirth, Job xxxviii. 8; Ps. xxii. 10. Having employed the metaphor of a parturient female, the prophet carries it on in this verse, strikingly depicting the condition of anguish and distress which the Jews had to anticipate before they should enjoy deliverance. The Babylonish captivity, and its happy termination, are predicted in express terms. Both were likewise expressly foretold by Isaiah, the contemporary of Micah, chap. xxxix. 7, xliii. 14, xlviii. 20. The repetition of שׁם, *there*, is emphatic. The inhabitants of Jerusalem, when removed from the city, should be located in the open country, till the whole were collected, and then they should all be conveyed to Babylon.

11. The nations here referred to were those which composed the army of Nebuchadnezzar, or which joined that army in its attack upon Jerusalem. The more immediate neighbors of the Jews are no doubt specially intended. Comp. Lam. ii. 16; Ezek. xxxv.; Obad. 12, 13. These defiled Jerusalem when they shed the blood of her citizens and profaned her sacred places. ב חזה is used, like ב ראה, Obad. 12, in an emphatic sense, to denote the malignant delight with which the enemies of the Jews feasted on their calamities. For the use of the feminine singular תחז with the dual masculine, comp. 2 Sam. x. 9; Job xx. 11. Nothing is more common in Arabic than to employ the feminine form of the verb when the agent is anything irrational or inanimate. The singular number is employed as the simpler form of the verb. It may be observed, however, that, instead of עיניו in the plural, four MSS., two of the most ancient editions, the Syr. and Targ., read עינו in the singular. The LXX. have the plural. Both תחזה and תחז are optative in force.

That say: Let her be profaned!
And: Let our eyes look upon Zion.
12 But, as for them, they know not the designs of Jehovah,
Neither do they understand his purpose:
For he shall collect them as sheaves into the threshing-floor.
13 Arise! thresh, O daughter of Zion!
For I will make thy horn iron,
And thy hoofs copper,
And thou shalt beat in pieces many nations;
Thou shalt devote their gains to Jehovah,
And their substance to the Lord of all the earth.
14 Assemble yourselves now, O daughter of troops!
We are besieged!

12. הֵמָּה is a nominative absolute, used for the sake of emphasis. The enemies of the Jews had not the most distant idea, that the object of Jehovah in permitting his people to be so treated was to recover them from idolatry, and thus prepare them for a triumphant restoration. The metaphor taken from the process of threshing out grain is frequently used by the prophets to denote the complete destruction of a people. Comp. Jer. li. 33. For the manner in which this process is carried on, see on Is. xxviii. 27, 28.

13. A continuation of the metaphor. Comp. for a real parallel, Is. xli. 15, 16. There is, however, a very natural instance of mixed metaphor, derived from the destructive power lodged in the horn of the ox, though it is not employed in threshing, which greatly adds to the force of the passage. That קַרְנֵךְ, horn, should here be employed to signify the horny substance forming the hoof of the ox, cannot be admitted. Comp. 1 Kings xxii. 11. The horn was a symbol of power exercised in subduing and punishing enemies. The Orientals give to Alexander the Great the epithet of ذو القرنين, bicornis; and the kings of Macedon were actually in the habit of wearing the horns of a ram in their casques. וְהַחֲרַמְתִּי I take to be the second person feminine, the Yod being a fragment of the old form of the personal pronoun אַתְּ, regularly preserved in the Syriac. Compare, for other instances, עָשִׂית, Ruth iii. 3; הֲלַכְתִּי, Jer. xxxi. 21, though they are pointed with a Sheva, and the Keri directs that they should be read עָשִׂית and הָלָכְתְּ. The LXX., Aquila, Symm., Theodot., the Syr., and Vulg., all have the second person. חֶרֶם, Arab. حَرَمَ, prohibuit; sacrum, quod non est promiscue usus; to make sacred, devote, whether in a good or a bad sense. As conquerors used to consecrate a portion of their spoils to their deities by hanging them up in their temples, so the triumphant Hebrews would employ the riches which they acquired by their victories in beautifying the temple of Jehovah, and supporting his worship. The Maccabean times are specially referred to.

14. I consider גְּדוּד, troop, to be a collective. Jerusalem is called a daughter of troops, on account of the great body of military quartered within her walls, and in the surrounding districts. That it is Jerusalem, and not the enemy, that is addressed, the close coherence of the forms with those of the preceding context sufficiently shows. For the paronomasia in תִּתְגֹּדְדִי בַּת־גְּדוּד, comp. Gen. xlix. 19. The common acceptation of גָּדַד, is to cut or make incisions; but that it also signifies to assemble as troops, see Jer. v. 7. Syr. ܓܘܕܐ, a portion or detachment of

With a rod they have smitten on the cheek
The judge of Israel!

an army. Though at עִיר the enemy is understood, it is better to construe it impersonally, and give it in our language in the passive. In שֵׁבֶט and שֹׁפֵט is another paronomasia. Most understand by the שֹׁפֵט, *judge*, Zedekiah, who was treated contumeliously by the Babylonians; but it seems preferable to refer it to some of the chief rulers of the Jews at the time of the siege of Jerusalem described by the prophet; or the term may be used collectively. The position of Hengstenberg and some others, that it is selected on purpose to mark a period during which no king of the house of David reigned, might be allowed, were it not for the influence of the foregoing שֵׁבֶט, with which it forms the paronomasia. Though the LXX. have rendered the term by φυλὰς, Aq., Symm., and Theod., have κριτήρ. The siege in question Michaelis thinks was that by Sosius, the Roman general, B. C. 37, when Antigonus, the last of the Asmonæan dynasty, was obliged to submit to the superior power. Whether this prince be specifically intended I shall not determine. So much is certain, that he was most contemptuously treated by Sosius; see Josephus, Bell. Jud. lib. i. cap. xviii. 2.

CHAPTER V.

HAVING just adverted to the calamitous circumstances in which the Jews should be placed at the commencement of the reign of Herod, the prophet foretells in a very explicit manner, the birth of the Messiah, which was to take place during the lifetime of that king, 1. A prediction is then introduced respecting the final dealings of God towards the nation previous to that illustrious event, 2, on which the permanent and universal nature of the new dispensation is announced, 3. The subject of the victories of the Jews over the Syro-Grecian armies is again taken up, 4-8; and the chapter concludes with threatenings both against the Jews in the time of Micah, and the enemies by whom they were to be punished, 9-15.

1 AND thou, Bethlehem Ephratha!
Art small to be among the thousands of Judah,

1. Michaelis remarks, "If not even a word was found in Matt. ii. 5, 6, explanatory of our text, I should believe the subject to be Christ, who was born in the reign of Herod. The whole thread of the prophecy in the preceding chapter leads me to him, and the time of his birth." The Messianic application of the prophecy was formally made by the Jewish Sanhedrim, in their official reply to Herod, Matt. ii. 5, 6; and is admitted both by the Rabbinical and the rationalistic interpreters, though, as might be expected, they differ as to the person of the Messiah. The Targum has, מִנָּךְ קֳדָמַי יִפּוֹק מְשִׁיחָא לְמֶהֱוֵי עָבֵיד שׁוּלְטָן עַל יִשְׂרָאֵל דִּי שְׁמֵיהּ אֲמִיר מִלְּקַדְמִין מִיּוֹמֵי עָלְמָא, *"From thee the Messiah shall come forth before me, to exercise dominion over Israel, whose name was announced long ago, from the days of*

Yet from thee shall He come forth to me
To be Ruler in Israel,

old." The position of Theodore of Mopsuesta, Grotius, Dathe, and some others, that Zerubbabel was intended, is now given up by all; and most interpreters of the German school find their notion of an *ideal* Messiah sufficiently convenient in explaining this and other passages, as it relieves them from all investigation in regard to positive historical personality. בֵּית־לֶחֶם, *Bethlehem*, literally, *the House of Bread*. Arab. بيت لحم, *Beit Lahm, the House of Flesh*. It was a small town in the tribe of Judah, built on the slope of a ridge, about six Roman miles to the west by south of Jerusalem, and originally celebrated as the birth-place of David, the first of the line of Jewish kings. אֶפְרָת, *Ephrath*, Gen. xlviii. 7, or, as it is commonly written, with the ה paragogic, אֶפְרָתָה, *Ephratha*, appears from the passage just cited to have been the original name of the place. The word has much the same signification as *Beth-lehem*, being derived from פָּרָה, *to be fruitful;* and no doubt the place received both names from the fertility of the region. Dr. Robinson observes respecting the present aspects of the town: "The many olive and fig orchards, and vineyards round about are marks of industry and thrift; and the adjacent fields, though stony and rough, produce nevertheless good crops of grain." Biblical Researches in Palestine, vol. ii. p. 161. The names occur as parables in the stanzas, Ruth iv. 11:—

עֲשֵׂה־חַיִל בְּאֶפְרָתָה
וּקְרָא־שֵׁם בְּבֵית לָחֶם׃

It was likewise called *Bethlehem Judah*, Judges xvii. 7, xix. 1; Ruth i. 1; Matt. ii. 5, in order, it is thought, to distinguish it from another place of the same name in the tribe of Zabulon, Josh. xix. 15. צָעִיר, as well as אַתָּה, is of the masculine gender, contrary to rule in Hebrew, but in accordance with Arabic usage, in which the names of cities are sometimes put in the masculine. In the present instance, however, the change was doubtless occasioned by בְּיִת, which is of that gender, being strongly prominent to the view of the prophet. Pocock, in the notes to his Porta Mosis, chap. ii., and in his commentary on the passage, labors hard to support the opinion of Tanchum and Abulwalid, that צָעִיר has the two contrary significations of *little* and *great;* but the opinion rests upon nothing beyond the construction which these writers have put upon the term as occurring in Jer. xlviii. 4, and Zech. xiii. 7, which passages, when closely examined, admit of no other signification being attached to the word but that of *little*, of *small note, or esteem*, though it may seem to be supported by the Targumic rendering זְעֵיר טַבְיָא in the former of these passages, and by ποιμένας the reading of the Alexandrian MS. of the LXX., and ܪܥܘܬܐ, that of the Syriac, in the latter. In none of the cognate dialects has the word the signification of greatness or dignity. צָעִיר לִהְיוֹת is literally *little in respect of being, little to exist, or be reckoned*. There is no occasion to resort to the hypothesis that לְ here forms a comparative, and is equivalent to מִן. What the prophet asserts is, that Bethlehem was positively little in point of size or population, to rank with the other subdivisions of the tribe of Judah. Comp. 1 Sam. xxiii. 23. The tribes were subdivided into מִשְׁפָּחוֹת, *families*, or *clans*, the chiliads or thousands of which had heads or princes, to whom, from this circumstance, was given the name of אַלְפֵי יִשְׂרָאֵל, רָאשֵׁי אֲלָפִים, *princes* and *heads of thousands*. It is highly probable that at the time to which the prophecy refers, if not in that of the prophet, the place might not have been able to muster a thousand men. No mention is made of it among the cities of Judah enumerated Josh. xv., though, with many others, it is found in the text of the LXX. Nor does it occur in the list, Neh. xi. 25,

Chap. V.   MICAH.   243

Whose comings forth have been of old,
From the ancient days.

etc. It is spoken of in the New Testament as Κώμη, *a village*, or *hamlet*, John vii. 42. In the present day its inhabitants are rated at eight hundred taxable men. See Dr. Robinson, *ut sup.* Yet, small and inconsiderable as Bethlehem was, it was to have the distinguished honor of giving birth to the Messiah.

" O sola magnarum urbium
Major Bethlem, cui contigit
Ducem salutis cœlitus
Incorporatum gignere."
Prudentius, Hymn. Epiph. 77.

Between the former and the latter half of the verse is a marked antithesis. In this respect, יֵצֵא and מוֹצָאֹתָיו, correspond; the former, designating the future *coming forth* of the Illustrious Ruler here predicted, when he should actually assume human nature; the latter, his ancient *comings forth*, when he created the world, and appeared to Moses and the patriarchs, and revealed to them the Divine will. The idea conveyed by the noun must be identical with that expressed by the verb. Abenezra, Abarbanel, Grotius, Hartmann, Rosenmüller, Gesenius, Hitzig, Maurer, and Ewald, give *origines* as the signification of מוֹצָאֹתָיו, and regard the term as referring to the Davidic extraction of the Messiah. This signification is likewise strenuously maintained by Hengstenberg; but, instead of finding any reference to the ancient family of David, he adopts the opinion that the object of the prophet is to teach the eternal existence of the Messiah. His position, however, is perfectly untenable, since nothing can be more incongruous than the ascription of locality to eternity, which he expressly does in the translation, " his goings forth (in the sense of places of going forth), are the ancient times, the days of eternity, *i. e.* the very ancient times." None of the passages which he alleges proves the local signification; they all describe the act, not the place or time of egress. מִן before קֶדֶם and in מִימֵי עוֹלָם, is used in its temporal acceptation, marking the

terminus a quo. The LXX. ἔξοδοι αὐτοῦ ἀπ' ἀρχῆς ἐξ ἡμερῶν αἰῶνος. Syriac ܘܡܦܩܢܗ ܡܢ ܪܝܫܝܬܐ ܡܢ ܝܘܡܬܐ ܕܥܠܡܐ, "*Whose going forth is from the beginning, from the days of the ages.*" Vulg. "*Et egressus ejus ab initio, a diebus æternitatis.*" The Arab. though unwarrantably free as a version, gives pretty much the true sense:

ومخارجه في اسرايل منذ ايام الدهر, "*Whose goings forth in Israel are from the days of the age.*" It is, however, not unlikely, that the words في اسرايل, have crept into the text from the preceding clause. Though קֶדֶם is used of past duration absolutely in reference to God, Deut. xxxiii. 27, yet it is most frequently employed to denote past, especially *ancient time*, and is synonymous with עוֹלָם, with which it occurs in poetic parallelisms. Comp. the Arab. قدم, *præcessit; tempus antiquum.* Syr. ܩܕܡ, *ante, coram.* In Ps. xliv. 2, יְמֵי קֶדֶם occurs, just as יְמֵי עוֹלָם does in the present verse; and in Ps. lxxvii. 6 we have יָמִים מִקֶּדֶם and שְׁנוֹת עוֹלָמִים corresponding to each other. Comp. also Micah vii. 14, 20; Mal. iii. 4. That the dogma of eternal generation or emanation is taught by our prophet, does not appear; but the actual preëxistence of our Saviour, and his active comings forth, in the most ancient times, for the accomplishment of the Divine purposes, he not obscurely teaches. Thus Piscator: " Verto egressiones, nempe egressiones a Deo Patre ad sanctos Patres Adamum, Noachum, Abrahamum, Isaacum, Jacobum, quibus apparuit seseque familiari sermone patefecit." For the interpretation of Calvin, that the eternal decree respecting the future birth of the Messiah is intended, there is no foundation whatever. The

2 Nevertheless he will give them up
   Till the time when she who is to bear hath brought forth,
   And the rest of his brethren
   Shall return to the sons of Israel.

term מֹשֵׁל, *Ruler*, here employed, is that used by David in his Messianic Ode, 2 Sam. xxiii. 3 : —

מוֹשֵׁל בָּאָדָם צַדִּיק
מוֹשֵׁל יִרְאַת אֱלֹהִים :

Comp. Jer. xxx. 21 : —

וְהָיָה אַדִּירוֹ מִמֶּנּוּ
וּמֹשְׁלוֹ מִקִּרְבּוֹ יֵצֵא
וְהִקְרַבְתִּיו וְנִגַּשׁ אֵלָי
כִּי מִי הוּא־זֶה עָרַב אֶת לִבּוֹ
לָגֶשֶׁת אֵלַי נְאֻם יְהוָה :

Comp. also Is. xi. 1-4. לִי, *to me*, is not without emphasis. The Messiah was to come for the express purpose of carrying into effect the will of his Father in the salvation of men; and though Israel is specially mentioned as the sphere of his rule, it is not to the exclusion of the Gentile world, as ver. 3, and numerous passages in other prophets clearly show.

For the verbal discrepancies between the Hebrew text of Micah, and the quotation Matt. ii. 6, the reader is referred to the commentators on the latter passage. It may suffice to remark here, that the Hebrew words cannot with any propriety be rendered interrogatively, as some have proposed, and that the quotation in question, made by the Sanhedrim, and not by the evangelist, is obviously given from memory, and not with any view to verbal accuracy.

2. Notwithstanding the glorious prospect afforded by the promise of the Messiah, it was not to supersede the state of suffering to which the nation was to be previously reduced on account of its sins. Into that state it was to be brought by the Chaldeans, and was not to be fully restored till about the time of his birth. The return from Babylon was only partial at first; but, encouraged by the prosperity which attended the reestablishment of the theocracy, others who resided in the East were induced to follow, and multitudes returned from Egypt and other parts, before the Christian era. The words יוֹלֵדָה יָלָדָה are susceptible of two interpretations. They may either be referred to the Jewish church, and regarded as descriptive of her deliverance from suffering, set forth under the metaphor of a travailing woman; or, they strictly and literally apply to the mother of the Messiah. The former interpretation is adopted by Lipman, Munster, Vatablus, Grotius, Drusius, Dathe, Justi, and others; the latter by the greater number of expositors—among other moderns, by Secker, Michaelis, Hartmann, Rosenmüller, Hitzig, Maurer, and Ewald. This construction of the passage alone suits the entire connection. It would appear altogether incongruous to introduce a tropical designation of the church, in a verse in which the Jewish people are more than once spoken of in language strictly literal. The birth of the Messiah, in so far as regards its place, and the preëxistence of his person, had been predicted ver. 1 : the prophet, who, as already noticed, was contemporary with Isaiah, and in all probability was acquainted with his celebrated prophecy respecting the עַלְמָה, Is. vii. 14, now further adverts to the interesting fact by a somewhat indefinite, but by no means obscure reference to his virgin mother. This view is further confirmed by the use of the pronominal affix in אֶחָיו, which unquestionably belongs to the Messiah, the immediate antecedent, and not, as a collective, to Israel, as given in the LXX. and Targ. By his "brethren" cannot be meant the Gentile believers, which some interpreters have alleged, referring in proof to Ps. xxii. 22 ; Heb. ii. 11; but his brethren according to the flesh, those who still remained in foreign parts, but who were to be brought back to Judea, in order that they might

CHAP. V.   MICAH.   245

3 And He shall stand, and feed in the strength of Jehovah,
In the majesty of the name of Jehovah his God.
And they shall continue;
For now shall He be great unto the ends of the earth.
4 And This Same shall be the peace.
When the Assyrian shall invade our land,
And tread our palaces,
We will raise against him seven shepherds,
And eight anointed men.
5 And they shall afflict the land of Assyria with the sword,
And the land of Nimrod at the entrances thereof:

be there to receive him, when he should come forth to be ruler in Israel. The preposition עַל conveys here the idea of superaddition. The foreign Jews were to be gathered *in addition* to those who had already been collected. It is thus more expressive than אֶל. That the phrase בְּנֵי יִשְׂרָאֵל, *the children of Israel*, is not here to be taken in its distinctive application to the ten tribes, but denotes the descendants of Jacob generally, may be inferred from the fact, that it is thus appropriated after the Babylonish captivity, the period to which the prophecy refers. It is well known that the Maccabæan coins bear the inscription, שֶׁקֶל יִשְׂרָאֵל, *the Shekel of Israel*. Comp. for this use of the term יִשְׂרָאֵל, ver. 1 of the present chapter.

3. The verb עָמַד signifies not simply *to stand*, but also to *stand firm, to endure, continue*. This latter acceptation is adopted here by many, who think it better suits the character of the predicted king, who is otherwise represented as *sitting* upon his throne, and not standing. But, as the following verb רָעָה, signifies *to feed* a flock, there is the greatest propriety in presenting him to view in the attitude of the good shepherd, who stands, that he may survey the whole of his sheep, and be in readiness to defend them against all attacks. Comp. Is. lxi. 5. The pastoral metaphor is beautifully expressive of royal care and protection. Comp. Iliad i. 263 :

Οἷον Πειρίθοόν τε, Δρύαντά τε, ποιμένα λαῶν,

where the scholiast has, βασιλέα ὄχλων. See for this use of the Hebrew verb רָעָה, 2 Sam. v. 2, vii. 7. The power and glory of the Messiah here predicted are those with which, as Mediator, he is invested. Comp. Is. xi. 2 ; Matt. xxviii. 19 ; Heb. ii. 7-9. Jehovah being called "his God," intimates his subordinate official relation. Comp. John xx. 17. If שֵׁם יְהֹוָה, *the name of Jehovah*, be not here a periphrasis for Jehovah himself, it may be regarded as descriptive of his attributes, or the character in which he hath revealed himself to mankind. The nominative to יָשֵׁבוּ must be the subjects over whom Messiah reigns, understood. These were to consist not of believing Jews only, but likewise of believing Gentiles in the remotest regions of the globe, as it follows in the verse. Comp. for אַפְסֵי אָרֶץ, "the ends of the earth," in reference to the amplitude of the kingdom of Christ, Ps. ii. 8, xxii. 28, lxxii. 8. The verb conveys the idea of security and permanence. Such was to be the character of the new dispensation. It remains to add on this verse, that instead of רָעָה, *to feed*, two MSS. and some printed editions read רָאָה, *to see*, while the LXX. and Arab. exhibit both readings; and that three MSS. and another originally, the Syr., Targ., and Vulg., read וְיָשֻׁבוּ or יָשֻׁבוּ, *they shall return*, or *be converted*, instead of the current reading יָשֵׁבוּ, *they shall remain*. The LXX. have ὑπάρξουσι.

4, 5. The words וְהָיָה זֶה שָׁלוֹם, *And This Same shall be the peace*, are inti-

And there shall be deliverance from the Assyrian,
When he shall invade our land,
And when he shall tread our borders.

mately connected with the preceding words, but have no relation to those which follow, except in so far as the victories there assumed were to pave the way for that state of the Jewish affairs during which the Messiah was to appear in the world. זֹאת, *This, This Same,* is used emphatically, with reference to the Messiah, who had just been spoken of. Comp. for a similar use of the pronoun, Gen. v. 29; Exod. xv. 2. שָׁלוֹם, *peace,* is put, by metonymy, for the author and introducer of reconciliation. Comp. Gen. xlix. 10; Is. ix. 5; Zech. ix. 10; Eph. ii. 14, 17; Col. i. 20. שִׁלֵּם, signifies *to restore things to their former state, to make restitution;* in Hiph. *to restore, or cause to be at peace.* Comp. the Arab. سلم, *redintegrare, sanare.* The substantive is without the article, as frequently in the prophetic writings, when the object is to impart energy to the language, by condensing the mode of expression. If אַשּׁוּר be taken to signify the ancient Assyrian empire, the reference will be to the threatened invasion in the time of the prophet; but this construction ill suits the connection, in which respect is had to the more distant future; and what follows, relative to the resistance of the Jews, does not agree with any successful events in the history of that people during the Assyrian rule. I cannot, therefore, but think, that the term is employed by our prophet to denote the empire of the Seleucidæ, founded by Seleucus, one of the generals of Alexander the Great, by whom he was invested with the government of Babylonia and Media, and who, under the title of King of Syria, subjugated all the countries from the Hellespont to India and the Jaxartes. On the same principle that Darius is called מֶלֶךְ אַשּׁוּר, *the king of Assyria,* Ezra vi. 22, though that empire had long ceased to exist, the title might be applied to Seleucus and his successors. To them,

during the period of their reign, belonged "the land of Assyria," which is also here called "the land of *Nimrod,*" because, according to the proper rendering of Gen. x. 11, that monarch went forth from Babylon into the country of Assyria, where he built Nineveh and other cities there named. According to this interpretation, the prophecy in these two verses relates to the noble and successful opposition which the Maccabees offered to Antiochus Epiphanes, when he marched against Jerusalem, pillaged the temple, and desecrated every object sacred in the estimation of the Jews. By rousing a spirit of patriotic piety in the breasts of their countrymen, they not only recovered their sacred city from the enemy, but, after a series of the most brilliant victories, drove him to the gates of his own fortified cities, and finally succeeded in securing the national independence. It is to this protracted, but triumphant struggle, the reference is made, Dan. xi. 32. The assertion of Hartmann, that אֶרֶץ־בָּבֶל is not Hebrew in its construction, and that, consequently, אַשּׁוּר is to be connected with שָׁלוֹם, is without foundation; for we meet with the very same construction in אִישׁ אוֹ אִשָּׁה כִּי יַפְלִא, Numb. vi. 2. Thus also in Arab. مدينتين اذا اتفقوا علي راي واحد اهلها, "*two cities when their inhabitants are of one accord,*" Locman, Fable I. The numbers *seven* and *eight* appear to be used to denote indefinitely a full and sufficient number, as in Eccles. xi. 2. "Give a portion to seven, and also to eight. Comp. also Job v. 18; Prov. vi. 16, xxx. 15, 18, 21; Amos i. 3, 6, 9, etc. So the Greek τρὶς καὶ τετράκις, and the Latin *ter quaterque.* Were they to be taken literally, there would be no great difficulty in selecting the number from the Maccabæan period; but the com-

CHAP. V.   MICAH.   247

6 And the remnant of Jacob shall be in the midst of many people,
  Like the dew from Jehovah;
  Like the small rain upon herbs,
  Which waiteth not for man,
  And tarrieth not for the sons of man.
7 Yea, the remnant of Jacob shall be among the nations,
  In the midst of many people,
  Like a lion among the beasts of the forest,
  Like a young lion among the flocks of sheep,
  Which, if he pass through, treadeth down and rendeth,
  And there is none to deliver.
8 Thy hand shall be high against thine adversaries,

parison of the above passages shows that such a process would be unwarranted. רֹעִים, *shepherds*, and נְסִיכֵי אָדָם, *princely men*, are synonymous, signifying those who took the lead in opposing the enemy, and who administered the affairs of the Jews at the time. Because נָסַךְ also signifies *to pour out a libation*, Michaelis is inclined to render the phrase נְסִיכֵי אָדָם, *sacrifices of men*, and to interpret it of such as sacrificed their life in defence of their country. Not only, however, is the parallelism opposed to this construction of the meaning, but also the use of נְסִיכִים in other passages. Thus Josh. xiii. 21, נְסִיכֵי סִיחוֹן, *princes* (Comp. Ver. *dukes*) *of Sihon*; and Ezek. xxxii. 30, נְסִיכֵי צָפוֹן, *there are the princes of the north*. The title properly signifies *anointed*, those who had been consecrated to their office by anointing with oil; and thus is equivalent to מְשִׁיחִים. In the present instance it is used tropically, without any reference to the ceremony. Syr. ܘܰܐܢܫܐ. Targ. אֲנָשֵׁי רַבְרְבֵי; Arab. عظماء من الناس, *great men*. רָעָה, *to feel*, being here used in connection with "the sword," must be taken metaphorically, and means to *consume*, *devastate*, or the like. To refer רָעַע to רָצַץ as its root, is altogether inadmissible. The repetition in these two verses possesses peculiar elegance. הֻצַּל is used impersonally.

Instead of גַּבְּנוֹ in the singular, גַּבֵּנוּ in the plural, is the reading of thirty-four MSS., originally four more; the Soncin., Brixian, and Complut. editions; the Soncin. Prophets, and all the ancient versions.

6, 7. The former of these verses depicts the beneficial influence which the remainder of the nation, after its restoration, should exert, by spreading the knowledge of the true God among the nations in the midst of which they were situated; their signal victories against such formidable armies, attracting attention to Him whom they worshipped, and to whom they ascribed their success. During the existence of the new Jewish state, the members of the theocracy had much intercourse with foreigners, multitudes of whom became proselytes to the faith of Jehovah, and were thus prepared to receive the gospel, when preached by the apostles. The idea of number lies both in טַל, *the dew*, and רְבִיבִים, *the rain*; and the sudden raising up of the Jews was to be as entirely a work of Divine providence, and independent of human aid, as the production of the material elements. The seventh verse describes the formidable character of the Jews in reference to the hostile nations by which they were attacked. For the accumulation and the rise in the meaning of the verbs עָבַר וְרָמַס וְטָרַף, comp. Exod. xv. 9: אָרִיק חַרְבִּי אֲשִׂיג אֲחַלֵּק שָׁלָל.

8. Here the prosperous aspect of the prophecy closes. The words are ad-

And all thine enemies shall be cut off.
9 And it shall be in that day, saith Jehovah,
That I will cut off thy horses from the midst of thee;
And I will destroy thy chariots.
10 I will cut off the cities of thy land,
And raze all thy fortresses,
11 I will cut off the sorceries from thy hand,
And thou shalt have no diviners.
12 I will cut off thy graven images and thy statues from the midst of thee,
And thou shalt no more worship the work of thine hands.
13 I will break down thine images of Astarte from the midst of thee,
And destroy thy cities.

dressed optatively to Jehovah, and may be considered as those either of the prophet, or as designed to be adopted by the Jewish church. Comp. Is. xxvi. 11. Her enemies were the enemies of Jehovah.

9–14. The prophet now returns to times nearer his own, and predicts the beneficial moral changes that were to be effected in the condition of his countrymen by the Babylonish conquest and captivity. They had, contrary to the express command of the Lord, Deut. xvii. 16, kept up a formidable body of cavalry, and war-chariots; trusted in their fortified cities; encouraged sorcery, and indulged in abominable idolatry. These were all to be removed, when the Jewish state was broken up; and after God had employed the heathen in punishing his apostate people, they in their turn should be punished for their obstinate adherence to idol worship, notwithstanding the testimony borne against their conduct by the Jews who lived among them. This portion of the chapter is strikingly parallel with Is. xlvii. 6–22. For עָרֵי בְצֻרֶיךָ, see on Is. xlvii. 9; for מִקְסָמִים, comp. קֹסְמִי, Is. iii. 6; and for מַצֵּבוֹתֶיךָ see on Is. xvii. 8. As עָרֶיךָ had already occurred in the acceptation of *cities*, ver. 10, we should scarcely expect it to be again used ver. 13. To remove the difficulty Michaelis compares the word with the Arab. عَرُوّة, *arbor semper virens*; Arnold, with the Arab. غار, *speluncus*; others propose to read עֵצֶיךָ, *woods*, i. e. groves, supposing the initial Yod to have been absorbed by that with which the preceding word terminates; while others would change the word into עֵדֶיךָ, *witnesses*, understanding thereby the statues etc., belonging to idol-worship. There seems, however, to be no absolute necessity for departing from the signification *cities*, only we thereby understand such as were specially appropriated to idolatrous uses, as Jerome suggests. Comp. עִיר בֵּית הַבַּעַל, *the city of the house*, or *temple of Baal*, 2 Kings x. 25, by which is meant a separate part of Samaria, where the temple was situated. This construction is required in order to form a parallelism with אֲשֵׁרֶיךָ, *images of Astarte*, occurring immediately before in the verse. In all the ancient versions the word is rendered by *cities*, except the Targum, in which it is translated *enemies*. Some refer the relative אֲשֶׁר at the end of ver. 14 to גּוֹיִם, and interpret, *unheard of vengeance*, but it is more natural to connect it with גּוֹיִם, *nations*, the immediate antecedent, and to regard the prophet as describing the refusal of the pagans, who had enjoyed opportunities of learning the true religion

6 : And I will execute vengeance in anger and in wrath,
Upon the nations which have not been obedient.

from the Jews, to listen to the instructions which had been tendered to them. Thus the Targ. עַמְמַיָּא דְּלָא קַבִּילוּ אָן‏
אוֹרָיְתָא, "*the peoples that have not received the doctrine of the law.*" LXX. ἐν τοῖς ἔθνεσιν, ἀνθ' ὧν οὐκ εἰσήκουσαν.

Syr. ܚܣܡܬܐ ܐܡܝܢ ܘܠܐ ܫܡܥܘ‎
the peoples who have not hearkened. In the same way Michaelis, Hartmann, Justi, Dathe, Hitzig, Maurer, Ewald.

CHAPTER VI.

It was not sufficient for the prophet to predict the punishments that were to be inflicted on the Jews; he was required to press the subject upon their attention, which he does in a very affecting manner, by calling a public court, in which the inanimate creation is summoned to supply evidence, 1, 2. An appeal is then made by Jehovah to the accused party, respecting his kindness to the nation from the earliest period of its history, 3-5. Convicted of guilt, the people are represented as deeply anxious to obtain, at any cost, reconciliation with God, 6, 7; and are pointed by the prophet to the only source whence it was to be obtained; while, at the same time, they are reminded of the high properties and obligations of true piety, 8. He next demands attention to the threatened judgments, 9; specifies some of the crimes on account of which they were to be brought upon them, 10-12; repeats the threatening, 13; shows the blasting effects of the Divine wrath upon all their undertakings, 14, 15; and traces the evil to its true source—the idolatries of the kingdom of Israel, 16.

1 Hear ye now what Jehovah saith :
Arise! plead in the presence of the mountains,
And let the hills hear thy voice.
2 Hear, O ye mountains! Jehovah's controversy,
And ye rocks, the foundations of the earth ;

1, 2. It is not unusual with the prophets to make appeals respecting the enormity of human guilt to the inanimate parts of creation, as if it were impossible for it not to inspire them with life, and call them forth as intelligent witnesses of what hath taken place in their presence. See Deut. xxxii. 1 ; Is. i. 2 ; Jer. ii. 12, 13. By a similar personification the mountains and durable foundations of the earth are here summoned to appear in the court of heaven. Jehovah, however, instead of bringing forward the charge, abdicates, as it were, his right, and leaves it to the guilty party to state the case. Comp. Is. xliii. 26. In the appeal to the lofty and ever-during mountains, in which the puny affairs of man could excite no prejudice, and which might therefore be regarded as quite impartial judges, there is something inexpressibly sublime. רִיב עִם הָרִים, does not mean, contend *with* the mountains, as if they were the party to be accused, but to carry on the cause in their presence. אֵת is here to be taken in the signification

For Jehovah hath a controversy with his people,
And will contend with Israel.
3 O my people! What have I done to thee?
With what have I wearied thee?
Testify against me.
4 Nay, I brought thee up from the land of Egypt,
And redeemed thee from the house of slaves;
And sent before thee Moses, Aaron and Miriam.
5 O my people! remember now how Balak the king of Moab consulted,
And how Balaam the son of Beor answered him;
[Remember what happened]
From Shittim to Gilgal,
That ye may know the benefits of Jehovah.

of *apud, coram*, and is equivalent to לִפְנֵי, *before*, just as the forms הִתְהַלֵּךְ אֶת־הָאֱלֹהִים, Gen. v. 24, and הִתְהַלֵּךְ אֶת־אָבִיו לִפְנֵי, xlviii. 15, are identical in meaning. אֶת־חַי, or as it is spelt אֶת־חָי in a great many MSS., and in four early editions, standing absolutely, must be taken as a substantive, and not as an adjective qualifying מִיסְדֵי אָרֶץ. Arab. اتن, *stetit, consistit;* اتان, *petra.* واتن, *est omne id, quod durat, et permanet sua in sede.* Schultens, Origg. Hebbr. p. 112. Instead of מוֹסְדֵי אָרֶץ, *the foundations of the earth,* the Arabs call the mountains اوتاد الارض, *the stakes,* or *posts of the earth.*

3, 4. The Israelites are asked, in the kindest and most affecting style, what ground of complaint they had against Jehovah, which could have induced them to act the part they did. Comp. Jer. ii. 5, 31. He had demanded of them nothing that was unreasonable. כִּי at the beginning of ver. 4, is very expressive, and is equivalent to *nay, on the contrary,* or the like. Instead of having done anything to alienate them, God had shown the utmost kindness to them from the beginning: not only rescuing them from Egyptian bondage, but providing them with inspired leaders. Miriam is mentioned, on account of the prominent part she took in celebrating the Divine interposition for their deliverance. She is called הַנְּבִיאָה, *the prophetess,* Exod. xv. 20, because she led the female chorus which rehearsed the inspired song of Moses. The Targ. on Micah adds: לְאַלָּפָא נְשַׁיָּא, *to instruct the women.* Comp. Numb. xi. 2.

5. The kindness of Jehovah to his people was manifested, not only in furnishing them with inspired teachers, but also in counteracting the designs of Balak, who wished to engage the prophetic influence of Balaam against them; for that avaricious prophet was compelled, contrary to the cherished desire of his heart, to pronounce blessings upon them instead of curses. See Numb. xxii. xxiii. xxiv. The words מִן הַשִּׁטִּים עַד הַגִּלְגָּל, *from Shittim to Gilgal,* are not to be constructed with those immediately preceding; for Balaam did not cross over Jordan to Gilgal, but was slain in the land of Midian, as we read Numb. xxxi. 8. Nor are we, with Ewald, to suppose them to be a marginal gloss; but have merely to supply the ellipsis זְכֹר מֶה הָיָה, *what happened,* and repeat זְכֹר, *remember,* from the first clause of the verse. To this effect the Targ. הֲלָא גְּבוּרָן אִתְעֲבִידָא לְכוֹן מִמֵּישַׁר שִׁטִּין עַד בֵּית גִּלְגָּלָא, "*Were not mighty deeds performed for you from the plain of Shittim to the house Gilgal?*" Thus also Mun-

6 With what shall I come before Jehovah?
With what shall I bow to the high God?
Shall I come before him with burnt offerings?
With calves of a year old?
7 Will Jehovah be satisfied with thousands of rams?
With ten thousand rivers of oil?
Shall I give my first-born for my transgression?
The fruit of my body for the sin of my soul?

ster, Vetablus, Grotius, Calvin, Dathe, De Wette, Michaelis, Hartmann, and others, There was a peculiar propriety in specifying these two places. *Shittim* was the name of a valley in the country of Moab, where on account of the impurities committed with the Midianitish women, twenty-four thousand Israelites were destroyed. The evil was so great that it might have caused the Lord to abandon them entirely; but he mercifully spared them as a people, miraculously divided the Jordan to afford them a passage, and gave them actual possession of Canaan, the land promised to their fathers. In proof of this last act of the Divine goodness, *Gilgal* is singled out from other places, because it was there they made their first encampment in the promised land. It was situated between Jericho and the Jordan, but no trace of its site now remains. צִדְקוֹת יְהֹוָה, *the benefits of Jehovah.* Comp. Jud. v. 11; 1 Sam. xii. 7; Ps. xxiv. 7. In this way the phrase is interpreted by Tanchum, Grotius, Drusius, and by most of the moderns. Calvin observes: "Per Justitias intelligit beneficia quemadmodum multis aliis locis; and paraphrases thus: " Ut ipsa experientia tibi demonstret quam verax, quam beneficus, quam misericors semper fuerit Deus erga genus vestrum."

6, 7. The Jews convicted of guilt, are represented as most anxious to propitiate the Divine favor. They could not deny the charges that had been brought against them; nor could they put in any plea of justification. They stood condemned before God and the universe. The language which they employ is not such as the prophet would have taught them, but such as well

accorded with the notions which were prevalent among them, some of which had been learned from their heathen neighbors. How much soever they might formerly have grudged the expense of prescribed offerings, they are now willing to bring the most costly and abundant, rams by thousands, and oil sufficient to fill myriads of rivers; nay, what is more, human victims, and of these the most endeared, their own offspring. In רִבְבוֹת נַחֲלֵי־שָׁמֶן, *myriads of torrents of oil,* is a double hyperbole, quite in the style of the Orientals. For רִבְבוֹת, as thus used, comp. 1 Sam xviii. 7; and for נַחֲלֵי־שָׁמֶן, Job xx. 17. The fact of the presentation of human sacrifices is fully established in the ancient history of all nations. This barbarous custom was especially prevalent among the Phœnicians, and was by them introduced into the north of Africa, where it continued till the proconsulate of Tiberius. According to Porphyry, the book of Sanchoniathon was full of examples of such sacrifices. That they obtained among the idolatrous Israelites is clear from Jer. xix. 5, xxxii. 35, who offered their children to Moloch or Saturn, after the example of their Phœnician neighbors. Eusebius, in his Præpar. Evangel. lib. iv. 16, enters at length into the subject; and adduces a passage from Philo Byblius which has a special bearing upon the present text: Ἔθος ἦν τοῖς παλαιοῖς, ἐν ταῖς μεγάλαις συμφοραῖς τῶν κινδύνων, ἀντὶ τῆς πάντων φθορᾶς ΤΟ ΗΓΑΠΗΜΕΝΟΝ ΤΩΝ ΤΕΚΝΩΝ τοὺς κρατοῦντας ἢ πόλεως ἢ ἔθνους, εἰς σφαγὴν ἐπιδιδόναι, λύτρον τοῖς τιμωροῖς δαίμοσι. "It was customary among the ancients, on calamitous or dangerous emergencies, for the rulers of the city or

8 He hath showed thee, O man! what is good:
And what doth Jehovah require of thee,
But to do justice, and love mercy,
And be diligent in walking with thy God?

the state, to prevent the destruction of all, to offer up the *most dearly beloved of their children*, as a ransom to divine vengeance." אצב is the future in Niphal of the root כפף, *to bend, bow one's self down*. Comp. Ps. lvii. 7, cxlv. 14. Instead of בְּרִבֲבוֹת־שָׁמֶן, *rivers of oil*, the LXX. who have χιμάρων πιόνων, or, as the Alex. MS. reads, ἀρνῶν, have read כְּבָרִים־שָׁמֵן, *fat sheep;* which rendering is followed by the Vulg. and Arab., but is unsupported by any other authority. The translator was evidently misled by an improper view of the parallelism.

8. The questions put in the preceding verses do not involve anything like irony, as Rosenmüller and Maurer imagine, but manifestly argue a deep anxiety about an atonement, and at the same time the grossest ignorance of what was necessary to constitute that atonement. In replying to them, the prophet first of all shows, that the ignorance of the people was culpable. They had been furnished with revelations of the mind of God upon the subject. הִגִּיד לְךָ, *He* (i. e. Jehovah) *hath shown* or *manifested it to thee;* or, the verb may be taken impersonally, and rendered in the passive: *It hath been shown thee*. No MS. supports אַגִּיד, *I will show*, the reading of the Syr., Vulg. and Arab. Had they searched the Divine records they could not have failed to discover, that, whatever prescriptions relative to sacrifices had been delivered to them, they had never been taught to attach to them any moral efficacy, but the contrary. Both reason and revelation combined to invest them with an ulterior reference. What that reference really was, the Apostle plainly teaches us, Heb. x. 1: Σκιὰν γὰρ ἔχων ὁ νόμος τῶν μελλόντων ΑΓΑΘΩΝ:— the שׁוּב־טוֹב of the prophet. Comp. Heb. ix. 23, where the sacrifice of Christ is, by way of eminence and distinction, called κρείττοναι θυσίαι.

Of this, the only intrinsically valuable atonement, the Levitical sacrifices, were ὑποδείγματα, *instructive examples*, or types, which were intended to suggest and foreshadow it; and, connected as they were with the progressive developments, which, from time to time, were made of the sacerdotal character, and the personal oblation of the Great Deliverer promised from the beginning, the worshippers were without excuse if they did not, like Abraham, rejoice in the anticipation of his day. Having referred the inquirer to the revealed method of reconciliation, with a tacit intimation of the importance of availing himself of it, Micah proceeds to describe the conduct which alone could meet with the divine approval. The piety required by Jehovah, he sums up under three heads : strict equity in all our transactions with our fellow men ; a heart set on 'doing them good, according to the claims which they have upon us : and diligent attention to everything belonging to converse with God. Comp. Deut. x. 12, 18. See also, as contrasting a right state of the heart and life with ceremonial services, 1 Sam. xv. 22 ; Is. i. 11-20 ; Jer. vii. 21-23 ; Amos v. 22-24 ; Hos. vi. 6. A still more compendious description of genuine religion is given by our Lord under the threefold division of κρίσις, ἔλεος and πίστις, Matt. xxiii. 23 ; or, as Luke has for the last, τὴν ἀγάπην τοῦ Θεοῦ, chap. xi. 42 ; which shows how completely mistaken Campbell is in referring it to the social virtues, and rendering it *fidelity*. There can be little doubt that Christ had the passage of Micah in his eye. טוֹב, Arab. صنع, *fecit, elaboravit in re aliqua; paravit;* also, *industrius et solers;* Syr. ܚܟܝܡ, *astutus, callidus;* Eth. ኀየለ, *validus, constans*

9   The voice of Jehovah crieth to the city,
    (And he who is wise will regard thy name)
    Hear ye the rod, and Him who hath appointed it.

fuit; to be apt, ready, diligent, to bend the mind to anything; here, to apply it carefully and sedulously to devotional and other spiritual exercises, which are essential to communion with God. Thus the LXX, ἕτοιμον εἶναι; Theod. ἀσφαλίζου: the fifth Greek version, φροντίζειν; the Syr. ܡܚܠܨ, *paratus;* Vulg. *solicitum.* The idea of *humility,* which is that adopted in our common version, seems to have been derived from the Arab. صنع فرسه, *to train* one's horse, *i. e.* by rendering him *submissive* and patient of restraint; hence فرس صنيع, *equus bene exercitatus.* See A. Schultens on Prov. xi. 2. While this grace is an indispensable attribute of true religion, and lies indeed at its very foundation, it is only one of the several important qualities of which it is composed. The term employed by the prophet, comprehends them all. Michaelis renders, *mit gewissenhafter sorgfalt,* "with conscientious solicitude." The comment of Jerome is not unworthy of notice;—"Ita præcipitur ut præparati simus ambulare cum Domino Deo nostro, nulla hora dormire, nullo tempore securi esse debemus, sed semper expectare patremfamilias venientem et diem formidare judicii, et in nocte hujus seculi dicere: ego dormio, et cor meum vigilat." וְתוּשִׁיָּה is the Hiphil Infinitive, used adverbially. Bps. Butler and Lowth, Mr. Peters, and some others, are of opinion that the sixth, seventh, and eighth verses contain a dialogue between Balak and Balaam; but there does not appear to be sufficient ground for it. The connection of these verses with verse fifth is not so close as they suppose.

9. On the ground of the foreseen determination of the Jews, notwithstanding their present professions of repentance, to persevere in a line of conduct diametrically opposite to that required by the Most High, the prophet proceeds to summon their attention to the certainty of the judgments that were to be inflicted. לָעִיר for לָעִיר, *to the city,* i. e. Jerusalem, by way of eminence. As she was preëminent in privilege, so she was also in regard to wickedness and guilt. תּוּשִׁיָּה Gesenius refers to an obsolete root יָשָׁה, which he thinks may probably have meant to *stand, stand out,* and so *to be.* From such a root both this noun, and יֵשׁ, *being, subsistence, substance,* may most naturally be derived. The significations will then be, *that which really is, something solid or substantial, real wisdom, wealth, power, security, deliverance,* or whatever else best agrees with the context. Comp. the Arab. وشى, in the acceptations *juvit restituitque ægrotum medicina; abundavit opibus* vir; وشاء, *opulentia, abundantia opum;* وشى, *largitus est.* The noun is used in parallelisms with חָכְמָה, *wisdom,* עֵצָה, *counsel,* עֶזְרָה, *assistance,* עֹז, *strength,* מָגֵן, *a shield,* etc. The LXX., who render it by ἀληθές, βοήθεια, ἰσχὺς, σωτηρία, ἀσφάλεια, βουλὴ, give in the present text the verb σώσει, as if they had read תּוֹשִׁיעַ, from יָשַׁע; but they may, after all, have attached the same signification to תּוּשִׁיָּה. The Syriac has ܡܠܦܢܘܬܐ, *doctrine;* the Targ. בַּעֲלֵי *teachers.* The construction of the word here will depend upon the reading of the following verb. If, with seven MSS., originally one more, and apparently another, now corrected, and one in the margin, the LXX., Syr., Targ., Vulg., and Arab., we read יִרְאֵי שְׁמֶךָ, *those who fear thy name,* the passage will best be rendered, *there will be safety* or *deliverance,* i. e. for such. In this case we have to supply the substantive verb, and the ellipsis of לְ, *to* or *for.* On the other hand, if we retain the current reading יִרְאֶה

10 Are there still in the house of the wicked treasures of wickedness,
   And the accursed scanty ephah?
11 Can I be innocent with wicked balances,
   And with a bag of deceitful weights?
12 Whose rich men are full of violence,
   And her inhabitants speak falsehood;

יִרְאֶה, *he shall see thy name*, we must, with our own, and other translators, understand אִישׁ before תּוּשִׁיָּה, and take the noun in the signification *solid*, or *sound wisdom*. That אִישׁ is frequently to be thus understood abstract nouns, comp. Ps. cix. 4, אֲנִי תְפִלָּה, *I am prayer*, for אֲנִי אִישׁ תְּפִלָּה, *I am a man of prayer*; Prov. xiii. 6, חַטָּאת, *sin*, for אִישׁ חַטָּאת, *the man of sin*, i. e. *the sinner*; xix. 15, עַצְלָה, *indolence*, for אִישׁ עָצֵל, *the man of indolence*, etc. What greatly favors the reading יִרְאֶה שְׁמֶךָ is its occurring only in this place, whereas יִרְאֶה שֵׁם, and other forms of יָרֵא with שֵׁם, are of frequent occurrence. It was quite natural for copyists and punctators to substitute the former for the latter, but not the latter for the former. As to the ancient versions, the LXX. may, as frequently, have translated from hearing, and thus have mistaken the pronunciation of יִרְאֶה for that of יִרְאֵי, which it so nearly resembled. The common reading best suits the connection. Before announcing his message, the prophet parenthetically declares, that, whatever might be the treatment it would receive from the bulk of the people, the truly wise would regard it as God's message, and having special respect to his revealed character as thereby disclosed, would find in it security and consolation in the approaching calamities. The *name* of the Lord is frequently used to express the sum total of the Divine attributes, and often stands for God himself. רָאָה, signifies not merely *to see*, but to *recognize practically, to experience*. 1 Sam. xxiv. 12; Ps. xxxiv. 13, lxxxix. 49; Lam. iii. 1. Contrasted with רָאָה שֵׁם, see Is. xxvi. 10; מִי רָאָה בְּגֵאוּת יְהוָֹה.

מַטֶּה, the LXX., Syr., Vulg., and among the moderns, Newcome and Ewald, take to signify *tribe*, or collectively *tribes*, and render in the vocative. The Targ. adopts a metaphorical signification, corresponding to that which attaches to שֵׁבֶט — rendering, מַלְכָּא וְשִׁלְטוֹנָא, *O King and Prince!* The acceptation *rod*, as emblematical of punishment, is best suited to the connection. Comp. Is. ix. 3, x. 5, 24. מַטֶּה is also variously translated and explained: some deriving it from the root עָדָה, *to adorn*; some from עוּד, *to testify*; some adopt the signification of the Arab. وَعَدَ, *minatus fuit*; while

עֵדָה, *congregation*. There is no necessity for departing from the ordinary signification of יָעַד, *to fix, appoint*. The only real difficulty lies in the feminine suffix ה, which does not grammatically agree with מַטֶּה; but even this may be removed by taking the suffix as a neuter, or as referring to רָעָה, *the calamity*, understood. Comp. Jer. ix. 11. Ewald, *höre Gemeine und wer sie bestellt!* "let the community hear, and he that appoints it," understanding thereby the king as principal ruler. Hitzig and Maurer, as in our common version, both make Jehovah the nominative to the verb. Comp. Jer. xlvii. 7.

10—12. Several crimes are here specified as a sample of those which abounded, and on account of which the Divine judgments were to be brought upon the land. For עוֹד at the beginning of a sentence, comp. Gen. xix. 12. Forty-nine MSS., thirteen more originally, and perhaps one other, with one in the margin, read הַאִשׁ *the man*, instead of הַאִשׁ; and this is also the reading of the Son-

Their tongue in their mouth is deceitful.
13 I will surely smite thee incurably,
Rendering thee desolate on account of thy sins.
14 Thou mayest eat, but thou shalt not be satisfied,
For thou shalt be inwardly depressed ;
Thou mayest remove, but thou shalt not rescue,
Or what thou rescuest I will give to the sword.
15 Thou mayest sow, but thou shalt not reap ;

cin., the Brixian, and five other printed editions, and has the approval of Jarchi, Abenezra, and Abarbanel, but it affords no suitable sense ; and with הָאֵשׁ in Kennicott's MS. 201, must be regarded as the result of interpretation. Owing to the same cause, numerous MSS. and editions have הָאֵשׁ. The LXX., Syr., and Vulg., have read הָאֵשׁ, *the fire*; but there cannot be any doubt, that it is only another form of הֵישׁ, there being merely an omission of the *Yod*, as there clearly is, 2 Sam. xiv. 19 ; and the *Aleph* corresponds to the same letter in the cognate forms : Chald. אִית, Syr. ܐܝܬ, Arab. أَيْسَ, *est, exsistit*. The ellipsis of בְּ before בְּיִת is not unfrequent. The Hebrews were much given to the falsification of their weights and measures, though such conduct was repeatedly prohibited by the law, Lev. xix. 35, 36 ; Deut. xxv. 13–16 ; and elsewhere severely condemned in their sacred writings. See Prov. xi. 1, xx. 10 ; and for the practice, comp. Ezek. xlv. 9, 10 ; Hos. xii. 8 ; Amos viii. 5. וְזַעֲמָהּ, *accursed*, from זָעַם, *to be angry, indignant*. This participial form presents the object as suffering the effects of anger, or as marked with the Divine displeasure. רָשָׁע, ver. 11, the LXX., Syr., and Targ., have read in the third person יְדַבֵּר, though the two last render it in the plural. As the MSS. show no variation, the present reading must be retained ; but as this verb is never used transitively in Kal, we cannot refer the nominative to God, and interpret it of his inquiring whether he could treat the persons in question as innocent, but must regard the prophet as putting the ques-

tion, for the sake of effect, into the mouth of one of themselves, and making him ask, how he could possibly lay claim to the character, while he had none but instruments of fraud in his possession ? the antecedent to אֲשֶׁר, *whose*, ver. 12, is עִיר, *city*, ver. 9.

13. In this, and the following verses, severe judgments are threatened against the people on account of their iniquitous practices. The LXX., Syr., Vulg., and Arab., render הֶחֱלֵיתִי, *I have begun*, or, *I will begin*, as if it were the Hiphil of חָלַל, but it is that of חָלָה, *to be in pain, sick*, etc. As here used with the infinitive of נָכָה, *to smite, inflict* punishment, it gives intensity to the threatening, and expresses the incurable nature of the punishment.

14. יֶשְׁחֲךָ, is not to be referred, with Simonis and Gesenius, to the Arab. وحش, *fame exinanitus fuit*, but to وشخ, *sequior, et imbecillis, infirmus;* and was most likely intended to express what we find in the Syr. ܡܟܬܫܐ, "*the diarrhœa* shall be within thee." The LXX. taking תַּסֵּג for יֶשְׁחֲךָ, renders, καὶ σκοτάσει ἐν σοι. תַּסֵּג is the apocopated Hiphil of נָסַג, *to remove*, and expresses the attempt to save goods by removing them out of the way of the enemy. All the ancient versions have adopted the signification of הִשִּׂיג with שׂ, *to seize, lay hold on*, but that conjugation of נָסַג, has also the signification, *to remove* anything. See Job xxiv 2.

15. תִּדְרֹךְ זַיִת. Oil was expressed from the olive, by stamping or treading it out with the foot, in the same way as

Thou mayest tread the olive, but thou shalt not pour out the oil;
And the grape of the new wine, but the wine thou shalt not drink;
16 The statutes of Omri are strictly kept,
And all the work of the house of Ahab,
And ye walk in their counsels;
That I may make thee desolate,
And the inhabitants thereof an object of hissing;
Therefore ye shall bear the reproach of my people.

grapes were trodden. Hence the name גַּת, Gethsemane, or the *oil-press*, Matt. xxvi. 36. Oil is indispensable to oriental comfort, being used for anointing the body, and perfuming the garments. It is also a very common ingredient in food.

16. Hartmann stumbles at the introduction of this verse; but it is quite in the manner of the prophet, to recur to the wicked character of his people. יִתְהַלֵּךְ is best rendered impersonally, though it refers to עַם, *people*, understood. Hithpael is here intensive of Piel. Omri is specially mentioned, because he was the founder of Samaria and the wicked house of Ahab, and a supporter of the superstitions of Jeroboam, 1 Kings xvi.

16–28. לְמַעַן, *in order that*. The Hebrews did not, indeed, commit the wickedness described with the intention of bringing upon themselves divine punishment; but the punishment was as certainly connected with the sin, in the purpose of God, as if its infliction had been the end at which they aimed. הֶרְפַּת עַמִּי תִשָּׂאוּ, *ye shall bear the reproach of my people*, i. e. your own reproach, that which you have deserved; only the meaning is so expressed, in order to derive a high aggravation of their guilt from the relation in which they stood to Jehovah. The LXX. have λαῶν, which intimates that they either read עַמִּים, or עַמָּי, as a defective masculine plural.

CHAPTER VII.

BEFORE concluding, the prophet once more reverts to the wickedness of his people, which he depicts with the darkest colors, 1–6. He then represents them in their state of captivity, brought to repentance, and confidently expecting the Divine interposition, which would be rendered the more conspicuous by the complete destruction of their enemies, 7–10. The restoration of Jerusalem, and the conversion of the hostile nations, are next predicted, 11, 12; while the previous desolation of Judea is traced to the sins of the inhabitants, 13. Turning to Jehovah, he prays for the undisturbed and prosperous condition of the restored nation, 14; to which a gracious response is given, 15. The overthrow of the nations hostile to the Jews, and their reverence for Jehovah, are then pointed out, 16, 17; and the prophecy closes with a sublime and exulting appeal to his gracious character, 18, and an assurance that the covenant people should experience the full accomplishment of the sacred engagements into which he had entered with their progenitors, 19, 20.

1 Alas for me!
For I am as when they gather the summer fruit.
As when the vintage is gleaned:
There is no cluster to eat,
No early fig which my soul desireth.
2 The pious hath perished from the land.
And there is none upright among men;
They all lie in wait for blood;
They hunt each other into the net.
3 For evil their hands are well prepared;
The prince asketh,

1. In no part of his prophecy does Micah so fearfully describe the universal corruption of manners which prevailed among the Jews as in the first six verses of this chapter. The picture is peculiarly applicable to their character in the wicked reign of Ahaz, during which the prophet flourished, and was awfully anticipative of that which they again exhibited during the reigns immediately preceding the captivity. The preposition כְּ in כְּאָסְפֵּי־קַיִץ כְּעֹלְלֹת בָּצִיר, denoting time as well as comparison, the two nouns in construction must be rendered as if they were verbs, though a literal translation would be, *the gatherings of the summer fruit*, and *the gleanings of the vintage*. For בְּכוּרָה, *the early fig*, see on Is. xxviii. 4. The prophet compares the strong desire which he felt to meet with a single pious man, to that eagerness with which the traveller looks in vain for one of those delicious figs after the summer has advanced.

2. Comp. Ps. xii. 1, xiv. 2; Is. lvii. 1. חָרֶם, rendered in most of the versions *destruction*, signifies also a *net*, which is so called from its *enclosing* or *shutting up* whatever it catches. Occurring, as it here does, in connection with the verb צוּד, *to hunt*, it is preferable to take it in this acceptation. The Orientals employed the net for hunting, as well as for fishing. The word is here in the accusative case.

3. This verse is very differently rendered by translators. The version of it which I have given appears to express as literally as possible the ideas, which,

it is generally admitted, the prophet intended to convey. הֵיטִיב is frequently used to express the doing of anything *well, skilfully, aptly*, and the like. Here it is intransitive. Ewald, with Michaelis, Vogel and Döderlein, mistakes the meaning of the clause altogether, when he explains it of endeavoring by bribery to prevail upon the magistrates to pronounce that to be good which in itself is evil. שָׁאַל, which he is obliged to convert into שֹׁאֵל, a Pual form, of which no example occurs in the Hebrew language, can only refer to the avaricious passion of the ruler. It it, therefore, the wickedness of their governors and judges, and not that of the people themselves, which the latter clauses of the verse describe. After שֹׁאֵל supply שֹׁחַד; and after שֹׁפֵט, שֹׁפֵט. The substantive הַוָּה, like the Arab. هَوَى, *desideravit, voluit*, has here the signification, *wish, desire, will*. See Schultens on Prov. x. 3; and the Koran ii. 87:

افكلما جاءكم رسول بما لا تهوى انفسكم, *" and whenever a messenger cometh to you with that which your souls desire not."* Comp. Ps. lii. 9; Prov. xi. 6; and for the cognate אָוַת נֶפֶשׁ, Deut. xii. 15, 20. עָבַת, signifies *to intertwine, bind together*, as the branches of trees, ropes, etc.; here, metaphorically, *to effect by united effort.* Comp. the Arab. عَبَسَ, *miscuit commiscuit*, Syr. ܚܠܛ, *concordavit.*

And the judge also, for a reward;
And the great man giveth utterance to the desire of his soul;
They combine to act perversely.
4 The best of them is like a prickly thorn;
The most upright is worse than a thorn hedge;
The day of thy watchmen, thy visitation cometh;
Now shall be their perplexity.
5 Place no faith in a companion;
Trust not a familiar friend;
From her that lieth in thy bosom
Guard the doors of thy mouth.
6 For the son despiseth his father;
The daughter riseth up against her mother;
The daughter-in-law against her mother-in-law:
A man's enemies are the members of his own family.

Dathe: *conjunctis viribus exequuntur.* The princes, judges, and great men, conspired to set aside all law and right in their treatment of the poor of the land. The suffix ה is to be taken as a neuter, and refers to the injustice practised by the rulers. Thus Calvin: "Deinde complicant ipsam pravitatem: hoc est hinc fit ut grassetur furiosa crudelitas, quoniam conspirant inter se gubernatores et qui volunt sibi acquirere peccandi licentiam: quasi contexerent inter se funes, confirmant hoc modo pravitatem."

4. Both טוב, *good*, and ישר, *upright*, are here used superlatively. Comp. for this use, Gen. xlv. 23; Is. i. 19; Exod. xv. 4. It frequently occurs in Arabic. חדק is now allowed to designate a species of *thorn*, and not a brier. As the מ now stands before מסוכה, it must be taken as an emphatic comparative, which derives its force, not from any adjective expressed, but from the noun to which it is prefixed, as in Ps. lxii. 10; Is. xli. 24; or it may have originally belonged as a suffix to the preceding noun ישר, in which case טובם and ישרם must have corresponded to each other, leaving an ellipsis of the כ which had just been used in כחדק. By "the day of thy watchmen," the period of calamity predicted by the prophets is meant. With this, the following פקדתך, *visitation*, is explicatively parallel. For יום מבוכה, *a day of perplexity*, see on Is. xxii. 5. The reference in ם is not to the watchmen, improperly interpreted by some of false prophets; nor is it to be confined to the persons of rank and office described ver. 3; but to the people generally.

5, 6. אלוף, Arab. الـيف, *familiaris socius*, from الـف, *conjunxit, sociavit,* etc., *a familiar*, and, by implication, a confidential, *friend*. מרעך, LXX. ἀτιμάζει. Comp. Deut. xxxii. 15. The root נבל, primarily signifies *to wither, fall off* as leaves, and tropically *to act wickedly, irreligiously,* as one that has fallen off from God. Comp. נבל, Ps. xiv. 1. נבלה, *an atrocious deed,* Gen. xxxiv. 7; Jud. xix. 23, 24. The state of things here described is that of the most wretched perfidiousness, anarchy, and confusion, in which the most intimate could have no confidence in each other, and the closest ties of relationship were violated and contemned. Comp. Jer. ix. 2–6. —ἀλλοτρίους ἀλλήλων εἶναι πάντας τοὺς μὴ σπουδαίους, καὶ γονεῖς τέκνων, καὶ ἀδελφοὺς ἀδελφῶν, οἰκείους οἰκείων. Diog. Laert. vii. 32. In language strikingly similar, Ovid describes the iron age:

7 But I will look for Jehovah;
I will wait for the God of my salvation;
My God will hear me.
8 Rejoice not over me, O mine enemy!
Though I have fallen, I shall rise again;
Though I sit in darkness, Jehovah is my light.
9 I will bear the indignation of Jehovah,
Because I have sinned against him;
Till he plead my cause, and give effect to my sentence;
He will bring me forth to the light;
I shall behold his righteousness.
10 Mine enemy also shall see it,
And shame shall cover her.
She that said to me, Where is Jehovah thy God?
Mine eyes shall behold her;

" Vivitur ex rapto; non hospes ab hospite tutus,
Non soror a genero; fratrum quoque gratia rara est.
Imminet exitio vir conjugis, illa mariti;
Lurida terribiles miscent aconita novercæ,
Filius ante diem patrios inquirit in annos."

Metamorph. i. 144.

Our Saviour appropriates the words to the treacherous and cruel treatment which he taught his disciples to expect from their nearest relatives, Matt. x. 35, 36; Luke xii. 53.

7. Having described the wickedness of the Jews, the prophet abruptly changes the scene, and introduces them to view in that state of captivity in Babylon in which it was to issue. There, at a distance from the land of their fathers, they are brought to repentance, and the exercise of true piety; and seeking again to their covenant God, they express the fullest confidence that he would in due time deliver them from banishment. צָפָה, here used in Piel, signifies to *look out* for an answer to prayer, divine aid, etc. Comp. Ps. v. 4.

8, 9. Who the enemy intended by the prophet is, cannot be positively decided. Some interpreters think Babylon; others, Edom. For the former, see Jer. l. 11; for the latter, Obad. 12; for both, Ps. cxxxvii. 7, 8. בַּת־בָּבֶל, *daughter of Babylon*, or בַּת־אֱדוֹם, *daughter of Edom*, for Babylon and Edom themselves, is understood in the feminine participle אֹיַבְתִּי, *mine enemy*. For the idiom, see on Is. i. 8. The Jews understand Rome as professing Christianity to be meant by the enemy. See Pococke on verses 9th and 10th. "Light" and "darkness" are used, as frequently, for prosperity and adversity. The 9th verse contains a beautiful specimen of submissiveness and patient endurance of suffering, from a humbling conviction of the demerit of sin; accompanied by the firm persuasion, that when the chastisement had answered its end, Jehovah would graciously afford deliverance. צְדָקָה, *righteousness*, is here to be understood with reference to the *kindness* or *favor* which God was to show to his people, in strict accordance with the tenor of his promises, rather than to the punishment of their enemies.

10. The deliverance of the Jews was to be the occasion of the destruction of their foes, who, because the former had no visible object of worship, and had been delivered into their power, tauntingly asked: אַיּוֹ יְהוָה אֱלֹהָיִךְ, *where is Jehovah thy God?* The feminine suffix refers to בַּת־צִיּוֹן, *daughter of Zion*, understood.

She shall now be trodden upon as the mire of the streets.
11 In the day when thy walls shall be rebuilt,
   In that day the decree shall be extended;
12 In that day they shall come to thee
   From Assyria to Egypt;
   Even from Egypt to the river,
   From sea to sea, and from mountain to mountain.

11, 12. Micah resumes the language of prophecy, and, addressing Jerusalem, announces her restoration, and the way that would be paved for the conversion of the surrounding hostile nations to the true religion. Such appears to me to be the meaning of these verses, which have been very variously interpreted. חֹק, *statute, decree, order, appointment,* LXX. νόμιμα, Symm. *ἐπιταγή*, Theod. *πρόσταγμα,* some refer to the tyrannical enactments of the Babylonians; some to the order of Artaxerxes, Ezra iv. 21; some to the punishment decreed upon the enemies of the Jews; some to the idolatrous statutes, with which the Jews complied; some to the boundary of the Holy Land; and some to the preaching of the gospel among all nations, of which last interpretation Calvin says: "Sed locus hic non patitus se ita violenter torqueri." Secker, Newcome, Vogel, Döderlein, and others, join חֹק to יִרְחַק, and form a reduplicate verb רָחַק־חֹק, of the whole; with whom, as to meaning, Gesenius agrees, who rejects חֹק altogether, and renders, *dies ille procul abest,* Thesaur. p. 1284. What would seem to determine the meaning of the term, as here used, is the light thrown upon רָחַק, *to be distant, remove to a distance,* etc., by the geographical specifications contained in verse 12th. The subject of both verses is sufficiently proved to be identical, by the repetition of הוּא יוֹם, *that day,* which indisputably is the יוֹם, *day,* spoken of at the beginning of verse 11th. Whatever the decree or command was, the effect of its promulgation was to be the coming of foreigners from different regions to the Jewish people, reassembling at Jerusalem, יָבוֹא עָדֶיךָ. The most natural construction is, that the decree of God respecting the political changes that were to take place, was not to be confined to Babylon, but was to be extended to all the countries round about Judea, in consequence of which great numbers would become proselytes to the Jewish faith. There is an ellipsis of the preposition בְּ, *in,* before יוֹם, *day,* in all the three instances in which it here occurs. וְ before עָדֶיךָ is not pleonastic, but is used, as in several other instances, after words which imply condition or time. See Exod. xvi. 6; 1 Sam. xxv. 27. יָבוֹא is used impersonally: "*one, they* shall come;" it is rendered in the plural in the LXX., Targ., and Arab., and one of Kennicott's MSS. reads יָבֹאוּ. That עָדֶיךָ has originally been עָדַיִךְ, the parallelism, compared with other instances of its occurrence, sufficiently shows. The change of ד into ר, and *vice versâ,* by transcribers, owing to their great resemblance to each other, is very common. For example in רְעֻאֵל and דְּעֻאֵל, 1 Chron. i. 6; דּוֹדָנִים and רוֹדָנִים, ver. 7; זְרֻדִים and זְרֻדִים, Ps. liv. 5; מַדְוֶה and מַרְוֶה, lxxxi. 7; יְעוּר and יָרוּץ, Prov. x. 32; and especially as corresponding to the present case, עָדֶיךָ and עָדַיִךְ, Ps. cxxxix. 20. The latter reading is found in fifteen MSS., has been originally in eleven more, and is in one printed edition. No objection can be taken from the preposition assuming the poetic form עָדֵי, while in the following sentence we have עַד; the same variety appears in אֶרֶץ and אָרֶץ, 1 Sam. xi. 7. It is also worthy of notice that the LXX. have read עָרֶיךָ at the beginning of the verse, as if it had been עָרַיִךְ, having rendered it *αἱ πόλεις σου.* By מָצוֹר, I understand *Egypt,* and not *fortification.* Comp. 2 Kings xix. 24, Is. xix. 6, on which see my note.

13 Nevertheless the land shall be desolate
On account of her inhabitants,
Because of the fruit of their doings.
14 Feed thy people with thy crook,
The flock of thine heritage;
That dwell alone in the wood, in the midst of Carmel;
Let them feed in Bashan and Gilead, as in ancient days.
15 As in the days of thy coming forth from Egypt,

Upon this construction, Assyria and Egypt are contrasted, just as they are Is. xix. 23, where the same subject is treated of in almost the same language. הָיְאֹר, the *river*, κατ' ἐξοχήν, *i. e.* the Euphrates, corresponding in the parallelism to אַשּׁוּר, *Assyria.* The Syr. and Targ. have mistaken צוּר in מִצּוּר, for *Tyre*; as the latter has מִן, for *Armenia.* The concluding words of the verse, יְרָם מַיִם וְהַר הָהָר, stand irregularly for וּמֵהַר עַד־הָר וּמִיָּם. It does not appear that any specific mountains are intended; the prophet describes in general terms the natural boundaries of the countries from which the persons spoken of were to come. For a prophetical illustration of these verses, see on Is. xix. 23-25.

13. The conjunctive וְ in וְהָיְתָה is used antithetically to introduce a sentence predictive of what should take place previous to the arrival of the events mentioned in the verses immediately preceding. It has the force of *but yet, nevertheless,* or the like. However bright the prospects which opened upon the Jews in futurity, they were not to forget the punishment that was to intervene, but ought to repent of their sins, to which it was to be traced as its cause. Some interpret הָאָרֶץ, *the land,* of Babylonia; but this construction seems less apt.

14. In the believing anticipation of the fulfilment of the Divine promises made to the covenant people, Micah addresses a prayer to Jehovah, which, though brief, is distinguished for the poetical elevation of its style, and the appropriateness of its petition. Like many other prayers in the Old Testament, it is prophetic in its aspect. The Jewish people are frequently spoken of under the metaphor of a flock, and Jehovah as their shepherd. See Ps. lxxx. 1. xcv. 7, c. 3. They are also often represented as his special heritage, Deut. iv. 20, vii. 6, xxxii. 9. Some understand לְבָדָד שֹׁכְנִי, *dwelling alone* or *solitarily,* as descriptive of the condition of the Jews in captivity, and יַעַר, *forest,* of the dangers and annoyances to which they were exposed while in that state. That it rather refers to the security and prosperity of their restored condition may fairly be concluded from the meaning of similar language in other passages. Thus, in the celebrated prophecy of Balaam, Num. xxiii. 9, which, in all probability, Micah had in view, we read, הֶן־עָם לְבָדָד יִשְׁכֹּן וּבַגּוֹיִם לֹא יִתְחַשָּׁב; *Behold! the people shall dwell alone, and shall not be reckoned among the nations.* Comp. Deut. xxxiii. 28; Jer. xlix. 31; and for יַעַר, as used figuratively for a place of safety and cool repose, see Ezek. xxxiv. 25. The meaning of the prophet is, that on being brought back to their own land, they should no longer be mixed with, and exposed to enemies, but live by themselves in a state of undisturbed tranquillity. For instances of the paragogic Yod affixed to participles, see Gen. xlix. 11; Deut. xxxiii. 16; Obad. 3; Zech. xi. 17. That the Carmel here mentioned must be the celebrated mountain on the coast of the Mediterranean, see on Amos i. 2. The regions of *Bashan* and *Gilead,* on the east of the Jordan, were likewise celebrated for their rich pasturage, and were, on this account, chosen by the tribes of Reuben and Gad, and the half tribe of Manasseh, Numb. xxxii.; Deut. iii. 12-17. Comp. as strictly parallel, Jer. l. 19.

15. The answer of Jehovah to the prophet's prayer, assuring the nation,

I will show them marvellous things.

16 The nations shall see it, and be ashamed of all their power;
They shall lay their hands upon their mouth;
Their ears shall become deaf.

17 They shall lick dust like the serpent;
Like reptiles of the earth they shall tremble from their hiding places;
They shall turn with fear towards Jehovah;
They shall be afraid of thee.

18 Who is a God like thee,
Pardoning iniquity, and passing by transgression,
In regard to the remnant of his heritage?
He retaineth not his anger for ever,
Because he delighteth in mercy.
He will again have compassion upon us,

that the same Almighty power which had interposed in so remarkable a manner for their deliverance from Egypt, would again wonderfully appear on their behalf. Comp. Jer. xvi. 14, 15. Such changes of person as in ךְ, *thy*, and מ, *him*, are common. The reference in both is to the people of the Jews.

16. The גְּבוּרָתָם, *power*, spoken of, is that of the hostile nations, of which they were so proud, and which they regarded as invincible, and not that of the Jews when restored, as Junius and Tremellius, Tarnovius, Stokes, and some others, have imagined. The latter half of the verse most graphically describes the silence, astonishment, and utter consternation, with which they should be seized. Com. Jud. xviii. 19; Job xxi. 5; Ps. cvii. 42; Is. lii. 15.

17. An equally graphic description of the state of degradation and terror to which the enemies were to be reduced. Comp. Ps. lxxii. 9; Is. xlix. 23, lxv. 25. For זֹחֲלֵי, *crawlers*, or *reptiles*, comp. Deut. xxxii. 24. The distinctive use of אֶל, *to* and מִן, *from* or *of*, as here used, shows that there is not a change of person in יִרְאוּךָ, and that the affix ךָ refers, not to Jehovah, but to the people of the Jews. The fear ultimately produced in the minds of their enemies was to be a religious fear or veneration which should attract them

towards Jehovah as its object. Comp. for this construction of פָּחַד אֶל, *to exercise reverential regard towards* God, Hos. iii. 5. Combined with the circumstances under which the nations were to acknowledge the supremacy of Jehovah, was their standing in awe of the political power of the Jews. See on Is. xix. 17.

18. Impelled by strong feelings of gratitude at the anticipated deliverance of his people, the prophet breaks out into a strain of the sublimest praise and admiration, and gives a description of the gracious character of God, unrivalled by any contained in the Scriptures. The phrase עֹבֵר עַל־פֶּשַׁע, *passing by transgression*, is a metaphor, taken from the conduct of a traveller who passes on without noticing an object to which he does not wish to give his attention. The idea which it communicates is not, that God is unobservant of sin, or that it is regarded by him as a matter of little or no importance, but that he does not mark it in particular cases with a view to punishment; that he does not punish, but forgive. Comp. Prov. xix. 11, Amos vii. 8, in which latter passage the verb alone is used. The opposite is expressed by שָׁמַר עָוֹן, *to watch iniquity*, Ps. cxxx. 3, *i. e.* to keep it in view in order to punish it. שְׁאֵרִית, *remnant*, does not necessarily imply a small or inconsiderable number,

Chap. VII. MICAH. 263

19 He will subdue our iniquities;
Yea, thou wilt cast all their sins into the depths of the sea.
20 Thou wilt grant the truth to Jacob,
The kindness to Abraham,
Which thou didst sware to our fathers
From the days of old.

but merely conveys the general notion of a surviving body of men: here it means those of the Jewish nation who should be alive at the termination of the captivity. חָפֵץ, *to delight*, according to the Arab. حفض, *flexit, inflexit*, lignum, *projecit*, properly expresses the *bent* or *propension* of the mind, or what we commonly call its *inclination* towards an object; hence *desire, affection, delight*. The combined force of חָפֵץ חֶסֶד, *bent on kindness*, is inimitable, the primary idea of חֶסֶד being that of *eager desire* or *love* towards an object. It is the term which is so often rendered *loving-kindness* in our common version.

19. This verse may be regarded as containing a beautiful epiphonema, in which the people of the Jews exultingly avow their full confidence in the forgiving mercy and subduing power of their God. שׁוּב, *to turn*, in יָשׁוּב יְרַחֲמֵנוּ, is, as usual before another verb, employed adverbially to signify *again*. God had often pitied and delivered his people. It is here intimated that his compassion was not exhausted, but should be exercised towards them anew. All the meaning found by Rosenmüller, Gesenius and Maurer, in יִכְבֹּשׁ עֲוֹנֹתֵינוּ, is that of disregarding or not avenging, but there is no ground for rejecting the radical idea of *trampling under foot as enemies*. Sin must ever be regarded as hostile to man. It is not only contrary to his interests, but it powerfully opposes and combats the moral principles of his nature, and the higher principles implanted by grace; and but for the counteracting energy of divine influence, must prove victorious. Without the subjugation of evil propensities, pardon would not be a blessing. If the idolatrous and rebellious disposition of the Jews had not been subdued during their stay in Babylon, they would not have been restored. The total and irrevocable forgiveness of sins is forcibly expressed by casting them into the depths of the sea. What is deposited there is completely hid from the view, and cannot in any way affect us. Instead of חַטֹּאתָם, *their* sins, five MSS. read חַטֹּאתֵינוּ, *our* sins, which is the reading of the LXX., Syr., Vulg., and Arab. It may, however, only be a correction; the change of person we have frequently had occasion to notice.

20. The return from captivity, while it furnished a striking specimen of the covenanted fidelity and kindness of Jehovah, was only preliminary to the infinitely greater display of these attributes in the mission of the Messiah, the Seed of Abraham in whom all the families of the earth were to be blessed. The words of this verse are quoted, with scarcely any variation, in the inspired song of Zacharias, with direct application to Him of whom his son had just been born to be the forerunner, Luke i. 72, 73. Before the names of the patriarchs, a verb signifying to *declare, promise*, or the like, is understood.

NAHUM.

PREFACE.

OWING to the paucity of information respecting the prophet Nahum, little can be said in regard to his life and times. All that we know of him personally is, that he was the native of a town or village called Elkosh, chap. i. 1.

The only historical data furnished by the book itself with respect to the period at which he flourished, are the following: the humiliation of the kingdoms of Israel and Judah, by the Assyrian power, chap. ii. 3; the final invasion of Judah by that power, i. 9, 11; and the conquest of Thebes in Upper Egypt, iii. 8–10. But the removal of the glory of the Hebrew kingdoms, to which reference is made, could only be that which was effected by Tiglath-pileser and Shalmaneser, by whom the Israelites were carried into captivity; when the Jews also were harassed and spoiled by the Syrians, as well as impoverished by the large sum of money paid by Ahaz to the former of these monarchs. See Is. vii.–ix.; 2 Chron. xxviii. Sargon, who appears to have succeeded Shalmaneser, not satisfied with the reduction of Phœnicia by that king, and fearing lest Egypt should prevail upon the conquered provinces of the west to join her in a confederacy against him, undertook an expedition into Africa; and, though history is silent as to the event, it would appear from chap. iii. 8–10, that the expedition proved so far successful, that he took Thebes, the celebrated metropolis of Upper Egypt. It was by his successor, Sennacherib, that the last attempt was made by the Assyrians to crush the Jewish people, which issued in the total defeat of their army.

Now, since the last of these events took place in the fourteenth year of Hezekiah, and the circumstances connected with it are clearly referred to by Nahum, partly prophetically, and partly as matter of historical notoriety, chap. i. 9–13, it follows that he must have lived in, or about the year B. C. 714. Jarchi, Abarbanel, Grotius, Junius and Tremelius, and Justi, place him in the reign of Manasseh, and some, as Ewald, would make him contemporary with Josiah; but Bp. Newton, Eichhorn, Bertholdt, Rosenmüller, Newcome, Horne, Gesenius, de Wette, Jahn, Gramberg, Winer, Maurer, and Knobel, unanimously agree with Jerome in referring his ministry to the latter half of the reign of Hezekiah. Neither the opinion of Josephus, that he foretold the destruction of Nineveh in the reign of Jotham, nor that of Clement of Alexandria, that he lived between Daniel and Ezekiel, has met with any supporters. But if, as is highly probable, he flourished in one of the latter years of Hezekiah, his prophecy must have been delivered nearly one hundred years before its accomplishment; for Nineveh was overthrown, and the Assyrian power destroyed, by the joint forces of Cyaxares and Nabopolassar, in the reign of Chyniladanus, B. C. 625.

Considerable difference of opinion obtains with respect to the birth-place of the prophet. That הָאֶלְקֹשִׁי, *the Elkoshite*, was designed to point out the place of his nativity, and not his paternity, as the Targumist interprets, is evident from a comparison of the form with similar instances of the Yod affixed, 1 Kings xvii. 1; Jer. xxix. 27; Micah i. 1. There are two cities of the name of Elkosh, each of which has had its advocates, as that which may lay claim to the honor of having given birth to Nahum. The one, القوش, *Elkosh*, is situated in Koordistan, on the east side of the Tigris, about three hours' journey to the north of Mosul, which lies on the same side of the river, opposite to Nunia, supposed to be the site of ancient Nineveh. It is inhabited by Chaldean or Nestorian Christians, and is a place of great resort by Jewish pilgrims, who firmly believe it to be the birth-place and the burial-place of the prophet, to whose tomb they pay special respect. It is, however, generally thought that the tradition which connects this place with his name is of later date; and that it owes its origin to the Jews or the Nestorians, who imagined that he must have lived near the principal scene of his prophecy; and that the name had been transferred to the place from a town so called in Palestine just as our colonists have given the name of towns in Britain to those which they have erected in America and Australia. The other place is *Elcesi*, or *Elkesi*, a village in Galilee, which was pointed out to Jerome as a place of note among the Jews, and which, though small, still exhibited some slight vestiges of more ancient buildings.* Eusebius mentions it in his account of Hebrew places; and Cyrill (ad cap. i. 1,) is positive as to its situation being in Palestine.† It has been thought, and not without reason, by some, that Capernaum, Heb. כְּפַר נַחוּם, most properly rendered *the village of Nahum*, derived its name from our prophet having resided in it, though he may have been born elsewhere in the vicinity, just as it is said to have been ἡ ἰδία πόλις of our Lord, though he was born at Bethlehem.

Where the prophet was when he delivered his predictions, is not specified; but, from his familiar reference to Lebanon, Carmel, and Bashan, it may be inferred that he prophesied in Palestine; while the very graphic manner in which he describes the appearance of Sennacherib and his army, chap. i. 9-12, would seem to indicate that he was either in, or very near to Jerusalem at the time. What goes to confirm this supposition, is the number of terms, phrases, etc., which he evidently borrowed from the lips of Isaiah. Comp. שֶׁטֶף עֹבֵר כָּלָה יַעֲשֶׂה, i. 8, and כָּלָה הָיֹא וְנֶחֱרָצָה, ver. 9, with שֶׁטֶף וְעָבַר, Is. viii. 8, and כָּלָה יַעֲשֶׂה, Is. x. 23; מְבֻקָה וּמְבוּקָה וּמְבֻלָּקָה, ii. 11, with בּוֹקֵק הָאָרֶץ וּבוֹלְקָהּ,

---

* "Porro quod additur, *Naum Elcesæi*, quidam putant Elcesæum patrem esse Naum, et secundum Hebræam traditionem etiam ipsum prophetam fuisse; quum Elcesi usque hodie in Galilæa viculus sit, parvus quidem et vix ruinis veterum ædificiorum indicans vestigia, sed tamen notus Judæis, et mihi quoque a circumducente monstratus." — *Hieron. Praf. in Naum*.

† τοῦ ἀπὸ τῆς Ἐλκεσέ· κώμη δὲ αὕτη πάντως που τῆς Ἰουδαίαν χώρας.

Is. xxiv. 1; בֹּקֵק־אֶרֶץ, הִתְלַלְלָה, ii. 11, with הִתְלְלָה עֲתֵי מָלֵא, Is. xxi. 3; מֵהֲבָאוּ צַל־הֶהָרִים רַגְלֵי, ii. 1, with הִנֵּה עַל־הֶהָרִים רַגְלֵי מְבַשֵּׂר מַשְׁמִיעַ שָׁלוֹם, Is. lii. 7, etc.

The subject of the prophecy is the destruction of Nineveh, which Nahum introduces, after having in the first chapter, and at the beginning of the second, depicted the desolate condition to which, in the righteous providence of God, the country of the ten tribes had been reduced by the Assyrian power; the invasion of Judah by Sennacherib, whose destruction, and that of his army, he predicts; and the joyful restoration of both the captivities to their own land, and the enjoyment of their former privileges. His object obviously was, to inspire his countrymen with the assurance, that, however alarming their circumstances might appear, exposed as they were to the formidable army of the great eastern conqueror, not only should his attempt fail, and his forces be entirely destroyed, but his capital itself should be taken, and his empire overturned. The book is not to be divided into three separate parts, or prophecies, composed at different times, as some have imagined, but is to be regarded as one entire poem, the unity of which is plainly discoverable throughout.

The style of Nahum is of a very high order. He is inferior to none of the minor prophets, and scarcely to Isaiah himself, in animation, boldness, and sublimity; or, to the extent and proportion of his book, in the variety, freshness, richness, elegance, and force of his imagery. The rhythm is regular and singularly beautiful; and with the exception of a few foreign or provincial words, his language possesses the highest degree of classical purity. His description of the Divine character at the commencement is truly majestic; that of the siege and fall of Nineveh inimitably graphic, vivid and impressive.

CHAPTER I.

THE prophet opens with a sublime description of the attributes and operations of Jehovah, with a view to inspire his people with confidence in his protection, 2–8. The Assyrians are then unexpectedly addressed and described, 9–11; and their destruction, together with the deliverance of the Jews connected with that event, are set forth in the language of triumph and exultation, 12–15.

1 THE SENTENCE OF NINEVEH:
The Book of the Vision of Nahum•the Elkoshite.
2 Jehovah is a jealous and avenging God;
Jehovah is an avenger and furious;
Jehovah is an avenger with respect to his adversaries;

1. For the meaning of אשׂא, see on Is. xiii. 1; and for the historical circumstances connected with *Nineveh*, see on Jonah i. 2. Between the time of the prophet just referred to and that of Nahum, there elapsed a period of about one hundred and fifty years. The inscription consists of two parts; the former of which is supposed by some to be from a later hand. If genuine, we should rather expect the order to have been reversed.

1. The exordium, which begins here and reaches to ver. 8, is highly magnificent. The repeated use of the Incommunicable Name, and of the particle נקם, *avenging* or *avenger*, gives great force to the commencement. Nothing can exceed in grandeur and sublimity the description which the prophet furnishes of the Divine character. The attributes of infinite purity, inflexible rectitude, irresistible power and boundless goodness, set forth and illustrated by images borrowed from the history of the Hebrews, the scenery of Palestine, and the more astounding phenomena of nature, present to view a God worthy of the profoundest reverence, the most unbounded confidence, and the most intensive love. How inferior the otherwise sublime description given of the anger of Jove by Æschylus:

χϑὼν σεσάλευται·
βρυχία δ' ἠχώ παραμυκᾶται
βροντῆς, ἕλικες δ' ἐκλάμπουσι
στεροπῆς ζάπυροι, στρόμβοι δὲ κόνιν
εἰλίσσουσι· σκιρτᾷ δ' ἀνέμων
πνεύματα πάντων, εἰς ἄλληλα
στάσιν ἀντίπνουν ἀποδεικνύμενα.
Prom. vinctus, 1089.

קנא, *jealous*, from קנא, *to be warm*, ζηλόω, *burn with zeal, anger, jealousy*. The term is here used ἀνϑρωποπαϑὼς, principally in the last of these acceptations, though not to the entire exclusion of the others. The term describes a keen feeling of injured right, coupled with a strong inclination to see justice done to the parties concerned. בעל חמה, lit. *a lord*, or *master of fury*, an idiom by which the possession of an attribute or quality is frequently expressed. Com. בעל החלמות *a master of dreams*, i. e. a dreamer; בעל הלשון, *a master of the tongue*, i. e. eloquent. In these verses the prophet appears to have an eye specially to the judgments which God had brought upon his country by means of the Assyrians, both when they carried away the ten tribes, and now when they had again rushed into the land, and taken the fortified cities of Judah. נטר, properly signifies *to watch, observe*, in a bad sense, *to mark for punishment*. Arab. نظر, *oculos con-*

He keepeth his anger for his enemies.
3 Jehovah is long-suffering, but great in power;
He will by no means treat them as innocent:
Jehovah hath his way in the whirl-wind and in the storm,
And the clouds are the dust of his feet.
4 He rebuketh the sea and maketh it dry,
He parcheth up all the rivers:
Bashan languisheth, and Carmel,
And the bloom of Lebanon languisheth.
5 The mountains quake at him,
And the hills are melted;
The earth heaves at its presence,
The world and all that inhabit it.
6 Before his indignation who can stand?
And who can subsist in the heat of his anger?
His fury is poured out like fire,
And the rocks are overthrown by him.
7 Jehovah is good, a fortress in the day of distress;
And knoweth those that trust in him.
8 But with an overflowing inundation

vertit ad rem; ܢܛܪ, *custodem et observatorem egit.* Comp. Ps. ciii. 9; Jer. iii. 5, 12; and נֹצֵר, Ps. cxxx. 3.

3. נקה לא ינקה, *holding pure will not hold pure*, i. e. will not treat as innocent those who are guilty, but, on the contrary, punish them according to their demerit. LXX. ἀθοῶν οὐκ ἀθοώσει. Com. Exod. xx. 7, xxxiv. 7. The idea conveyed by the metaphor, *the clouds are the dust of his feet*, is exceedingly sublime. Large and majestic as the clouds may be, in reference to God, they are but as the most minute particles of dust raised by the feet in walking. אבק, signifies *light dust* or powder, what is easily raised.

4. What is here predicated of Jehovah is attributed to our Saviour, Luke viii. 24: ἐπιτίμησε—τῷ κλύδωνι τοῦ ὕδατος. The action involves omnipotence. ויבשהו is a contracted form of the Piel, for וייבשהו, as ויגל for ויגלה, Lam. iii. 33, in both of which the radical Yod gives its vowel to the preformative letter.

5 There is no authority for rendering

נשאה, *to be burnt up:* none of the MSS. or ancient versions directing us to any root signifying *to burn*. The verb is likewise thus rendered in our common version, 2 Sam. v. 21, but the marginal reading is, *took them away.* The Targ. indeed has חריבת, *vastata est*, but the LXX. render ἀνεστάλη. Symm. ἐκινήθη. The Syr. ܙܥ, *shaketh.* Vulg. *contremuit.* The root is נשא, *to raise, lift up*; intransitively, *to lift up one's self*; and appropriately expresses here the raising or heaving of the ground by an earthquake.

6. The *pouring out* of wrath, *like fire*, would seem to be a comparison taken from volcanoes, which pour out furiously their streams of liquid fire over the circumjacent regions. The breaking in pieces of the rocks, in the following hemistich, confirms this idea. Comp. Jer. li. 25, 26.

7, 8. There is a marked antithesis in these two verses, in the course of which the prophet arrives at his main topic, the destruction of Nineveh. Ver. 7 beauti-

He will effect a consummation of her place,
And darkness shall pursue his enemies.
9 What devise ye against Jehovah?
He will effect a consummation;
Distress shall not twice arise.

fully depicts the safety and happiness of those who make God their refuge, how severe soever may be the calamity which threatens or may have overtaken them; and was primarily intended to administer comfort to the pious Jews in the prospect of the Assyrian attack by Sennacherib. יֹדֵעַ, *to know*, is here, as frequently, taken in the sense of *knowing* with *regard, kindness*, or *love*. Comp. Ps. i. 6, cxliv. 3; Amos iii. 2. In בְּשֶׁטֶף עֹבֵר, the metaphor of a river impetuously overflowing its banks, rushing into the adjacent country, and passing through, carrying all before it, is employed to denote the ruthless invasion of a country by a hostile and powerful army. It is used by Isaiah, chap. viii. 8, to describe the resistless entrance of the Assyrian army into Palestine; and here Nahum appropriates the language for the purpose of describing the triumphant progress of the Medo-Babylonian troops when advancing towards Nineveh. He not only beholds, in prophetic vision, their approach to the devoted city, but announces its complete destruction. It is usual with the prophets, as it is with the Oriental poets, when powerfully affected, to introduce into their discourse persons or objects as acting, without having previously named them. See on Is. xiii. 2; and comp. מְקוֹמָהּ, ver. 11 of the present chapter. See Nordheimer's Heb. Gram., § 867. They, as it were, take it for granted, that every one must, like themselves, clearly perceive the reference. On this principle there can be no difficulty in accounting for the feminine pronominal affix in מְקוֹמָהּ, "*her* place," *i. e.* the place of Nineveh, the עִיר, *city*, or metropolis of Assyria, the overthrow of which the prophet was afterwards to describe, and which he here merely touches upon by way of anticipation. The use of מָקוֹם, *place*, is not without emphasis. Comp. chap. iii. 17. Those who desire to see the difference of opinion existing both among ancient and modern writers respecting the actual site of Nineveh, may consult Bochart, Phaleg. lib. iv. cap. xx. Lucian, speaking of it, says, ἡ Νῖνος μὲν ἀπόλωλεν ἤδη, καὶ οὐδὲν ἴχνος ἔτι λειπὸν αὐτῆς, οὐδ᾽ ἂν εἴπῃς ὅπου ποτ᾽ ἦν. Dialog. entitled Ἐπισκοποῦντες. Bochart, referring to the city of the name mentioned by Ammianus, expresses himself thus: Merito dubitatur an restaurata fuerit eo *in loco*, in quo prius condita." In the Hebrew MSS. there is no various reading of מְקוֹמָהּ; but the rendering of the LXX., τοὺς ἐπεγειρομένους, and of Aq., ἀντισταμένων, supported by Theod. and the fifth Greek version, would indicate, that their authors read קָמֶיהָ, or מְקִימֶיהָ, in favor of which אֹיְבָיו in the following hemistich might be adduced. The Syriac, however, Vulg., and Symm., read with the received text.

9. By a sudden apostrophe Nahum here turns to the invaders, and boldly challenges them to account for their temerity in daring to oppose themselves to Jehovah. On which he repeats what he had declared in the preceding verse respecting the total destruction of the Assyrian power, and adds, for the special encouragement of the Jews, that it should never annoy them again. The parallel to this brief apostrophe we have more at length, Is. xxxvii. 23–29. For the force of פַּעֲמַיִם, *twice*, comp. רַק אַתְכֶם יָדַעְתִּי וְלֹא אֶשְׁנֶה, 1 Sam. xxvi. 8. That the renewal of the affliction does not refer to any supposable future overthrow of the Assyrians, as Michaelis, Rosenmüller, Hitzig, Ewald, and others maintain, but to any further calamity to be apprehended

10 For though they are closely interwoven as thorns,
   And thoroughly soaked with their wine,
   They shall be consumed like stubble fully dry.
11 From thee he came forth,
   The deviser of mischief against Jehovah,
   The wicked counsellor.
12 Thus saith Jehovah:
   Though they are complete and so very numerous,
   Yet in this state they shall be cut down,
   And he shall pass away:

from them by the Jews, appears from ver. 12 to be the true construction of the meaning.

10. However strong and vigorous the Assyrian army might be, its complete destruction would easily be effected by Jehovah. עַד, *to, even to,* is here used as a comparative particle of degree: *to the same degree as,* or *like* thorns. Comp. 1 Chron. iv. 27. Briers and thorns are employed by the prophets to denote the soldiers composing a hostile army. See Is. x. 17, xxvii. 4. The metaphor is here taken from a thicket of thorns, the prickly branches of which are so closely intertwined as to present an impenetrable front to those who would enter it. Such were the celebrated military phalanxes of antiquity, consisting of bodies of troops armed with long spears, and arranged in the form of a square. The other metaphor is taken from drunkards who drench or saturate themselves with wine, and denotes the degree of moisture which those thorny warriors possessed, and by which they were prepared to resist the action of fire. No account is to be made of the reading שָׂרֵי, *princes,* which Newcome adopts from the Targ. and Syr. It is found in no Heb. MS. אָכַל, *to eat,* is often used to express consumption by fire. The application of the language of this and the preceding verse to the literal inundation of the Tigris, the drunkenness of the Assyrian camp, and the burning of the palace, etc., at Nineveh by Sardanapalus, as related by Diodorus Siculus, lib. ii., is not justified either by the import and usage of the terms, or by chronology, the catastrophe described by Nahum not having taken place till long after the time of that monarch.

11. מִמֵּךְ, *from thee,* O Nineveh! in the feminine. Sennacherib, whose machinations against Jehovah had been adverted to ver. 9, is here intended. The Heb. בְלִיַּעַל, frequently rendered in our common version *Belial,* properly signifies *worthlessness, inutility,* and by implication, *badness* in a moral sense, *wickedness.* Hence the idiomatic combinations, אִישׁ בְלִיַּעַל, *a man of Belial,* a wicked man; בֶּן־בְלִיַּעַל, *a son of Belial,* a bad man; בַּת־בְלִיַּעַל, *a daughter of Belial,* a wicked woman. The word is compounded of בְּלִי, *without,* and יַעַל, *profit.*

12. Another description of the formidable appearance of the hostile army, accompanied with a prediction of its sudden and complete annihilation, the flight of Sennacherib, and the future immunity of the Jews from an invasion on the part of the Assyrians. שְׁלֵמִים, *complete,* expresses the unbroken condition of the army of the enemy, and their being fully provided with everything requisite for the successful siege of Jerusalem. The word may also be designed to convey the idea of mental completeness, *i. e.* in this connection, *security, martial courage.* Thus Kimchi, לֹא יִפְחֲדוּ מֵאִישׁ כִּי כֹל גִּבְּרוּ גְבָרִים, *they are not afraid of man, for they have subdued all the countries.* וְכֵן, as used the second time, signifies *thus, so, in this state, as thus con-*

Though I have afflicted thee,
I will afflict thee no more.
13 For now I will break his yoke from off thee,
And burst thy bands asunder.
14   And with respect to thee, Jehovah hath commanded:
There shall no more be sown any of thy name;
From the house of thy gods I will cut off the graven and the
molten image;

stituted. The change of number from the plural נְגֹזּוּ, "*they* are, or shall be cut down," to עָבָר, "*he* passeth away," is obviously intended to distinguish between the overthrow of the Assyrian army, and the immediate departure of Sennacherib to his own land. The nominative to עָבָר is רֹעֵץ בְּלֹעֵץ in the preceding verse. גזז, *to cut,* or *mow down,* is a metaphor derived from the hay harvest, and forcibly sets forth the sudden and entire destruction of an army. See for the historical facts, 2 Kings xix. 35; Is. xxxvii. 36, 37. At the close of the verse, Jehovah directs the discourse to his people, graciously assuring them that, though he had employed the Assyrian power to punish them, he would do so no more. Newcome, almost entirely on the authority of the LXX., improperly changes אִם שְׁלֵמִים וְכֵן רַבִּים וְכֵן נָגֹזּוּ into אִם מֹשֵׁל מַיִם רַבִּים כֵּן גֻזַל וְכֵן עָבָר, "Though the Ruler of many waters has thus ravaged, and thus passed through." That these ancient translators did, from hearing שְׁלֵמִים אִם read as מֹשֵׁל מַיִם, render, κατάρχων ὑδάτων πολλῶν, there can be no doubt; but then, they place the words in apposition with τάδε λέγει κύριος; and make the Lord, and not the king of Assyria, to be "the ruler of many waters." The Syr. following the LXX., only changing the singular into the plural, has ܪܺܝܫܶܐ ܕ݁ܡܰܝܳܐ ܣܰܓܺܝܶܐܐ "respecting the heads of many waters." עִתִּיתִךְ is merely a defective reading of עִנִּיתִיךְ, which is found in a number of MSS., and in some

editions. The object of the verb is *Judah,* understood, which Jehovah here kindly addresses, and not Nineveh, as Michaelis and Hitzig suppose. The Jews are addressed as a female, as they are in the words חָגִּי יְהוּדָה חַגַּיִךְ שַׁלְּמִי נְדָרָיִךְ, *Celebrate thy festivals, O Judah! perform thy vows.* Chap. ii. 1. On the introduction of a predicate without previous mention of the subject, see on ver. 8. The meaning is, that the Jews were to be no more afflicted by the Assyrians, and not that Divine judgments were never afterwards to be inflicted upon them by others.

13. The suffix ךְ has here the same reference as in the preceding verse, and in מֹטֵהוּ, "*his* yoke," to the king of Assyria. Comp. Is. x. 27; Jer. ii. 20. For מֹטֵהוּ, some think the LXX. and Vulg. read מַטֵּהוּ, which is the reading of several MSS.; but they both signify a *staff* or *pole;* only the former denotes what is placed on the neck, in order to bear a burden.

14. We have here another apostrophe to the Assyrian monarch, announcing to him, that his dynasty should not be perpetuated, that his favorite idols should be destroyed, that the very temple in which he worshipped them should become his grave. When it is said, that "no more of thy name shall be sown," the meaning is not, that none of his sons should succeed him in the government, but that his dynasty should cease on the arrival of the event predicted by Nahum, the destruction of Nineveh. The Medes being great enemies to idolatry, those of them who composed the army of Cyax-

I will make it thy grave,
Because thou art worthless.

ares would take singular pleasure in destroying the idols which they found in the chief temple at Nineveh. No mention is made in history of the sepulture of Sennacherib, but we are expressly told, 2 Kings xix. 37, Is. xxxvii. 38, that he was slain by two of his sons while in the act of worship in the temple of Nisroch his god; and there can be no doubt that it is to this event reference is here made. אָשִׂים stands elliptically for אָשִׂים־אֹתוֹ, *I will make it*, i. e. the temple of thy gods, *thy grave*. Some take קַלּוֹתָ, *thou art light*, in the same sense in which the Chaldee תְּקַל is used Dan. v. 27, but without sufficient ground in Hebrew usage. In application to persons it always signifies to be the object of shame or disgrace. Though to be buried in a temple naturally conveys to our minds the idea of honorable interment, it is otherwise here, owing to the peculiar circumstances of the case.

CHAPTER II.

AFTER prophetically describing the joyful announcement of the overthrow of the Assyrian power, 1; and calling upon the Jews manfully to defend Jerusalem against the attack of Sennacherib, in the assurance that there would be a glorious restoration of the whole Hebrew people, 2, 3; the prophet arrives at his main subject, the destruction of Nineveh, the siege and capture of which he portrays with graphic minuteness, and in the most sublime and vivid manner, 4–11. In a beautiful allegory he then, with triumphant sarcasm, asks where was now the residence of the once conquering and rapacious monarch? 12, 13; after which, Jehovah is introduced, expressly declaring that he would assuredly perform what he had inspired his servant to predict.

---

1 BEHOLD! upon the mountains are the feet of him that announceth good,
That publisheth peace:
Celebrate thy feasts, O Judah! perform thy vows,
For the wicked shall no more pass through thee;
He is entirely cut off.

1. Some interpreters refer these words to the messengers which should arrive from the East, announcing to the inhabitants of Judah the joyful intelligence of the destruction of Nineveh, which had been briefly hinted at in the course of the preceding chapter; but it better accords with the spirit and bearing of the immediate connection to apply them to what took place on the miraculous deliverance of Jerusalem, recorded Is. xxxvii. 36. They are almost identical, so far as they go, with the language of Isaiah, chap. lii. 7, relative to the return from Babylon. During the Assyrian invasion, the inhabitants of Judah were cut

2   The disperser hath come up before thee;
    Keep the fortress, watch the way,
    Make fast the loins,
    Strengthen thee with power to the utmost.
3   For Jehovah will restore the excellency of Jacob,
    As he will the excellency of Israel; ·
    Though the emptiers have emptied them,
    And destroyed their branches.
4   The shield of his heroes is dyed red,

off from all access to the metropolis; now, they would be at liberty to proceed thither as usual, in order to observe their religious rites. בְּלִיַּעַל, *Belial*, doubtless means the same as יוֹעֵץ בְּלִיָּעַל, *wicked counsellor*, chap. i. 11; *i. e.* as there explained, Sennacherib. Restricted as the declaration here made must necessarily be to this monarch, the passage is nowise at variance with the fact, that Manasseh was for a time in the power of the Assyrians, 2 Chron. xxxiii. 11.

2. Most moderns adopt the interpretation of Jerome, who is of opinion, that the prophet here turns to Nineveh, and directs the attention of her monarch to the approach of the Medo-Babylonish army. I rather think with Abarbanel, Kimchi, Jarchi, Hezel, Dathe, and others, that the words are addressed to Hezekiah, and the inhabitants of Jerusalem, for the purpose of inspiring them with courage to hold out during the Assyrian attack.

מֵפִיץ, from פּוּץ. Arab. فيص, *abiit, peregrinatus fuit*, *to scatter, disperse*, properly signifies *the Disperser*, and is appropriately applied to the king of Assyria, by whose army the inhabitants of the different countries which it invaded were scattered from their abodes. Some prefer rendering the word by *hammer*, and compare Prov. xxv. 18, and Jer. li. 20, in the latter of which passages we have מַפֵּץ from נָפַץ, *to break in pieces, disperse*, etc., rendered in our common version *battle-axe*. The address is beautifully abrupt, and derives great force from the use of the Infinitive instead of the Imperative of all the four verbs which here occur. The fuller forms would be נָצוֹר מְצוּרָה, צָפֹה תְצַפֶּה, נָצוֹר תְּצוּר, etc., form a paronomasia.

3. Further to encourage the inhabitants of Jerusalem, a promise is here given of the restoration of the Hebrew people to their former independence and glory. גְּאוֹן יַעֲקֹב, etc., is not to be interpreted of the pride of the Hebrews, nor of the proud and insulting conduct of their enemies towards them; but, as in Ps. xlvii. 5; Amos vi. 8, it means the land of Canaan, as distinguished above all other countries. This land, as the prophet immediately adds, had been spoiled by the Assyrians, who had not only carried away the ten tribes into captivity, but taken the fortified cities of Judah; but it was again to be restored, partly on the destruction of the Assyrians, and completely on the return from Babylon. שׁוּב, *to return*, has here the force of the Hiphil הֵשִׁיב, *to restore*, as in Numb. x. 36; Ps. lxxxv. 5. Connected as this verb is with the future, implied in the abbreviated form יְצַו, etc., in the preceding verse, it is to be rendered in this tense. *Jacob* and *Israel* are, as frequently, put for the people of the two kingdoms. The devastation effected by the Assyrians is described by a metaphor taken from the pruning of vines, or the cutting off of the young twigs or shoots. Parallel to the promise made in this verse is that given by Isaiah, chap. xxxvii. 31, 32.

4. The prophet now proceeds to describe the siege and capture of Nineveh,

The warriors are clothed with scarlet;
The chariots are furnished with fiery scythes,
In the day of his preparation;
And the cypresses are brandished.

which involved the downfall of the Assyrian empire. The formidable, terrific, and invincible appearance of the Medo-Babylonish army is first noticed. גִּבֹּרֵיהוּ, *his heroes*, i. e. the mighty men of Cyaxares. The suffix is the less frequent form, instead of יו, but represents more of the primitive pronoun הֵם, of which both are fragments. מְאָדָּם is the Pual participle of אָדַם, *to be red;* and is applied to the shields, to intimate that they were dyed red. The bull's hide with which they were commonly covered was easily susceptible of this process; and, on being anointed with oil, would shine brightly. See on Is. xxi. 6. This interpretation of the word, which is confirmed by the meaning of the corresponding principle, in the following hemistich, is preferable to that which would make it express the idea of *fiery, sparkling*, or the like. "Bloodstained is altogether to be rejected. The LXX. mistaking מְאָדָּם for מֵאָדָם, preposterously render ὅπλα δυναστείας αὐτῶν ἐξ ἀνθρώπων. מְתֻלָּעִים, lit. *are crimsoned*, is a ἅπαξ λεγ., but is the Pual participial form, and is evidently derived from תּוֹלָע, the name specially used to denote the *coccus,* or *worm* which was used in dying, to give to cloth a deep scarlet color. The manufacture of such stuffs was chiefly carried on by the Tyrians and Lydians. The LXX. have also mistaken this word for מְהַלְּכִים, ἐμπαίζοντας, in which they are followed by the Syr. Pollux describes the Medes as wearing a cloth called *Sarages*, which was of scarlet color, striped with white; Σάραγης, Μήδων τι φόρημα, πορφυροῦς, μεσόλευκος χιτών. Lib. i. cap. 13. בְּאֵשׁ פְּלָדֹת, *with fiery scythes.* That פְּלָדֹת stands here by transposition of the first two letters for לַפִּדֹת, cannot be admitted; the plural of לַפִּיד, *a lamp,* or *torch,* being always לַפִּידִים, in the masculine, so that the Syr., Targ., etc., give an erroneous interpretation. פְּלָדָה, *iron, steel.* Syr. ܦܘܠܕܐ the same. Com. Arab. فلذ, *secuit, in partes concidit.* فولاذ, *ferrum durum, chalybs.* مفلوذ, *e chalybe confectus*, de gladio. For the manufactury of swords of the finest steel, not only Damascus but certain towns on the east of the Caucasus have long been celebrated; and that this compound metal is of high antiquity, is universally allowed. Its name, *Chalybs*, is derived from the Chalybes, a people bordering on the Euxine sea. It is doubtless what the prophet Jeremiah means by בַּרְזֶל מִצָּפוֹן, *iron from the North*, and which he distinguishes from בַּרְזֶל, *common iron*, chap. xv. 12. Now there appears to be no part of the war-chariots entitled to the character of irons flashing with fire, but the falces or scythes, which were "fixed at right angles to the axle, and turned downwards, or inserted parallel to the axle into the felly of the wheel, so as to revolve, when the chariot was put in motion, with thrice the velocity of the chariot itself; and sometimes also projecting from the extremities of the axle." Dr. William Smith's Dict. of Greek and Roman Antiquities, art. *Falx.* The ἅρματα δρεπανηφόρα were justly reckoned among the most terrific implements of ancient warfare, as they mowed down all that came in their way. The אֵשׁ *fire* of these scythes was the coruscations produced by their excessive brightness and the rapidity of their motion. Instead of בְּאֵשׁ, "*with fire*," seven MSS., originally one more, and the Soncin. edition of the Prophets, read כְּאֵשׁ "*like fire.*" The suffix in הֲכִינוֹ may either form an

Chap. II.   NAHUM.   275

5 The chariots dash madly on the commons,
   They run furiously in the open places;
   Their appearance is like that of torches,
   They flash like lightnings.
6   He remembers his nobles;
   They stumble in their march;

accusative to הָרֶכֶב, or the genitive of an agent not mentioned — the hostile commander. The latter construction is preferable, as it refers *the day of his preparation* to the period fixed upon by the general for commencing the attack. It would only be then that the scythes would be fixed in the chariots: it being not only useless but dangerous to have them attached at other times. By בְּרוֹשִׁים, *cypresses*, are meant *spears* or *lances*, the staves of which were made of the branches of the cypress. The LXX., followed by the Syr. and Arab., have taken the word for פָּרָשִׁים, *horsemen*, rendering it οἱ ἱππεῖς, which Michaelis is inclined to prefer, and Newcome has actually adopted. There is, however, no just cause for stumbling at the boldness of the figure. Homer, describing the spear of Achilles, calls it an *ash*:

'Ἐκ δ' ἄρα σύριγγος πατρώϊον ἐσπάσατ' ἔγχος,
Βριθὺ μέγα στιβαρόν· τὸ μὲν οὐ δύνατ' ἄλλος Ἀχαιῶν
Πάλλειν, ἀλλά μιν οἶος ἐπίστατο πῆλαι Ἀχιλλεύς,
Πηλιάδα ΜΕΛΙΗΝ, κ. τ. λ.
                Iliad. xix. 387—390.

Hesiod also designates the lance ἐλάτη, *a pine*, Scut. Herc. 188; and Virgil uses the *fir* for the spear of Camilla:

———— "cujus apertum
Adversi longâ transverberat *abiete* pectus."   *Æneid*. xi. 667.

יְרוֹעָלוּ, a ἅπαξ λεγ., from the root רָעַל, Syr. ܪܥܠ, *tremuit, to move tremulously, wave, shake*; hence רַעַל and תַּרְעֵלָה, *trembling*, Zech. xii. 2; Ps. lx. 5. The reference seems to be to the custom of the spear-men to wave their lances before engaging in battle, for the purpose of evincing their eagerness for the contest.

5. This verse Ewald explains of the preparations made by the Ninevites for the defence of the city; but the war-chariots could not be used within the walls: they could only be effective in the open field. חוּצוֹת signifies not merely streets, as being *without* the houses of a city, but also the *out-fields* or *commons* without the city itself. Comp. Job v. 10; Ps. cxliv. 13; Prov. viii. 26. In like manner רְחֹבוֹת, as its parallel, denotes any wide or open spaces in the suburbs without the gates. Comp. 2 Chron. xxxii. 6; Ps. cxliv. 14. הִתְהוֹלֵל signifies *to act the part of a madman, to show one's self violent, rage*, and the like. The reduplicate form יִשְׁתַּקְשְׁקוּן is obviously intended to give great force to the expression; on which account, to render it *run up and down* is too weak. I have added *furiously*, which makes this hemistich better agree with the preceding. Nor is the reduplication of the third radical of רוּץ, *to run*, in Piel, וִירוֹצֵצוּ, without a corresponding degree of energy. It expresses the rapid zig-zag course of the chariots, resembling the quick flashing of lightning. As רֶכֶב is masculine, the feminine suffix in מַרְאֵיהֶן must be taken for a neuter, or regarded as an instance of neglected gender.

6. The king of Nineveh is here represented as roused from a profound stupor; and, contriving the necessary means of defence, as first of all turning his attention to his principal officers, whom he summons to their posts. Michaelis, Maurer, and others, think that by these

They hasten to her wall,
And the defence is prepared.
7 The flood-gates are opened,
And the place is dissolved,
Though firmly established.
8 She is made bare; she is carried up,
While her handmaids moan like doves,
And smite upon their hearts.

officers, the generals commanding in the provinces are intended; but it is more likely the prophet means the military leaders within the city, since it is represented in the preceding verses as already invested by the enemy; and they are spoken of as hastening to the wall, and not to the city, which the former interpretation would require. זָכַר is here used, not in the sense of simply recollecting, or calling to mind, but with the accessory idea of carrying out or giving effect to the recollection, in regard to the object of remembrance. It therefore implies, that the monarch ordered them to occupy each his place in the defence of Nineveh. On receiving the orders, they make such haste, that they and their troops stumble while marching to the walls. Instead of ה in הֲכִינוּ‎, eight of De Rossi's MSS., another originally, the Brixian, and another ancient edition, exhibit the local ה, which is supported by the Targ., Syr., and Arab. By the סֹכֵךְ, *protector*, or *protection*, here mentioned, some understand the *vinea*, or the *testudo*, military coverings used by the besiegers of a city, under the shelter of which they might safely carry on their operations in undermining, or otherwise destroying the walls. As, however, the term is here applied to something employed by those who acted on the defensive, it cannot be so interpreted. In all probability, some kind of breastwork, composed of the interwoven boughs and branches of trees, erected between the towers upon the walls, is intended. According to Diodorus Siculus, Nineveh had fifteen hundred towers, each of which was two hundred feet high. סָכַךְ signifies to *weave, intertwine, fence,* and the like, and so to *protect, shelter.* LXX. καὶ ἑτοιμάσουσι τὰς προφυλακὰς αὐτῶν. Syr. ܚܣܢ̈ܐ, *fortifications*. Targ. מִגְדְּלַיָּא, *towers*.

7. Though it is not unusual in Hebrew to represent invading armies or multitudes of people under the image of floods or waters, an interpretation adopted here by Rosenmüller, De Wette, and others, there does not appear to be sufficient ground to depart from the literal meaning. By נַהֲרוֹת, *rivers*, or *streams*, are meant the canals dug from the Tigris, which intersected the city, and more especially those which afforded a supply of water for the defence of the palace. The gates or sluices of these canals were doubtless strongly constructed, to prevent a greater influx of water than what was required; but having upon the present occasion been burst open by the besiegers, the waters of the Tigris rushed in, and completely inundating the royal residence, dissolved and ruined it. The verb נָמוֹג describes the physical effects of the inundation, not metaphorically those produced by the event upon the minds of the inhabitants.

8. הֻצַּב has occasioned a great diversity of interpretations. Gesenius, dissatisfied with all those derived from its being the Hophal of נָצַב, to *place, settle, fix,* has recourse to a new root, צָצַב, which he borrows from the Arab. ضَبَّ, *fluxit*, *stillavit*, aqua, ضَبَّ, *fudit, effudit*; and,

9 Though Nineveh hath been like a pool of water,
   From the most ancient time,
   Yet they are fleeing :
   " Stop ! stop ! " but none looketh back.
10 Plunder the silver, plunder the gold ;
   There is no end to the store ;
   There is abundance of all covetable vessels.
11 Emptiness and emptiedness and void,
   Heart-melting and tottering of knees ;
   There is intense pain in all loins,
   And all faces withdraw their color.

then removing the word to the end of the preceding verse, reads thus, נָהֵיבַל הֲקִימָה וְהָצַב, *the palace is dissolved and made to flow away.* That the verb is to be connected with the preceding הֲקִימָה, the gender at once shows ; but there is no necessity of departing from the usual signification of יָצַב, *to place, fix, stand firmly* ; in Hiph. *to cause to stand, establish.* However strongly the place might have been constructed, it would not be able to resist the fury of the water. ו has here the force of *though, and though.* Comp. וְהִיא חֲבֵרְתֶךָ, Mal. iii. 14. The nominative to the feminines גֻּלְּתָה and הֻעֲלָתָה is Nineveh understood. The first of these verbs some render, *is carried into captivity ;* but this signification is confined to the Kal and Hiphil conjugations. It here describes the ignominy with which the Ninevites were treated, when, stripped of everything, they were forced from their capital. Comp. Is. xlvii. 3. Nineveh is represented as a queen degraded from her dignity ; and led away captive by the enemy ; her female slaves following and deploring her fate. That the queen of Nineveh herself, supposed to be here called *Huzzab*, is intended, in a position which cannot be sustained, though adopted by several interpreters, and recently by Ewald. Persons are never introduced by name into prophecy, except for some important purpose, as in the case of Cyrus. For נָהַג, *to pant, sigh, moan,* comp. the Arab. ﻧﻬﺞ, *graviter, continuo an-*

helavit, vix interrupto spiritu ; Syriac ܓܥܐ, *clamavit, rugiit.*

9. The comparison of the population of Nineveh to a collection of water is here appropriate. מִימֵי הִיא is an antiquated mode of expressing the feminine pronominal affix — the absolute form of the pronoun being retained instead of the fragmental הָ being attached to the noun, מִימֵי־הִיא ; lit. *from her days, i. e.* during the whole period of her existence, or, from the most ancient time. The prophet compares the royal city to a reservoir of water, on account of the confluence of people from the surrounding provinces. All who could make their escape, now took to flight, and no entreaties could induce them to remain.

10. Nahum here apostrophizes the victorious enemy. They had now only to possess themselves of the immense riches which had been abandoned by the inhabitants, or which they might plunder at pleasure. The repetition of the verb בֹּזּוּ gives force to the diction. תְּכוּנָה, from כּוּן, in Hiphil, *to set up, prepare ;* anything *laid up, prepared,* and *ready for use,* as costly garments, ornaments, etc. Comp. Job xxvii. 16. LXX. τοῦ κόσμου αὐτῆς. Vulg. *divitiarum.* Targ. אוֹצְרָא *treasures.* כָּבֹד, followed by מִן, is here a nominative absolute : as for the abundance, it consists of, etc.

11. The three synonymes בּוּקָה מְבוּקָה וּמְבֻלָּקָה, all from roots signifying to

12   Where is the den of the lionesses?
     And the feeding-place of the young lions?
     Where the lion and the lioness walked,
     The lion's cub also, and none disturbed them.
13   The lion tore for the supply of his cubs,
     And strangled for his lionesses;
     He filled his dens with prey,
     And his habitations with rapine.
14   Behold! I am against thee, saith Jehovah of hosts;
     I will burn her chariots into smoke;
     The sword shall devour thy young lions,
     And I will cut off thy prey from the land:
     The voice of thy messengers shall be heard no more.

empty, empty out, are exquisitely chosen, and from their increase in length, as well as from their similarity both in sound and meaning, give great force to the expression of total desolation — the idea here intended to be conveyed. Gesenius considers them to be onomatopoetic, imitating the sound of emptying out a bottle. Comp. Is. xxiv. 1, for the etymology of the verbs בוּק and בָּלַק ; and for a similar use of words varied in form, but nearly alike in sound, Is. xxiv. 3, 4, xxix. 2; Ezek. xxxiii. 29; Zeph. i. 15. חַלְחָלָה, an intensive form, from חוּל, *to be in pain*. For מָה־גַּם see on Joel ii. 6.

12-14. A beautiful allegory, setting forth the rapacious, irresistible, and luxurious character of the king of Assyria, and the destruction of Nineveh, the seat of his empire, with all his armies, and their means of supply. In the last verse the literal is intermixed with the figurative. Comp. for the metaphor, Is. v. 29; Jer. ii. 15. אִם, in ver. 12, has the force of *that which;* דַּי, ver. 13, *a sufficiency, supply*, etc. טֶרֶף and טִרְפָּה are employed idiomatically in the two genders to express different kinds of prey. Comp. Is. iii. 1. For בֶעָשָׁן the Targ. has בְּאֶשָּׁתָא, *with fire*. The meaning is, that such should be the number of chariots consumed, that the smoke arising from the fire in which they were to be burnt, should be visible to all. Comp. Ps. xxxvii. 20. The MSS. and editions differ in their punctuation of מַלְאָכֵכֵה, but there can be little doubt that it is a defective reading, for מַלְאָכֶיךָ. Comp. מַלְאָכָה, Ps. cxxxix. 5. The Syr. and LXX. have read מַעְבָּדֶיךָ, "thy works."

CHAPTER III.

THE prophet, resuming his description of the siege of Nineveh, 1-3, traces it to her idolatry as its cause, 4, and repeats the divine denunciations which he had introduced chap. ii. 13, ver. 5-7. He then, to aggravate her misery, points her to the once formidable and celebrated, but now conquered and desolate Thebes, 8-10, declaring that such should likewise be her fate, 11–13; calls upon her sarcastically to make every preparation for her defence, but assuring her that it would be of no avail, 14, 15; and concludes by contrasting with the number of merchants, princes, and generals, which she once possessed, the miserable, remediless state of ruin to which she was to be reduced, 16–19.

---

1 Wo to the city of blood!
She is wholly filled with deceit and violence;
The prey is not removed.
2 The sound of the whip, and the sound of the rattling of the wheels,
The horses prancing, and the chariots bounding;
3 The mounting of horsemen, the gleaming of swords,
And the lightning of spears;
The multitude of slain,
And the mass of corpses;
There is no end to the carcasses;
They stumble over their carcasses :
4 Because of the multitude of the whoredoms of the harlot,
The very graceful mistress of enchantments;

1. A portraiture of the atrocious character of the Ninevites. בֵּית דָּמִים form an asyndeton. The non-removal of the prey refers to the fact, that the Assyrians had not restored the ten tribes. .

2, 3. The description which the prophet here gives of the approach of the enemy, his attack on the city, and the slaughter of the besieged, is exquisitely graphic. Every translator must acknowledge with Jerome : "Tam pulchra juxta Hebraicum et pictura similis ad prœlium se preparantis exercitus descriptio est, ut omnis meus sermo sit vilior." The passage is unrivalled by any other, either in sacred or profane literature. Comp. however Jer. xlvii. 3. דָּהַר occurs only here, but in Judges v. 22, we find דַּהֲרוֹת אַבִּירָיו, *the charges of his mighty* warriors, in connection with סוּס, *the war-horse.* It would seem to have some affinity to the Arab. دَهَرَجَ, *celeriter incessit,* and expresses the *coursing* or *prancing* of the cavalry, when rapidly advancing to the attack. Their eagerness the LXX. expresses by rendering it διώκοντος. Syr. ܐܵܨ, *ebullivit, anhelavit.* D. Kimchi: דָּרְסַת הַסּוּס בְּכֹחַ וּמְהַלֵּךְ, *the powerful trampling or prancing of the horse and his course.* The collectives require to be rendered in the plural. קוֹל is not to be understood as repeated before סוּס and the following substantive. Instead of מְדַלֵּג or מְדַלֵּק, as it is read in some of the old editions, the Keri, many MSS., and the Soncin., Brix., and Complut. editions, read מְדַלְּגִים, which is favored by the renderings of the LXX. and Vulg.

4. The idolatrous practices of the Ninevites, and the means which they employed to seduce others to worship their gods, are here represented as the principal cause of their destruction. At the same time, the commerce, luxury, etc. which they carried to the greatest height, are not to be excluded; for in making contracts and treaties with the more powerful of their neighbors, they not only employed these as inducements, but did not scruple to deliver into their power, nations and tribes that were un-

Who sold nations through her fornications,
And tribes through her enchantments.
5 Behold! I am against thee, saith Jehovah of hosts:
I will throw up thy skirts upon thy face,
And show the nations thy nakedness,
And the kingdoms thy shame.
6 I will cast abominable things upon thee,
And disgrace thee;
And will make thee a gazing-stock.
7 And every one that seeth thee shall flee from thee
And shall say, Nineveh is destroyed!
Who will commiserate her?
Whence shall I seek comforters for thee?
8 Art thou better than No-Ammon,
That dwelt in the rivers,
That had water around her;

able to defend themselves. Comp. Joel iii. 3, 6–8; Amos i. 6. The metaphor of an unchaste female, and the seductive arts which she employs, is not unfrequent in the prophets.

5, 6. The language of commination here used, is suggested by the metaphor of an harlot, employed in the preceding verse. It would seem to refer to an ancient mode of punishing strumpets, by stripping them of all their gaudy attire, and exposing them, covered with mud and filth, to the gaze of insulting spectators. The abhorrent character of the figure constitutes the very reason of its selection. Comp. Ezek. xvi. 37–41. The בְ in בְּאִי is the Caph veritatis. LXX. εἰς παράδειγμα.

7. הָאִי carries out the idea implied in אִי, ver. 6. It is in the plural, but is followed by a singular verb, to agree with כֹּל. Comp. for the sentiment Is. li. 19.

8. נֹא אָמוֹן, No Amon, Egyp. ΠΟΖ ΔⲘΟⲬⲚ, the lion, or portion of Amon, thus etymologically the LXX. μερίδα, Ἀμμών, though in Ezek. xxx. 15, they render Διόσπολις, i. e. the residence or possession of the Egyptian deity known by the name of Jupiter Ammon. The statement of Macrobius, that he was the representative of the sun, is confirmed by the name of Amon-Re, i. e. "Amon, the Sun," being given to him in Egyptian inscriptions. On Egyptian monuments this god is represented by the figure of a man sitting upon a chair, with a ram's head, or by that of an entire ram. In Jer. xlvi. 25, we have נֹא אָמוֹן, Amon of No, where, as well as in the present passage in Nahum, our translators have regarded אָמוֹן as equivalent to הָמוֹן, a multitude. Bochart, Schroeder, and some others, have contended that Διόσπολις, near Mendes, in Lower Egypt, is intended, but all the later commentators are in favor of Thebes. The Targum preposterously renders, אֲלֶכְּסַנְדְּרִיָּא רַבְּתָא, Alexandria the Great, which Jerome, deferring to his Rabbi, has adopted in the Vulg. The city, which from its being the principal seat of his worship, was called by the Greeks Διόσπολις, is the celebrated Thebes, the ancient capital of Upper Egypt, situated on both sides of the Nile, about two hundred and sixty miles south of Cairo. It was renowned for its hundred

Whose strength was in the sea;
Her wall was on the sea?
9 Cush strengthened her, and Egypt,
With countless hosts;
Put and the Lybians were thine auxiliaries.

gates, and was of such extent, that its remaining ruins still describe a circuit of twenty-seven miles:

——————— οὐδ' ὅσα Θήβας
Αἰγυπτίας, ὅθι πλεῖστα δόμοις ἐν κτήματα κεῖται,
Αἵ δ' ἑκατόμπυλοί εἰσι, διηκόσιοι δ' ἀν' ἑκάστην
Ἀνέρες ἐξοιχνεῦσι σὺν ἵπποισιν καὶ ὄχεσ-
φιν.   Iliad. ix. 381.

Of the magnificent ruins, the most remarkable are the temples of Luxor and Karnac, on the eastern side of the river. The architecture is of the most gigantic and superior description. Fragments of colossal obelisks and statues are found in every direction. The stupendous colonade at Luxor is in the highest degree imposing; but the grand hall of the temple at Karnac is of surpassing interest. Wilkinson, in his Thebes, p. 174, describes it as "one hundred and seventy feet by three hundred and twenty-nine, supported, by a central avenue of twelve massive columns, sixty-six feet high, (without the pedestal and abacus,) and twelve in diameter, besides one hundred and twenty-two of smaller or rather less gigantic dimensions, forty-one feet nine inches in height, and twenty-seven feet six inches in circumference, distributed in seven lines on either side of the former." The walls of the temples are covered with hieroglyphics, chiefly representing the victories gained by the Egyptian kings over their enemies. One of the walls exhibits the result of the expedition of Shishak against Jerusalem, 1 Kings xiv. 25, etc.; 2 Chron. xii. 2-9, in the leading away of the Jewish captives.

Of the conquest of this famous city, here referred to by Nahum, no mention is made in profane history, but it not improbably took place on the advance of the Assyrian army under Sargon, in the year B. C. 714. See on Is. xx. It was afterwards taken by Cambyses, B. C. 525, and its ruin completed by Ptolemy Lathyrus, B. C. 81. According to the representation of our prophet, Nineveh, could not vie with it either in point of grandeur or of strength. They both possessed the advantage of mighty rivers for their defence — a circumstance to which he gives a special prominence, as it was that on which the inhabitants placed great dependance. By ם־, sea, is meant the Nile; see on Is. xix. 5; by יארים, streams, the same as יארי מצר, Nah. ii. 7, viz. the canals by which the water of the river was carried round or through the principal parts of the city. Ewald proposes to connect ם־ with מים, thus, מים־ים, and renders from sea to sea, which he attempts to justify by appealing to Micah vii. 12, but the cases are not parallel. חיל־ stands elliptically for חֵיל־מָה. The preposition מ in מים expresses the material out of which the defence was made; and the triple reference to the Nile as a sea, in this verse, indicates the great importance which attached to it as a means of protecting the city.

9. Not only was Thebes strong by nature and art, and in the number of her native troops; she also possessed immense military resources in her African auxiliaries. For כוש, Cush, see on Is. xi. 11. פוט, Put, Egypt. ⲫⲁⲓⲁⲧ, the region immediately to the west of Lower Egypt, and conterminous with Lybia Proper, with the inhabitants of which, it is here mentioned. Gesenius derives the name from פוט or ⲫⲓⲧ,

10 Yet she became an exile,
    She went into captivity;
    Her young children also were dashed in pieces,
    At the top of all the streets;
    They cast lots for her honorable men,
    And all her great men were bound with chains.
11   Thou also shalt be drunken,
    Thou shalt hide thyself,
    Thou also shalt seek a refuge from the enemy.
12 All thy fortresses are like fig-trees with early figs;
    If they shake them, they fall into the mouth of the eater.
13 Behold! thy people are as women in the midst of thee;
    The gates of thy land shall be thrown wide open to thine enemies;
    Fire shall consume thy barriers,
14   Draw water for the siege;

a bow, and thinks the people were so called from their being expert as archers. That they were descended from Ham, see Gen. x. 6. Josephus speaks of them as Mauritanians, Antiqq. i. 6, 2; and the river of the same name, which he describes as flowing through their country, is called *Fut* by Pliny, v. 1, and *Phtuth* by Ptolemy, iv. 1. They are spoken of as forming part of the Egyptian army, Jer. xlvi. 9, and as being in the Syrian marine, Ezek. xxvii. 10. Winer's Real W. B. ii. p. 308. לוּבִים, *Lybians*, the inhabitants of Africa to the south and west of the former country, stretching as far as Numidia. Hitzig, on Is. lxvi. 19, has endeavored in vain to establish the hypothesis that the people of Nubia are meant. Comp. 2 Chron. xii. 3, xvi. 8. מִצְרַיִם, *Egypt*, is here taken for Lower Egypt, as distinguished from the Upper, of which Thebes was itself the capital. There is no reason, with some, to change the ך in בְּעֶזְרָתֵךְ into ה, though the LXX. and Syr. have the third person. The prophet concludes his description by apostrophizing Thebes. בְּ is the *Beth essentiæ*.

10, 11. If the celebrated metropolis of Egypt, with all its means of defence, was captured, and its inhabitants subjected to all the cruelities and indignities usually inflicted by the victors, what was there in Nineveh to claim exemption? Instead of תִּשְׁכְּרִי, *to drink, be intoxicated*, a mode of speech not uncommon in the prophets, denoting participation in severe punishment, Newcome, without authority, reads תִּשָּׂכְרִי, *to hire*, and renders, *thou shalt become an hireling*. In 1 Sam. ii. 5, to which he refers, the latter, and not the former verb, occurs.

12, 13. Two figures strikingly expressive of the extreme ease with which the Assyrians should be subdued. For the former, see on Is. xxviii. 4; and comp. Rev. vi. 13; for the latter, Is. xix. 16; Jer. l. 37. עִם, *with*, in the phrase הִפִּילוּ עַל פִּי אוֹכֵל denotes *accompaniment*, etc.; the phrase itself is equivalent to הִפִּילוּ לְפִי אֹכֵל אֶת־פְּרִיהֶם. Thus the LXX. συκαῖ σκοποὺς ἔχοντες. Comp. for this rare use of the preposition, 1 Sam. xvii. 42. בְּרִיחָיִךְ, Michaelis translates *thy fugitives*, but as fugitives are always represented as perishing by the sword, and never by fire, the signification *barriers* must be retained.

14. The prophet ironically summons the Ninevites to make every effort in

Strengthen thy fortifications;
Enter the mire, and tread the clay;
Repair the brick-kiln.
15 There shall the fire consume thee,
The sword shall cut thee off;
It shall consume thee like the licking locust;
Be thou numerous as the licking locusts;
Be thou numerous as the swarming locusts.
16 Thou hast increased thy merchants more than the stars of heaven;
The licking locusts spread themselves out,
And took their flight.
17 Thy princes were as the swarming locusts,
And thy satraps as the largest locusts;
That encamp in the hedges in the cold day;
The sun ariseth, then they flee,
And the place where they are is unknown.
18 Thy shepherds slumber, O king of Assyria!

the way of preparing for a long and vigorous defence of the metropolis itself. As water is one of the first necessaries, it behooved them to see to it, that the cisterns, etc., were well filled. They were also to put the fortifications in a perfect state.

15–17. שָׁם, *there*, points emphatically to the fortified city. The nominative to הִתְכַּבֵּד is the masculine noun עַם, *people*, *i. e.* the inhabitants; that to הִתְכַּבְּדִי, the feminine עִיר, *city*, understood. Instead, however, of הִתְכַּבֵּד, six MSS., originally four more, and one by correction, read הִתְכַּבְּדִי. For the names of the locusts which here occur, see on Joel i. 4, and Amos vii. 1. The reduplication of גּוֹב בְּגֹבָי, *locust of locusts*, is designed to express the largest or most formidable of that kind of insect. For the plural form גֹּבָי, see on Amos vii. 1. מִנְּזָרַיִךְ is a ἅπαξ λεγ., derived from נָזַר, *to consecrate, separate* and *devote* to a high or noble office; hence נֶזֶר, *prince*, נֵזֶר, *consecration, diadem*. It denotes here the princes, crowned with diadems, who formed the glory of the Assyrian court. Thus Kimchi: שָׂרַיִךְ אֲשֶׁר נֵזֶר וַעֲטָרָה עַל רָאשֵׁיהֶם, "Princes with diadems and crowns on their heads." The Arab. مَنِيش, *monitor, i. e.* counsellor, is less apt, as the comparison to the locusts shows. Six of De Rossi's MSS. and three ancient editions omit the Dagesh in the Nun. The parallel term טִפְסָרַיִךְ occurs only here, and in Jer. li. 27, in the singular טִפְסָר. It is obviously a foreign word, and is in all probability compounded of what we still find in the Persic, تاو, or تاب, *strength, power,* and سر, *chief, captain, prince.* It occurs in the Targum of Jonathan, Deut. xxviii. 12, as the name of a superior angel. For other derivations see Gesen. Thesaur. *in voc.* Dr. Lee prefers deriving it from the Chald. טָב, *egregius,* and שַׂר, *dux.* Whatever might be the power of these princes and generals, and whatever number of troops they might have at their command, they would on the approach of the enemy, betake themselves to flight, and leave Nineveh to her own defence. No trace of them would be found.

18. The masculine suffixes in this and

Thy nobles have lain down;
Thy people are dispersed upon the mountains,
And there is none that collected them.
19 There is no alleviation of thy ruin;
Thy wound is grievous;
All that hear the report of thee
Shall clap their hands at thee,
For upon whom did not thy wickedness unceasingly pass?

the following verse, refer to the king of Assyria. The רֹעִים, *shepherds*, were the *satraps* or *viceroys* appointed to govern the provinces under the king of Assyria; the אַדִּירִים were the *nobles*, who as parallel with the רֹעִים, are to be regarded under the same image. See Jer. xxv. 34, where *principals* would have been better than *principal* in our common version. יִשְׁכְּנוּ, corresponding to נָמוּ, *they slumber*, is a *vox pregnans*, implying, not only that they had lain down, but that they were taking rest or were asleep. פּוּשׁ is cognate with פּוּץ, to *scatter*, *disperse*, Arab. فَشَا, *propagata et multiplicata sunt pecora*, but is not to be substituted for it, as some propose. Comp. the Arab. نفش, *pastum noctu incesserunt cameli aut oves sine pastore*. The figure is carried on throughout the verse.

19. אֵין כֵּהָה, lit. *nothing* of *infirmity*, by litotes, for *powerful*, *great* is thy breach. The deliverance of the king of Nineveh was utterly hopeless. Nothing remained but for the prophet to announce his end, and the joy which the surrounding states would express at the irretrievable ruin of an empire, whose iron sway had been so extended, and whose cruel oppressions had been unintermitting.

HABAKKUK.

PREFACE.

OF the prophet Habakkuk, we possess no information but what is purely apocryphal. The position of Delitzsch, founded upon the subscription, chap. iii. 19, that he was of the tribe of Levi, and engaged in the temple service, is too precarious to warrant its adoption. The statement made in the inscription to Bel and the Dragon in the LXX., which has been preserved from the Tetrapla of Origen, in the Codex Chisianus, ἐκ προφητείας 'Αμβακοὺμ υἱοῦ 'Ιησοῦ ἐκ τῆς φυλῆς Λευί, may be nothing more than conjecture. Considerable difference of opinion obtains respecting the time at which he flourished — the Rabbins; Grotius, Kalinsky, Kofod, Jahn, and Wahl, placing him in the first years of Manasseh; Friedrich, De Wette, Bertholdt, Justi, and Wolf, in the period of the exile; while Usher, Newcome, Eichhorn, Horne, Winer, Maurer, and Ewald, are of opinion that he prophesied in the reign of Jehoiachin, about 608—604 before Christ. This last hypothesis seems best supported, since the Chaldeans are spoken of chap. i. 5, 6, as being upon the point of invading Judah, but not as having actually entered it. The position of Rosenmüller, that chap. i. was composed under Jehoiakim, chap. ii. under Jehoiachin, and chap. iii. under Zedekiah, is altogether gratuitous. The whole forms one prophecy, and does not admit of being thus dissected.

The book embraces the wickedness of the Jews which demanded the infliction of punishment, the infliction of this punishment by the Chaldeans, the destruction of the latter in their turn, and an ode composed by the prophet in anticipation of the consequent deliverance of his people. Its position immediately after Nahum is most appropriate, setting forth the judgments of God inflicted by and upon the Chaldeans, just as the latter treated of those to be inflicted upon the Assyrians. The two prophets take up separately what Isaiah had expatiated upon at large.

In point of general style, Habakkuk is universally allowed to occupy a very distinguished place among the Hebrew prophets, and is surpassed by none of them in dignity and sublimity. Whatever he may occasionally have in common with previous writers, he works up in his own peculiar manner, and is evidently no servile copyist or imitator. His figures are well chosen, and fully carried out. His expressions are bold and animated; his descriptions graphic and pointed. The parallelisms are for the most part regular and complete. The lyric ode contained in chap. iii. is justly esteemed one of the most splendid and magnificent within the whole compass of Hebrew poetry. See the introduction to that chapter.

The words מִשְׁפָּט, i. 9 עָצֵב, ii. 6, and חֲקִיקָה, ii. 16, are peculiar to this prophet.

CHAPTER I.

THE prophet commences by briefly, yet emphatically and pathetically, setting forth the cause of the Chaldean invasion, which was to form the burden of his prophecy — the great wickedness which abounded in the Jewish nation at the time he flourished, 2-4. He then introduces Jehovah summoning attention to that invasion as the awful punishment of such wickedness, 5; describes, in a very graphic manner, the appearance, character, and operations of the invaders, 6-11; and then, by a sudden transition, expostulates with God, on account of the severity of the judgment, which threatened the annihilation of the Jewish people, 12-17.

---

1 THE Sentence, which Habakkuk the prophet saw.
2 How long shall I cry, O Jehovah! And thou hearest not?
  How long shall I cry to thee of violence, and thou savest not?
3 Why dost thou permit me to see wickedness,
  And beholdest misery?

1. For the signification of נָבִיא, see on Is. xiii. 1; and for the form הַחָזוֹן, compare הֶחָזוּי, Jer. v. 30, xxiii. 14.

2. The evils complained of in this and the two following verses, are, by many interpreters, considered to be those consequent upon the invasion of Judea by the Chaldeans. Such a construction, however, breaks up the symmetry of the connection, as marked by ver. 5, and leaves out of view the wickedness of the Jews as the cause of the calamity, contrary to the universal custom of the Hebrew prophets. They were the intestine broils, litigations, and acts of oppression, which sprang up in the kingdom of Judah, after the death of the pious reformer Josiah, and had been long the subject of complaint on the part of Habakkuk. That such was the state of things at that time is evident from Jer. xxii. 2, 13. The argument in favor of the contrary hypothesis, derived from the recurrence of the words הֶחָזוֹן, עָמָל, etc., and the phrase לֹא תִשְׁמָע, etc., in the following part of the chapter, with undoubted application to the Chaldeans, is of no weight, since they are rather to be regarded as modes of expression familiar to the prophet, than indicative of identity of subject. The influence of עַד־אָנָה, how long, upon the Preterite and Future tenses in this verse, so modifies them as to give them the force of a present time, though the one includes what had taken place down to such time, and the other, the possibility of its being still carried forward into the future. Because חָמָס, violence, occurs without a preposition, Hitzig thinks it was what was done to the prophet himself; but it is better, with Kimchi, to suppose an ellipsis of מִפְּנֵי, or, to supply עַל, on account of, because of, with the Targum. Comp. Job xix. 7; Jer. xx. 8. שָׁוַע and זָעַק are synonymes, but the latter is the more expressive of the two.

3. Some, regarding תַּרְאֵנִי and תַּבִּיט as strictly parallel, understand the suffix נִי to be omitted in the latter verb, and render: Why dost thou cause me to see wickedness, and make me look upon wrong? but תַּבִּיט, though the Hiphil conjugation, is never used in a causative sense. Besides, לְהַבִּיט, and not תַּבִּיט, is the proper synonyme, corresponding to

Chap. I.   HABAKKUK.   287

Destruction and violence are before me;
Contention and strife exalt themselves.
4 On this account the law faileth,
And true judgment goeth not forth;
Because the wicked circumvent the righteous,
Therefore perverted judgment goeth forth.

תִּרְאֵנִי. Between the two clauses, the prophet introduces Jehovah, with whom he expostulates, as an inactive spectator of the evil, because his providence did not interfere for its removal, and it was allowed, unavenged, to take its course. The expostulation thus gains in force, and scope is afforded for the striking contrast, ver. 5, in which the Most High is represented as interposing for the punishment of the wicked. מִדִּין יֵצֵא has been variously explained. The LXX., taking מִדִּין for מֵדִין, render it ὁ κριτὴς λαμβάνει; which the Syriac explains, ܘܕܝܢܐ ܩܒܠ ܡܘܗܒܬܐ, the judge taketh a bribe. Abenezra translates thus; וַיְהִי אֲנָשֵׁי רִיב וּמָדוֹן אֲשֶׁר יִשְׂאוּ רֹאשׁ, and there are men of strife and contention who lift up their head. The structure of the sentence, however, obliges us to regard יֵצֵא as parallel to תֵּרַד, so that it stands in the same relation to מִדִּין, that the substantive verb does to רִיב. The nouns in both cases are nominatives to the verbs, and יֵצֵא is here to be taken intransitively in the sense of exalting or raising one's self up. Comp. Ps. lxxxix. 10; Hos. xiii. 1; Nah. i. 5. Thus Dahl, combining the two nouns, Und Hader, und Gezank erheben sich; and Perschke, Es gibt Streit, und Zwist erhebet sich. The language is descriptive of the prevalence of a litigious spirit, in consequence of which no one was permitted quietly to possess or enjoy his rights. What was not seized upon by main force, was obtained by perversion of law.

4. עַל־כֵּן, therefore, on this account, refers not to the state of things set forth in the verse immediately preceding, but to Jehovah's forbearing to punish, spoken of ver. 2. Of the law, which ought to have been maintained in all its vital energy, it is said תָּפוּג, it chilleth, groweth frigid, languisheth, faileth; by which is meant, that it was not enforced, but left, as it were, to grow stiff and torpid, from want of use. The words, וְלֹא־יֵצֵא לָנֶצַח מִשְׁפָּט, may either be rendered, judgment, i. e., what is strictly and properly such, righteous judgment never goeth forth; or, judgment goeth not forth according to truth; לָנֶצַח, signifying to perpetuity, for ever, and, with a negative, never, like לֹא לַאֲמִתּוֹ, and truly, according to truth. Comp. the Arab. ضَحٌ, sincerus fidelis fuit; and the Eth. ኢንጹሕ: purus, mundus fuit. The latter signification of the word is that adopted by the Syr. ܘܠܐ ܢܦܩ ܕܝܢܐ ܒܫܪܪܐ, and judgment goeth not forth in purity; and is approved by Sheltinga, Hesselberg, Wolf, Rosenmüller, De Wette, Winer, Gesenius, Lee, and Ewald, chiefly on the ground of מִשְׁפָּט מְעֻקָּל, wrong or perverted judgment, occurring, as a contrasted formula, at the close of the verse. By the going forth of judgment is meant the publication of legal decisions delivered by a judge. In the time of the prophet, justice was utterly corrupted, in consequence of which there was no security either for person or property. מַכְתִּיר, from כָּתַר, to surround, is here used in a bad sense, to express the ensnaring of a person by fraud and artifice; it depicts the windings of intrigue, and is best rendered by circumvent. Thus Dathe: cum impius pium circumvenit. מְעֻקָּל, distorted, perverse, wrong, from the root

5 Look among the nations, and behold!
Be ye greatly astonished;
For I will perform a work in your days,
Which ye will not believe, though it should be told you.
6 For, behold! I will raise up the Chaldeans,
That bitter and impetuous nation;
Which traverseth the wide regions of the earth,
To seize upon habitations belonging not to it.

פָּעַל. Comp. the Syr. ܦܥܠ, *pervertit*, Arab. عَقَلَ, *constrinxit, distortos habuit pedes*; عَقْلَاء, *distortio linguæ in loquendo*. LXX. κρίμα διεστραμμένον.

5. By a sudden apostrophe Jehovah calls upon the Jews, in anticipation of the punishment which their sins deserved, and which should assuredly be inflicted upon them, to direct their attention to the events that were taking place among the surrounding nations. Nabopolassar had already destroyed the mighty empire of Assyria and founded the Chaldeo-Babylonian rule; he had made himself so formidable, that Necho found it necessary to march an army against him, in order to check his progress; and though defeated at Megiddo, he had, in conjunction with his son Nebuchadnezzar, gained a complete victory over the Egyptians at Carchemish. These events were calculated to alarm the Jews, whose country lay between the dominions of the two contending powers; but, accustomed as they were to confide in Egypt, and in the sacred localities of their own capital, Is. xxxi. 1; Jer. vii. 4, and being in alliance with the Chaldeans, they were indisposed to listen to, and treated with the utmost incredulity, any predictions which described their overthrow by that people. Such overthrow God claims as his work, though he might employ men as his instruments in effecting it. רָאָה and חָבַשׁ are frequently combined as here for the sake of effect. The phrase בַּגּוֹיִם, *among the nations*, is translated by the LXX. οἱ καταφρονηταί,

ye despisers, in which they are followed by the Syr. and Arab.; and this rendering is adopted by Paul in his quotation of the verse, Acts xiii. 41. On the other hand, the Targ. חֲזוֹ בְעַמְמַיָּא, Aquila, Symm., Theod., and Vulg. *aspicite in gentibus*, which is sustained by all the Heb. MSS. that have been collated, except five of Kennicott's, which have גוֹיִם, *nations*, without the preposition. To account for the rendering of the LXX., some are of opinion that instead of בַּגּוֹיִם, they must have read בֹּגְדִים, בֹּגְדִים, or בּוֹזִים; others, with Pococke, in his Porta Mosis, chap. iii., suggest a supposititious root, בָּגָה, the corresponding Arabic بَغَى, signifying, *injustus fuit, superbe, insolenter se gessit*; most unjustifiably insisting on the preference of some such reading to that of the Hebrew text. With respect to the quotation, Acts xiii. 41, it was obviously made by the apostle on account of the exact similarity of the case of the Jews in his day, both as regards the destruction of Jerusalem by the Romans, and the incredulity of the nation in reference to that event. "Paulus fideliter accommodat in usum suum Prophetæ verba, quia sicuti semel minatus fuerat Deus per prophetam suam Habacuc, ita etiam semper fuit sui similis." Calvin, *in loc*. The double form, הִתַּמְּהוּ תְּמָהוּ, is used for intensity. הִתַּמְּהוּ is the Hithpael for הִתְמַהְמְהוּ. Comp. הִתְמַהְמְהוּ וּתְמָהוּ, Is. xxix. 9, and my note on that verse. Before פָּעַל subaud. אֲנִי.

6. Now follows a lengthened and fearful description of the character and op-

7 It is terrible and dreadful;
   Its judgment and its dignity are from itself.
8 Swifter than leopards are its horses,
   And lighter than evening wolves;
   Its horses spread proudly along;
   Yea, its horse that come from afar:
   They fly like an eagle hastening to devour.
9 It cometh entirely for violence;
   The aspect of their faces is like the east wind;
   It collecteth the captives as sand.

erations of the instrument which Jehovah would employ in executing his work. הִנְנִי מֵקִים, which has unquestionably the force of the future, must be referred to the special *raising up* of the Chaldeans to undertake the expedition against Judea, and not to their organization as a political power, since they had already been upwards of twenty years in possession of such power under Nabopolassar. On this account, some prefer rendering the phrase, *Behold! I will excite.* For an account of this people, see on Is. xxiii. 23. In הַמַּר וְהַנִּמְהָר is a paronomasia. By מַר, *bitter*, the fierce and cruel disposition of the Chaldeans is expressed; comp. Jer. l. 42; by נִמְהָר, *rash, hasty,* the rapidity or impetuosity of their operations. In the latter part of the verse, their widely extended conquests under Nebuchadnezzar are clearly predicted.

7. שְׂאֵת, the LXX. render λῆμμα, Symm. δόγμα, Vulg. *onus,* Syr. ܩܘܠܐ, *vision.* Targ. גְּזֵרָה, *decree* or *sentence,* all deriving it from נָשָׂא, in the sense of קוֹל נָשָׂא, *to lift up,* or utter anything with *the voice,* and regarding it as equivalent to מַשָּׂא, from the same root. The signification *decree,* though approved by Hesselberg, De Wette, Winer, and Gesenius, is less appropriate than that of *dignity,* which is that of our common version, and is adopted by Hitzig, Maurer, and Ewald. Comp. Gen. xlix. 3; Job xiii. 11; Ps. lxii. 5. שְׂאֵת nowhere occurs in reference to a judicial decree. What

the prophet has in view appears to be the self-assumed political superiority of the Chaldeans in the Babylonian empire. As they had raised themselves to this dignity, so they would permit none to share in their counsels and determinations, but would act in the most arbitrary manner.

8. Frequent reference is made in Scripture to the "evening wolves," on account of the sudden ravages which, in the keenness of their hunger, they commit on the flocks at that time of the day. See Gen. xlix. 27; Jer. v. 6; Zeph. iii. 3; and comp. Virgil's Georg. iii. 537, iv. 431; and the Æneid, ii. 355, ix. 59. The LXX. render improperly, λύκους τῆς 'Αραβίας. פּוּשׁ, from the root פּוּשׁ, having here the signification of the Arab. فاش, *superbivit, gloriatus fuit,* describes the proud and spirited mien of the horses composing the Chaldean cavalry. Comp. the inimitable description of the Arabian war-horse, Job xxxix. 19-24. The meaning of the two last lines of the verse is, that the eagerness of the cavalry to plunder the Jews should be so great, that they would make no account of the fatigue occasioned by the length of their march.

9, 10. נְבֹה is the less correct orthography of כֹּל, which occurs several times in the course of the Hebrew Bible. The affix refers to כִּי, ver. 6. So great was to be the invading army, that it would seem as if it were composed of the entire

10 It maketh a mockery of kings,
  And princes are a laughter to it;
  It smileth at every fortress;
  It heapeth up earth and taketh it.
11 Then it gaineth fresh spirit;

nation. Considerable difficulty has been experienced in the interpretation of the words, מְגַמַּת פְּנֵיהֶם קָדִימָה. By the LXX. the ἅπαξ λεγ. מְגַמַּת is rendered ἀνθεστηκότας; by Symm. πρόσοψις; by the Syr. ܨܘܼܦܳܐ, *aspect*; by the Targ. מְקַבֵּל, *front*, what is opposite to anything. The Vulg. omits the word altogether, obviously on the principle of its being sufficiently expressed by *facies* immediately following. With these Abenezra and Kimchi agree; and thus also generally, Munster, Vatablus, Pagninus, Castalio, Calvin and others. On the other hand, Gesenius derives the word from the suppositious root גָּמָא, Arab. جمع, *to congregate, heap up*, and renders it *host, troop*; but, as Lee observes, *the host of their faces* is anything but Hebrew phraseology. Rosenmüller, Lee, Maurer, Hitzig, and Ewald, derive it from the same root in the significations, *impetus, desire*, a *striving after*; Ger. *streben*: while our own, and some other modern translators, adopt the idea of *absorption, supping up*, etc. from the signification of גָּמָא, גָּמָה. Considering the marked and independent coincidence of the ancient versions above quoted, borne out, as they are, by the Arab. جمّ, *adparuit; quod de re quavis extrinsicus apparet; corpus rei, seu res individua existans et conspicua*, I cannot but regard *aspect* or *appearance* as the term best adapted to convey the meaning of the prophet. קָדִימָה, in every other passage in which it occurs, has the signification of *eastward*, and it is taken in this acceptation by Abarbanel, Parkhurst, Dahl, Wolff, and Hitzig, who explain it either of the direction in which the Chaldeans would return home with their booty, or of their first coming down along the coast of the Mediterranean, and then turning direct east upon the Jews. Both constructions are forced. Gesenius renders *forwards*, and gives the whole sentence thus: *the host of their faces is forwards*. Here again I prefer the rendering of Symm. ἄνεμος καύσων; the Targ. כְּרוּחַ קִדּוּם, קָדִים, the Vulg. *ventus urens*, which, or *east wind*, its equivalent, is the rendering of many of the moderns. It is true, that the east wind is elsewhere uniformly expressed by קָדִים, without the ה; but this letter seems clearly to be here used paragogically, just as it is in נִבְנְתָה, לַיְלָה, לַיְלָה, the primitive forms of which are אֵפֹן, בֵּן, לֵיל. In some instances, indeed, it is the ה directive, indicating motion towards the quarter specified, but in others it has lost all such power. For the east wind, or samoom, see on Is. xxvii. 8. Nothing could more appropriately describe the terrific appearance of the destructive Chaldean army, than this phenomenon, which occasions awful devastation in the regions over which it passes. The collecting of the captives *like sand*, which the prophet immediately adds, corroborates the opinion that the samoom is intended, as it is frequently accompanied with whirlwinds of sand, which is collected and carried with great rapidity across the desert. The 10th verse sets forth the haughty, fearless, and irresistible character of the Chaldeans. The last clause of the verse describes the throwing up of walls or batteries before fortified cities, from which to attack them. עָפָר seldom signifies fine dust; it is more commonly used of *earth* generally, including clay, mire, etc.

11. אָז, τότε, usually, rendered *then*,

It passeth onward, and contracteth guilt, [saying,]
Is this his power through his God?
12   Art not Thou from eternity,
   O Jehovah! my God, my Holy One?
   We shall not die:
   O Jehovah! thou hast appointed it for judgment.
   O Rock! thou hast ordained it for correction.
13 Thou art of purer eyes than to regard evil;
   Thou canst not behold injustice.
   Why dost thou behold the plunderers?
   Why art thou silent when the wicked destroyeth
   Him that is more righteous than he?
14 And makest men as the fishes of the sea,

has here the force of *thereupon*, marking the transition from what had just been described to what immediately follows, and their intimate connection with each other. וַיֶּהִי is the accusative to עָמָל, which denoting *to succeed, exchange, change, renew*, etc., the phrase means, to assume, or gain a fresh accession of courage or military spirit. For this signification of חָלַף, comp. Josh. ii. 11, v. 1. Elated by the fortresses they had taken, and the victories they had won in heathen countries, the Chaldeans are represented as passing onwards into Judea; and treating with contempt the puny resistance made to them by the Jews, asking sarcastically, "Is this all your boasted power conceded to you by the God in whom you confide?" Comp. Is. x. 10, 11, xxxvi. 19, 20; Ps. lxxix. 10, cxv. 2. The aggravated guilt which they contracted (אָשֵׁם) lay in their vilifying Jehovah, by speaking of him as incapable of protecting his people. This simple construction of the verse at once frees it from the numerous difficulties with which it has been clogged by interpreters, and gives peculiar force to the interrogatory appeal in that which follows. The ellipsis of לֵאמֹר is of frequent occurrence in Hebrew. The absence of the interrogative ה is more seldom; but comp. Gen. xxvii. 24, זֶה אַתָּה for הַאַתָּה זֶה; 2 Sam. vii. 19, זֹאת, *this is*, for הֲזֹאת, *is this*;

and xvi. 17, זֶה חַסְדְּךָ אֶת־רֵעֶךָ, "*This is* thy kindness to thy friend," for, *Is this*, etc.

12. The contemptuous manner in which the enemy had treated the Most High calls forth an impassioned appeal from the prophet, in which he vindicates the eternal existence and purity of Jehovah, as that God who had formerly wrought deliverance for his people, and who was now employing the Chaldeans, not for their annihilation, but only for their punishment and correction. Since צוּר, *Rock*, is elsewhere used metaphorically of God, I have retained it in the translation. See on Is. xxvi. 4. It is here parallel to יְהוָה. The Tikkun Sopherim לֹא תָמוּת is unsupported by any authority.

13. Habakkuk resumes the expostulatory mode of address which he had employed, verses 2, 3. The בּוֹגְדִים, *plunderers*, were the Chaldeans who had been the allies of the Jews, but now treated them with violence. Comp. Is. xxi. 2, and xxiv. 16. The LXX., Syr., and Arab., have nothing corresponding to מִמֶּנּוּ; but it is expressed in Aquil., Sym., Theod., the Targ., and Vulg. Wicked as the Jews were, they were righteous in comparison of the Babylonians. Comp. for the sentiment, Ezek. xvi. 51, 52.

14. God is often said to do what he permits to be done by others. וַתַּעֲשֶׂה is

As the reptiles which have no ruler?
15 It bringeth up all with its hook,
   It gathereth them into its net,
   It collecteth them into its drag;
   Therefore it rejoiceth and exulteth.
16 Therefore it sacrificeth to its net,
   And burneth incense to its drag;
   Because through them its portion is fat,
   And its food fattened meat.
17 Is it for this it emptieth its net,
   And spareth not to slay the nations continually?

used of aquatic animals, such as crabs and other shell-fish, Ps. civ. 25, a sense which the parallelism and connection here require.

15–17. הלב is allowed by all to be here the accusative, though it was, in the same position, the nominative, ver. 9. Converting the simile employed in the preceding verse into a metaphor, the prophet describes the rapacity of the Chaldeans, the indiscriminate and universal havoc which they would effect, and their proud confidence in their own prowess. הֶעֱלָה, an unusual punctuation for הֶעֱלָה. The hook, the net, and the drag, are separately mentioned, to indicate that every means would be employed in taking captives, and whatever else came in their way. To their arms, signified by these implements of fishers, they rendered divine honors, ascribing to them solely the success which they had in war. Comp. Justin. 43. 3. "Ab origine rerum pro diis immortalibus veteras coluere." Lucian in Trag. Σκύθαι μὲν ἀκινάδῃ θύουσι. By the emptying of the net, ver. 17, is meant the depositing of the captives, etc., in Babylon, in order to go forth to fresh conquest and plunder. It is strongly implied in the questions with which the chapter concludes, that God would not permit the Chaldeans to proceed in their selfish conquests without a check, but the answer is reserved for the sequel.

CHAPTER II.

This chapter contains an introductory statement respecting the waiting posture in which the prophet placed himself, in order to obtain a divine revelation in reference to the fate of his people and of the Chaldeans, their oppressors, 1; a command which he received to commit legibly to writing the revelation which was about to be made to him, 2; an assurance, that though the prophecy should not be fulfilled immediately, yet it would certainly be at length accomplished, 3; and a contrasted description of the two different classes of the Jews to whom it was to be communicated, 4. The insolence of the Chaldeans, and their insatiable lust of conquest, are next set forth, 5; on which the proper משׁל, sentence, or prophetical denunciation, commences, in the form of a taunt on the part of the nations, in which they anticipate the downfall of that hostile power, 6–8; and the punishment of its rapacity, 9–11; of its cruelty and injustice, with a special view to the universal spread of true religion, 12-14; of its wanton and sanguinary wars, 15-17, and of its absurd and fruitless idolatry, 18, 19. The last verse of the chapter beautifully contrasts with the two preceding, by representing Jehovah as the only God, entitled to universal submission and homage.

---

1 I WILL stand upon my watch-post,
And station myself upon the fortress,
And will look out to see what he will say to me,
And what I shall reply in regard to my argument.

1. מִשְׁמֶרֶת properly signifies *observance, guard, watch,* from שָׁמַר, *to watch, observe, preserve,* etc., but here, as a concrete, the *place,* or *post of observation.* Comp. Is. xxi. 8, where it is similarly used, with מִצְפֶּה for its parallel. Thus the Syr. ܡܰܛܰܪܬܝ, *my place.* From the use of מָצוֹר in the corresponding hemistich, it is obvious that the post of a sentinel or watchman appointed to keep an eye upon what may transpire without a fortified city, is that from which the idea is here borrowed. It has been questioned whether our prophet has any real locality in view, or whether the words are to be understood metaphorically. The former is advocated by Hitzig, who after describing it as a high and steep point, such as a tower, and comparing 2 Kings ix. 17, 2 Sam. xviii. 24, says "Here, in a solitary position, far from the bustle and noise of men, with his eye directed towards heaven, and his collected spirit fixed upon God, he looks out for revelations." With the exception, however, of Wolff, who preceded him, the hypothesis has met with no approbation. All that the passage seems to teach is, that Habakkuk, anxious to ascertain the Divine purpose relative to the enemies of his people, brought his mind into such a state of holy expectancy as was favorable to the reception of supernatural communications. צָפָה, *to look about,* from which מָצִיא, a *speculator, watchman,* is derived, as likewise מִצְפֶּה, a *watch-tower,* is employed, as here in Piel, to express the looking out for an answer to prayer, Ps. v. 4. The paragogic ה of the Futures, marks the intensity of his desire. The formula בְּ, which the Syr. and Targ. render ܡܡܰܠܶܠ ܥܰܡܝ, יְדַבֵּר בִּי, in the sense of speaking or conversing *with* a person, the LXX. give by λαλήσει ἐν ἐμοί, " will speak *in* me." That the preposition בְּ is here purposely used, in preference to אֶל, לְ, עִם, or אֵת, to denote the *internal* mode of the Divine communication which the prophet received, has been maintained by some who compare רוּחַ יְהֹוָה דִּבֶּר־בִּי, "the Spirit of Jehovah spake *in* me," 2 Sam. xxiii. 2 ; Num. xii. 6, and particularly Zech. i. 9, 13, 14, ii. 2, 7, iv. 1, 4, 5, v. 5, 10, vi. 4, where the interpreting angel that addressed him in vision is uniformly styled הַמַּלְאָךְ הַדֹּבֵר בִּי, *the Angel that spake in me,* which the LXX. as uniformly render ὁ λαλῶν ἐν ἐμοί. This view was anciently expressed by Jerome, who says, " Sed et hoc notandum, ex eo quod dixerat, ut videam quid loquatur in me, propheticam visionem et eloquium Dei non extrinsicus ad Prophetas fieri, sed intrinsicus et interiori homini respondere." The same construction is put upon the phrase by Delitzsch, in his able commentary on our prophet. But it seems after all more than doubtful whether any such construction can fairly be put upon the phrase in most of the passages in which it occurs. In 2 Sam. xxiii. 2, it may be admitted, though

2   And Jehovah answered me and said:
    Write the vision and make it plain on tablets,
    That he who readeth it may run.

through or *by* will equally well suit. The other declarations made Num. xii. 6, show that it cannot there be so understood, while what Moses states, taken in connection with 1 Samuel xxv. 39, and the passages in Zechariah, goes to prove that if any stress at all is to be laid upon the preposition, it must be regarded as conveying the idea of *familiar* or *intimate* communication. In הִתְבָּרֵךְ, the suffix is not to be taken passively, but actively; *i. e.* the הִתְבָּרֵךְ, *argument, complaint, reproof*, or in what way soever the word may be rendered, was not any employed by others, but what the prophet himself hath employed in the preceding chapter. What he was desirous of obtaining, was an answer to the statement which he had there made respecting the Divine conduct in permitting the Chaldeans to multiply their conquests without end. Maurer: "causa querimoniæ meæ."

2. חָזוֹן, the *vision*, or prophetic matter which was about to be communicated to the prophet. That the idea of *digging, boring*, or *graving*, is to be attached to בָּאֵר, the position of the verb in such connection clearly forbids. Had the character of the writing been durability, such an idea might fitly have been expressed by a word signifying to *grave* or *dig deep*, into a hard substance, but as it is unquestionably legibility that is intended, we are compelled to understand the verb as relative to כְּתֹב, and that either as a new Imperative, or as an adverbial Infinitive qualifying it. In the latter case the clause should be rendered, *Write the vision, and that clearly*. Thus the LXX.: Γράψον ὅρασιν, καὶ σαφῶς. The Targ. has בְּכְתָב בְּרִיר וּמְפָרַשׁ, with which the Syr. so far agrees, rendering the verb by ܦܫܩ, *to explain*. Comp.—בָּאֵר הֵיטֵב—בַּבְּאֵר, *write*—

very plainly, Deut. xxvii. 8. The command therefore, has respect to the size, and not to the depth of the writing. הַלֻּחוֹת, *tables*, having the article, Ewald thinks the prophet refers to the tables which were openly exhibited in the market-place, on which public announcements were graven in large and clear characters, in common use among the people. The article, however, may only designate the tables which were to be employed for the purpose. It may merely indicate these as definite in the mind of the speaker. This is often the case in Hebrew, when it cannot be rendered by the definite article in other languages. For the writing tablets of the ancients, see on Is. viii. 1. The LXX. have πυξίον, *boxwood*. The reason why the prophecy should be easily legible, is stated to be, that whosoever read it might run and publish it to all within his reach. It was a joyful message to the Jews, involving as it did the destruction of their oppressor, and their own consequent deliverance. Compare Dan. xii. 4, יְשֹׁטְטוּ רַבִּים וְתִרְבֶּה הַדָּעַת, "Many shall run to and fro," viz. with the explanation of the prophecy when unsealed, "and knowledge shall be increased." The two passages are remarkably parallel as to their general meaning, though the times and events to which they refer are totally different. Comp. also Rev. xxii. 17, Καὶ ὁ ἀκούων εἰπάτω· Ἔρχου ! יָרוּץ, *to run*, is equivalent to נָבָא, *to prophesy*, Jer. xxiii. 21, obviously on the principle that those who were charged with a divine message were to use all despatch in making it known. The common interpretation, indeed, represents the meaning to consist in the writing being so large as to be easily read even by persons who were hasting past it. But in order to bear this construction, the words must read thus: לְמַעַן יִקְרָא בּוֹ הָיָה,

3 For the vision is still for an appointed time,
But it shall speak at the end, and not lie;
Though it should delay, wait for it,
For it will surely come, and not tarry.

that the runner, or, *he that runneth, may read it*. Besides, such an addition would scarcely be requisite after בָּא, and certainly would not correspond to the force of לְמַעַן, *in order that*, with which the hemistich commences.

3. The particles כִּי, and וְ, in יָפֵחַ, are correlative. מוֹעֵד, from יָעַד, *to fix, appoint*, denotes, in such connection, a season or period of time definitely fixed in the purpose of God for the occurrence of the predicted events. It is frequently employed by Daniel in this acceptation, along with קֵץ, *the end*, or termination of the state of the things comprehended in the prophecy. Comp. Dan. viii. 17, 19, xi. 27, 35; and somewhat similar phraseology, chap. viii. 26, x. 14. The term obviously implies that the period was still future, which is also expressed by the use of עוֹד, *still, yet*. This adverb is too closely connected in sense with מוֹעֵד, to admit of the rendering of Michaelis: "There will still come a vision, which shall determine the time;" which he refers to Jeremiah's prophecy of the seventy years. יָפֵחַ has been variously translated. LXX. ἀνατελεῖ; Syr. [ܢܐܙܠ]; *to come*; Vulg. *apparebit*; Targ. מְזֻמַּן, *prepared*. As, like its cognates יָפֵחַ and יָפִיחַ, the root פּוּחַ, of which יָפֵחַ is the future in Hiphil, signifies *to breathe, blow, puff*, Michaelis, Bauer, Stäudlin, De Wette, Hesselberg, Maurer, Winer, Hitzig, Ewald, and Hengstenberg, in his Psalms, vol. i. p. 255, contend, that it is here to be taken in the acceptation of *panting, hasting, eagerly moving forward* to an object, and that the meaning is, that the prophecy hastened to its accomplishment. Such construction, however, requires us to attach to קֵץ the idea of the object or objects on which a prophecy terminates, the end or extreme point beyond which its import does not extend. But the word nowhere occurs in this acceptation, but, as Delitzsch has shown, it always designates, in a prophetico-chronological sense, *the time of the end*, whatever may be the compass of events to which reference may be had. Besides, לַקֵּץ and לְמוֹעֵד are so obviously parallel, that they do not admit of being differently construed. לַקֵּץ here, is only an abbreviation of the phrase לְקֵץ־יָמִין, Dan. viii. 17, of which we have again a varied form in לְמוֹעֵד קֵץ, ver. 19. I therefore agree with Abarbanel, Jarchi, Kimchi, Vatablus, Calvin, Coccius, Rosenmüller, Wolff, and Delitzsch, in assigning to יָפֵחַ in this place the acceptation of *speaking, breathing out words*, in which acceptation the verb is used Prov. xii. 17, xiv. 5, 25, xix. 5, 9. This interpretation derives support from the antithetical כָּזָב לֹא, in which the idea of speaking is obviously implied. The meaning of the verse will accordingly be, that though the destruction of the Chaldean power, about to be predicted, was not to take place immediately, yet it was definitely fixed in the Divine counsel, and would infallibly happen at the termination of the period appointed for the exercise of its oppression, and for the deliverance of the captive Hebrews; it was to be an object of confident expectation, though his arrival might be somewhat protracted. For יְמַהְמֵהַּ, see on Is. xxix. 9. לֹא יְבַזֵּב, is emphatic, denoting the certainty of the event. אָחַר, signifies *to stay long*, and intimates that the predicted event would not be protracted to any great length. Instead of לֹא יְאַחֵר, upwards of forty of Kennicott and De Rossi's MSS., four ancient editions, the LXX., Aquil., Syr., Targ., and Vulg., read לֹא יְאַחֵר.

4   Behold the proud! his soul is not right within him;
   But the righteous shall live by his faith.

4. Most interpreters apply the former hemistich of this verse to the Chaldeans, supposing the denunciation against them to begin here; but its coherence with the preceding verse is too close to admit of this construction, while the latter hemistich, were such application admitted, would awkwardly interrupt the prophecy at its very commencement. On the other hand, the whole verse most naturally and appropriately applies to the Jewish people, and contains a description of those who would proudly reject the prophetic vision, and of those who would give it a cordial reception: the two members forming a marked and striking antithesis. עֻפְּלָה, of which עֻפְּלָה may either be the third feminine singular of Pual, or a noun formed from that part of the verb, occurs elsewhere only in Hiphil, Num. xiv. 44; but it is evident, from the use of the derivative עֹפֶל, as denoting a *swelling*, *tumor*, *mount*, *hill*, etc., and the comparison of the context of both passages, that it is employed metaphorically to express the idea of *mental inflation*, *elation*, *pride*, *presumption*, or the like. Such Hebrew usage supports the relation of the verb to the Arab. غَفِلَ, *tumore laboravit*, rather than to غَفَلَ, *neglexit vel omisit rem, per socordiam non curavit*, for which Pococke contends at great length in his Porta Mosis; though the rendering of the LXX. ὑποστείληται, and that of Aquila, νωχελευόμενου, may both be referred to the radical notion conveyed by this root. Its reference to עָפֵל, *to set*, *become dark* as proposed by Abarbanel, and approved by Deutsch and Wolff, cannot be sustained. Nor must it be overlooked, that though the following words, לֹא־יָשְׁרָה בוֹ נַפְשׁוֹ, are not to be regarded as epexegetical of the term in question, they nevertheless appear to have been suggested by it. יָשַׁר signifies not only to be *straight* or *right*, in opposition to being *crooked*, but also, *even*, *level*, *plain*, *smooth*, in opposition to what is *rough*, *rugged*, and *difficult*. See 1 Kings vi. 35; Ezra viii. 21; Ps. v. 9; Prov. xxiii. 31, where יִתְהַלֵּךְ בְּמֵישָׁרִים means, goeth *sweetly* or *pleasantly down*, or as Jerome gives it, *ingreditur blande; De Dieu, subit facillime*. Com. the Arab. سهل, *facilis fuit res; facilitas, lenitas*. Of the reading עֻפְּלָה, found in one of Kennicott's MSS., or עֻפָּלָה, as it is written in another, no account is to be made, though in his Dissert. Gen. § 72, that author prefers it to that which is attested by all the other codices. The Syr. ܥܘܠܐ, *wickedness*, is founded upon a mistake of עֻפְּלָה for עָפְלָה. עָפְלָה I consider to be an abstract noun, used elliptically for אִישׁ עָפְלָה, *a man of arrogance* or *presumption*, and so to be rendered adjectively, the *proud*, *presumptuous*, etc. For instances of similar ellipsis, comp. אֲנִי תְפִלָּה, *I am prayer*, for אֲנִי אִישׁ תְּפִלָּה, *I am a man of prayer*, Ps. cix. 4; זָדוֹן, *arrogance*, for אִישׁ זָדוֹן, *man of arrogance*, i. e. arrogant, Jer. l. 31, 32; Dan. ix. 23. אַתָּה חֲמוּדוֹת, *thou art delights*, for אִישׁ חֲמוּדוֹת אַתָּה, *thou art a man of delights*, i. e. greatly beloved, as it is expressed in full, chap. x. 11, 19. See on Micah vi. 9. The term is thus strictly antithetical to צַדִּיק, *the just*, in the following hemistich, precisely as the predicate לֹא־יָשְׁרָה בוֹ נַפְשׁוֹ, *his soul is not right within him*, is to צַדִּיק בֶּאֱמוּנָתוֹ יִחְיֶה, *by his faith he shall live*. With respect to this latter point of antithesis, it must be evident, that, as יִחְיֶה, the latter predicate, signifies not merely *to live*, but *to live well*, *be happy*, the former must convey the idea of its opposite. This was clearly perceived by Luther, who often discovers a wonderful sagacity in seizing upon the meaning of a passage, though in his translation he may not adhere to the strict significations

5 Moreover wine is treacherous;

of single words. He renders the words thus: *Siehe wer halsstarrig ist, der wird keine Ruhe in seinem Herzen haben.* "Behold he who is stubborn shall have no tranquillity in his heart." So also Gesenius: "Lo, the lofty-minded, his soul is not tranquil within him." Maurer: "*Non planus, complanatus, compositus, tranquillus, etc., est animus ejus.*" To this interpretation I adhere, as best meeting the exigency of the passage. While those Jews who, elated by false views of security, refused to listen to the Divine message should have their security disturbed, and their minds agitated by the calamities with which they would be visited, such as lived righteously before God and men, should experience true happiness in the exercise of faith in that message, and others which God might communicate to them by his prophets. Thus a Lapide: "*Incredulus habet animam, id est vitam, non rectam, sed distortam, anxiam, miseram, et infelicem; justus autem in fide et spe sua agit vitam rectam, puta lætam, quietam, sanctam et felicem.*" בו, *in*, or *within him*, is added to show that the verb יָשְׁרָה is not to be taken here as referring to anything of an objective character, such as the Divine estimation, agreeably to the meaning of the phrase יָשָׁר בְּעֵינֵי יְהוָֹה, *to be right in the sight of Jehovah*, but must be understood as marking the subjective sphere of the predicate. For the fullest view of the various constructions, both logical and philological, that have been put upon this verse, I refer the more curious reader to Delitzsch. From the discrepancy existing between the Hebrew, and the version of the LXX., some have argued a corruption of the former, and have proposed emendations; but the difference has arisen either from a desire on the part of these translators to render the sense plainer, or from their mistaking one letter for another that is similar. They render, ἐὰν ὑποστείληται οὐκ εὐδοκεῖ ἡ ψυχή μου ἐν αὐτῷ. ὁ δὲ δίκαιος ἐκ πίστεως μου ζήσεται. To such rendering, its quotation by Paul in Heb. x. 38, gives no sanction, since he not unfrequently quotes passages from that version containing renderings to which there never could have been anything corresponding in the Hebrew text. In the present instance he takes a liberty with the version itself, placing the latter part of the verse first, and the former last, and omitting μου after πίστις. Nor, it must further be observed, is it his intention either here, or in Rom. i. 17, and Gal. iii. 11, in employing the words, ὁ δίκαιος ἐκ πίστεως ζήσεται, to maintain, that the doctrine of justification by faith in Christ is taught by Habakkuk; he merely applies the principle laid down by the prophet respecting the instrumentality of faith in securing the safety and happiness of the pious portion of the Jewish people to the subject of which he is treating — the influence of faith in the gospel scheme of salvation. As צַדִּיק is the nominative absolute, בֶּאֱמוּנָתוֹ cannot be connected with it, except in regard to the pronominal reference, but must be joined with יִחְיֶה, *as for the righteous, he shall live by his faith.* From the circumstance, however, that the two former words are, in most MSS. and editions, joined by the accents Merca and Tiphca, while the latter, as a disjunctive, separates the second from the third, it might seem that the Rabbins construed the clause thus: *but the just by his faith, shall live.* And this construction would seem to confirm the hypothesis that in his quotation, Rom. i. 17, Gal. iii. 11, the Apostle connects ἐκ πίστεως with ὁ δίκαιος, and not with ζήσεται; but as quoted by him, Heb. x. 38, the former division of the words alone suits the connection, in which his object evidently is to show the necessity of faith as a means of perseverance under all the afflictions and persecutions of the christian life. See Owen on the passage.

5. The two first lines of this verse partake of the nature of a proverb, being

The haughty man stayeth not at home,
Because he enlargeth his desire as Sheol;
He is even as death, and cannot be satisfied;
He gathered for himself all the nations,
And collecteth for himself all the people,

6 Shall not all these utter an ode against him,
A song of derisive taunt against him, and say:
Wo to him that increaseth that which is not his!
How long?
And ladeth himself with many pledges!

expressed in a short and pithy manner, and admitting of general application. It is, however, obvious from the connection with what follows, that they are introduced with special reference to the Chaldean power, the nefarious conduct of which the prophet immediately proceeds to describe. The phrase הַיַּיִן בֹּגֵד, *wine is a deceiver*, has its parallel, Prov. xxx. 1, לֵץ הַיַּיִן, *wine is a mocker*. יָהִיר occurs only here, and Prov. xxi. 24, where, from its connection with זֵד, *proud*, as its synonyme, it clearly signifies *elated, haughty*, LXX. ἀλαζών. Chald. יְהִיר, as used by the Rabbins, *superbivit*. See Buxt. *in voc.* Thus also in the Nazaræan Syr. ܝܗܝܪ, Ethpa. *superbivit*. There is, therefore, no necessity for recurring to the Arab., the attempted derivations from which are very precarious. The introductory particles וְאַף כִּי are designed to connect the proper prophecy with what had just been developed of the vision, as that which formed the most important part of it. אַף is expressive of addition, and כִּי of certainty. That the prophet has his eye upon the intemperance to which the Babylonians were greatly addicted, there can be little doubt. Comp. Dan. v.; with Herod. i. 191; Xenoph. Cyrop. vii. 5, 15. "Babylonii maxime in vinum et quæ ebrietatem sequuntur effusi sunt." Curtius, v. 1. How strikingly was the deceptive character of wine exemplified in the case of Belshazzar! נָוָה, primarily signifies to *dwell, remain at rest*, which signification better suits the present passage than the secondary one of *being decorous, proper*, etc., adopted by the Vulg., Ewald, and some others. Still it is a question, whether the not remaining tranquil is to be viewed as a voluntary or as an involuntary act. The Targ., Rashi, Kimchi, Ben-Melec, De Wette, Justi, Maurer, and Delitzsch, refer it to the forcible ejection for the Babylonians: Abenezra, Abarbanel, Rosenmüller, Wolff, Wahl, Gesenius, and Hitzig, to their restless disposition, by which they were continually impelled to go forth upon new expeditions of conquest. The latter seems, from what follows, to be the preferable interpretation. For תִּרְהַב בָּהּ נַפְשׁוֹ, see on Is. v. 14, and comp. Prov. xxvii. 20, xxx. 15. The insatiable desire of conquest, which specially showed itself in the reign of Nebuchadnezzar, is here forcibly predicted. כָּל־הַגּוֹיִם and כָּל־הָעַמִּים must be restricted to all the nations with which the Jews were familiar.

6. Comp. Is. xiv. 4, and see my notes on מָשָׁל as there occurring. מְלִיצָה occurs only here, and Prov. i. 6, in which verse also all the three synonymes מָשָׁל, מְלִיצָה, and חִידָה are found. It properly signifies *derision, taunt, scorn*, from לוּץ, *to stammer, speak barbarously or unintelligibly;* hence *to mock, deride;* and thus the substantive obtained the acceptation, *taunt, taunting song.* LXX. σκοτεινὸν λόγον. In the later Hebrew the word is used to denote poetry in general. חִידָה means *oratio inflexa, per-*

7 Shall not they rise up suddenly that have lent thee on usury?
And awake that shall shake thee violently?
And thou shalt become their prey.
8 Because thou hast plundered many nations,

plexa, an enigma, highly figurative and difficult language, requiring acuteness and ingenuity fully to understand it. Comp. the Arab, حَانٌ, حُونٌ, *superavit negotii difficultatem*. Delitzsch not unaptly instances the words עַבְטִיט, ver. 6, נִשְׁךְ, ver. 7, and קִיקָלוֹן, ver. 16, as enigmata of this description. The derisive ode or song commences immediately, and occupies the rest of the chapter. It consists of five stanzas, the three first of which are composed of three verses each, the fourth of four verses, and the last of two. Each stanza has its distinct and appropriate subject; and with the exception of the last, they all commence with הוֹי, *wo*, the denunciative interjection; and have each a verse at the close, beginning with כִּי; thus forming an organic whole of singular force and beauty. וְיֹאמַר is to be taken impersonally or collectively. עַבְטִיט has been variously interpreted. Several of the Rabbins, the Syr., Vulg., and after them Luther, and other translators, take it to be compounded of עַב, *dense*, and טִיט, *clay*, which ten of Kennicott's MSS. read as two words, and most commentators who follow them suppose riches or earthly goods to be meant: but it is more in accordance with the grammatical form of the word to regard it as a quadriliteral noun, from the root עָבַט, *to exchange, give a pledge;* in Hiph., *to lend on a pledge*. The signification of the noun is thus correctly given by Lee: "*an accumulation of pledges* in the hand of an unfeeling usurer." The form is that of קְטַלְטֵל as in חֲבַלְבֵּל from חֶבֶל; בַּמְרִיר or בְּמְרִיר from בְּמֵר; סַגְרִיר from סָגַר; פְּצַצְפֵּץ from פָּצַץ. The reduplication expresses intensity or augmentation. Maurer, *copia pignorum captorum*, an interpretation already given by Nic. Fuller in

his Miscell. Sac. lib. v. cap. viii. The Chaldean power is thus represented as a rapacious and cruel usurer, who had accumulated the property of others, and from whom it would again be taken. Comp. Deut. xxiv. 10–13, for the use of עָבַט, and the law against cruelty in usurers. The hypothesis of Delitzsch, that עַבְטִיט is, as an enigmatical term, to be understood both as a compound, and as a quadriliteral, is not in keeping with his usual good sense.

7. פֶּתַע, *suddenly*, corresponds to עַד־מָתַי, *how long?* in the preceding verse, and not improbably refers to the unexpectedness of the attack made upon Babylon by the Medes and Persians. See on Is. xxi. 3, 4. נָשַׁךְ properly signifies *to bite*, and thus it is rendered in most versions. Some translate, *oppress;* but, since it likewise signifies *to lend on usury*, there can be little doubt the prophet intended it to be understood in this acceptation, as a striking antithesis to עַבְטִיט at the close of the preceding verse. Comp. the Aram. נְכַת, ܢܟܬ, *momordit, usuras exegit.* Arab. قرض, the same. The same mode of speech was not unknown both to the Greeks and Romans. Aristoph. Nub. i. 12, δακνόμενος ὑπὸ τῶν χρεῶν. Lucan. i. 171, *usura vorax.* The meaning is, that as the Babylonians had cruelly amassed the property of others, so other nations, like devouring usurers, would unmercifully deprive them of all they had acquired. יְקִיצוּ, defective for יְקִיצוּ, as in Jud. xvi. 20. מְזַעְזְעֶיךָ, the Phil. participle of זוּעַ, *to shake, agitate.* The reduplicate form conveys the idea of violent or excessive agitation. The allusion is to the violent seizure of a debtor by his creditor. See Matt. xviii. 28.

8. The remainder of the nations con-

All the remainder of the people shall plunder thee;
Because of the blood of men, and of the violence done to the earth,
To the city and all that dwell in it.

9 Wo to him that procureth wicked gain for his house,
That he may establish his nest on high,
To be preserved from the power of calamity.

10 Thou hast devised what is a disgrace to thy house,
Cutting off many people, and sinning against thyself.

11 For the stone crieth out from the wall,
And the brick from the timber answereth it;

sisted of those who had escaped the devastation of the Chaldeans. The terms *man*, *earth*, and *city*, are to be understood generally, and are not to be restricted to the Jews, with their country and its metropolis. חָמַס־אֶרֶץ is the genitive of object.

9. In the stanza, comprising this and the two following verses, the avarice and selfishness of the Chaldeans are denounced. The phrase בָּצַע בֶּצַע is very common in Hebrew. The verb denotes *to cut*, or *break off*, as the Orientals, especially the Chinese do, pieces of silver and other metals in their money transactions with each other. Hence it came to be applied, in a bad sense, to such as were greedily occupied with such transactions, and its derivative בֶּצַע, to signify *wicked gain, lucre*. To mark it, in the present instance, as specially atrocious, רָע, *wicked*, is added. בֵּית, *house*, stands here for the royal family; קֵן, *nest*, for the *arx regia*, to express its inaccessible height, the allusion being taken from the nest of the eagle, which is built on high rocks, difficult of access. See Job xxxix. 27, and comp. Numb. xxiv. 21; Jer. xlix. 16.

10. "Thou hast devised disgrace to thy house," means thy schemes and projects shall issue in the infamy of thy family. Instead of קְצוֹת, the infinitive of קָצָה, the ancient versions have read קָצוֹתָ, the preterite of קָצַץ. The infinitive may either follow in construction

יָעַץ preceding, or the following יָשׁוּב. I have adopted the latter, and rendered it participially. It properly denotes the direct aim of the action predicted by the preceding finite verb. For the last clause, comp. Prov. viii. 36, xx. 2.

11. An exquisite instance of bold and daring personification, by which the materials used in the construction of the royal palace, and other sumptuous buildings, at Babylon, are introduced as responsively complaining of the injustice which they had suffered, either in their having been taken from their original owners, or in their being made subservient to the scenes of wickedness that were enacted in their presence. Comp. Luke xix. 40. The Targ. adds to the first line, בְּלָא דִינָא עַל, *because violence has been done to it*. כָּפִיס occurs only here, but from the signification of the cognate Syr. ܟܦܣ, *connexuit*, it has been supposed to mean the *cross beam* by which the walls of a building are held together. Thus Sym., Theod., and the 5th vers., σύνδεσμος, LXX. κάνθαρος, *scarabæus*, but which some think was originally κανθήριον, which Vitruvius explains as signifying a cross-beam. Arab. من الشبجرة, والوتد, *the pin from the wood.* According to the Mishnah, the word signifies *a half brick*, which Parchon also gives as the meaning. He thus describes it: בריס ע׳ לבנים קטנים עשויין בבשון בכלי חרס ובוניס בהת

12   Wo to him that buildeth a town through bloodshed,
     And establisheth a city through injustice.
13   Behold! is it not from Jehovah of hosts?
     So that the people shall labor for the very fire;
     Yea, the nations shall weary themselves for mere vanity.
14   For the earth shall be filled
     With the knowledge of the glory of Jehovah,
     As the waters cover the sea.
15   Wo to him that giveth drink to his neighbor,
     Pouring out thy wrath, and making him drunk;
     In order to look upon their nakedness.

הבנים, *small bricks prepared in the kiln, like pottery, and used in building edifices.* This interpretation is confirmed by the rendering of Aquila, μάζα, *what is baked,* and by the abundant use of bricks by the Babylonians, which are still visible in the ruins of their city. Citing this passage in the Taanith, Rashi explains it to be "half a brick which is usually laid between two layers of wood," Delitzsch. That it was not the wood itself is evident from the following מֵעֵץ, *from* or *out of the wood,* except we take the preposition as indicating the material of which the beam consisted. In this latter case, the words should be rendered, *And the wooden beam answereth it;* but against such construction the parallel מִקִּיר, *out of the wall,* is an insuperable objection.

12, 13. The subject of the third stanza, which begins here, was naturally suggested by the concluding verse of the preceding. The riches which enabled the king of Babylon to rebuild and enlarge the royal city, were procured in the bloody wars in which he had engaged; and the works themselves were carried up by people from different parts of the empire, and by captives from other nations. The preposition מִן prefixed in מֵאֵת יְהוָה, points out the ultimate cause of the destruction of the Babylonian empire — the overruling providence of God, who, in order to give prominence to his resistless omnipotence, is designated

יְהוָה צְבָאוֹת, *Jehovah of hosts.* For this epithet, see on Is. i. 9. בְּדֵי is not a poetic form for בְּ, but is intensive, דַּי, signifying *sufficiency, abundance.* The preposition here points out the final issue or result of the labor and fatigue connected with the erections in question, the conflagration and depopulation of the city of Babylon. The last two lines of verse 13 are found in Jer. li. 58; only אַךְ and רִיק have exchanged places, יִיעֲפוּ stands for יִעֲפוּ, and the defective form וְיָגְעוּ for וְיִיגְעוּ. For the destruction by fire, comp. Jer. li. 30, 58; for her desolation, ver. 43. Hitzig, from the mere circumstance of the use of the same terms Micah vii. 10, applies the prophecy to Jehoiakim!

14. This verse is clearly predictive of the gospel dispensation, to the introduction of which the destruction of the Babylonian power was indispensable, inasmuch as it involved the deliverance of the Jews from captivity, and their re-occupation of their own land before the advent of the Messiah. See on Is. xi. 9, 11, the former of which verses contains a similar prediction of the same event. יָם *sea,* is used for *the bed of the sea.*

15. The commencement of the fourth stanza. Though the idea of the shameless conduct of drunkards, here depicted, may have been borrowed from the profligate manners of the Babylonian court, yet the language is not to be taken lit-

16 Thou art filled with shame, not with glory;
Drink thou also, and show thyself uncircumcised;
The cup of Jehovah's right hand shall come round to thee,
And great ignominy shall be upon thy glory.

erally, as if the prophet were describing such manners, but, as the sequel shows, is applied allegorically to the state of stupefaction, prostration, and exposure, to which the conquered nations were reduced by the Chaldeans. See on Is. li. 17, 20; and comp. Ps. lxxv. 8; Jer. xxv. 15-28, xlix. 12, li. 7; Ezek. xxiii. 31, 32; Rev. xiv. 10, xvi. 9, xviii. 6. רְעֵה is a collective, and thus is equivalent to רֵעָיו in the plural, which is required to agree with the suffix in מְעוֹרֵיהֶם. The latter noun is derived from עוּר Arab. عَارَ, to be naked, as its synonyme עֶרְוָה is from עָרָה. In הֵעָרֵל is a change from the third person to the second, for the sake of effect. There not being anything in the ancient Greek versions corresponding to the ך, is no ground for its rejection, since their authors frequently took liberties even when professedly most verbal. חֵמָה is not the construct of חֵמָה or חֵמֶת, bottle, but of חֵמָה, heat, or wrath. Comp. בְּאַרְצָם הַגְּדוֹלָה, Is. lxiii. 6, and li. 17; Jer. xxv. 15; Rev. xvi. 19. Delitzsch attempts in vain to set aside the signification of pour, as inhering in the root שָׁפַךְ; Arab. سَفَكَ, effudit. Cognate

שָׁפַךְ. Targ. סְבַע. סְבַע is the infinitive used instead of the participle. The language of the concluding clause of the verse is expressive of the deepest humiliation on the one hand, and of the most haughty wantonness on the other.

16. The preposition in מִדְּבַשׁ is negative, as in אָרַבְתָּ רַע מִטּוֹב, Ps. lii. 5. The full force of the hemistich is, "Thou art satiated, but it is with shame, not with glory." Kimchi and others, comparing הִתְרַעֲלָה כּוֹס, Is. li. 17, and רַע

רַע, Zech. xii. 2, suppose that in הֵעָרֵל, be thou uncircumcised, there is a transposition of the letters ע and ר, and that the verb has originally been הֵרָעֵל, reel or stagger. And thus the LXX. (καρδία σαλεύθητι καὶ σείσθητι) have interpreted it, and have been followed by the Arab., Syr., and Vulg. There is, however, such a manifest agreement with מְעוֹרֵיהֶם, pudenda eorum, at the close of the preceding verse, that the interpretation cannot be admitted. In the mouth of a Hebrew no term could have expressed more ineffable contempt. Comp. 1 Sam. xvii. 36. As the Chaldeans had treated the nations which they conquered in the most disgusting manner, so they, in their turn, should be similarly treated. To express the certainty of the event, the verbs are in the imperative. See on Is. vi. 10. תִּסּוֹב is the future in Niphal, and conveys the idea of the cup of suffering being transferred from one nation to another, each in its turn, being made to drink of it. Comp. Jer. xxv. 6; Lam. iv. 21. קִיקָלוֹן, the Vulg. renders, vomitus ignominiæ, as if compounded of קִיא for קוֹא, vomit, and קָלוֹן, shame. In nine MSS. it is read as two words, and this etymology is approved by most Jewish and Christian interpreters. It is, however, more in accordance with the genius of the Hebrew language, to regard it as a reduplicate form of קָלוֹן, employed for the sake of intensity, after the form קְטַלְטַל: only instead of קַלְקָלוֹן we have the softer קִיקָלוֹן. Comp. the Syr.

ܢ݁ܩܰܠܩܶܠ for קִלְקֵל. Thus the LXX. ἀτιμία; Syr. ܨܰܥܪܳܐ; Targ. קְלָנָא. The glory of the Babylonians was to be completely eclipsed by the deep disgrace in which they should be involved.

17 For the violence done to Lebanon shall cover thee,
   As the destruction of beasts terrifieth them;
   Because of the blood of men, and the violence done to the
      earth,
   To the city, and all that dwell in it.
18 What profiteth the graven image which its maker graveth —
   The molten image, and the teacher of falsehood?
   In which the maker of his work trusteth —
   Making dumb idols.
19   Woe to him that saith to the wood, Awake!
   Wake up! to the dumb stone.
   It teach! There it is,

17. חֲמַס לְבָנוֹן and חֲמַס־אֶרֶץ are genitives of object. That Lebanon is not here to be understood literally, but figuratively, of Jerusalem, seems fully established by the prophetic style in other passages, especially Jer. xxii. 23; Ezek. xvii. 3, 12; Zech. xi. 1. The aptness of the figure consists partly in the circumstance, that cedars from that mountain were employed in the construction of the temple and other houses in Jerusalem, 1 Kings vi. 9, 10, 18, vii. 2, ix. 10, 11; 2 Chron. i. 15; and partly in its stateliness and grandeur as the metropolis. Against this interpretation, the objections do not apply which Delitzsch makes to the opinion of those who maintain that by Lebanon the land of Palestine is meant. כָּסָה, to cover, is used emphatically to express the completeness of the destruction which should overtake the Chaldeans. Similar violence to that which they had exercised should be brought upon themselves. The וְ in וְשֹׁד is a particle of comparison, retaining, indeed, its ordinary conjunctive power, but also introducing a clause designed to illustrate the preceding. Of this idiom, the following are instances: אָדָם לְעָמָל יוּלָד וּבְנֵי רֶשֶׁף יַגְבִּיהוּ עוּף, Man is born to trouble, AND (AS) birds of prey fly aloft, Job v. 7. כִּי־אֹזֶן מִלִּין תִּבְחָן וְחֵךְ יִטְעַם לֶאֱכֹל, For the ear trieth words, AND (AS) the palate tasteth food. This construction entirely obviates the difficulty which

necessarily attaches to the attempts that have been made to interpret the בְּהֵמוֹת, beasts, of the inhabitants of Palestine. The prophet compares the confusion and destruction which should come upon the enemy of the Jews to those experienced by the wild beasts when brought into circumstances from which they cannot escape. חָתַת signifies to be broken, broken in pieces, destroyed, confounded, terrified. In the present form יְחִיתַן, the Yod is substituted for the Dagesh in the regular form יְחִתַּן, as תָּתְּמוּ for תַּתְמוּ, Is. xxxiii. 1. The Nun appended is not paragogic, but the verbal suffix of the third feminine plural, agreeing with בְּהֵמוֹת. There is no sufficient ground for changing ן into ם, though the authors of some of the ancient versions may have thus read. For the last clause, see on verse 8.

18, 19. These verses expose the folly of idolatry to which the Babylonians were wholly addicted. It might be supposed, from all the other stanzas having been introduced by a denunciatory הוֹי, wo, that a transposition has here taken place, and that the nineteenth ought to be read before the eighteenth: and Green has thus placed them in his translation; but there is a manifest propriety in anticipating the inutility of idols, in close connection with what the prophet had just announced respecting the downfall of Babylon, before delivering his

Overlaid with gold and silver,
But there is no breath at all within it.
20 But Jehovah is in his holy temple;
Keep silence before him all the earth.

denunciation against their worshippers themselves. בְּ, in both instances, is used as a relative pronoun, as in Gen. iii. 19. iv. 26; Is. lvii. 20. The idol is called "a teacher of falsehood," on account of the lying oracles that were connected with its worship. For these verses, compare Is. xliv. 9–20; Jer. x. In the latter part of the nineteenth verse, the language is highly and pointedly ironical. הוּא יוֹרֶה, *it teach!* is an emphatic form of putting a question which requires a negative reply. יוֹרֶה forms a paronomasia with מוֹרֶה in the preceding verse. הִנֵּה הוּא, *there it is.* Such is the force of the interjection הִנֵּה in this place — it not being followed as usual by the accusative, but for the sake of making the idol more prominent, by the nominative case.

20. In striking contrast with the utter nihility of idols, Jehovah is here introduced, at the close of the prophecy, as the invisible Lord of all, occupying his celestial temple, whence he is ever ready to interpose his omnipotence for the deliverance and protection of his people and the destruction of their enemies. Comp. Is. xxvi. 21. Such a God it becomes all to adore in solemn and profound silence. Ps. lxxvi. 8, 9; Zeph. i. 7; Zech. ii. 13.

CHAPTER III.

Though forming a distinct whole, this chapter is intimately connected with the two preceding, the subjects contained in which it presupposes, and is evidently designed to afford consolation to the Jews during the national calamities there anticipated. It exhibits a regular ode beginning with a brief but simple and appropriate exordium; after which follows the main subject, which is treated in a manner perfectly free and unrestrained, as the different topics rose one after another in the powerfully excited mind of the prophet; and finishes with an epigrammatic resumption of the point first adverted to in the introduction, and the practical lesson which the piece was intended to teach.

With respect to the body of the ode, interpreters are greatly divided in opinion. The Fathers generally, and after them many Catholic commentators, and among Protestants, Cocceius, Bengel, Roos, and others, apply the whole chapter, with certain modifications, to New Testament times, and subject it to all the uncertainty of imaginary interpretation. But the principal point of disagreement relates to the theophania, or Divine interposition, so sublimely set forth. ver. 3—15. According to the Targum, Abarbanel, Abenezra, Tarnovius, Munster, Clarius, Drusius, Schnurrer, Herder, Michaelis, Green, Lowth, Tingstadius, Eichhorn, Justi, Hesselberg, Ackermann, and Ewald, the prophet adverts to the wonderful displays of the power and majesty of God during the early history of the Hebrews. Maurer, Hitzig, and Delitzsch, on the other hand, contend that the future interposition of Jehovah for the destruction of the Chaldeans, is what he exclusively contemplates. The last-mentioned author has not only gone at great length, and with much minuteness, into the subject, but appears to have exhausted all his critical and exegetical ingenuity in his attempt to establish his hypothesis. Taking for granted that יָבֹא, ver. 3, cannot, by any possibility, be construed otherwise than to express the strict futurity of the advent predicated, he proceeds to show, from what he considers to be the organic structure of the ode; from the connection of שָׁמַעְתִּי and וַתִּרְגַּז, ver. 16; and from certain features of the picture itself, that what he calls the lyric-prophetical view is alone to be admitted. I must, however, confess, that after a careful examination of his arguments, I can discover nothing in them that goes to overturn the historical position adopted by the numerous writers above mentioned. That nothing in the shape of a regular and specific recital of distinct facts is exhibited in the tableau, cannot fairly be urged against this interpretation, since such a recital would ill accord with the enthusiasm and impetuosity which are so characteristic of the ode as a species of poetry. The abrupt and rapid transitions of the prophet did not admit of more than a slight, though sublimely figurative allusion, to one or two localities, which it was necessary to specify, in order to call up the general scene of events to the mind of the reader: all the rest is left to be supplied by his familiar acquaintance with the sacred national records. What he aims at is to produce a powerful impression by condensing, within the shortest possible limits, a view of the *magnalia Dei*, as exhibited in these records. And this he does by giving utterance to the total impression which they produced upon his own mind, rather than by furnishing a detailed historical description. Regarding the composition in this light, the obscurity and apparent incoherence which attach to certain parts of it are at once accounted for.

As parallels to this ode, we may adduce Deut. xxxiii. 2—5; Jud. v. 4, 5; Ps. lxvlii. 7, 8, lxxvii. 13—20, cxiv.; Is. lxiii. 11—14. That the Holy Spirit availed himself, so to speak, of some of these passages in presenting the subject to the view of the prophet, there can, I think, be little doubt. The agreement in point of phraseology, especially as it respects Ps. lxxvii. is most palpable. Some, indeed, have maintained the priority of our ode to the Psalm; but Delitzsch has proved, by an elaborate collation of passages and expressions, that this hypothesis is entirely without foundation, and that Habakkuk had the Psalm brought to his mind, just as he had the song of Moses called up to his recollection.

The following description of this sublime ode, by the master pen of Bishop Lowth, is not more beautiful than just: "The prophet, indeed, illustrates this subject throughout with equal magnificence; selecting from such an assemblage of miraculous incidents, the most noble and important, displaying them in the most splendid colors, and embellishing them with the sublimest imagery, figures, and diction, the dignity of which is so heightened and recommended by the superior elegance of the conclusion, that were it not for a few shades, which the hand of time has apparently cast over it in two or three passages, no composition of the kind, would, I believe, appear more elegant or more perfect than this poem." Lect. xxviii. Whether the hand of time has really cast any shades over it will appear in the sequel.

That it was designed for use in public worship, appears both from the inscription and the subscription, as well as from the musical term סֶלָה, *Selah*, occurring verses 3, 9, 13.

The chapter begins with the title and introduction, ver. 1, 2. Habakkuk then represents Jehovah as appearing in glorious majesty on Sinai, 3, 4; describes the ravages of the plague in the desert, 5; the consternation into which the nations were thrown by the victorious approach of the Hebrews to Canaan, and their wars with the inhabitants, 6—10; specially refers to the celestial phenomenon at Gibeon, 11; and then sets forth the auspicious results of the interposition of God on behalf of his people, 12—15. The prophet concludes by resuming the subject of the introduction, 16; and strongly asserting his unshaken confidence in God in the midst of anticipated calamity, 17—19.

---

1   A PRAYER of Habakkuk, the prophet: with triumphal music.

1. תְּפִלָּה, usually rendered *prayers*, comprehends all kinds of devotional composition, whether abounding in petitions, supplications, etc., or not. Hence it is applied to all the Psalms of David collectively, Ps. lxxii. 20; and is otherwise

2 O Jehovah! I heard the report of thee, I was afraid;
O Jehovah! revive thy work in the midst of the years;

only used in the inscriptions of Psalms xvii. lxxxvi. xc. cii. cxlii. The term is derived from בָּדַל, *to separate, distinguish;* cognate to פָּלָה; and so *to form an opinion or judgment, to judge, give a verdict.* In Hithpael the verb signifies to apply to a judge for a favorable decision, to *supplicate, pray,* etc.; and is employed at the commencement of the song of Hannah, 1 Sam. ii. 1. Though the only precatory sentences are those contained in ver. 2, yet there are several instances of direct address to God, which impart to the ode one of the characteristic feature of prayer. The Lamed prefixed in לִתְפִלָּה is that of authorship. עַל שִׁגְיֹנוֹת. That this is a musical term seems beyond dispute, from similar terms occurring in the titles of the psalms, such as עַל־הַשְּׁמִינִית, עַל אַיֶּלֶת הַשַּׁחַר, etc. For the explanation of the noun, which only occurs here, and in the singular שִׁגָּיוֹן, in the title of Ps. vii., different methods have been proposed. Bauer, Herder, Perschke, De Wette, Rosenmüller, Lee, Hitzig, and Maurer, have recourse to the Arabic شَكَى, *anxius, tristis, mæstus fuit,* and render עַל־שִׁגְיֹנוֹת, *after the manner of elegies,* but there seems no reason deducible either from the present ode or from the Psalm, why they should be thus characterized, or why they should be sung to a plaintive tune, but the contrary. Others, as Wahl, Justi, Gesenius, derive the word from the Syriac ܫܓܐ, in Pael, ܫܰܓܺܝ, *cecinit,* whence ܫܰܓܺܝܳܐ, *carmen, cantus,* to which it has justly been objected, that it is too vague and indefinite to admit of adoption. The LXX, indeed, have ψαλμός in the Psalm, and here ᾠδῆς; but without any apparent reference to the specific meaning of the term. Other philologists more reasonably content themselves with שָׁגָה, an indigenous Hebrew verb in common use, signifying *to err, wander, reel,* etc. This interpretation Aquila, Symm., and the fifth Greek version so far support, rendering ἐπὶ ἀγνοημάτων, which Jerome adopts, on the principle that שָׁגָה signifies to *sin through ignorance.* To this derivation Hengstenberg has recently given his adhesion (Comm. on Psalms, vol. i. p. 144), but most preposterously affirms, that in our ode the sins or crimes of the Chaldeans are intended. There is nothing either in the Psalm or in the song of Habakkuk to warrant the appropriation of any such signification of the term. The most probable explanation is that given by Delitzsch, who is of opinion that שִׁגָּיוֹן means a *dithyrambos,* or *cantio erratica,* a species of rhythmical composition, which, from its enthusiastic irregularity, is admirably adapted for songs of victory or triumph. It is obvious, however, from the established use of the preposition עַל *upon, after the manner of,* or *accompanied with,* in the titles of the Psalms, that the plural שִׁגְיֹנוֹת, to which, in like manner, it is here prefixed, must be understood as describing a corresponding kind of music with which the ode was to be accompanied. The translation of Theodotion, ὑπὲρ τῶν ἑκουσιασμῶν, *i. e.* as Jerome interprets the words, *pro voluntariis,* has, in all probability, some such reference.

2. The שֵׁמַע, *report* of Jehovah, here referred to by the prophet, does not mean what God had communicated to him, but a report *respecting* Jehovah, or the punishment which he had threatened to inflict upon the Jews for their sins. The genitive is that of object. That it cannot refer to what follows in the ode is certain, since the exhibition there given of the Divine interposition for the overthrow of the enemies of his people was calculated to inspire the prophet with joy, and not with the fear of which

In the midst of the years make it known:
In wrath remember mercy.
3   God came from Teman;
     The Holy One from mount Paran: *Pause*.

he declares he was conscious. His prayer also, that while punishment was being inflicted, God would exercise pity, shows that the Jews, and not the Chaldeans, were to be the subjects of the infliction. It may, therefore, be regarded as certain, that what he has in view is the prediction chap. i. 6–11. The fear with which the prophet was seized, he particularly describes ver. 16. By פָּעָלְךָ, *thy work*, Abarbanel, Kimchi, Schnurrer, Justi, and some others, understand the Jews, on the ground that they are designated the פֹּעַל, *work* of Jehovah's hands, Is. xlv. 11; but the simple occurrence of the same word, irrespective of the specific claims of the connection, cannot justify such a construction of the meaning. In chap. i. 5, the term is used of the Divine judgment upon the Jews, as it also is Is. v. 12, and of that upon their enemies, Ps. lxiv. 9. This latter sense, which involves the exercise of the power and goodness of God on behalf of his people, alone suits the present context. Comp. Ps. xc. 16. What the prophet prays for is the renewal of such interposition. This he expresses by the strong term חַיֵּהוּ, *quicken, restore to life*, which suggests the idea of a cessation of the avenging and delivering power of the Most High. It had been, in regard to its exertion, as if it had been dead, and required to be called forth afresh into action. Thus Jarchi: חייהו פעלך הראשון שהייתה נפרע לנו מאויבינו בקרב שני הצרה שאנו שרויים בם חייהו כלומר עוררהו והשיבהו. *Thy former work, when thou didst avenge us of our enemies, in the midst of the years of the calamity in which we live, revive it*, i. e. *rouse it up, cause it to return*. Comp. Is. li. 9, 10. No stress is to be laid on the phrase בְּקֶרֶב שָׁנִים, *in the midst of the years*, from which Bengel deduced so much fanciful support to his chronological calculations; maintaining that the middle point of the years of the world is meant. שָׁנִים are unquestionably the *years*, or period of affliction, which was to come upon the Jewish people. בְּקֶרֶב is not to be taken in the strict acceptation of the middle point of any given period of time, but is, as frequently, only a more emphatic prepositive form, instead of בְּ, *in*. The meaning, therefore, simply is, During the period of suffering, or, in the course of our punishment by the Chaldeans, interpose for our deliverance. Symm. ἐντὸς τῶν ἐνιαυτῶν. To give pathos to the language, the phrase is repeated; and תּוֹדִיעַ is added, as synonymous with תְּחַיֵּהוּ, the suffix of which is to be understood, though not expressed. The verb יָדַע, *to know*, is here used in the sense of experiencing, knowing by experience. הוֹדִיעַ, the infinitive, is to be regarded as an accusative. Comp. Ps. xxv. 6: זְכֹר־רַחֲמֶיךָ יְהוָה וַחֲסָדֶיךָ כִּי מֵעוֹלָם הֵמָּה. It is merely necessary to exhibit the version of this verse as now found in the text of the LXX. to show that it can only have originated in the amalgamation of different readings, some of them probably marginal glosses, and that it would be most unwarrantable to attempt any correction of the Hebrew text by it: Κύριε, εἰσακήκοα τὴν ἀκοήν σου, καὶ ἐφοβήθην, κατενόησα τὰ ἔργα σοῦ καὶ ἐξέστην· ἐν μέσῳ δύο ζώων γνωσθήσῃ, ἐν τῷ ἐγγίζειν τὰ ἔτη ἐπιγνωσθήσῃ, ἐν τῷ παρεῖναι τὸν καιρὸν ἀναδειχθήσῃ, ἐν τῷ ταραχθῆναι τὴν ψυχήν μου, ἐν ὀργῇ ἐλέους μνησθήσῃ.

3. אֱלוֹהַּ is not used by any of the minor prophets except Habakkuk, and by him only here, and chap. i. 11. It occurs four times in Daniel, and once in Isaiah, but never in Jeremiah or Ezekiel. There is no foundation whatever for the

His splendor covered the heavens,
And the earth was full of his praise.

position assumed by Gesenius and some others, that this use of the singular belongs to the later Hebrew, though it is allowed to belong to the poetic diction. It is employed *forty* times in the book of Job, one of the most ancient specimens of Hebrew composition extant, and twice by Moses, Deut. xxxii. קָדוֹשׁ, *Holy*, which is here parallel to אֱלוֹהַּ, *God*, also occurs in this application to express the absolute purity of the Divine Being, Job vi. 10; Is. xl. 25; and in the plural, קְדֹשִׁים, Prov. ix. 10, xxx. 3; Hos. xii. 1. Delitzsch contends, that, as יָבֹא is uninfluenced by any preceding preterite, it cannot possibly be taken otherwise than as strictly future in signification, as it is in form. But this is not the only instance in which the future stands absolutely at the commencement of a sentence or paragraph, yet clearly indicating a past transaction. Thus Num. xxiii. 7, יַנְחֵנִי בָלָק מְלֶךְ־אֲרָם; Jud. ii. 1, אַעֲלֶה; אֶרֶץ מִצְרַיִם; 2 Sam. iii. 33, יָמוּת; יֹאבַד יוֹם אִוָּלֶד בּוֹ Job iii. 3, אֶעֱנֶה מְעַצְּבֵיהֶם הַסֶּלַע; Ps. lxxx. 9, &c. The idiom, in these and similar cases, is sufficiently accounted for on the principle that the speaker places himself, in imagination, anterior to the action expressed by the verb, and thus, regarding it as still future, puts the verb in that tense. Having prayed that God would remember the mercy which he had shown to his people in ancient days, the prophet has his mind carried back to their affliction in Egypt, in their deliverance from which that mercy was signally displayed; and assuming that as his point of observation, he proceeds at once to describe the Theophania as future in regard to such position. The past, thus implied, though not expressed, as completely modifies a future tense, as if a preterite, or any qualifying particle, had preceded it. תֵּימָן, *Teman*, the LXX. retain as a proper name: the Targ., Syr., Theod., Vulg., and many modern versions read, *the south*. The word is doubtless to be taken as designating the country to the south of Judea, and east of Idumea, in which latter country Mount Paran (הַר־פָּארָן) was situated. Some, indeed, have endeavored to identify this mountain with Sinai, on the ground that وادي فيران, *Wady Pheiran*, which extends north-west from Sinai, is the same as מִדְבַּר־פָּארָן, *the desert of Paran*, mentioned in Scripture. But although this desert might have stretched so far towards the south-west as to touch upon the Wady, and so give it the name, it is certain, from Paran being mentioned in connection with Kadesh and Beersheba, that the wilderness of that name extended to the southern confines of Palestine, including the mountainous region to the west of the Ghor, or great valley stretching from the Dead Sea to the Elanitic gulf. In 1 Kings xi. 18, it is spoken of as lying between Midian and Egypt. From Sinai occurring along with Seir and Paran, Deut. xxxiii. 2, and with Seir and the country of Edom, Jud. v. 4, 5, it is probable that Habakkuk here alludes to the regions to the south of Palestine generally, as the theatre of the Divine manifestations to Israel, only, like Moses and Deborah, specifying the two points nearer to that country. In this view, his omission of Sinia, which they notice, is not of material moment. The glorious displays of the power and majesty of Jehovah which had been made in that quarter occupied his thoughts, and inspired him with feelings of the most exalted devotion. סֶלָה, *Selah*. This word, which occurs thrice in this ode, and seventy-three times in the Psalms, has been variously interpreted. That it is a musical sign is now almost universally admitted. It is found at the end of certain sections, or stropes, and always at the close of a verse,

4 The brightness was like that of the sun,
Rays streamed from his hand,
Yet the concealment of his glory was there.

except Hab. iii. 3, 9 ; Ps. lv. 20, lvii. 4; where however, as always, it ends the hemistich. Sometimes it occurs at the end of a Psalm, as Ps. iii. ix. and xxiv. The current, and apparently the traditionary interpretation, is that of the Targ. לְעָלְמִין ; Aq. ἀεί ; Symm. sometimes εἰς τὸν αἰῶνα ; Theod. sometimes εἰς τέλος ; the V. Greek version, διαπαντός ; but Symm. and Theod. most commonly coincide with the LXX., who uniformly render, διάψαλμα. This last translation is decidedly entitled to the preference, in so far as it confines the idea to the music, though the exact meaning even of this Greek term has been matter of dispute. Suidas, however, seems to come nearest to the mark, when he gives as its meaning μέλους ἐναλλαγή, a change of the modulation, and with him Hesychius agrees, explaining it by μέλους διαλλαγή. The hypothesis that סֶלָה is merely an abbreviation, consisting of the initial letters of three Hebrew words, is altogether gratuitous, there not being the least shadow of evidence that the Jews, in ancient times, ever employed abbreviations. Pfeiffer, in his work, Die Musik der Alten Hebr. p. 17, proposes to explain the term by the Arab شلّ, membrum, or section ; Prof. Lee, by صَلَوٰ, صَلَاة, which he renders, Dei invocatio, and derives from صلى, he blessed; but neither of the derivations will suit all the passages in which it occurs. Indeed, bless! or praise! would come in most incongruously in such connections as Ps. vii. 5, xxxix. 5, 11; lii. 3. Of the two Hebrew roots to which the word has been referred, סָלַל, to raise, elevate, and סָלָה, which, besides signifying to raise, has been supposed to be equivalent to שָׁלָה, to rest, pause, the latter, on the whole, seems to deserve the preference. There are several instances in which the letter שׁ has been softened into ס, as in שִׂרְיָן and סִרְיָן ; שֶׂה and סֶה ; just as, in most cases, we find it expressed in Arabic by س. This derivation, in which Gesenius finally acquiesced, has been approved of by Delitzsch and Hengstenberg. The term may be regarded as a substantive, signifying silence or pause; designed, in all probability, to command a cessation of the song or chant, while the instruments either repeated what had just been played, or introduced an interlude between the parts. At the end of a psalm it may have been intended to prevent a repetition on the part of the singers, while the instrumental music continued. Having, by a solemn pause, prepared the mind for the contemplation of the manifested glory of Jehovah, the prophet proceeds to describe this glory in the most sublime and magnificent language. By נֹגַהּ splendor or brightness, as the Targ., Kimchi, and Hitzig interpret; nor does it here express the actual praises of the inhabitants of the earth produced by the effulgence of Deity, for the effect of this effulgence is described, ver. 6, to be fear and trembling; but matter of praise, or the glory which was calculated to call forth universal adoration.

4. By אוֹר we are not here to understand light simply, but the sun as the source of light. Comp. Job xxxi. 26, xxxvii. 21. The Kametz of the article in כ renders the noun more definite. תִּהְיֶה, which Heidenheim would connect with הָאָרֶץ and Hitzig with תְּהִלָּה, in the preceding verse, can have no other nominative than נֹגַהּ, which, like other substantives in the Oriental languages, expressive of fire or light, is conceived to be of the feminine gender, or it may be regarded as neuter in signification.

5 Before him went the plague;
 The burning pestilence followed him.
6 He stood, and made the earth to tremble;
 He looked, and caused the nations to shake;
 The old mountains were shattered in pieces,
 The ancient hills sank down —
 His ancient ways.

and so taking the feminine of the verb. That by קַרְנַיִם, *horns*, we are here to understand *rays*, is obvious from the connection, from the comparison of the rising sun scattering his rays upon the earth to the gazelle, Ps. xxii. 1, and from its being common with the Arabs to compare them to the horns of that animal. Thus the Arab. قَرْن, *cornu animalis, latus superior pars solis, primi radiis solis.* Kamoos and Djauhari. Hence, the verb קָרַן signifies to *emit rays*, Exod. xxxiv. 29, 30, 35. Though in the dual, the noun, like others of that number which describe objects naturally existing in pairs, is here expressive of the plural. Comp. אַרְבַּע רַגְלַיִם, Lev. xi. 23; שְׁלשׁ שָׁנַיִם, 1 Sam. ii. 13; כָּל־בִּרְכַּיִם, Ezek. xxi. 12; and see my note on Is. vi. 2; צִבְעַת יָדָיו, Zech. iii. 9. The phrase מִיָּדוֹ *from his hand*, is equivalent to מִמֶּנּוּ, *from him*; and a verb of flowing, streaming, or the like, must be supplied. לוֹ is the dative of possession. שָׁם, *there*, refers to the scene of splendor just described, which, though so excessively bright, instead of exhibiting the Divine glory, only veiled or concealed it. Comp. Ps. civ. 2. The LXX., Syr., Aq., and Symm., have read וַיָּשֶׂם, *and he put*, instead of שָׁם, *and there*, and are followed by Hitzig and Maurer, but this rendering is less apt. עֹז, in such connection denotes *majesty* or *glory* rather than *power*. Comp. Ps. cxxxii. 8, lxxviii. 61. For עֻזֹּה many MSS. read עֻזּוֹ, the regular affix. Whether the substratum of the vivid representation here furnished of the glorious majesty of of Jehovah be the symbol of the Divine presence exhibited upon Mount Sinai, Exod. xxiv. 17, or the Shekinah which accompanied the Hebrews through the desert, chap. xvi. 7, 10; Lev. ix. 23, xl. 35, etc., cannot be determined. See on ver. 3.

5. דֶּבֶר, from דָּבַר, *to inflame*, has two leading significations, that of *lightning*, or *flame*, and that of *hot*, or *burning fever*. The latter is required in the present case to correspond to דֶּבֶר, *plague* in the preceding hemistich: a circumstance which forbids the adoption of the precarious rendering, *birds of prey*, though supported by the Syr., Aq., Symm., Theod., the V. Greek version, Michaelis, Schnurrer, Herder, Kofod. Dahl, Rosenmüller, and others; as well as that of *lightning*, adopted by Kalinsky, Wahl, Bauer and others; and *burning coals*, as in our common version. Thus Kimchi: רשף כמו דבר, וחצינך בפול בעלבות סגות, וכן ולחמי רשף, והוא חלי הקדחת שהוא חמה חסורפת ימיתתו מהר, *i. e.* "רשף corresponds to דבר, the same thing being expressed in different words. The word has the same signification. Deut. xxxii. 24, and denotes the fever, which consists in a burning heat, and speedily causes death." The Vulg. has, "Et egredietur *diabolus* ante pedes ejus!" לְרַגְלָיו יֵצֵא or חֶלֶף, means to *track* or *follow* any one. Here it is opposed to לְפָנָיו, *before him*. What the prophet has in view, would seem to be the plagues with which the enemies of the Hebrews were visited, of which we have an instance 1 Sam. v. 9, 11.

6. עָמַד וַיְמֹדֶד, forms an easy and elegant paronomasia, and, at the same time, exhibits one of the boldest, most abrupt,

7 I saw the tents of Cushan in trouble;
The tent-curtains of Midian trembled.
8 Was it against the rivers it burned, O Jehovah?

and sublime turns to be found in sacred poetry. While Jehovah is marching forth for the deliverance of his people, he stops all of a sudden in his progress, the immediate effects of which are universal consternation and terror. Nature, in her strongest and most ancient formations, is broken in pieces before him. The inhabitants of the earth tremble at his look. מָדַד may either be the Poel of מוד , *to measure,* or the Pilel of מוט, which, like the Arab. مَاسَ, signifies *to be agitated* The latter derivation best suits the connection. LXX. ἐσαλεύθη ἡ γῆ. Targ. אָזְעַת אַרְעָא . Arab. تَزَعْزَعَتِ الْأَرْضُ. Comp. the cognate מוט. Thus Gesenius, Lee, Maurer, Ewald, Heidenheim, Hesselberg, Delitzsch. The primary idea conveyed by רגז is that of *bounding, springing up,* as a person does when overtaken by sudden fear. In רִפְצֵץ we have all the force of intensive verbs, heightened in effect by the harsh sound of the reduplicated Tzade. פוץ signifies *to break* or *dash in pieces,* and also *to scatter, disperse.* For הַרְרֵי־עַד and גִּבְעוֹת עוֹלָם, comp. Gen. xlix. 26; Deut. xxxiii. 15. הֲלִיכוֹת עוֹלָם לוֹ , *His ancient ways,* I consider to be epexegetical of the preceding; and הֲלִיכוֹת is to be taken in the same sense as דְּרָכִים in the sentence הוּא רֵאשִׁית דַּרְכֵי־אֵל , Job xl. 19, which describes the hippopotamus as "the first or principal of *the ways of God,*" *i. e.* his creative acts, his works. The words may be resolved into הֲלִיכוֹת אֲשֶׁר עוֹלָם לוֹ , or into הֲלִיכוֹת עוֹלָמוֹ . The mountains which Jehovah had created of old, and which had resisted the revolutions of ages, were now shattered in pieces, and dissipated like dust before him. The irresistibility of his power, and the utter imbecility of the most formidable enemies of his people, are the ideas conveyed by the language of the prophet.

7. תַּחַת אָוֶן , " *under* affliction," is more expressive than בְּאָוֶן, " *in* affliction," as it suggests the idea of a heavy load by which those spoken of were oppressed. כּוּשָׁן , *Cushan,* is now generally admitted to be the same as כּוּשׁ , *Cush,* as לוֹטָן , *Lotan,* Gen. xxxvi. 20, is only another form of לוֹט , *Lot ;* but whether it be intended to designate the African or the Arabian Cush is disputed. Gesenius, Maurer, Delitzsch, and others, contend for the former; but the connection of the name with that of מִדְיָן, *Midian,* is decidedly in favor of the latter. For a satisfactory refutation of the position adopted by Gesenius, that *Cush,* and all the tribes connected with this name, are only to be sought in Africa, see Robinson's Calmet, art. *Cush.* That any reference to Cushan-rishathaim, Jud. iii. 10, is intended, does not appear. *Midian* appears to have stretched from the eastern shores of the Elanitic Gulf to Mount Sinai, and the frontiers of Moab. Edrisi speaks of a town called مَدْيَن , *Madian,* about five days' journey from Ailah, or Akabah, and six from Tubuk. The "tents" and "curtains" describe the nomadic mode of life as still found among the Bedawin of the Arabian deserts. יְרִיעוֹת , *the coverings of the tents,* so called from their tremulous motion when hanging down like curtains and affected by the wind. The word is here used merely as a synonym of אֹהָלִים , *tents ;* and both are put by metonymy for the persons dwelling in them.

8. The prophet rising in his graphic description of the ancient manifestations of Jehovah, now by a bold apostrophe inquires why the rivers were affected by them? Was it on account of any cause in the rivers? The implied answer is, No; and the true cause is assigned at the

Was thine anger against the rivers?
Was thy wrath against the sea?
That thou didst ride upon thy horses,
In thy chariots of victory.
9 Naked and bared was thy bow,
"Sevens of spears" was the word: *Pause.*
Thou didst cleave the earth into rivers.

close of the verse — the safe and victorious deliverance of the Israelites from Egypt, and their introduction into Canaan. יִהְיֶה is in the vocative, and the subject of the verb חָרָה is אַפֶּךָ, in the second hemistich. בַּנְּהָרִים, *the rivers,* mean the waters of the Red Sea, and the Jordan, which were dried up to allow them to pass over on foot. The former is not indeed a river, but may not inaptly be included under the term, on account of the *flowing* of the tide, which is said to rise at Suez to about the height of seven feet. On the miraculous division of the sea, recorded Exod. xiv., it was made to go or *flow* back the whole night, ver. 21. For the application of נָהָר to the stream tide of the Mediterranean, See Jonah ii. 4. That the rivers of Cush should be intended is altogether out of the question. Specifically, however, to mark out the Red Sea, it is afterwards expressly called יָם in the third hemistich. Comp. as parallel with the present verse, Exod. xv.; Ps. lxxvii. 13, cxiv. 3, 5. Jehovah is here, and in the following verses, represented as a mighty and victorious warrior, giving orders to his army, and, in triumphant progress, carrying all before him. Comp. Exod. xv. 3, xiv. 14. אַף, *anger,* and עֶבְרָה, *wrath,* are synonymes, only the latter is the stronger of the two, signifying unrestrained indignation; from עָבַר, *to pass over,* or *beyond a boundary.* By "horses" and "chariots," there is no necessity for our understanding either the angels, or thunder and lightning, as some would interpret. They are merely figurative expressions, designed to carry out the metaphor adopted from military operations. In the phrase מַרְכְּבֹתֶיךָ יְשׁוּעָה, supply עַל, *upon,* before the former word, and repeat מֶרְכְּבוֹת, *chariots,* before the latter. Comp. for instances of similar construction, מִצְוֹת חֵיל, 2 Sam. xxii. 33. דִּרְכֵּי זַעַם, Ps. lxxi. 7; בְּרָכָה יָמִים, Ezek. xvi. 27.—יְשׁוּעָה has in such connection, the specific signification of *victory,* though the idea of *salvation* or *deliverance,* as the result, is not to be lost sight of.

9. The combination עֶרְיָה תֵעוֹר, which forms a paronomasia, determines the signification of עוּר, as here employed, to be that of being *bare* or *naked,* and not that of *rousing* or *exciting.* For though the Piel עוֹרֵר is used of the lifting up of a spear, there would be no propriety in thus applying it to a bow: whereas the substantive עֶרְיָה, *nakedness,* having just been employed, nothing was more natural than to add תֵעוֹר, *to be bared* — עוּר being thus cognate in signification with עָרָה, from which עֶרְיָה is derived, and with עָרַר. עָרָה is used adjectively, as in וַיֹּאמֶר עָרֹם יָעֹר, Ezek. xvi. 7. תֵעוֹר is not the second, but the third person singular in Niphal, having for its nominative קֶשֶׁת, which is of the common gender. Some of the moderns have explained קֶשֶׁת, of the *rainbow,* than which nothing can be conceived more incongruously out of place in a passage containing a sublime poetical description of warlike operations. The making bare the bow, refers to the removal of the cover in which it was carefully wrapped, to prevent its receiving injury, or of such a leathern case as the γωρυτὸς, κωρυτὸς *corytus,* of the Greeks and Romans. Of the following words, שְׁבֻעוֹת מַטּוֹת אֹמֶר,

10 The mountains saw thee, they were in pain;
   The inundation of water overflowed;
   The abyss uttered its voice,
   It raised its hands on high.

upwards of one hundred different interpretations have been proposed. That which I have adopted appears to me best to suit the connection. It keeps up the spirit of the poem, and is fully justified on the simplest and most legitimate etymological grounds. That שְׁבֻעוֹת cannot signify *oaths*, is determined by the circumstance that "the oaths of the tribes," the rendering of our common version, affords no tolerable sense as here introduced, whether we regard the tribes as the persons swearing, or as those to whom oaths were sworn. The other signification of שְׁבֻעָה, is *seven*, a *heptade*, or what is made up of seven. It is elsewhere literally applied only to this number of weeks; but in connection with language so highly figurative as that of our prophet in the present chapter, no objection can reasonably be taken against its being used otherwise than as a designation of time. It appears to have been appropriated by him, to express the *perfection, fulness*, or *abundance*, of the number, instead of the usual numeral שֶׁבַע or שִׁבְעָה, when employed symbolically as a sacred and indefinite number. מַטֶּה signifies a *tribe*, but also, as שֵׁבֶט, 2 Sam. xviii. 14, a *lance* or *spear*; and that the latter signification is that in which Habakkuk here uses it may be inferred from his using it in this acceptation in the 14th verse. Thus the Syr. ܒ̇ܠܰܘ. אֹמֶר has been variously rendered by *word, promise, epicinium, commander*, etc. I take it in the first of these significations, as specifically designating the military order, or word of command. Compare Ps. lxviii. 12. אֲדֹנָי יִתֶּן־אֹמֶר, "the Lord gave *the word*," etc. Thus, אֹמֶר, like the Arab. اَمَرَ, signifies to *order, command*. The meaning of the

prophet will therefore be, that Jehovah prepared his bow for battle, and ordered numerous spears to be produced; in other words, that he brought the most formidable and effective instrumentality to bear against the enemies of his people. The nominative to תִּבְקַע is not אֶרֶץ, as some would construe the words, but קַשְׁתְּךָ understood from the suffix in קַשְׁתֶּךָ. Comp. יְבַקַּע צֻרִים בַּמִּדְבָּר, Ps. lxxviii. 15. Before נְהָרוֹת supply לְ or בְּ; to cleave *into* rivers. The effect of the Divine command is sublimely represented under the idea of that which is frequently produced by earthquakes, when immense quantities of water gush out of the fissures, and flow like rivers through the country. The whole verse is distinguished for its sublimity and beauty; and the sentiment conveyed in the two first lines was regarded as so weighty that a סֶלָה, *Selah*, or *pause*, is added, to give time for its producing its proper effect before supplementing the concluding line.

10. The mountains being the most prominent objects on the surface of the globe, Habakkuk reiterates, in a somewhat different form, what he had expressed, ver. 6, in order to preserve the impression of the tremendous character of the transactions, to illustrate which they had been figuratively introduced. In the former case רָאָה is used of Jehovah; in this, of the mountains, which are, by a bold figure, represented as inspired with life, and capable of taking sensible cognizance of the manifestations of Deity. To express the instantaneous character of the effect, יָחִילוּ, *they quaked*, is put in the future. The root חוּל or חִיל properly signifies *to twist, writhe*, as with pain, and is frequently used of a woman in travail. It is also employed in the sense of *quaking* or *trembling*, which idea is conveyed by it in this place.

11 Sun and moon stood back in their habitation
At the light of thine arrows which flew,
At the glittering brightness of thy lance.
12 Indignant thou didst march through the earth;
Wrathful thou didst tread down the nations.
13 Thou wentest forth for the deliverance of thy people,

"Silvarum juga cœpta moveri
Adventante Deo." *Virgil.*

זֶרֶם מַיִם, *a torrent of water*, i. e. an extremely heavy rain, in contradistinction from זֶרֶם בָּרָד, *a hail storm*, Is. xxviii. 2. רוּם, *elevation*, is used adverbially. By יָדֵיהוּ, the elongated pronominal form of יָדָיו, *its hands*, is meant the waves of the ocean. תְּהוֹם, *the ocean*, its antecedent, is of both genders. The whole of nature is here exhibited as thrown into consternation at the approach of God. The mountains tremble; the heavens pour down sweeping torrents of rain; the sea roars, and causes its billows to "run mountains high." Comp. Ps. lxxvii. 17.

11. שֶׁמֶשׁ יָרֵחַ form an asyndeton, and are probably so put for the sake of effect. In many MSS., however, the ellipsis of the ו is supplied. The paragogic ה in זְבֻלָה, is that of *direction* or *motion*, and the idea which it conveys, as here used with the verb עָמַד, is not that the sun and moon remained stationary in a part of the firmament, which is represented as their dwelling or habitation, but that they *stood back* or *withdrew* into that locality. It was usual with the Arabian astronomers to assign houses or chambers to the celestial orbs. Thus منزل, *mansio, domus*, is the name of the signs of the Zodiac; and فلك البروج, *the circle of the palaces* which the sun occupies. Job, likewise, speaks of חַדְרֵי תֵמָן, *the chambers of the south*, antithetically with the northern constellations, ch. ix. 9; as also of מְזָרוֹת, chap. xxxviii. 32, the same as מַזָּלוֹת, *inns* or *lodgings*, 2 Kings xxiii. 5. That specific reference is made to what is recorded Josh. x. 12, is, after the Targ., very generally admitted; but, though it were granted that the event there described may have suggested the language of the prophet, yet the point of view in which he presents the heavenly luminaries is altogether different. In the history, the construction to be put upon their standing still or being arrested in their course, is obviously their continuing to shine, in order to afford light to Joshua, while following up his victory over the enemy; whereas, in the present connection, they are sublimely introduced as retiring into their abode before the brighter refulgence of the arrows and lances employed in the conflict. So completely were they eclipsed by this refulgence, that it seemed as if they had set. Schnurrer and Justi interpret the language of their remaining in their habitation, in the sense of not rising, but the ה of motion is directly opposed to such construction. The ל in לְאוֹר and לְנֹגַהּ is the dative of cause, as in לְזֹאת יֶחֱרַד לִבִּי, "*at*, or *owing to* this, my heart trembled," Job xxxvii. 1. Supply אֵשׁ before יְהַלֵּכוּ, which is put in Piel for the purpose of marking the velocity of the motion of the arrows. The words אוֹר and נֹגַהּ, which are elsewhere used of the light of the sun and the moon respectively, are here transferred to the glitter of the weapons specified.

12. צָעַד, *to march*, is used of the solemn and majestic proceeding of Jehovah before the Hebrews, Judges v. 4; Ps. lxviii. 8. דּוּשׁ, *to thresh* or *tread down*, is applied metaphorically to the destruction of enemies, Micah iv. 13.

13. Having described, in language of

For the deliverance of thine anointed;
Thou dashedst in pieces the head of the house of the wicked,
Laying bare the foundation to the very neck: *Pause.*

the most sublime and terrible import, the manifestations of Jehovah in reference to his enemies, Habakkuk now proceeds to specify in express terms the end which they were designed to answer, viz., the deliverance and safety of his chosen people; and then depicts their fatal effects in the destruction of every hostile power. The second לְיֵשַׁע is employed instead of the infinitive לְהוֹשִׁיעַ, and thus governs the accusative אֶת־מְשִׁיחֶךָ. These last words Aq. and the author of the fifth Greek version render εἰς σωτηρίαν σὺν Χριστῷ σου, and the Vulg. *in salutem cum Christo tuo*, which has led many interpreters, both ancient and modern, to refer מְשִׁיחֶךָ, *the anointed*, to our Saviour. This construction of the passage is adopted even by Delitzsch, on the principle that as the term here designates the regal office of those who were of the Davidic dynasty, and Christ is represented as the greatest king of that family, consequently THE ANOINTED by way of eminence, he is to be regarded as included in the prophetic reference. By the law of parallelism, however, we are compelled to identify מְשִׁיחֶךָ, *thine anointed*, with עַמֶּךָ, *thy people*, in the preceding hemistich. The noun is thus a collective, and is rendered in the plural by the LXX. τοὺς χριστούς σου, or, as in the Alex. MS., τοὺς ἐκλεκτούς σου. The plural מְשִׁיחֶיךָ is actually found in two of Kennicott's MSS., and apparently in two more: in one of De Rossi's and two more originally. It is denied, indeed, by Delitzsch, that מָשִׁיחַ, *anointed*, is ever used of the people of Israel; and certainly none of the passages which have usually been adduced in support of this application of the term, can be fairly vindicated to it, except, perhaps, Ps. xxviii. 8, where מְשִׁיחוֹ corresponds to לָמוֹ or לְעַמּוֹ, according to the reading of six MSS., originally three more, and the rendering of the LXX., Syr., Vulg., Arab. Still, as the Hebrews were מַמְלֶכֶת כֹּהֲנִים, *a kingdom of priests*, Exod. xix. 6, they may with as much propriety be said to have been anointed, as the patriarchs are, 1 Chron. xvi. 22; Ps. cv. 15. The term, as thus applied, expresses their destination. The Dagesh forte is found in the initial ר of ראֹשׁ in some editions, and is one of the few instances of its occurrence in this letter, contrary to rule. Comp. 1 Sam. i. 6, x. 24; 2 Kings vi. 32; Prov. iii. 8, xiv. 10; Song v. 2; Jer. xxxix. 12; Ezek. xvi. 4. Delitzsch accounts for it on the principle of the word being short, and occurring after a Milel. The prepositive מ in מִבֵּית intimates, that the ruler here spoken of as the head, was not merely *over* the house, which the simple construct form would have expressed, but that he sprung *from* it. It is most probable that one or other of the Canaanitish kings is intended; perhaps Jabin, whose city Hazor is said to have been רֹאשׁ, *the head* of all the confederate kings, Josh. xi. 10; and was the most formidable of all the kings with whom the Hebrews had to contend, Judges iv. 3, 13. The general sense of the concluding hemistich is apparent; but considerable difficulty attaches to the interpretation of צַוָּאר, *neck*, as here connected with יְסוֹד, *foundation*. This connection is so strongly marked by the force of the preposition עַד, *even to*, that the former substantive cannot be separated from the latter, and referred to some supposable higher part of the figurative building. It must, from the structure of the language, describe the very lowest part of the foundation, or that on which the foundation itself rests; but how either of these could be called *the neck*, it is impossible to conceive. There is, therefore, very great probability in the conjecture of Cappel-

14 Thou piercedst with his own spears the chief of his captains,
That rushed on like a tempest to scatter me;
Whose joy it was to devour the poor in secret.
15 Thou wentest with thy horses through the sea,
The boiling up of many waters.
16 I heard, and my inward parts trembled,

lus, which has been approved by Herder, Green, and some others, that instead of צַוָּאר, *neck*, the text originally read צוּר, *rock*, which makes all plain. Both words are derived from the same root; and צַוָּאר occurs with the א, Neh. iii. 5. All the MSS. and versions support the present reading. עָרוֹת is the infinitive absolute, which is often employed in the prosecution of a statement, instead of the finite form of the verb. The historical facts which the prophet here poetically describes, appear evidently to be those narrated Josh. xi.; Judges iv., involving the complete destruction of the Canaanitish nations, and more especially the discomfiture of Sisera, celebrated by Deborah in her splendid triumphal song, Judges v.

14. After a solemn pause, marked by סֶלָה. *Selah*, Habakkuk prosecutes his subject, which still embraces the discomfiture of the enemies of Israel. מַטָּיו, *his own spears*, the same as רְמָחָיו, ver. 9. Interpreters are divided in regard to the signification of פְּרָזָו, or, as it is in the Keri, and in the text of a great number of MSS., and of four of the early editions, פְּרָזָיו. The traditionary interpretation is that of *villagers*, or the inhabitants of the country; hence *hordes*, which Delitzsch adopts, and explains it of armies or soldiers. Thus the Vulg., *capiti bellatorum ejus*. Perschke, Gesenius, Ewald, and other moderns, however, derive the word from the Arab. فرز, *segregavit, discrevit, modum præscripsit, statuit*, etc., and explain it of *judges, captains*, etc., which appears to be the more appropriate meaning. Thus the LXX., δυνάσται; the Syr. ܡܫܠܛܢܐ;

just as the former in the Vatican codex render the cognate noun פְּרָזוֹן, Judges v. 7, 11, by δυνατοί, and the Vulg. by *fortes*. The pronominal suffix refers to רָשָׁע, *the wicked*, in the preceding verse. Before יִסְעֲרוּ supply אֲשֶׁר. In using the first personal suffix singular in the following verb, the prophet so identifies himself with his people as to represent what was aimed at them as designed for him. Comp. ch. i. 12. The nominative to עֲלִיצֻתָם is פְּרָזָיו, *his captains*. In the last hemistich, the object of comparison is the robber who lies in wait for the poor defenceless traveller, and exults when he sees him approach. Such was the exultation of the Canaanitish chiefs when the Israelites entered the country. Comp. Ps. x. 8—10.

15. בְּסוּסֶיךָ must either be taken as an accusative absolute, *as to thy horses;* or it must have a בְּ supplied before it. The latter I have adopted as the easier mode of resolving the form. חֹמֶר describes here the boiling up or foaming of the sea in a storm. The immediate connection, however, shows, that what the prophet has in view is not the Red Sea, but the hostile army of the Canaanites, which presented a furious and impenetrable aspect to the Hebrews. Through this army Jehovah is represented as *walking* with his warriors, as if a general were coolly to march his cavalry through the thickest of a proud and vaunting foe, which he knew would prove utterly powerless in the attack. Comp. Ps. ii. 4, where Jehovah is said to *smile* at the puny attempts of his enemies.

16. Having finished the poetic rehearsal of the mighty acts of Jehovah on behalf of his people in ancient times,

At the sound my lips quivered;
Rottenness entered my bones,
I trembled in my place:
Yet I shall have rest in the day of distress,
When the people that shall attack us come up.
17 Though the fig-tree should not blossom,

which he had composed in order to inspire the pious with unshaken confidence in him as their covenant God, Habakkuk reverts to the fear which had seized him on hearing of the judgments that were inflicted upon his country by the Chaldeans. שָׁמַעְתִּי וַתִּרְגַּז בִּטְנִי is a varied repetition of יְהוָה שָׁמַעְתִּי שִׁמְעֲךָ יָרֵאתִי, ver. 2. Instead of there entering into a description of his feelings, he broke out in an earnest prayer that God would exercise pity toward Israel, from which there was an easy transition to the ancient Divine interpositions. He now describes those feelings in very forcible and affecting language. קוֹל, *the voice*, is to be referred to the Divine threatening recorded chap. i. 6. The quivering of the prophet's lips is merely expressive of the effect of the fear with which he was seized, and has no reference to his delivery of the threatening. תַּחְתַּי, literally *under me*, i. e. *my under parts, limbs*, or the like. Comp. the Arab. يَكْسِت, *pars inferior.* LXX. ὑποκάτωθέν μου ἐταράχθη ἡ ἕξις μου. The Syr. ܪ̈ܓܠܝ *my knees*. Jarchi and Kimchi בִּמְקוֹמִי, *in my place*. אֲשֶׁר אָנוּחַ has been variously rendered, "That I may rest;" "That I must expect;" "O that I might rest;" "Yet I shall rest," or "have rest." The last construction is alone suitable. אֲשֶׁר, which the LXX. have entirely omitted, is here a conjunction, connecting the following clauses with those which are antecedent to it, but obviously intended to qualify what had been there expressed. It thus forms a particle of transition from one class of circumstances to another of a different character. See Noldius, *sub voce*. Deeply as the prophet was affected, and overpowering as were the feelings of apprehension with which he anticipated the awful calamity that was coming upon his people, he did not abandon himself to despair, but, on the contrary, consoled his mind with the assurance, that God, in whom he trusted, would keep him in perfect peace in the day of trial. Nothing can be more uncritical than the emendation of אָנוּחַ into אָגִיחַ, proposed by Houbigant, the verb גּוּחַ or גִּיחַ having no such signification as that which he ascribes to it. The preposition לְ in לְיוֹם צָרָה and לַעֲלוֹת is to be taken as signifying the time when the events were to happen; in לַעַם it is the sign of the genitive; so that לַעֲלוֹת עַם is equivalent to עֲלוֹת עַם, *the coming up of the people.* The infinitive is the infinitive construct. By the *people*, the Chaldeans are meant. They are, as usual, said to *come up*, because of the elevated position of Jerusalem, both in a local and a religio-political point of view. Comp. 2 Kings xxiv. 1. Before יְגוּדֶנּוּ supply אֲשֶׁר. The verb גּוּד, like its cognate גָּדַד, signifies to *cut*, or *break in* upon an enemy, *attack*. Hence the substantive גְּדוּד, a *troop* or *band* of warriors, chiefly used of such as engage in plundering expeditions. It is the very term employed in the account given us of the fulfilment of the prophecy, 2 Kings xxiv. 2; "And the Lord sent against him אֶת־גְּדוּדֵי כַשְׂדִּים, the *bands* of the Chaldeans," etc.

17, 18. From a statement of the assurance which he possessed of the mental tranquillity which he should enjoy during the anticipated calamity, Habakkuk rises to a triumphant assertion of the holy joy and exultation which would be

And there should be no produce on the vines;
Though the fruit of the olive should fail,
And the fields should yield no food;
Though the flocks should be cut off from the fold,
And there should be no cattle in the stalls:
18 Yet I will exult in Jehovah;
I will be joyful in the God of my salvation.
19 Jehovah the Lord is my strength;
He will make my feet like those of gazelles,

vouchsafed to him amidst all the desolation to which his country might be subjected. The desolation here so graphically and forcibly described, is that which was to be effected by the Chaldeans, whose army would consume or destroy the best and most necessary productions of the land; not only seizing upon the cattle, and devouring the fruits of the earth, but so injuring the trees as to render them incapable of yielding any produce. The passage contains the most beautiful exhibition of the power of true religion to be found in the Bible. The language is that of a mind weaned from earthly enjoyments, and habituated to find the highest fruition of its desires in God. When every earthly stream is dried up, it has an infinite supply in his all-sufficient and exhaustless fulness. No affliction, however severe or trying, can cut the believer off from this blessed resource. On the contrary, its tendency is to bring him into closer contact with it. מַעֲשֵׂה is not the *labor* bestowed upon the olive-tree, but the *fruit* which the tree produces. Comp. the phrase עֹשֶׂה פְּרִי, *to make* or *produce fruit*. The irregular construction of the singular masculine עָשָׂה with the feminine plural שְׁדֵמוֹת is to be accounted for on the principle, that in the mind of the prophet both number and gender had merged in the totality and impressiveness of his subject. Comp. אֹכֶל נִבְזֶה, Is. xvi. 8. It is what is commonly called, *constructio ad sensum*. Some would refer כִּחֵשׁ to an obsolete root כָּחַשׁ, which they take

to be cognate with כָּחַד, *to burn;* but it seems preferable to regard it as a derivative like שָׁדֶה, both signifying a *smooth* or *level field*, such as was prepared for grain or vines: from שָׁדַד, *to break*, and שָׁדָה, *to be level*, as ground is which is broken up and levelled by the plough, the hoe, and the harrow. גָּזַר is here used intransitively, and is equivalent to the Niphal נִגְזַר. מִכְלָה stands for מִכְלָאָה, just as מִרְיָה for מִרְיָאָה, and מְקֻמָּה for מְקֻמָּאָה or מַשְׁקָה. The root is כָּלָא, *to shut up, confine*. אֶצְבָּלוֹת and עֲצָלוֹת are synonymes in the elongated future—the ה directive expressing the strong bent of the mind towards the exercise. The words בֵּאלֹהֵי יִשְׁעִי are rendered in the Vulg. *in Deo Jesu meo!* The LXX. have ἐπὶ τῷ Θεῷ τῷ σωτῆρί μου.

19. The formula יְהוָה אֲדֹנָי, instead of אֲדֹנָי יְהוָה, is of infrequent occurrence. Comp. Ps. lxviii. 21, cxl. 8. The language of this verse is found in Ps. xviii. 33, 34; and in part, Deut. xxxii. 13; Is. lviii. 14. It expresses the confident hope that Jehovah would prove the support and defence of the prophet, and of all who made Him the object of their trust, and that he would grant them complete deliverance from their enemies, and restore them to the full and undisturbed possession of their own land. אַיָּלָה, *the gazelle*, is so swift-footed, that grey-hounds are liable to be killed by over-exertion in the chase. בָּמוֹתַי, *my high places*, stands for בָּמוֹת אֶרֶץ, *the heights of my country*. Except for purposes of warfare, the elevated parts

And cause me to walk on my heights.
To the precentor, with my stringed instruments.

of a land are the last that are occupied. The present is the only instance in which a musical direction is placed at the end of a psalm or ode. לַמְנַצֵּחַ, which occurs fifty-five times in the titles to the Psalms, is derived from the root נָצַח, *to overcome, excel, take the lead, direct, superintend, preside*, etc. It is used in reference to the *prefects* or *overseers*, whom Solomon appointed over the workmen, 2 Chron. ii. 2, 18 ; and specially of the *masters* or *directors* of the music employed in the temple, 1 Chron. xv. 21 ; Neh. xii. 42. By the LXX. לַמְנַצֵּחַ is almost always rendered εἰς τὸ τέλος ; Aq. τῷ νικοποιῷ ; Symm. ἐπινίκιον ; Theod. εἰς τὸ νίκος ; Targ. לְשַׁבָּחָא . In 2 Chron. ii. 17, however, the LXX. render the noun by ἐργοδιώκτης, and ver. 1, and xxxiv. 13, by ἐπιστάτης. The form is that of the participle in Piel, the לְ taking the Patach of the article — a circumstance which shows that it cannot be, as some have supposed, an infinitive. נְגִינָה (from נָגַן, נָגַג, to *strike* the strings, *play* on a stringed instrument, and then, generally, to *perform either vocal or instrumental music*, but chiefly the latter) signifies what is thus performed : *music, melody, song*, and also the stringed instruments with which it was accompanied. The preposition בְּ is that of accompaniment. Delitzsch infers from the use of the affix in נְגִינוֹתַי , *my* music, that the prophet himself was to take an active part in the performance of it ; and further, from this circumstance, that he was of the tribe of Levi, and engaged in carrying on the temple music. But these inferences cannot be sustained, since, if the reasoning were valid, it would equally prove that Hezekiah must have belonged to that tribe, and been thus officially engaged : for he uses the very same form : נְגִינוֹתַי , " *my* stringed instruments," Is. xxxviii. 20. On what ground either the prophet or the king claimed these instruments, it is impossible to determine. The conjecture of Schnurrer, that נְגִינוֹתַי was originally נְגִינָתִי , and that the termination וֹתַ is merely paragogic as in רַבָּתִי , is overturned by the fact, that this paragogic form is never found except when the word in which it appears is in the construct state.

ZEPHANIAH.

PREFACE.

ALL that we know of Zephaniah is furnished by the title to his book, in which it is stated that he was the son of Cushi, grandson of Gedaliah, great grandson of Amariah, and great great grandson of Hezekiah. As in no other instance do we find the pedigree of a prophet carried so far back, it has not unfairly been inferred that he belonged to a family of considerable respectability.* Whether, however, the Hezekiah there mentioned were the king of that name, or some other person of note so called, cannot be determined with certainty. The circumstance that the words, " king of Judah," are not added to the proper name, rather militates against the position that he was descended from that monarch, since this addition always occurs when primary reference is made to any of the Jewish kings; and, what is specially to the present point, when such reference is made to Hezekiah. See Prov. xxv. 1; Is. xxxviii. 9. The number of generations also forms an objection against the hypothesis, since it is scarcely possible to make room for them in the short space of time which elapsed between Hezekiah and Josiah.

As our prophet is stated, chap. i. 1, to have received his prophecies in the days of Josiah, he must have flourished between the years B. C. 642, and B. C. 611. This statement is corroborated by certain circumstances in the book itself. For instance, he predicts the fall of Nineveh, and the overthrow of the Assyrian empire; consequently he must have prophesied prior to the year B. C. 625, when these events took place; i. e., in the former half of the reign of Josiah. The mention, too, of the destruction of " the *remnant* of Baal," chap. i. 4, evidently implies, that the abolition of idolatry had been carried on to a considerable extent, but had not yet been completed. Now this exactly tallies with the state of things in Judah from the twelfth to the eighteenth year of Josiah; for though this monarch began, in the former of these years, to effect a reformation, it was not till the latter that it was prosecuted with more successful results. If, therefore, we suppose that Zephaniah delivered his predictions between these two terms, we shall not be wide of the mark. To the objection, that no mention is made of him or his labors in the historical books, which we might expect on the ground of the valuable service he must have rendered to the zealous monarch, it is sufficient to reply,

---

* Οὐκ ἄσημος ὢν τὸ κατὰ σάρκα γένος. — *Cyril, Præf. ad Zeph.*

that the same objection would lie against the prophetical existence of Jeremiah at the same period, though we know that he then flourished at Jerusalem, under the very eye of his sovereign. The mention made of "the king's sons," chap. i. 8, cannot be urged in favor of a later date; for it is altogether uncertain whether we are not to understand by the phrase the princes of the royal house generally, or such of the royal children as should be alive at the time of the fulfilment of the prophecy. The connection and manner in which they are introduced favor the latter construction.

The predictions contained in the book are chiefly directed against the Jews, on account of their idolatry, and other sins of which they were guilty. The awful judgments to be executed upon them and the neighboring nations by the Chaldeans are denounced with great force and effect. Hitzig, indeed, has recently revived the opinion advocated by Cramer and Eichhorn, that the invasion of these countries by the Scythians, about the year B. C. 630, whose incursion into Western Asia is described by Herodotus, i. 102, is what the prophet has in his eye; but the Jews appear to have been so little affected by their progress, that it by no means corresponds to that of the enemy described by Zephaniah, in the course of which not only Judea, but the adjacent countries were to be entirely laid waste. His predictions received their accomplishment during the successes of Nebuchadnezzar. Towards the close of the book the restoration and prosperity of the Jewish people are introduced.

In respect to style, Zephaniah is not distinguished either for sublimity or elegance. His rhythm frequently sinks down into a kind of prose; but many of the censures that have been passed upon his language are either without foundation, or much exaggerated. In point of purity it rivals that of any of the prophets. He has much in common with his contemporary Jeremiah, and some, after Isidore, have regarded him as his abbreviator. A careful comparison of the two, however, proves the futility of this hypothesis. Occasionally he borrows the language of former prophets. Comp. chap. ii. 14, with Is. xiii. 21, xxxiv. 11; chap. ii. 15, with Is. xlii. 8.

CHAPTER I.

The prophet begins by announcing the universality of the judgments which God was about to bring upon the land, 2, 3; specifies the different classes of transgressors whose conduct had merited the infliction of these judgments, 4—6; and calls attention to the speedy approach, and the features of the period of punishment, which he intermingles with further descriptions of the character of the ungodly, 7—13. He then dwells upon the awfully calamitous nature of the visitation, and points out the impossibility of escape, 14—18.

---

1   The word of Jehovah which was communicated to Zephaniah the son of Cushi, the son of Gedaliah, the son of Amariah, the son of Hizkiah, in the days of Josiah the son of Amon, king of Judah:
2   I will utterly take away everything from the face of the land, Saith Jehovah.
3   I will take away man and beast;
I will take away the birds of heaven, and the fishes of the sea,
And the cause of stumbling along with the wicked;
And I will cut off man from the face of the land,
Saith Jehovah.
4   I will also stretch forth my hand against Judah,

1. See the Preface.

2, 3. אָסֹף, which is variously employed in Scripture in the sense of *gathering, collecting*, etc., is here used, as in Jud. xviii. 25; 1 Sam. xv. 6; Ps. xxvi. 9; Ezek. xxxiv. 29, to denote *the taking away* by death, or other violent means; *to destroy*. Thus Jarchi, עניינו כלייה, its signification is *destruction*." What clearly shows this, is the use of the cognate verb סוּף, *to scrape*, or *sweep off*, in the form אָסֵף=אֹסֵף, which the Rabbi just mentioned erroneously takes to be the Hiphil of אָסַף, by elision for אַאֲסֵף. The latter verb is never used in Hiphil; but the same combination of the two verbs in the infinitive and finite forms occurs Jer. viii. 13, אָסֹף אֲסִיפֵם. Compare for similar usage אָרוֹשׁ יְדוֹשֶׁנּוּ, Is. xxviii. 28; בֹּזֹז יָבֹז, Jer. xlix. 9. The enumeration of particulars is designed to augment the fearful and universal character of the punishment. מִכְשֵׁלֹת does

not appear to differ in this connection from מִכְשׁוֹל, *a stumbling block, cause of moral offence*, what occasions, excites to, or promotes sin. Syr. ܡܟܫܘܠܐ; Symm. τὰ σκάνδαλα. There can be no doubt that the different objects and rites of idolatrous worship are what the prophet has in view. Thus Jarchi, חֵטְא עֲבוֹדַת זָרוֹת. The repetition of אָסֹף shows the prophecy had special reference to human beings, as the guilty party. The particle אֶת before הָרְשָׁעִים has the signification of *with, together with*, thus denoting accompaniment. Comp. Jud. i. 16. The idols and their worshippers were to be involved in one common destruction. Newcome improperly renders אֶת as a sign of the genitive.

4. To stretch forth the hand against any one, means not merely to threaten, but to exert one's power to his injury. הַמָּקוֹם הַזֶּה, *this place*, means Jerusa-

And against all the inhabitants of Jerusalem;
And will cut off from this place the remnant of Baal,
The name of the idolatrous with that of the other priests;
5 And those that worship the host of heaven on the roofs,
And those that worship and swear to Jehovah,
And swear by their king;

Iem. By שְׁאָר הַבַּעַל, *the remnant,* or *rest of Baal,* we are to understand the statues, images, etc, dedicated to the chief domestic and tutelary god of the Phœnicians, to whose worship the Hebrews were addicted as early as the time of the Judges (ii. 13), and among whom it afterwards spread more and more, especially in the ten tribes. Altars and high places were reared to this deity by Manasseh, even in the temple of Jehovah itself, 2 Kings xxi. 3, 5, 7; 2 Chron. xxxiii. 3, 7. These Josiah destroyed in the reformation which he undertook in the twelfth year of his reign, 2 Chron. xxxiv. 4; but it appears from this passage of our prophet, compared with 2 Chron. xxxiv. 8, that idols continued to be worshipped, most probably in places which were more remote from public observation, or which had been formed after the destruction of the others, and the cessation of the reformation referred to. Marckius and Gesenius interpret the phrase שְׁאָר הַבַּעַל, of *the people of Baal,* but this seems less probable. The phrase corresponds to מִבְּלִילוֹת in the preceding verse, and is in like manner immediately followed by the אֵת of accompaniment, pointing out the persons that encouraged idolatry. For שְׁאָר the LXX., who have τὰ ὀνόματα, must have read שֵׁמוֹת, or they may have been misled by the שֵׁם following. שֵׁם, however, is found in two of Kennicott's MSS., and in the margin of another. Upwards of twenty MSS., four ancient editions, and all the versions read וְאֶת שֵׁם, instead of עִם אֵת. For הַכְּמָרִים, *the idolatrous priests,* see on Hos. x. 5. Both in the ancient and in the latter Hebrew, the term כֹּהֵן is used of the *priests* of idols, as well as of those belonging to Jehovah. See Gen. xli. 45, 50; 1 Kings xiii. 2, 33; 2 Kings x. 19, xi. 18. It may to some appear doubtful whether the former be not here intended; but as such are undeniably included in the כְּמָרִים, it is more probable that in using the term כֹּהֲנִים, the prophet had in his eye those who were professedly priests of the true God, but who, instead of checking, or endeavoring to eradicate idolatry, encouraged it by their indifference, or the inconsistency of their conduct in other respects. Comp. Jer. ii. 8, v. 31. The Targ. renders פָּלְחֵיהוֹן עִם כּוּמְרֵיהוֹן, *their worshippers with their priests.* Neither were he left in the land by the Chaldeans. Their very names were to be forgotten.

5. Having directed his prophecy against the priests, the prophet now denounces those of the people who indulged in idolatrous practices. He first takes up those who were the votaries of Sabiism, or the worship of the heavenly bodies: a system which had, at an early period, become extensively prevalent, and continued to exert its influence, not only over the nomades of Arabia, but over the philosophers and wise men of the East; but which, in whatever form or degree it obtained, had the lamentable effect of deifying the creature, and obscuring the existence, claims, and glory of the Creator. That it was adopted, and its rites practised to a great extent by the Jews, appears from 2 Kings xxiii. 5, 6; Jer. vii. 17, 18, xliv. 17—19, 25. The גַּגּוֹת, *roofs* or house-tops, in the East are flat, and are used for various purposes. The idolaters may have chosen them for secrecy in the time of the prophet, or they may have selected them for the purpose of obtaining a fuller view of the plane-

6 And those that have turned back from Jehovah,
 And that neither seek Jehovah nor apply to him.
7 Keep silence before the Lord Jehovah,
 For the day of Jehovah is near;
 For Jehovah hath prepared a sacrifice,
 He hath consecrated those whom he hath invited.
8 And it shall come to pass on the day of Jehovah's sacrifice,
 That I will punish the princes and the king's sons,
 And all that wear foreign apparel.

tary objects of their worship. Jer. xix. 13, xxxii. 29. The planet to which they specially burnt incense on the roofs of their houses is supposed to have been the Moon, or it was more probably Venus, called מְלֶכֶת הַשָּׁמַיִם, "the Queen of heaven," Jer. vii. 17, 18, 19, 25. The prophet next instances a mongrel class of worshippers, such as professed attachment to Jehovah, as the national God, but, at the same time, were devoted to the service of *Moloch*, whom in reality, they regarded and honored as *their king*. For the forms מֹלֶךְ, מַלְכָּם, מִלְכֹּם, see on Amos v. 26, and Gesenius under the word מֶלֶךְ. Instead of immediately connecting these opposite objects of worship with the participle הַמִּשְׁתַּחֲוִים, as he had done in the preceding clause, Zephaniah stops short, as if uncertain how to describe the persons whom he had in view, and then proceeds to characterize them as combining, by acts of solemn profession, the worship of the true God with that of Moloch. Comp. 1 Kings xviii. 21. נִשְׁבַּע בְּ, *to swear by* a deity, means to acknowledge him in a public, solemn, and binding manner; openly to pledge one's self to his service.

6. This verse is more comprehensive in its import, being descriptive of all who were in any way guilty of defection from Jehovah, and lived in total neglect of him and his ways.

7. For הַס מִפְּנֵי, comp. Hab. ii. 20; Zech. ii. 13. In the symbolical language of prophecy, a sacrifice denotes the slaughter or destruction of an army or people. In the words הִקְדִּישׁ קְרֻאָיו,

he hath consecrated his called ones, however, there is no allusion to guests invited to partake of a sacrificial feast, as there unquestionably is Ezek. xxxix. 17—20; Rev. xix. 17, 18. The קְרֻאִים, *called ones*, were the Chaldeans, who, as the Divine army, or the instruments of his retributive justice, were *called* into the field against the enemies of the Most High. In this sense Cyrus is said to have been *called*, Is. xli. 9, xlviii. 15. Comp. also Is. xiii. 3, and my note there, in which קִדֵּשׁ, *to sanctify, consecrate*, is explained of the selection of troops for war, and the religious rites engaged in when they set out upon the military expedition.

8. That by the phrase בְּנֵי הַמֶּלֶךְ, *the sons of the king*, we are to understand the immediate children of Josiah, does not appear. He could not have had sons of an age sufficiently mature at the time the prophet uttered his prediction, to allow of their contracting guilt to such a degree as that which the connection necessarily requires; for he could not himself have been above seventeen years old. It may either mean the princes of the royal house generally, or the children of the king who should be on the throne at the time of the accomplishment of the prophecy. That the latter supposition is the more probable, appears from 2 Kings xxv. 7, where it is stated, that the king of Babylon slew the sons of Zedekiah before his eyes. By those that wore foreign attire, the prophet means the rich and great generally, who, in violation of an express ordinance relative to national

9 I will also punish all who leap over the threshold in that day,
Who fill the house of their lord with violence and deceit.
10 And it shall come to pass in that day, saith Jehovah,
That there shall be the sound of crying from the fish-gate,
And of wailing from the second,
And of great destruction from the hills.
11 Howl, ye inhabitants of the Mortar!
For all the people of Canaan are destroyed;
All who are laden with money are cut off.

costume, which was designed to preserve them distinct from other people, Numb. xv. 37—40, arrayed themselves in the more costly and gorgeous garb of idolaters, and thus more easily mixed with them in the performance of their idolatrous rites.

9. Because the priests of Dagon abstained from treading on the threshold of his temple, 1 Sam. v. 5, it has been by some inferred that Zephaniah alludes here to some such superstitious custom as practised by the Jews. Thus the Targ. כָּל דִּמְהַלְּבִין בְּנִימוּסֵי פְלִשְׁתָּאֵי, *all who walk in the laws of the Philistines.* But this construction has little to support it beyond the simple occurrence of the word מִפְתָּן, *threshold,* in both passages; for in Samuel it is merely said, לֹא יִדְרְכוּ — מִפְתַּן דָּגוֹן, "they *tread* or *walk* not over the threshold of Dagon;" whereas the language of the prophet, הַדּוֹלֵג עַל־הַמִּפְתָּן, "*him that leapeth* over the threshold,*" is expressive of a more violent action; and as the parallel hemistich shows, characterizes the eagerness with which the servants of the great rushed out of their palaces in order to seize upon the property of others, and thereby increase the wealth of their masters. If we may apply the signification of the cognate word in Arab. دَلَجَ, *principio, or sub finem noctis iter fecit,* we should interpret the term as denoting their setting out on their predatory expeditions under cloud of night. Thus, as to the general sense, the Syr. ܟܠ ܐܝܠܝܢ ܕܡܗܠܟܝܢ, *all who com-*

mit violence and plunder. Kimchi explains the word of their forcibly entering the houses of the poor, and robbing them of their goods.

10, 11. These verses describe the state of Jerusalem when besieged by Nebuchadnezzar. שַׁעַר הַדָּגִים, *the fish-gate,* occurs 2 Chron. xxxiii. 14; Neh. iii. 3, xii. 39; but there is nothing in these passages by which we can determine its exact position. From the name it might be inferred, that it was situated either on the north or the north-east side of the city, that being the direction from which those would arrive who brought fish from Tiberias and the Jordan, and corresponded to what is now called the Damascus Gate, or to that of St. Stephen. It was from this side, being that which was most accessible, that Jerusalem was attacked by the enemy. That מִשְׁנֶה, *the second,* is not to be referred to שַׁעַר, *gate,* as its antecedent, but to עִיר, *city,* understood, appears from Neh. xi. 9, where we have in full הָעִיר מִשְׁנֶה, *the second city,* i. e. the second division of the city. Ewald renders the word by *Neustadt,* "Newtown." In all probability it was what was afterwards called Akra, or the lower city, which lay to the north of the ancient city on Mount Zion, and was separated from it by the Tyropœon, a valley which ran down between them to the present pool of Siloam. In our common version the word is improperly rendered *college,* 2 Kings xxii. 14, 2 Chron. xxxiv. 22, after the interpretation of the Rabbins. The גְּבָעוֹת, *hills,* here mentioned, were not those around the city, such as

12 And it shall come to pass at that time
That I will search Jerusalem with lights,
And punish the men who are hardened on their lees,
Who say in their hearts,
Jehovah will not do good, neither will he do evil.
13 And their wealth shall become a spoil,
And their houses a desolation;
They may build houses, but they shall not inhabit them,
And plant vineyards, but they shall not drink the wine of them.
14 The great day of Jehovah is near;

the Mount of Olives, the Mount of Evil Counsel, etc., but Zion, Moriah, Ophel, and other elevated localities within the walls, occupied by the temple, the royal palace, and the houses of the richer portion of the inhabitants. The prophet graphically represents the progress of the Chaldeans, from the gate at which they entered, into the second division of the city, until they had ultimately taken possession of the whole, and destroyed the principal buildings. This destruction is very appropriately expressed by the noun שֶׁבֶר, from שָׁבַר, *to break, break in pieces*, 2 Kings xxv. 4, 8, 9. מַכְתֵּשׁ is not a proper name, as the article prefixed shows, but an appellative, signifying *mortar*, from כָּתַשׁ, *to bray, pound*. See Prov. xxvii. 22. It appears to have been applied, from its resemblance to that vessel, to one or other of the valleys in or about Jerusalem. Theod. ἐν τῷ βάθει. Aq. εἰς τὸν ὅλμον. According to the Targum, נַחֲלָא דְקִדְרוֹן, it was that through which the brook Kidron flows. Others think it was the Tyropœon, the locality of the bazaars, where the merchants carried on their business. From what follows in the verse, the latter is most probably the true interpretation. It is thought by some that the term was purposely chosen by the prophet, on account of its resemblance in sound to מִקְדָּשׁ, *a holy place*, and that Jerusalem itself is meant; but this word is exclusively appropriated to the tabernacle, or temple, and other sacred places, and never to the city, though it is called עִיר הַקֹּדֶשׁ,

the Holy City, just as it is still known in the East by the names القدس, *El-Kuds*, and بيت المقدس, *Beit-el-Mukeddes*, of similar signification. By עַם כְּנַעַן, *the people of Canaan*, the prophet does not mean the inhabitants of Canaan generally, nor Phœnician merchants in particular, who carried on trade with those of Jerusalem, but ironically the Jerusalem merchants themselves, who not only resembled the former in their modes of acquiring gain, but adopted their idolatrous manners and customs. See on Hos. xii. 8.

12. The Divine judgments were to reach those who practised wickedness in the most hidden places, and in the most covert manner. This is metaphorically expressed by searching out with lights what is concealed in the dark. The metaphor following is taken from the firm crust which is formed on the surface of fermented liquors when they have been long left in an undisturbed state. קָפָא, signifies, *to contract, become concrete, hard*, etc., and strikingly expresses the hardened state of the rich who have settled down into infidelity and atheism. Comp. Jer. xlviii. 11. Their practical denial of a superintending and governing providence is expressed in so many words at the end of the verse.

It is here implied that those of whom the prophet speaks would go on building and planting till the judgment of God overtook them, and deprived them of all their property. Comp. Matt. xxiv. 38, 39.

14. מְמַהֵר is not the participle in Piel,

It is near and hasteth greatly;
The sound of the day of Jehovah:
There the mighty man shrieketh bitterly.
15 That day is a day of indignation,
A day of trouble and distress,
A day of desolation and ruin,
A day of darkness and gloom,
A day of clouds and obscurity;
16 A day of the trumpet and the war-shout,
Against the fortified cities,
And against the lofty towers.
17 And I will bring trouble upon men,
So that they shall walk as the blind;
Because they have sinned against Jehovah,
Their blood shall be poured out as dust,
And their flesh shall be as dung.
18 Neither their silver nor their gold
Shall be able to rescue them
In the day of Jehovah's indignation;
But the whole land shall be consumed
By the fire of his jealousy:
For a consummation altogether sudden will he make

with the affirmative Mem rejected, but the infinitive of the same conjugation, used as an abbreviated form of מָהֵר‎ יְמַהֵר‎. מַר‎, *bitter*, is here used adverbially. So irresistible should be the attack of the Chaldeans, that the Jewish warrior would be compelled to abandon himself to shrieks of hopeless grief.

15, 16. A beautiful amplification, for the purpose of aggravating the character of the calamity. Passages somewhat similar occur in the prophets, but none equal to this. צָרָה וּמְצוּקָה‎, as well as שֹׁאָה וּמְשׁוֹאָה‎, are instances of paronomasia. Comp. Job xv. 24, xxx. 3, xxxviii. 27. הַפִּנּוֹת וְהַגְּבֹהוֹת‎ form a Hendiadys, and describe the high towers or turrets, at the angles of fortified walls. Gesenius assumes an obsolete root פָּנַן‎, *to separate, divide into classes*, as that from which פִּנָּה‎, *a turret*, is derived; but there is no occasion to depart from its usual derivation from the Piel of פָּנָה‎, *to cause to turn*. It thus signifies what is at the *turning, corner*, or angle of a building, and that whether at the top or the bottom. Tacitus, describing the walls of Jerusalem, says: "Per artem obliquos et introrsum sinuatos, ut latera oppugnantium ad ictus, patescerent." Hist. lib. v. cap. 11, § 5.

17. לְחֻם‎, or, as in some MSS. and editions, לְחֻם‎, *flesh*. Arab. لَحْم‎, *caro*. Root לָחַם‎, *to eat*. שָׁפַךְ‎ may, by zeugma, be made to govern לְחֻמָם‎ as well as דָּמָם‎, but it is preferable to supply the substantive verb after לְחֻמָם‎. For the latter figure, comp. Job xx. 7.

18. גַּם — גַּם‎, *also — also*, meaning both the one and the other. As here with a negative, *neither — nor*. "Fire"

Of all the inhabitants of the land.

is often used figuratively to denote war, because of its devastating effects. Is. x. 16, xxvi. 11. אֵת is to be taken in the sense of *wholly, entirely, altogether.*

CHAPTER II.

A solemn admonition is now given to the Jewish people to repent during the short space of time that would be allotted to them before the Chaldean invasion, 1, 2; followed by an exhortation to the pious to persevere in their devotedness to God, and the interests of righteousness, 3. The prophet then proceeds to foretell the destruction of those nations which had always been hostile to the Jews, as the Philistines, 4—7; the Moabites and Ammonites, 8—10; parenthetically. the idols of the nations, 11; the Ethiopians, 12; and the Assyrians, 13—15.

---

1 BEND yourselves, and be ye bent,
 O nation not desired!
2 Before the birth of the decree;
 The day passeth away as chaff;
 Before there come upon you the burning anger of Jehovah;
 Before there come upon you the day of anger of Jehovah.

---

1. הִתְקוֹשְׁשׁוּ וָקוֹשּׁוּ, the Hithpolel and Kal conjugations joined for the sake of intensity. Comp. Is. xxiv. 19. The words have been variously rendered. LXX. συνάχθητε καὶ συνδέθητε. Vulg. *convenite et congregamini.* De Wette, *prüfet euch, ja prüfet.* Gesenius, *collect yourselves and be ye collected;* i. e. collect your thoughts, look into your own mind, prove yourselves; thus agreeing with De Wette, after the interpretation of Pagninus, Vatablus, Coccoius, and others. Ewald, *erbleichet und bleichet.* Most refer to קַשׁ as the root, which signifies in Poel to collect *stubble, wood,* etc. ; but it is never used with respect to human beings. I prefer deriving it from קוֹשׁ, *to bend, be bent.* Arab. قوس. II. *incurvavit arcus more; incurvatus fuit senex.* Hence קֶשֶׁת, *a bow,* from its being bent.

Bend yourselves, and be ye bent, will then be the proper rendering. Comp. the use of שָׁחָה, *to bow down,* Is. lx. 14. The prophet calls the Jews to deep humility before God on account of their manifold sins. Because כָּסַף signifies *to be pale,* Gesenius renders the words הַגּוֹי לֹא נִכְסָף, *O nation not ashamed!* but כָּסַף never denotes to be pale from a feeling of shame, but as the effect of desire, the verb everywhere else expressing the idea of *pining, longing,* being intensely desirous of any object. The phrase לֹא נִכְסָף, *not desired,* is here used by litotes for *abominated, hated.*

2. The Divine decree or purpose of punishment announced in the preceding chapter, is here tropically represented as a pregnant female near the time of her delivery. The words כְּטֶרֶם עֲבֹר יוֹם, *as*

3 Seek ye Jehovah, all ye humble of the land,
   Who perform his judgments;
   Seek righteousness, seek humility,
   If perhaps ye may be hid
   In the day of the anger of Jehovah.
4 For Gaza shall be forsaken,
   And Askelon a desolation;
   As for Ashdod, they shall drive her out at noon-day,
   And Ekron shall be rooted up.
5 Woe to the inhabitants of the line of the sea!
   The nation of Kerethites!
   The word of Jehovah is against you;
   O Canaan! the land of the Philistines,
   I will destroy thee, that there shall be no inhabitant.

chaff the day passeth, do not refer to the coming of the period of calamity, but the rapid lapse of the time of repentance. The image of chaff is always used of that which flies quickly away, never of what comes to any one. They are introduced parenthetically. The sentence בְּטֶרֶם לֹא־יָבוֹא עֲלֵיכֶם חֲרוֹן אַף יְהוָה is wanting in six of Kennicott's MSS., probably in two more, and originally in eight of De Rossi's. It is also omitted in the Arabic version. The declaration, with the trifling change of a single word, is properly repeated for the sake of emphasis.

3. The prophet here addresses himself to the afflicted and humble among his people, from whom some hope of a better state of things might be expected. אוּלַי, rendered *perhaps*, is not intended to express a doubt respecting the safety of the pious, but the extreme difficulty of escaping the threatened judgment. The poor of the land were left by Nebuzar-adan to be vine-dressers and husbandmen. 2 Kings xxv. 12.

4. The connective force of the particle כִּי, *for*, with which this verse commences, lies in the universality of the calamity which was about to come, not upon the Jews only, but upon all the nations with which they had been brought into contact. There would be no country to which they might flee for safety, for all were to be visited by the Chaldeans. For the cities of the Philistines here specified, see on the parallel prophecy, Amos i. 6—8; and Is. xx. 1. צָהֳרַיִם, *the meridian* or *noon*, being the hottest part of the day, is generally spent by the Orientals in sleep, and is the less likely time for any military operations to be carried on. 2 Sam. iv. 5; Jer. vi. 4, xv. 8. The paronomasias, עַזָּה עֲזוּבָה and עֶקְרוֹן תֵּעָקֵר, are not to be overlooked.

5. This and the two following verses contain an amplification of the prediction against the Philistines. חֶבֶל הַיָּם, LXX. τὸ σχοίνισμα τῆς θαλάσσης, *the line of the sea*, i. e. the *region* or *coast* along the sea-shore, and so called from the custom of using a cord or line in measuring off or dividing a territory. Comp. with the same application, חוֹף הַיָּם, *the coast of the sea*, Jer. xlvii. 7; Ezek. xxv. 16. By גּוֹי כְּרֵתִים, *nation of Cretians*, we are not to understand the actual inhabitants of Crete, but the Philistines, a nation descended from those who originally emigrated from that island, and took possession of the south-west coast of Palestine. פְּלִשְׁתִּים, the name of *the Philistines*, properly signifies *the emigrants*, from פָּלַשׁ. Eth. ፈለጠ,

6 And the line of the sea shall be pastures,
With cisterns for shepherds,
And folds for sheep.

7 Yea, the line shall be for the remnant of the house of Judah.
Thereupon shall they feed;
In the houses of Askelon shall they lie down at even;
For Jehovah their God shall visit them,
And reverse their captivity.

8 I have heard the reproach of Moab,
And the revilings of the sons of Ammon,
Who have reviled my people,
And carried themselves haughtily against their border.

9 Wherefore, as I live, saith Jehovah of hosts,
The God of Israel:
Surely Moab shall be as Sodom,
And the sons of Ammon as Gomorrah;
A region of overrunning brambles and salt pits,
And a perpetual desolation;
The remnant of my people shall plunder them,
And the residue of my nation shall possess them.

10 This shall happen to them for their pride,
Because they reproached and carried themselves haughtily,
Against the people of Jehovah of hosts.

to rove, migrate. According to Stephen of Byzantium, Gaza was originally called *Minoa*, after Minos, king of Crete, who, with his two brothers, Arakus and Rhadamanthus, undertook an expedition to the coast, and gave the city his own name. Comp. Deut. ii. 23; 1 Sam. xxx. 14; Jer. xlvii. 4; Ezek. xxv. 16; Amos ix. 7. כְּנַעַן, *Canaan*, which is not only employed to designate the whole country taken possession of by the Hebrews, but more specially Phœnicia, is here to be understood as restricted to the country of the Philistines.

6. It is thought by some that there is an allusion to בְּאֵרוֹת in the word כְּרֹת, which properly signifies *wells* or *cisterns*, from כָּרָה, *to dig*. Instead of continuing to be a thickly populated and well cultivated country, the land of the Philistines should be converted into a region fit only to be occupied by nomades.

7. Instead of being any longer annoyed by the Philistines, the Jews, restored to their land, would occupy the territory as described in the preceding verse.

8—10. Comp. the parallel prophecies against Moab, Is. xv. xvi.; Jer. xlviii.; Amos ii. 1—3; and Ammon, Jer. xlix, 1—6; Amos i. 13—15. הִגְדִּיל עַל means *to carry one's self haughtily against* any one. There is no occasion to supply פֶּה or any other noun. The suffix in גְּבוּלָם has עַמִּי for its antecedent. The formulas חַי אָנִי, *I living*, or *as I live*, ver. 9, and חַי יְהֹוָה, חַי אֱלֹהִים, *as Jehovah, as God liveth*, are solemn modes of expression, by which the Divine Existence is pledged for the certainty of the declarations which they introduce. מִמְשַׁק, *a drawing*, or *extending out*, from מָשַׁק, cognate מָשַׁךְ, *to draw out, extend*. As connected with *bramble*, it denotes the *overspreading* or *overrunning* of that

Chap. II.   ZEPHANIAH.   331

11 Jehovah is to be feared above all the gods of the earth,
   For he will cause them to waste away;
   And all the inhabitants of the maritime regions
   Shall worship him — each from his place.
12   Also ye, O ye Cushites!
   Shall be slain by my sword.
13 And he will stretch forth his hand over the north,
   And destroy Assyria;
   He will also make Nineveh waste,
   An arid region like the desert.
14 And flocks shall lie down in the midst of her;
   All the wild beasts of the nations;
   Both the pelican and the porcupine
   Shall take up their abode in her capitals;
   A voice shall sing in the windows,

shrub. מְבְרֵה מֶלַח, *a pit* or excavation, such as are found in the vicinity of the Dead Sea, in which, when it overflows in spring, its water is collected, and pure salt obtained by evaporation. The idea conveyed by both metaphors is that of sterility and desolation.

11. This verse connects so slightly with the preceding, and, as the former part is usually rendered, affords so little suitable a sense, that I cannot but regard the suffix in עֲלֵיהֶם as possessing an anticipative pronominal reference to אֱלֹהֵי הָאָרֶץ, *the gods of the earth*, with respect to whom Jehovah was to show himself worthy of exclusive veneration by effecting their destruction. In Hebrew poetry the pronoun or pronominal affix frequently occurs before the noun. See on Is. xxviii. 26. While announcing the destruction of the surrounding idolatrous nations, the prophet was inspired to predict the gradual, but certain destruction of idolatry universally throughout the earth. The period predicted should be one in which all peculiarity of local worship would cease, and Divine worship be acceptable wherever presented in sincerity and truth. Comp. Mal. i. 11; John iv. 21—24; 1 Cor. i. 2. For the phrase גּוֹיֵא עֲלֵי־הֶם, comp. Ps. xcvi.

4. The מ prefixed in מִמְּקוֹמוֹ, expresses simply the locality in which the persons spoken of resided. Compare מִבֵּית, מְקֹדֶם, מְיָמִין מִגְּוּאל, etc. רָזָה, Arab. رزي, *to make thin, lean, diminish*, cause to waste away, and to *destroy*. LXX. ἐξολοθρεύσει. The knowledge and worship of the true God were to be extended not only over the vast continental regions of the globe, but over those which bordered on, or existed in the sea. In אִיֵּי הַיָּם, *the isles*, or *maritime regions*, there is, as usual, a special reference to the West; though in connection with כֹּל, *all*, the universality of such regions is intended. The passage is strictly Messianic, since the accomplishment of the prediction has been, and is being effected by means of the gospel.

12. For כּוּשׁ, *Cush*, see on Is. xi. 11, xviii. 1. The prophecy received its fulfilment when Nebuchadnezzar invaded and conquered Egypt, with whose military operations and fate the Ethiopians were more or less mixed up. Jer. xlvi. 9; Ezek. xxx. 5, 9. There is, indeed, reason to think that Egypt herself is designed to be included in the term as here employed.

13—15. From the remote South into

Desolation shall be in the thresholds,
For the cedar-work is laid bare.
15 This is the exulting city which dwelt securely,
Which said in her heart,
I am, and besides me there is none.
How she is become desolate!
A resting-place for wild beasts!
Every one that passeth by her shall hiss,
He shall shake his hand.

which the prophet had carried his hearers, he turns suddenly back to the North, where there still existed a mighty empire, which must of necessity be overthrown, before the Divine sword, i. e. the arms of Babylon, could reach the countries against which he had denounced the judgments of God. This empire was the Assyrian, which was drawing towards its end, and was actually subverted when Nineveh was taken and destroyed by Cyaxares and Nabopolassar, B. C. 625. It is this catastrophe, with its disastrous consequences, which Zephaniah so graphically describes in these verses. So completely was the celebrated metropolis of the ancient world to be desolated, that not even the Nomades would seek a temporary shelter among her ruins. They should only be inhabited by the wild beasts of the desert. That by צִיִּים we are to understand herds of savage animals, and not flocks of sheep, goats, etc., is apparent from the mention made in the parallelism of כָּל־חַיְתוֹ־גוֹי, *every wild beast of the nation* גוֹי, *nation*, has by some been thought to stand poetically for a collection of animals, just as עַם, *people*, does, Prov. xxx. 25, 26; but it is rather to be regarded as synonymous with אֶרֶץ, *land, country;* only restricting it to the particular country in which Nineveh had been situated; so that the phrase will be equivalent to חַיְתוֹ־אֶרֶץ, Gen. i. 24. The LXX. render πάντα τὰ θηρία τῆς γῆς. Targ. כָּל חַיְוַת בָּרָא, *all the beasts of the field.* The ו in חַיְתוֹ is merely paragogic. For קָאַת and קִפֹּד, see on Is. xxxiv. 11. Some interpret לִילִית of the Arab غُول, *the demon of the desert,* and convert חָרְבָּה, *desolation,* into עֹרֵב, *raven,* but without sufficient ground. See Maurer, who, in opposition to Hitzig, takes both words in their usual acceptation. עָרָה, the Piel of עָרָה, is here used impersonally, and is best rendered in the passive. בַּפְתּוֹר, *chapiter,* see on Amos ix. 1. By אֲרָזָה is meant the wainscoting and fine carved *cedar work* with which the walls, ceiling, etc., of the houses were ornamented. For the language of pride and carnal security expressed in ver. 15, comp. Is. xlvii. 8.

CHAPTER III.

HAVING digressed to predict the fate of the surrounding nations, Zephaniah returns to his own countrymen, and specially directs his prophecy against Jerusalem, the leading persons in which had persevered in wickedness in spite of all the warnings which they had received, 1—7. After addressing the pious members of the theocracy, and encouraging them to wait for the development of the Divine purposes, 8, he proceeds to predict the conversion of the Gentiles, 9, and of the Jews, 10; describes their character when converted, 11—13; congratulates them on their deliverance, and enjoyment of the presence of their heavenly King, 14—17; and concludes by adverting to the circumstances connected with their return to Palestine after their conversion, 18—20.

1 Wo to the rebellious and polluted,
   The oppressing city!
2 She listened not to the voice,
   She received not instruction;
   She trusted not in Jehovah,
   She drew not near to her God.
3 Her princes in the midst of her
   Are roaring lions;
   Her judges are evening wolves;
   They gnaw no bones in the morning.
4 Her prophets are vain-glorious,
   Hypocritical men;
   Her priests profane what is sacred;
   They do violence to the law.

1. It has been thought by some that in מֹרְאָה, *rebellious*, as here applied to Jerusalem, there is a play upon the name of מֹרִיָּה, *Moriah*, on which the temple was built. If so, it was calculated to suggest to the minds of the Jews the gross inconsistency of their laying claim to any connection with that sacred place, while they obstinately refused to obey the law of God. The root is מָרָא, cognate with מָרָה, *to prove refractory, rebel*. The LXX. rendering the word by ἐπιφανής, *illustrious*, have doubtless mistaken it as coming from רָאָה, *to see;* as the Syr. likewise has done, rendering ܐܝܕܝܥܐ, *noted, celebrated.* יוֹנָה, the Benon. participle of יָנָה, *to rage, be cruel, oppressive*, etc. What the prophet has in his eye is the rage and cruelty with which the idolatrous inhabitants persecuted such as adhered to the worship and service of Jehovah, as well as their oppression of the widows, orphans, etc. See Jer. xxii. 3.

2—4. Not only did the inhabitants generally refuse to receive instruction from the Lord, and alienate their affections from him and his service, but the rulers, both civil and ecclesiastical, evinced the grossest dereliction of duty, and the most flagrant inconsistency of character. זְאֵבֵי עֶרֶב, *evening wolves*, i. e. wolves which come forth from the forests or other lurking places in the evening, and, greedy with hunger, seize or devour during the night, whatever animals they fall in with. Comp. Hab. i. 8, λύκοι νυκτερινοί, Oppian. Cynoget. 3, 266. The voracious and insatiable cupidity of the judges is further expressed by לֹא גָרְמוּ לַבֹּקֶר, *nothing is craunched in the morning;* i. e. all is devoured in the night, and not so much as a bone left to be gnawed in the morning. גָּרַם is here used impersonally. Thus, as to the

5 Jehovah, the righteous One, is in the midst of her,
  He doeth no injustice;
  Every morning he bringeth his judgment to light,
  It is not lacking;
  But the unjust know no shame.
6   I have cut off the nations;
  Their corner-stones are laid waste;
  I have made their streets desolate,
  Without any one passing through them.
  Their cities are destroyed; they are without a man;
  There is no inhabitant.
7 I said: Only fear me;
  Receive instruction;
  That her habitation might not be cut off,
  According to all that I had appointed concerning her:
  But they rose up early;
  They corrupted all their doings.

sense, the LXX. and Vulg. οὐχ ὑπολίποντο; *non relinquebant.* The prophets, instead of evincing that gravity and humility which became those who professed to deliver Divine messages, were פֹּחֲזִים, *light* and *vain-glorious* persons, trifling with the most serious subjects, and carrying themselves haughtily towards others. The verb פָּחַז properly signifies to *boil up* like water. Comp. Gen. xlix. 4; Jud. ix. 4; Jer. xxiii. 32. Arab. كَسَل, *superbivit.* The priests were equally corrupt. They made no distinction between the holy and profane, and distorted the meaning of the law, when expounding it to the people. Comp. Ezek. xxii. 26, where similar language is used, and explained.

5. Jehovah had his residence in the temple, connected with the daily worship, in which were those unfailing revelations of the rectitude of his character that brought to view a glorious pattern, which it was the duty of the Jews to imitate; but, hardened in wickedness, they were conscious of no feelings of shame. בַּבֹּקֶר בַּבֹּקֶר, *in the morning in the morning,* i. e. according to a common Hebrew idiom, *every morning.*

6. Besides the plentiful instruction with which the inhabitants of Jerusalem had been furnished by the public institutions that existed among them, and from which they might conclude what punishment they had to expect if they persisted in sin, they had examples from which to take warning in the desolate condition to which other nations had been reduced on account of their wickedness. Under the long and happy reign of Josiah, the Jews enjoyed rest and tranquillity until the last year, while other neighboring nations were laid waste; for it was during his reign that the great incursion of the Scythians into western Asia took place, while Judea was spared. Michaelis. פִּנָּה is here to be taken in its literal acceptation of *corner-stone,* but the ruin or desolation of the building resting upon it is implied. נִצְדּוּ is the Niphal of צָדָה, *to cut down, lay waste.*

7. תִּירְאִי and תִּקְחִי are both futures used as imperatives. In מְעוֹנָהּ and פָּקַדְתִּי is a change, by no means uncommon, of the second person to the third. In כֹּל there is an ellipsis of כְּ, *according to*

Chap. III.   ZEPHANIAH.   335

8   Nevertheless, wait for me, saith Jehovah,
      In the day when I rise for the prey;
      For my determination is to assemble the nations,
      To gather the kingdoms;
      To pour out upon them my fury,
      All the heat of my anger;
      For by the fire of my jealousy
      The whole earth shall be consumed.
9   For then I will turn to the nations a pure language,
      That they may all invoke the name of Jehovah;
      That they may serve him with one accord.

עַל חָקַם is not to be here taken in the sense of punishing, but of *appointing* for punishment. Comp. Jer. xv. 3. The appointed and threatened judgments should be averted from Jerusalem, if the inhabitants would only turn from their evil ways, and walk in the fear of the Lord. Such was the announcement which he graciously made to them by his servants the prophets; but, instead of reforming, they addicted themselves more sedulously and entirely to the practice of iniquity. הִשְׁכִּים, *to rise early*, is frequently used in the Hebrew Scriptures in a tropical sense, to indicate that a person does anything with preparedness or full purpose of mind. The primary idea conveyed by the verb seems to be that of placing the burdens on the shoulders of camels, etc., before setting out on a journey, which, in the East, is done very early in the morning. Root שָׁכֵם, *shoulder*, Eth. ባጀለ ; *bajulavit.* ኣጀለ ; *onus imposuit humeris.*

8. Most expositors interpret the words חַכּוּ לִי, *expect* or *wait for me*, as if they were addressed to the profligate characters described in the preceding verse, but this construction is admissible only on the principle of their being applied ironically, since the phrase is never used except in a good sense. Yet even this but ill suits the entire connection. I consider them to form an apostrophe to the pious among the Jews, calling upon them to look forward, amid all the calamities which were approaching, to the glorious period which these calamities were designed to usher in, and which the prophet specially describes in the following verses. The LXX., and all the other Greek versions, as also the Syr., render עֵד, by *testimony* or *witness;* a signification which only attaches to the letters when pointed עֵד. The signification of *prey* is more appropriate here. Compare for this signification Gen. xlix. 27; Is. xxxiii. 23. What is meant by rising up to the prey is explained in the following clause of the verse. Indeed, the very derivation of the word from עָדָה, *to pass on in a hostile manner*, to *rush upon, attack;* Arab. عَدَا, irruit in aliquem; عَدُوّ, *inimici, hostes;* at once suggests the ideas of conflict and destruction.

9. From this verse to the end of the book the prophecy relates exclusively to Messianic times. The שָׂפָה בְרוּרָה, *purified lip* or *language*, means the profession of pure religion, a language freed from the polluted names of idols, and of every abomination connected with their worship. As this was to be realized by the nations, the עַמִּים, as distinguished from the Jews, it follows that the spread of Christianity, and the consequent subversion of idolatry throughout the world, are here specifically predicted. This prediction, however, has hitherto been only partially fulfilled. By the gospel, indeed, idolatry has been dislodged from many

10 From beyond the rivers of Cush,
My suppliants, the daughter of my dispersed,
Shall bring my offering.

parts of the globe, but its place has to a great extent been occupied by the pollutions of antichristian systems of worship, while vast regions are still the scenes of varied and most degrading idolatrous abominations. And, as to the unity so strikingly expressed by אֶחָד שְׁכֶם, *one shoulder*, whatever there may be of that real substantial unity which binds all true believers to Christ as their Head, and to one another as members of the same family, there is still a deplorable want of the visible manifestation of oneness in obeying the laws of Christ, and obeying the ordinances of his house. These laws are spoken of as a burden, Matt. xi. 20; Acts xv. 28; Rev. ii. 24; and the metaphor here employed by the prophet is taken from two persons jointly carrying a burden between them, shoulder to shoulder. Compare the use of ὁμοθυμαδὸν, Acts i. 14; ii. 1, 46; iv. 24; v. 12; xv. 25; Rom. xv. 6. What has prevented the outward visibility of the unity of believers has been, that some of them have added burdens of their own to that of the Redeemer, while others have submitted to those imposed by men professing to be acting by his authority, but who have had no Scripture warranty for their pretensions. Until there is a return to an unanimous adherence to the simplicity which is in Christ, there can be no such unity as that taught in this verse. Yet for such the Bible teaches us to look ; and it behooves every Christian to do whatever lies in his power, in order to bring about so blessed a consummation. Comp. 2 Cor. vi. 14, Μὴ γίνεσθε ἑτεροζυγοῦντες ἀπίστοις; and 1 Cor. i. 10, ἦτε δὲ κατηρτισμένοι ἐν τῷ αὐτῷ νοΐ καὶ ἐν τῇ αὐτῇ γνώμῃ.

10. Having foretold the conversion of the Gentiles, the prophet in this verse predicts that of the Jews; quite in accordance with other passages of Scripture, in which they are placed in juxta-position with each other. עֲתָרַי, *my suppliants*, from עָתַר, *to burn incense to a divinity; pray, supplicate.* Arab. عَطَرَ, *bonos odores spiravit.* Syr. ܥܛܪ. *fumavit odore suavi.* Comp. Rev. v. 8, where the prayers of saints are called θυμιάματα, odors or incense, and Ps. cxli. 2, where David compares his prayer to קְטֹרֶת, the Hebrew synonyme for *incense*. Who the worshippers are, the prophet explains in the following words : בַּת־פּוּצַי, *the daughter of my dispersed*, i. e. by a common Hebrew idiom, my dispersed people, the Jews; and the locality in which we are directed to look for them is מֵעֵבֶר לְנַהֲרֵי־כוּשׁ, *beyond the rivers of Cush*, i. e. Ethiopia or Abyssinia itself, the rivers of which enclose it on the north. See on Is. xviii. 1, where the same phraseology occurs, but where the Ethiopians, and not the Jews, are the subjects of the prophecy. It is a well ascertained fact, though all the historical circumstances with which it is connected have not yet been brought to light, that there has long existed in the west of Abyssinia, a people called *Falashas*, or emigrants (from the Eth. ፈለሰ ፡ *to migrate;* hence ፈላሲ ፡ *a sojourner, stranger*, the root from which פְּלִשְׁתִּי, *Philistine*, is derived, and for the same reason), who maintain that they derived their origin from Palestine, and all of whom profess the Jewish religion. They are identified, as to physical traits, not with the African races living in Ethiopia, but with the tribes of Arabia. They have their own government conceded to them by the Negus, or king of Ethiopia. When Bruce was there they had a Jewish king named Gideon, and his queen, Judith. Considering how greatly the

11   In that day thou shalt not be ashamed
On account of all thy doings,
By which thou hast transgressed against me;
For then I will remove from the midst of thee
Thy proud exulters;
And thou shalt no more be haughty in my holy mountain.
12   And I will leave in the midst of thee
An humble and poor people.
And they shall trust in the name of Jehovah.
13   The residue of Israel shall not commit injustice;
They shall not speak lies;
Neither shall a deceitful tongue be found in their mouth;
But they shall feed and lie down,
And none shall make them afraid.
14   Rejoice, O daughter of Zion!
Shout, O Israel!
Be joyful and exult with all thy heart,
O daughter of Jerusalem!
15   Jehovah hath removed thy judgments;

Christianity of Abyssinia has been mixed up with Judaism, there is every reason to believe that most of the early converts in that country belonged to this very people. That the Falashas are part of the dispersed people whose conversion is here predicted, I can have no doubt. They are singled out as a separate portion of the scattered seed of Abraham, most probably on account of the peculiar circumstances in which they have lived during the dispersion. Their bringing of Jehovah's offering does not necessarily imply that they are, on their conversion, to come with gifts to Jerusalem; all that is intended may only be מִנְחָה טְהוֹרָה, *the pure offering*, which, under the new dispensation, was to be presented in every place. See Mal. i. 11; and comp. ver. 9.

11—13. These verses contain a description of restored and regenerated Israel. The not being ashamed of their sinful practices does not mean their not feeling a compunctious sense of their intrinsic odiousness and demerits, but is expressive of the great change that should take place in the outward condition of the Jews. That condition into which they have been brought by their obstinate rebellion against Jehovah and his Messiah, is one of disgrace. When recovered out of it, all the marks of shame and infamy shall be removed. The Pharisaic spirit of pride, and the vain confidence in the temple and the temple worship, which proved the ruin of the nation, shall be taken away. The converted residue shall be a people humble and poor in spirit, Matt. v. 3, xi. 5, and of a truly righteous and upright character; and having fled for refuge to the hope set before them in the gospel, shall be safe under the protecting care of their heavenly Father.

14. A call to the converted Israelites, restored to their own land, and especially to the inhabitants of Jerusalem, to exult in their distinguished experience of the Divine loving-kindness.

15. This and the following verses furnish the reasons why the Jews should indulge in exultation. פָּנָה, in Kal, *to turn*; in Piel, *to cause to turn out of the*

He hath cleared away thine enemies;
The King of Israel, Jehovah, is in the midst of thee,
Thou shalt see calamity no more.

16 In that day it shall be said to Jerusalem, Fear not
O Zion! let not thy hands be feeble;

17 Jehovah thy God is in the midst of thee,
The Mighty One, that will save;
He will rejoice over thee with gladness,
He will be silent in his love!
He will exult over thee with a shout of joy.

18 I will gather those that are grieved for the festivals,
(They were of thee;)
Burdened with reproach for her sake.

19 Behold! I will deal with all thine oppressors at that time,

---

way, remove, destroy. Instead of אֹיְבֵךְ, *thine enemy,* thirty-two MSS., originally six more, and two by correction, read אֹיְבַיִךְ, *thine enemies,* which reading is also supported by two early editions, the Babyl. Talmud, and all the versions. For תִּרְאִי, sixty-eight MSS., and among these some of the most accurate Spanish, read תִּירְאִי. In the full enjoyment of the presence of their God, the converted Jews should have nothing to fear.

17. A beautiful description of the delight which Jehovah shall take in his recovered people, and of their consequent and continuous happiness. The phrase יַחֲרִישׁ בְּאַהֲבָתוֹ has occasioned some difficulty to interpreters. Houbigant, after the LXX. and Syr., and following him Newcome, and recently Ewald, propose to read יְחַדֵּשׁ, "*he will renew* his love;" but this verb nowhere occurs in Hiphil, and the conjectural emendation is wholly unnecessary. חָרַשׁ, *to be dumb, keep silence,* has the same signification in Hiphil, *to be silent, not to speak,* and is here very appropriately employed to express the non-remembrance of iniquity. Justly as God might set the sins of his people before them, he, in the exercise of his love, makes no mention of them, having freely forgiven them for the sake of the atonement made by his only-begotten Son. Comp. Ps. xxxii. 2; Jer. xxxi. 34; Ezek. xxxiii. 16.

18. נוּגֵי, of which נִבְגִּים is the Niphal participle, has two significations, that of being *pained* or *grieved,* and that of being *separated, removed,* etc. Both derivations may be supported by the Arab. وَجِيَ, *doluit,* and Conj. iv. *procul a se avertit.* The former, which is here most approved, fully meets the exigency of the passage, and may be said to imply the latter. The Jews, in a state which rendered it impossible for them to celebrate their sacred festivals at Jerusalem, are represented as filled with grief when they reflected on the privileges of their ancestors. מוֹעֵד, *festival,* is here a noun of multitude. עָלֶיהָ, *on her account,* is introduced, for the sake of emphasis, between the words מַשְׂאֵת חֶרְפָּה, *the lifting up,* or *utterance of reproach,* which would otherwise have appeared in the construct state. By metonymy, the Jews, who are the objects of such reproach, are intended. Comp. Micah vi. 16. The feminine suffix in עָלֶיהָ refers to Jerusalem or Zion, understood: the change of person is, as frequently, for the sake of effect. The various reading עָלַי, though supported by more than twelve MSS., the Targ. and Syr., is most probably an emendation.

19. עָשָׂה אֵת, means *to deal with,* in

And will save her that halteth,
And collect the expelled,
And make them a praise and a name,
In every country where they have been put to shame
20 At that time I will bring you in,
Even at the time when I collect you;
Yea, I will make you a name and a praise
Among all the nations of the earth,
When I reverse your captivity in their sight,
Saith Jehovah.

the way of retribution or punishment. Vulg. *interficiam.* Targ. אֲנָא עָבֵיד גְּמִירָא עַם, *I will make an end of.* The restoration of the Jews is uniformly represented as taking place in connection with the destruction of those nations that are hostile to the cause of God, and that shall, in a special manner, oppose the accomplishment of his purpose respecting the final deliverance of that long depressed and scattered, yet beloved people. Comp. Is. lix. 17—21, lxvi. 15, 16. צֹלֵעָה, *halting,* and נִדָּחָה, *driven away, cast out,* express the deplorable circumstances of the Jews during the dispersion; and the verbal forms indicate that such shall be their condition till the time of restoration. The illustrious character of that restoration, however, shall redound to the celebrity of the covenant people in all the countries where they have been the objects of reproach and ignominy. אֶרֶץ, *land,* is used collectively for אֲרָצוֹת, *lands,* and אֶרֶץ בָּשְׁתָּם, *the land of their shame,* means the countries in which they have been the objects of contumely and disgrace. Ezek. xxxiv. 29. The occurrence of the article in הָאָרֶץ, which is in construction with בָּשְׁתָּם, is contrary to rule, but is otherwise not without examples. See Josh. iii. 17; 1 Sam. ii. 13; 2 Kings vii. 13. In such cases, however, the article is generally repeated before the following noun. See Josh. viii. 11; Jer. xxv. 26. Some would account for the irregularity by an understood repetition of the noun, thus, בְּכָל־הָאָרֶץ אֶרֶץ בָּשְׁתָּם.

20. After אָבִיא אֶתְכֶם supply בְּאַרְצָכֶם. The ו in וּבְעֵת is exegetical. The period of the reintroduction of the Jews into their own land is here rendered distinguishingly prominent by repeated and pointed reference. So wonderful, however, shall be the circumstances connected with the event, that they shall scarcely believe it when it happens, how greatly and how long soever they may have desired it. Jehovah, to remove all doubts, declares that he will bring it about *before their eyes;* i. e. it shall certainly become the object of their delightful contemplation.

HAGGAI.

PREFACE.

It is generally thought that the prophet Haggai was among the Hebrew exiles who returned with Zerubbabel, and Joshua the high priest, from Babylon in the year B. C. 536, when Cyrus granted them their liberty, and ordered them to be furnished with what was necessary for the restoration of the temple at Jerusalem. His book itself vouches for the fact that he prophesied in the reign of Darius Hystaspis, who ascended the Persian throne B. C. 521. Having been interrupted in building the temple by an interdict, which the Samaritans obtained from Smerdis the usurper, the Jews became in some measure indifferent to the work; and when Darius came to the throne, an event which must have deprived the prohibition of all authority, instead of vigorously recommencing their labors, the more influential persons among them pretended that, as the prophecy of the seventy years applied to the temple as well as to the captivity in Babylon, and they were only yet in the sixty-eighth year, the proper time for rebuilding it had not arrived, and gave their whole attention to the erection of splendid mansions for themselves.

To rouse them from their selfish indifference to the claims of religion, Haggai and Zechariah were commissioned, in the second year of Darius, i. e. B. C. 520, to deliver to them rousing appeals from Jehovah. These appeals had the desired effect, and the work proceeded with vigor.

The book is made up of five messages, which were all delivered, at successive periods, within the short space of three months. They are so exceedingly brief, that they are, not without reason, supposed to be only a summary or epitome of the original discourses.

The style of Haggai is not distinguished by any peculiar excellence; yet he is not destitute of pathos and vehemence, when reproving his countrymen for their negligence, and exhorting them to the performance of duty. To these, the interrogatory form which he frequently adopts, in no small degree contributes. He is not without elevation when predicting the future. Certain portions of the book are purely historical; and the rest, though exhibiting more or less of the parallelism of members which characterizes the usual prophetic style, are but faintly rhythmic l. The phrases, נאם יהוה ; שימו לבבכם, are frequently repeated. נאם יהוה occurs not less than thrice in a single verse, chap. ii. 4.

כאחד, ii. 3; משפט אחת, ii. 6; ארץ עם, ii. 16, are peculiar, and indicate the Chaldee age.

CHAPTER I.

THE prophet calls the attention of the principal civil and ecclesiastical authorities to the negligence of the people in not building the temple, 1—4; directs that of the people to this as the cause of their want of outward prosperity, 5—11; and subjoins a notice respecting the success with which the delivery of his message was accompanied.

1   IN the second year of Darius the king, in the sixth month, on the first day of the month, the word of the Lord was communicated through Haggai the prophet to Zerubbabel, the son of Shealtiel, governor of Judah, and to Joshua, the son of Josedech, the high priest, saying:

1. The Darius here mentioned is Darius the son of Hystaspis, of the family of the Achæmenidæ, who, in consequence of an oracle, was raised to the throne of Persia, on the death of the usurper Smerdis, B.C. 521, and reigned thirty-six years. That this must be the monarch intended is obvious from the facts, that Darius the Mede, mentioned Dan. v. 31, ix. 1, lived before the return of the Jews from Babylon; and that Darius Nothus and Darius Codomannus flourished, the former ninety-three years after the completion of the temple, and the latter at a much later period. Darius Hystaspis is represented by Herodotus as a mild and benevolent ruler. He protected the Jews from the opposition of their enemies, and carried into effect the edict of Cyrus, Ezra vi. The name דָּרְיָוֶשׁ, Daryavesh, or, as it appears in the cuneiform inscriptions of Persepolis, Daryawus, is derived by Lassen (üb. d. Keilform. Inschriften, p. 158), from the root darh, to preserve, with the affirmative awu, the s being the sign of the nominative; and thus signifies conservator. Comp. Herodotus, vi. 98, where the signification ἑρξείης, coercer, is given to the name. The date in the prophecy is taken from the reign of this monarch, because at the time he swayed his sceptre over all the countries with which the Jews were brought into contact, from Lybia in Egypt, and the frontiers of Europe, to the Oxus and the Indus on the east. The months specified by Haggai and Zechariah are those not of the Persian, but of the Hebrew year. See Zech. i. 7, vii. 1, viii. 19. Zerubbabel, whose Chaldee name was Sheshbazzar, Ezra i. 8, v. 14; comp. v. 16, iii. 8, 10, was the grandson (בֵּן is used by Haggai in its more extended signification) of Shealtiel, of the royal house of David, 1 Chron. iii. 9—19. Cyrus committed to his care the sacred vessels of the temple, and appointed him governor of the colony which returned to Judea. The title of פֶּחָה, prefect or governor, by which he is designated, is applied to persons bearing rule in provinces or divisions of the Persian empire of less extent and importance than satrapies. Comp. the Pracrit. Pakkha, and the present Turkish Pasha, though the latter word, باشا, Basha, is rather to be referred to باش, Bash, head, commander, ruler. Joshua the high priest is repeatedly mentioned in the book of Zechariah, as presiding over the Jewish affairs at the same time with Zerubbabel. That הַכֹּהֵן הַגָּדוֹל, the high priest, is to be connected, not with the more proximate, but with the more remote noun, i. e. with יְהוֹשֻׁעַ, Joshua, is clear, not only from the sim-

2 Thus saith Jehovah of hosts:
This people say, The time is not come,
The time for the house of Jehovah to be built.
3   Yea, the word of Jehovah was communicated through Haggai the prophet, saying:
4 Is it time for you, O ye,
To dwell in your wainscoted houses,
And this house lie waste?
5   Now, therefore, thus saith Jehovah of hosts:
Consider your ways.
6 Ye have sown much, but brought in little;
Ye have eaten, but not had enough;
Ye have drunk, but not to the full;
Ye have put on clothing, but none is warm;

ilar coherence of עֵת, but from all other instances in which offices and genealogical statements are blended.

2. Simple as are the words לֹא עֵת בֹּא ׳וגו עֵת, the construction is somewhat difficult, owing to the position of the infinitive בֹּא. Either we must, with Hitzig, give to the former עֵת the points עַתָּה=עֵת, *now*, as in Ps. lxxiv. 6; Ezek. xxiii. 43; or convert בֹּא into בָּא of the preterite, as one of De Rossi's MSS. reads, and agreeably to the rendering of the LXX., Syr., Vulg., Targ., and Arab.; or, what is preferable, regard בֹּא as put absolutely for the purpose of more emphatically expressing the sentiment that the time was not yet *really* come in which to erect the temple. As two of the seventy years' captivity had yet to elapse, the colony which had arrived at Jerusalem encouraged themselves in their neglect of present duty, by assuming that the building of the temple was included in the calculation, and that, till the full time had expired, they were under no obligation to recommence the work.

4. Repeating the word עֵת, *time*, which he had employed twice, verse 2, the prophet makes an appeal full of point and cogency to those whom he addresses. The use of אַתֶּם before לָכֶם adds to the force of the language. סָפַן signifies to cover, *cover over*, *wainscot*, or overlay with boards, so that what is predicated of the houses is not to be confined to the ceiling, but must be extended to the walls which were thus covered, at once for comfort and ornament. How beautifully the feelings of David, 2 Sam. vii. 2, contrast with those of the persons reproved by Haggai.

5. The ו in וְעַתָּה is inferential, while עַתָּה is employed, not in its temporal acceptation, but argumentatively, as in Ps. ii. 10. שִׂימוּ לְבַבְכֶם עַל־דַּרְכֵיכֶם, lit. *place your heart upon your ways*, an idiomatic, but very expressive mode of speech. Comp. ver. 7, and ii. 18, twice, in the elliptical form שִׂימוּ לְבַבְכֶם.

6. זָרַע, אָכוֹל, שָׁתוֹ and לָבוֹשׁ, are historical infinitives, which carry forward the force of the finite form in זְרַעְתֶּם at the commencement of the verse, and, at the same time, give a greater degree of prominence to the actions which they express. Nothing prospered, and nothing could be expected to prosper, while the Jews were living in the flagrant neglect of their duty. They had brought property with them from Babylon, with which they had erected splendid houses for themselves, but God blasted their agricultural and other expectations; and they had nothing in prospect but a sea-

And he that earneth wages, earneth them
 To put them into a purse with holes.
7 Thus saith Jehovah of hosts:
 Consider your ways.
8 Go up to the mountain, and bring wood,
 And build the house, and I will take pleasure in it,
 That I may be glorified, saith Jehovah.
9 Ye looked for much, but, behold! little;
 And ye brought it home, and I blew upon it.
 Wherefore? saith Jehovah of hosts.
 Because of my house which lieth waste,
 And ye run each to his own house.
10 Therefore, it is on your account the heavens withhold the dew,
 And the earth withholdeth her produce.
11 And I have called for drought,

son of scarcity and want. The necessaries of life were already become so dear, that those who wrought for day's wages parted with all that they earned, as if they had put it into a bag or purse with holes. נָקוּב, *bored* or *perforated*.

7. A reiteration of the exhortation contained in ver. 5.

8. The reason why the Jews are called to provide wood only is thought by Jerome to be, that the walls of the temple remained standing; but this hypothesis is contradicted by repeated statements in the books of Ezra and Zechariah, as well as in Haggai ii. 18, in which express mention is made of laying its foundations. It rather seems to have been on account of the time which would be necessary to procure the article in question from Lebanon, since it required first to be hewn down, and afterwards transported by sea to Joppa. By הָהָר, *the mountain*, Rosenmüller thinks Moriah is meant; Hitzig, the mountainous country in the vicinity of Jerusalem; but it is more natural to interpret the term of Lebanon, whence the wood was actually fetched. It is true the Jews themselves did not go to that mountain for the timber; it was conveyed by the Zidonians and Tyrians, Ezra iii. 7; but persons are often said to do what they perform through the instrumentality of others. For וְאֶכָּבְדָה, the textual reading, which should be pointed וְאֶכָּבֵדָה, the Keri has וְאֶכָּבְדָה. The copula ו marks here the end to be obtained, or the result that would follow the performance of the enjoined duty. In such cases the future has the force of a potential mood.

9. פָּנֹה, the infinitive absolute, as in ver. 6. Even the small crop which was reaped had no sooner been brought into the barns or granaries, than it was dissipated. Their running each to his own house is expressive of the eagerness with which the Jews pursued their own affairs, and sought for self-indulgence. בֵּיתִי and בֵּיתוֹ stand here in striking contrast.

10. עֲלֵיכֶם is not to be referred to the heavens, and so rendered *over you*, but *on your account*, *for your sake*. Comp. לָכֵן בִּגְלַלְכֶם, Micah iii. 12. The meaning is, on account of your neglecting to build the temple. The preposition in מֵעַל, following כָּלָא, signifies *with respect to*, but does not require to be translated.

11. In the use of חֹרֶב, *drought*, there is an obvious reference to חָרֵב, *dry, waste, desolate*, verses 4 and 9. They form a paronomasia. The lengthened

Upon the land, and upon the mountains,
Upon the grain, and upon the new wine,
Upon the oil, and upon what the ground bringeth forth,
Upon man and upon beast,
And upon all the labor of the hands.

12   Then Zerubbabel, the son of Shealtiel, and Joshua, the son of Josedech the high priest, and all the residue of the people, hearkened to the voice of Jehovah their God, and to the words of Haggai the prophet, according as Jehovah their God had sent him; and the people feared Jehovah.

13   Then spake Haggai, the messenger of Jehovah, in the message of Jehovah to the people:
I am with you, saith Jehovah.

14   And Jehovah stirred up the spirit of Zerubbabel, the son of Shealtiel, governor of Judah, and the spirit of Joshua, the son of Josedech the high priest, and the spirit of all the rest of the people, and they came and did the work in the house of

15   Jehovah of hosts, their God, on the twenty-fourth day of the sixth month, in the second year of Darius the king.

amplification is employed in order to add to the force of the threatening. The LXX., supposing it to be incongruous to speak of bringing a drought upon *man and beast*, read חֶרֶב instead of חֹרֶב, and rendered the word by μάχαιραν, *a sword*, not adverting to the circumstance that the latter term was still less applicable to the other subjects here enumerated. What the prophet threatens is a universal drought, the effects of which would specially be experienced by living creatures.

12. The prophet now describes the happy effect which was produced by the message which he had just delivered. All the people who had returned united with their rulers in rendering obedience to the Divine command.

13. To encourage them to proceed in the path of obedience on which they had entered, Haggai delivers to them the brief, but most cheering promise, אֲנִי אִתְּכֶם נְאֻם יְהוָֹה, *I am with you, saith Jehovah*.

14. הֵעִיר רוּחַ, *to excite, or stir up the spirit* of any one (comp. Ezra i. 1, 5), means to render him inclined effectively to undertake the performance of any act, or to pursue a certain line of conduct.

15. From the date here assigned it appears, that most of the month elapsed before the work was fairly undertaken. Several of the early editions of the Hebrew Bible, as also the London Polyglot, improperly place this verse at the beginning of the next chapter.

CHAPTER II.

THIS chapter contains three different oracles of the prophet. The first, designed to encourage the people and their leaders to proceed with the building of the temple, by considerations derived from the Divine presence, 1—4; from their national covenant continuing in force, and that of the prophetic and gracious influences of the Holy Spirit, 5; from the advent of the person and kingdom of the Messiah, 6, 7; and from the universal proprietorship of Jehovah, the glory of the Messiah, and the reconciliation which he should effect, 8, 9. The second oracle cautions them against intermission in their labors, by showing that if they did so, nothing they did could be acceptable to God, 11—14; and by referring them to the infelicitous state of their affairs before the late revival, 15—18; and promises them prosperity, 19. The third is addressed to Zerubbabel individually, to animate and encourage him in conducting the work.

1 In the seventh month, on the twenty-first day of the month, the word of Jehovah was communicated through Haggai the
2 prophet, saying: Speak now to Zerubbabel, the son of Shealtiel, the governor of Judah, and to Joshua, the son of Josedech, the high priest, and to the rest of the people, saying:
3 Who is there among you that remaineth,
That saw this house in its former glory?
And how do ye see it now?
Is it not, compared with it, as nothing in your eyes?
4 Yet now be strong, O Zerubbabel! saith Jehovah;
And be strong, O Joshua! son of Josedech, the high priest;
Be ye strong, also, all ye people of the land!
Saith Jehovah of hosts, and work:
For I am with you, saith Jehovah of hosts.
5 The covenant which I made with you,

1, 2. This oracle was delivered nearly a month after the rebuilding of the temple had commenced, and was evidently designed to remove the despondency in which some of the people indulged, and to animate them to prosecute the work.

3. It appears from Ezra iii. 13, that there were many present at the laying of the foundation of the second temple, who had seen the first. To such of them as were still alive, few as they must have been, Haggai appeals respecting the disparity between the two, in regard to the rough and unpromising appearance of the new structure, contrasted with the elegant and splendid aspect of that of Solomon, previous to its destruction by the Chaldeans. הַנִּשְׁאָר is not in apposition

with בָּכֶם, but connects with the interrogative מִי. The phrase כָּמֹהוּ כְּאַיִן is peculiar, but not difficult of resolution, the word for temple being understood.

4. The comparison instituted in the preceding verse, so far from being designed to discourage those to whom the appeal was made, was on the contrary intended to inspire them with confidence in their covenant God, whose prerogative it is to call things that are not as though they were. It is tacitly implied, that whatever might be the estimate they might make of the work, it was very different with respect to his. Comp. Zech. viii. 6. And what is here only implied is expressly declared ver. 9.

5. The government of אֶת־הַדָּבָר has

When ye went forth out of Egypt,
And my Spirit remain among you:
Fear not.
6 For thus saith Jehovah of hosts:
Yet once, within a little,
And I will shake the heavens, and the earth,
And the sea, and the dry land,

unnecessarily puzzled interpreters. Ewald thinks the sentence is incomplete, and would supply זִכְרוּ, *remember*. Hengstenberg actually supplies the word in a parenthesis. Maurer endeavors to make it out to be an accusative *modi* s. *normæ*, and explains, *secundum illud verbum:* and connects it with the preceding verse, thus: I am with you, *according to that word*, etc.; and so our own translators, after Calvin. Rosenmüller would supply עִמִּי from the preceding verse. The particle אֶת I consider to be prefixed to הַדָּבָר, in order to give it a greater degree of prominence, and to be equivalent to *that* or *the same* covenant, etc.; while אֶת־הַדָּבָר, together with רוּחִי, form the nominative to the participle עֹמֶדֶת; only, as separated from it by the intervening predicate "אֲנִי בְּרִתִּי וגו, the participle is put in the feminine singular, to agree with רוּחִי, the nearer antecedent. For this use of אֶת before the nominative, though rare, see Neh. ix. 19. הֶעָנָן לֹא־סָר אֶת־עַמּוּד, *the pillar of cloud did not depart*, etc.; ver. 34, וְאֶת־מְלָכֵינוּ לֹא־עָשׂוּ, *And our kings — have not kept*, etc.: Dan. ix. 13, אֵת כָּל־הָרָעָה הַזֹּאת בָּאָה עָלֵינוּ, *All this evil hath come upon us*. דָּבָר, *word* or *matter*, is here employed to denote the Sinaic Covenant, as the accompanying verb כָּרַת, *to cut*, or *make a covenant* obviously shows. Notwithstanding the flagrant violation of that covenant of which the Jews had been guilty, on account of which they had been punished in Babylon, it still continued in all its force. They possessed it in its written form, and thus had the pledge which Jehovah had given them, that he was their covenant God, and would confer blessings upon the obedient. They also had his רוּחַ, the spirit of inspiration in the prophets who were raised up in the midst of them to declare his will, and call to the discharge of duty, Ezra, v. 1; and of efficient influence to induce them to listen to, and enable them to comply with such call, Zech. iv. 6; Hag. i. 14.

6. In this and the following verse the Jews are encouraged to proceed with the work by the assurance that Jehovah would, as the Governor among the nations, in a brief space, exert his Almighty power in effecting a great revolution in the state of the kingdoms of this world, preparatory to the establishment of the kingdom of the Messiah. This mighty change is first described in the usual figurative language of prophecy, as a convulsion of the physical universe, and then literally as a convulsion of all nations. In the phrase עוֹד אַחַת מְעַט, it is only the numeral אַחַת which occasions any difficulty. The combination עַד מְעַט, *yet a little*, i. e. time, occurs more than once. See Ps. xxxvii. 10; Is. xxix. 17; Jer. li. 33. But that here presented being peculiar to this passage, naturally suggests some peculiarity in the meaning. Most supply פַּעַם, *time*, after the LXX. ἔτι ἅπαξ, quoted and reasoned upon, Heb. xii. 26, 27, and the Syr. ܚܕܐ ܙܒܢ. Comp. for אַחַת פַּעַם, *one time, once*, Josh. vi. 3; 1 Sam. xxvi. 8; and for the ellipsis of פַּעַם, where אַחַת stands by itself, as here, Exod. xxx. 10; Job. xl. 5; Ps. lxii. 12, lxxxix. 36. And certainly, as מְעַט, *little*, is designed to express *brevity of time*,

7 Yea, I will shake all the nations,
And the things desired by all the nations shall come;

nothing can be more appropriate than such construction. Hengstenberg labors hard to bring the idea of brevity of time out of אחת, but fails to produce any examples to confirm his hypothesis. What the prophet has in view appears to be the convulsions which were yet to take place in the Persian and Greek empires, some of which were soon to commence, but all of which were more proximately, or more remotely connected with the complete establishment of the Jews in their own land, and the splendor of their temple as erected by Herod. The previous convulsion, implied in the phrase *yet once*, does not appear to be the shaking, etc., which took place at the giving of the law on Sinai, but the violent change which had lately taken place in the condition of the Babylonian empire, just as that yet to come is not to be extended to the downfall of the Roman empire, the destruction of Antichrist, etc., but must be confined to events which were to happen before the coming of Christ. We have only to call to mind the wars of the Persians in Asia Minor, Greece, Egypt, and other parts; and those of Alexander and his successors which followed, till the period when the establishment of the power of the Romans at length gave peace to the world, in order to read, in legible characters, the fulfilment of the present prophecy. Nor does the comment of the writer of the Epistle to the Hebrews require any other application of it. His object is to show that the dispensation or kingdom of the Messiah is stable and immovable; and in order to illustrate His point, he introduces, by way of contrast, the natural phenomena which took place on the promulgation of the Sinaic covenant, as described by Moses, and the political phenomena predicted by Haggai, all of which indicated the mutable character of the elements upon which they were exerted. That the prophet intended to include the dissolution of the Jewish state in his prediction, does not appear; indeed, the reference to such an event must have increased the despondency of his people, instead of inspiring them with hope and courage, which formed his only object in addressing them.

7. Having figuratively set forth the great political changes which were still to take place among the nations before the introduction of the kingdom of the Messiah, Haggai here repeats his prediction in literal terms, and then at once announces the arrival of the eagerly expected blessings of that kingdom. The passage has long been regarded as one of the principal prophecies relative to the time of the Redeemer's advent. That it was so applied by some of the early Jewish Rabbins, is undeniable. Thus in the chapter of the Talmudic treatise Sanhedrin, entitled חלק, the following interpretation is given as that of Rabbi Akiba, who flourished before the time of Jerome: מימט מלכות ארך לחם לישראל לאחר חרבן ולאחר אותו מלכות הנני מרעיש שמים וארץ ויבא משיח, *For a little I will give the kingdom to Israel, after our desolation, and after the kingdom, behold I will shake heaven and earth, and* MESSIAH SHALL COME. The rendering of the Vulg. supports the same view: "Et veniet Desideratus cunctis Gentibus." Leo Juda : " Et veniet qui desideratur ab omnibus gentibus." Dathe: "Et deinde veniet gentibus omnibus expetendus." On the other hand, Kimchi, Vatablus, Calvin, Ribera, Drusius, Gataker, Vitringa, and others, render : " The Gentiles shall come with their delightful things," *i. e.* their silver, gold, precious stones, etc. Some, violently, " Come *to* the desire," etc., meaning thereby Jerusalem. Most of the moderns, rejecting this construction as altogether unwarranted, translate after the LXX. ἥξει τὰ ἐκλεκτὰ πάντων τῶν ἐθνῶν, "the choice things," or "the pleas-

And I will fill this house with glory,
Saith Jehovah of hosts.

ant things of all nations shall come."
Ewald: "dass die liebsten aller Völker
kommen;" *i. e.* "That the most lovely
of all people may come." Hengstenberg, who renders, "the beauty of all
the heathen," is at great pains in endeavoring to make good his translation,
which he interprets of what he says is
always beautiful among them — all their
costly good things. But he fails alike
in his attempt to set aside the idea of
desire as expressed by חֶמְדַּת, and in
that to prove that the prophet here foretells
the rich contributions which the
heathen would bring into the church.
That the root חָמַד, primarily and most
commonly signifies *to desire* or *covet*, both
in a good and a bad sense, must be evident
to every one who will take the
trouble to consult the Hebrew concordance;
and that חֶמְדַּת, which is derived
from it, signifies *desire, an object of desire*,
see the Lexicons of Gesenius and
Lee. This acceptation must be vindicated
to 1 Sam. ix. 20. וּלְמִי כָּל־חֶמְדַּת
יִשְׂרָאֵל; to 2 Chron. xxi. 20, בְּלֹא חֶמְדָּה;
and to Dan. xi. 37, חֶמְדַּת נָשִׁים.
The want of concord in וּבָאוּ חֶמְדַּת
כָּל־הַגּוֹיִם, the verb expressing the
predicate, being in the plural masculine,
while חֶמְדַּת, the subject of the proposition,
is in the singular feminine, occasions
no small difficulty, and presents an
insuperable objection to the usual Messianic
interpretation. That בָּאוּ should
have been produced by zeugma with
חֶמְדַּת, is totally unsupported by analogy,
just as a plural of excellence in
verbs is equally without example. The
only practicable solution warranted by
grammatical usage, consists in assuming
חֶמְדַּת to be a collective noun, conveying
a plural idea, the gender of which
not having yet presented itself to the
mind of the prophet when he enunciated
the verb, he naturally expressed it in the
masculine as the more worthy gender.
The construction in such cases is *ad sen-*

sum; i. e. it is not formal, but logical.
The proper translation, therefore, of
וּבָאוּ חֶמְדַּת כָּל־הַגּוֹיִם will be, *And*, or,
*And then the things desired by all nations
shall come.* The Genitive being the Genitive
of object, must be thus expressed.
Now these objects of desire on the part
of all nations, cannot mean their riches,
for no such riches were brought to Jerusalem
by all the nations — the gifts
bestowed by some few of the heathen
princes after the time of Alexander not
in any degree exhausting the force of the
language here employed. Neither could
the prospect of contributions in more remote
future time have operated in the
way of encouragement upon the minds
of those whom the prophet addressed, so
as to induce them to proceed with their
work. The objects in question, therefore,
must have been of a higher order —
τὰ μελλόντα ἀγαθά, *the good things to
come,* i. e. the blessings of the New Covenant.
There was found to pervade the
minds of the heathen, a deep and dark
feeling of the necessity of supernatural
light and influence. Bewildered in the
mazes of error and superstition, they
could find nothing satisfactory respecting
the Divine Being, pardon, emancipation
from the power of moral evil, and a future
state of existence; and more or less
earnestly desired to obtain information in
regard to these important and necessary
points. To adduce only one testimony
from among many to be found in ancient
pagan writers. Socrates, endeavoring to
satisfy the mind of Alcibiades on the
subject of acceptable worship, says: ἀναγκαῖον
οὖν ἐστι περιμένειν ἕως ἄν τις μάθῃ
ὡς δεῖ πρὸς θεοὺς καὶ πρὸς ἀνθρώπους διακεῖσθαι,
*It is therefore necessary to wait
till some one may teach us how it behooves
us to conduct ourselves, both towards the
gods and men.* To which Alcibiades responds:
πότε οὖν παρέσται ὁ χρόνος οὗτος
ὦ Σώκρατες; καὶ τίς ὁ παιδεύσων; ἥδιστα
γὰρ ἄν μοι δοκῶ ἰδεῖν τοῦτον τὸν ἄνθρωπον

8 Mine is the silver, and mine is the gold,
Saith Jehovah of hosts.
9 The glory of this latter house shall be greater than that of the former,
Saith Jehovah of hosts.

τίς ἐστιν; *When shall that time arrive, O Socrates? and who shall that Teacher be? for most eagerly do I wish to see such a man.* — Plato, Alcibiades, ii. near the end. And, as the time of the Redeemer's advent drew near, there was a general expectation of a Teacher and Deliverer, not only in the Jewish nation, but throughout the world. To Christ, as the Light of the world, and to the spiritual blessings which flow through his mediation, the prophecy strictly applies; and, with this reference, was admirably calculated to stimulate the Jews to perseverance in building the temple, with which was inseparably connected the restoration of their ancient polity, during the existence of which the Messiah was to appear. The "glory" with which the temple was to be filled, was not the rich and splendid furniture, etc., but a resplendence, consisting in the manifestation of Jehovah himself. Comp. Zech. ii. 5, with Ezek. xliii. 4, 5; Exod. xl. 34, 35; 1 Kings viii. 11.

8. The Jews needed to be under no concern about the means requisite for the erection of the temple. The earth is the Lord's and the fulness thereof, so that whatever amount of earthly riches was wanted, he would in his providence supply. The declaration contained in this verse is introduced parenthetically, to relieve their minds from any momentary anxiety, arising out of the circumstances in which, as a poor and despised people, they were placed.

9. The LXX. refer the terms הָאַחֲרוֹן, *the latter*, and הָרִאשׁוֹן, *the former*, not to הַבַּיִת הַזֶּה, *this house*, but to כָּבוֹד, *the glory*. And thus Hitzig, Maurer, and Ewald; but Ezra iii. 12, determines to the contrary. The glory here predicted was to be greater than that of the former temple, not merely in degree, but in kind. That the second temple, even as renewed and beautified by Herod, at all equalled in magnificence that of Solomon, there is no reason to believe. This must appear on comparing the description given of the former by Josephus, Antiq. Jud. lib. xv. cap. xi., with that furnished of the latter, 1 Kings vi. vii. 13—50. In point of size, indeed, the temple of Herod exceeded the structure erected by the celebrated Jewish monarch; but this was all. The statement made by Josephus, Bell. Jud. lib. vi. cap. iv. 8, that it was the most admirable of all the works he had seen or heard of, does not include Solomon's temple, but has respect to other erections in different parts of the world. But if the second house was inferior in point of sumptuousness to the former, and wanted, as the Jews admit, the Urim and Thummim, the ark, the pot of manna, Aaron's rod, and the visible glory, which was the symbol of the Divine presence, it follows that the greater glory by which it was to be distinguished, must denote something altogether different in kind, and which could only be supplied by Him, in whose person the glory of God appeared, 2 Cor. iv. 6, who is the "Brightness of the Divine glory," Heb. i. 2; whose glory was beheld as that of the only-begotten of the Father, John i. 14; who could say of himself, "that in this place is one greater than the temple," Matt. xii. 6; and who sat in it daily teaching, Matt. xxvi. 55. In support of this interpretation, and indeed of the Messianic character of the entire prophecy, ver. 7, 9, the declaration made in the concluding clause of the latter verse may with all propriety be adduced. When "peace" is spoken of in an absolute sense, in the prophets, it

And in this place I will give peace,
Saith Jehovah of hosts.

10 On the twenty-fourth of the ninth month, in the second year of Darius, the word of Jehovah was communicated through
11 Haggai the prophet, saying: Thus saith Jehovah of hosts: Ask now the priests as to the law, saying: If any one should carry
12 sacred flesh in the skirt of his garment, and touch with his skirt bread, or pottage, or wine, or oil, or any eatable, shall it be
13 holy? And the priests answered and said, No. Then said Haggai: If any one who is unclean on account of a dead body, should touch any of these, shall it be unclean? And the priests
14 answered and said, It shall be unclean. Then Haggai continued, and said:

Thus hath this people, and thus hath this nation been,
Before me, saith Jehovah;

denotes the reconciliation between God and sinful men, to be effected by the Messiah. Comp. Is. ix. 6, 7, liii. 5, lvii. 19; Micah v. 5; Zech. vi. 13; with Luke ii. 14; Acts x. 36; Rom. v. 1; Eph. ii. 14, 17. This peace was to be granted בַּמָּקוֹם הַזֶּה, *in this place*, i. e. in Jerusalem. It was there the Messiah made peace through the blood of his cross, Col. i. 20. It has with some been matter of dispute, whether the temple erected by Zerubbabel, and that built by Herod, are to be regarded as identical, or whether the latter is not to be considered as a third temple. Strictly and architecturally considered, that of Herod was entirely new, for he caused that of Zerubbabel to be taken down to the very foundations; but in the popular and religious language they were identical; just as Josephus speaks of those built by Solomon and Zerubbabel as one, Bell. Jud. lib. vi. cap. iv. 8. Accordingly nothing is more customary than for Jewish writers to speak of only the first and the second temple. In the present verse, Haggai is to be understood as speaking in an architectural sense, inasmuch as the second temple was then being actually built.

10. This prophecy was delivered rather more than two months after that contained in the preceding verses of the chapter.

11—13. To convince his countrymen of the impossibility of their conduct being well-pleasing to God, and of their obtaining his blessing, while in any one point they neglected to comply with his will, the prophet directs them to consult the priests on two legal questions; the one, relative to the communication of ceremonial sanctity to any object, by its having been brought in contact with what had been sanctified; and the other, respecting the communication of ceremonial impurity by one who was himself impure. The former was denied; the latter affirmed. Whatever the Jews might otherwise rightly perform, would not compensate for their neglect in building the temple; on the contrary, their neglect in this matter would taint or vitiate all their other actions. Comp. in illustration of these questions, Lev. vi. 27; Numb. vi. 6, xix. 13; in which latter passages the abbreviated form נֶפֶשׁ, *a dead body*, is expressed in full by נֶפֶשׁ מֵת, or by נֶפֶשׁ אָדָם אֲשֶׁר־יָמוּת.

14. The application of the legal decisions of the priests to the case of the Jews, who had neglected the building of the temple. It describes them, not as they

And thus hath been every work of their hands,
And what they have offered there hath been unclean.
15 And now consider, I beseech you,
From this day and backward,
Before one stone was laid upon another
In the temple of Jehovah.
16 Since these days were,
One came to a heap of twenty sheaves,
And there were but ten;
One came to the vat to draw fifty purahs,
And there were but twenty.
17 I smote you with blight, and mildew, and hail,
In all the labors of your hands;
Yet ye turned not to me,
Saith Jehovah.
18 Consider, I beseech you,
From this day backward,
From the twenty-fourth day of the ninth month,
From the day when the temple of Jehovah was founded,
Consider!
19 Is the seed still in the granary?

now were, engaged in the work, but as they had been, and is designed to put them upon their guard against falling back into the same state. The adverb שָׁם, *there*, points graphically to the altar, which had been erected at Jerusalem, and which was, in all probability, within view of the audience which the prophet addressed. Ezra iii. 3.

15—17. The Jews are earnestly exhorted to reflect upon the state of their affairs during the period in which they had intermitted the work. God had frowned upon them, and rendered them infelicitous. מַעְלָה, a substantive, with the local ה, used adverbially. Properly it signifies *upward*, being derived from עָלָה, *to ascend;* but used, as here, of time, it means *back, backwards.* In הֱיוֹתָם, the word יָמִים, *days,* is understood. בָּא is to be taken impersonally. At עֲרֵמַת עֶשְׂרִים, *a heap of twenty,* supply אֲלֻמּוֹת or עֳמָרִים, *sheaves.* פּוּרָה, which is used for the wine-press itself,

Is. lxiii. 3, is here employed to denote a liquid measure in which the wine was drawn out. LXX. μετρητής. The quantity being unknown, I have retained the original word. For ver. 17, comp. Amos iv. 9, where we have the words לֹא־שַׁבְתֶּם עָדַי, *ye turned not unto me,* instead of אֵין־אֶתְכֶם אֵלַי, used by Haggai, in which there is an ellipsis of the participle שָׁבִים. For this use of אֵת, as a nominative, or as indicating the subject of discourse, see on ver. 5. In ver. 18, the exhortation is once and again reiterated for the sake of effect; and to render it still more definite, the exact date is added to the formula הַיּוֹם הַזֶּה, *this day,* which had been employed ver. 15. מַעְלָה is here to be taken, as in that verse, in reference to past time, and not, as the Vulg., Hitzig, etc., in reference to the future.

19. To the question put at the beginning of the verse, a negative is to be given. The seed was no longer in the

And as yet the vine, and the fig-tree,
And the pomegranate, and the olive have borne nothing;
From this day will I bestow the blessing.

20 And the word of Jehovah was communicated a second time to Haggai on the twenty-fourth day of the month, saying:
21 Speak to Zerubbabel, the governor of Judah, saying:
I will shake the heavens and the earth,
22 I will overthrow the throne of kingdoms,
I will destroy the strength of the kingdoms of the nations,
And overthrow the chariots and those who ride in them;
The horses, also, and their riders shall come down,
Each by the sword of another.
23 In that day, saith Jehovah of hosts,
I will take thee, O Zerubbabel! the son of Shealtiel,
My servant, saith Jehovah,

granary. It had been sown in the course of the month, and there were no signs of its springing up any more than there were of the produce of the fruit-trees. Jehovah had formerly blasted their harvest; but now that the people were diligently engaged in building his temple, they might confidently calculate upon one of plenty. He gives them a positive promise to this effect. The repetition of מִן־הַיּוֹם הַזֶּה, *from this day,* which had been twice used in the preceding verses, gives emphasis to the declaration. עַד, usually signifying *until,* is here employed in the sense of *while,* or *as yet,* as in Judges iii. 26; 2 Kings ix. 22; Job. i. 18, where it corresponds to עוֹד in verses 16 and 17.

20—23. These verses contain a special message to Zerubbabel, in which there is a repetition of the prediction, somewhat amplified, respecting the revolutions that were about to take place, which had been delivered in verses 6 and 7. In ver. 22, the verb יָרַד, *to go* or *come down,* is equivalent to נָפַל, *to fall.* That the promise made, ver. 23, cannot be viewed as having respect to Zerubbabel in his individual capacity, has been thought to be quite obvious from the fact, that he lived upwards of an hundred years before the time of Alexander, who overturned the Persian throne, and subdued the rest of Asia; but the predicted convulsions did not commence with the conquests of that monarch. Many of them took place during the reign of Darius, whose arms were carried not only into Scythia, Asia Minor, and Greece, but, according to Herodotus, into India. It is, therefore, not at all improbable that Zerubbabel survived several of these wars, and thus lived in the beginning of הַיּוֹם הַהוּא, *that day,* or the period in the course of which the prophecy was to be fulfilled; and as the Persians occasionally experienced serious reverses, as, for instance, in the Scythian expedition, it was natural for the Jews who were under the protection of Darius, to have their minds unsettled by apprehensions respecting the ultimate state of their affairs. To inspire them with confidence, Jehovah here assures their governor of his regard and protection amid all the commotions that might take place in the surrounding nations. לָקַח, *to take,* is merely employed for the purpose of introducing the action expressed by the following verb. For שַׂמְתִּיךָ כַחוֹתָם, *I will place thee as a signet,* comp. Song viii. 6; Jer. xxii. 24. חוֹתָם, from חָתַם, *to seal,* or *close by sealing,* signifies a *ring* with *the seal* or *signet* in it, with which the impression

And will make thee as a signet;
For in thee I take pleasure,
Saith Jehovah of hosts.

was made. Seals were commonly made of silver, but sometimes of the most precious stones, and, consequently, held in high estimation by their owners. Being worn on one of the fingers of the right hand, they were likewise objects of constant inspection and care. In all these points of view Zerubbabel was to be regarded by God. He was to be an object of his incessant care and delight. The latter idea is more definitely expressed by the addition בְּחַרְתִּי — בְּךָ בָחַר, signifying not only to *try* objects, and then to *select* what is valuable, but also to *take pleasure* in what is thus selected.

ZECHARIAH.

PREFACE.

ZECHARIAH was of a sacerdotal family. His father Berechiah was a son of Iddo, one of the priests who returned with Zerubbabel and Joshua from Babylon. Neh. xii. 4. When he is said to have been the *son* of Iddo, Ezra v. 1, vi. 14, the word בן is used, according to a common Hebrew idiom, in the sense of grandson. He must have been born in Babylonia, and been young, rather than otherwise, at the time of his arrival in Judea. He was contemporary with Haggai, and, like him, received his prophetic commission in the second year of Darius Hystaspis, B. C. 520, only the latter began his ministry two months earlier. Both prophets were employed in encouraging Zerubbabel and Joshua to carry forward the building of the temple, which had been intermitted through the selfish and worldly spirit of the returned exiles — a spirit which they boldly and variously reproved.

The most remarkable portion of the book is that containing the first six chapters. It consists of a series of visions which were vouchsafed to the prophet in the course of a single night, in which, by means of symbolical representations, the dispensations of Divine Providence relative to the nations that had oppressed the Jews, the entire removal of idolatry from the latter, the re-establishment of the city and temple of Jerusalem, and the certainty of the Messiah's advent, were strikingly and impressively revealed.

The next portion contains the seventh and eighth chapters, and contains an answer to a question which the inhabitants of Bethel had proposed respecting the observance of a certain fast, together with important ethical matter necessarily arising out of the subject.

The remaining six chapters contain predictions respecting the expedition of Alexander the Great along the west coast of Palestine to Egypt; the Divine protection of the Jews both at that time, and in that of the Maccabees; the advent, sufferings, and reign of the Messiah; the destruction of Jerusalem by the Romans, and dissolution of the Jewish polity; the sufferings of the Jews during the dispersion; their conversion and restoration; and the sacred character of their worship, in which the Gentiles shall join, after the destruction of the wicked confederacy which will be opposed to their final establishment in Canaan.

The authenticity of this last portion has been, and still is, strongly contested. Not only has it been denied to be the production of Zechariah, but

PREFACE TO ZECHARIAH. 355

it has been broken up into fragments, the independent authorship of which has been vindicated to as many anonymous authors. The first who ventured upon such a denial was Joseph Mede, whose opinion was adopted by Hammond, Kidder, Whiston, and Bridge, and more recently by Secker and Newcome in this country, and on the continent by Flügge, Döderlein, J. D. Michaelis, Seiler, Eichhorn, Bauer, Bertholdt, Forberg, Rosenmüller, Gramberg, Hitzig, Credner, Maurer, Ewald, and Knobel. The authenticity, on the other hand, has been maintained by Carpzovius, Blaney, Jahn, Beckhaus, Koester, Hengstenberg, and Burger.

The principal objection is taken to the language and character of the materials, as being very different from those which are found to distinguish what is universally allowed to have been written by Zechariah. To this, however, it has been replied, that granting such to be the case, there may have elapsed a long period of time between the composition of the former and latter portions of the book, during which any observable change in the style of the prophet might have taken place. It is evident, from there being no reference whatever in the chapters in question to the completion of the temple and the restoration of the Jewish affairs after the captivity, that, if they had not been written previously, they must have been composed long after these events had become matter of history, and in circumstances altogether different from those which occupied the attention of the prophet at the commencement of his ministry.

That these chapters were written long before, and, indeed, during the existence of the two kingdoms of Judah and Israel, is a position maintained by most of those who dispute their authenticity; but it is based upon too feeble and precarious a foundation to recommend it to the adoption of any who will impartially examine into all the circumstances of the case. The mere mention of Judah and Ephraim, upon which so much stress is laid, can yield it no real support. Not the smallest hint is anywhere dropped which would lead us to infer the existence, at the time, of a separate political or religious establishment in the northern part of Palestine; nor is there anything, but the contrary, to induce the conclusion that a king reigned in Judah in the days of the author. That Ephraim should be spoken of as existing after the captivity, cannot be matter of surprise, when it is considered, that a very large, if not the larger, portion of the ten tribes availed themselves of the liberty granted by the Persians to the Jews in Babylon, and likewise returned to the land of their fathers. This view of the subject is confirmed by the application of the term "Israel" to all the tribes, chap. xii. 1, just as it is used in the identical formula Mal. i. 1. Compare Mal. ii. 11, 12, iii. 6. The few references to a return relate to those Jews which were in a state of banishment or slavery under the Græco-Syrian and Græco-Egyptian kings. The historical circumstances connected with the Egyptian expedition of Alexander are so strongly marked in the prophetic announcements, that they cannot without violence be identified with any previous events. The absence, too, of the slightest allusion to the Babylonish captivity, either in the way of threatening or warning, while the prophet minutely describes the character of the Jewish rulers, and the condition of the Jewish people, in immediate connection with the sufferings of the Messiah, the destruction of Jerusalem, and the consequent fate of the people, goes convincingly to show that the captivity must have taken place, and that the whole of this portion of the book has respect to times future to those in which he flourished. So strongly, indeed, has this feature of the case presented itself to Eichhorn, and other sharp-sighted critics, that, rejecting, as their neology compelled them to do, all ideas of actual prophecy, they scruple not to affirm that the disputed chapters must have been composed in the days of Alexander, Antiochus, Epiphanes, or Hyrcanus I. It also deserves notice that no reference whatever is made to the existence of royal government among the Jews, at the time the author wrote, or to any circumstances in the history of that people previous to the captivity.

When, therefore, the difference both in regard to time and subject-matter are taken into consideration, it must be regarded as sufficient to account for any difference of style that may be detected. It is, however, after all, a question whether there really does exist such a difference in this respect, as that to which it has become so fashionable to appeal. Be it that the introductory formulas which occur in the first eight chapters do not occur in the last six, the objection, if fully carried out, would go in like manner to dismember the Book of Amos, and assign its composition at least to three different authors. The first two chapters of that prophet, it may be alleged, cannot have been written by the same person that wrote the three which follow, since in the former every prediction is ushered in by the marked formula, "Thus saith Jehovah," whereas in the latter no such formula occurs, but another equally marked: "Hear ye this word." And upon the same principle, the seventh and eighth chapters must have come from the pen of a third writer, since the distinguishing formula there is, "Thus hath Jehovah showed me."

The very peculiar character of the first six chapters of Zechariah, is such as to exclude all comparison of any other portion with it, while the more adorned and poetical style of the concluding chapters, which is so admirably adapted to the subjects treated of, ought equally to be regarded as exempting them from the category of comparison. In these no dates were requisite, though they were in the former, in which they occupy their appropriate place in necessary connection with the events which transpired at the time. With respect to the titles, chap. ix. 1, and xii. 1, they are precisely such as might be expected to mark the strictly prophetic matter to which they are prefixed. The exactly parallel title, Malachi, i. 1, naturally suggests the idea, that they belong to a common period, especially as nothing analogous is found in any of the earlier prophets.

On the whole, I cannot but regard the objections to the authenticity of the disputed chapters as the offspring either of a holy jealousy for the honor of the Evangelist Matthew, who attributes chapter xi. 12, 13, to Jeremiah, and not to Zechariah,* or of a spirit of wanton and unbridled hypercriticism,

---

* See Comment. on the passage.

which would unsettle everything, in order to satisfy the claims of certain favorite principles of interpretation that may happen to be in vogue.

In point of style, our prophet varies, according to the nature of his subjects, and the manner in which they were presented to his mind. He now expresses himself in simple conversational prose, now in poetry. At one time he abounds in the language of symbols; at another in that of direct prophetical announcement. His symbols are, for the most part, enigmatical, and require the explanations which accompany them. His prose resembles most that of Ezekiel; it is diffuse, uniform and repetitious. His prophetic poetry possesses much of the elevation and dignity to be found in the earlier prophets, with whose writings he appears to have been familiar; only his rhythmus is sometimes harsh and unequal, while his parallelisms are destitute of that symmetry and finish, which form some of the principal beauties of Hebrew poetry.

CHAPTER I.

In the first six verses, which serve as a general introduction to the whole book, the prophet is charged to warn the Jews by the consequences which resulted from the impenitence of their forefathers, not to be backward in complying with the Divine will. We have then the first of the prophetic visions, with which Zechariah was favored, containing a symbolical representation of the tranquil condition of the world at the time, 7—11; followed by an expostulation respecting the desolate state of Judea, 12, 13, and gracious promises of its restoration, 14—17. The last four verses set forth, by appropriate symbols, in a second vision, for the encouragement of the Jews, the destruction of the hostile powers by which they had been attacked, at different periods of their history.

---

1 In the eighth month, in the second year of Darius, the word of Jehovah was communicated to Zechariah (the son of Berechiah, the son of Iddo,) the prophet, saying:
2 Jehovah hath been greatly displeased with your fathers.
3 Say therefore unto them,
Thus saith Jehovah of hosts:
Return unto me, saith Jehovah of hosts,
And I will return unto you, saith Jehovah of hosts.

---

1. See preface, and on Haggai i. 1.

2 The special object which the prophet has in view in this and the following verses, is to call those Jews who had returned from Babylon to Jerusalem, to repent of the selfish negligence which they evinced in regard to the building of the temple. Comp. Hag. i. 4, 5, 7. This repentance is urged upon them by the consideration of the severe punishment which had overtaken their fathers. The argument is of the kind called enthymeme, in which the antecedent only is expressed, and the consequent proposition is left to be supplied by the reader. "Jehovah hath been very angry with your fathers, and so he will be with you, except ye repent and reform your conduct." קָצַף קֶצֶף. The construction of a verb with a noun derived from it, is found in other languages, as μάχεσθαι μάχην, gaudere gaudium; but its frequency in the Hebrew is such as to entitle it to be regarded as one of its idioms; and, generally, it expresses augmentation or intensity. Hence the LXX. render here, ὠργίσθη — ὀργὴν μεγάλην; and the Syr. [Syriac]. In ver. 15, the intensity is still more strongly marked by the addition of גְּדוֹלָה, great: — קָצַפְתִּי גָדוֹל אֶת קָצֶף. The persons addressed in אֲבוֹתֵיכֶם, your fathers, are the Jews to whom the prophet had been sent. There is no occasion, with Blayney, to suppose that the text is defective.

3. The ו in וְאָמַרְתָּ is not merely continuative, but argumentative, and inferential. For the defective form אֲלֵהֶם, twenty-eight MSS., and three editions read אֲלֵיהֶם in full. The phrase יְהֹוָה צְבָאוֹת, Jehovah of hosts, is of unusually frequent occurrence in the eight first chapters of this book, and in that of Haggai, written about the same time. In the last six chapters, however, it occurs not fewer than nine times. See on Is. i. 9. Its use appears to have been designed to inspire the mind with unshaken confidence in the supreme and

4 Be not like your fathers,
  To whom the former prophets cried, saying,
  Thus saith Jehovah of hosts:
  Turn now from your evil ways,
  And from your evil practices;
  But they did not hearken,
  Neither did they give heed to me, saith Jehovah.
5 As for your fathers, where are they?
  And as for the prophets, do they live forever?
6 But my words, and my decrees,
  Which I gave in charge to my servants the prophets,

irresistible power of God. The ו in אֲשֶׁר marks the apodosis, and has the force of *and then*, or *in that case*. Comp. James iv. 8.

4. The prophets here referred to are those who lived before the captivity, and the fathers are those who lived in their time, whose wicked practices had brought upon the nation that dire calamity. The appropriation of the phrase נְבִיאִים הָרִאשֹׁנִים, *the former prophets*, as a designation of the books of Joshua, Judges, Samuel, and Kings, is of much later date. The returned Jews are here reminded that the same announcement which was made to them had been made to their ancestors, and that they might have escaped all the evil by a timely repentance, to which Zechariah now urgently calls them. The former ו in מַעַלְלֵיכֶם is marked in the margin as redundant, and is omitted in the text of more than twenty MSS. and some printed editions. The plural of מַעֲלָל, viz. מַעֲלָלִים, is the only form in which the word occurs. Comp. ver. 6.

5. Jerome refers הַנְּבִיאִים to the false prophets by whom the Jews who lived before the captivity had been deceived — an interpretation which appears to have been suggested by Jer. xxxvii. 19: "Where are now your prophets, which prophesied unto you, saying, The king of Babylon shall not come against you, nor against this land?" The most natural construction of the verse, however, is that which connects it closely with what goes before, and identifies "the prophets" here spoken of with "the former prophets" there mentioned, just as the "fathers" in both verses correspond to each other. The question, אֲבוֹתֵיכֶם, *where are they?* is equivalent to אֵינָם, *they are not;* i. e. in the land of the living. This the following question clearly shows. In Hebrew, simple interrogatives frequently imply the contrary: so that the language of the prophet is equivalent to "your fathers are no more, neither do the prophets live forever." The latter declaration seems to involve the idea, "but my words never fail," as it follows in ver. 6. This had been proved by the fulfilment of the Divine threatenings in the mournful experience of their fathers, and would again be proved in theirs, except they repented, which idea is amplified in the following verse.

6. חֻקַּי, *my decrees*, i. e. my firm and determined purposes to punish your fathers, if they did not repent, which I communicated to them by the prophets. The root is חָקַק, *to hack, cut, cut* letters, etc., *in* stone or other hard substances. Thus laws were originally written on tablets, and hung up for public inspection. The confession made in this verse is that which the captives were compelled to make by the sufferings which they endured in Babylon. How far their תְּשׁוּבָה, *conversion*, extended we are not informed.

Did they not overtake your fathers?
So that they turned and said,
According as Jehovah of hosts proposed to do to us,
According to our ways, and according to our practices,
So hath he dealt with us.

7 On the twenty-fourth day of the eleventh month, which is the month of Shebat, in the second year of Darius, the word of Jehovah was communicated to Zechariah (the son of Berechiah, the son of Iddo), the prophet, saying:

8 I saw by night, and behold a man riding upon a red horse,

It is, however, generally admitted that, as regards the great body of the nation, it involved the entire abandonment of idolatry. That שׁוּב is here to be strictly taken as signifying *to turn, return* from evil to good, and not according to its idiomatic usage before another verb, as simply expressing the repetition of the action described by such verb, is required by the exigency of the passage. בְּאָמְרָם and כֵּן are *correlates*; the כְּ repeated, qualifies a subordinate, but important part of the proposition.

7. From this part of the book to chap. vi. 8, we have a series of eight symbolical visions, the language of which is exceedingly simple, but, in many cases, the interpretation is matter of no small difficulty. The general plan on which it is constructed, is, first to present to view the symbol or hieroglyphic, and then, on a question being put respecting its import, to furnish the interpretation. Though the visions are described as distinct from each other, the one following the other in regular succession, yet they are so closely connected as to form one grand whole; and, as we learn from ver. 8, were all presented to the mind of the prophet in the course of a single night. The period of these nocturnal revelations was between two and three months after the prophet first received his commission. Comp. ver. 1. שְׁבָט, *Shebat*, is the eleventh month of the Jewish year, extending from the new moon in February to the new moon in March. Like other names of the months, the word is Chaldee; Syr. ܫܒܛ; Arab. شباط and شباط. The etymology is not certain; but the resemblance of the word to the Hebrew שֵׁבֶט, *a shoot, rod, staff*, suggests the idea of the month being so called because it was that in which the trees began to put forth their shoots or sprouts. As the following statement does not contain the identical words merely of the communications made to the prophet, but an account of the scenes with all their accompanying circumstances, the formula לֵאמֹר must be taken as signifying, "to the following effect," "as follows," or the like.

VISION I.

8. It has been doubted whether the article ה in הַלַּיְלָה is to be regarded as definitely marking the particular night on which the visions were vouchsafed to the prophet, or whether it is not rather to be taken as expressing the adverbial determination of the noun — *in the night*, or, *by night*. The latter seems preferable. Comp. בַּלַּיְלָה, Job v. 14. The person here described as riding upon a red horse, is spoken of as אִישׁ, *a man*, *i. e.* in the shape or appearance of a man; for that an angel, and not a human being, is intended, is evident from verses 11 and 12, in which he is expressly called "the angel of Jehovah." And that he was no ordinary angel, but the Divine Mediator, the Angel of the Covenant,

and he stood among the myrtles in the shade, and behind him

and of the presence of Jehovah, will not be denied by any who have rendered themselves familiar with the attributes and circumstances in connection with which the Person so designated is presented to view, both in our prophet and in other parts of the Old Testament. One of the most remarkable of these circumstances, is his being identified with Jehovah himself. This Gesenius, so far from denying, or attempting to explain away, expressly asserts both in his Thesaurus, and in the last edition of his Hebrew Lexicon, under the word מַלְאָךְ. "Sometimes," he writes, "the same divine appearance, which at one time is called מַלְאַךְ יְהוָה, is afterwards called simply יְהוָה, as Gen. xvi. 7, et seq. coll. v. 13; xxii. 11; coll. 12; xxi. 11, coll. 16; Exod. iii. 2, coll. 5; Jud. vi. 14, coll. 22; xiii. 18, coll. 22. This is to be so understood, that the *Angel of God* is here nothing else than the invisible Deity itself, which thus unveils itself to mortal eyes; see J. H. Michaelis de Angelo Dei, Hal. 1702. Tholuck, Comment. zum Ev. Johannis, p. 36. Hence Oriental translators, as Saadias, Abusaides, and the Chaldee-Samaritan, wherever Jehovah himself is said to appear upon earth, always put for the name of God, the *Angel of God*." See the very satisfactory observations of Dr. M'Caul on this subject, in his translation of Kimchi on Zechariah, pp. 9—27, in which he has shown that there is but one being who is called in Scripture מַלְאַךְ יְהוָה, *the Angel of Jehovah;* that the proper name of this one Being is יְהוָה, *Jehovah;* that this Being says of himself, distinctly and unequivocally, that He is the God whom Jacob worshipped, the God of Abraham, Isaac, and Jacob; and that some of the Rabbins themselves have been compelled to admit the facts. See also Dr. J. Pye Smith's Scripture Testimony to the Messiah, vol. i. pp. 445—463; and Stonard on Zechariah, pp. 15—19. In the Babylonian Talmud, Sanhedrin, fol. 93, col. 1, the following brief exposition is given of the man here referred to by the prophet: "This man is no other than the Holy One, blessed be He; for it is said, 'The Lord is a man of war.'" The position of this Captain of the Lord's host, is stated to be " among the myrtles which were in the shady valley." Many conjectures have been advanced respecting both the myrtles and the valley, but, in my opinion, they are all gratuitous, since it does not appear that these objects were designed to be symbolically understood, but are merely added as incidental circumstances, to give vivacity and force to the representation. מְצֻלָּה being always used, like מְצוֹלָה and צוּלָה, of *depth* in reference to water or mire, it is clear from the connection that such cannot be the signification of מְצֻלָה, which is a derivative, not from צוּל, *to sink, be deep,* but from צָלַל, *to be shaded, darkened;* hence *the shade* or *shady place,* probably that of a mountain. Such derivation is indicated by the Dagesh compensative in the Lamed, and is supported by the renderings of the LXX. and Syr. κατασκίων, ܡܛܠܠܐ. Hitzig and Ewald, comparing the Arab. مظلة, *umbraculum, tentorium,* interpret the word as meaning tent or tabernacle, and suppose heaven, as the dwelling-place of Jehovah, to be intended; but the exegesis is far-fetched and inept. Equally unsatisfactory is the attempt of the latter of these writers to palm upon הֲדַסִּים the signification of הָרִים, *mountains,* by comparing the term with הֲדַר, *height,* Is. xlv. 2. Τῶν ὀρέων of the LXX. must have originated in their having mistaken הֲדַסִּים for הָרִים, or it may be an interpretation derived from chap. vi. 1. Behind the rider, who appears as their leader or captain, follow three companies of horsemen, distinguished from each other by the color of the horses. It is not to be inferred, that, because סוּסִים, *horses,* only are mentioned, we are to

9 were horses that were red, bay and white. Then I said, What are these, my lord? And the angel who spake with me, said

conceive of them as being presented to view without their riders. This is evident from the reply given by the riders, ver. 11. סוּס, like our English *horse*, is sometimes used in a military sense, to denote cavalry. Still, as the color of the horses forms an important feature in the representation, they must have been especially prominent to the mental vision of the prophet. On a comparison of the present verse with chap. vi. 1—8, and Rev. vi. 2—8, it will appear that horses with their riders are employed in the symbolical language of Scripture to denote dispensations of divine providence. The peculiar nature of the dispensations is indicated by the color of the horses, and the armor and appearance of the riders. *Red*, the color first mentioned, being that of fire and blood, is the appropriate symbol of war and bloodshed. That of the second company of horses is expressed by שְׂרֻקִּים, *bay*, or *brown*, perhaps not differing from what is commonly called *chestnut*. See Bochart, Hieroz. tom. i. lib. ii. cap. 7. What induces the belief that this color is meant is, that שְׂרֵקִים signify vines which bear purple, or dark colored grapes. Comp. the Arab. شَقْرَة, *rufus color*; أَشْقَر, *valde rubens seu rufus camelus*. The LXX. ψαροί; Vulg. *varii*. The addition, καὶ ποικίλοι, in the text of the LXX. is doubtless a gloss. This color is symbolical of a middle state of things — a dispensation neither characterized by bloodshed, nor by victory and joyous prosperity, which the *white* color is universally allowed to represent. From what is stated, ver. 11, it is obvious we cannot interpret the dispensations, thus emblematically set forth, of events still future at the time of the vision. The different cohorts speak of their commission as already fulfilled. The colors must, therefore, denote the Medo-Persian war, in which the Babylonian empire was subverted; the mixed or transition state of affairs which followed; and the complete establishment of the new dynasty in the room of the tyrannical power by which the Jews had been enslaved. In consideration of the awful vengeance which had been inflicted upon that power, the color of the horse on which the commander rode is represented as being red, rather than bay or white — evidently with the design of affecting the minds of the Jews with a sense of the great deliverance which had been wrought for them by their Divine Protector.

9. Marckius, Ch. B. Michaelis, Rosenmüller, Maurer, and Ewald, are of opinion, that the angel here spoken of is identical with the man riding on the horse mentioned in the preceding verse, but the contrary is properly maintained by Vitringa and Hengstenberg, as a comparison with ver. 10 is sufficient to show. Though the angel who made the communications to the prophet had not been formerly mentioned, he had presented himself to him, or stood beside him, ready to discharge the duties of his office. This angel is uniformly spoken of as הַמַּלְאָךְ הַדֹּבֵר בִּי, *the angel that spake with me*. See verses 13, 14, chap. ii. 2, 7, iv. 1, 4, 8, v. 5, 10, vi. 4. The language is peculiar to our prophet; and from the office specially assigned to the angel, he is usually called the *angelus interpres*, or the *angelus collocutor*. That stress is to be laid upon the use of the preposition בְּ following the verb דִּבֶּר, *to speak*, as if it were designed to mark the *internal* character of communications made by the angel to the prophet — a position maintained by Jerome, Ewald, Delitzsch, and some others — cannot be satisfactorily made out. The utmost that can be conceded respecting the force of the preposition, in such connection, is its expressing the familiarity or intimacy of the intercourse between the Divine mes-

10 to me, I will show thee what these are. And the man that
stood among the myrtles answered and said, These are they
11 whom Jehovah hath sent to walk to and fro through the earth.
And they answered the Angel of Jehovah that stood among the
myrtles, and said, We have walked to and fro through the earth,
and, behold! the whole earth sitteth still and is tranquil.
12 Then the Angel of Jehovah answered and said: O Jehovah
of hosts! how long wilt thou not compassionate Jerusalem, and
the cities of Judah, with which thou hast been angry these
13 seventy years? And Jehovah answered the angel who spake

senger and the prophet. When the angel says אַרְאֶךָ, *I will show*, or *cause thee to see* these things, the reference is to a mental perception or understanding of their meaning.

10, 11. עָנָה, signifies to *commence* or *proceed* to speak, as well as *to answer*. Comp. the use of ἀποκρίνομαι in the New Testament. Instead of the requisite information being communicated by the interpreting angel, it is imparted by the Angel of Jehovah himself, and by those who acted under his command. Because the phraseology הִתְהַלֵּךְ בָּאָרֶץ is almost identical with that employed to describe the roaming of Satan through the earth, Job. i. 7, ii. 2, it has been inferred that the horsemen represent celestial spirits sent forth for the execution of the divine purposes; but the ground is too precarious to admit of any such theory being built upon it, as a comparison with Rev. vi. 2—8, is sufficient to show. The simple occurrence of the same terms cannot of itself justify this interpretation. From the reply being given to the Angel of Jehovah, we may conclude, that he had signified to them that they should make their report for the information of the prophet. In consequence of their several operations, the obstacles had been removed out of the way which prevented the restoration of the Jews; the wars in which the Persians had been engaged had ceased; and, at the time the prophet had the vision, in the second year of Darius, universal peace obtained in all the regions with which the people of God had any connection. For the use of שָׁקַט to denote a state of tranquillity after war, comp. Jud. v. 26. A similar combination of יֹשֵׁב with שָׁלֵו occurs ch. vii. 7, and is intended to express the profound character of the peace which was then enjoyed.

12. עָנָה, *to answer*, is here, as in other instances, used in the simple acceptation of speaking, or continuing a discourse. The language is that of intercessory expostulation. While all the heathen nations around Judea enjoyed prosperity, that country was still much in the same state in which it had been during the captivity. Some of the captives had returned, but they were too few to produce anything like a marked change in its circumstances. Vitringa, Stonard, and some others, without sufficient reason, think that a different term of seventy years is here intended from that predicted Jer. xxv. 11, xxix. 10. What in reality were the years of indignation upon the cities, but the years of the captivity of their inhabitants? זֶה שִׁבְעִים שָׁנָה, "*these* seventy years," express emphatically the period during which the captivity had continued. Two of these years, dating from the destruction of Jerusalem by Nebuchadnezzar, had yet nearly to run before the expiration of the predicted period, so that the language of the expostulation is most appropriate, when viewed as calculated to meet the feelings of the Jewish people.

13. That it is the same being who is styled מַלְאַךְ יְהוָֹה, *the Angel of Jeho-*

14 with me with good and comfortable words. And the angel who
    spake with me said to me, Cry, saying,
        Thus saith Jehovah of hosts:
        I am zealous for Jerusalem,
        And for Zion, with great zeal;
15 And I am very greatly displeased
        With the nations that are at ease;
        Because I was a little displeased,
        And they helped forward the affliction.
16 Wherefore, thus saith Jehovah:
        I have returned to Jerusalem in compassion:
        My house shall be built in her, saith Jehovah of hosts,
        And a line shall be stretched out over Jerusalem.
17 Cry again, saying,
        Thus saith Jehovah of hosts:
        My cities shall yet overflow with prosperity;
        For Jehovah will yet comfort Zion,
        And will yet take pleasure in Jerusalem.

vah, that is here designated by the incommunicable name יְהֹוָה, *Jehovah*, just as in the passages quoted by Gesenius, ver. 8, seems past dispute. As the Divine Mediator, after having made intercession with the Father, who is addressed by the title יְהֹוָה צְבָאוֹת, *Jehovah of hosts*, he communicates to the interpreting angel the consolatory answer which was to be made to the prophet. דְּבָרִים נִחֻמִים, are in apposition: lit. *words, consolations*, i. e. consolatory words. LXX. λόγους παρακλητικούς. Comp. Is. lvii. 18; Hos. xi. 8.

14. This and the three following verses contain the consolatory words just referred to, which the prophet is commanded by the interpreting angel to communicate to the Jews. קָנָא construed with בְּ, or with the accusative, signifies *to envy, be jealous, indignant at* any person or thing; with לְ as here, it is taken in a good sense, *to be zealous for* anything, *actively to interest one's self on behalf* of any one. Comp. Numb. xxv. 11, 13; 2 Sam. xxi. 2; 1 Kings xix. 10.

15. The adjective שַׁאֲנָן signifies not merely *to be at rest*, as the whole earth is described, ver. 11, but, in a bad sense *to live at ease, be carnally secure*. The enemies of the Jews had not simply executed the Divine indignation against that people, but they had done it wantonly. Such seems to be the force of עָזְרוּ לְרָעָה.

16. The building of the temple had been begun, but it still lay for the most part in ruins, and was not finished till the sixth year of Darius. See Ezra vi. 15. קָוֶה, for which the Keri has, by emendation, the more usual form קָו, occurs 1 Kings vii. 23; Jer. xxxi. 39.

17. Few as were the inhabitants of Judea at the time of the vision, the land was speedily re-occupied; and the population had greatly increased by the time of the Maccabees. Josephus informs us, that, overflowing with numbers, Jerusalem gradually crept beyond its walls, till a fourth hill, called Bezetha, was covered with habitations. פוּץ, Arab. فاض, فيض, *effusus fuit, to overflow*. That the overflowing, however, is to be interpreted of prosperity, and not of the

CHAP. I.   ZECHARIAH.   365

18 Then I lifted up my eyes and looked, and, behold! four horns.
19 And I said to the angel who spake with me, What are these?
And he answered me, These are the horns which have scat-
20 tered Judah, Israel and Jerusalem. And Jehovah showed me
21 four workmen. Then I said, What are these coming to do?
And he spake, saying, These are the horns which have scattered

inhabitants, appears from the מ, indicating the subject-matter, being prefixed to טוב.

VISION II.

18, 19. (Heb. ii. 1, 2.) This vision is so intimately connected with the preceding that the break in the Hebrew Bible here, occasioned by the commencement of a new chapter, is very unhappy. As usual in these visions, the hieroglyphic is first presented. קֶרֶן, *a horn*, is the symbol of a kingdom, or political power, the figure being taken from bulls, and other horned animals having their strength in their horns. Thus the ten horns of the fourth beast in Daniel's vision, are symbolical of the ten kingdoms into which the Roman empire was divided on the overthrow of the imperial throne, chap. vii. 20; and in the representation made of the same subject to John, the ten horns of the seven-headed beast are said to have upon them ten crowns, Rev. xiii. 1, xvii. 3. Comp. ver. 12, where it is expressly stated, that "the ten horns which thou sawest are ten kings," *i. e.* kingdoms, the ruling power being put for the whole government. The powers referred to by Zechariah were those which had been hostile to the Jews, and had scattered them abroad from their own land. Jerome, Kimchi, Abarbanel, Vatablus, and others, have been led by the occurrence of the number *four*, to interpret the horns of the Babylonian, Persian, Grecian, and Roman empires; but to this exegesis it has justly been objected, that of these powers two were not yet in existence, and cannot be prophetically spoken of, because the hostility described was that which had already taken place. Neither is it true that the Jews were scattered by the Persian power as they had been by the Babylonian. What took place under Darius Ochus cannot be taken into the account here. The number is rather to be referred to the four quarters of the earth in their immediate relation to Palestine. Comp. chap. ii. 6. Thus Theodoret, Clarius, Ribera, Sanchez, à Castro, Munster, Calvin, Newcome, Rosenmüller, Hitzig, and Maurer. "Jerusalem" is added to render the description more emphatic, being the metropolis, the site of the temple, and the royal residence.

20, 21. (Heb. ii. 3, 4.) Here, again, the same Divine Person is called יְהֹוָה, who was formerly spoken of as מַלְאַךְ יְהֹוָה. See on ver. 13. חָרָשִׁים, *workmen* in iron, brass, stone, or wood, from חָרַשׁ, *to cut, grave, fabricate*. From the special employment assigned to these artificers, we may not inaptly compare חָרָשֵׁי מַשְׁחִית, *workmen of destruction*, which is rendered in our common version, "skilful to destroy," Ezek. xxi. 36. The attempt of Blaney to justify his rendering the word by *ploughmen*, first suggested by Michaelis, must be regarded as a failure. On the inquiry being made, what these artificers were coming to do, a reply is given, which further describes the tyranny exercised over the Hebrew people, and then states that they were the instruments commissioned to destroy the hostile powers. By again pressing the number *four*, interpreters have involved themselves in inextricable difficulties. All that is meant to be conveyed, is the adequacy of the means employed to effect the punishment of the nations which had afflicted the people of God. That no appeal can be made, in illustration,

Judah, so that no man lifted up his head; but these are come to terrify them, to throw down the horns of the nations, which raised the horn against the land of Judah to scatter it.

to the history of the four great monarchies, is proved by the fact that the workmen are represented as distinct from the horns, whereas these monarchies successively destroyed each other. The rabbinical reference to the days of the Messiah is altogether aside from the point, as is likewise the reference which some have made to angels. There can be no doubt that the several human instrumentalities are intended, which God called into operation to crush the powers in the different countries around Palestine, by which it had been invaded, and its inhabitants carried away captive. The conjecture of Blaney, who would read הֶחֱרִיד instead of הַחֲרִיד, and, changing the punctuation of אֵת into אֵת, renders, "to sharpen their coulter," has not been approved. Nor is anything of the kind necessary. Terror implies a sense of inferiority, weakness, and exposure to suffering, and is here appropriately represented, as a precursor of that overthrow to which the enemies of the Jews were to be subjected. Comp. Jud. viii. 12 ; 1 Sam. xiv. 15; Ezek. xxx. 9. יָדָה signifies to *throw, cast, stretch,* the particular manner of which is to be determined by the context. Here that of *casting down*, or *effecting an overthrow*, is the mode most naturally suggested. The signification *to handle, exercise the hand,* which some have proposed, is less apt, יָד, *hand*, being derived from the verb, and not the verb from the noun. אֶרֶץ, *land*, is here, as frequently, put for its inhabitants.

CHAPTER II.

In a third vision, a man with a measuring line is represented as going forth to take the dimensions of Jerusalem with a view to its restoration to its former condition, ver. 1—3; an act which is virtually declared to be unnecessary, by the prediction that such should be the increase of the population, and such their prosperity, that the city should extend, like unwalled towns, into the surrounding localities; and that, under the immediate protection of Jehovah, walls would be altogether unnecessary, 4, 5. In the faith of this prophetic announcement, and with a view to their escape from the judgment which was still about to be inflicted upon Babylon, the Jews which remained in that city are summoned to return from their captivity, 6, 7; an assurance of Divine protection, and of the destruction of their enemies, is given them, 8, 9; and they are cheered by the promises, that Jehovah would again make Jerusalem his residence, and effect, in connection with the restoration of his people, the conversion of many nations to the true religion, 10, 12. A solemn call to universal reverence concludes the scene.

Then I lifted up my eyes, and looked, and, behold! a man

VISION III.

1—4. (Heb. ii. 5—7.) The measurement here specified was not that of the houses, but of the whole extent of the city. Jerusalem is not here considered as already rebuilt, as Stonard supposes,

2 with a measuring line in his hand. And I said: Whither art thou going? And he said to me, To measure Jerusalem, to see
3 how much is the breadth thereof, and how much is the length thereof. And, behold! the angel who spake with me went forth,
4 and another angel came forth to meet him. And he said to him, Run, speak to this young man, saying,
 Jerusalem shall be inhabited into the open country,
 Because of the multitude of men and cattle in the midst of her.
5 And I will be to her, saith Jehovah,
 A wall of fire around,
 And will be the glory in the midst of her.

The dimensions are those of the city before its destruction by the Chaldeans, and were now being taken, in order to ascertain the extent of the work that was to be effected in its complete restoration. The symbolical action was calculated to encourage the Jews to proceed with the building of the temple which they had commenced. Who the measurer was has been disputed. Jarchi, J. H. Michaelis, Rosenmüller, are of opinion that the *angelus interpres* is intended. Hengstenberg thinks that, in all probability, he is none other than the Angel of Jehovah himself. But for neither of these opinions is there sufficient foundation, any more than there is for the supposition of Blayney, that he was Nehemiah. He appears to be merely an additional person introduced in the scenic representation, for the purpose of calling forth, by the significant action which he was about to undertake, the important information contained in the following part of the chapter. יָצָא, as twice used here, has reference to two different localities: in the former instance, in which it is employed of the interpreting angel, the presence of the prophet is the *terminus a quo*; in the latter, that of the Angel of Jehovah. In opposition to the hypothesis of the Rabbins, Vatablus, Ribera, à Lapide, Drusius, Blayney, Rosenmüller, Hengstenberg, and Knobel, who maintain that Zechariah himself is meant by הַנַּעַר הַלָּז, *this young man*, and argue from it, that the prophet was of youthful age at the time he had the vision, I cannot but concur with Stonard, Hitzig, Maurer, and Ewald, in thinking, that the person intended is the man with the measuring line, spoken of vers. 1, 2. The verb רוּץ, *run*, implies the necessity of despatch, which could only have been occasioned by the intended procedure of the measurer. He is arrested in his progress, and virtually told, that the former dimensions of the city would be totally inadequate to contain the number of its inhabitants. פְּרָזוֹת תֵּשֵׁב יְרוּשָׁלִַם, lit. *Jerusalem shall dwell*, or *inhabit open places*, i. e. the inhabitants will not confine themselves within her walls, but will occupy the localities in the open country around. Thus Symm. ἀτειχίστως; Jarchi and Jerome, מַצִּיב חֹמָה, *absque muro*. Comp. 1 Sam. vi. 18, where כֹּפֶר הַפְּרָזִי, *the country village*, is contrasted with עִיר מִבְצָר, *a fortified city*. See also Esth. ix. 19; Ezek. xxxviii. 11.

5. (Heb. ver. 9.) Though "the wall of fire," and "the glory," are doubtless both to be taken figuratively, the former denoting certain protection, and the latter, illustrious displays of the Divine presence in affording all needful supplies of grace, strength, and comfort, we are not hence to conclude with Stonard, that more is meant by the city than the literal Jerusalem, as the centre of the restored theocracy. The entire connection, and all the circumstances of the prophecy, demand this limitation.

6   Ho! ho! flee from the north country, saith Jehovah,
   For as the winds of heaven
   Have I spread you abroad, saith Jehovah.
7   Ho! deliver thyself, O Zion!
   That dwellest with the daughter of Babylon.
8   For thus saith Jehovah of hosts:

6, 7. (Heb. 10, 11.) It is generally thought that the urgent calls here given to those Jews who still remained in Babylon, were designed to induce them to leave that devoted city before its approaching siege and capture by Darius. In all probability many of them had acquired wealth, and might have been induced to remain in the enjoyment of their possessions. It was necessary that such should take the alarm, and, with the rest of their countrymen, avail themselves without delay of the opportunity they now had of returning to their own land. The urgency of the call is expressed by the repetitious form, הוֹי הוֹי, *Ho! Ho!* which occurs, so far as I am aware, in no other part of Scripture. The verbs קוּם, *arise*, שְׁמַע, *hear*, or the like, being readily suggested by the interjection, will account for the use of the conjunctive Vau in וְנֻסוּ. The land of the north is Babylon, and the regions adjacent. See Jer. vi. 22, xvi. 15. Between the former and the latter clause of the verse there seems, at first sight, a palpable discrepancy. How, it may be asked, could the scattering of the Jews like the four winds of heaven be a reason why those, in particular, who lived in the north quarter should return? But this apparent incoherence has originated in the supposition that the prophet here asserts the dispersion of that people into the four quarters of the globe. Had this, however, been his meaning, he would have employed לְ after the verb, as in Ezek. xvii. 21. Nor can such construction be supported by substituting the various reading בְּ, viz. בְּאַרְבַּע, instead of כְּ; for the words could then only properly be rendered, "I have scattered you *by*," and not "*in*" or "*into* the four winds." This reading, though supported by fifteen MSS., originally by seven more, and perhaps by another, by thirteen printed editions, and by the Syr. and Vulg., is inferior in point of authority to that of the Textus Receptus. The meaning seems to be, that the scattering of the Hebrew people had been so violent and extensive, that it could only be fitly compared to the force and effect of the combined winds of heaven being brought to bear upon any object susceptible of dispersion. The scattering had been most severely felt by those resident at the time of the vision in Babylon, and other regions in that quarter; on which account it is described with special reference to them. כִּי is here used, not as a causative, but as a concessive participle, as in Gen. viii. 21; Exod. xiii. 17. Nothing can be more forced, or unsuited to the connection, than the interpretation, which assumes that פֵּרַשְׂתִּי is future in signification, and that the words contain a prediction of a future spreading abroad of the Jews as missionaries among the heathen. What can be conceived more incongruous, than a return of the Jews from Babylon, induced by the motive of a still more extended dispersion among the nations of the earth, without the smallest hint of this as their destination! By צִיּוֹן, *Zion*, are meant the inhabitants of Jerusalem, at that time still in Babylon. The words יוֹשֶׁבֶת בַּת־בָּבֶל are not in apposition, but in construction, and are equivalent to *Habitatrix Babelis.* For this idiomatic use of בַּת see on Is. i. 8. Comp. יוֹשֶׁבֶת בַּת־מִצְרַיִם, Jer. xlvi. 19.

8. (Heb. 12.) Some suppose the prophet to be the person who here speaks of himself as having been sent; others, the

After the glory he hath sent me
To the nations which spoiled you;
Surely he that toucheth you
Toucheth the pupil of his eye.
9 For, behold! I will shake my fist at them,

angel mentioned ver. 4; but that the Messiah is intended, must be inferred from what is predicated of him, ver. 9, that he would shake his hand at the nations which had afflicted the Jews. Comp. Is. xlviii. 16, where the divine mission of the Second Person of the Trinity is described in parallel language. Blayney, Newcome, Gesenius, Hitzig, Maurer, and Ewald, strangely concur in rendering אַחַר כָּבוֹד שְׁלָחָֽנִי, *He hath sent me after glory*, in the sense of, with a view to acquire it. In no other passage, however, is אַחַר employed, except as an adverb or preposition of place or time; nor is it ever connected as a preposition with שָׁלַח. This verb is not even here construed with it, but with the preposition אֶל immediately following. It can only, therefore, be employed to denote the posteriority of the mission specified to the restoration of the glorious presence of the manifested Jehovah to his recovered people. Thus the LXX. ὀπίσω δοξοῦς. Syr. ܟ݁ܳܕ݂ ܐܶܡܰܪ, *after the glory*, which is falsely rendered in the London Polyglott, *ad prosequendum honorem*. Targ. בָּתַר יְקָרָא דַאֲמִיר לְאַיְתָאָה עֲלֵיכוֹן, *after the glory which he hath promised to bring to you*. Vulg. *post gloriam*. Such exegesis is most naturally suggested by the use of כָּבוֹד, *glory*, ver. 5. After what had been there promised should have been accomplished, the Divine Legate had a commission to punish the nations in the immediate vicinity of the Holy Land, such as the Moabites, Idumeans, Ammonites, Philistines, and Syrians, by whom the Jews had been attacked and plundered on various occasions, and especially on that of the Chaldean invasion. The Jews in Babylon needed, therefore, to be under no apprehension from these enemies, and might return with confidence to their own land. The tender regard which Jehovah cherished for them, is expressed with exquisite beauty in the concluding clause of the verse. No member of the body is more susceptible of pain, or more vigilantly protected, than the eye, especially the pupil, or aperture through which the rays of light pass to the retina. בָּבָה, in the phrase בָּבַת עַיִן, *the pupil of the eye*, Gesenius now derives from בָּבַב, *to bore, make hollow*, and considers it to stand for נִבְבָה, *a hole gate*, like the Arab. بَاب; but his former etymology is preferable, according to which it is to be derived from בָּבָה, Arab. بَابَا, *dixit baba*, Gr. παππάζειν, to say *papa*, spoken of a child. Hence the Arab. بُوبُو, *booboo* (the origin of our English booby), *puellus, boy*. The phrase thus corresponds to the other Hebrew mode of expressing the same thing, אִישׁוֹן עַיִן, *the little man of the eye*, Deut. xxxii. 10; Prov. vii. 2. Both modes of expression, بُوَيْوُ عَيْنٍ and إِبْسَانُ الْعَيْنِ, are used in Arabic; and the Arabs say in language quite parallel to that of the prophet, هُوَ أَعَزُّ عِنْدِي مِنْ بُوبُو عَيْنِي, *He is dearer to me than the pupil of mine eye*. Both modes are more expressive than the Latin of Catullus; *multo quod carius illi est oculis*, or, *ni te plus oculis meis amarem*. The pronominal affix in עֵינוֹ, *his eye*, is to be referred to יְהוָה צְבָאוֹת, Jehovah of hosts, at the beginning of the verse, the nominative to שְׁלָחַנִי, and not with Kimchi, Blayney, Stonard, and others, to the enemy himself.

9. (Heb. 13.) For the phrase מֵנִיף יָד, comp. Is. xi. 15, xix. 16. It is indica-

And they shall be a spoil to their slaves:
And ye shall know that Jehovah of hosts hath sent me.
10 Sing and rejoice, O daughter of Zion!
For, behold! I come,
And I will dwell in the midst of thee, saith Jehovah.
11 And many nations shall join themselves to Jehovah in that day,
And shall become my people;
And I will dwell in the midst of thee,
And thou shalt know that Jehovah of hosts hath sent me unto thee.
12 And Jehovah shall possess Judah his portion,
In the holy land;
And shall again take pleasure in Jerusalem.
13 Let all flesh be silent before Jehovah,
For he is roused from his holy habitation.

tive of the threatening attitude of Jehovah when about to inflict vengeance upon his enemies. By עַבְדֵיהֶם, *their slaves*, are meant the Jews, whom the nations, either by capture or purchase, had brought into a state of slavery. Comp. Is. xiv. 2. יָדַע, here and in ver. 11, signifies, as frequently, *to know by experience*.

10, 11. (Heb. 14, 15.) The divine residence here predicted, must be interpreted of that which took place during the sojourn of the Son of God in the land of Judea. The almost entire identity of the language here employed, with that used chap. ix. 9, where, in like manner, the daughter of Zion is called to hail the advent of her King, compels to this conclusion. Comp. Ps. xl. 7; Is. xl. 9, 10. So evidently is this the only fair construction of the meaning, that Kimchi himself refers the passage לְעָתִיד בִּימֵי הַמָּשִׁיחַ, *to future events in the times of the Messiah*. The phrases הַיּוֹם הַהוּא, בַּיָּמִים הָהֵם, *that day, those days*, frequently point out the period of his manifestation and reign. With this appearance and residence of the Messiah are connected, as their consequents, the extensive conversion of the heathen nations and their being constituted a people devoted to his service and glory. The repetition of the prediction relative to his residence in Zion, is designed to express the certainty of the event.

12. (Heb. 16.) As mention had just been made of the adoption of the nations to be the people of the Messiah, the prophet, to preclude the idea, that the Jews were no more to enjoy that privilege, proceeds to describe a future period, during which they should again be the objects of the Divine favor and delight. Restored to the Holy Land, they shall again be the possession of the Lord. Comp. Exod. xxxiv. 9; Deut. iv. 20, ix. 26, 29, xxxii. 9. The ideas suggested by their being the possession of Jehovah are those of their being the objects of his regard and care. Ps. xxviii. 9.

13. (Heb. 17.) A call to universal reverence and submission in prospect of the wonderful interpositions of Jehovah on behalf of his church. Comp. Ps. lxxvi. 8, 9; Zeph. i. 7.

CHAPTER III.

IN this chapter a fourth vision is described, in which Joshua the high priest is represented as occupying his official position in the Divine presence at Jerusalem, but opposed in his attempt to recommence the service of Jehovah, by Satan, who accused him of being disqualified for the discharge of his functions, ver. 1. The accusation is met by a reprimand, drawn from the Divine purpose to restore Jerusalem, and the narrow escape which the priesthood had had from total extinction, 2. The guilt attaching to the high priest, in his representative capacity, and its removal, is next figuratively set forth, 3—5. He has then a solemn charge delivered to him, followed by a conditional promise, 6, 7; after which we have a prediction of the Messiah, as a security that the punishment of the Jews would be entirely removed, their temple completely restored, and a period of prosperity introduced, 8—10.

1 AND he showed me Joshua the high priest, standing before the Angel of Jehovah, and the Adversary standing on his right hand to oppose him.

VISION IV.

1. The nominative to וַיַּרְאֵנִי is the interpreting angel, understood. Comp. ch. i. 9. As the phrase עָמַד לִפְנֵי, *to stand before*, is sometimes used of appearing before a judge, Numb. xxxv. 12; Deut. xix. 17; 1 Kings iii. 16; it has been inferred that we have here the representation of a judicial transaction, an exegesis which is supposed to derive confirmation from the circumstance of an accuser being mentioned in the following verse. But as the person here described is the high priest, and the phrase in question is that which is appropriated to express the position of the priests when ministering to Jehovah, Deut. x. 8; 2 Chron. xxix. 11; Ezek. xliv. 15; it is more natural to conclude that Joshua is here represented as having entered the new temple which was in the course of erection, and taken his position in front of the altar before the holy of holies. The high priest not only entered the most sacred place once a year on the day of atonement, but was authorized to perform all the duties of the ordinary priests; so that he may here be conceived of as about to offer sacrifice for the people, when he was opposed by Satan. That the altar of burnt offering was erected before the building of the temple was proceeded with, is clear, from Ezra iii. 2, 3, 6, 7. The מַלְאַךְ יְהֹוָה, before whom Joshua stood, was no other than יְהֹוָה himself, as ver. 2 evidently shows. It has been matter of dispute, whether by הַשָּׂטָן we are here to understand the great enemy of God and man ὁ ἀντίδικος, 1 Pet. v. 8; ὁ κατήγωρ, Rev. xii. 1❿; or, whether a human adversary or adversaries are intended. Those who advocate the latter position think that Sanballat, or some other enemy of the Jews, is meant; but the emphatic form of the term, investing it, as it does, with the nature of a proper name (Gesen. Heb. Gram. § 107, 2), decidedly favors the former interpretation. We find this name given to the chief of the evil spirits in the book of Job, the most ancient in the Bible. See chap. i. and ii. Some have compared Ps. cix. 6, but the parallel term רָשָׁע is against such construction in that passage. From the identity of the phraseology, however, which represents the adversary as taking his place at the right hand of the accused, it has been concluded, that it was customary in the Jewish courts for the accuser to assume this position. What the ground of opposition on the part of Satan was, we are not here informed; but if

2   And Jehovah said to the Adversary,
    Jehovah rebuke thee, O Adversary!
    Even Jehovah that taketh delight in Jerusalem, rebuke thee;
    Is not this a brand snatched from the fire?
3   Now Joshua was clothed with filthy garments, and he stood
4   before the Angel. And he answered and spake to those that
    stood before him, saying, Remove the filthy garments from him.
    And he said to him, See! I have caused thine iniquity to pass

the construction put by some eminent commentators upon Jude 9, which resolves "the body of Moses," there mentioned, into the Jewish church, and supposes the apostle to refer to the passage before us, be the true one (and of this I cannot entertain a doubt), it will follow, that the character of the Jewish people, as not having been legally purified from their idolatries, and the backwardness which they evinced in rebuilding the temple, were urged as pleas against them. It is true, the opposition is said to have been made to Joshua; but it must be remembered that he appears here, not in his personal, but in his official character, as the representative of the whole body of the people.

2. Almost all the commentators, even Maurer and Hitzig, agree in the opinion, that the incommunicable name יְהֹוָה, Jehovah, is here given to the angel spoken of in the preceding verse. See on ch. i. 8. So obvious did this appear to the Syriac translator, from the spirit of the context, that he renders ܡܠܐܟܗ ܕܡܪܝܐ, the Angel of the Lord, a rendering which Newcome would, very uncritically, have admitted into the text. The interpretation of Rosenmüller, "vocatur legatus de nomine principis sui," is a pure fiction, and directly opposed to Scripture usage. The verb גָּעַר signifies to chide, rebuke, so as to silence those who are the objects of the reproof, and restrain them from carrying their designs into effect. It is repeated for the sake of emphasis, to express the absolute certainty that the machinations of Satan should prove utterly abortive. In the reference to the Divine choice of Jerusalem, there is a recognition of the promise, ch. i. 17, ii. 12. The pointed interrogation has respect to Joshua, and forcibly, though tacitly, conveys the idea, that his deliverance, and that of the people whom he represented, from the destruction which threatened them in Babylon, was the result of sudden and efficient interposition on the part of Jehovah. It was not, therefore, for a moment to be supposed that he would now withdraw his favor from them, and abandon them to their enemies. He had rescued them, in order that they might be preserved.

3, 4. Because the Romans used to clothe persons who were accused in a sordid dress, Drusius and others have imagined that the idea of a criminal is still kept up. That the filthy garments in which Joshua appeared were symbolical of the guilt and punishment of the Jews, seems beyond dispute; just as their removal, and his investment with splendid attire, indicates a state of restoration to the full enjoyment of their religious privileges. צוֹאָה, filth, is used metaphorically to denote the moral pollution contracted by sin. See Prov. xxx. 12; Is. iv. 4. He is represented as appearing in the squalid garments in which he had returned from a state of captivity in Babylon, and as having restored to him the gorgeous dress of the high priest. מַחֲלָצוֹת, costly or splendid habiliments, such as were worn on special occasions, and put off as soon as the occasion was over. See on Is. iii. 22. Those who are here commanded to change the dress of

5 away from thee, and I will invest thee with costly habiliments. He then said, Let them place a pure mitre upon his head. And they placed the pure mitre upon his head, and invested him with
6 the habiliments. Then the Angel of Jehovah stood up. And the Angel of Jehovah protested to Joshua, saying:
7 Thus saith Jehovah of hosts:
If thou wilt walk in my ways,
And if thou wilt observe my charge,
Then thou shalt both judge my house,

Joshua are not, as Ewald supposes, attendant priests, but attendant angels. The nominative to וַיַּעַן and יִגְעַר is יְחוָֹה, and not יְהוֹשֻׁעַ. עָוֹן הֶעֱבִיר does not mean, as Gesenius interprets, to let iniquity or sin pass by, but to *remove its guilt* or *punishment*, and thus effectively to remit or forgive. This guilt or punishment is represented as having lain as a heavy load upon Joshua, and to have been removed מֵעָלָיו, *from upon him*. הַלְבֵּשׁ is not to be changed into אַלְבֵּשׁ, as in the Targ. and Syr., but is to be regarded as a not unusual elliptical form of the idiomatic הַלְבֵּשׁ אֶלְבָּשׁ.

5. The punctuation וָאֹמַר is obviously incorrect, since it introduces the prophet as taking a part in the transactions exhibited in the vision, which is altogether foreign to the position he occupied. The word should be pointed וַיֹּאמֶר, and has been so read by the Targ., Syr., and Vulg. translators. צָנִיף, *tiara*, or *turban*, is used instead of מִצְנֶפֶת, the term employed in the Pentateuch to denote this part of the high priest's dress. LXX. κίδαρις. At בְּגָדִים the adjective טְהוֹרִים is to be supplied from the preceding, or the article may be understood. עֹמֵד is more appropriately rendered "stood up," than, as in our common version, "stood by." The latter rendering presents the Angel of Jehovah to view as a simple spectator; the former in the solemn posture of one who is about to deliver an important charge. And this, as the following verses show, was precisely the character in which he appeared. He had been sitting upon his throne, but now rises to announce the divine decree respecting the responsible duties which devolved upon Joshua in his sacerdotal capacity. I do not agree with Dr. Stonard, who supposes that the Angel assumed the character and position of a witness. The participial form of the verb is adopted for the purpose of varying the style.

6, 7. הֵעִיד, as here used in Hiphil, signifies, *to make a solemn declaration.* LXX. διεμαρτύρατο. Targ. and Syr. אַסְהֵד. Vulg. *contestabatur.* מִשְׁמַרְתִּי, *my charge*, means the laws, prescriptions, or rites, which I have given in charge, namely, the Mosaic Institute. Obedience to this the high priest was bound to render himself, and upon him supremely devolved the obligation to see that it was obeyed by others. מִשְׁמֶרֶת, from שָׁמַר, *to guard, keep, observe*, is frequently used by Moses to denote the *office, duty,* or *charge*, to which the priests were to attend. See Lev. viii. 35; Numb. i. 53, iii. 28, 31, 32, 38. By the "house" of the Lord here, we are not to understand the temple, as some have imagined, but the people of Israel, viewed as composing his household or family. Comp. Numb. xii. 7; Hos. viii. 1, ix. 15. דִּין, *to judge*, is always employed in reference to persons; never with respect to things. There appears to be in the declaration here made, an anticipation of the part which the sacerdotal family of Joshua was to take in the government of the Jewish state. מַהְלְכִים is the Hiphil participle of הָלַךְ, just as מַחֲלְמִים is of חָלַם, Jer. xxix. 8; and מַעֲוְרִים of עָוַר,

And keep my courts,
And I will give thee guides among those who are standing by.
Hear now, O Joshua! the high priest,
Thou and thy companions that sit before thee;

2 Chron. xxviii. 23. It must, therefore, signify *those who cause to go* or *walk, leaders, conductors, guides*. Who these were we are not informed, farther than that they were standing in the presence of the Angel, and were pointed at by him. Some have thought that the subordinate priests who attended upon Joshua are intended; but such interpretation is altogether unsuitable to the dignified character which, as high priest, he sustained. As none but superior beings could be his leaders or conductors, it follows that the angels must be meant. This view is confirmed by the circumstance of their being represented as "standing," namely, in the presence of Jehovah, ready to execute his behests, whereas the subordinate priests are spoken of in the following verse as "sitting" before Joshua. The import of the promise is, that he and his successors in office should enjoy the care, direction, and aid of celestial spirits in the management of the national affairs. Munster, Vatablus, Rosenmüller, Ewald, and Hitzig, take מַהְלְכִים to be the plural of the noun מַהֲלָךְ, *a walk*, or *walking place*; but this affords no appropriate sense, except it be referred to the heavenly state — a construction put upon the clause by the Targum, Kimchi, and several Christian interpreters, but which is little suited to the language of the connection, and is a mode of representation otherwise foreign to Scripture.

8. The companions of Joshua were the ordinary priests, who were associated with him for the purpose of carrying on the service of the temple. They are represented as "sitting before" him, not at the time the words are addressed to him, for they are spoken of in the third person, but usually, when consulting together about religious matters. On such occasions he occupied a more elevated seat or throne as their president, while they sat on chairs or benches before him. By אַנְשֵׁי מוֹפֵת, *men of sign*, or *portent*, are meant *symbolical men*, persons prefiguring, or foreshadowing some person or persons still future. Comp. Is. viii. 18, xx. 3; Ezek. xii. 6, xxiv. 27. That only one person is here referred to as typified by the Jewish priests, and that this one person is none other than the Messiah, the following clause of the verse incontrovertibly shows. In their sacerdotal character, and in the presentation of sacrifices before Jehovah, they foreshadowed the High Priest of our profession, Christ Jesus, and the one sacrifice which he offered for sins, when he presented himself as a propitiatory victim in the room of the guilty. For the derivation of מוֹפֵת, see on Joel ii. 30. Though הֵמָּה, *they are*, refers immediately to the subordinate priests, we are not to suppose that Joshua is excluded, or that he was not a symbolical person as well as they. This use of the third person of the pronoun instead of the second is not without example. See Zeph. ii. 12. The author of the Targum admits that by צֶמַח, *Branch*, the MESSIAH is meant. His words are, עַבְדִּי מְשִׁיחָא דְיִתְגְּלֵי, "My Servant, the Messiah who shall be revealed." The same interpretation is found in other Jewish authorities, as both Kimchi and Rashi admit. Some few Christian interpreters, among whom Grotius and Blayney, adopting the opinion of the two Rabbins just mentioned, suppose Zerubbabel to be intended; but in my opinion very preposterously, for that prince was already in existence, and in the full exercise of his official duties; whereas the person to whom Jehovah refers had not yet appeared. Even Gesenius, Hitzig, and Maurer, make no scru-

(For they are typical persons)
For, behold! I will introduce my servant THE BRANCH.
9 For, behold! the stone which I have laid before Joshua,
Upon the one stone shall be seven eyes:
Behold! I will form the sculpture thereof,

ple in applying the title to the Messiah. It is that given to him, Is. iv. 2; Jer. xxiii. 5, xxxiii. 15; and Zech. vi. 12; and is equivalent to *Son*. See on Is. iv. 2, where it is shown that in the writings of the ancient Persians, "the *branch*" of any one means his son, or one of his posterity. The verb צָמַח, from which the noun is derived, signifies to *spring forth* or *up*, as plants; but the LXX. have adopted the word ἀνατολή, which expresses the *sun-rise*. Hence the Saviour is called ἀνατολὴ ἐξ ὕψους, "the Dayspring from on high," Luke i. 78. Comp. Mal. iv. 2, where וְזָרְחָה שֶׁמֶשׁ צְדָקָה, "the Sun of righteousness shall arise," is rendered by the LXX. ἀνατελεῖ ἥλιος δικαιοσύνης. The Vulg. *adducam servum meum orientem*. For עַבְדִּי, *my servant*, as a designation of the Messiah, comp. Is. xlii. 1—7, xlix. 1—9, l. 5—10, lii. 13—liii.; and see my Comm. on the first of these passages.

9. Most interpreters regard this verse as a continuation of the subject treated of at the close of the preceding, and explain the אֶבֶן, *stone*, of the Messiah in accordance with such passages as Ps. cxviii. 22; Is. xxviii. 16. This view is largely insisted upon by Stonard; but what, in my judgment, renders it altogether untenable, is the circumstance that the stone is spoken of as having been laid *before*, or *in the presence of*, Joshua — language which can with no propriety be employed with reference to the Messiah. Neither can the reference be to הָאֶבֶן הַבְּדִיל, *the plummet*, spoken of ch. iv. 10, that being represented as in the hand of Zerubbabel, and not placed or laid before his associate in the government. I cannot, therefore, imagine any other stone to be here intended than the foundation stone of the temple, which had been laid by Zerubbabel in the presence of Joshua and his brethren the priests, who celebrated the joyful event in songs of praise to Jehovah. Ezra iii. 8—13. When it is said, that upon this "one stone" were "seven eyes," we are not to conclude that they were exhibited upon it. The meaning is, that they were directed towards it, or intent and fixed upon it, as an object of special attention and care. While with us an eye is the hieroglyphic of Divine Providence, the Hebrews, to express the perfection of knowledge and wisdom in which all its affairs are conducted, employed the hieroglyphic of "*seven eyes*," — seven, in the Oriental style, denoting fulness or perfection. Such symbolic representations were common among the Persians. Comp. Rev. i. 4, v. 6. Jehovah here declares, that the erection of the temple, the commencement of which had been made, in the course of his providence, by the laying of the foundation, should be an object of his special care and regard. . For עַיִן עַל, *the eye being upon* any person or thing, as denoting the exercise of kind and vigilant care, see Ps. xxxii. 8. The attempt of Vitringa and Blayney to explain עֵינַיִם, of *fountains*, and so apply the passage to living waters flowing from Christ as the antitype of the rock smitten in the wilderness is a complete failure. The singular עַיִן, signifies, indeed, *fountain* as well as *eye*, but it is a settled principle of Hebrew grammar than when *fountains* are intended, the plural feminine is uniformly employed, just as the dual עֵינַיִם is as uniformly and exclusively used to express *eyes*. See for the principle, Gesen. Lehrgeb. pp. 539, 540. That the dual is employed to express things that exist in pairs, even when more

Saith Jehovah of hosts;
And I will remove the punishment of that land in one day.
10 In that day, saith Jehovah of hosts,
Ye shall each invite his neighbor,
Under the vine, and under the fig tree.

than two is intended, see on Is. vi. 2. הִנְנִי מְפַתֵּחַ פִּתֻּחָהּ, *Behold! I will form the sculpture thereof;* lit. "I will open the opening thereof." What kind of architectural ornaments are hereby intended, it is impossible to say; but that they were cut out or engraven in the foundation-stone, the exigency of the place requires, except we regard the stone as here used by synecdoche for the whole temple, in which case reference will be had to the finishing off of the structure, the foundation of which had been laid in the presence of Joshua. LXX. ὀρύσσω βόθρον. Syr. ࡀࡇ ࡐࡕࡇ ࡀࡍࡀ ࡌࡐࡕࡇ. "Behold, I open the gates of it." מוּשׁ is here used in Kal, but with a causative signification: *to remove, cause to depart.* עָוֹן is to be understood, not of iniquity, but of the punishment of iniquity —

the troubles and sufferings to which the Jews were subjected on account of it. Thus the iniquity of Sodom, Gen. xix. 15, was the punishment to be inflicted upon it; and that of Babylon, Jer. li. 6, the same. The land of Judea had borne its punishment during the captivity, but was now to be occupied and cultivated. To sufferings the Jews were still exposed on the part of their enemies, who caused an interruption of the building of the temple, and prevented the comfortable settlement of the people in their own land. For their encouragement Jehovah promises to put an end to their distress, בְּיוֹם אֶחָד, *in one day;* i. e. soon, in the shortest space of time. הָאָרֶץ הַהִיא is specifically the land of Palestine.

10. A promise of the tranquillity and social enjoyment that were to be experienced by the restored Hebrews.

CHAPTER IV.

UNDER the symbol of a golden candlestick is represented the pure and flourishing state of the Jewish church as restored after the captivity, 1–3. The signification of this symbol the prophet is left to find out, 4, 5; only a clue is given him in the message which he was commissioned to deliver relative to the completion of the temple, in spite of the formidable difficulties which interposed, and to the Messiah who was to come after the temple was in a finished state, 6, 7. He was further instructed to announce the certainty of the former event, on the ground that Zerubbabel, who superintended the work, was under the special care of Divine Providence, which should so arrange the course of human affairs as to render them subservient to the undertaking, 8–10. Under the additional symbol of two olive trees, which supplied the candlestick with the necessary oil, are represented Joshua and Zerubbabel, the two principal official persons in the new state, 11–14.

---

1   AND the angel who spake with me awoke me again, like one

VISION V.

1. We are not to conclude from the use of the verb שׁוּב at the beginning of this verse, that the communicating angel had removed to a distance from the prophet, and now returned to him.

2 who is waked out of his sleep. And he said to me, What dost thou see? And I said, I see, and behold! a candlestick wholly of gold, and its bowl upon the top of it, and its seven lamps

When employed by itself, שוּב certainly signifies *to return;* but, according to a common Hebrew idiom, when used before another verb, it merely indicates the repetition of the action expressed by such verb. See Gen. xxvi. 18, xxx. 31; 2 Kings i. 11, 13. Connecting the verb in this manner with וַיְעִירֵנִי, reference will be had, not to any absence of the angel, but to his renewed excitement of the prophet to give his attention to another vision which was to be presented to his view. He had become so absorbed in the contemplation of the preceding vision, that he required to be roused, as in the case of a person in profound sleep.

2. Instead of the second וַיֹּאמֶר, a vast number of the MSS. read correctly וָאֹמַר, as the word is found also in some of the earliest editions. Many MSS. and several printed editions exhibit גֻּלָּה without Mappick in the ה, and thus bring the word into accordance with the feminine form, as occurring in the following verse. It has been thus read by the LXX. and Syr.; still it seems preferable to regard it as a masculine noun, and read גֻּלָּהּ, with the pronominal affix. It signifies an oil-cup, bowl, or basin, and was placed at the top of the candlestick for the purpose of supplying with oil the small tubes or pipes leading to the several lamps. Considerable difficulty has been found in endeavoring to account for the double numeral form שִׁבְעָה וְשִׁבְעָה, *seven and seven.* Some think the number is to be multiplied by itself, and rendered forty-nine; but this is not only abhorrent from the representation otherwise given of the candlestick, but is unwarranted by Hebrew usage. Others, as Stonard, take the words in a distributive sense, and make the number to be fourteen, understanding by *seven and seven,* twice seven. To this hypothesis, however, the copulative Vau forms an insuperable objection, since it conveys the idea not of distribution merely, but also that of diversity or variety. The instance adduced from 1 Kings viii. 65, is not exactly parallel, as the noun is there repeated, which is not the case in Zechariah; nor, so far as I can find, do we meet with any instance parallel to שִׁבְעָה וְשִׁבְעָה מוּצָקוֹת. Our translators remove the one seven, and place it before "lamps;" but such construction is altogether unwarranted, and, indeed, they appear to have placed only a qualified reliance upon it, for they render in the margin, *seven several pipes.* There is every reason to suspect that the former שִׁבְעָה is an interpolation which has found its way into some ancient MSS. and been copied into all the rest. This suspicion is confirmed by two circumstances. The word occurs only once both in the LXX. and the Vulg. The former renders: καὶ ἑπτὰ ἐπαρυστρίδες τοῖς λύχνοις τοῖς ἐπάνω αὐτῆς; the latter, *et septem infusoria lucernis, quæ erant super caput ejus.* The other circumstance is, that, as in conformity to the number of lamps belonging to the candelabrum in the tabernacle, Exod. xxv. 37, from which the symbol was evidently borrowed, it is expressly stated, that there were only שִׁבְעָה נֵרוֹת, *seven lamps* attached to that presented to view in the vision, we cannot conceive of there being to each two pipes or conductors for the oil. The קָנִים, *reeds* or *tubes* of Moses, Exod. xxv. 32, 33, 35, xxxvii. 18, and the מוּצָקוֹת, *pipes* or *tubes* of Zechariah, both signify the same objects, *viz.,* those used for conveying the oil into the lamps. The latter word is derived from יָצַק *to pour* or *flow.* Vulg. *infusoria.* That the candlestick was symbolical of the Jewish church cannot be doubted. Comp. Rev. i. 20; xi. 4, where the same symbol is used in reference to Christian churches. The idea which it

3 upon it, and seven pipes to the lamps which are upon the top
of it. And two olive trees beside it, one on the right side of
4 the bowl, and one on the left side of it. And I addressed my-
5 self farther to the angel who spake with me, saying, What are
these, my lord? And the angel who spake with me answered
6 and said to me, Dost thou not know what these are? And I
said, No, my lord. And he answered and spake to me, saying,
This is the word of Jehovah to Zerubbabel, saying:
>   Not by might, nor by power,
>   But by my Spirit, saith Jehovah of hosts.
7 Who art thou, O great mountain?
    Before Zerubbabel thou shalt become a plain:

conveys is that such churches are placed in the world for the sake of its illumination. Thus it was with the Jewish church in the midst of the surrounding darkness of Paganism; and thus it hath been with Christian churches in every age of their history.

3. Of what the two olive-trees were emblematical, we learn from ver. 14.

4, 5. עָנָה, like ἀποκρίνομαι in the New Testament, signifies to *proceed* or *begin to speak*, as well as to answer. It is obviously thus used at the beginning of ver. 4. Comp. chap. i. 10. While the angel had it in commission to explain what was meant by these trees, he was to reserve the explanation till after he had made certain communications relative to the building of the temple, and the advent of Messiah.

6. From the purport of the message which the prophet was to deliver to Zerubbabel, it may be inferred that he was laboring under despondency, produced by the consideration of the powerful opposition with which he had to contend, the greatness of the undertaking in which he had embarked, and the inadequacy of the human means which he had at his disposal. Between חַיִל and כֹּחַ there is no clearly defined difference of meaning. They are both used equally of physical and of mental and moral *power;* and are here employed as synonymes, to express the idea that human might, of whatever

description, was of no account with the Almighty; that he can effect his purposes by few as well as by many, by those whom the world accounts foolish as well as by those of superior intellect; and that it is by the exercise of his own spiritual agency exciting to action, and sustaining and giving efficiency to it, that its performance is secured. There seems to be here a reference to what we read, Haggai, ii. 5: "My Spirit remaineth among you: fear ye not." The truth, however, is of universal application, and is clearly taught in the New Testament in reference to the conversion of sinners, 1 Cor. iii. 6; 2 Cor. x. 4; Eph. i. 19: Col. i. 12.

7. However lowly the feelings entertained by Zerubbabel, he is here taught by the sublime and noble figure of the depression of a large mountain into a level plain, that none of the formidable impediments which he apprehended, should, in the smallest degree, obstruct his progress מִי, *who,* sometimes refers to things, yet so as to include the idea of the human agency connected with them. Before לִפְנֵי־זְרֻבָּבֶל supply הָיָה or תִּהְיֶה. The interpretation of Stonard, who applies the mountain to the Christian church, is altogether forced and inept. By אֶבֶן הָרֹאשָׁה is meant, not any stone uniting the two sides of a building at the top, but the *lapis angularis,* or foundation stone, on which at the angle both rest, and which, being necessarily much

And he shall bring forth the Chief Stone,
With shouts of Grace! Grace to it!
8 And the word of Jehovah was communicated to me saying,
9 The hands of Zerubbabel have founded this house,
And his hands shall finish it:
And ye shall know that Jehovah of hosts hath sent me to you.
10 For who hath despised the day of small things?

larger and more ponderous, as well as more serviceable than any other, was fully entitled to the distinctive character of *the chief* or *principal stone.* The foundations of the literal temple having already been laid by Zerubbabel, it must be obvious, that the language is merely borrowed from that event, and that his attention is directed to Him of whom David had prophesied as אֶבֶן רֹאשׁ פִּנָּה, the *chief* or *principal corner stone,* Ps. cxviii. 26, and who is called in the New Testament, Κεφαλὴ γωνίας, and Λίθος ἀκρογωνιαῖος. Symm. renders: τόν λίθον τὸν ἄκρον; Theod. τὸν λίθον τὸν πρῶτον; Aq. τὸν λίθον τὸν πρωτεύοντα; all conveying the idea of the primary or principal stone of the building. The LXX. mistaking הָרֹאשָׁה for וְיָרַשׁ, render, τὸν λίθον τῆς κληρονομίας. The nominative to הוֹצִיא is not Zerubbabel, but Jehovah. This was perceived by the Targumist, who puts the same Messianic interpretation upon the passage, paraphrasing it thus: וְיִגְלֵי בֵית מְשִׁיחֵיהּ דַּאֲמִיר שְׁמֵיהּ מִלְּקַדְמִין וְיִשְׁלוֹט בְּכָל מַלְכְּוָתָא, *And he shall reveal his Messiah, who was named of old, and he shall rule over all kingdoms.* The introduction of this stone was to be accompanied with acclamations of "Grace, Grace to it." תְּשֻׁאוֹת, *shouts* or *acclamations,* from נָשָׁא, *to make a noise, shout aloud,* cry as a crowd; hence the noun came to signify the shouting of a multitude. The repetition of חֵן, *favor* or *grace,* is for the sake of intensity; and the ascriptions of this favor to the stone (לָהּ) implies that it was possessed of this quality, and was to be the medium or means of its conveyance to others. This prediction was clearly ful-

filled in our Redeemer. "*Grace,*" or *favor,* "was poured through his lips." Ps. xlv. 8. At his birth the תְּשֻׁאוֹת, acclamations of the heavenly choir, were, "Glory to God in the highest, on earth peace, goodwill toward men." Luke ii. 14. As he approached Jerusalem, the multitudes were loud in their acclaims of "Hosanna to the Son of David. Blesssed be he that cometh in the name of the Lord! Hosanna in the highest." Nor is the phrase, "The *grace* of our Lord Jesus Christ," of unfrequent occurrence in the New Testament. The usual application of the words to the completion of the work of grace in the soul of a believer, or to the addition of the last convert to the church, is quite incongruous. Whatever grace is possessed by the people of God is altogether derived, and is not to be ascribed to themselves, but to him to whom alone they are indebted for its communication. It may farther be observed, that perhaps the repetition in the phrase חֵן חֵן, *Grace, Grace,* may have been intended to express the infinite value of the Corner Stone. In Prov. xvii. 8, we read that "a gift is אֶבֶן חֵן, *a precious stone* in the eyes of him that hath it;" and one of the qualities of a stone laid for a foundation in Zion is, that it is יְקָרַת, *precious.* Is. xxviii. 16.

9, 10. כִּי is the Preterite of Piel. בָּצַע signifies *to cut, cut off, bring to an end, finish,* in which last acceptation it is here used. The verse contains a positive assurance that the temple should be completed by Zerubbabel. "The day of small things" means the short period which had elapsed since the Jews had begun to rebuild the temple, and the

For those seven eyes of Jehovah
Which run to and fro through the whole earth rejoiced,
When they saw the plummet in the hand of Zerubbabel.

11   Then I proceeded and said to him, What are these two olive-trees on the right side of the candlestick, and on the left of it?
12   And I proceeded a second time, and said to him, What are the two branches of the olive-trees, which, by means of the two
13   tubes of gold, empty the golden liquid out of themselves? And
14   he spake to me, saying, Knowest thou not what these are? And

commencement, which had been inconsiderable and inauspicious. The efforts bore no proportion to the magnitude of the undertaking, and could only provoke the scorn and contempt of unbelievers. בָּזָה is derived from בָּזָה, as בַּז is from בָּזַז; only with the signification of בּוּז and בָּזָה, *to despise.* בָּזַז otherwise signifies *to plunder, spoil.* With the human estimate of the enterprise, forcibly expressed in the interrogative form, that of Jehovah is strikingly contrasted. His eyes rejoiced when they saw the work marked out by Zerubbabel with the plummet. This instrument was called אֶבֶן הַבְּדִיל, *the stone of separation,* because it consisted of the alloy of lead or tin, which was *separated* by smelting from the silver ore with which it was combined. The Vau prefixed in וְרָאוּ is to be rendered *when,* as in וּמַלְכֵּי, Judges xix. 1. The nominative to וְרָאוּ שָׂמְחוּ is שִׁבְעָה־אֵלֶּה, with which עֵינֵי יְהוָה is in apposition. This, which appears to me to be the only tenable construction, is that given in the margin by our Translators. It relieves the passage from the burden of fanciful conjectures which had been advanced in regard to the meaning, and brings out the simple but encouraging truth, that, how much soever men might despise the commencement of the work in which Zerubbabel and his compatriots were engaged, it was the object of peculiar regard and delight to Divine Providence, which was acquainted with all human designs, and from its universal activity could not only defeat the machinations of enemies, but command the agency of those who should help forward the cause of truth and righteousness. Comp. chap. iii. 9; 2 Chron. xvi. 9; Prov. xv. 3.

11, 12. It is not a little remarkable that the prophet had to put the question three times respecting the two olive-trees, before he received any reply; first, ver. 4; a second time ver. 11; and a third time ver. 12. The question is varied each time, and becomes at last minute and particular. The reason seems to be, that it could scarcely be conceived possible for him not to understand their symbolical reference to the two most remarkable persons with whom he was conversant, Joshua and Zerubbabel. צַנְתְּרָה, *a branch.* LXX. κλάδος, so called from its resemblance to an *ear* of grain. צַנְתְּרָה, *a tube* or *canal,* through which oil or any other liquid is poured. The etymology of this quadriliteral is uncertain. LXX. μυξωτῆρες. With the tubes the two branches were exhibited as connected, to indicate the source whence the candlestick was supplied with oil. By הַזָּהָב, *the gold,* is meant the oil, which is so called because its purity and brightness resembled those of gold.

14. שְׁנֵי בְנֵי־הַיִּצְהָר, *two sons of oil,* i. e. two anointed ones, Joshua and Zerubbabel, who are so called, because, when installed into office, they had oil poured upon their heads as a symbol of the gifts and influences of the Holy Spirit, which alone could fit them rightly to discharge their important functions. Their services to the new state were of such value that they might well be rep-

I said, No, my lord. Then he said, These are the two anointed ones, that stand before the Lord of the whole earth.

resented as furnishing it instrumentally with what was necessary for enabling it to answer the purposes of its establishment. עַל־כָּל־הָאָרֶץ is elliptical for — הָעֹמְדִים עַל־כָּל־הָאָרֶץ, *who stand before.* The phrase expresses the posture of servants waiting to receive orders from their masters.

CHAPTER V.

THE two visions exhibited in this chapter are of a very different character from any of the foregoing, and were designed to furnish striking and instructive warnings to such of the Jews as might refuse to render obedience to the law of God, and might not have been thoroughly weaned from idolatry. In verses 1–4, is the description of a flying roll, presented to the view of the prophet, on which were inscribed the threatenings of the Divine law, which still remained in all their force, and were ever ready to be executed upon transgressors. In verses 5–11, the means are emblematically set forth which Jehovah had employed for the entire removal of idolatry from the Holy Land, and its abandonment to mingle with its native elements in Babylon — the land of graven images.

1 AND I again raised my eyes, and looked, and, behold! a fly-
2 ing roll. And he said to me, What seest thou? And I said, I see a flying roll, the length of which is twenty cubits, and the

VISION VI.

1. For the adverbial use of שׁוּב see on chap. iv. 1. מְגִלָּה, *a volume* or *roll*, from the root גָּלַל, *to roll*. The ancients wrote upon the inner bark of trees, which was rolled up for the sake of convenience, and for the better preservation of the writing. They also used rolls of papyrus and of the dressed skins of animals. Aq. and Theod. render the word by διφθέρα, a skin or parchment; Symm. by κεφαλίς, the term by which the LXX. have rendered it, Ps. xl. 8. Mistaking מְגִלָּה for מַגָּל, they have here translated it δρέπανον, *a scythe* or *sickle*.

2. The roll here described was of large dimensions, more than ten yards in length, by upwards of five in breadth. To compose such a roll several skins had to be sewed together, as we find to be the case with the Jewish Megillahs, or rolls containing the Pentateuch and other portions of the Old Testament, read in the synagogue at the present day. One of these synagogue rolls, preserved in the British Museum, contains the Pentateuch, written on forty brown African skins. In the Rabbinical division of the books of the Old Testament, the title of the five Megilloth is given to those of the Song of Solomon, Ruth, Lamentations, Ecclesiastes, and Esther; but in Ps. xl. 8, the term מְגִלָּה is applied by way of eminence to the roll or book of the law. The large size of the roll seems to have been intended to indicate the number of the curses which it contained. The circumstance, that the di-

3 breadth of it ten cubits. And he said to me, This is the curse which goeth forth over the face of the whole land; for every one that stealeth shall be cleared away on this side, according to it, and every one that sweareth shall be cleared away on that 4 side, according to it. I bring it forth, saith Jehovah of hosts, and it shall enter the house of him that stealeth, and the house of him that sweareth falsely by my name, and it shall continue in the midst of his house, and destroy it, and its wood, and its stones.

mensions of the roll correspond to those of the porch of the temple, 1 Kings vi. 3, seems rather to be accidental than intended to convey any specific instruction. The participle עָפָה, *flying*, expresses the velocity with which the judgments denounced in the volume would come upon the wicked.

3. הָאָלָה זֹאת, *this is*, or signifies, represents the curse, a phrase altogether parallel with that used by our Lord when instituting the sacred supper: τοῦτο ἔστι τὸ σῶμά μου; in Heb. זֹאת גְוִיָתִי, *this is*, i. e. represents my body. אָלָה, *curse*, is to be taken as a collective, comprehending all the curses denounced against transgressors of the Divine law. After מִזֶּה וּמִזֶּה supply מֵאֵת יְהֹוָה, "from the presence of Jehovah." Because מִזֶּה וּמִזֶּה, *on this side and on that*, is used when the writing of the law on both sides of the tables is spoken of, Exod. xxxii. 15, Abenezra, Kimchi, Rosenmüller, Hengstenberg, and some other interpreters, have argued in favor of the position, that the roll, like that of Ezek. ii. 9, 10, was also written in this manner; but the immediate construction of the pronoun with כָּמוֹהָ in both instances shows that it cannot be maintained. Reference is had to the place where the transgressor may be. From that place, whether on the right hand or on the left, he should be swept away by the Divine judgment. Nowhere should he find protection. The curse went forth over the whole land. It has been properly remarked, that an individual example of transgression is selected from each of the two tables of the law: הַגֹּנֵב, *he who stealeth*, standing for those who break the rule of duty in regard to their neighbor; and הַנִּשְׁבָּע, *he who sweareth*, for those who are guilty of a violation of such duties as have immediate reference to God. נִקָּה is not to be taken here in the sense of *treating as innocent*, but with the signification of *emptying, clearing, sweeping clean away*. Comp. Is. iii. 26; Jer. xxx. 11. It is in the Niphal conjugation, the form of which is the same as that of Piel. The ancient translators are at fault here, having mistaken נִקָּה for נָקִי. Thus the LXX. ἐκδικηθήσεται; Symm. δίκην δώσῃ. Nor can the rendering of Stonard, "] l adeth not guilty," be sustained. כָּמוֹהָ, *like*, or *according to it*, if fully expressed, would be כַּכָּתוּב בָּהּ, *according as it is written*, referring to the curse or threatening inscribed upon the roll. Thus Jerome, *sicut ibi scriptum est*.

4. The pronominal affix in הוֹצֵאתִיהָ refers to הָאָלָה in the preceding verse. לִשְׁמִי לַשֶּׁקֶר is an aggravation of נִשְׁבָּע. The punctuation of לָנֶה is irregular for לָן, the third feminine of the preterite of לוּן, which one of De Rossi's MSS. exhibits. לוּן not merely signifies to *turn aside and spend the night* in any place, but also to *remain permanently*. See Ps. xlix. 13. כְּלִלַתְהוּ=כִּלְּתָה. A like curse was pronounced by the Delphic oracle against perjury:

——— Κραιπνὸς δὲ μετέρχεται,
εἰσόκε πᾶσαν,
Συμμάρψας ὀλέσει γενεὴν καὶ οἶκον
ἅπαντα.   Herodot. vi. 86.

5 Then the angel who spake with me came forth, and said to
   me, Raise thine eyes, now, and look what this is that cometh
6 forth. And I said, What is it? And he said, This is the ephah
   that cometh forth. He said, moreover, This is their appearance
7 in all the land. And, behold! a round piece of lead, and there
8 was a woman sitting in the midst of the ephah. And he said,

VISION VII.

5. וַתֵּצֵא, *came forth*, i. e. came again into view to explain the new vision.

6. The ephah was one of the larger Jewish corn measures, containing about an English bushel, or seven gallons and a half. The LXX. give it simply by τὸ μετρόν. Symm. leaves it untranslated, οἰφί, which presents it pretty much in its Egyptian form, which was ⳙⳘⳘⳘⳘ. Comp. the Arab. وَيْبَة. Some have supposed that it is not to be specifically understood of the measure so called, on the ground that such a measure could not have contained the woman mentioned ver. 7; but the assumption is altogether gratuitous, since there is no necessity for maintaining that the female represented was actually in appearance of the ordinary size. There is equally little foundation for the interpretation of the Targum, that the use of false measures was intended by this item of the vision. עֵינָם, *their eye*, has been variously regarded by different translators and expositors. The LXX., Arab., and Syr., have read עֲוֺנָם, *their iniquity*, which many think much more suited to the connection, but this reading is supported by only one of De Rossi's MSS. It is clear from what Jerome says on the subject, that the text was the same in his day as we have it at present. The latter reading is adopted by Houbigant, Newcome, and others of the same school. That עַיִן signifies *appearance*, or that which presents itself to the *eye*, is fully established by reference to Lev. xiii. 55; Numb. xi. 7; Ezek. i. 4, 7, x. 9; and this signification is appropriately applicable in the present passage. Hengstenberg, taking the word in its primary acceptation, considers the meaning to be that *their eye* was universally set on evil; it was the effort of the whole people to fill up the measure of their sins, and thereby bring upon themselves a full measure of divine punishment. When it is said that the ephah (for this is the nominative to the latter זֹאת, *this is*), was their appearance, the language is metonymical; the container being used for the thing contained, *i. e.* הָרִשְׁעָה, *wickedness*, or idolatry, as further explained, ver. 8.

7. The כִּכָּר contracted for כְּרָרָה, *what is round* or *globular*, from כָּרַר, *to go round*, was the heaviest weight in use among the Hebrews, being equal to 3000 shekels, or, according to Jahn, 125 pounds, English troy weight. Luther renders it here by *centner*, or *hundredweight*; but it is obviously to be taken, not in its strict estimate as a measure, but in its etymological import, as signifying a flat, roundish lump or cake of lead, yet not without some respect to its heaviness, in consideration of the end it was designed to serve — the security of the woman in the vessel over which it was placed. To express the idea of weight it is called אֶבֶן, *a stone*, in the following verse. נִשֵׂאת is the feminine participle in Niphal. זֹאת does not refer to the talent or weight going before, but to אִשָּׁה immediately following, and is equivalent to *there was*. The woman was placed in the ephah in order to be conveyed to Babylon.

8. By רִשְׁעָה in this place is meant idolatry, which was the most flagrant kind of *wickedness* with respect to God, and the fruitful parent of every other

This is wickedness. And he threw her down in the midst of the ephah, and threw the weight of lead on the mouth of it. 9 Then I raised my eyes and looked, and, behold! two women came forth, and the wind was in their wings, for they had wings like the wings of a stork; and they bore away the ephah be- 10 tween earth and heaven. Then I said to the angel who spake 11 with me, Whither are these conveying the ephah? And he said to me, To build for it a house in the land of Shinar; for it shall be set up, and placed there on its own base.

species of iniquity. To mark it more emphatically, the article is prefixed. הָרִשְׁעָה, as used both times, conveys the idea of a forcible action. In the preceding verse the woman is represented as already sitting in the midst of the ephah; the action here described may either be carried back to a period pre- ceding the vision, or it may be intended to indicate what was further done, in order to cause her to occupy a lower position in the vessel, so as to allow of the leaden cover being thrown over her. The latter is the more probable inter- pretation. Jarchi is of opinion that the feminine suffix in פִּיהָ, her mouth, refers to the woman; but it can alone with propriety be referred to the ephah.

9. The two females here mentioned are regarded by Maurer and Hengsten- berg as merely belonging, by way of col- oring, to the symbol as such, two persons being required to carry so large a measure as the ephah. I should rather, however, infer that the Assyrian and Babylonian powers are intended, by which, as instru- ments, God removed idolatry in the per- sons of the apostate Hebrews out of the holy land. By their having the wind in their wings is conveyed the idea of the celerity of their motion. הַחֲסִידָה, the stork, so called from the affection which both the parent bird and her young show to each other. Aq., who frequently gives the etymology of Hebrew words, renders it 'Ερωδίος, in which he is followed by Theod. and Symm. This Greek term is derived from ἔρως, love. The large wings of the stork greatly accelerate its flight, when aided by the wind. In יִתְּשֶׂנָה is an elision of the letter א, the third radi- cal, for וַתִּשֶּׂאנָה, which is found in a great number of MSS. and some of the earliest printed editions.

10. Instead of the defective orthogra- phy מוּבִלוֹת, many MSS. and some edi- tions read in full, מוֹבִילוֹת.

11. אֶרֶץ שִׁנְעָר, the land of Shinar, is rendered in the LXX. γῇ Βαβυλῶνος, and in the Targ. מְדִינַת בָּבֶל, which is the proper interpretation. הֻכַן is to be con- strued with בַּיִת, and הֻנִיחָה with אֵפָה, including the idea of the woman, or of idolatry, of which she was the symbol. To the latter also the affix in מְכֻנָתָהּ belongs.

In this striking hieroglyphic we are taught how idolatry, with all its accom- panying atrocities, was removed from the land of the Hebrews, which it had des- ecrated, to a country devoted to it, and where it was to commingle with its native elements, never to be re-imported into Canaan. How exactly has the pre- diction been fulfilled! From the time of the captivity to the present, a period of more than two thousand years, the Hebrew people have never once lapsed into idolatry! The whole vision was intended to convince them of the great- ness of the evil.

CHAPTER VI.

HAVING warned the Jews against indulging in the evil practices which had occasioned their removal to Babylon, Jehovah now, in another vision, exhibits to their view the warlike and unsettled state of political affairs in the immediate future, during the reigns of Darius, and his successors, 1—8. Most commentators seem to have concurred in the opinion expressed by Munster: " Hæc visio est valde obscura." The symbols are in themselves simple, consisting of four chariots drawn by horses of different colors, which issue from between two mountains of copper, and proceed in different directions with respect to the land of Palestine. That they betoken certain dispensations of Divine Providence, in reference to the nations by which the Jews were immediately surrounded, and by whose fate they were more or less affected, appears to be the most consistent position that can be assumed in interpreting them, especially as such is the application of similar symbols elsewhere in the prophetic records. The colors of the horses denote, as usual, the character of these dispensations, as either calamitous, prosperous, or mixed. Comp. chap. i. 8; Rev. vi.

This vision, which is the last, is followed by a splendid prophecy of the Messiah in his co-ordinate offices of Priest and King, to typify which the symbolical action of making two crowns and placing them upon the head of Joshua, is ordained by Divine authority, 9—15.

1 AND I raised my eyes again, and looked, and, behold! four chariots came forth from between two mountains, and the moun-
2 tains were mountains of copper. In the first chariot were red
3 horses; and in the second chariot black horses; and in the third chariot white horses; and in the fourth chariot were piebald

1. For the idiom וָאָשֻׁב וָאֶשָּׂא, see on ch. iv. 1. Considering that the events referred to are those of war, it is most natural to infer that war-chariots are here intended. By mountains of copper are meant solid, strong and durable mountains, such as those in which copper and other metals are ordinarily found. Comp. Jer. i. 18. Of what these mountains were designed to be the symbols, or whether they are introduced merely as an ornamental part of the vision, have been matters of dispute. I am strongly inclined to regard them as emblems of the Medes and Persians, and thus corresponding to the two horns of the ram which are employed by Daniel to denote the same people. See chap. viii. 3, 4. From between these, or from the powerful empire which they formed, the instruments of Divine Providence were to proceed to execute his purposes in punishing the nations. That mountains are employed in the figurative language of prophecy to signify kingdoms or governments, see Is. ii. 2, xli. 15; Jer. li. 25; Dan. ii. 35.

2, 3. The *red* horses are symbolical of war and bloodshed; the *black*, of general calamity and distress; the *white*, of victory and prosperity; and the *piebald grays*, of a dispensation, mixed in its character, partly prosperous, and partly adverse. The last word, אֲמֻצִּים, would seem most naturally to be referrible to the root אָמֵץ, *to be strong, active*, etc.; and this mode of solution would at once be satisfactory were there no qualifying circumstances in the immediate context to require another interpretation. But as all the other terms here employed in describing the horses are expressive of colors, we should expect something of the same character to be intended by the

4 gray horses. I then proceeded and said to the angel who spake
5 with me, What are these, my lord? And the angel answered
   and said to me, These are the four spirits of heaven, coming
6 forth from presenting themselves before the Lord of the whole
   earth. That and the black horses in it are going forth into the
   north country; and the white go forth to the west of them; and

word in question. I, therefore, prefer adopting a derivation from the Arab. وَمَضَ, *leviter splenduit*, and regard it as qualifying בְּרֻדִּים, immediately preceding. Thus, the Targ. קְטַמְיָן, *ash-colored gray;* so that the most appropriate rendering of the two terms will be *spotted*, or *piebald grays.*

5. Though the phrase אַרְבַּע רוּחוֹת הַשָּׁמַיִם is that employed chap. ii. 10, (Heb.) to denote the four quarters of the horizon, yet, that it cannot have this meaning in the present instance, is evident from its being added that the רוּחוֹת are such as had taken their station, or presented themselves before the Lord, in order to receive their commissions for the execution of his will. In our common version, therefore, the words are properly rendered as to the meaning, *spirits of the heavens;* or, as we now commonly say, *celestial spirits,* thereby meaning angels. These are represented, as in Job i. 6; ii. 1, as employed by God to carry into effect his high behests, which they receive in his immediate presence, and then proceed to the different quarters of the globe in which the special operations of Divine Providence are to be carried forward.

6. By אֶרֶץ צָפוֹן, *the north country,* we are to understand, as usual, the land of Babylon. Comp. Jer. iii. 18, vi. 22, x. 22, xlvi. 10; Zech. ii. 10. Though that empire had been subdued by Cyrus, yet the Babylonians revolted in the beginning of the fifth year of Darius, on which that monarch besieged them with all his forces; and, after much devastation, completely depopulated it, and reduced it to solitude. To set forth symbolically this fearful event, black-colored horses are represented as conveying into the country the executioner of the Divine indignation upon that devoted people. It is remarkable that the red-colored horses, which had been introduced into the vision, ver. 2, are entirely passed over. The reason may, perhaps, be, that, disastrous as was the final destruction of Babylon, it was unaccompanied with anything like the quantity of bloodshed which characterized the battles of conflicting armies in the open field, though at the commencement there was every appearance of much blood being shed. Notwithstanding, therefore, the chariot with the red horses appeared along with the others, it seems to be intimated, by no further notice having been taken of it, that it was not employed. The *white* horses, denoting victory and prosperity, point out the successes of Darius in different parts of Greece, which, though checked by the battle of Marathon, contributed to the strengthening of his power in that quarter. The phrase, אֶל־אַחֲרֵיהֶם, literally means *behind them,* but geographically, *to the west of them.* That it is to be so taken here, the use of אֶל, *to,* corresponding with the use of the same preposition after the verb, both before and after in the verse, sufficiently shows. The dappled horses were symbolical of the varied condition of the Persian affairs, which followed the battle of Marathon, especially the changes which took place on the death of Darius, and the expedition of Xerxes for the reduction of Egypt. This last circumstance is particularly pointed at in the reference, אֶרֶץ הַתֵּימָן, *the country of the South.* That by תֵּימָן, *Teman,* we are not here to understand the city or region so called on the east of Idumea, but a land to the

7 the piebald go forth to the south country. And the grays went forth, and asked to go to walk to and fro through the land; and he said, Go, walk to and fro through the land; and they walked to and fro through the land.

8 Then he summoned me and said to me, See, those that went to the north country have appeased my anger in the north country.

9 And the word of Jehovah was communicated to me, saying:

10 Take from the captivity, from Heldai, from Tobijah, and from

south of Palestine, is obvious from the article being prefixed, and from a comparison of the use of the term in such passages as the following, Job ix. 9; Is. xliii. 6. It is synonymous with יָמִין, on the right hand, which geographically means *the South*, and here specifically signifies Egypt, to express which Daniel uses the word נֶגֶב, chap. xi. 40.

7. הָאָרֶץ, *the land* here referred to, but not described by any qualifying epithet, must be understood of the country of Palestine, the peculiar features of the dispensation of Providence with respect to which are marked by two circumstances: the gray color of the horses, which indicated the mixed state of the Jewish affairs till the time of Artaxerxes Mnemon; and the form of the verb הָלַךְ, *to go* or *walk*, which is in Hithpael, and signifies *to go about*, or *to walk up and down*. They were not to be molested by the hostile incursion of foreign armies, but neither were they to be free from annoyances. Accordingly, we find them involved in troubles by Sanballat, and other chiefs of the Samaritans; and, as the Persian army marched through Palestine to attack the Egyptians in the reign of Darius Nothus, the inhabitants must have been exposed to numerous inconveniences, which they could not but feel the more severely, owing to their having only just begun to take possession of their patrimonial inheritances. On the other hand, the appointment of Nehemiah to be governor of Judea, and other favors conferred by the Persian monarch, were calculated to mitigate

their distress, and inspire them with the hope of a complete and happy restoration to the enjoyment of their ancient privileges. These dappled horses supply the place of the red, specified ver. 2, but are omitted in the explanation, ver. 6, so that the number of chariots is still four.

8. The nominative to וַיַּזְעֵק must either be Jehovah, or the Angel of Jehovah, understood as the pronominal affix in רוּחִי, "*my* anger," shows. That among other significations רוּחַ has that of *anger*, see Jud. viii. 3; Eccles. x. 4; Is. xxxiii. 11. The phrase, הֵנִיחַ רוּחַ, *to cause anger to rest*, is equivalent to הֵנִיחַ חֵמָה, Ezek. v. 13, xvi. 42, xxiv. 13; and means *to satisfy, pacify*. The final judgment having been inflicted upon Babylon, the Divine displeasure should no more be manifested in that direction.

The tendency of the whole vision was to assure the Jews of the care and protection of their covenant God, and thus lead them to exercise confidence in him, while prosecuting the restoration of the temple and their former institutions.

9—11. Here commences a separate prophecy, calculated, like the preceding vision, to stimulate the Jews in their work. That what was commanded was actually performed by the prophet, and that it was not done in vision, seems the only tenable construction that can be put upon it. The infinitive לָקוֹחַ, at the beginning of the 9th verse, is to be taken in connection with the finite form of the same verb at that of the 11th, both having כֶּסֶף וְזָהָב for their object.

Jedaiah, who are come from Babylon, and enter thou on that
11 day, yea, enter the house of Josiah the son of Zephaniah; yea, take silver and gold, and make crowns, and place them upon the head of Joshua, the son of Josedech, the high priest; and speak
12 to him, saying, Thus speaketh Jehovah of hosts, saying:

The preposition which is prefixed to the following nouns is not to be taken partitively, as if *some* of the captivity, and *one* of each of the families, the heads of which are supposed to be here specified, were meant, but is used in its primary and most common signification. The persons named appear to have formed a deputation from the גוֹלָה, *captives* still remaining in Babylon, who had sent them with contributions in gold and silver to help forward the building of the temple at Jerusalem. These deputies had deposited their gifts in the house of Josiah, to which the prophet is commanded to repair and take what was necessary for making the two crowns which were to be placed on the head of the high priest. It is not improbable that Josiah was public treasurer at the time. The language of Zechariah is here more heavy and verbose than usual, which has occasioned some difficulty to interpreters. Instead of בָּאוּ מֵאֵת אֲשֶׁר, two of Kennicott's MSS., the LXX., Syr., and Targ., read בָּא in the singular, and restrict the declaration to Josiah, mentioned immediately before; but there can be little doubt that this various reading is merely an emendation of some copyist, who took Josiah, and not the three persons spoken of at the beginning of the verse, to be the subject of the predicate. To remove the ambiguity, our translators have properly connected the words immediately with the names of the persons to whom they belong. Hengstenberg contends that only *one* crown is intended, and that the plural form עֲטָרוֹת, is to be referred to several small crowns or diadems of which it consisted. With many other interpreters, he adduces in support of the opinion the διαδήματα πολλὰ, *many crowns*, which are described as being upon the head of the Saviour, Rev. xix. 12; but the reference there is purely to the crown of a conqueror, composed of many diadems, which Christ is represented as wearing, as a symbol of the numerous victories he had won over the enemies of his church. It appears, however, essential to the thing signified, namely, the priestly and regal offices, that they should have been distinct crowns, in which case either the one may have been placed upon the head of Joshua after the other, or they may have been joined together so as to form a double crown, and so placed upon his head at once. What favors the latter view of the subject is the circumstance, that the plural עֲטָרוֹת is construed with תִּהְיֶה, the singular of the substantive verb, ver. 14. Maurer not inaptly illustrates this by a reference to the triple crown or the tiara of the popes, by which they arrogate to themselves a higher degree of dignity than that of Him whose servants they profess to be.

12. The symbolical action performed upon Joshua as representative of the Messiah is here followed by an explanatory prophecy, in which his person, offices, and work are distinctly set forth. For the signification of צֶמַח, BRANCH, see on Is. iv. 2. That the Messiah is meant must be evident to all who will impartially compare Is. iv. 2; Jer. xxiii. 5, xxxiii. 15; Zech. iii. 8. Thus the Targ. expounds: הָא גַבְרָא מְשִׁיחָא שְׁמֵהּ עָתִיד דְיִתְגְלֵי, "Behold the Man, MESSIAH is his name; who is to be revealed." The same view is taken by Moses Hadarsan: הגיאל אם־אקים מכם אין לו אב שנ׳ הנה, איש צמח שמו ומתחתיו יצמח, "The Redeemer whom I will raise up from you shall have no father, as it is said; Behold the man, whose name is Zemach,

Behold the man whose name is THE BRANCH,
For he shall grow up out of his place,
And he shall build the temple of Jehovah.
13 Even he shall build the temple of Jehovah,
And he shall bear the glory;

and he shall grow up from his place." The Rabbins Jarchi, Abenezra, and Kimchi, and after them, Bauer and Ewald, suppose Zerubbabel to be intended. The last-mentioned writer, after the example of Eichhorn and Theiner, conjectures that, instead of יְהוֹשֻׁעַ בֶּן־, *on the head of Joshua*, the text has originally read, בְּרֹאשׁ זְרֻבָּבֶל וּבְרֹאשׁ יְהוֹשֻׁעַ, *on the head of Zerubbabel, and on the head of Joshua*. But who does not perceive that this conjecture is to be traced to the mere love of hypothesis. Maurer scruples not to regard it as doing violence to the passage. The application of the words to Zerubbabel is decidedly rejected by Abarbanel, notwithstanding his bigoted hostility to the Messianic interpretations. The words of the text can apply to no one who was not a priest; for it is expressly declared that such was to be the official character of him who is the subject of discourse. And that neither Joshua nor any of his descendants could be meant, is evident from the fact, that they could not exercise the regal power, none of them being entitled to occupy the throne. Simon Maccabæus, to whom Michaelis applies the prophecy, never filled the kingly office; he was merely commander of the army, and civil governor, subject to the kings of Syria. Instead of building the temple, as is here predicted of the Branch, he erected a splendid palace for himself on the mountain on which the temple stood. Nor did the work of repairing it, after it had been pillaged by Antiochus Epiphanes, devolve upon him, but upon his brother Judas. Besides, the declaration that the Branch should be invested with the honor or glory connected with the building of the temple, would be at variance with the uniform ascription of the glory of all great undertakings to Jehovah and not to man, wherever in Scripture such works are represented as carried on under the special direction of the Most High. In the phrase, וּמִתַּחְתָּיו יִצְמָח, *and he shall sprout forth from his place*, while there is a direct reference to the name צֶמַח, here given to the Messiah, there seems to be no very indistinct allusion to the miraculous conception. תַּחְתָּיו, *his place*, the place which was peculiar to him. The interpretation, that "under him there shall be growth," which is adopted by Cyril, Jerome, Luther, Calovius, Hitzig, Maurer, and Ewald, applying it to the church, the body of believers, or the affairs of Messiah's kingdom, is to be rejected on the ground of its not being warranted by Scripture usage. By הֵיכַל יְהוָֹה, *the temple of Jehovah*, which the Messiah was to build, the material temple then in the course of erection cannot be understood, for that was to be carried on and completed by Zerubbabel, chap. iv. 9. But, as we have just seen, Zerubbabel and the Branch are not identical. We are, therefore, compelled to interpret the phrase in application to the New Testament church, which is frequently spoken of as a temple, 1 Cor. iii. 17; 2 Cor. vi. 16; Eph. ii. 22; 2 Thess. ii. 4; and respecting which the Messiah himself declares, "Upon this rock will I build my church, and the gates of hell shall not prevail against it." Matt. xvi. 18.

13. The repetition וְהוּא יִבְנֶה אֶת־הֵיכַל יְהוָֹה is not, as has been conjectured, to be ascribed to an error of some transcriber, and on the authority of the LXX., Arab., and Syr., to be expunged as superfluous, but is singularly in its place, as giving a high degree of emphasis to the statement made respecting the personal work of the Messiah. The

And he shall sit and rule upon his throne,
And shall be a priest upon his throne,
And the counsel of peace shall be between them both.

14 And the crowns shall be for Helem and for Tobijah, and for Jedaiah, and for Hen the son of Zephaniah, for a memorial in

erection of the spiritual temple was to be effected exclusively through his mediation. With the declaration, that he should "bear the glory," compare Ps. xxi. 5, cii. 16; Is. lii. 13; Heb. ii. 9. The declaration has reference to the crowns, the insignia of glory and majesty, which were to be placed on the head of Joshua. In the following clauses of the verse the union of the regal and sacerdotal offices in the person of the Messiah is distinctly set forth, thus exhibiting the peculiar feature of the Melchizedekian priesthood, Gen. xiv. 18; Ps. cx. 4; Heb. v. 6, 10, vi. 20, vii. While our Lord continues to officiate in the heavenly temple as the Great High Priest of his people, ever living to make intercession for them, he exercises his mediatorial rule over the world and the church — that over the former being rendered subservient to the administration of that which he exercises over the latter. Vitringa, Reuss, Dr. McCaul, and others, refer the pronominal affix in בְּכִסְאוֹ, "*his* throne," to Jehovah, or the Deity absolutely considered, but, in my opinion, without sufficient ground. The natural construction requires the person who is prominently before the reader to be the object of reference. The rendering of Newcome, Hitzig, and Ewald, "and a priest shall be upon his throne," is forced and unwarranted; the Vau clearly connecting the substantive verb with the preceding verbs יֵשֵׁב and וּמָשַׁל, the nominative to which is הוּא, the Branch, or Messiah. The nominatives to שְׁנֵיהֶם, "them both," are neither Jehovah and the Messiah, as maintained both by ancient and by many modern interpreters, among others, Cocceius, De Dieu, Vitringa, Bengel, Reuss, Dr. Mc Caul, and Dr. J. Pye Smith; nor Jews

and Gentiles, as Dr. Stonard strangely interprets; but the כְּהֻנָּה, *priesthood*, and the מֶמְשָׁלָה, *regal dignity*, which had just been mentioned as unitedly exercised by the Branch. Thus Jerome, Marckius, Drusius, Lowth, Dathe, Rosenmüller, Hengstenberg, and others. The reason assigned by Dathe forms an insurmountable objection to the first opinion: "Quoniam enim Deus in toto hoc loco loquitur, affixum tertiæ personæ in שְׁנֵיהֶם non potest ad Jovam referre." The same objection lies against the reference of the affix in בְּכִסְאוֹ to Jehovah. By עֲצַת שָׁלוֹם, *the counsel* or *purpose of peace*, is to be understood the glorious scheme of reconciliation between God and man, effected by the joint exercise of the sacerdotal and regal offices of the Lord Jesus Christ. Comp. Is. ix. 6; Micah v. 5; Eph. ii. 14—17; Col. i. 20, 21; Heb. xiii. 20.

14. *Helem* is, in all probability, the same as *Heldia*, ver. 10, and *Hen* another name of *Josiah*, there also mentioned. There seems no ground for rendering חֵן, *favor*, and interpreting it of the hospitality shown to the deputies by Josiah; the construction adopted by Hengstenberg, Maurer and Ewald. The words וְהָעֲטָרֹת תִּהְיֶה לְחֵלֶם, *the crowns shall be to Helem*, etc., do not mean that they were to belong to the persons specified, but that they were to be for a memorial to them of the symbolical act that had just taken place, and were for this purpose to be deposited in the temple, where it is possible they remained till the Messiah, as high priest and king of his people, had taken possession of his mediatorial throne, when temple, and crowns, and the whole Jewish polity, were taken or destroyed by the Romans.

15 the temple of Jehovah. And those who are far off shall come and build in the temple of Jehovah; and ye shall know that Jehovah of hosts hath sent me to you. And it shall come to pass, if ye will diligently obey the voice of Jehovah your God * * * *

15. This verse contains a striking prophecy of the calling of the Gentiles, together with a solemn warning to the Jews, in which, the sentence being left unfinished, their rejection in consequence of unbelief is forcibly implied. It is a striking instance of ἀποσιώπησι.

CHAPTER VII.

This and the following chapter are occupied with replies to questions which had been proposed for solution, relative to certain fasts which the Jews had observed, but which they supposed might no longer be binding after the restoration of their prosperity, 1—3. From this circumstance Zechariah is commanded to take occasion to reprove them for their selfish observance of the days appointed for fasting, 4—7; to enforce attention to the weightier matters of the law. 8—10; and to warn them, by placing before them the rebellious conduct of their fathers, and the punishment with which it had been visited, 11—14.

1 AND it came to pass in the fourth year of Darius the king, that the word of Jehovah was communicated to Zechariah on
2 the fourth day of the ninth month, which is Chislev; when Bethel sent Sherezer, Regem-melech and his men, to conciliate

1. The occurrence here described took place two years later than those described in the preceding chapters. בְּכִסְלֵו, *Chislev,* the name of the ninth month of the Hebrews, which corresponds to part of November and part of December. Some think it is of Persic origin, but the idea of *torpor, rigidity, stiffness,* which is conveyed by the Heb. כָּסַל, is sufficient to justify its being referred to this root; such being the character assumed by nature in the course of this month. The ב prefixed may be regarded as the *Beth essentiæ.*
2. The words וַיִּשְׁלַח בֵּית־אֵל have occasioned considerable perplexity to interpreters. Some of the earlier Jews took *Bethel* to be the name of a person. Lightfoot supposes that it means the congregation of the Jews who had remained in Babylon. To the same effect Michaelis, "The congregation of God at Sharezer," though he acknowledges he had no idea of the geographical position of the city so called. Hengstenberg and Maurer think the people of the Jews are intended. The Vulg., Grotius, Dathe, Newcome, De Wette, and Arnheim, supply אֶל before the word, and render, "to the house of God." The LXX., Syr., Targ., Drusius, Blayney, Hitzig, and Ewald, regard it as the name of the city so called, in the tribe of Benjamin; only the ancient versions just specified repre-

3 the regard of Jehovah, speaking to the priests which were in the house of Jehovah of hosts, and to the prophets, saying: Shall I weep in the fifth month, separating myself as I have done these many years?
4 Then the word of Jehovah of hosts was communicated to me, saying: Speak to all the people of the land, and to the priests,
5 saying, When ye fasted and mourned in the fifth and in the seventh month, even those seventy years, was it at all to me that
6 ye fasted? And when ye ate, and when ye drank, was it not

sent it as the place to which the deputation was sent. Against the interpretation which explains it of the temple, there lies the insuperable objection, that that sacred edifice is uniformly called בֵּית יְהֹוָה, *the house of Jehovah*, — never בֵּית־אֵל, *the house of God;* and that it should have been so designated after the recovery of the Jews from idolatry is altogether incredible, considering the infamy attached to the city so named. I entirely concur in the last opinion, which refers it to the city of Bethel, which is used by metonymy for its inhabitants. The word occupies its proper place as the nominative to the verb, which cannot here be taken impersonally, as such construction would exclude all reference to those who sent the deputation, a circumstance not to be reconciled with the express specification of the names of the persons who composed it. לְחַלּוֹת, lit. *to stroke the face, to ingratiate onself with another, conciliate his regard.*

3. The city having been introduced in the preceding verse as sending the deputation, speaks here in the first person singular. Comp. 1 Sam. x. 10; 2 Sam. xx. 19; Zech. viii. 21. The question related to the continuance of the fast in the *fifth* month, which had been instituted to commemorate the destruction of Jerusalem by the Chaldeans. As the city was now being restored, it was presumed there would no longer be any necessity for keeping up the humiliating memorial. הַאֶבְכֶּה is not simply, *Shall I fast!* but, *Shall I continue to fast!* The following words indicate, that it

was felt to be a tedious and irksome performance of duty. The persons speaking were thoroughly weary of it. הִנָּזֵר, the infinitive in Niphal of נָזַר, *to separate, consecrate, vow;* in Niphal, to *abstain* from food, and the ordinary employments of life.

5, 6. Though the question had been proposed by the leading men of a single city only, yet the burden was generally felt, on which account the prophet is directed to address the Divine reply to all the inhabitants of the land, the priests not excepted, who appear to have been desirous of getting rid of the fast as well as others. Their fasts had not been performed from a purely religious motive, but were self-righteous and hypocritical. While they observed them, they neglected the weightier matters of the law. At צֹמְתֻּנִי is an ellipsis of the finite form of the same verb. In הֲצוֹם צַמְתֻּנִי אָנִי there is a double idiom, which renders it peculiarly emphatic. Not only is the finite form used after the infinitive of the same verb; but the nominative of the personal pronoun is employed after the usual verbal suffix. Comp. Gen. xxvii. 34. בֵּרְכֵנִי גַם אָנִי. The fast in the *seventh* month was in commemoration of the murder of Gedaliah, and those who were with him at Mispah. See 2 Kings xxv. 25, 26; Jer. xli. 1—3. Neither in fasting nor in feasting had the Jews any regard to Jehovah, but did all from self-interested motives. The feasting referred to is that which took place on the festival days, which were always days of rejoicing.

7 ye that ate, and ye that drank? Are not these the words which Jehovah proclaimed by the former prophets, when Jerusalem was inhabited and at peace, and her cities around her, when both the south and the plain were inhabited?

8 And the word of Jehovah was communicated to Zechariah, saying,

9 Thus spake Jehovah of hosts, saying:
Execute true judgment,
And show kindness and mercy one to another;

10 Oppress not the widow and the orphan,
The stranger and the poor;
And think not in your heart of the injury
Which one hath done to another.

11 But they refused to attend,
And turned their back rebelliously;
They made their ears heavy,
That they might not hear.

12 They made their heart an adamant,
That they might not hear the law,
Nor the words which Jehovah sent by his Spirit
Through the former prophets;
And there was great wrath from Jehovah of hosts.

13 And it came to pass,
When he called and they would not hear,
So they called, and I would not hear,
Saith Jehovah of hosts,

---

7. The former prophets had taught the worthlessness of attention to meats and drinks while God was forgotten, and the weightier matters of his law neglected. If the Jews had listened to, and complied with, the messages of the prophets, none of the evils which had come upon them would have been inflicted. For "the former prophets," see on chap. i. 4. By the "south and the plain," are meant the southern and western parts of Judah.

9. אָמַר is here to be taken in the strictly past tense, as the beginning of the 11th verse clearly shows.

10. Though אִישׁ intervenes between רֵעֵהוּ and אָחִיו they are to be regarded as in construction. Comp. Is. xix. 8;

Hos. xiv. 3. No one was to harbor any feelings of resentment against another for any injury he might have done him.

11. נָתַן כָּתֵף, *to give the shoulder*, is equivalent to turning the back upon any one. The cause of such action is traced to a refractory, rebellious, and intractable disposition. The מ prefixed in מִשְּׁמֹעַ is privative.

12. שָׁמִיר signifies both a *thorn* and a *diamond*, from the Arab. ﺷﻤﺮ, *to pierce*. Here the idea of hardness is that conveyed by its use. In בְּיַד הַנְּבִיאִים the double agency by which the Divine will was communicated is recognized — that of the inspiring Spirit, and that of the instruments inspired.

14 But tossed them among all the nations which they knew not,
And the land was desolate after them;
No one passed through or returned,
For they had made the land of delight desolate.

14. אֶפָּרֵם is an anomalous form, after the Aramæan manner, according to which Zēre is placed where there would otherwise be a movable Sheva. Regularly, it would be אֲפָרֵם. It is of the Piel conjugation. אֶרֶץ חֶמְדָּה, *the land of delight*, Canaan. Comp. Jer. iii. 19. Maurer proposes to take וַיְשַׁמּוּ impersonally. Others more properly consider the Jews to be the nominative, who by their crimes, had brought judgments upon the land.

CHAPTER VIII.

THIS chapter is a continuation of the subject introduced and treated of in the preceding. Having shown the awful consequences of disregarding the Divine will, which had been clearly announced by the prophets, God promises the renewal of his favor towards those who had returned from the captivity. Restored to purity, 3, Jerusalem should enjoy security and prosperity to a degree far exceeding the conceptions of those whom the prophet addressed, 4—6. Those who were still in heathen countries should be brought back, and share in the general prosperity, 7—17 The chapter closes with a direct answer to the question relating to the fasts, and a prediction of the great number of proselytes that should be made to the true religion by the display of the Divine goodness towards the Jews, 18—23.

1 AND the word of Jehovah was communicated to me, saying:
2 Thus saith Jehovah of hosts:
I have been zealous for Zion with great zeal,
Yea, with great indignation have I been zealous for her.
3 Thus saith Jehovah, I am returned to Zion,
And will dwell in the midst of Jerusalem;
And Jerusalem shall be called, The city of truth,
And the mountain of Jehovah of hosts, The holy mountain.
4 Thus saith Jehovah of hosts:

1. Before לֵאמֹר the word אֵלַי, *to me*, is found in thirty-three Heb. MSS.; it has been in ten more originally, and is now in three by correction; it is the reading of the Soncin., Brixian, and Complutensian editions, and is supported by the Syr. and Targ.

2. Comp. i. 14, 15.
3. Comp. Is. i. 26, and the remarks there made on the idiomatic use of קָרָא, *to call*.
4, 5. These verses beautifully depict the security and happiness of the inhabitants of Jerusalem. Longevity and a

Aged men and aged women shall yet be sitting in the streets
   of Jerusalem,
   Each man with his staff in his hand for very age;
5 And the streets of the city shall be filled
   With boys and girls, playing in the streets of it.
6 Thus saith Jehovah of hosts:
   Though it should be wonderful
   In the eyes of the remnant of this people in those days,
   Should it also be wonderful in my eyes?
   Saith Jehovah of hosts.
7 Thus saith Jehovah of hosts:
   Behold, I will deliver my people
   From the land of the rising,
   And from the land of the setting of the sun,
8 And I will bring them, and they shall dwell in the midst of
   Jerusalem,
   And they shall become my people,
   And I will become their God,
   In truth and in righteousness.
9 Thus saith Jehovah of hosts:

numerous offspring were specially promised under the old dispensation, but uniformly in connection with obedience to the law. Deut. iv. 40, v. 16, 33, vi. 2, xxxiii. 6, 24; Is. lxv. 20. The idea conveyed by מְשַׂחֲקִים in such connection is exquisite. What can be more gratifying to the uncorrupted simplicity of human feelings, than to witness a number of young children enjoying their innocent gambols? For a contrary state of things, see Jer. vi. 11, ix. 21.

6. פָּלָא, though like its cognate פָּלָה, is not used in Kal, yet, from its significations in Niphal, Piel, Hiphal, and Hithpael, it cannot be doubted that it must have conveyed the idea of *separation, distinction, difficulty;* hence in Niphal, it signifies *to be distinguished, to stand out prominently,* from common events, to be *impossible* to human power, to be *miraculous.* נִפְלָאוֹת, the participial noun, is often used for miraculous occurrences. בַּיָּמִים הָהֵם, *in those days,* i. e. at the time when I fulfil my promise. To justify the rendering of our common version,

"in *these* days," the Hebrew should have been בַּיָּמִים הָאֵלֶּה. See ver. 9.

7. The east and west are here put as parts for the whole. The meaning is, I will deliver my people from every region whither they have been scattered. Were there any reason to believe that the prophecy has respect to a restoration of the Jews yet future, there would be a singular propriety in the use of מִבוֹא, הַשֶּׁמֶשׁ, *the setting of the sun,* the Jews being now, for the most part, found in countries to the west of Jerusalem; but there is every reason to conclude that it has an exclusive reference to what was to take place soon after it was delivered. Vast numbers were carried away captive after the time of Alexander. Not fewer than 100,000 were carried by Ptolemy to Egypt, and were settled in Alexandria and Cyrene.

The words בֶּאֱמֶת וּבִצְדָקָה belong to both the members of the sentence, and express the reality and sincerity of the relation on both sides.

9. תֶּחֱזַקְנָה יְדֵיכֶם, *let your hands be*

Let your hands be strong,
Ye that hear in these days
These words from the mouth of the prophets,
Which were spoken on the day when the foundation was laid
Of the house of Jehovah of hosts,
The temple, in order to its being built
10 For before those days
There was no hire for man,
Neither was there any hire for beast;
And to him that went out or came in
There was no peace, because of the enemy:
Yea, I sent all men each against another.
11 But now I will not be as in the former days
To the residue of this people,
Saith Jehovah of hosts.
12 For the seed shall be prosperous,
The vine shall yield her fruit,
And the earth shall yield her produce,
And the heavens shall yield their dew,
And I will cause the residue of this people
To possess all these things.
13 And it shall come to pass,
As ye have been a curse among the nations,
O house of Judah, and house of Israel,

strong, a figurative mode of expression, denoting, *courage, resolution, effort.* Jud. vii. 11; 2 Sam. xvi. 21. The prophets here referred to were Haggai and Zechariah. See Ezra v. 1, 2. The words which the people heard were those of consolation and encouragement. Haggai ii. 18, 19. After אֲשֶׁר subaud. דִּבְרֵי.

. 10. Such was the danger to which the Jews were exposed before the actual commencement of building the temple, that all intercourse between the city and the country was interrupted. The Samaritans pressed sore upon them, and annoyed them in every possible way. See Ezra iv. 1—5. By צַר is not meant *affliction*, θλίψις, *tribulatio*, as the Eng., LXX., and Vulg.; but the *enemy*, or as we have it, צָרֵי יְהוּדָה וּבִנְיָמִין, *the enemies of Judah and Benjamin*, Ezra iv. 1

In the last clause of the verse reference is had to the intestine broils and contentions which prevailed.

11, 12. וְעַתָּה stands forcibly in contrast with לִפְנֵי at the beginning of the preceding verse. The providence of God brought about a complete change in the circumstances of the Jews who had returned. As they obeyed his voice and prosecuted his work, he gave them outward tranquillity, and prospered their agricultural pursuits. After זֶרַע הַשָּׁלוֹם, *the seed of prosperity*, i. e. healthy, prosperous seed, such as would not fail, supply יִהְיֶה, *there shall be.* Their fields should not be trodden down by the enemy, nor suffer from drought, mildew, locusts, and other calamities.

13. By the Jews being a curse and a blessing, is not meant that they were the

So I will deliver you, and ye shall be a blessing:
Fear not, let your hands be strong.
14 For thus saith Jehovah of hosts:
As I purposed to afflict you,
When your fathers provoked me to wrath,
Saith Jehovah of hosts, and I repented not;
15 So again I have purposed, in these days,
To do good to Jerusalem and the house of Judah:
Fear ye not.
16 These are the things which ye shall do:
Speak truth one to another;
Execute true and sound judgment in your gates.
17 And think not in your hearts of the injury
Which one hath done to another;
And love not the false oath;
For all these are things that I hate,
Saith Jehovah.
18 And the word of Jehovah of hosts was communicated to me,
19 saying, Thus saith Jehovah of hosts: The fast of the fourth month, and the fast of the fifth, and the fast of the seventh, and the fast of the tenth, shall become joy and gladness to the

instruments of communicating either evil or good to the nations, but that they themselves experienced either the one or the other. They were subjects of the curse and the blessing. "The house of Israel," or the ten tribes, as distinguished from "the house of Judah," shared in the happy fulfilment of the prophecy. It follows, that they also returned to Palestine, בַּיָּמִים הָאֵלֶּה, in the very days to which it refers. All attempts to discover them at more recent periods have proved utterly fruitless; and the idea that they must still exist somewhere in the world, and are still to be restored in their tribal state, has arisen from a misconstruction of those prophecies which refer to the return from Babylon.

14, 15. An amplification of what had been stated in the preceding verse.

16, 17. These verses contain a virtual and instructive reply to the question relative to the celebration of the fast, chap. vii. 3. It was not in such merely external, ritual, or ceremonial observances that Jehovah delighted, but in the love and practice of moral rectitude. The "gate" was, and still is, the forum in the East. מִשְׁפַּט שָׁלוֹם means *sound, wholesome judgment*. אִישׁ, in ver. 17, is wanting in three MSS., originally in two more, and now by correction in one; in the LXX. Syr. and Arab.

19. Now follows a formal reply to the question just referred to. The fast of the *fourth* month was on account of the taking of Jerusalem, Jer. xxxix. 2, lii. 5—7; that of the *tenth* was in commemoration of the commencement of the siege, Jer. lii. 4. For the other two fasts, see on chap. vii. 3 and 5. The Jews are distinctly informed that these fasts should be turned into festivals of joy. The ו in וְהָיְתָה is adversative, having the force of — but in order that ye may enjoy the predicted and promised blessing, see that ye be sincere before me, and live in harmony among yourselves.

house of Judah, even cheerful festivals; but love ye truth and
20 peace. Thus saith Jehovah of hosts:
21   There shall yet come people,
    And the inhabitants of many cities,
    And the inhabitants of one shall go to another, saying,
    Let us go speedily to conciliate the regard of Jehovah,
    And to seek Jehovah of hosts:
    I will go, even I also.
22 Yea, many people and mighty nations shall come
    To seek Jehovah of hosts in Jerusalem,
    And to conciliate the regard of Jehovah.
23   Thus saith Jehovah of hosts:
    In those days ten men,
    Out of all the nations,
    Shall take hold, shall even take hold

20. The prophecy concludes with the announcement that, in consequence of the distinguished favor shown to the Jewish people after their restoration to their own land, multitudes of Gentiles should be induced to embrace the worship of Jehovah. Just before the appearance of Christ, the heathen began powerfully to feel the emptiness of their false religions, and the unsatisfactoriness of their systems of philosophy, and many of them, who were brought into contact with the people of God, found in their religion, with all its imperfections, a satisfaction which they had sought in vain from any other quarter. It is evident, from various parts of the Acts of the Apostles, that proselytes were numerous in their day. Between לְ and אֶל, supply יְהִי. Two MSS., the LXX. and Arab. read רַבִּים, *many*, after עַמִּים, which in all probability existed originally in the text.

21. The second אַחַת is equivalent to אֶחָת. Comp. Exod. xvii. 12, xviii. 4.

23. אִישׁ is redundant. *Ten* is put as a round number, or a definite for an indefinite, but indicating many rather than few. Comp. Gen. xxxi. 7; Mic. v. 5. מִכֹּל לְשֹׁנוֹת הַגּוֹיִם, *of all the languages of the nations*, means, of all the nations speaking different languages. Comp.

כָּל־הַגּוֹיִם וְהַלְּשֹׁנוֹת, *all the nations and the languages*, Is. lxvi. 18. See also Gen. x. 5, 20; Dan. iii. 7; Rev. v. 9, vii. 9, xiii. 7. *To take hold of the skirt*, is not intended to convey the idea of entreaty, or the gesture of application for assistance, but is significant of a feeling of inferiority, and a desire to enjoy the happy privileges possessed by another. The Gentile nations would be anxious to participate in the blessings of the theocracy. The repetition of the verb יַחֲזִיקוּ is emphatic. אִישׁ יְהוּדִי, *a man, a Jew*, is merely a periphrasis for *a Jew*. Comp. ἀνὴρ Ἰουδαῖος, Acts x. 28. The prophecy is generally regarded as having respect to something yet future, and is often interpreted of the instrumentality of the Jews when converted in effecting the conversion of the world. I can find no such reference in the passage. "Jerusalem" cannot be understood otherwise than literally, just as the term "Jew" is to be so understood; but, according to our Lord's doctrine respecting the New Dispensation, that city is no longer the place where men are exclusively to worship the Father, John iv. 21—23. Incense and a pure offering are now presented to his name in every place where his people assemble in the name of Jesus

Of the skirt of a Jew, saying,
We will go with you;
For we have heard that God is with you.

end with a view to his glory, Mal. i. 10, 11. It was otherwise before the advent of Christ. Jerusalem was the place which Jehovah had chosen to put his name there, and thither all his true worshippers were expected to come to the great festivals, in whatever country they might reside. Thus, the treasurer of Candace went all the way from Abyssinia, Acts viii. 27; and thus numbers from all parts of the Roman empire assembled in that city at the first Pentecost after our Saviour's resurrection. As the Hellenistic Jews and the Gentile proselytes travelled along in companies, they could not but excite the curiosity of the pagans through whose countries and cities they passed; and celebrated as the metropolis of Judea had become for the favors conferred upon it by some of the greatest monarchs of the times immediately gone by, and for the prosperity and warlike prowess of the Jewish people, it was impossible that it should not attract the attention of the surrounding nations to the character and claims of the God who was there adored, and who accorded such blessings to his worshippers.

CHAPTER IX.

For the arguments in opposition to, and those in favor of, the authenticity of that portion of the book of Zechariah which begins with this chapter, and comprises it and the remaining chapters, see the Preface.

Having in prophetic vision exhibited some of the more remarkable events connected with the continued rule of the Persians, Zechariah now proceeds to predict those which were to take place under that of the Greeks, during the military expeditions of Alexander and his successors, in so far as they had a bearing upon the affairs of the Jews. He describes the conquest of Syria after the battle of Issus, 1; and the progress of the army of Alexander along the coast of the Mediterranean, involving the capture of the principal cities of the Phœnicians and Philistines, but leaving the Jews unmolested, through the protecting care of Jehovah, 2—8. He then contrasts with the character and military achievements of that conqueror the qualities which should distinguish the Messiah and his kingdom, whom he expressly predicts, 9, 10. After which he resumes the thread of his historical discourse, and describes the wars of the Maccabees with Antiochus Epiphanes, and the victory and prosperity with which they were followed, 11—17.

1 THE sentence of the word of Jehovah,
Against the land of Hadrach,

1. For the signification of מַשָּׂא, see on Is. xiii. 1. The combination מַשָּׂא דְבַר־יְהֹוָה, occurs only here, chap. xii. 1, and Mal. i. 1. As דָּבָר occurs in the sense of *oracle*, and מַשָּׂא signifies what is taken up and uttered by the voice, the

And Damascus shall be its resting place,
When towards Jehovah shall be the eye of man,
And of all the tribes of Israel.

phrase might be rendered, *The announcement of the oracle of Jehovah;* but it is better for the sake of uniformity to retain the term *sentence,* which I have adopted in my translation of Isaiah. With respect to חַדְרָךְ, *Hadrach,* it is uncertain whether it was intended to denote a country, a city, or a king. The last is the most probable, on the ground that it is not likely that the name either of a country or its metropolis, in a region near Damascus, would have entirely disappeared from the pages of history. But no such name has been found in any Arabic work either of history or geography. Joseph Abassus, indeed, a native of that country, informed Michaelis that there was a place so called at the distance of some miles from Damascus; that it was now of small consequence, but had once been a city of great celebrity; but there is every reason to believe that if he did not intend to impose upon his learned interrogator, the place he had in view was אֶדְרֶעִי, in Arabic ادرعات, called by Eusebius Ἀδραά, and by Ptolemy Ἄδρα. It lay about thirty miles from Damascus. The same remark applies to the statement of Rabbi Jose, mentioned by Kimchi in his Comm. on this verse, that he was from Damascus, and that there was a place there, of which the name was Hadrach. The Rabbins consider the term to be a compound appellative of the Messiah, who was to be חַד, *sharp* or *severe* towards the Gentiles, but רַךְ, *tender* towards Israel! Hengstenberg, who treats on the subject at large in his Christology, vol. ii. pp. 69—77, Keith's Translation, denies that it is a proper name at all, and regards it as a symbolical appellation of the Persian empire, which he thinks Zechariah would not designate by its proper name for fear of offending the government under which he lived. His reasoning in support of his hypothesis is very unsatisfactory, and his construction of לֵב קָמָי, Jer. li. 1, is perfectly ridiculous. I am compelled to acquiesce in the opinion, that a king of this name is meant, as the most probable of those that have been advanced, especially as the phrase, "the land of a king," is not without example in Scripture; see Neh. ix. 22; and very much suspect that the word הַדְרָךְ, *Hadrach,* is after all only a corruption of הֲדַד, the common name of the kings of Syria, though such corruption must have taken place at a very early period, for it was found in the copy from which the version of the LXX. was made. The affix in מְנֻחָתֹה is רָבָר in the preceding hemistich. Damascus was to be the place in which the Divine word or sentence was to rest or settle; in other words, where the threatened punishment would permanently be inflicted. That ancient city was taken by Alexander the Great after the battle at Issus, and formed part of the kingdom of the Seleucidæ, from whom it passed into the hands of the Romans. The native rule, which thus ceased on the Greek conquest, was never afterwards recovered. Several commentators, following the ancient versions, render the words, כִּי לַיהוָֹה עֵין אָדָם וְכֹל שִׁבְטֵי יִשְׂרָאֵל, *for the eye of Jehovah is upon men and all the tribes of Israel,* and explain them with reference to the universal judgments which the providence of God had brought or would bring upon the people in and around Palestine. But it is more natural to regard עֵין in construction with אָדָם וגו׳, The reference will then be to the effect produced upon the minds of others as well as of the Israelites, by the success and progress of the army of Alexander. Apprehensive of danger, they should be compelled to look to Jehovah alone for deliverance. When Alexander threat-

2 Hamath also which is contiguous to it;
   Tyre and Zidon, though she be very wise.
3 Yea, though Tyre hath built a fortress for herself,
   And heaped up silver as dust,
   And fine gold as the mud of the streets;
4 Behold, Jehovah will dispossess her,
   And strike her wealth into the sea,
   And she herself shall be burned with fire.
5 Askelon shall see it and be afraid;
   Gaza also, and shall be in great pain;

ened to punish the Jews on account of the refusal of Jaddua the high priest to swear fealty to him, they were thrown into the greatest consternation, and offered many sacrifices and prayers to God for deliverance. כִּי is here used as a particle of time.

2. *Hamath* was the capital of a kingdom of the same name, which lay between Zobah and Rehob, and to the north of Damascus. It was called by the Greeks Epiphania, but is now known by its ancient name, which it has all along retained among the natives. That the kingdom was conterminous to that of which Damascus was the metropolis is here expressed by תִּגְבָּל־בָּהּ, the feminine affix referring to אֶרֶץ, *land*, in the preceding verse. The whole of Syria was subjugated by the Greeks, or submitted to Alexander. *Tyre* and *Zidon*, which lay directly in the way of that monarch, as he marched along the coast of the Mediterranean towards Egypt, are next mentioned. See on Is. xxiii. The latter city voluntarily surrendered, and had Abdolonymus appointed as viceroy. Though originally the chief of all the Phœnician cities, and the mother of many colonies, yet at the time here referred to, she had become far inferior to Tyre, and quite sunk in comparison with her; on which account the predicate חָכְמָה מְאֹד, *she is very wise*, though, in point of position, it might seem to belong to צִידוֹן, *Zidon*, is nevertheless to be referred to צֹר, *Tyre*, as the more important of the two cities. The Tyrians,

who had long been celebrated for their worldly wisdom, Ezek. xxviii. 3, 4, 5, 12, 17, gave a specimen of it on the approach of the Grecian monarch. On his intimating that he wished to offer sacrifice in the temple of Hercules, they replied that the ancient and true temple of that god was at Old Tyre on the continent, and sent him a crown of gold in testimony of their respect for so great a conqueror; hoping by these means to induce him to pass on without visiting their island.

3. This verse is graphically descriptive of the insular and strongly fortified position of New Tyre, at the distance of seven hundred paces from the shore, and of the immense stores of wealth which it contained as the great emporium of Phœnician commerce. Ezek. xxvii.

4. Instead of אֲדֹנָי, many MSS., and some of them the best of the Spanish, read יְהֹוָה, which I have adopted as the true lection. Here is set forth the conquest of Tyre by Alexander, who constructed a causeway with the rubbish of Old Tyre from the shore to the island, and after a siege of seven months took the city by storm, put eight thousand of the inhabitants, who had not taken flight to Carthage, to the sword, sold thirteen thousand into slavery, crucified two thousand, and after plundering the city, burnt it to ashes. Jahn's Heb. Commonwealth, sect. 70.

5. It may easily be imagined what terror the news of the fall of Tyre must have struck into the inhabitants of the

And Ekron, because her expectation hath made her ashamed;
The king shall perish from Gaza,
And Askelon shall not be inhabited.
6 A foreigner shall sit as ruler in Ashdod,
And I will cut off the pride of the Philistines.
7 I will remove his blood from his mouth,
And his abominations from between his teeth;
And he, even he, shall be left for our God,
And shall be as a prince in Judah,
And Ekron shall be as a Jebusite.

cities further along the coast southward, who knew the destination and route of the victorious army. The prophet accordingly precedes the march of the conqueror from Phœnicia into Philistia. The principal cities of the Philistines are here enumerated. *Gath* only is omitted, owing, probably, to its being farther inland, and thus lying somewhat out of the route of the army. For *Ashkelon*, see on Amos i. 8. For *Gaza* and *Ekron*, on Amos i. 6. Ekron, lying farthest north of these cities, is represented as exercising confidence in Tyre. While that city withstood the attack, she might expect Alexander to be arrested in his course, and hope that he would give up his plan of invading Egypt. But when it fell, her hopes were gone. History is silent respecting the fate of these cities on occasion of the present expedition, but of Gaza it is recorded, that it resisted, and was captured after a siege of two months. Not fewer than ten thousand of the inhabitants were put to death, and the rest were sold into slavery. Betis, the commander or governor of the city, was bound to a chariot with thongs thrust through the soles of his feet, and in this manner dragged around the city. It is not improbable, that it is specially to this circumstance that the words מֶלֶךְ מֵעַזָּה אָבַד, *the king shall perish from Gaza*, refer. The title of king is frequently used in Scripture in a subordinate sense, to denote any chief ruler or governor. See Gen. xiv. 2.

6. For *Ashdod*, see on Amos i. 8. The word מַמְזֵר, which occurs only here and Deut. xxiii. 2, has been considered of uncertain etymology. Lee thinks it may probably be a compound of מִן, *from*, עַם, *a people*, and זָר, *a foreigner;* but this conjecture, however ingenious, is not warranted by Hebrew usage. In Deut. the LXX. render it by ἐκ πόρνης, *one born of a whore*, but ἀλλογενεῖς, *a different race or people*, best suits both passages. See Blayney. According to the form, it must be regarded as the Hiphil participle of מָזַר, a root not occurring in the Hebrew Scriptures, but signifying in more modern Hebrew, *to mix*. Comp. the Arab. مذر, *corruptus fuit*. Hengstenberg renders, *rabble*. By גְאוֹן, *the pride* of the Philistines, we are to understand the splendor of their cities, especially of their temples.

7. This verse contains a prediction of the future conversion of the Philistines to the knowledge and service of the true God. The pronominal affix ו refers to מַמְזֵר, the foreign prince, as does הוּא, *he*, further on in the verse. Their abandonment of idolatry, and their embracing the true religion, is represented by their no longer drinking blood, and eating things sacrificed to idols, both of which were common among the pagans, but prohibited by the Mosaic law, Numb. xxv. 2; Lev. vii. 26, xvii. 10, 12; and by the apostles, Acts xv. 29. It is implied that what the ruler did, would be done by the citizens subject to his power. He was to belong to God, as one who had

8 And I will encamp about my house because of the army,
Both when it passeth through, and when it returneth;
And no oppressor shall pass through them any more.
For now do I look with mine eyes.
9 Rejoice greatly, O daughter of Zion!
Shout aloud, O daughter of Jerusalem!
Behold thy King will come to thee;
Righteous, and having salvation,

joined himself to him by an act of self-dedication. Comp. Is. xliv. 5, lvi. 3. On his becoming a Jewish proselyte, he should be regarded as sustaining the dignity of one of the princes of Judah; no distinction should exist between them. The same idea is expressed in the parallel clause. The Jebusites were the original inhabitants of Jerusalem, who, on their subjugation by David, were incorporated among the Jews, and enjoyed their privileges. 2 Sam. xxiv. 16, etc.

8. For צָבָא, the Keri has the proper orthography צָבָא, *a host*, or *army*. Jehovah here promises to afford protection to the Jews (called, as in Hos. viii. 1, בֵּית יְהֹוָה, *the house of Jehovah*). They were not to be injured by the army of Alexander, either on its march to or from Egypt, a promise which was fulfilled to the letter; for while that monarch punished the Samaritans, he showed great favor to the Jews. Nor was any foreign oppressor to invade their land, as the Assyrians and Chaldeans had done, during the period which was to intervene before the advent of the Messiah, predicted in the verse immediately following. They were, indeed, subject to much suffering, both from the Egyptian and the Syrian kings, especially from Antiochus Epiphanes, but their nationality was not destroyed, and the evils to which they were exposed only paved the way for the Maccabean victories, and the establishment of the Asmonean dynasty. For this preservation they were indebted to the providence of God which watched over them for good. This is emphatically expressed in the last clause of the verse.

9. From the great Grecian conqueror, and the temporal protection which Jehovah would accord to his people, the prophet abruptly, and in the most sublime and animated strain, calls the attention of the Jews to a Royal Personage of a very different character, the MESSIAH, meek and righteous, the Prince and pattern of peace, and the Author of spiritual salvation to all his subjects. His advent was to be accompanied by such glorious results, that it was to be hailed with the most joyful anticipation. That the subject of the prophecy is the Messiah, is not only established by the inspired authority of the Evangelist Matthew, chap. xxi. 4, but has the suffrages of all the early Jewish authorities. It was not till the twelfth century that it was otherwise interpreted. Thus the Book of Zohar: ובגינה אתמר על משיח עני ורוכב על חמור. "On this account it is said of Messiah, Lowly and riding upon an ass;" a statement which is repeated in the same work. The same construction is put upon the passage by Joshua Ben Levi, Saadias Gaon, and others. The testimonies will be found in Wetstein on Matt. xxi. 4, who says in reference to them: "Magno consensu Judæi dictum Zachariæ de Messia interpretantur." And Solomon Jarchi has the ingenuousness to acknowledge, אי אפשר לפותרו אלא על המשיח, that "it is impossible to interpret it of any other than the Messiah." Of Him as the king of Zion it is predicted that he should be צַדִּיק, *righteous*, a quality frequently ascribed to him in the Old Testament. See Is. xlv. 21, liii. 11; Jer. xxiii. 5,

Lowly, and riding upon an ass,
Even upon a colt the foal of an ass.

xxxiii. 15; Mal. iv. 2. With respect to נֹושָׁע, or, as it is pointed in some copies, נוֹשָׁע, of which Kimchi approves, on the ground of its being the preterite converted into the future by the ו conversive, most modern commentators construe it as strictly passive in signification, and the more orthodox interpret it with reference to Christ's deliverance from the grave, after his sufferings upon the cross, rendering the passage, "righteous and saved." But to such construction it must be objected, first, that the passive signification does not suit the connection. If the people had been the nominative to the verb, this signification would have been admissible; but it is the king who is here described, and to speak of him as saved or delivered without any reference to previous danger or suffering, would be most inappropriate. There is, therefore, a real *exigentia loci:* the context imperatively requires the verb to be understood in an active sense. Secondly, though the usual signification of Niphal is passive, yet there are numerous instances in which verbs of that conjugation have a reflexive signification, which represent the agent as showing himself possessed of the quality of the action, or in which the signification is purely active, especially verbs, which are not used in Kal. Thus נֶאְדָּר, *to show one's self glorious;* נִכְבַּד, *to show one's self obstinate, to murmur, complain;* נִבָּא, *to prophecy;* נִכְסַף, *to desire greatly;* נִקְרַב, *to approach;* נִשְׁבַּע, *to swear;* נִשְׁמַע, *to obey,* show one's self obedient; נִשְׁעַן, *to lean,* etc. And thus in the present case נוֹשָׁע, *showing himself a Saviour, having salvation, saving, a Saviour.* Thirdly, that the verb is so to be interpreted here the combination of the term with צַדִּיק, *righteous,* clearly shows; for it occupies the same position in relation to that adjective, which the active participle רֹכֵב, *riding,* does to עָנִי, *lowly,* in the following clause of the verse. As

in the latter case the Messiah's riding upon an ass was a proof or manifestation of his humility, so, in the former, his actually having salvation for others was a manifestation of his possessing that righteousness which was indispensable for the justification of the guilty. See 1 Cor. i. 30; 2 Cor. v. 21; Phil. iii. 8, 9; 1 John ii. 2. As the one feature contrasted with the haughty character of the Grecian conqueror, so the other contrasted with the cruelties that were inflicted by him on the cities which he captured. The Son of Man came not to destroy men's lives, but to save them. Fourthly, all the ancient versions render the verb actively. LXX. σώζων, Targ. פָּרִיק, Syr. ܦܳܪܽܘܩܳܐ, Vulg. *Salvator.* That עָנִי, is here to be taken in the sense of *meek, lowly,* and not in that of *poor,* or *afflicted,* the connection sufficiently shows. Thus the LXX. πραΰς. In proof of the mild and gentle character of the Messiah's reign, he is represented as riding upon an ass, which, though not in the East the degraded and despised animal which it is with us, being used by princes and other persons of rank, is nevertheless comparatively so as regards the horse, and specially contrasts with the war-horse in the following verse. It was proverbially the symbol of peace, so that what the prophet here describes was at once calculated to inspire the mind with the conviction that the King of whom he spake was none other than the Prince of Peace, predicted Is. ix. 6. The ו in וְעַל עַיִר, "*and upon a colt,*" is exegetical of the preceding. Comp. Gen. xlix. 11. אֲתֹנוֹת, *she-asses,* docs not, as Michaelis would have it, convey the idea of the pedigree of the colt, as one of excellent breed, whose mothers could be traced back through several generations, but is merely an idiomatic form, the plural being used for the singular. Comp. הַרְרֵי אֲרָרָט, *mountains, of Ara-*

10 And I will cut off the chariots from Ephraim,
And the horse from Jerusalem;
The battle-bow also shall be cut off;
And he shall speak peace to the nations;
And his rule shall be from sea to sea,
And from the river to the ends of the earth.
11   As for thee also, by the blood of thy covenant,
I will send forth thy prisoners out of the pit

rat, i. e. *one* of the mountains, etc., Gen. viii. 4. עָרֵי גִלְעָד, *cities of Gilead*, i. e. one of them, Jud. xii. 7. For the fulfilment of the prophecy, see Matt. xxi. 4, and the Commentators on that passage.

10. This verse contains a distinct announcement of the nature and extent of the Messiah's reign. Instead of leading forth the Jews to battle and conquest, as their Rabbins have long taught them to believe, he was in his providence completely to disarm them, and render them incapable of engaging in hostile conflict. How literally this was accomplished their history subsequent to the destruction of Jerusalem by the Romans convincingly shows. The reign of the Messiah was not to be that of a worldly conqueror, like Alexander, nor was it to be confined, as to its boundaries, within the narrow limits of Palestine; but it was to be that under which the inestimable blessing of peace was preëminently to be enjoyed; it was to embrace the Gentiles, who had been excluded from the commonwealth of Israel; and, in point of extent, was to cover a vastly greater portion of territory than ever was possessed by the warrior of Macedon. On the circumstance that *Ephraim* is here mentioned, no valid argument can be built in favor of the hypothesis that this prophecy must have been delivered before the captivity of the ten tribes, since it is evidently the design of the prophet merely to describe the whole land of Canaan, the northern part of which still went by the ancient name, in contradistinction from *Judah*, which is here designated from Jerusalem, the capital. דִּבֶּר שָׁלוֹם, *to speak peace*, means to announce the message of the reconciliation effected by the Messiah. From the express inclusion of the גּוֹיִם, *nations*, among those who were to enjoy the benefits of the spiritual reign of the King of Zion, it is manifest that whatever may have been the originally restricted sense of מִיָּם עַד־יָם וּמִנָּהָר עַד־אַפְסֵי־אָרֶץ, as descriptive of the utmost bounds of the Hebrew kingdom, the words must here be taken in the widest possible extent of meaning, just as in Ps. lxxii. 8, where it is declared in the connection, that *all nations* should serve the Messiah.

11. Having been led by his predictions respecting the expedition of Alexander in the direction of Egypt, to exhibit in boldest contrast the character and reign of the Prince of Peace, Zechariah returns to the subject which he had in hand — the state of the Jewish people in the times succeeding the captivity in Babylon. גַּם, *also*, connects what follows with verses 6—8. The feminine pronoun אַתְּ refers to בַּת־צִיּוֹן, or בַּת־יְרוּשָׁלָ͏ִם, ver. 9. The covenant here called בְּרִיתֵךְ, *thy covenant*, means the covenant made with the Hebrews at Sinai, and ratified by the sprinkling of the blood of the victims slain upon the occasion. By that act the nation was consecrated as a peculiar people to Jehovah, and taken under his special protection. The covenant is called theirs, because it had their government and happiness for its object. In virtue of the blood then shed, it is here declared that their covenant God would release such

In which there is no water.
12 Return ye to the strong-hold, ye prisoners of hope,
   Even to-day I declare I will render to thee double;
13 For I have bent Judah for myself,
   I have filled the bow with Ephraim,
   And raised up thy sons, O Zion!
   Against thy sons, O Greece!
   And made thee as the sword of a hero.

of them as were still captives in foreign lands. By אֲסִירֵי is meant, not prisoners whom the Jews had taken, but such of their own nation as were in the condition just described. After the death of Alexander many thousands of Jews were in a state of exile in Egypt, and many thousands more in that of actual slavery in Greece and other parts of the East. Their condition is described as that of prisoners confined in dungeons, which were commonly cisterns without water. See Jer. xxxviii. 6; Gen. xxxvii. 24. In consequence of the mud which remained in them, they were exceedingly noxious to health, and those consigned to them were considered as subjects of the deepest misery. בִּלַּחְתִּי is not here the proper preterite, as some interpreters construe it, but the prophetic future, which is thrown into the form of the preterite to express the certainty of the event.

12. With the Divine promise of release is connected the duty of the captives to embrace the opportunity afforded them of returning to their own land, where they should enjoy the protection and favor of the Most High. בִּצָּרוֹן occurs only in this place. It is derived from בָּצַר, *to cut off*, to prevent the approach of an enemy, to erect an inaccessible fortification; hence the signification of the noun, *strong-hold*, or *fortress*. LXX. ὀχύρωμα. It forcibly contrasts with בוֹר, *the pit*, in the preceding verse, and for this reason is not to be interpreted of Jerusalem considered as again fortified, but is used figuratively to express the security and prosperity which those should enjoy who returned from captivity. Though captives, their condition was not hopeless. They were not to abandon themselves to despair, but to exercise confidence in the promise of God that he would assuredly deliver them, nor were they to wait for the arrival of any distant period when they might return as a body; even then (הַיּוֹם גַּם) they might individually avail themselves of the invitation, and share in the blessings. The abundance of these blessings is expressed by the term מִשְׁנֶה, *double*, which is elsewhere similarly employed to convey the idea of full or ample compensation, Is. lxi. 7. There is no foundation for the opinion of Michaelis, adopted by Blayney, who takes מִגֶּד to be a noun having the signification of מֶגֶד, *something precious*, and not the participle of Hiphil.

13. The declaration here made, that Jehovah would lead forth the Hebrews to military operations, and crown these operations with success, cannot be reconciled with the statement made ver. 10, on any other principle but that which refers them to two totally different periods of time. The one, as explained above, is predictive of the condition to which the nation was to be reduced after the advent of Messiah, instead of having become, under his reign, as they vainly expected, the conquerors of the world; the other sets forth the successful wars in which they would engage with the Grecian rulers of Syria under the command of the Maccabees. The prophecy is parallel with that of Daniel, chap. xi. 32. For the fulfilment see 1 Macc. i.

14 And Jehovah shall appear on their behalf,
And his arrows shall go forth as lightning;
Yea, the Lord Jehovah shall blow the trumpet,
And march in the storms of the south.
15 Jehovah of hosts shall protect them,
And they shall devour, and tread down the sling stones;
They shall drink, they shall be noisy, as those who drink wine;
They shall be full as the bowl,
As the corners of the altar.
16 And Jehovah their God shall save his people,
He shall save them as sheep in that day;
For they shall be as the stones of a crown,
Carrying themselves highly over his land.

62, ii. 41—43, iii. 33, etc. By a bold and expressive figure, the Hebrews are represented as the bows and arrows of Jehovah, the military implements which he would employ in resisting and overcoming the Grecians under Antiochus Epiphanes. By בְּנֵי־יָוָן, *the sons of Greece*, we are to understand, not the Greeks resident in Ionia or Greece, but those composing the army of the monarch just mentioned. Grotius remarks, that at the time here referred to, the Jews were accustomed to call the kings both of Syria and Egypt, מַלְכֵי־יָוָן, *kings of Greece*, because they were of Grecian extraction.

14. Here commences a number of special promises of Divine interposition and protection. Considering what the Jews had experienced from hostile armies, it was necessary to disarm their fears by such assurances, that God was on their side. He is represented as appearing in the thunderstorm, with the lightnings of which his arrows are compared, and with the noise of its thunders, the sound of his trumpet, summoning to the attack. For " the storms of the south," see on Is. xxi. 1.

15. After אָכְלוּ, *they shall eat*, supply בָּשָׂר, *flesh*, i. e. of their enemies; and after שָׁתוּ supply דָּם, their *blood*. This highly figurative language is frequently employed in Scripture to express the destruction of enemies in battle. כְּמוֹ־יַיִן, *like wine*, is elliptical for כְּמוֹ־שֹׁתֵי־יַיִן, *like those who drink wine*. Before הָמוּ, thirty-two MSS., originally four more, three by correction, eight printed editions, and the Rabbins Nathan, Kimchi, and Abarbanel, supply the conjunctive ו. By אַבְנֵי־קֶלַע, *sling-stones*, the enemies are meant, as clearly appears from the contrasted form of expression, אַבְנֵי־נֵזֶר, *stones of a crown*, descriptive of the Jews, in the following verse. The phrase conveys the idea of feebleness and contempt. The stones used for slinging are otherwise of no use or value. Carrying forward the idea of blood, reference is made to מִזְרָק, the *bowl*, which was used to receive that of the sacrifices, and to זָוִית, the corners of the altar, on the horns of which it was sprinkled. Abundant as was the blood thus shed and sprinkled should be that of the enemies of the Hebrews.

16. For כְּצֹאן עַמּוֹ, *as sheep, his people*, comp. כְּצֹאן עֶדְרוֹ. The words are neither in construction, nor in apposition, but are to be separated, so as to connect עַמּוֹ with הוֹשִׁיעַ, understood as repeated from the beginning of the verse. By אַבְנֵי־נֵזֶר, *crown stones*, are meant the precious stones or gems which were set in crowns, and were of great value. The elevation of these, and consequently of the crown which contained them, was

17 For how great is his goodness! and how great his beauty!
   Corn shall cause the young men to thrive,
   And new wine the maids.

strongly indicative of victory. For בָּנ in the acceptation of being *high*, comp. the Arab. نَصَّ, *elevavit rem;* in the viii. Conj. *elatus fuit;* نَصّ, *elevatus thronus.*

17. The affix in שׁוּבוֹ and יָפְיוֹ is most naturally to be associated with that in אֲדֹנָיו at the close of the preceding verse, and referred to Jehovah. The meaning is, the goodness and beauty which he bestows. Compare Jer. xxxi. 12; Ps. xxv. 7. יְנוֹבֵב, though occurring in the latter half, is common to both parts of the sentence. Piel has here the causative power of Hiphil. The root is נוּב, to sprout, *germinate, grow up.* The prophet refers to the plenty which there should be in the land after the destruction of the enemy. The drinking of must by young females is peculiar to this passage; but its being here expressly sanctioned by Divine authority, furnishes an unanswerable argument against those who would interdict all use of the fruit of the vine. תִּירוֹשׁ, *new wine* or *must,* so called from יָרַשׁ, *to take possession of,* because when taken to excess, it gains the mastery over the person who indulges in it.

CHAPTER X.

This chapter continues the subject with which the preceding concluded. The Hebrews are exhorted to apply to Jehovah for the constant supply of temporal blessings, 1, and are warned against an imitation of the conduct of their forefathers, who had recourse to false oracles, on account of which they and their rulers had been carried into captivity, 2, 3. Promises are then made of government by rulers of their own nation, and the victorious operations of their armies, 4, 5; the complete re-establishment of the theocracy, 6, 7; the restoration of such of the nation as still remained in foreign countries, especially in the East, and in Egypt, 8—11; and the chapter concludes with an assurance of the security and happiness which they should enjoy under the divine protection, 12.

1 Ask ye from Jehovah rain in the time of the latter rain:
  Jehovah maketh the lightnings,
  And giveth them the heavy rain,
  To every one grass in the field.
2 Surely the household gods spake vanity,

1. This verse stands in the closest connection with the preceding. חֲזִיזִים, *lightnings,* the precursors of rain. מְטַר־גֶּשֶׁם, lit. *rain of heavy rain,* i. e. plentiful rain. Comp. Job xxxvii. 6, where the same words occur, only their order is inverted.

2. הַתְּרָפִים, *the teraphim,* or house-

And the diviners saw a lie;
They told false dreams,
They gave vapor for comfort;
Therefore they wandered as sheep;
They were afflicted because there was no shepherd.

3 My anger burned against the shepherds,
And I punished the he-goats;
Nevertheless Jehovah of hosts hath visited his flock, the house of Judah,
And made them as his splendid horse in war.

4 From him shall be the corner-stone,
From him the peg,
From him the battle-bow,

hold gods, are opposed to Jehovah in the preceding verse. The term occurs only in the plural, and is of uncertain derivation. Gesenius refers it to the Arab. ڗنف, *to live in comfort*, and considers it as signifying the indicators or givers of pleasure or happiness; Lee to the Eth. ተርፈ ፡ *reliquus, superfuit*, and thinks *relics* are meant. They appear to have had the form of the human body, and to have been consulted as oracles. See on Hos. iii. 4. The preterites and futures, which are intermixed, are all to be taken in the strictly past time, reference being had to the evils which had prevailed among the Jews, on account of which they had been carried away to Babylon, and against any further indulgence in which they are here warned. They were exposed afresh to the influence of idolatrous practices by their intercourse with the Syro-Grecian and Egyptian troops, which repeatedly traversed the land. Antiochus Epiphanes actually set up a heathen idol in the temple at Jerusalem, and ordered temples and altars to be erected in the different cities throughout the country.

3. The verb פָּקַד is here used both in a good and a bad sense; followed by the preposition עַל, it signifies to *visit for evil, to punish;* governing the accusative, *to visit with good*. The ו in יִפְקֹד is prop-

erly the ו conversive, so that אֶפְקוֹד is to be rendered in the preterite, to agree with הֶחָרָה. By "he-goats" are meant the chiefs or leaders of the nation. יָשִׂים all the versions render, as if it had been וַיָּשֶׂם, in the preterite, which the connection requires. The "shepherds" and "he-goats" are used synonymously of the civil rulers. In the middle of this verse is a sudden transition from the calamitous condition to which the Jews had been reduced as a punishment for their sins, to that of prosperity and military prowess to which they were raised in the time of the Maccabees. In the preceding chapter they had been set forth under the images of the bows and arrows; here they are represented under that of the battle-horse. The horse selected by the commander of an army on which to ride at its head, was stately and richly caparisoned. The כ in כְּסוּס is the Caph veritatis.

4. מִמֶּנּוּ thrice repeated, possesses much emphasis. The nominative is יְהוָֹה in the preceding verse. The Hebrews were not now to be subject to governors of foreign extraction or appointment, but were to be independent, enjoying the benefits of a native rule. By פִּנָּה, *corner-stone*, is meant the prince or governor, on whom the political edifice may be said metaphorically to rest. The word is derived from פָּנָה, *to turn*, and primarily

From him shall go forth each and every ruler.
5 And as heroes shall they trample the enemy
In the mud of the streets in battle;
They shall fight, for Jehovah is with them,
And put to shame the riders on horses.
6 I will strengthen the house of Judah,
And deliver the house of Joseph,
And will settle them, because I have pitied them;
And they shall be as if I had not cast them off;
For I Jehovah am their God, and will answer them.
7 And Ephraim shall be as a hero,
And their heart shall rejoice, as those who drink wine;
Their sons shall see it and be glad;
Their heart shall exult in Jehovah.
8 I will whistle for them and gather them,

signifies a *turning-point, angle* or *corner* of a building. With us a nail would be an insignificant image, but יָתֵד, the Oriental nail, is a large peg in the inside of a room, wrought into the wall when the house is built, and on which is hung all kinds of household stuff, together with the different implements of war. See on Is. xxii. 23. One of these, *the bow*, is mentioned immediately after, and stands for the whole. נוֹגֵשׂ is used here simply in the sense of *ruler*. Compare the Eth. ንጉሥ ፡ *king*.

5. Supply אֹיְבִים, *enemies*, as the object to בְּטִיט, *trampling*, and compare Is. xiv. 25, lxiii. 6. רֹכְבֵי סוּסִים refer to the numerous cavalry which composed the chief strength of the Syro-Grecian army (see 1 Macc. iii. 39), but which were put to the route by a mere handful of Jews.

6. "The house of Joseph" stands for the ten tribes, in contradistinction to those of Judah and Benjamin, to which is given the name of "Judah" as the more important of the two. It is clear from the reference thus made, that part, if not most of all the tribes, returned and took possession of their patrimonial lands after the captivity. הוֹשַׁבְתִּים is a mixed form, supposed by Kimchi, Abarbanel, and some others, to have been artificially compounded of הֲשִׁיבֹתִים, the Hiphil of שׁוּב, *to return*, and הוֹשַׁבְתִּים, the Hiphil of יָשַׁב, *to sit* or *dwell*, in order to express in one word both verbs as used by Jeremiah, וַהֲשִׁבֹתִים אֶל־הַמָּקוֹם הַזֶּה וְהֹשַׁבְתִּים לָבֶטַח, chap. xxxii. 37; but it is far more probable that the word is a corruption of הוֹשַׁבְתִּים, introduced through inadvertence by some transcriber. Such is, indeed, the reading of many MSS. and of four printed editions, and is supported by the LXX. κατοικιῶ. The reading הֲשִׁיבֹתִים, has the support of the Syr., Vulg., and Targ., but is less suitable to the connection.

7. As the state of things here described was brought about by the heroic conduct of Ephraim, it is obvious the return from the captivity cannot be intended, for the Hebrews were altogether passive on that occasion. The reason why special mention is here made of the ten tribes may be their longer rejection by the Lord, and the exiled state in which many of them still were in the days of the prophet. אֶפְרַיִם, as a collective noun, is the nominative to וְהָיָה. For בְּמוֹ־יַיִן see on chap. ix. 15.

8. An express promise of the restoration, settlement, and increase of the ten

> For I have redeemed them,
> And they shall increase, as they did increase.
> 9 Though I have scattered them among the nations,
> Yet they shall remember me in the distant regions,
> And shall live with their children and return.
> 10 I will bring them back from the land of Egypt,
> And gather them from Assyria;
> And I will bring them to the land of Bashan and Lebanon,
> And room shall not be found for them.
> 11 And he shall pass over the sea,
> He shall cleave and smite the waves of the sea,
> And all the deeps of the river shall dry up;
> The pride of Assyria shall be brought down,
> And the sceptre of Egypt shall depart.

tribes, many of whom were still at that time in a state of exile. They were to be brought back to Palestine, and placed in a condition in which they should be able to act valiantly in defence of their country. The verb שָׁרַק signifies *to whistle*, or give a shrill sound, as those who keep bees do, who, by means of a whistle, or pipe, call them out from and back to their hives. See on Is. v. 26. Josephus informs us, that two hundred years after the time here referred to, Galilee was peopled to an amazing extent, studded with cities, towns, and villages; and adds, that the villages were not what were usually called by that name, but contained, some of them, fifteen thousand inhabitants. Jewish Wars, book iii. ch. iii. § 2.

9. The first two Vaus are employed antithetically, the former having the signification of *though* or *indeed;* the latter, that of *but* or *yet*. יָרַע cannot here mean *saved*, as Hengstenberg contends, but must be rendered *scattered*, which the verb primarily signifies, and the connection here requires. The last clause of the verse indicates the settled enjoyment of chartered privileges as before the dispersion, when the Hebrews should return to their own land.

10. We have no historical account of any specific removal of any belonging to the ten tribes into Egypt, but it cannot be doubted that, as in the case of the Jews in the time of Jeremiah, many of them betook themselves to that country for refuge on the invasion of Tiglathpileser; and when Ptolemy attempted to seize the whole of Syria, and carried away 100,000 captives, whom he settled in Alexandria and Cyrene, vast numbers of them must have consisted of the descendants of those Israelites who had returned from the Eastern captivity. Those who had remained in the East were also to return. Comp. Is. xi. 11. יִמָּצֵא has here the signification of there being *sufficient* or *enough*, as in Kal, Numb. xi. 22; Jud. xxi. 14. מָקוֹם, *room*, or *place*, is understood. So great should be the number of inhabitants, that the territory, however ample and fertile, would not be able to furnish them with the necessary supplies.

11. There is here an allusion to the original deliverance of the Hebrew people at the Red Sea. Comp. Is. xi. 15. The Divine interposition in behalf of those who were still in Egypt is not expressly compared with what then took place, but such comparison is implied. צָרָה has been variously rendered. The LXX. στενῇ, Vulg. *freto*, Syr. اܘܠܨܢܐ, *angustia*, Calvin, *afflictio*, Hengstenberg,

12 And I will strengthen them through Jehovah,
And they shall walk up and down in his name,
Saith Jehovah.

the distress, Blayney, *Tyre*, Hitzig, *Zara*, by which he understands the Nile. The difficulty is at once removed by taking צרה as a verb, with the Aramaic signification of צרא, גזר, *cut, cleave, divide.* Comp. the Arab. صرى, *resecuit, amputavit.* In which case three verbs, having Jehovah understood as their nominative, will follow in regular order: וְעָבַר בַּיָּם צָרָה וְהִכָּה בַיָּם גַּלִּים. *And he shall pass over the sea; he shall cleave and smite the waves of the sea.* The last words are literally, *he shall smite the sea into waves;* or, *as to the sea, he will smite its waves.* Comp. Exod. xiv. 16, 21; Is. xi. 15, 16. That by "the river,"

the Nile, and not the Euphrates, is meant, the use of the Egyptian word יְאֹר places beyond dispute. See on Is. xix. 6. With respect to אַשּׁוּר, *Ashur*, it may justly be queried whether the Syro-Greek kingdom be not intended — that kingdom occupying not only the territory which belonged to ancient Assyria, but extending still further towards the east. The pride of that power, as well as the Egypto-Greek sceptre, was to be swept away.

12. The phrase, הִתְהַלֵּךְ בְּשֵׁם, *to walk in the name* of a deity, is a Hebrew mode of speech, descriptive of a course of action pursued in accordance with his character and will. Comp. Micah iv. 5.

CHAPTER XI.

It is obvious, from the nature of the predictions contained in this and the following chapters, that they must have been delivered at a time subsequent to the erection of the temple. As they are exclusively occupied with denunciations of evil against the Jews, with the exception of interjected prophecies of the Messiah, and one relative to the final deliverance of the covenant people, they must have dispirited rather than encouraged those who were engaged in building the sacred edifice. It may be said, indeed, that there were many carnal and secure persons among the Jews, who required to be warned, and that the following denunciations were designed for their benefit; but, as the predictions do not relate to the times in which those persons lived, it is not conceivable how they could have so appropriated them as to derive effectual advantage from them. Besides, they contain no instances of direct address, or personal application of the truths delivered, such as we find in the other prophets when addressing themselves to their contemporaries for their immediate benefit. It may, therefore, be concluded, that they were communicated by Zechariah on some occasion or occasions of which we have no knowledge.

The scenes here depicted lay in the more distant future. In the present chapter the prophet furnishes a bold figurative description of the destruction of the temple by the Romans, and the utter consternation into which the priests and rulers of the people should thereby be thrown, 1—3. He then describes certain symbolical actions performed by him in vision, by which he personated the Messiah who had been promised as the Shepherd of his people, setting forth his commission to teach and rule them, 4; their deplorable condition in consequence of the rapacious disposition of their leaders, 5; and the judgments that should overtake them in consequence of their wickedness, 6. Under the emblems of two staves the relation of the whole nation to God, as their protector, and the relation of the different tribes among themselves are exhibited, and the cessation of these relations is pointed out by the act of breaking the staves, 7—14. The three last verses set forth the character of Herod, and the judgment of God upon him for his wickedness.

1 Open, O Lebanon! thy gates,
That the fire may devour thy cedars.
2 Howl, ye cypresses! for the cedars have fallen,
Because the magnificent are destroyed:
Howl, ye oaks of Bashan! for the fortified forest hath come down.
3 There is the sound of the howling of the shepherds,
Because their magnificence is destroyed;
There is the sound of the roaring of young lions,
Because the pride of Jordan is destroyed.

1. Some interpret this verse literally of the locality so called; others understand it figuratively, but apply it either to Jerusalem, or to the whole land of Palestine. The construction which most commends itself is that which applies it to the temple restrictively. Such is the ancient rabbinical interpretation. To the same effect is the remarkable declaration of Rabbi Johanan Ben Zakkai: "O sanctuary, sanctuary! why dost thou trouble thyself? I know of thee that thine end is to be left desolate, for Zechariah, the son of Iddo, has prophesied against thee long ago. Open thy doors, O Lebanon, that the fire may devour thy cedars." Talmud, Bab. Yoma. fol. 39, col. 2. This interpretation seems to be referred to by Josephus, in his Jewish Wars, bk. vi. ch. v. § 3. The temple might with all propriety be figuratively called Lebanon, not only because the cedars with which it was built were brought from that mountain, but because as Lebanon was the most stately and magnificent of all in the vicinity of Palestine, so the temple was the most glorious of all objects in or about Jerusalem. Its gates were kept carefully shut against all who had no right to thread its courts. Now it was to become a prey to the flames. The prediction received its literal fulfilment in spite of the utmost solicitude of the Roman general to preserve the edifice. In vain did he attempt to save it from the flames, so that in a short time it was entirely consumed.

2. בְּרוֹשׁ, *the cypress*, was greatly inferior to the *cedar*, but was employed for the floor and ceilings of the temple. "The oaks of Bashan" were also used for purposes of building. These terms, however, are likewise to be interpreted figuratively of the priests and rulers of the temple, its superior and inferior officers, together with the judges of the people. אַדִּיר is used both of animate and inanimate objects. It is here employed to denote those who were elevated in dignity and magnificent in apparel. Comp. אַדִּירֵי הַצֹּאן. By יַעַר הַבָּצוּר, *the fortified* or *inaccessible forest*, is meant Jerusalem, the houses of which were numerous and close together as the trees of the forest, and round which the Jews had thrown up a wall of great strength. Comp. Micah iii. 12. For בְּצוּרוֹ, many MSS., and two early editions, read בְּצִירוֹ, which is only another form to express the same thing.

3. The Jewish rulers are called "shepherds," with reference to their office, and "young lions," in regard to their fierce and rapacious disposition. The אַדֶּרֶת, was the *magnificence* of the temple of which they boasted. Comp. Mark xiii. 1; Luke xxi. 5. גְּאוֹן הַיַּרְדֵּן, *the pride of Jordan*, i. e. the thickets which ornament its banks, and furnish excellent lairs for lions, has the same figurative reference, and is selected to correspond to the young lions immediately preceding. Comp. Jer. xii. 5, xlix. 19. The leaders of the Jews are represented as indulging in loud wailings of despair, on account of the destruction of their temple and polity.

4   Thus saith Jehovah my God,
    Feed the sheep of slaughter;
5   Whose possessors kill them, and are not held guilty;
    And each of those who sell them saith,
    Blessed be Jehovah, I am enriched;
    And none of whose shepherds spareth them.

4, 5. The prophet now proceeds to point out the cause of the destruction which he had figuratively described, and that of the people which was connected with it — the obstinate refusal of their rulers to receive the doctrine of the Messiah. By צֹאן הַהֲרֵגָה, *the sheep of slaughter*, are meant the people devoted to destruction. Comp. צֹאן טִבְחָה, Ps. xliv. 23. At the fall of Jerusalem not fewer than 1,100,000 Jews perished, and near a million and a half altogether in the course of the war. It has been questioned, who is the person directed in this verse to assume the office of a shepherd, and who declares, ver. 7, that he performed the duties of that office? Frischmuth, Marckius, Michaelis, and others, are of opinion that it is the Messiah, and, unquestionably, if ultimate reference be had to him, this is the true interpretation; but it is equally clear that the prophet is to be regarded as having received the commission, and performed, in vision, what was enjoined upon him. What proves this, is the putting into the hands of the same person the instruments of a foolish shepherd, ver. 15, an action which can with no propriety be referred to the Messiah. On this principle, most of the difficulties connected with the exegesis of the intervening verses vanish. Zechariah had all the transactions presented to his view in prophetic vision, but what he describes was actually done, not in his own personal history, or in any outward occurrences between him and the Jews of his time, but in the personal history and office of the Messiah whom he personated. He did not really feed or teach those who were to be slain, but the Messiah and his apostles did; and had the Jews believed their message, the awful calamity would have been averted. The hypothesis of a prophetic vision was first advanced by Maimonides, and is ably supported by Hengstenberg, in his Christology, and by Dr. McCaul, in his translation of Kimchi on our prophet. That by the buyers and sellers of the Jewish people, we are not to understand the Romans, but their own unprincipled teachers and rulers, the facts of the case show. The corresponding term רֹעֵיהֶם, *their shepherds*, is merely expletive of what the same persons were officially. The avarice of the Pharisees was excessive, yet they had the barefaced hypocrisy to thank God for their ill gotten wealth, and because they were not punished, they imagined they might persevere with impunity. The construction of the plural nouns מֹכְרֵיהֶן, קֹנֵיהֶן, and רֹעֵיהֶם, with the singulars יֹאמַר and יַחְמוֹל, cannot, with any propriety, be accounted for on the principle advanced by Hengstenberg, that Jehovah himself was the principal actor, and that the wicked rulers were merely his instruments. It is only a more emphatic mode of construction, by which each of the individuals specified in the plural is represented as performing the action, see Gen. xxvii. 29; Exod. xxxi. 14; Prov. iii. 18. The masculine affix הֶם refers to the people, strictly so taken; the feminine הֶן, to them considered under the idea of the sheep that were to be fed, צֹאן being of the common gender. There is, therefore, no ground for correcting the text by changing רֹעֵיהֶם into רֹעֵיהֶן, the reading of fifteen MSS. and some printed editions.

6 For I will no more spare the inhabitants of the land, saith
Jehovah,
But behold! I will deliver the men,
Each into the hand of his neighbor, and into the hand of his
king;
And they shall destroy the land,
And I will not deliver them out of their hand.
7 And I fed the sheep of slaughter, truly miserable sheep!

6. The particle כִּי, *for*, connects what follows with the command, ver. 4. The Jews were no longer to have Divine pity extended to them, but were to be abandoned to all the evils of civil discord, and to the oppressions of a foreign rule. That the king here referred to was the Roman emperor, is obvious from the acknowledgment of the Jews themselves: "We have no king but Cæsar." John xix. 15. The verb כָּתַת, *to beat*, or *dash in pieces*, is most appropriately chosen to express the destructive measures adopted by the Romans, by which the Jewish polity was broken up. The nominative is the troops of the foreign ruler that had just been spoken of.

7. The prophet declares, in the name of the Messiah, that he executed the task committed to him. This was fulfilled during the personal ministry of our Lord. לָכֵן עֲנִיֵּי הַצֹּאן have been variously rendered. LXX. εἰς τὴν Χαναανῖτιν. Syr. ܡܛܠ ܡܣܟܢܐ ܕܓܙܪܐ, *the little ones on account of the collection of the sheep.* Vulg. *propter hoc ó paupere egregis.* Leo Juda, *adeoque pauperes gregis.* Tremellius and Junius, *vos* inquam, *ó pauperes gregis.* Schmid, J. H. Michaelis, Newcome, Hitzig, and others, *propter vos, o miseri gregis.* Maurer, *pavi igitur miserrimus ovium.* Arnheim, fürwahr die elendesten der Heerde. Ewald, wirklich die unglücklichsten Schafe. The only real difficulty lies in the word לָכֵן. The LXX. have read it, and the following word, as one, thus, לִכְנַעֲנֵי, and made

Canaanite of it. This rendering is adopted by Blayney, only he attaches to the term the idea of merchant, which it sometimes has (*among those who trafficked with the flock*), and explains it of the buyers and sellers of the flock, described ver. 5. The interpretation is so far specious, and is approved by Jahn, but cannot be philologically sustained. Some take לָכֵן for the infinitive in Hiphal of כּוּן, which furnishes no tolerable sense; others, for the dative of the second personal feminine pronoun, supposing the Segol to have been changed into a Tzêre, but this is liable to the same objection. Most regard it as the particle לָכֵן, and construe it either with its causal, or its adversative signification; but neither do any of the interpretations thus brought out satisfactorily meet the exigencies of the case. I cannot help thinking that the ל is here redundant, as it is in many instances, and that we must construe כֵּן, as in ver. 11, where it occurs without the ל. The term is properly a participial noun, derived from כּוּן, in the sense of the Arab. كون, *esse*, and implies *reality, certainty*, or the like, but admits of being variously rendered, according to the context in which it is found. See Lee's Heb. Lex. *in voc.* And thus it is understood by Kimchi, Jarchi, Castalio, De Dieu, Drusius, Storr, Dathe, Arnheim, De Wette, and Ewald. Even were the ל retained, the same result would be brought out, the rendering in this case being, *with respect to truth*, i. e. *truly*; just as in לָנֶצַח, *with respect to perpetuity*, i. e. *forever*. The words עֲנִיֵּי הַצֹּאן are the superlative of con-

And I took to myself two crooks; the one I called Grace, and
8 the other I called Bands, and I fed the sheep. And I cut off
the three shepherds within one month; and my soul loathed
9 them, and their soul also rejected me. So that I said:
I will not feed you;
That which is dying, let it die;
And that which is being cut off, let it be cut off;
And as for the rest, let them eat each the flesh of another.

struction, as in רָעֵי גוֹיִם, *the most wicked of nations*, Ezek. vii. 24; מִבְחַר בְּרֹשָׁיו, *the choicest of his cypresses*, Jer. xxxvii. 7; or, what is quite parallel with the present case, צְעִירֵי הַצֹּאן, rendered in our common version, *the least of the flock*. The article is as usual to be referred to the former of the two nouns, and both might be rendered, *the most miserable of sheep*, or *the most miserable sheep*. Such was the state to which the Jewish people were reduced in the days of our Lord. They were ἐσκυλμένοι καὶ ἐῤῥιμένοι, ὡσεὶ πρόβατα μὴ ἔχοντα ποιμένα. Matt. ix. 36. They were *worried* and *harassed* in every possible way, πρόβατα ἀπολωλότα, Matt. x. 6. The two staves were symbolical of the different modes of treatment which the Hebrews had experienced under the guidance and protection of the providence of God. One of them was called נֹעַם, *Grace*, or *Favor*, to indicate the kindness of Jehovah to them in restraining the surrounding nations from overpowering them, and carrying them again into captivity. See ver. 10. To the other was given the name of חֹבְלִים, which Drusius, Marckius, the Dutch translators, and others, render *Binders*, but better, *Bands*, expressing the ties which unite parties together. The LXX., Aq., Symm., σχοίνισμα; Vulg. *funiculi*; Maurer, *conjuncti, fœderati*. Reference is had to the fraternal confederacy into which the Jews and Israelites had entered with each other after the return from Babylon. See ver. 14. The last clause of the verse is a repetition of the first, for the sake of emphasis.

8. Who "the three shepherds" here definitely pointed out were, cannot be determined with certainty. All kinds of interpretations have been given, from Moses, Aaron, and Miriam, suggested to Jerome, by his Hebrew Rabbi, to the Roman emperors Galbus, Otho, and Vitellius, in Calmet. The only construction which is at all entitled to any notice, is that which regards the language as descriptive of the three orders of rulers in the Jewish state — the priests, the teachers of the law, and the civil magistrates. These were the persons of influence by whom the affairs of the nation were conducted, and to whose wickedness, which reached its culminating point when they crucified the Lord of Glory, the destruction of the state is to be ascribed. יֶרַח אֶחָד, *one month*, doubtless refers to the last period of the siege of Jerusalem, when everything was thrown into confusion, and all authority came to an end. כָּחַד, *to hide, conceal;* in Hiphil, as here, ἀφανίζειν, *to cause to disappear, to cause to cease with respect to office, to remove from it*. The last two lines of the verse point out the mutual dissatisfaction and disgust with which the wicked rulers and the Messiah regarded each other. בָּחַל, occurs only here, and Prov. xx. 21. Comp. the cognate root בָּעַל, *to reject*, and the Arab. بَحَلَ, *impulsus valadus, propulsio vehemens*; بَحَلَ, *maledixit*, III. *execratus fuit*.

9. The entire abandonment of the Hebrew people is here most affectingly set forth. For the threefold destruction here predicted, comp. Jer. xv. 1, 2,

10   I then took my crook Grace, and cut it asunder in order to
11 break my covenant which I had made with all the nations. And
it was broken in that day, and the miserable sheep that gave
heed to me, knew of a truth that it was the word of Jehovah.
12 And I said to them, If it be good in your eyes, give my reward;
13 and if not, forbear. So they weighed my reward, thirty pieces
of silver. And Jehovah said to me, Cast it to the potter, the

xxxiv. 17; Ezek. vi. 12. And for the fulfilment, see Josephus.

10. By this symbolical action, the removal of the restraint which Jehovah had exercised over the nations, whereby the destruction of the Jewish people had been prevented, is strikingly represented. The exercise of restraint with respect to hostile forces is elsewhere spoken of under the idea of a covenant. See Job v. 23; Ezek. xxxiv. 25; Hos. ii. 18. When this restraint was removed, the Romans invaded Judea, and destroyed the city and polity of the ancient people of God. That by עַמִּים, *people* or *nations*, we are to understand foreign nations, and not the Hebrew tribes, is now agreed among the best interpreters.

11. The anticipated accomplishment of the prediction, and the conviction wrought in the minds of the pious portion of the Jewish people, that the prediction was indeed divine. For the force of כֵּן see on ver. 7. The LXX. again join the two words, and render, οἱ Χαναναῖοι.

12, 13. On the question of the application of these verses to the circumstances narrated Matt. xxvii. 7—10, a very decided difference of opinion has obtained. This difference has been occasioned, partly by the fact of certain discrepancies existing between the accounts which they furnish of the transactions, and partly by the more important consideration that the Evangelist expressly ascribes the words which he quotes to Jeremiah, and not to Zechariah. With respect to the former of these points, it may, to a considerable extent, be obviated by the general observation, that the discrepances are not greater than we meet with in several other quotations made from the Old Testament by the writers of the New, and are by no means such as to affect the end which either the prophet or the Evangelist had in view. In producing the citation, the latter had his eye more intent upon the historical circumstances which he had just detailed, than upon the strict grammatical construction and verbality of the language employed in the prophecy. He fixes upon the principal points, the despicable price at which the Messiah had been sold, and the appropriation of the money as a compensation to the potter for the possession of his field; and having faithfully exhibited these to the view of his readers, he is less solicitous about the wording of the prophet. The very changes which he introduces into the phraseology are such as his position in the character of an historian required. Thus, instead of אֲשֶׁר יָקַרְתִּי מֵעֲלֵיהֶם, *at which I was estimated by them*, Matthew has ὃν ἐτιμήσαντο ἀπὸ υἱῶν Ἰσραήλ, *at which he was estimated by the sons of Israel*. Instead of וָאֶקְחָה שְׁלֹשִׁים הַכֶּסֶף, *And I took the thirty pieces of silver*, we find, καὶ ἔλαβον τὰ τριάκοντα ἀργύρια, *and they took the thirty pieces of silver*. Instead of וָאַשְׁלִיךְ אֹתוֹ, *and I threw it*, the Gospel has, καὶ ἔδωκαν αὐτά, *and they gave them*. The freedom with which the Evangelist renders שָׁלַךְ by δίδωμι is the more noticeable, since he employs the participle ῥίψας in reference to the same subject in the fifth verse, where, at the same time, he renders בֵּית יְהוָֹה by ἐν τῷ ναῷ. The conjecture of some that יוֹצֵר, *potter*, is a corruption of אוֹצָר,

splendid price at which I was estimated by them! And I took

treasurer, is worse than gratuitous, as the latter word nowhere occurs in Hebrew in reference to such an office, and as the potter was the most suitable person to whom to cast the despicable sum, occupying as he did a workshop in the valley of Hinnom, Jer. xviii. 1, 3, xix. 2, which was held in abomination by the Jews. That the Evangelist should have ascribed the prediction to Jeremiah has proved a source of great perplexity to critics. No person who has read the passage in Zechariah can peruse that in Matthew without at once being reminded of it. And so exactly do they tally in every important point, that no doubt of their relationship can for a moment be entertained. On the other hand, no such passage is to be found in any part of the prophecies of Jeremiah. The solution of the difficulty proposed by Hengstenberg, that it was the object of our prophet to bring forward to view the predictions contained in Jer. xviii. xix., in order to point out the destruction of Jerusalem by the Romans, and that on this ground the Evangelist might, with all propriety, ascribe the authorship to Jeremiah, is very unsatisfactory; and we are shut up to one or other of the following conclusions: First, that the one name was substituted for the other by a *lapsus memoriæ*. Secondly, that the portion of the book of Zechariah, in which the words are found, though now bearing his name, was actually written by Jeremiah, and by some means or other, to us unknown, has been appended to the real prophecies of Zechariah. Thirdly, that the citation is made from an apocryphal book of the prophet Jeremiah. Or lastly, that there is a corruption of the name in the Greek text of Matthew. The first of these positions will not be admitted by any who believe in the plenary inspiration of the Apostles; a doctrine fully established on Scripture authority, and which, if denied, would completely annihilate our confidence in their testimony. If their memory might fail, or they might be mistaken in one instance, such might be the case in hundreds. For a refutation of the second hypothesis, see the Preface, in which it is shown that there is no solid foundation for the opinion, that the last six chapters of Zechariah were not written by that prophet. With respect to the third supposition, it cannot be denied that there was an apocryphal book of Jeremiah, containing an analogous passage. Jerome found it among the Nazarenes, and a portion of it still exists in a Sahidic Lectionary, in the Codex Huntingtonianus 5, in the Bodleian Library, Oxford, and in the Coptic language in the MS. 51 fol. in the library of St. Germain in Paris. The words are as follows: "Jeremiah spake again to Pashur, Ye and your fathers have resisted the truth, and your sons, which shall come after you, will commit more grievous sins than ye. For they will give the price of him that is valued, and do injury to him that maketh the sick whole, and forgiving iniquity. And they will take thirty pieces of silver, the price which the children of Israel have given. They have given them for the potter's field, as the Lord commanded. And thus it shall be spoken: The sentence of eternal punishment shall fall upon them, and upon their children, because they have shed innocent blood." But who does not perceive in this fragment the clumsy attempt of one of the early Christians to support the cause of truth by what was deemed a harmless fraud? Jerome at once rejected it as spurious, and expresses his belief that Matthew made his citation from Zechariah. It only remains that we assume a corruption in the Greek text of the Evangelist. That a variety of reading exists has long been matter of notoriety. Augustine mentions, that in his time some MSS. omitted the name of Ἰερεμίου. It is also omitted in the MS. 33, 157; in the Syriac, which is the most ancient of

the thirty pieces of silver, and cast them into the house of Jehovah, to the potter.
14 Then I cut asunder my second crook Bands, in order to break the brotherhood between Judah and Israel.
15 And Jehovah said to me, Take to thee yet the instruments of a foolish shepherd;
16 For, behold, I will raise up a shepherd in the land;
Those which are perishing he will not visit,
That which strayeth he will not seek,
That which is wounded he will not heal,
That which standeth he will not nourish;

all the versions; in the Polyglott Persic, and in a Persic MS. in my possession, bearing date A. D. 1057; in the modern Greek; in the Verona and Vercelli Latin MSS. and in a Latin MS. of Luc. Brug. The Greek MS. 22, reads Ζαχαρίου, as also do the Philoxenian Syriac in the margin, and an Arabic MS. quoted by Bengel. Origen and Eusebius were in favor of this reading. I think it very probable that Matthew did not insert either name, but simply wrote in his Hebrew Gospel, בְּיַד הַנָּבִיא, *by the prophet*, just as in chap. i. 22, ii. 5, 15, xiii. 35, xxi. 4, xxvii. 35; and that his Greek translator, mistaking ד in בְּיַד for ר, read בְּיַר, which he considered to be a contraction for בְּיִרְמְיָהוּ, and so rendered it διὰ Ἱερεμίου τοῦ προφήτου. This reading having found its way into the first Greek MS., will account for its all but universal propagation. Another conjecture supposes Ἱρίου to have been written by some early copyist instead of Ζρίου. I only add, that there can be no doubt the passage in question existed in the book of Zechariah in the Jewish canon in the days of the Evangelist, since it is found to occupy that place in the text of the LXX. which was formed three hundred years previously.

14. For the meaning of הַחֹבְלִים *Bands*, see on ver. 7. The circumstances here predicted were those of the utter breaking up of the social condition of the Hebrews. This dissolution was in no small degree brought about by the internal dissensions which prevailed among themselves, the rage of the different parties against each other, and the barbarities that they practised, which none could have indulged in but such as had their hearts steeled against every feeling of brotherhood or humanity. "Yet by these men," says Josephus, "the ancient prediction seemed rapidly drawing to its fulfilment: That when civil war should break out in the city, and the temple be profaned by the hands of native Jews, the city should be taken, and the temple burned with fire."

15. עוֹד, *again*, refers back to what is recorded ver. 7. The כֵּלִים, here as a collective in the singular כְּלִי, were the articles usually belonging to shepherds, viz. a crook, a bag or wallet containing food, a pipe or reed, a knife, etc. Instead of כְּלִי, one of De Rossi's MSS., the Halle Bible of 1720, the Vatican copy of the LXX., the Syr., Vulg., and Arab., read כְּלִי, the punctuation of the plural. אֱוִלִי, *foolish*, by implication *wicked*, as wickedness is often represented in Scripture as folly.

16. מֵקִים is employed here, like similar verbs in Hiphil, to denote not any direct moral excitement to action, but the operation of concurring circumstances, under the Divine government, in consequence of which certain events are brought about by responsible human agency. הַנִּכְחָדוֹת, *those that are perishing*, the Niphal participle of כָּחַד,

But he will eat the flesh of the fat,
And will break off their hoofs.

17 Woe to the worthless shepherd, that leaveth the flock;
The sword shall be upon his arm,
And upon his right eye;
His arm shall be utterly palsied,
And his right eye utterly darkened.

which in Hiphal and Niphal signifies *to cut off or be destroyed*. נַעַר is not to be taken in the sense of *young*, as it is interpreted by Kimchi and Hitzig, since it is never so used, except with reference to human beings, but signifies *expulsion*, that which has been *cast out*, by implication, *strayed, wandered*. Comp. the Arabic نَفَىٰ, *repulsus, in fugam versus*.

הַנִּצָּבָה, *that which standeth still*. נָצַב properly signifies *to set* or *place*, in Niphal, *to stand, stand firm, be strong, firm, sound*; and thus the LXX. here ὁλόκληρον, but this interpretation is quite at variance with the exigency of the place, which requires the idea of *weakness* rather than *strength* to be expressed. And this the verb naturally suggests, reference being had to the *standing*, or *standing still* of sheep that are obliged, through weakness or faintness, to lag behind. Comp. the Arabic نصب *posuit, fixit*, and then *dolore affecit, lassus fuit, laboravit*. Such it devolves upon the shepherd to provide with necessary nourishment, or, as it is here expressed, כַּלְכֵּל, *to sustain, furnish with provisions*. Root כּוּל, *to measure grain*. The words אֲשֶׁר־תִכָּחֵד נַעַר are expressive of the greatest cruelty, being descriptive of an act which must not only occasion the most acute pain, but disable the animals, and prevent their going about in quest of pasture. Who the ruler here depicted is, cannot with certainty be determined. If taken as pointing to an individual king, there is none to whom it will more aptly apply than to Herod, who was totally regardless of the real interest of the Jews, and whose reign was marked by the perpetration of the most shameful and barbarous cruelties. What goes to confirm this view is the circumstance of his being said to be raised up "*in* the land."

17. This denunciation seems to be directed against the wicked rulers of the Jews who might be in office between the time of the prophet, and that of the dissolution of the Jewish state, rather than against the person referred to in the preceding verse. The י in רֹעִי is not the pronominal affix, but the poetic paragogic, as in' the following עֹזְבִי, and other participles. See Gen. xlix. 11; Deut. xxxiii. 16; Ps. cxiv. 8, cxxiii. 1. רֹעִי הָאֱלִיל, *the worthless* or *good-for-nothing shepherd*. Comp. Job xiii. 4. The root must unquestionably have been אָלַל. Comp. בְּלִיל from בָּלַל; סָבִיב from סָבַב. The character described is that of negligence, arising from the total absence of a sense of official claims, and of personal responsibility. The rest of the verse from חֶרֶב onward, is to be taken optatively. The doom imprecated is truly awful — an utter deprivation of power and intelligence.

CHAPTER XII.

THIS chapter contains a series of predictions, which relate to the future restoration of the scattered people of the Jews, the destruction of whose national polity, and their consequent wretchedness, had been so graphically set forth in that which precedes it. On their return to their own land, Jerusalem shall prove formidable to the nations that oppose them, 2—4, having a regular government, by which, in reliance upon Jehovah, the inhabitants shall be protected, 5, 6. To prevent the inhabitants of the metropolis from glorying over their brethren in the country, the latter shall be first delivered from their invaders, 7; but Jerusalem being the principal point of attack, special promises of deliverance are made to it, 8, 9. When the Jews shall have been collected, and delivered from the opposing powers, there will be a remarkable effusion of the influences of the Holy Spirit, in consequence of which a season of great and universal mourning, on account of the crucifixion of the Messiah, will be observed, each family bewailing separately the guilt entailed upon it by the nefarious deed, 10—14.

As might be expected to be the case with unfulfilled prophecy, a considerable degree of obscurity necessarily attaches to certain portions of this and the two following chapters; but the leading features of the Divine dealings with the Jews in times yet future, are marked with a sufficient degree of distinctness to enable us to form a general idea of the circumstances in which they will be placed.

---

1 THE Sentence of the word of Jehovah concerning Israel;
Saith Jehovah, who stretcheth forth the heavens,
Who layeth the foundations of the earth,
And formeth the spirit of man within him:
2 Behold, I will make Jerusalem a cup of intoxication
To all the people around;

1. That מַשָּׂא does not necessarily involve a sentence of judgment, see on Is. xiii. 1; and for the entire phrase, מַשָּׂא דְבַר־יְהוָֹה, see on chap. ix. 1. That it cannot be so taken here is manifest from the connection. Hengstenberg, in order to establish the contrary hypothesis, is obliged to have recourse to the desperate resort of interpreting *Israel* of the enemies of God! The term is obviously employed in its original acceptation, as designating the whole Hebrew people. With no other reference could it have been introduced. To remove all the doubts which unbelief might suggest respecting the possibility of the deliverance here predicted, a sublime description is given of the omnipotent Creator by whom it would be effected, than which no introduction could have been more appropriate. For יֹצֵר רוּחַ־אֱנוֹשׁ, compare Πατὴρ τῶν πνευμάτων, Heb. xii. 9, and Numb. xvi. 22, xxvii. 16; and for the several predicates, Is. xlii. 5.

2. סַף רַעַל, some render a *shaking threshold*, in imitation of the LXX. ὡς πρόθυρα σαλευόμενα, and interpret the declaration here made of the concussion which Jerusalem should receive from the attack of the enemy; but it is more natural to regard the phrase as only another form for כּוֹס הַתַּרְעֵלָה, Is. li. 17, 22, by which is meant a cup filled with intoxicating liquors, causing those who drink it to *reel* and stagger to their injury. Root רָעַל, *to shake, reel, stagger*. The attempt of Hengstenberg to deny that סַף is ever used to denote *a cup*, is a com-

And also with Judah it shall be thus,
In the siege of Jerusalem.
3 And it shall be in that day, I will make Jerusalem
A burdensome stone to all people,
All that lift it shall be cut in pieces:
Yet all the nations of the earth shall be gathered against it.
4 In that day, saith Jehovah,
I will smite every horse with consternation,
And his rider with madness;
But upon the house of Judah I will keep my eyes open,
While I will smite every horse of the people with blindness.
5 And the chiefs of Judah shall say in their heart,
My strength is the inhabitants of Jerusalem,
Through Jehovah of hosts their God.

plete failure, as must be obvious to any one who will take the trouble to consult the Concordance. The second part of the verse has occasioned no small perplexity to interpreters. The chief difficulty is created by the position of the preposition בְּ in the phrase בַּם יְרוּשָׁלַ͏ִם־עַל. The Targ., Jerome, Kimchi, Drusius, Rosenmüller, Hitzig, Maurer, and Ewald, suppose the meaning to be, that the inhabitants of Judah would be compelled to join the enemies in the attack upon Jerusalem, and with them share in the punishment: making בְּכָל־עַמִּים the nominative to יִהְיֶה. But this interpretation ill suits the context, in the whole of which Judah is represented as triumphant, and not as placed in the degrading position of auxiliaries in a war against its own capital. I consider the preposition to be here used for the purpose of conveying the idea of addition or accompaniment, so that, connecting Judah with Jerusalem, it represents the former, as well as the latter, as a cup of intoxication to the invaders. See for this use of עַל, Gen. xxxii. 12; Exod. xxxv. 22; Job xxxviii. 32. In support of this interpretation, see especially ver. 6. The same result will be brought out, if we take עַל in the acceptation *in reference to, with respect to;*

thus: "And with respect to Judah it shall also be in the siege;" *i. e.* Judah shall also be a cup, etc.

3. Another metaphor employed like the preceding to represent the victory which the Jews shall obtain over their enemies, whose attack will only issue in their own injury. Jerome mentions it as a custom, which still obtained in his time, in Palestine, for young men to try their strength by lifting enormous stones so high from the ground, as to place them upon their heads. It may be from such an exercise that the metaphor is borrowed. שָׂרֹט describes the cuts or gashes made by the sharp edges or corners of the stones thus employed. Though exposed to the punishment here predicated, the nations shall confidently advance to the attack. The confederacy against the Jews will be universal in its character.

4. While Jehovah will specially interpose for the discomfiture of the enemy by rendering their cavalry incapable of performing any effective service, he will exercise the greatest watchfulness over his people.

5. אַמְצָה is a substantive, but occurs only this once. The LXX. have read אֶמְצָא, and render εὑρήσομεν. The successful resistance offered to the enemy by

6 In that day I will make the chiefs of Judah
Like a fire pot among sticks of wood,
And like a torch of fire in a sheaf,
And they shall consume all the people around,
On the right hand and on the left;
For Jerusalem shall occupy her place in Jerusalem.
7 And Jehovah shall deliver the tents of Judah first,
In order that the splendor of the house of David,
And the splendor of the inhabitants of Jerusalem,
May not be magnified above Judah.
8 In that day Jehovah shall protect the inhabitants of Jerusalem:
So that he that stumbleth among them in that day shall be as David,
And the house of David shall be as God,
As the Angel of Jehovah before them.

the inhabitants of the metropolis, will inspire those of the country with the assurance, that, through the Divine aid, they shall obtain deliverance. לׁו , which is the Dative of advantage, stands collectively for לָמוֹ . Two MSS. and the Targ. read לְמוֹשֵׁב, but no doubt from correction. In two other MSS. לׁו is omitted.

6. *Jerusalem*, in the first instance, stands for the inhabitants. After the Jews shall have completely routed their enemies, they shall dwell in peace in their own land, and in the city of their ancient solemnities. Houbigant proposes to change וְיָשְׁבָה, as occurring the second time, into בִּכְלָיו , but, like most of his other conjectures, the change is not based upon any authority. One MS., the Arab, and the Greek MS. Pachom, omit the word altogether.

7. The inhabitants of the country being more exposed to the evils of the war than those in the fortified city, shall be the first to experience the Divine help. Standing in antithesis with the capital, their comparative helplessness is clearly implied; and the reason for the preference being given to them is assigned to be the prevention of that spirit of pride and self-exaltation, in which the inhabitants of a royal metropolis are too prone to indulge. The reading בָּרִאשֹׁנָה , "*as at the first*," which is found in two MSS., and is the original reading of three more, and is favored by the LXX., Arab., Syr., and Vulg., is not entitled to consideration.

8. A gracious promise of Divine assistance, supported, with admirable effect, by a beautiful climax. From the circumstance, that the LXX. have in several instances rendered אֱלֹהִים , by *angels*, some interpreters have supposed that the term is to be so understood here. The more enlightened moderns, however, discard this signification altogether. See Gesenius, Thesaurus Ling. Heb. p. 95, and Lee's Heb. Lex. p. 32. What clearly shows that no such idea can attach to the word in this place is the corrective phrase, כְּמַלְאַךְ יְהוָה , *as the Angel of Jehovah*, immediately following. The house of David was to be as God, yet not as God in the abstract, of which no proper conception can be formed, but as God manifested to men in his glorious forthcomings under the ancient dispensation, in the Divine Person of the Son, who went before the children of Israel as their Almighty leader and Protector, and to whom are vindicated the

9 And it shall be in that day,
  I will seek to destroy all the nations
  That come against Jerusalem.
10 And I will pour out upon the house of David,
  And upon the inhabitants of Jerusalem,
  A spirit of grace and of gracious supplications,
  And they shall look unto me whom they have pierced,

sum total of the Divine attributes. See Exod. xxxii. 34; where the words אֶמְחֶה‎ לְךָ‎ form the type of מַלְאָכִי‎ יִהְיֶה‎ לִפְנֵיכֶם‎, here adopted by Zechariah. Compare also Exod. xxxiii. 15, xxiii. 21; Is. lxiii. 9; Mal. iii. 1; and my Comment. on Zech. i. 11.

9. אֲבַקֵּשׁ‎ לְהַשְׁמִיד‎, *I will seek to destroy*, is spoken *more humano*, but conveys no idea of weakness in the speaker. "Summo studio ero attentus. Calvin.

10. We have here a clear and definite prophecy of the future conversion of the Jews, in consequence of a special and extraordinary outpouring of the influences of the Holy Spirit. Nothing that has hitherto taken place in the history of that people can be regarded as in any degree answering to the description here furnished, not even the numerous conversions that accompanied the Apostolic preaching on the day of Pentecost, and subsequently as narrated in the Acts. By רוּחַ‎, *spirit*, is not meant a gracious and prayerful disposition produced in the minds of the Jews, but the Divine influence itself by which that disposition will be created. It is called "spirit" by metonomy of cause for effect. חֵן‎ and תַּחֲנוּנִים‎ are from the same root, חָנַן‎, *to regard with favor, exercise mercy*, etc. The verb נָבַט‎, here used in Hiphil, is intensive in signification: *to look to*, or *regard with fixed attention*, to contemplate *with deep interest*, and with believing expectation. Such is the nature of that act of the mind which is exerted by every converted sinner, when the Saviour is spiritually discerned. In the case of the Jews there will be a special recognition of him as the Messiah whom their ancestors crucified, and whose deed they have appropriated by their personal unbelief and opposition to the truth of the Gospel, but whom they will then regard as all their salvation and all their desire. The textual reading אֵלַי‎, in the phrase וְהִבִּיטוּ‎ אֵלַי‎, "they shall look to ME," has been the subject of much controversy. It is found in most MSS., and among these the best, and is supported by the LXX., Aq., Symm., Theod., Syr., Targ., Vulg., and Arab. It is the more difficult reading, and one which has always proved revolting to the mind of a Jew, as there is no other antecedent to whom it can be referred than יְהֹוָה‎, JEHOVAH, verses 1 and 4. In order to avoid this reference, Kimchi gives to the following words, אֵת‎ אֲשֶׁר‎ דָּקָרוּ‎, the interpretation, *because they pierced*, leaving it undetermined who was pierced. But this construction is altogether inadmissible, as it deprives the verb of its accusative case, which is expressed in every other instance in which it occurs. It has accordingly been condemned by Abenezra, Abarbanel, Alschech, and other Rabbins. The rendering given to דָּקָרוּ‎ by the LXX. κατωρχήσαντο, *they insulted*, has been eagerly seized upon by some, especially by Theiner, Rosenmüller, Eichhorn, Gesenius, De Wette, Winer, and by none more than Maurer, who is at great pains to prove that, like נָקַב‎ and נָבַב‎, the verb דָּקַר‎ is to be taken in the metaphorical sense of *blaspheming* or *cursing*. Against such interpretation it is justly objected that this verb, which occurs in ten other passages, is never used except in the literal acceptation of piercing the body. It

And they shall lament for him,
As one lamenteth for an only son,
And be in bitterness for him,
As one is in bitterness for a first-born.

is thus used in chap. xiii. 3, of this very book. The same objection lies against the metaphorical sense of *grieving* or *provoking*, which even Calvin adopted, though he admits that the prophecy was literally fulfilled in Christ.

That the passage has a Messianic reference has been admitted both by the ancient and the more modern Jews. In the Gemara of Jerusalem, written sometime in the third century, we read : תריך אמוריך חד אמר זה הספידו של משיח וחורנה אמר זה הספידו של יצר הרע. *Two opinions are expressed: one states that they mourned on account of Messiah, and another that they mourned on account of corrupt nature.* A similar passage occurs in the Gemara of Babylon, Tract Succoth, fol. 52, col. 1, in which the words of Zechariah are cited, after the declaration respecting the mourning: בשלמא למאן דאמר על משיח בן יוסף שנהרג . *May he be in peace who refers it to Messiah the son of Joseph, who shall be slain.* See also the commentaries of Abarbanel and Abenezra, who give the same interpretation, as also does the Talkut Chasdash, fol. 24 : כי אחרי שידקר יונה שהוא משיח בי יוסף אחרי כי יבא דויד דהיינו משיח בן דויד . *For after they have pierced Jonah, who is Messiah the son of Joseph, then David will come, Messiah the son of David.* Hengstenberg's Christol. vol. iii. p. 222. The fiction of two Messiahs, one the son of Joseph, who should suffer and die, and another the son of David, who should prove victorious and reign forever, was invented purely with a view to reconcile those passages which describe the Messiah now as suffering, and now as reigning in glory, and thus to evade the Christian application of them to our Saviour.

It only remains to inquire how the Jews, who did not acquiesce in the interpretation adopted by Kimchi, have endeavored to get rid of the pronominal reference in אֵלַי . To this the reply is : By changing the reading into אֵלָיו , which, however, they did not at first venture to insert into the text, but merely gave it as the Keri, or corrected reading in the margin. This Keri, however, is only found in sixteen of Kennicott's and De Rossi's MSS. ; but at length a more daring step was taken by receiving it into the text itself, in which it is found in thirty-four of Kennicott's MSS., originally in three more, perhaps in five others, and now by correction in six ; in six of De Rossi's own, in two more originally, now in five others, and in twenty collated by him in other libraries. Of this insertion a serious complaint is made by Raymundus Martini, in his Pugio Fidei, p. 411, Leipsic, 1687, fol. And so ashamed have Lipmann, Abarbanel, and other Rabbins been of it, that they pass it entirely by in their controversies with the Christians, or candidly acknowledge that it is not to be regarded as forming any part of the sacred text. It is much to be regretted, that while it has been rejected by the best Jewish and Christian critics, the most free-thinking of the German school not excepted, it should have been adopted by Newcome and Boothroyd, who accordingly translate: "They shall look unto HIM whom they have pierced." It is true, they may seem to have the sanction of the Evangelist John, who quotes the passage thus : Ὄψονται εἰς ὃν ἐξεκέντησαν, xix. 37, and employs the words, καὶ οἵτινες αὐτὸν ἐξεκέντησαν, Rev. i. 7 ; but it must be obvious that he gives the prophecy historically, as having been literally fulfilled in Jesus of Nazareth, without designing to exhibit the exact wording of the prophet. See on Zech. xi. 12, 13.

11 In that day there shall be great lamentation in Jerusalem,
   As the lamentation of Hadad-rimmon in the valley of Megiddon.
12 And the land shall lament, every family apart;
   The family of the house of David apart, and their wives apart;
   The family of the house of Nathan apart, and their wives apart;
13 The family of the house of Levi apart, and their wives apart;
   The family of Shimei apart, and their wives apart;
14 All the families that are left,
   Every family apart, and their wives apart.

It might be supposed that אֶל being the true reading, לְ, and not יִלְ, would be required in the following sentence; but the use of the expletive phrase אֶת אֶרֶץ, necessarily led to the change of construction. הֵמַר is the infinitive of Hiphil, which carries forward the description instead of the finite form. It is here used intransitively; the root is מָרַר. The verb סָפַד signifies primarily *to beat*; then, as a sign of intense grief, *to smite* or *beat* the breast. There being usually great wailing and lamentation connected with such significant action in the East, it is also used to denote the noise made by mourners. The instances selected for illustration are of the most tender and touching kind.

11. To represent the greatness and universality of the lamentation which he describes, the prophet compares it to the greatest ever known among the Jews, viz. that which took place on the death of the excellent king Josiah, the result of the wound which he received at Hadad-rimmon. 2 Kings xxiii. 29; 2 Chron. xxxv. 23—25. See also the Lamentations of Jeremiah, composed on the occasion. Hadad-rimmon was the name of a place in the great plain of Esdraelon, near Megiddo, and was probably so called after the Syrian idol of that name. In the time of Jerome it was called Maximianopolis.

12—14. In these verses the universal character of the mourning is described, while, at the same time, its particular and individual features are likewise set forth. To show that all will be the subjects of it, the prophet begins with the descendants of David, and then proceeds to those of the priests, on account of the influence which their example would have on the rest of the people. Instead of Shimei, the LXX. have Συμεών, supposing that a tribal division was intended; and some have thought that שַׁמּוּעַ, *Shammua*, one of the sons of David, 2 Sam. v. 14, is meant; but it is more natural to regard the individual as one of the sons of Levi, who is classed along with that patriarch, just as Nathan, one of the sons of David, is with him, ver. 12. For שִׁמְעִי, *Shimei*, see Numb. iii. 18, 21, in which latter verse מִשְׁפַּחַת הַשִּׁמְעִי, *the family of the Shimeites*, occurs just as in Zechariah. It is implied in the last verse, that some families shall have become extinct at the period referred to. The men and women mourning apart has reference to the Jewish custom, according to which not only did the females dwell in separate apartments from the males, but also worshipped separately.

CHAPTER XIII.

This chapter contains a continuation of the prophecy respecting the future conversion of the Jews, ver. 1; predictions relating to the entire abolition of idolatry and false doctrine, 2—6; a resumption of the subject of the Messiah's sufferings, 7; and an account of the destruction of the greater part of the Jews during the Roman war, the preservation of the rest, and their ultimate restoration, 8, 9.

---

1 In that day there shall be a fountain opened
To the house of David, and to the inhabitants of Jerusalem,
For guilt and for uncleanness.
2 And it shall be in that day, saith Jehovah of hosts,
I will cut off the names of the idols from the earth;
And they shall not be remembered any more.
And I will also cause the prophets and the unclean spirit
To pass away from the earth.

1. This verse is intimately connected with the subject of the concluding verses of the preceding chapter. It is designed to relieve the anxious and troubled minds of the penitents there described. מָקוֹר, a *well*, or *fountain*, from קוּר, *to dig;* not, perhaps, without reference to chap. xii. 10. חַטָּאת, *guilt*, from חָטָא, *to miss a mark* or *way, to sin;* hence the substantive comes to signify the *guilt* contracted by sinning, the *punishment* to which it exposes the transgressor, and *a sin offering*, for the purpose of making expiation. That it is here to be taken in the sense of *guilt*, is shown by the accompanying term נִדָּה, *uncleanness*, or the impurity contracted by sin. That moral, and not ceremonial guilt and pollution are intended, the circumstances of the case evince; and the Jews are taught, that their deliverance from these is not to be effected by the Levitical sacrifices and purifications, but by the cleansing influence flowing from the death of the Messiah. See Heb. ix. 13, 14; 1 John i. 7. The verse exhibits the two grand doctrines of the gospel: justification and sanctification. The fountain here spoken of was opened when the Redeemer presented his sacrifice on the cross; but the Jews, with comparatively few exceptions, after the apostolic age, have shut it against themselves by their impenitence and unbelief. When, however, these shall be removed by the outpouring of Divine influence, promised, chap. xii. 10, they shall find it נִפְתָּח, *opened*, full, and overflowing with all spiritual blessings.

2. As no idolatry has existed among the Jews since their return from Babylon, and it is in the highest degree improbable that they will ever fall into it again, הָאָרֶץ should not be rendered, as in our common version, *the land*, but *the earth;* so that this and the following verses describe the total extinction of that horrible evil, and all the other systems of superstition and false religion which now impose upon the human family, together with those who teach and defend them. By רוּחַ הַטֻּמְאָה, *the spirit of impurity,* is meant a person pretending to inspiration, and in league with Satan, the god of this world, to whom, in contradistinction to רוּחַ הַקֹּדֶשׁ, *the spirit of holiness*, the

3 So that should any one still prophesy,
His father and his mother — his parents
Shall say to him, Thou shalt not live;
For thou speakest falsehood in the name of Jehovah;
And his father and his mother — his parents
Shall thrust him through when he prophesieth.
4 And it shall be in that day,
That the prophets shall be ashamed,
Every one of his vision, when he prophesieth;
And they shall not wear a hairy garment to deceive.
5 But each shall say, I am not a prophet,
I am a tiller of the ground;
For I have been in a state of slavery from my youth.
6 Then shall it be said to him,
What are these wounds in thy hands?
And he will say,
Those with which I have been wounded in the house of my
friends,

designation may well be applied. Compare πνεῦμα πύθωνος, Acts xvi. 16; τὸ πνεῦμα τῆς πλάνης, 1 John, iv. 6; and especially, καὶ ἐκ τοῦ στόματος τοῦ ψευδοπροφήτου πνεύματα τρία ἀκάθαρτα, Rev. xvi. 13.

3. There is in this verse a recognition of the law against those who seduced others to idolatry, Deut. xiii. 6—11. הוֹרָיו *parents.* יָלַד, signifies both to *beget*, and to *bear* children. The evil here denounced will not be connived at even by the nearest relatives. The tenderest parental feelings shall give place to the infliction of merited punishment.

4, 5. The shame with which false teachers shall be covered is here set forth. The hairy mantle, the garb of the ancient prophets, and that of certain orders of monks still, which is assumed in order to inspire the multitude with an impression of the superior sanctity of those by whom they are worn, shall be thrown aside, as dangerous to appear in. The false prophets wished to pass off as those who had really been invested with a Divine commission. The form of the infinitive הִנָּבְאֹתוֹ, is according to the analogy of verbs in לה. To the singular וַיֹּאמַר, at the beginning of ver. 5, each of the prophets previously mentioned is the nominative. הִקְנַנִי, lit. *one sold me as a slave,* but taken in connection with the following, מִנְּעוּרָי, *from my youth,* it signifies to be held in a state of slavery, to be a slave. The speaker declares that he had always been in a condition of life with which the exercise of the prophetic office was altogether incompatible. אָדָם, which some translators have preposterously retained as the proper name, *Adam,* is here used impersonally, precisely as the German *man,* and is best rendered into English by the passive of the accompanying verb.

6. This verse is commonly applied to the sufferings of Christ, but without any further ground than its mere proximity to that which follows, in which he and his sufferings are clearly predicted. In no tolerable sense could the Jews be called his מְאַהֲבִים, *lovers,* or *friends;* on the contrary, they hated both him and his Father. The words connect with the preceding thus: The false prophet, though he might rid himself of his idol-

7   Awake, O sword! against my shepherd,
    And against the man who is united to me,
    Saith Jehovah of hosts:

atrous vestments, would not be able to efface the marks that had been made on his hands in honor of the idol which he served, yet as it was customary to cut and maim the body, especially the hand, in token of grief for departed relatives, he might hope to escape detection by attributing his scars to the latter cause.

7. Various opinions have been formed respecting the person here referred to. Calvin thought he was Zechariah himself, as representative of all the prophets, and that the prophecy referred only indirectly to Christ. Grotius, Eichhorn, Bauer, and Jahn, apply it to Judas Maccabeus; Maurer to Jehoiakim; Ewald to Pekah; Hitzig to the pretended prophets spoken of in the preceding verses! The only satisfactory solution of the question is that which regards the words as directly and exclusively prophetic of the person and sufferings of the Messiah. This solution is induced not only by our Saviour's express appropriation of them to himself, Matt. xxvi. 31, but also by the manifest identity of the subject treated with that exhibited chap. xi. 4, 7, 10—14. The same subject there handled is resumed, and treated, just as it is there, in connection with the downfall of the Jewish state. The prophecy contained in this and the following verses has no coherence with what immediately precedes, and was evidently delivered upon a different occasion. A new section may, therefore, be considered as commencing here, though it only extends to chap. xiv. 5. The language employed is altogether peculiar. Not only is the Messiah designated the Shepherd of Jehovah, to indicate the relation in which he stood to the Father in the economy of redemption, but he is described as עֲמִיתִי גֶּבֶר, *the man of his union*; *i. e.* conjoined or closely united to him. The term translated *man*, is not that usually employed in Hebrew, which in such construction would merely be idiomatic, but גֶּבֶר, *a strong*, or *mighty man*, one who is such by way of eminence. עָמִית is used elsewhere only in the Pentateuch, namely, in Lev. v. 21, xviii. 20, xix. 11, 15, 17, xxiv. 19, xxv. 14, 15, 17; in all which passages it is employed to denote persons who were united together under common laws, for the enjoyment of common rights and privileges. It is derived from עָמַת, cognate with עָמַד, *to bind, bind together, unite in society*; Arab. ـمع *communis fuit, communem fecit rem*: hence the derivates עַם, a people, *i. e.* those united for their common interest; עֻמָּה, *conjunction, communion, association*; עִם, the conjunction *with*, indicating *accompaniment, society*. The renderings of the versions vary. LXX. ἄνδρα πολίτην μου. Aq. ἄνδρα σύμφυλόν μου. Symm. ἄνδρα τοῦ λαοῦ μου. Theod. ἄνδρα πλησίον μου. Syr. ܐܢܫ ܚܒܪܝ, *the man my friend*. Targ. שְׁלֻטָנָא חַבְרֵיהּ דִּבְּחִיתֵּיהּ דְּדָמֵי לֵיהּ, *the ruler his companion, his associate who is like him*. Vulg. *virum cohærentem mihi*. Leo Juda, *virum coæqualem mihi*. Hengstenberg, *a man, my nearest relation*. Burger, *mon confident*. De Wette, den Mann meines Gleichen, *the man my equal*. Arnheim, dem Manne, den ich mir zugesellt, *the man whom I have associated with myself*. The two last are the more remarkable, coming, as they do, the one from a Rationalist, and the other from a Jew. The idea expressed by the latter I conceive to be precisely what was intended by the Holy Spirit, by whom the words were indited. But of whom can this association be predicated, except of Him whose human

Smite the shepherd, and the sheep shall be scattered,
But I will turn back my hand upon the little ones.
8 And it shall be that in all the land,
Saith Jehovah,
Two parts therein shall be cut off and expire,
But the third part shall be left in it.
9 And I will cause the third part to go through the fire,

nature was assumed into the most intimate and perfect union with the Divine —IMMANUEL, who was one with the Father, and who could say, "He that hath seen me, hath seen the Father! The union or association is that of the two natures, and not that of the Divine nature or substance. This the use of the word גֶּבֶר, *man*, clearly proves. To the objection, that the words cannot be applied to our Saviour, since he was not cut off by a *sword*, it has been sufficiently replied, that חֶרֶב, *sword*, is here used figuratively for any means of taking away human life, just as in Exod. v. 21; 2 Sam. xii. 9, compared with 2 Sam. xi. 24. That the wicked Jews are intended, see Ps. xvii. 13, where the wicked are called the sword of Jehovah. They are regarded as in a state of sleep or inactivity, and are summoned to perpetrate the awful deed. According to an idiom common in the Hebrew prophets, the imperative is used instead of the future, in order to express with greater force the certainty of the event. See my note on Is. vi. 10. For a parallel instance of the personification of the sword, see Jer. xlvii. 6, 7. As חֶרֶב is feminine, and הַךְ masculine, Hitzig would refer the latter to the human agent handling the sword, but the irregularity in point of gender is sufficiently accounted for by the remoteness of the antecedent. הַךְ, *smite*, is quoted, Matt. xxvi. 31, as if it were אַךְ, *I will smite*, the first person singular of the future in Hiphil. There is no diversity of reading in the Hebrew MSS., but the Ald. and Pachom. MSS. of the LXX. read πατάξον, instead of πατάξω, which the Evangelist Matthew and Mark have copied. The difference is unimportant, yet there seems to be more propriety in the reading הַךְ, with reference to the sword addressed in the preceding clause, than in connecting this verb, whatever may be supposed to have been its form, with what follows in the verse. Comparing the present verse with chap. xi. 4, 7, and especially with what is predicted in the two following verses of the present chapter, in which the same subject is continued, it is evident the צֹאן, *sheep*, or *flock*, cannot be restricted to the disciples of Christ. The circumstances, however, in reference to which our Saviour appropriated the prophecy, afforded a striking type of the dispersion of the Jewish people, which is that intended by Zechariah. The disciples as Jews formed part of the flock which the good shepherd was commissioned to feed, but they, together with the Jewish Christians, converted by their ministry, who formed the first church at Jerusalem, were the צֹעֲרִים, *little ones*, on whom the Lord promises to turn back his hand, in order to protect them in the time of calamity. That the phrase הֵשִׁיב יָד עַל, *to turn*, or *turn back the hand*, upon any one, is used in a good as well as in a bad sense, see on Is. i. 25.

8, 9. In these verses are predicted the destruction of two-thirds of the inhabitants of Judea by the Roman arms, and by the famine and pestilence, the usual concomitants of war in the East, and the preservation of the remaining third part, which, after having been submitted to very trying and afflictive processes, should come forth out of the furnace a regenerated and spiritual people. The

And will refine them as silver is refined,
And will try them as gold is tried;
It shall invoke my name, and I will answer it,
I will say, It is my people;
And it shall say, Jehovah is my God.

former was fulfilled not only during what is commonly called the Jewish war, but also, to a fearful extent, under more than one of the succeeding emperors; the processes pointed at in the latter have been more or less carried forward ever since, but are, it is to be hoped, soon to terminate in the conversion of the Jews to God. Then shall they enter into a new relation to him, according to the terms of the better covenant, Jer. xxxi. 33; Heb. viii. 10, 11.

CHAPTER XIV.

IN the first two verses of this chapter the destruction of Jerusalem by the Romans and the calamities consequent upon that event are set forth; after which the destruction of the forces composing the hostile army is predicted, 3. A promise of special interposition in behalf of the people of God is then given, by which effectual provision is made for their escape, 4, 5. The prophet next describes a period of great calamity, which is to give place to one of unmixed and perennial happiness, 6, 7; when the means of spiritual life and enjoyment shall be universal and continual, 8; and the true God the exclusive object of obedience and worship, 9; and while every barrier to the free intercourse of Christians throughout the world shall be removed, special honor will be conceded to Jerusalem as the metropolis of converted Israel, 10, 11. The dreadful judgments to be inflicted on their final enemies, and the complete discomfiture of these enemies, are depicted, 12—15: after which follow predictions respecting an annual visit which all the nations shall pay to Jerusalem, 16; the punishment of those which neglect to perform it, 17—19; and the universally holy character which shall distinguish her inhabitants, their occupations and services, 20, 21.

1 BEHOLD the day of Jehovah cometh,
And thy spoil shall be divided in the midst of thee.
2 For I will collect all the nations against Jerusalem to battle,

1. For the phraseology יוֹם בָּא לַיהֹוָה, comp. Is. xxii. 5. The criticism of Hengstenberg, who denies that it is equivalent to בָּא יוֹם יְהֹוָה, is without any foundation. By the day of Jehovah is meant the period of the infliction of judgment. See, in reference to the same event which is here predicted, Joel ii. 31, iii. 14; Mal. iv. 1, 5. By the spoil of Jerusalem is meant all that her inhabitants had accumulated, and which would be fit spoil for the enemy, especially the treasures of the temple. Notwithstanding all that was consumed by fire, the plunder obtained by the Romans was so great, that gold fell in Syria to half its former value.

2. All the nations here mean soldiers from all the different nations forming

And the city shall be taken,
And the houses plundered, and the women ravished;
And half the city shall go forth into captivity,
But the rest of the people shall not be cut off from the city.
3 And Jehovah shall go forth,
And fight with those nations,
As in the day when he fought
In the day of battle.
4 And his feet shall stand in that day
On the mount of Olives, which is before Jerusalem on the east;
And the mount of Olives shall be split in its midst,
Toward the east and toward the west,
Into a very great valley;
Half of the mountain shall recede towards the north,
And half of it towards the south.
5 And ye shall flee to the valley of my mountains,
For the valley of the mountains shall reach to Azal;
Yea, ye shall flee as ye fled from the earthquake,
In the days of Uzziah, king of Judah;

the Roman empire, which composed the army of Titus. The verse contains a fearful description of the capture of Jerusalem under the command of that general. After its destruction, the more distinguished, handsome, and able-bodied Jews were sold into slavery, or condemned to work in the mines; but the poorer and more contemptible sort were permitted to remain among the ruins. As usual, where הִשָּׁגַלְנָה occurs in the text the Keri has תִּשָּׁכַבְנָה, for the sake of euphemism. The latter word has found its way into a great many MSS.

3. The Roman power was doomed in its turn to destruction. Formidable as it might appear, Jehovah would in his providence overthrow it, as he had done the enemies of his people in former ages. Comp. Exod. xiv. 14, xv. 3, etc.

4, 5. These verses convey, in language of the most beautiful poetical imagery, the assurance of the effectual means of escape that should be provided for the truly pious. We accordingly learn from Eusebius, that on the breaking out of the Jewish war, the Christian church at Jerusalem, in obedience to the warning of our Saviour, Matt. xxiv. 16, fled to Pella, a city beyond Jordan, where they lived in safety. As the mount of Olives lay in their way, it is represented as cleaving into two halves, in order to make a passage for them. Comp. chap. iv. 7. הָרַי is not to be considered as the less usual form of the masculine plural, but as a proper plural with the pronominal affix. Jehovah calls them *his*, because he had formed them, by cleaving Olivet into two. The valley lay between them. אָצַל was the proper name of a place, close to one of the gates on the east side of Jerusalem, to which the cleft or valley was to extend westward, so as at once to admit those who should flee from the enemy. Most commentators think of some locality to the east of the mount of Olives, but far less aptly. The word properly signifies to *join* or *be joined to*, *be at the side*, *near*. Its proximity to the city must have originated the name. For וְנַסְתֶּם, *ye shall flee*, we find the reading וְנִסְתַּם, *shall be stopped up*, in four of De Rossi's MSS. and in

For Jehovah my God shall come,
And all the holy ones with thee.
6   And it shall be in that day
That there shall not be the light of the precious orbs,
But condensed darkness.
7   But there shall be one day,

the margin of Bomberg's Hebrew Bible; but, though supported by the LXX., Arab., Targ., Symm., and the other Greek interpreters, it is utterly to be rejected, as unsuited to the connection. The very opposite of what would thus be expressed, is required. Yet it is adopted by Blayney and Boothroyd! We have nothing in Scripture relative to the earthquake here referred to except as a date, Amos i. 1. Instead of עִמָּךְ, *with thee*, nearly forty MSS. and all the versions read עִמּוֹ, *with him;* and instead of קְדֹשִׁים, *the holy ones*, one MS., the Syr., Arab., and Targ., read קְדֹשָׁיו, *his holy ones.* To refer עִמָּךְ, with the Rabbins, Drusius, and Blayney, to Jerusalem, is quite inadmissible, since such construction affords no tolerable sense. The change of person was occasioned by a sudden transition in the mind of the prophet to the Lord, whom he addresses as present. For the application of this part of the prophecy, compare the parallel prediction of our Lord himself, Matt. xxiv. 30, 31, where those whom Zechariah designates קְדֹשִׁים, *holy ones*, are called τοὺς ἀγγέλους αὐτοῦ. That a future personal and pre-millennial advent of the Redeemer is here taught, I cannot find.

6. Now follows the prediction of a period of unmitigated calamity, which may be regarded as comprehending the long centuries of oppression, cruelty, mockery, and scorn, to which the Jews have been subjected ever since the destruction of Jerusalem. It has also, for the most part, been a period during which the gross darkness of superstition and delusion has reigned over the land of their fathers. יִקָּפְאוּן יְקָרוֹת have been

variously rendered and interpreted. LXX. ψύχος καὶ πάγος. Vulg. *frigus et gelu.* Syr. ⟨Syriac⟩, *cold and ice.* Thus also Maurer, and several other moderns. But whatever connection there may be between the absence of light and the production of cold and ice in the depth of winter, the contrast is not so natural as that between light and darkness. Besides, יְקָרוֹת cannot with any show of truth be rendered *cold.* It is an adjective plural from the root יָקַר, *to be precious, valuable, costly.* The idea of *cold* rests upon no better authority than a mere Rabbinical conjecture embodied in the Keri of Prov. xvii. 27, which exhibits יְקַר רוּחַ, instead of וְקַר רוּחַ, the proper and only term suitable in such connection. That יְקָרוֹת may fitly be understood as designating the celestial luminaries, whence we obtain what, in common parlance, we call "the *precious* light of heaven," will appear on comparing Job xxxi. 26, where the moon is described as יָקָר הֹלֵךְ, *walking preciously* or *splendidly* across the heavens. With Prof. Lee, (Heb. Lex. p. 533,) I read אוֹר יְקָרוֹת in construction, placing the accent on the latter of the two words, instead of retaining it over the former. קִפָּאוֹן properly signifies *congelation, condensation, excessive density*, from קָפָא, *to draw together, contract, become thick, dense*, and the like. Blayney renders, *thick fog.* The textual reading יִקַּפְּאוּן, *they shall withdraw themselves*, is inferior to that of the Keri יִקָּפָּאוֹן, which is found in the text of one hundred and thirty-four of Kennicott's MSS., and in twenty-two more originally, in nine of De Rossi's Spanish MSS., which are

(It is known to Jehovah),
When it shall not be day and night;
For at the time of the evening there shall be light.
8 And it shall be in that day
That living waters shall proceed from Jerusalem,
Half of them to the Eastern sea,
And half of them to the Western sea;
In summer and in winter shall it be.

reckoned the best in the Soncin., Brixian, and Complutensian editions, and in Machzors of the fifteenth and sixteenth centuries. None of the ancient versions employ a verb.

7. Another period is here predicted, but one entirely different from the preceding — a day altogether *unique*, יוֹם אֶחָד, *one peculiar day*, the only one of its kind. See Gesenius in אֶחָד, No. 5. Its peculiarity is to consist in the absence of the alternations of day and night. It is to be all day — a period of entire freedom from war, oppression and other outward evils which induce affliction and wretchedness, interrupt the peace of the church, and prevent the spread of truth and righteousness. Νὺξ γὰρ οὐκ ἔσται ἐκεῖ, Rev. xxii. 25. לְעֵת־עֶרֶב, *the time of the evening*, does not refer to the close of the happy period just described, but to that of the preceding period of afflictive darkness. At the very time when a dark and gloomy day is expected to give way to a night of still greater darkness and obscurity, light shall suddenly break forth, the light of the one long day, which is to be interrupted by no night. That this period is that of the Millennium, or the thousand years, the circumstances of which are described Rev. xx. 3—7, I cannot entertain a doubt. The time of its commencement has been variously but fruitlessly calculated. The knowledge of it the Father hath reserved in his own power. "It is known to Jehovah," and, by implication, to him alone.

8. מַיִם חַיִּים, *living*, i. e. *running, perennial, refreshing, and salubrious water*, in opposition to that which is stagnant and noxious. הַיָּם הַקַּדְמֹנִי, *the Eastern sea*, i. e. the Asphaltitic Lake; and יָם הָאַחֲרוֹן, *the Western sea*, i. e. the Mediterranean; so called because when a person resident at Jerusalem faces the East, which is the primary point of the horizon with the Orientals, the Dead Sea is *before* him, (מִקַּדְמָיו), and the Mediterranean (אַחֲרוֹן) *behind* him. The more important portions of the globe lying to the east and west of Jerusalem, there is an obvious propriety in the selection of these two directions. The declaration that these waters are to flow בַּקַּיִץ וּבָחֹרֶף, is expressive of constancy. They shall neither be dried up by the heat of summer, nor congealed by the frost of winter. The LXX. have ἐν θέρει καὶ ἐν ἔαρι, "in summer and in spring," which is to be accounted for on the ground that what was winter in more northerly regions, was spring in Egypt, in which country that version was made. In the figurative language of Scripture, water is not only used as an emblem of purification, but also for the purpose of representing the means of spiritual life, refreshment, and fertility —the doctrines and ordinances of the gospel. The descendants of Abraham, restored to their own land, and become his children in the faith, will go forth, full of zeal and spiritual activity, as missionaries to other nations, to promote revivals in the churches of Christ by rehearsing what great things God hath done for them, and to carry on the work of conversion among those nations and tribes that shall not then have been turned to the Lord.

9 And Jehovah shall become king over all the earth;
In that day Jehovah alone shall be,
And his name alone.
10 And all the earth shall be changed
As it were into the plain from Geba to Rimmon,
South of Jerusalem;
And she shall be exalted,
And be inhabited in her place,
From the gate of Benjamin
· To the place of the former gate,
To the gate of the corners;
And from the tower of Hananeel
To the king's wine-vats.

9. In consequence of the universal spread of the Gospel, the multiplicity of heathen gods will be swept away from the face of the earth, the unity of Jehovah universally acknowledged, and the glorious harmony of those attributes which constitute his one Divine character (שְׁמוֹ, *his name*) clearly discovered, and heartily adored. According to the ordinary mode of translating the words יִהְיֶה יְהוָה אֶחָד וּשְׁמוֹ אֶחָד, *there shall be one Lord and his name one*, they may seem clogged with little or no difficulty, as the true God is thus set forth in opposition to the "gods many and lords many" of the heathen; but we have only to introduce the incommunicable name JEHOVAH into the translation when the greatest incongruity at once appears. If we then render, *there shall be one Jehovah*, the conclusion is inevitable, that previous to the predicted period, there must have existed more Jehovahs than one. Or, if we render, *Jehovah shall be one*, we make the passage teach either that Jehovah was not one before, or, that he will no longer be three, or triune — Father, Son, and Holy Ghost, in the undivided unity of the Godhead. All ambiguity, however, will at once be removed, if אֶחָד be taken adverbially, and rendered *only, alone*, or the like. And thus I conceive it must be rendered in the primary article of the inspired creed of the Hebrews: יְחִיֶה אֱלֹהֵינוּ יְהוָה אֶחָד, JEHOVAH *is our God*, JEHOVAH *alone*. The doctrine, therefore, taught in the present verse is simply that Jehovah shall be the only existing object of religious worship and obedience, and no characteristics but his be any longer recognized as divine.

10, 11. These verses intimate that every obstruction shall be removed which prevents the free and full flow of the living waters throughout the world. What is high shall be levelled, and what is low shall be elevated. This idea was suggested by the natural impossibility of water flowing in a westerly direction from Jerusalem to the Mediterranean, owing to the hilly country which intervenes. In יִסֹּב we have a rather unusual signification of סָבַב, *to be turned*, i. e. *changed*. The verb חָפַךְ is ordinarily used to express what is here intended. גֶּבַע, *Geba*, was a Levitical city in the tribe of Benjamin, near to Gibeah, on the northern border of the kingdom of Judah. רִמּוֹן, *Rimmon*, was a town in the tribe of Simeon, in the south of Palestine, and to be distinguished from the rock Rimmon, to the north-east of Michmash. הָעֲרָבָה, *the Arabah*, is the level or plain of the Jordan, extending from the lake of Tiberias to the Elanitic gulf, · though in the present day this name is only applied to that part of it which lies

11 And they shall dwell in her,
   And there shall be no more curse,
   And Jerusalem shall dwell in safety.
12 And this shall be the plague
   With which Jehovah will plague all the people
   That shall fight against Jerusalem;
   Their flesh shall consume away
   While they stand upon their feet,
   And their eyes shall consume away in their sockets,
   And their tongue shall consume away in their mouth.
13 And it shall be in that day
   That there shall be great confusion from Jehovah among them,
   So that each shall seize the hand of another,
   And his hand shall be raised against the hand of another;
14 And Judah also shall fight in Jerusalem,
   And the wealth of all the nations around shall be collected,
   Gold, and silver, and garments, in great abundance.
15 And the plague of the horses,
   The mules, the camels, and the asses,
   And all the cattle which shall be in those camps,
   Shall be even as this plague.
16   And it shall be

to the south of the Dead Sea. The nominative to רָאָה and רָבָה, is not הָאָרֶץ, but יְרוּשָׁלַיִם, immediately preceding. For the orthography of רָאָה, comp. Hos. x. 14, and other passages in which the א is inserted as a *mater lectionis*. Great uncertainty exists relative to the exact position of some of the places here mentioned. חֶרֶם is used as in Mal. iii. 24, in the acceptation, *curse*. LXX. ἀνάθεμα. Comp. πᾶν κατανάθεμα οὐκ ἔσται ἔτι, Rev. xxii. 3. There will be no more any civil or national punishments inflicted on account of sin, these having been rendered unnecessary by the universal prevalence of righteousness and truth.

12--15. The hostile powers whose punishment is here denounced are those which shall form the great final confederacy. Com. Is. lix. 18; Ezek. xxxviii., xxxix.; Rev. xix. The representation of the punishment is the most horrible that can be imagined — a living skeleton, rapidly wasting away! From what is stated ver. 14, it appears that the Jews (יְהוּדָה, *Judah*), shall not only defend themselves at Jerusalem, but make a successful attack upon the enemy. נִלְחַם בְּ, when used in reference to place, signifies to fight *at* or *in* such place. LXX. παρατάξεται ἐν Ἰερουσαλήμ. בְּגִבְעָה — נִבְחֲמָה, Jud. v. 19. The collection of the wealth of the surrounding nations, refers to the gathering of the rich spoil of the contingents furnished by them to compose the hostile army. The entire encampments of the enemy, including the cavalry and beasts of burden, were all to share in the awful catastrophe. Whether God will employ the plague and other destructive diseases for the annihilation of the enemies of his people, time must show. The genitive in מְהוּמַת יְהֹוָה, is that of cause, *a consternation sent* or *produced by Jehovah*.

16—18. מֵאֵת מִשְׁפְּחוֹת, lit. *from the*

That the whole residue of all the nations
That shall come up against Jerusalem,
Shall go up from year to year
To worship the king, Jehovah of hosts,
And to celebrate the feast of tabernacles.
17 And it shall be that those who go not up
Of the families of the earth to Jerusalem,

sufficiency of a year in a year, i. e. when time has fully satisfied the claims of one year and enters upon another. It is only an idiomatic mode of expressing *from year to year*, or *annually*. What is here predicted is expressly restricted to the particular nations which shall have engaged in the last great attack upon the Jews. And, though the language of the following verse may appear to be more general, yet the circumstances of the context require the restriction to be carried forward beyond the limits of the present. Still, however, even with this restriction, the prophecy cannot, without manifest absurdity, be interpreted of the totality of the inhabitants of the nations in question. Let steam vessels and railroads be multiplied to any imaginable extent, the idea of the possibility of conveying such immense numbers to Palestine cannot be entertained. Or, supposing them to have been conveyed thither, few of them would after all have an opportunity of worshipping at Jerusalem during the short period allotted for the Feast of Tabernacles. Not only would the country be too small to contain their encampments, and to furnish them with necessary provisions, but the pressure, noise, and bustle of the crowds would be such as to destroy everything in the shape of devotional propriety and enjoyment. I cannot, therefore, but take the meaning to be, that the nations in question will go up to Jerusalem in the persons of their representatives, just as in former times the Jews resident in foreign countries had those who went to the annual festivals in their name, or on their behalf. Why the Egyptians should be specially introduced. ver. 18, it is difficult to determine, except it be, that as their country is watered by the Nile, and is not dependent for fertility upon rain falling in the country itself, they might be considered as exempt from the threatened plague of drought. But, if the rains fail in Ethiopia, it will in effect be the same as if they fail in Egypt itself. After the words עֲלֵיהֶם לֹא, the repetition of הַגֶּשֶׁם, *the rain*, from the end of the preceding verse, is understood.

It is worthy of notice, that the Feast of Tabernacles or Booths is the only one of all the Jewish festivals which is represented in this prophecy as being observed at the period therein specified. No mention is made of the great day of Atonement, the Passover, the Pentecost, etc. These have all been superseded by their fulfilment as types in the substantial blessings of the Christian economy. Their re-establishment would be a denial of the reality or efficacy of their antitypes. It may, however, be asked, Why should the Feast of Tabernacles form an exception? To this it may be replied, first, that such a festival may be observed without any compromise of the principles of the New Dispensation. Secondly, it may be considered as peculiarly adapted to the retrospections of the converted Jews, who will have to commemorate the sojourn of their fathers, not merely for forty years in the wilderness, but their sojourn for two thousand years in the countries of the dispersion. And thirdly, it may serve as a striking memento to them, that, though they have been restored to the rest of Canaan, they are still only strangers and pilgrims upon the earth, and that there yet remaineth a rest for the people of God. In this

To worship the King, Jehovah of hosts,
Upon them there shall be no rain.
18 And if the family of Egypt should not go up, nor come,
Upon them also there shall be none;
There shall be upon them the plague,
With which Jehovah shall plague the nations,
That will not go up
To celebrate the feast of tabernacles.
19 This shall be the punishment of Egypt,
And the punishment of all the nations
That will not go up
To celebrate the feast of tabernacles.
20   In that day there shall be upon the bells of the horses,
HOLINESS TO JEHOVAH;
And the pots in the house of Jehovah
Shall be as the bowls before the altar.

point of view, believing Gentiles, who may go up to the festival, can find no difficulty in celebrating it with them to their mutual edification. That the sacrifices which were offered at that feast, or any other animal sacrifices, will then be renewed, is a position, to maintain which would be to counteract the express design, and contradict the express declarations of the dispensation of grace.

It may be said, that Ezekiel gives a full description of the re-establishment of the sacrificial system and of the whole of the temple worship. Nothing can be more certain. But when was this re-establishment to take place? Any one who will only cursorily examine the commencement of the fortieth chapter of that prophet will at once perceive, that, though it follows immediately after chapters relating to the destruction of Gog and Magog, it was nevertheless delivered to the prophet not fewer than *thirteen* years afterwards, and may, therefore, naturally be expected to refer to a subject altogether different. That subject I conceive to be the restoration of the temple and the temple worship after the return from Babylon — a subject which cannot but have lain near the heart of the exiles, and worthy to be made the theme of prophecy, but which is nowhere else referred to in the book of Ezekiel. Difficulty there may be in making the measurements there given agree with those specified by Josephus as the dimensions of the second temple; but far greater difficulties attach to every attempt to refer them to a temple still future, or to view them as wholly emblematical.

19. The connection shows that חַטָּאת is not here to be taken in the sense of *sin*, but of the *punishment of sin*. Comp. Lam. iii. 38, iv. 6.

20. The מְצִלּוֹת were small metallic plates, suspended from the necks or heads of horses and camels, for the sake of ornament, and making a tinkling noise by striking against each other like cymbals. Root צָלַל, to *tingle, tinkle*. As the inscription קֹדֶשׁ־לַיהוָה, HOLINESS TO JEHOVAH, was the sacred symbol engraven upon the golden crown of the Jewish High Priest, the design of the prophecy is evidently to teach, that when the Jews shall be restored to their own land, there shall be no greater degree of holiness attaching to what was formerly accounted most sacred, than what will attach to the ornamental trappings of the horses. Devotion of person and

21 Yea every pot in Jerusalem and in Judah
Shall be holiness to Jehovah of hosts;
And all who slaughter shall come,
And take of them and boil in them,
And there shall no more be a Canaanite
In the house of Jehovah of hosts in that day.

property to the service of God will be the only holiness then recognized. Ceremonial sanctity shall no longer exist. The same thing is expressed in the second clause of the verse. The vessels in which the flesh was cooked, and which were accounted the meanest about the temple, shall, as to the degree of holiness, be upon a par with those which had been destined for the most sacred purpose, namely, the reception of the blood of the sacrificial victims. All distinction shall be done away.

21. The same idea is here more fully carried out. Not only the common utensils used by the priests, but those employed for cooking in private houses, both at Jerusalem and throughout the country, shall all be regarded as equally holy. From its being expressly stated, that the flesh of the animals to be slaughtered is to be boiled in the pots, and no mention is made of the sprinkling of the blood, it must be inferred that killing for food, and not for sacrifice, is what the prophet has in view. Considering what stumbling-blocks a mercenary and covetous priesthood has ever proved to the world, and to what a fearful extent the ministry in holy things has been made a matter of merchandise, there is great force in the declaration with which the prophet closes: "There shall no more be a *Canaanite* in the house of Jehovah!" By כְּנַעֲנִי, *Canaanite,* is meant a *merchant;* the Phœnicians, who inhabited the northern part of Canaan, having been the most celebrated merchants of antiquity. See for this acceptation of the term, Job xl. 30; Prov. xxxi. 24; Is. xxiii. 8. It is here used metaphorically.

MALACHI.

MALACHI (מַלְאָכִי, *Messenger*), is the last of all the Hebrew prophets, but we are left in profound ignorance respecting his personal history, and can only judge of the circumstances of his times from what is contained in his book. According to the tradition of the synagogue, he lived after the prophets Haggai and Zechariah, and was contemporary with Nehemiah. This statement is fully borne out by the affinity of the book written by the prophet, with that written by the patriot. Both presuppose the temple to have been already built. The same condition of the Jews is described. They both condemn foreign marriages, and enforce the due payment of tythes, which had been neglected. They likewise correct abuses which had crept in with respect to the sacrifices, and reprove their countrymen for their want of sympathy with the poor.

In all probability, Malachi occupied the same place with respect to Nehemiah, which Haggai and Zechariah did with respect to Zerubbabel. That the former was assisted in the discharge of his duties by prophets, may be inferred from the charge brought against him by Sanballat, Neh. vi. 7. He may therefore be conceived of as having flourished somewhere about the year B. C. 420. His book is composed of a series of spirited castigations, in which the persons accused are introduced as repelling the charges, but thereby only affording occasion for a fuller exposure, and a more severe reproof of their conduct. Both priests and people are unsparingly reprimanded, and while they are threatened with divine judgments, encouragement is held out to such as walked in the fear of the Lord. His predictions respecting John the Baptist, the Messiah, and the destruction of the Jewish polity, are clear and unequivocal.

Considering the late age in which he lived, the language of Malachi is pure; his style possesses much in common with the old prophets, but is distinguished more by its animation, than by its rhythmus or grandeur.

CHAPTER I.

WITH a view to work a conviction of ingratitude in the minds of his countrymen, the prophet begins by setting forth the peculiar favor which Jehovah had shown to them as a people in contradistinction to the Edomites, 1—5. He then reproaches the priests for their unworthy conduct in presenting the refuse of the animals in sacrifice, 6—8; charges them with a mercenary spirit, and threatens to reject them, and supply their place with true worshippers from among the most distant heathen, 9—11; and concludes with a renewed reprimand, and the denunciation of a curse upon those who practised deception with respect to the offerings, 12—14.

---

1 THE Sentence of Jehovah's oracle to Israel by Malachi.
2 . I have loved you, saith Jehovah,
Yet ye say, Wherein hast thou loved us?
Was not Esau brother to Jacob? saith Jehovah,
Yet I loved Jacob,

1. For the formula מַשָּׂא דְבַר־יְהֹוָה, see on Zech. ix. 1. That מַלְאָכִי, *Malachi*, is the proper name of the prophet, and not a mere official appellative, as the LXX., Vitringa, and others, interpret, may safely be inferred from the analogy of the title with others prefixed to the prophetical writings. As for the form of the name, Vitringa, Hiller, Michaelis, and Gesenius, take it to be compounded of מַלְאָךְ and יָהּ, of which they consider י to be a contraction, and accordingly explain the name as meaning *The Messenger of Jehovah*. To this, however, it has been objected, that no examples of an abbreviation of the Divine name to this extent are to be found; and, therefore, it has been deemed more natural to regard the י as the pronominal affix of the first person singular, and to render, *My Messenger*. This latter solution has been adopted by Hengstenberg, who labors in vain to establish a connection between the name of the prophet, and the same word as occurring in its official signification, chap. iii. 1. The form appears to be really nothing more than an instance of what Ewald calls "the last and newest mode of deriving adjectives from nouns," and denoting origin or source. Compare כְּתָרִי, עִבְרִי, צָבָאִי, רַגְלִי, דְּבָרִי, סוּפִי, etc. יִשְׂרָאֵל, *Israel*, is here used to denote the whole of the twelve tribes, which had returned to their native land, Jer. l. 4, 5, 19, 20.

2, 3. The sovereign benevolence of Jehovah, and the ingratitude of the Hebrews in the time of the prophet, are strikingly contrasted. To the petulant question, "Wherein hast thou loved us?" which is only the first of a series which are put in the course of the book, the answer is direct and conclusive — in showing greater kindness to their progenitor Jacob, than he had done to his brother Esau. The temporal advantages of Palestine were vastly superior to those of Idumea, which was comparatively a sterile and desert country; and the Jews had, besides, experienced distinguished favor in having been restored to their land, and had prosperity conferred upon them, while the Edomites, who had suffered from the invasion of their country by the Chaldeans, five years after the capture of Jerusalem, had not been restored. It is to the desolations occasioned by this invasion that reference is

3 But I hated Esau,
  And made his mountains a desolation,
  And his heritage abodes of the desert.
4 Because Edom saith, We are impoverished,
  But we will rebuild the desolate places;
  Thus saith Jehovah of hosts,
  They may build, but I will overthrow;
  And men shall call them, The border of wickedness,
  And, The people against whom Jehovah is indignant forever.
5 And your eyes shall see, and ye shall say,
  Let Jehovah be magnified, from the border of Israel.
6   A son honoreth his father,
  And a servant his master:
  If then I be a father, where is my honor?
  And if I be a master, where is my fear?
  Saith Jehovah of hosts to you, O ye priests,
  That despise my name; yet ye say,
  Wherein have we despised thy name?

made ver. 3. שָׂנֵא, *to hate*, is here used in a comparative sense, qualifying the preceding verb אָהַב, *to love*. As the opposite of love is hatred, when there is only an inferior degree of the former exhibited, the object of it is regarded as being hated rather than loved. See for this idiom, Gen. xxix. 30, 31; Deut. xxi. 15, 16; Prov. xiii. 24; Matt. vi. 24; Luke xiv. 26, compared with Matt. x. 37. תַּנּוֹת is considered by some to be the feminine of תַּנִּים, and is rendered *serpents, jackals*, or the like; but it is preferable to adopt the derivation from the Arabic, تَنَّ, *substitit, habitavit.* Hence تَنَّةٌ, *habitatio, mansio.* By the "habitations of the desert," are meant deserted, ruined dwellings, such as are still found in great abundance in Idumea. The phrase is parallel to שְׁמָמָה in the preceding hemistich, and corresponds to the חֳרָבוֹת, *waste places*, or ruins, ver. 4.

4, 5. Every attempt on the part of the Idumeans to recover themselves, and enjoy permanent prosperity, should prove abortive, and their continually depressed condition should afford additional proof to the Israelites of the kindness of God towards his own people. גְּבוּל, *boundary*, is here used in the sense of *territory*, or the space marked out by the surrounding boundaries. Comp. Gen. x. 19; Numb. xxi. 24. מֵעַל לִגְבוּל יִשְׂרָאֵל, according to Rosenmüller, Hitzig, Maurer, and Ewald, means *beyond the Hebrew territory*, — construing the words with יִגְדַּל, but it seems more natural to connect them with אֲשֶׁר תֹּאמְרוּ. Ye who dwell upon the land of Israel shall say from the locality you occupy, and to which, through Divine goodness, ye have been restored, Jehovah be magnified. The ל prefixed to גְּבוּל, adds nothing to the force of the preceding preposition. See Gesen. in מֵעַל.

6. Upon the fact of the respect usually shown by inferiors to their superiors, Jehovah had a right to expect that honor and reverence which corresponded to the high position which he occupied as Author and Moral Governor of the universe. These having, however, been withheld,

7 In offering polluted bread upon my altar;
   But ye say, Wherein have we polluted thee?
   In your saying, The table of Jehovah is contemptible.
8 When ye offer the blind for sacrifice, is it not evil?
   And when ye offer the lame and the sick, is it not evil?
   Present it now to thy governor;
   Will he be satisfied with thee,
   Or accept thy person? saith Jehovah of hosts.
9 Now, then, conciliate the regard of Jehovah, that he may pity us:
   This hath been by your means;
   Will he accept your persons? saith Jehovah of hosts.
10   Who is there even among you that would shut the doors?
   Yea, ye will not kindle the fire on my altar for nought.
   I have no pleasure in you, saith Jehovah of hosts,
   Neither will I accept an offering at your hand.
11 But from the rising of the sun to its setting,
   My name shall be great among the nations;
   And in every place, incense shall be offered to my name,
   And a pure offering;

chiefly owing to the irreligious and profane conduct of the priests, the charge is principally laid against them.

7. That לֶחֶם, *bread*, or *food*, is here to be taken as the Arab. ꜰꜱꜱ, *caro*, in the sense of *animal flesh*, is obvious, from its being presented on the מִזְבֵּחַ, *altar of sacrifice*, to which also the שֻׁלְחָן, *table*, must be referred, and not to the table of shew-bread. Contempt of sacred things involves contempt of Him to whom they appertain.

8. Another *argumentum ad hominem.* The priests had the effrontery to present to Jehovah what they would not have dared to offer to their civil governor. To offer animals with any blemish, was expressly prohibited in the law. Lev. xxii. 22, 24; Deut. xv. 21.

9. How much soever the words וְעַתָּה חַלּוּ־נָא פְנֵי־אֵל וִיחָנֵנוּ, may at first sight appear to contain a serious exhortation to the priests to repent of their wicked conduct, and to pray for the Divine favor to themselves and the people, yet the connection requires them to be understood ironically. No prayers or supplications of theirs could avail anything while they presented such unlawful sacrifices. This is expressly declared in the form of a pointed interrogation at the close of the verse. הֲיִשָּׂא מִכֶּם פָּנִים is a more emphatic form, instead of הֲיִשָּׂא אֶת־פְּנֵיכֶם.

10, 11. The rendering of the LXX., adopted by Newcome, "Surely the doors shall be closed against you," cannot be admitted. The authority for the change of מִי, *who*, into כִּי, *surely*, is of no weight; and the verb סָגַר is never construed with בְּ, in order to express the idea of exclusion. Such was the avaricious disposition of the priests, that they would not perform even the most trivial services without payment. How could such expect to be acceptable to God? These verses contain an explicit prediction of the rejection of the Jewish worship, and of the reception of the Gentiles to perform spiritual worship in the Church of the Lord. His name, which the priests had treated with contempt,

For my name shall be great among the nations,
Saith Jehovah of hosts.
12 But ye have profaned it by your saying,
The table of Jehovah is polluted,
And its fruit, even his food, is contemptible.
13   Ye have also said, What a weariness!
And have contemned it, saith Jehovah of hosts;
And ye have brought the torn, and the lame, and the sick,
Yea, ye have brought the offering;
Should I accept it at your hand? saith Jehovah.
14 But cursed be the deceiver, who hath a male in his flock,
And voweth, and sacrificeth to Jehovah that which is corrupt;
For I am a great king, saith Jehovah of hosts,
And my name shall be feared among the nations.

ver. 6, should receive universal homage among the nations that had been addicted to idolatry, and who were now the objects of abomination on the part of the Jews. The sacrificial terms are transferred from their original application to ceremonial objects and acts, to such as are spiritual, agreeably to the nature of the new economy. Comp. John iv. 20—24; Heb. xiii. 10, 15, 16; 1 Pet. ii. 5. All that Hitzig can discover in these verses is, that God was worshipped by all nations, under the different names of Jehovah, Ormuzd, Zeus, etc. ! ! !

12—14. A renewal of the charge against the priests, nearly in the same words. מִתְאֵלָּה is an abbreviated form for מָה תְּלָאָה. Comp. מָצָה, Exod. iv. 2; נֻבֲלוּ, Is. iii. 15. אוֹתוֹ, *it*, after הֲחָחָם, refers to אֲבָלָהּ in the preceding verse, and is not to be changed into אוֹתִי, *me*, as proposed in the Tikkune Sopherim. The ו in וְאֶת־הָחֳלֶה is omitted in ninety-three MSS., in seven printed editions, and in all the versions except the Syriac. Though it is not said that the מִנְחָה, *meat offering*, consisted of inferior ingredients, yet it is either implied, or the idea is intended to be conveyed, that the presentation of the other sacrifices rendered this, however pure in itself, unacceptable to God. Hitzig and Maurer regard מֻשְׁחָת to be a contraction of the feminine מָשְׁחֶתֶת; but I should rather think it ought to be pointed מָשְׁחָת, as in Lev. xxii. 25, where it occurs, in application to the same subject, in the masculine gender. Many MSS. and some of the early editions read לָהֶם instead of לֵאלֹהַי, which has no doubt been substituted for it by some superstitious Jewish scribe.

CHAPTER II.

The prophet continues to urge the charge against the priests, warning them that if they did not reform, they should be deprived of all enjoyment, and rendered the objects of shame and contempt, 1—4. The original institution, and the sacred nature and obligations of the priestly office, are then brought forward, with which to contrast the baseness of their conduct in violating its responsibilities; and the section closes with another threatening of punishment, 5—9. In a new section the prophet takes up the subject of divorce, and marriage with foreign women, and severely reproves the priests for the evil example which they had set in this respect, 10—16. They are finally charged with teaching immoral doctrine, 17.

1 AND now, unto you is this charge, O ye priests!
2 If ye will not hearken, nor lay it to heart,
   To give glory to my name, saith Jehovah of hosts;
   I will send the curse among you, and will curse your blessing,
   Yea, I will curse them singly,
   Because ye lay it not to heart.
3 Behold! I will rebuke the seed to your hurt,
   And I will scatter dung upon your faces,
   The dung of your festivals;
   And ye shall be taken away with it.
4 And ye shall know that I have sent you to this charge,
   Because my covenant was with Levi, saith Jehovah of hosts.
5 My covenant of life and peace was with him,
   And I gave them to him,
   For the fear which he showed for me,
   And the awe in which he stood of my name.

2. הַמְּאֵרָה is emphatic, and doubtless has reference to Deut. xxvii. 15, etc. The feminine suffix in אָרוֹתִיהָ is to be taken distributively, with reference to the בִּרְכוֹת, *blessings*, immediately preceding.

3. The ל in לָכֶם is that of the *Dativus incommodi*, "to your detriment or disadvantage." זֶרַע, *seed*, is not to be changed into זְרוֹעַ, and rendered *shoulder*, as Houbigant and Newcome do, merely on the authority of the LXX. There is great force in the reference to the dung of the festivals, as the maw, which contained it, belonged to the priests, Deut. xviii. 3. אֶל in אֵלָיו has the signification of *with, together with*, as in Lam. iii. 41. Such usage, however, is rare. נָשָׂא is to be taken impersonally.

4. יָדַע, *to know*, has here the signification, to *know by experience*, to feel

the consequences of transgression. From the words which follow, we must infer that knowledge issuing in reformation of conduct is meant. On no other condition could the Levitical covenant continue in force.

5. In this and the following verses the prophet forcibly contrasts with the base and unworthy conduct of the priests, the noble character of their progenitor, with whom officially Jehovah had entered into covenant. The reference, however, is not to Levi personally, but to Phinchas, Numb. xxv. 12, 13, where we have an account of this covenant, there called בְּרִיתִי שָׁלוֹם, *my covenant of peace*, and בְּרִית כְּהֻנַּת עוֹלָם, *the covenant of an everlasting priesthood*. Both ideas are expressed in the present verse, and the meaning is, that the covenant was secured in perpetuity. Before הַחַיִּים וְהַשָּׁלוֹם the word בְּרִית is understood from the

6 The law of truth was in his mouth;
   No iniquity was found in his lips;
   He walked with me in peace and uprightness,
   And turned many from iniquity.
7 For the lips of the priest should preserve knowledge,
   And men should seek the law at his mouth,
   For he is the messenger of Jehovah of hosts.
8 But, as for you, ye have departed from the way,
   Ye have made many to stumble in the law;
   Ye have corrupted the covenant of Levi, saith Jehovah of hosts.
9 Therefore have I also rendered you contemptible and base to all
      the people;
   Forasmuch as ye have not observed my ways,
   And have acted partially in the law.
10   Have we not all one Father?

preceding. מִיְרָא, *fear* or *reverence*, is here the accusative absolute. נִחַת is the Niphal of חָתַת, *to be terrified, dismayed*. This verb is here purposely employed to express the extraordinary degree of profound and holy awe with which Phinehas was inspired when zealously vindicating the honor of Jehovah.

6, 7. A comprehensive and beautiful description of the character and spiritual duties of Phinehas, which ought to have been realized in the persons and ministrations of all his successors in office, and which suggests topics of the most serious self-examination to all who engage in the work of the Christian ministry. The higher and more important functions of the sacerdotal office are here recognized, to the exclusion of such as were merely ceremonial. These the priests in the days of Malachi had neglected, while they discharged the latter in a perfunctory and niggardly manner. That תּוֹרָה is not here to be rendered *doctrine*, but is to be taken in its appropriated sense of *law*, appears from the use of the term in the two following verses. מִצְוָה is in the accusative case, with which יְבַקְשׁוּ, as in other instances of passive verbs, does not agree in number. See Gesen. Gram. § 140, 1 b. The priests were the ordinary expounders of the law to the people; it was only on special and extraordinary occasions that the prophets gave their decision. Each of them was, therefore, to be regarded as מַלְאָךְ, a *messenger*, or interpreter of the Divine will.

8. The character of the priests whom Malachi was sent to reprove was the very reverse of that exhibited by Phinehas. Not only did they violate the law themselves, but, as is universally the case, induced others by their bad example to violate it likewise. They thus forfeited all right to the sacerdotal immunities of the Levitical covenant.

9. וְגַם־אֲנִי is strikingly antithetical to וְאַתֶּם at the beginning of ver. 8. The priests are here threatened with a retribution corresponding to their base and contemptible character, an additional and aggravating feature of which is added, *viz.* partiality in the decisions which they gave on points of law. Instead of הָעָם, *the people*, twenty-three MSS., and a few printed editions, the LXX., Targ., Arab., and Hexapl. Syr., read הָעַמִּים, *the peoples* or *nations*, but much less appropriately.

10. The prophet now proceeds to administer reproof to the people, and especially to the priests, for their flagrant

Hath not one God created us?
Wherefore do we act unfaithfully one to another,
Profaning the covenant of our fathers?
11 Judah hath acted unfaithfully;
And an abominable thing hath been done in Israel and in Jerusalem;
For Judah hath profaned that which was holy to Jehovah,
That which he loved,
And hath married the daughter of a strange god.
12 Jehovah will cut off the man that doeth this,
Him that watcheth, and him that answereth,
From the tents of Jacob,
And him that presenteth an offering to Jehovah of hosts.

violation of the law, which prohibited intermarriages with foreigners. See Exod. xxxiv. 16; Deut. vii. 3. For the historical account of this violation, see Ezra ix. 1, 2; Neh. xiii. 23—31. That by אָב אֶחָד, one Father, we are to understand Jehovah, and not Abraham, or Jacob, as some have supposed, is determined by the force of the parallelism, in which we have the corresponding and elucidatory phrase אֵל אֶחָד, one God. As the Jews put away their wives, that they might marry others, they are here distinctly taught that both males and females stood in the same relation to God as their common Father and Creator. He had an equal propriety in them, and when the men acted the part for which they are here reproved, they acted unjustly by their Maker. But, in addition to this, they broke the covenant made with their fathers, which interdicted such practices. אָח, brother, is not here to be pressed, as if reference were had to the father of the female who had been repudiated. אִישׁ בְּאָחִיו is the usual idiom, one against another. Comp. 1 Thess. iv. 6. The questions so pointedly put at the commencement of this verse are highly condemnatory of that degradation which is experienced by Oriental females. Not only do most of the Mohammedans deny them the privilege of immortality, but the Jews universally to this day give thanks every morning — the man, that God has not made him a woman; and the woman, that God has made her כִּרְצוֹנוֹ, according to his pleasure.

11. The nominative to בָּגְדָה is יְהוּדָה, understood in חִלֵּל. By קֹדֶשׁ יְהוָה, the holiness of Jehovah, is meant the people of the Hebrews, who were separated to be a people devoted to his service. Comp. זֶרַע הַקֹּדֶשׁ, the holy seed, Ezra ix. 2; and קֹדֶשׁ יִשְׂרָאֵל לַיהוָה, Israel is holiness, i. e. holy to Jehovah, Jer. ii. 3. For אֲשֶׁר אָהֵב comp. Ps. xlvii. 5. "The daughter of a strange god" means an idolatress, a female addicted to the worship of a false deity.

12. עֵר וְעֹנֶה has been variously rendered. The LXX. mistaking עֵר for עֵד, have ἕως καὶ ταπεινωθῇ. Vulg. magistrum et discipulum. Targ. בַּר וּבַר בַּר, son and son's son. Syr. ܒܪ ܘܒܪ ܒܪܗ, both his son and his son's son. Thus also Abarbanel, Sachs, Ewald, and others. The phrase is obviously, from its very form, like עֶצֶם וְעָצוּם, גֵּר וְגֵר, proverbial, and has its parallel in the Arabic ولیس بها داع ولا مجیب There is not in the city a caller, nor is there a responder. Life of Timur, quoted by Gesenius in his Thesaur. p. 1004. Turkish, هم اویانغ هم جواب

13 And this ye have done a second time,
    Covering the altar of Jehovah with tears,
    With weeping and groaning,
    So that there is no longer any regard paid to the offering,
    Nor is it favorably received at your hand,
14 Yet ye say, Wherefore?
    Because Jehovah was witness
    Between thee and the wife of thy youth;
    To whom thou hast acted unfaithfully,
    Though she was thy companion and covenanted wife.
15 Yet did he not make one?
    Though he had the residue of the spirit;
    And why the one?
    That he might seek a godly seed;
    Therefore take heed to your spirit,
    That none act unfaithfully to the wife of his youth.

ايلني, both the *watcher, and the answerer*. The meaning is, that *none* should be left alive; all should be cut off. Gesenius thinks that the reference is probably to the Levites who kept watch in the temple by night, and who called and responded to each other at certain intervals; but the mention that is made of "the tents of Jacob" immediately after, shows that the words are not to be thus restricted. ער is the participle of עור, *to wake, be awake*.

13. שֵׁנִית is to be taken strictly in the sense of *a second time*. Measures had been adopted to cure the evil in the time of Ezra, chap. ix. x.; but the Jews had relapsed into the same sin of marrying foreign wives in that of Nehemiah, and it is this latter which the prophet here reproves. Neh. xiii. 23—31. The language implies an aggravation of the offence. The crying and weeping were those of the Jewish wives who had been repudiated by their husbands.

14. The legitimate marriages had been contracted with special appeal to Jehovah as witness of the transaction. The phrase אֵשֶׁת נְעוּרֶיךָ, *the wife of thy youth*, has reference to the early marriages among the Hebrews. In Poland, at the present day, they marry at the age of thirteen and fourteen, and the females still younger.

15, 16. Michaelis, Hitzig, Maurer, and Hengstenberg, concur in the opinion expressed in the Targum, and adopted by most of the Rabbins, that by אֶחָד, *one*, and הָאֶחָד, *the one*, Abraham is intended; and maintain, that what is here stated, was designed to repel an objection raised by the priests, viz., that Abraham took an Egyptian female in addition to Sarah. The prophet, according to them, admits the fact, but denies the consequence, by showing that Abraham still retained the Spirit of God, because his object in contracting this alliance was to obtain the seed which God had promised him, and not to gratify carnal passion, to which the evil here condemned was to be traced. Ewald refers אֶחָד, *one*, to God, considering the term to be used here in the same sense as in ver. 10, but fails in giving a satisfactory explanation of the passage. Nor does the other interpretation at all do justice to its claims; so that we are shut up to the conclusion, that by הָאֶחָד, *the one*, we are to understand בָּשָׂר אֶחָד, the *one flesh*, or conju-

16 For I hate divorce, saith Jehovah, the God of Israel,
And for a man to cover over his garment with violence,
Saith Jehovah of hosts;
Therefore take heed to your spirit,
That ye act not unfaithfully.
17 Ye have wearied Jehovah with your words,
Yet ye say, Wherein have we wearied him?
In your saying, Every one that doeth evil
Is good in the sight of Jehovah, and he delighteth in them;
Or, Where is the God of justice?

gal body into which the first couple were formed, Gen. ii. Instead of forming only two into one, the Creator might have given to Adam many wives. There was no lack of spiritual existence from which to furnish them with intelligent souls. When he gave to Eve such an existence, he did not exhaust the immense fountain of being. There remained all with which the human race hath been furnished throughout its generations. What, then, the prophet asks, was the design of the restriction? to this he replies, the securing of a pious offspring. Divorces and polygamy have ever been unfavorable to the education of children. It is only by the harmonious and loving attention bestowed by parents upon their children, that they can be expected to be brought up in the fear of God. The reply bore hard upon the priests who had married idolatrous wives. In such a connection there was everything to counteract and destroy the interests of piety.

16. עָלָה should be pointed עָלָיו, with the personal pronoun אֲנִי understood. By לְבוּשׁ, garment, it is now generally admitted we are to understand the *wife*, who had the most glaring injustice done to her by giving her a divorce, or by taking one or more in addition to her. Thus the Arab. لبس, *texit, induit; لباس, vestimentum, " conjux tum mulier viri, tum vir mulieris, quod sibi invicem pro tegumento sunt."* Freytag. Accordingly we read in the Koran, Sur. 183, respecting the wives: هن لباس لكم ولنتم لباس لهن, *they are your garment, and you are theirs.* In the ecclesiastical language of the East, matrimony was called τὸ θνητὸν καὶ δουλικὸν ἱμάτιον.

17. The old objection taken against the providence of God from the afflictions of the righteous, and the prosperity of the wicked.

CHAPTER III.

This chapter commences with a lucid prophecy of John the Baptist, as the forerunner of the Messiah, and of the Messiah himself, who was, as he had long been, the object of delightful expectation to the Jews, 1. The aspect of his advent in regard to the wicked, and especially to the ungodly priesthood, is next introduced, together with the severe judgments that were to be brought upon the nation, 2—6. The people are then reproved for having withheld the legal tithes and offerings, and are promised a profusion of blessings in case of repentance, 7—12. To the infidel objection that there is no utility in religion, seeing the wicked prosper, while the godly are oppressed, the prophet replies by pointing to the day of retribution, when all should be treated according to their character, which would then be fully disclosed, 13—18.

1 BEHOLD! I will send my messenger,
And he shall prepare the way before me,
And suddenly there shall come to his temple
The Lord whom ye seek,

1. That by מַלְאָכִי, *my messenger*, we are to understand John the Baptist, is placed beyond dispute by the appropriation of the words of the prophecy to him, Mark i. 1. Comp. Is. xl. 3. Hengstenberg strangely gives in to the notion of Eichhorn and Theiner, that the collective body of the prophets is intended, though he thinks that the idea of the messenger chiefly concentrates in John. Not one of his five reasons is at all satisfactory. The office of this messenger is described as preparing the way for the Messiah. The language is borrowed from the custom of sending pioneers before an Eastern monarch, to cut through rocks, and forests, and remove every impediment that might obstruct his course. פָּנָה, which in Kal is never transitive, signifies in Piel *to clear, clear away, put in order, prepare*. This John did by preaching repentance, and announcing the near approach of the kingdom of God. Comp. chap. iv. 5. In this prophecy of the Messiah are three palpable and incontrovertible proofs of his divinity. First, he is identified with Jehovah: "he shall prepare the way before ME"—"saith Jehovah." Secondly, He is represented as the Proprietor of the temple. Thirdly, He is characterized as הָאָדוֹן, THE SOVEREIGN, a title nowhere given in this form to any except Jehovah. In its anarthrous state the noun אָדוֹן is applicable to any owner, possessor, or ruler, and it is applied in the construct state to Jehovah as אֲדוֹן כָּל־הָאָרֶץ, *the Possessor of the whole earth*, Josh. iii. 11, 13; but when it takes the article, as here, it is used κατ' ἐξοχήν, and exclusively of the Divine Being. See Exod. xxiii. 17, xxxiv. 23. Is. i. 24, iii. 1, x. 16, 33, xix. 4; See Dr. J. Pye Smith's Messiah, vol. i. pp. 442—444. Abenezra thus explains the term, and identifies the Sovereign Lord with the Angel spoken of immediately after: הָאָדוֹן הוּא הַכָּבוֹד הוּא מַלְאָךְ הַבְּרִית כִּי הַטַּעַם כָּפוּל, *The Lord is both the Divine Majesty, and the Angel of the Covenant, for the sentence is doubled*. It is likewise admitted in Mashmiah Jeshua, fol. 76, אֶפְשָׁר לְפָרֵשׁ הָאָדוֹן עַל מֶלֶךְ הַמָּשִׁיחַ, *The Lord may be explained of the King Messiah;* and Kimchi not only, with Abenezra, identifies the Lord and the Angel, but applies both to the Messiah: הָאָדוֹן הוּא מֶלֶךְ הַמָּשִׁיחַ וְהוּא מַלְאַךְ הַבְּרִית, *The Lord is the King Messiah, he is also the Angel of the Covenant;* though, in order to elude the Christian application of the passage, he suggests another interpretation, according to which Elijah is meant. It has been questioned, whether the phrase מַלְאַךְ הַבְּרִית, *the Messenger of the Covenant*, is to be viewed retrospectively or prospectively; in other words, whether it be the Old or the New Covenant to which reference is made. Considering the fact, that in such parallel forms as לֻחוֹת הַבְּרִית, *the tables of the covenant*, אֲרוֹן הַבְּרִית, *the ark of the covenant*, סֵפֶר הַבְּרִית, *the book of the covenant*, דַּם הַבְּרִית, *the blood of the covenant*, etc., the ancient dispensation which Je-

Even the Messenger of the covenant, in whom ye delight,
Behold! he shall come, saith Jehovah of hosts.
2 But who may endure the day of his coming?
And who may stand when he appeareth?
For he is like the fire of the refiner,
And like the soap of the fullers;
3 And he shall sit, refining and purifying the silver;
He shall purify the sons of Levi,
And refine them like gold and like silver,
That they may present to Jehovah an offering in righteousness.
4 Then shall the offering of Judah and Jerusalem
Be pleasing to Jehovah,

hovah granted to the Hebrews at Sinai is intended, it would seem natural to infer that מַלְאַךְ הַבְּרִית is to be understood in the same way. This view of the subject would seem to be corroborated by the circumstances, that a מַלְאָךְ, *Angel* or *Messenger*, who is said to possess the Divine name, *i. e.* whatever is distinctive of Deity, is frequently spoken of under that economy; that He is represented as leading the Israelites out of Egypt, giving them the law, and superintending the whole of the theocracy. All the theophanies or manifestations of the invisible Deity were made in his Person. He was the proper nuncius sent to reveal the will of the Father. Moses was only a θεράπων, עֶבֶד, or servant employed by him, while he was God manifested in glory. I can put no other consistent construction upon such passages as the following: Gen. xlviii. 15, 16; Exod. iii. 2—15, xxiii. 20, 21; Is. lxiii. 9; Zech. i. ii. iii. vi.; Acts vii. 38; Heb. xi. 26, xii. 26. In strict consistency with the representations of Scripture, therefore, the Messiah may be called the *Messenger* of that ancient economy of which he was the Founder and Head. Most interpreters, however, understand the New Covenant, or the dispensation of grace, with special reference to Heb. ix. 15, where our Saviour is called διαθήκης καινῆς μεσίτης, *the Mediator of the New Covenant*; among others, Grotius, Rosenmüller, and Gesenius. The Jews may be said to have sought and delighted in the Messiah, because he was the object of national expectation and desire, though the great body of them formed no higher conception of him than that of an earthly monarch, under whose reign they should enjoy a profusion of temporal blessings. When it is declared that he should come "*suddenly*" to his temple, it is not implied that he was to come in or near the times of the prophet, but merely that his coming would be sudden and unexpected in the circumstances under which it took place.

2—4. Employing a strong metallurgic metaphor, the prophet shows that the Covenant Messenger would be very different from that which the carnal Jews expected. Instead of flattering their prejudices, and gratifying their wishes, he would, by his pure and heart-searching doctrines, subject their principles and conduct to the severest test. Those of the priests should be specially tried. The object he was to have in view in this trial, was their purification, that they might serve him in righteousness. Matt. iii. 12; John xv. 3. And such was the result with respect to many of them. "A great company of the priests were obedient to the faith," Acts vi. 7. The influence of their conversion upon the people must have been very great, though we have no information respecting it in

As in the days of old,
And as in the former years.

5 But I will draw nigh to you for judgment,
And will be a swift witness
Against the sorcerers, and against the adulterers,
And against those who swear to a falsehood,
And against those who wrest the wages of the hireling,
The widow and the orphan,
Who turn aside the stranger as to his right,
And fear not me, saith Jehovah of hosts.

6 Because I am Jehovah, I change not;
Therefore ye sons of Jacob are not consumed.

7 Even from the days of your fathers
Ye have departed from my statutes, and have not kept them;
Return to me, and I will return to you,
Saith Jehovah of hosts.
But ye say, Wherewith shall we return?

8 Will a man defraud God?
Yet ye have defrauded me.
But ye say, Wherein have we defrauded thee?
In the tithes and the oblations.

9 Ye are cursed with the curse;
For ye — the whole nation — have defrauded me.

10 Bring ye all the tithes into the storehouse,

the Acts. The religious services of the churches composed of Jewish converts in Jerusalem and throughout Judea, are represented as peculiarly well-pleasing to God. For the meaning of מִנְחָה, *offering*, as here used, comp. chap. i. 10, 11.

5. Malachi here returns to his own times, and threatens his ungodly contemporaries with divine judgment, speedily to be executed upon them. Magic greatly prevailed among the Jews after the captivity, as did also the other crimes here specified. How much they obtained in the time of our Lord, we learn from the Evangelists and Josephus. The prophet traces them all back to their true source — absence of the fear of God. After וּבְעֹשְׁקֵי, the phrase בְּשָׂמִי is found in nineteen MSS., in some printed editions, and in the LXX., Syr., Hexapl., and Arab.

6. As the incommunicable name יְהוָֹה, JEHOVAH, implies a futurity of reference with respect to the communication of blessings (see on Hos. xii. 5), the Divine immutability secured the preservation of the Jewish people from destruction, notwithstanding their flagrant wickedness, till he had accomplished all his purposes of mercy.

7. The ל in לְמִימֵי is prosthetic, with somewhat of its temporal signification. There was still mercy in store for the Jews, if they only would repent.

8. קָבַע, which occurs only in our prophet, and in Prov. xxii. 23, signifies *to cover, do anything covertly, defraud*. Comp. the Arab. قبع, *retrahit*, قابع, *occultus*.

9. Comp. chap. ii. 2.

10. עַד־בְּלִי־דָי, *usque ad defectum*

That there may be meat in my house,
And try me now with this, saith Jehovah of hosts,
Whether I will not open for you the windows of heaven,
And pour out a blessing for you,
Till there shall be a superabundance.
11 And I will rebuke the devourer for your sake,
And he shall not destroy the fruits of your ground;
Neither shall your vine in the field be unfruitful,
Saith Jehovah of hosts.
12 And all the nations shall pronounce you happy,
For ye shall be a delightful land,
Saith Jehovah of hosts.
13   Your words against me have been hard, saith Jehovah;
But ye say, What have we spoken against thee?
14 Ye have said:
It is vain to serve God;
And what profit is it that we keep his ordinance,
And that we walk mournfully before Jehovah of hosts?
15 For now we pronounce the proud happy;
They also that work wickedness are built up;
They even tempt God, yet they are delivered.
16   Then they that feared Jehovah
Conversed one with another;
And Jehovah hearkened, and heard,

sufficientiæ, i. e. not as Gesenius explains it, till my abundance be exhausted, which being impossible, the phrase is equivalent to, *forever, without end;* but where sufficiency can have no more place, more than sufficient, superabundantly. To this effect Jerome, Winer, De Wette, Hitzig, and Maurer.

11. By the אכל, *devourer*, noxious animals and insects are meant, especially the locusts. שכל properly signifies *to cause abortion, render childless*, and metaphorically, to make barren or *unfruitful*, when spoken of trees.

13—15. חזק signifies to *bind fast, make firm*, and, in a bad sense, *to be hard, obstinate*, or the like. Such was the language of the Jews against Jehovah. Comp. Jude 15, περὶ πάντων τῶν σκληρῶν ὧν ἐλάλησαν κατ' αὐτοῦ. Some

awful specimens of their hard speeches are here exhibited, in which the usual objection against the rectitude of Providence is dressed up in some of its more taking forms. Comp. Job xxi. 14, 15; Ps. lxxiii. 1—14. בחן is here used like נסה in the bad sense of tempting, or braving the Most High by presumptuous speeches and conduct. The walking mournfully has reference to their going about in sackcloth and ashes, pretending to sorrow on account of their sins. קדר, *to be dirty*, to go about in filthy garments, like persons who mourn; such being universally the custom in the East.

16. אז, *then*, specially marks the time in which the impious conversations were being held. Here נדברו beautifully contrasts with the same term in the thirteenth verse. The verb is in Niphal, to

And a book of remembrance was written before him,
For those that feared Jehovah,
And thought upon his name.
17 And they shall be a peculiar treasure to me, saith Jehovah of hosts,
In the day which I have appointed;
And I will be kind to them
As a father is kind to his son who serveth him.
18 Then shall ye again perceive the difference
Between the righteous and the wicked,
Between him that serveth God,
And him that serveth him not.

express the reciprocal or conversational character of the language. As the ungodly did not confine their hard speeches to the mere utterance of them to such individuals as they might happen to meet, but made their infidel objections the subject of mutual discussion, so the pious are here represented as holding mutual converse respecting the interests of truth and godliness. It does not appear that Niphal ever has the frequentative signification, expressed in our common version. The writing of a book of remembrance is a metaphor borrowed from the custom at the Persian court of entering in a record the names of any who have rendered service to the king, with an account of the nature of such service. See Esther vi. 1, 2.

17. סְגֻלָּה is to be construed with וְהָיוּ לִי , and עֹשֶׂה is connected by means of אֲשֶׁר with יוֹם. The phrase עָשָׂה יוֹם, *to make a day*, which occurs chap. iv. 3; Ps. cxviii. 24, means to *fix, ordain, appoint*, such a period for the execution of a special purpose. סְגֻלָּה, signifies *private, special*, or *peculiar property*. סָגַל , like the kindred root סָגַר , has the primary signification of *shutting up, closing*,

and then, secondarily, that of *getting*, or *acquiring*, what is shut up, in order to its being carefully preserved. Hence the idea of what is peculiarly valuable or precious. The term is applied to the people of Israel, Exod. xix. 5; Deut. vii. 6, xiv. 2, xxvi. 18. It is used of the choice treasure of kings, etc., Eccles. ii. 8. It is expressive of the high estimation in which God holds his people, and, in this connection, of their perfect safety in the day of judgment.

18. שׁוּב is used idiomatically in connection with רָאָה to express the repetition of the action, the idea of which is conveyed by the latter verb. Notwithstanding the charge brought by the wicked against the providence of God, as if he treated all alike, the righteous had already had opportunities of perceiving from observation and experience, that the position was false, viewed in application to the entire state and circumstances of the different characters; but they should have another and most convincing proof in the salvation of all who loved and feared the Lord, and in the overthrow and destruction of his enemies.

CHAPTER IV.

Most editions of the Hebrew Bible, and most of the MSS., exhibit this concluding portion of the book as a continuation of the third chapter. Not a few MSS., however, leave a blank space before it, and several editions make a separate chapter of it. As this division obtains in all the versions, it is more convenient to retain it.

The chapter continues the threatenings against the Jewish unbelievers, 1; exhibits a luminous prophecy of the Messiah, and the prosperity of his people, 2, 3; and concludes with a solemn call to the Jews, to observe the institutes of the old economy, till the forerunner of the Messiah should appear, when the Jewish polity should be destroyed, and a new and better dispensation established, 4—6.

1   For, behold! the day cometh, it shall burn as an oven,
    And all the proud, and every one that doeth wickedly, shall be stubble,
    And the day that cometh shall burn them up,
    Saith Jehovah of hosts;
    That it may not leave them either root or branch.
2   But unto you that fear my name,
    The Sun of righteousness shall arise,

1. Instead of רֶשַׁע עֹשֵׂה, nearly eighty MSS., the most ancient and several other editions, the Babylon, Talmud, the LXX., Syr., and Targ., read עֹשֵׂי רִשְׁעָה in the plural. The phrase שֹׁרֶשׁ וְעָנָף, *root or branch*, is proverbial, and signifies *any*, the least remnant. The persons referred to were to be consigned to utter destruction. The Targhum has בַּר וּבַר בַּר , *son or son's son*.

2. The term שֶׁמֶשׁ , *Sun*, is metaphorically applied to God, Ps. lxxxiv. 11, on account of that luminary being the most glorious and beneficent object which meets the human eye. It is with good reason supposed to be thus used of the Messiah in the declaration, 2 Sam. xxiii. 4:

וּבְאוֹר בֹּקֶר יִזְרַח־שָׁמֶשׁ,

"And as the morning light he shall arise — a Sun."

In the present verse there can be no doubt with respect to the application. Our Lord is elsewhere called אוֹר , *Light*, which in Hebrew poetry is used of the sun, as the source of light. See Is. ix. 1, xlix. 6 ; John i. 9, viii. 12. What the sun is to the natural world, that the Messiah is to the moral. The invaluable spiritual blessings which he dispenses are all comprehended under the two heads here specified — righteousness and moral health. Comp. Is. lvii. 19. Both of these are indispensably requisite to the happiness of our guilty and depraved race, and from no other quarter can they be obtained, than from Him, "who of God is made unto us wisdom, and righteousness, and sanctification, and redemption." 1 Cor. i. 30. By "wings" we are to understand the *beams* of the sun, on account of the velocity and expansion with which they spread over the

And there shall be healing in his wings;
And ye shall go forth and leap as calves of the stall.
3 And ye shall tread down the wicked;
Surely they shall be ashes under the soles of your feet,
In the day which I have appointed, saith Jehovah of hosts.
4 Remember ye the law of Moses my servant,
Which I gave him in charge in Horeb for all Israel,
The statutes and the judgments.
5 Behold! I will send to you Elijah the prophet,

earth. Comp. Ps. cxxxix. 9. Those for whose immediate benefit the Sun of righteousness was to arise, were such as "feared the name" of Jehovah — like Simeon, who was δίκαιος καὶ εὐλαβής, righteous and *devout*, waiting for the consolation of Israel. Luke ii. 25. נצא, *to go forth*, is here used in the sense of escaping from the judgment to be inflicted upon the unbelieving part of the Jewish nation. This the Jewish Christians did when they left Jerusalem, and proceeded to Pella, where they were preserved in safety. וּשׁ, signifies *to spread, take a wide range*, and is used of the proud prancing of horses, and as here of the leaping and sporting of calves. The simile is designed to convey the ideas of freedom from outward restraint, and the enjoyment of self-conscious hilarity.

3. This verse expresses the depressed condition to which the Jews were to be reduced after the destruction of their polity, contrasted with the prosperous condition of those who embraced Christianity, and who were no longer subject to oppression on the part of their unbelieving brethren.

4. As the law and the prophets were to remain in force till the appearance of John the Baptist, no prophet intervening after Malachi to make any further communications of the Divine will, it was necessary to pay the closest attention to the enactments and observances of the Mosaic institute. That there were no more inspired messengers under the Old Economy may be inferred, not only from the nature of the injunction here given, especially as taken in connection with the promise of a new messenger in the following verse, but also from Ecclesiasticus xlix. 10, where, after mentioning Jeremiah and Ezekiel, the author closes with τῶν δώδεκα προφητῶν, *the twelve prophets*, as the last in the category.

5. The coherence of this verse with the first clause of chap. iii. is too palpable to be overlooked. Accordingly, the Jews in the time of Jerome interpreted the messenger of Jehovah there predicted, of Elijah the Tishbite, as they explain the present verse to this day, believing, that as the ancient prophet ascended into heaven both as to body and soul, he is destined to reappear in the same upon earth before the advent of Messiah the Son of David. That Elijah here presented to view is to be understood ideally and not historically, and that the individual personally intended is John the Baptist, are positions the certainty of which is rendered indubitable by the repeated declarations of our Lord. When John denied that he was Elias, John i. 21, he is to be understood as making the denial in reference to the personal sense of the term as employed in the question that had been proposed to him. The historical theory is entirely set aside by the express testimony of the angel, Luke i. 17, according to which all that is meant by Malachi is, that the forerunner of the Messiah was to come "in the spirit and power of Elias." Like that prophet, he was to be endowed with extraordinary

Before the great and terrible day of Jehovah come:
6 And he shall turn the heart of the fathers to the children,

power and energy, to fit him for the great work of reformation which his ministry was designed to effect. Adverting to the erroneous Jewish notion, which even then obtained, relative to the appearance of Elijah in person, our Lord says of John, "If ye will receive it, αὐτός ἐστιν 'Ηλίας ὁ μέλλων ἔρχεσθαι, he is Elias who was to come," Matt. xi. 17. And when the disciples asked him, "Why do the Scribes then say that Elias must first come? he replied, Elias shall, indeed, first come and restore all things. But I say unto you that 'Ηλίας ἤδη ἦλθε, Elias is already come, and they knew him not, but have done unto him whatsoever they listed." Matt. xvii. 10—13. Upon the circumstance that our Lord uses the future tense, ἔρχεται, shall come, some Christian interpreters have attempted to establish the hypothesis, that the prophecy is still to be fulfilled before his second advent; but he is obviously speaking in the style of language employed by the prophet, to whom the event was future, and in adaptation to the opinion of the Scribes, though he immediately corrects what was erroneous in their notion, declaring that the event was no longer future, but had actually taken place in the person and ministry of John. It is truly surprising that any should persist in giving to the prophecy an aspect still future, in the very face of an exposition at once positive and infallible. That John the Baptist was נָבִיא, a prophet, Christ admits, though he at the same time declares, that he was "more than a prophet." Matt. xi. 9. The "great and terrible day of Jehovah" was the dreadful period of his judgment, effecting the destruction of Jerusalem by the Romans. Comp. Joel ii. 31.

6. The design of the ministry of John is described as consisting in the production of universal peace and concord. Family feuds had increased to an enormous extent by the time of John the Baptist, the removal of which by genuine repentance and reformation of conduct might be taken as a specimen of the ἀποκατάστασις, or restoration of things to a better state throughout Judea. Some have proposed to take the preposition לְ, to, as equivalent to עִם, with, a signification which it sometimes has, and so to explain the passage as simply predicting the universality of the conversion spoken of; but such an interpretation would introduce an intolerable tautology into the language of the prophet, and be at variance with the construction put upon it by the angel, Luke i. 17, in which only one member of the sentence is quoted. With respect to the extent of the effects produced by John's ministry, there can be no doubt it was very great. Not only did immense multitudes come to his baptism, confessing their sins, but the great body of the common people appear to have been prepared by him for the labors of our blessed Lord himself, and thus the foundation was laid for the recovery of tens of thousands from Judaism to the faith of the gospel, previous to the destruction of Jerusalem. See Acts xxi. 20.

The prophecy, and with it the entire Old Testament, closes with the awful alternative — the denunciation of the Divine curse, to be realized in the extermination of the impenitent Jews from their own land. חֵרֶם signifies utter destruction, from חָרַם, to shut or stop up, exclude from common use, place under a ban, devote to destruction. It is one of the most fearful words in use among the Jews, and was specially applied to the extermination of the Canaanites, whose cities were razed to the foundations, and their inhabitants utterly destroyed. Under this ban, the land of Palestine has lain ever since the capture

And the heart of the children to the fathers,
Lest I come and smite the land with a curse.

of Jerusalem; and the sufferings to which, in consequence, the Jews have been subjected are truly appalling; but incomparably more dreadful is the New Testament חֵרֶם —ANAΘEMA, MAPAN AΘA! 1 Cor. xvi. 22.

WARREN F. DRAPER,
PUBLISHER AND BOOKSELLER
ANDOVER, MASS.,

PUBLISHES AND OFFERS FOR SALE THE FOLLOWING WORKS, WHICH WILL BE SENT, POSTPAID, ON RECEIPT OF THE SUMS AFFIXED.

WORKS OF W. G. T. SHEDD, recently Professor of Ecclesiastical History in Andover Theological Seminary.

Few clearer and more penetrating minds can be found in our country than that of Prof. Shedd. And besides, he writes with a chaste and sturdy eloquence, transparent as crystal; so that if he goes DEEP, we love to follow him. If the mind gets dull, or dry and ungovernable, put it to grappling with these masterly productions.—*Congregational Herald, Chicago.*

DISCOURSES AND ESSAYS. 324 pp. 12mo. $1.50.

CONTENTS.—The Method and Influence of Theological Studies.—The True Nature of the Beautiful, and its Relation to Culture.—The Characteristics and Importance of a Natural Rhetoric.—The Nature and Influence of the Historic Spirit.—The Relation of Language and Style to Thought.—The Doctrine of Original Sin.—The Atonement, a Satisfaction for the Ethical Nature of both God and Man.

These elaborate articles are written in a lucid and racy style, and invest with a rare interest the themes of which they treat.—*Bibliotheca Sacra.*

LECTURES UPON THE PHILOSOPHY OF HISTORY. 128 pp. 12mo. 75c.

CONTENTS.—The abstract Idea of History.—The Nature and Definition of Secular History.—Nature and Definition of Church History.—The Verifying Test in Church History.

Professor Shedd has already achieved a high reputation for the union of philosophic insight with genuine scholarship, of depth and clearness of thought with force and elegance of style, and for profound views of sin and grace, cherished not merely on theoretical, but still more on moral and experimental grounds.—*Princeton Review.*

GUERICKE'S CHURCH HISTORY. Translated. 449 pp. 8vo. $2.75.

This volume includes the period of the ANCIENT CHURCH (the first six centuries, A. C.), or the Apostolic and Patristic Church.

Here is a Manual of Church History which may be confidently recommended, without reserve or qualification, to students belonging to all evangelical churches. Guericke is thoroughly Orthodox. His evangelical belief and feeling give him a lively and appreciative interest in the internal history of the Church; he devotes special attention to the development of doctrines, and presents the range of thought and substance of opinion distinguishing the works of the principal writers in successive ages of the Church. Guericke's manual is complete in the particular lines of history he has chosen, and is a most useful and reliable book for the theological class-room. Professor Shedd has wisely translated with freedom, and has improved the structure of the work.—*Nonconformist.*

OUTLINES OF A SYSTEMATIC RHETORIC. From the German of DR. FRANCIS THEREMIN. Third and Revised Edition, with an Introductory Essay by the translator. pp. 216. 12mo. $1.00.

This is a work of much solid value. It is adapted to advanced students, and can be read and reread with advantage by professed public speakers, however accomplished they may be in the important art of persuasion. This edition is an improvement upon the other, containing a new introductory essay, illustrating the leading position of the work, and a series of questions adapting it to the use of the student.—*Boston Recorder.*

THE CONFESSIONS OF ST. AUGUSTINE. Edited, with an Introduction. $1.50.

"Prof. Shedd has earned our heartfelt thanks for this elegant edition of Augustine's Confessions. The book is profitable for the Christian to study, and we would commend it as a daily companion in the closet of the intelligent believer who desires to be taught the way to holiness through communion of the Spirit. Prof. Shedd's Introduction is a masterly essay, which itself is a volume for attentive reading. It ought to be read before the book is begun. Thorough, searching, and discriminating beyond the facts it communicates, its instructions and hints are suggestive and invaluable."—*N. Y. Observer.*

"We have long wanted to see just such an edition of Augustine's Confessions. The editor has done a public service in introducing it; and its typographical beauty is no small recommendation of it."—*Presbyterian.*

WORKS OF MOSES STUART, late Professor in Andover Theological Seminary.

COMMENTARY ON THE EPISTLE TO THE ROMANS. Third Edition.
Edited and revised by PROF. R. D. C. ROBBINS. 12mo. pp. 544. $2.25.

"His Commentary on the Romans is the most elaborate of all his works. It has elicited more discussions than any of his other exegetical volumes. It is the result of long-continued, patient thought. It expresses, in clear style, his maturest conclusions. It has the animating influence of an original treatise, written on a novel plan, and under a sense of personal responsibility. Regarding it in all its relations, its antecedents and consequents, we pronounce it the most important Commentary which has appeared in this country on this Epistle.—*Bib. Sacra.*

"We heartily commend this work to all students of the Bible. The production of one of the first Biblical scholars of our age, on the most important of all the doctrinal books of the New Testament, it deserves the careful study, not only of those who agree with Prof. Stuart in his theological and exegetical principles, but of those who earnestly dissent from some of his views in both respects."—*Watchman and Reflector.*

"This contribution by Prof. Stuart has justly taken a high place among the Commentaries on the Epistle to the Romans, and, with his other works, will always be held in high estimation by the student of the Sacred Scriptures."—*New York Observer.*

COMMENTARY ON THE EPISTLE TO THE HEBREWS. Edited and revised by PROF. R. D. C. ROBBINS. 12mo. pp. 570. $2.25.

"It is a rich treasure for the student of the original. As a commentator, Prof. Stuart was especially arduous and faithful in following up the thought and displaying the connection of a passage, and his work as a scholar will bear comparison with any that have since appeared on either side of the Atlantic."—*American Presbyterian.*

"This Commentary is classical, both as to its literary and its theological merits. The edition before us is very skilfully edited by Professor Robbins, and gives in full Dr. Stuart's text, with additions bringing it down to the present day."—*Episcopal Recorder.*

"We have always regarded this excellent Commentary as the happiest effort of the late Andover Professor. It seems to us well-nigh to exhaust the subjects which the author comprehended in his plan."—*Boston Recorder.*

COMMENTARY ON THE APOCALYSE. 2 vols. 8vo. pp. 504, 504. $4.

COMMENTARY ON THE BOOK OF PROVERBS. 12mo. pp. 432. $1.75.

"This is the last work from the pen of Professor Stuart. Both this Commentary and the one preceding it, on Ecclesiastes, exhibit a mellowness of spirit which savors of the good man ripening for heaven; and the style is more condensed, and, in that respect, more agreeable, than in some of the works which were written in the unabated freshness and exuberant vigor of his mind. In learning and critical acumen they are equal to his former works. No English reader, we venture to say, can elsewhere find so complete a philological exposition of these two important books of the Old Testament."—*Bib. Sacra.*

COMMENTARY ON ECCLESIASTES. Second Edition. Edited and revised by R. D. C. ROBBINS, Professor in Middlebury College. 12mo. pp. 346. $1.50.

The Introduction discusses the general nature of the book; its special design and method, diction, authority, credit, and general history; ancient and modern versions, and commentaries. The Commentary is strictly and minutely exegetical.

MISCELLANIES. pp. 369. 12mo. $1.00.

CONTENTS.—I. Letters to Dr. Channing on the Trinity.—II. Two Sermons on the Atonement.—Sacramental Sermon on the Lamb of God.—IV. Dedication Sermon.—Real Christianity.—V. Letter to Dr. Channing on Religious Liberty.—VI. Supplementary Notes and Postscripts.

HEBREW GRAMMAR; Translated from Gesenius. 8vo. $1.00.

ANDOVER PUBLICATIONS.

COMMENTARIES (*Critical and Grammatical*) OF C. J. ELLICOTT, Bishop of Gloucester and Bristol.

The Commentaries of Prof. Ellicott supply an urgent want in their sphere of criticism. Prof. Stowe says of them, in his Notice to the Commentary on the Galatians: "It is the crowning excellence of these Commentaries that they are exactly what they profess to be, — *critical* and *grammatical*, and therefore in the best sense of the term, *exegetical* . . . . . His results are worthy of all confidence. He is more careful than Tischendorf, slower and more steadily deliberate than Alford, and more patiently laborious than any other living New Testament critic, with the exception, perhaps, of Tregelles."

"They [Ellicott's Commentaries] have set the first example in this country [England] of a thorough and fearless examination of the grammatical and philological requirements of every word of the Sacred Text. I do not know of anything superior to them, in their own particular line, in Germany; and they add, what, alas! is so seldom found in this country, profound reverence for the matter and subjects on which the author is laboring; nor is their value lessened by Mr. Ellicott's having confined himself for the most part to one department of a commentator's work, — the grammatical and philological." — *Dean Alford.*

COMMENTARY ON GALATIANS. With an Introductory Notice by C. E. STOWE, Professor in Andover Theological Seminary. 8vo. pp. 183. $1.75.

"We have never met with a learned commentary on any book of the New Testament so nearly perfect in every respect as the 'Commentary on the Epistle to the Galatians,' by Prof. Ellicott, of King's College, London — learned, devout, and orthodox." — *Independent.*

"We would recommend all scholars of the original Scriptures who seek directness, luminous brevity, the absence of everything irrelevant to strict grammatical inquiry, with a concise and yet very complete view of the opinions of others, to possess themselves of Ellicott's Commentaries." — *American Presbyterian.*

COMMENTARY ON EPHESIANS. 8vo. pp. 190. $1.75.

COMMENTARY ON THESSALONIANS. 8vo. pp. 171. $1.75.

COMMENTARY ON THE PASTORAL EPISTLES. 8vo. pp. 265. $2.50.

COMMENTARY ON PHILIPPIANS, COLOSSIANS, AND PHILEMON. $2.50.

HENDERSON ON THE MINOR PROPHETS. THE BOOK OF THE TWELVE Minor Prophets. Translated from the Original Hebrew. With a Commentary, Critical, Philological, and Exegetical. By E. HENDERSON, D.D. With a Biographical Sketch of the Author, by E. P. BARROWS, Hitchcock Professor in Andover Theological Seminary. 8vo. pp. 490. $4.00.

"This Commentary on the Minor Prophets, like that on the Prophecy of Isaiah, has been highly and deservedly esteemed by professional scholars, and has been of great service to the working ministry. We are happy to welcome it in an American edition, very neatly printed." — *Bib. Sacra.*

"The American publisher issues this valuable work with the consent and approbation of the author, obtained from himself before his death. It is published in substantial and elegant style, clear white paper and beautiful type. The work is invaluable for its philological research and critical acumen. The notes are learned, reliable, and practical, and the volume deserves a place in every theological student's library." — *American Presbyterian, etc.*

"This is probably the best Commentary extant on the Minor Prophets. The work is worthy of a place in the library of every scholar and every diligent and earnest reader of the Bible." — *Christian Chronicle.*

MISCELLANEOUS.

WORKS OF LEONARD WOODS, late Professor in Andover Theological Seminary: comprising Lectures, Letters, Essays, and Sermons. 5 vols. 8vo. $12.00.

LECTURES ON INFANT BAPTISM. By Leonard Woods, late Professor in Andover Theological Seminary. Boards. 35 cents.

AUGUSTINISM AND PELAGIANISM. By G. F. WIGGERS, D.D. Translated from the German, by PROF. R. EMERSON, D.D. pp. 383. 8vo. $1.50.

CARLYLE'S LATTER-DAY PAMPHLETS. 12mo. pp. 427. $1.00.
CONTENTS.— The Present Time. — Model Prisons. — Downing Street. — The New Downing Street. — Stump Orator. — Parliaments. — Hudson's Statue. — Jesuitism.

HISTORICAL DEVELOPMENT OF SPECULATIVE PHILOSOPHY FROM KANT to Hegel. From the German of Dr. H. M. CHALYBAEUS. With an Introductory Note by SIR WILLIAM HAMILTON. pp. 413. 12mo. $1.25.

THE DEBATE BETWEEN THE CHURCH AND SCIENCE; or, The Ancient Hebraic Idea of the Six Days of Creation. With an Essay on the Literary Character of TAYLER LEWIS. 12mo. pp. 437. $1.25.

"We wish in this notice to state concisely our impressions of an important and remarkable book...... The first impression which the volume has given us is of a certain *chivalry* and nobleness...... The next is of a pervading *modesty*..... An impression equally strong is that of *reverence*...... Then of extraordinary *patience* both of thought and composition. ..... *Exactness* of reasoning is another undeniable feature of the volume ...... The *learning* of the volume, though not paraded in any fulness of notes or references, is yet quite sufficient for the purposes of the argument. .... One more merit of the volume we mention, — its wonderful *suggestiveness*. — *North American Review*."

ERSKINE ON THE INTERNAL EVIDENCE FOR THE TRUTH OF REVEALED Religion. Third American, from the Fifth Edinburg Edition. pp. 139. 16mo. 75 cts.

"The entire treatise cannot fail to commend the positions which it advocates to intelligent and considerate minds. It is one of the best, perhaps THE best, of all the discussions of this momentous subject." — *Congregationalist*.

"This argument of Erskine for the Internal Evidence of the Truth of Revealed Religion, is the most compact, natural, and convincing we have ever read from any author." — *Chris. Chron.*

"No man ought to consider himself as having studied theology unless he has read, and pondered, and read again, 'Erskine on the Internal Evidence.'" — *Independent*.

HYMNS AND CHOIRS; OR, THE MATTER AND THE MANNER OF THE Service of Song in the House of the Lord. By AUSTIN PHELPS and EDWARDS A. PARK, Professors at Andover, and DANIEL L. FURBER, Pastor at Newton. 12mo. pp. 425. $1.50.

This volume describes the true design and character of Hymns; it comments on their rhetorical structure and style; points out the proper method of uttering them in public worship; and the most important principles and rules for congregational singing.

PLUTARCHUS DE SERA NUMINIS VINDICTA; Plutarch on the Delay of the Deity in the Punishment of the Wicked. With Notes by H. B. HACKETT, Professor of Biblical Literature in Newton Theological Institution. pp. 172. 12mo. 60 cents.

PUNCHARD'S VIEW OF CONGREGATIONALISM, its Principles and Doctrines, the Testimony of Ecclesiastical History in its favor, its Practice and its advantages. With an Introductory Essay by R. S. STORRS, D.D. Second edition. 16mo. pp. 331. 60 cents.

THEOLOGIA GERMANICA. Which setteth forth many fair lineaments of Divine Truth, and saith very lofty and lovely things touching a Perfect Life. Edited by DR. PFEIFFER, from the only complete manuscript yet known. Translated from the German by SUSANNA WINKWORTH. With a Preface by the REV. CHARLES KINGSLEY, Rector of Eversley; and a Letter to the Translator, by the CHEVALIER BUNSEN, D.D., D. C. L., etc.; and an Introduction by PROF. CALVIN E. STOWE, D. D. 275 pp. 16mo. Cloth, $1.50.

This treatise was discovered by Luther, who first brought it into notice by an edition which he published in 1516, of which he says: "And I will say, though it be boasting of myself, and 'I speak as a fool,' that, next to the Bible and St. Augustine, no book hath ever come into my hands whence I have learnt, or would wish to learn, more of what God and Christ, and man, and all things, are."

THE ANGEL OVER THE RIGHT SHOULDER. By the author of "Sunny Side." 18mo. pp. 20. 40 cts.

WORKS OF JESSE APPLETON, D.D., late Professor of Bowdoin
College, embracing his Course of Theological Letters, his Academic Addresses, and a selection from his Sermons, with a Memoir of his Life and Character. 2 vols. 8vo. $3.00.

WRITINGS OF PROF. B. B. EDWARDS. With a Memoir by PROF. EDWARDS A. PARK. 2 vols. 12mo. $2.50.

BIBLE HISTORY OF PRAYER. By C. A. Goodrich. 12mo. pp. 384. $1.25.
The aim of this little volume is to embody an account of the delightful and successful intercourse of believers with heaven for some four thousand years. The author has indulged a good deal in narrative, opening and explaining the circumstances which gave birth to the several prayers.

MESSIANIC PROPHECY AND THE LIFE OF CHRIST. By W. S. Kennedy. 12mo. pp. 484. $1.25.
"The plan of the author is to collect all the prophecies of the Old Testament referring to the Messiah, with appropriate comments and reflections, and then to pursue the subject through the New Testament in the life of Christ as he appeared among men. The reader will find the results of Hengstenberg and Neander here gathered up, and presented in a readable shape." — *The Presbyterian.*

MONOD'S DISCOURSES ON THE LIFE OF ST. PAUL. Translated from the French, by Rev. J. H. MYERS, D.D. 12mo. pp. 191. 90 cts.
"The aim of the author is to present an estimate of the character, labors, and writings of the Apostle Paul in the light of an example, and to apply the principles which actuated him, and which he maintained, to Christians of the present day."— *Boston Journal.*

"This little volume we regard as a very valuable addition to what may be called the 'Literature of the Apostle Paul.' The number of books that have been composed upon St. Paul is one of the many proofs of his greatness, both by nature and grace. But, of them all, there is not a more vital and appreciating book than this of Monod. Original and suggestive, thoughts are continually struck out upon collateral subjects, while yet the the principal aim of the work is never lost sight of. The account of the physique of the apostle, in its relations to eloquence (p. 115, *seq.*), will interest the preacher. The translation is faithful and elegant; reproducing, in no ordinary degree, the finer and more intangible qualities in the style of a vivid and commanding orator." — *Bib. Sacra.*

SCHAUFFLER'S MEDITATIONS ON THE LAST DAYS OF CHRIST. 12mo. pp. 439. $1.25.
The first sixteen chapters of the book consist of Meditations on the last days of Christ, preached in the midst of plague and death, by Rev. Dr. Schauffler, at Constantinople; the second part, of eight sermons on the 17th chapter of John, is a practical exposition of that chapter.

SELECT SERMONS OF REV. WORTHINGTON SMITH, D. D. With a Memoir of his Life, by REV. JOSEPH TORREY, D. D., Professor in the University of Vermont. 12mo. pp. 380. $1.25.
"This is a memorial volume of Dr. Smith, late President of Vermont University, and was prepared at the request of many of his friends. An interesting Memoir of his Life, edited by Joseph Torrey, D. D., Professor of Intellectual and Moral Philosophy, introduces the Sermons.

VENEMA'S INSTITUTES OF THEOLOGY. Translated by REV. A. W. BROWN, Edinburgh. 532 pp. 8vo. Fine edition. $3.00.

PAMPHLETS. A variety of Sermons, Addresses, and Essays; some of which have become very rare. Catalogues furnished.

CLASSICAL WORKS AND TEXT-BOOKS.

POLITICAL ECONOMY. Designed as a Text-book for Colleges. By JOHN BASCOM, A.M., Professor in Williams College. 12mo. pp. 366. $1.50.
"It goes over the whole ground in a logical order. The matter is perspicuously arranged under distinct chapters and sections; it is a compendious exhibition of the principles of the science without prolonged disquisitions on particular points, and it is printed in the style for which the Andover Press has long been deservedly celebrated." — *Princeton Review.*

Just Published.

A
CRITICAL AND EXEGETICAL COMMENTARY
ON
THE BOOK OF GENESIS,
WITH A NEW TRANSLATION.

BY JAMES G. MURPHY, LL.D., T.C.D.,
Professor of Hebrew, Belfast.

WITH A PREFACE BY J. P. THOMPSON, D.D.,
NEW YORK CITY.

One Vol. 8vo. pp. 535. Price $3.50.

We cannot better describe this excellent Commentary than by quoting from the Preface of Rev. Dr. Thompson.

"In introducing to the American public Dr. Murphy's Commentary on Genesis, I would commend it as a timely antidote to much of the negative and destructive criticism upon the Pentateuch which has so largely obtained in Germany, and of late in England also, rather than as a complete solution of the many and vexed questions in language, in science, and in history which pertain to the so-called "Books of Moses." The merits of Dr. Murphy's work are a nice critical analysis of the text, a candid consideration of all alleged difficulties, a common-sense view of the principles of interpretation, and a philosophical clearness and comprehensiveness in the statement of inference or of doctrine. It consists of an exact literal translation of such passages as contain either verbal or grammatical difficulties, and of a critical and exegetical commentary, based upon the grammatical construction of the text, and framed in view of the best lights of modern criticism and science. Thus, in the narratives of the creation and the deluge, our author unfolds step by step the literal meaning of the sacred writer, and evolves from the Hebrew a sense which well accords with the facts of astronomical and geological science....

"In character, Dr. Murphy has the simplicity of the true scholar, and the devout and humble spirit of the true disciple of Christ."

THE ESSAYS OF THE LATE ARCHBISHOP WHATELY
ON SOME OF THE DIFFICULTIES IN
THE WRITINGS OF THE APOSTLE PAUL,
AND IN OTHER PARTS OF THE NEW TESTAMENT.

12mo. pp. 376. Tinted Paper. Extra Cloth, Gilt. Price, $2.00.

Either of the above will be sent by mail, post paid, on receipt of the sum named.

W. F. DRAPER, Publisher,
Andover, Mass.

www.ingramcontent.com/pod-product-compliance
Lightning Source LLC
Chambersburg PA
CBHW021419300426
44114CB00010B/563